ENCYCLOPEDIA
OF
PSYCHOLOGY

Volume 3

ENCYCLOPEDIA
OF
PSYCHOLOGY

Editors

H. J. Eysenck, London

and

W. Arnold, Würzburg
R. Meili, Berne

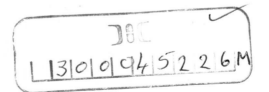

ENCYCLOPEDIA
OF
PSYCHOLOGY

Volume Three

Phas to Z

Search Press · London

1972
SEARCH PRESS LIMITED
85 Gloucester Road, London SW7 4SU

Executive Editor

J. Cumming

Any patents, trade marks or trade names, of pharmaceutical preparations, psychological tests and so on, which appear in this Encyclopedia, are cited only by way of example. The presence or absence of any manufacturer's name or that of any product, or the order of appearance of any cited, is no indication of any judgment passed on the same, and does not show that any substance, formula or test etc. is free.

© 1972 by Herder KG, West Germany
Printed in Great Britain at The Pitman Press, Bath
ISBN   0   85532   282   9

AUTHORS OF SHORTER ARTICLES
KEY TO INITIALS

A.A.	A. Anastasi	*C.Bü.*	C. Bühler
A.B.	A. Broadhurst	*C.C.*	C. Cherry
A.Ba.	A. Bandura	*C.D.F.*	C. D. Frith
A.Be.	A. Bellebaum	*C.G.*	C. Guttmann
A.B.K.	A. B. Kristofferson	*C.G.H.*	C. G. Hoyos
A.D.B.C.	A. D. B. Clarke	*C.M.*	C. Münkel
A.E.B.	A. E. Bergin	*C.N.*	C. Nahoum
A.E.L.	A. E. Lányi	*C.S.*	C. Scharfetter
A.E.M.	A. E. Maxwell	*D.B.*	D. Bartussek
A.F.	A. Friedemann	*D.E.*	D. Eaves
A.G.	A. Gubser	*D.E.B.*	D. E. Berlyne
A.H.	A. Hajos	*D.F.*	D. Furneaux
A.Hi.	A. Hicklin	*D.G.*	D. Görlitz
A.J.Y.	A. J. Yates	*D.P.*	D. Pfau
A.K.	A. Karsten	*D.V.*	D. Vaitl
A.L.	A. Lang	*D.Vo.*	D. Vormfelde
A.N.S.	A. N. Sokolov	*E.D.*	E. David
A.R.	A. Rausche	*E.F.K.*	E. Furch-Krafft
A.R.L.	A. R. Luria	*E.G.W.*	E. G. Wehner
A.R.-S.	A. Rocheblave-Spenlé	*E.H.*	E. Heineken
A.S.-M.	A. Schmidt-Mummendey	*E.J.*	E. Jorswieck
A.T.	A. Tanda	*E.L.*	E. Lehmann
A.Th.	A. Thomas	*E.L.H.*	E. L. Hartley
A.V.	A. Vergote	*E.M.*	E. Mittenecker
A.W.	A. Wellek	*E.M.-L.*	E. Müller-Luckmann
A.W.-F.	A. Weill-Fassima	*E.N.-N.*	E. Noelle-Neumann
A.Y.	A. Yates	*E.N.S.*	E. N. Sokolov
B.B.	B. Brooker	*E.R.*	E. Rausch
B.H.	B. Heinze	*E.R.H.*	E. R. Hilgard
B.J.U.	B. J. Underwood	*E.U.*	E. Ullrich
B.L.	B. Louis	*E.W.*	E. Wehner
B.R.	B. Rollett	*F.B.*	F. Bomio
B.S.	B. Schmidt	*F.Bu.*	F. Buggle
B.Sp.	B. Spiegel	*F.-C.S.*	F.-C. Schubert
B.T.	B. Tschanz	*F.H.*	F. Haeberlin
B.W.	B. Wittlich	*F.J.*	F. Jodelet
C.B.	C. Brinkmann	*F.K.*	F. Keller

F.Ki.	F. Kiener	*H.J.B.*	H. J. Butcher
F.Kl.	F. Klix	*H.J.En.*	H. J. Engels
F.K.I.	F. K. Illyés	*H.-J.E.*	H.-J. Eysenck
F.M.	F. Merz	*H.-J.K.*	H.-J. Kornadt
F.Ma.	F. Mattejat	*H.-J.S.*	H.-J. Steingrüber
F.N.	F. Novak	*H.-J.Sch.*	H.-J. Schneider
F.S.	F. Süllwold	*H.K.*	H. Knauer
F.Sch.	F. Schumer	*H.Kr.*	H. Kreitler
F.W.	F. Wesley	*H.L.*	H. Lippert
G.A.	G. Arnold	*H.M.*	H. Maisch
G.B.	G. Bachmair	*H.Ma.*	H. Mandl
G.B.T.	G. B. Trasler	*H.Me.*	H. Meister
G.C.M.	G. C. Mialaret	*H.N.G.*	H. N. Genius
G.D.	G. Debus	*H.P.*	H. Pick
G.D.W.	G. D. Wilson	*H.R.*	H. Riedel
G.E.	G. Erdmann	*H.Ro.*	H. Roth
G.G.	G. Guttmann	*H.Rr.*	H. Rohracher
G.H.	G. Huber	*H.R.B.*	H. R. Blackwell
G.J.	G. Jones	*H.S.*	H. Schmalfuss
G.K.	G. Kaulfush	*H.Sa.*	H. Sattes
G.Ka.	G. Kanizsa	*H.Schr.*	H. Schröder
G.Ki.	G. Kaminski	*H.T.*	H. Tajfel
G.K.S.	G. K. Stürup	*H.W.*	H. Wagenknecht
G.L.	G. Lischke	*H.Z.*	H. Zemanek
G.Li.	G. Lienert	*H.Zu.*	H. Zumkley
G.M.	G. Mikula	*I.B.*	I. Bilodeau
G.Mi.	G. Mitze	*I.L.*	I. Lindner
G.P.	G. Prystav	*I.M.*	I. Martin
G.R.W.M.	G. R. W. Marschner	*I.M.D.*	I. M. Deusinger
G.S.	G. Stocker	*I.O.*	I. Oswald
G.Sch.	G. Schilling	*J.B.*	J. Beloff
G.S.S.	G. S. Spinks	*J.Bi.*	J. Birren
G.T.	G. Trasler	*J.Br.*	J. Brožek
H.A.M.	H. A. Murray	*J.B.G.*	J. B. Grize
H.C.H.	H. C. Holland	*J.B.-H.*	J. Bar-Hillel
H.D.	H. Dumoulin	*J.B.L.*	J. B. Lotz
H.D.S.	H. D. Schmidt	*J.C.*	J. Cumming
H.E.	H. Ehrhardt	*J.Co.*	J. Cohen
H.F.	H. Frank	*J.D.*	J. Drösler
H.G.	H. Giessen	*J.D.H.*	J. D. Hundleby
H.H.	H. Haase	*J.D.T.*	J. D. Teasdale
H.He.	H. Hediger	*J.Fa.*	J. Fahrenberg
H.H.J.K.	H. H. J. Keil	*J.F.*	J. Friedrichs
H.I.	H. Illner	*J.F.U.*	J. F. Ullmann
H.-J.A.	H.-J. Aebi	*J.G.*	J. Griffiths
H.-J.Au.	H.-J. Autrum	*J.L.*	J. Leplat

J.L.H.	J. L. Horn	*M.-J.B.*	M.-J. Borel
J.L.I.	J. Lopez Ibor	*M.L.*	M. Lorr
J.M.	J. Mields	*M.Mo.*	M. Monjé
J.Ma.	J. Maxwell	*M.R.*	M. Reinhardt
J.Me.	J. Maisonneuve	*M.S.*	M. Spreng
J.-M.F.	J.-M. Faverge	*M.Sa.*	M. Sachs
J.N.	J. Nitsch	*M.Y.*	M. Yela
J.O.	J. Osterland	*N.K.*	N. Kogan
J.P.	J. Price	*N.S.-R.*	N. Schmidt-Relenberg
J.R.	J. Rudert	*O.S.*	O. Schrappe
J.R.N.	J. R. Nuttin	*O.T.*	O. Topič
J.S.	J. Schenk	*O.W.*	O. White
J.W.	J. Wittkowski	*P.B.*	P. Braun
J.Wi.	J. Wilcock	*P.-B.H.*	P.-B. Heinrich
J.Wo.	J. Wolpe	*P.C.W.*	P. C. Wason
J.Z.	J. Zoltobrocki	*P.D.*	P. Dietsch
J.Zu.	J. Zubin	*P.G.*	P. Graw
K.D.G.	K. D. Graf	*P.G.B.*	P. Gomez Bosque
K.D.N.	K. D. Nissen	*P.J.*	P. Jankowski
K.-D.S.	K.-D. Stoll	*P.L.*	P. Leyhausen
K.E.	K. Eyferth	*P.Le.*	P. Ley
K.E.G.	K. E. Grossmann	*P.L.B.*	P. L. Broadhurst
K.E.P.	K. E. Pelzer	*P.M.*	P. Müller
K.F.	K. Fiedler	*P.Ma.*	P. Malrieu
K.Fo.	K. Foppa	*P.Mc.K.*	P. McKellar
K.G.	K. Grossmann	*P.S.*	P. Steck
K.H.P.	K. H. Plattig	*P.Sch.*	P. Schmidt
K.M.	K. Mizushima	*P.T.*	P. Tholey
K.Mi.	K. Mierke	*P.V.*	P. Vernon
K.P.	K. Pawlik	*P.W.B.*	P. W. Bradshaw
K.T.	K. Thomas	*P.Z.*	P. Zimmermann
K.W.	K. Weltner	*R.A.S.*	R. A. Stamm
L.A.	L. Ancona	*R.A.St.*	R. A. Sternbach
L.B.	L. Blöschl	*R.B.C.*	R. B. Cattell
L.J.I.	L. J. Issing	*R.C.*	R. Chocholle
L.J.P.	L. J. Pongratz	*R.C.B.*	R. C. Bolles
L.S.	L. Shaw	*R.C.P.*	R. C. Pagès
M.A.	M. Amelang	*R.D.*	R. Droz
M.Ad.	M. Adler	*R.D.H.*	R. D. Hare
M.B.	M. Brambring	*R.G.*	R. Glaser
M.Ba.	M. Bartl	*R.H.*	R. Hetherington
M.Bo.	M. Boss	*R.Hä.*	R. Hänni
M.H.	M. Haider	*R.K.*	R. Kirchhoff
M.Ha.	M. Hamilton	*R.L.*	R. Lynn
M.He.	M. Henke	*R.M.*	R. Meili
M.Ho.	M. Hofer	*R.M.C.*	R. M. Church

MAIN ABBREVIATIONS USED IN THIS WORK

AA = Achievement age
abb. = abbreviation
ACh = Acetylcholine
ACTH = Adrenocorticotrophic hormone
AL = Adaptation level
Am. = American
ANS = Autonomic nervous system
ant. = antonym
anthropol. = anthropological
A.P.A. = American Psychological Association
AQ = Achievement quotient
b. = born
biol. = biological
CA = Chronological age
c. = *circa* = about
cc = cubic centimeter (centimetre)
cf. = *confer* = compare
ch., chs = chapter(s)
CFF = Critical flicker frequency
chem. = chemical
CNS = Central nervous system
cps = cycles per second
CR = Conditioned response
CS = Conditioned stimulus
d. = died
db = decibel
d.f. = degrees of freedom
DNA = Desoxyribonucleic acid
E., Es = Experimenter(s)
EA = Educational age
Ed., Eds = Editor(s)
ed. cit. = edition cited
EEG = Electroencephalogram
e.g. = *exempli gratia* = for example
EKG = Electrocardiogram
Eng. = English
EQ = Educational quotient
ERG = Electroretinogram
esp. = especially
ESP = Extrasensory perception
et al. = *et alii* = and others
etc. = *et cetera* = and so forth

et seq. = *et sequens, sequentia* = and the following
ex., exs = example(s)
f., ff. = and the following
FFF = Flicker-fusion frequency
fig., figs = figure(s)
fn. = footnote
Fre. = French
GABA = Gamma-amino-butyric acid
GAS = General adaptation syndrome
Ger. = German
Gr. = Greek
GSR = Galvanic skin response
Hz. = Hertzian wave
Ib. = *ibidem* = in the same place
Id. = *idem* = the same person(s)
i.e. = *id est* = that is
introd. = introduction by
IQ = Intelligence quotient
IRM = Innate releasing mechanism
It. = Italian
IU = Interval of uncertainty
j.n.d. = Just-noticeable difference
Lat. = Latin
loc. cit. = *loco citato* = in the place (passage) cited
m. = meter (metre)
MA = Mental age
math. = mathematical
med. = medical
min. = minute
mm. = millimeter (millimetre)
n.d. = no date
No., Nos = number(s)
n.p. = no place of publication
n.s. = new series
NS = Nervous system
O = Observer
op. cit. = *opere citato* = in the work cited
o.s. = old series
OT = Occupational therapy
p = probability
p., pp. = page(s)

PE	= Probable error	S., Ss	= Subject(s)
philol.	= philological	SD	= Standard deviation
philos.	= philosophical	SE	= Standard error
phys.	= physical	sec.	= second(s)
physiol.	= physiological	sect.	= section
PR	= Percentile rank	ser.	= series
pref.	= preface	S-R	= Stimulus-response
q.v.	= *quod vide* = which see	stat.	= statistical
R	= Response	syn.	= synonym
REM	= Rapid eye movement	TAT	= Thematic Apperception Test
resp.	= respectively	TE	= Trial-and-error learning
rev.	= revised by	trans.	= translation
RI	= Retroactive inhibition	UR	= Unconditioned response
RNA	= Ribonucleic acid	US	= Unconditioned stimulus
rpm	= revolutions per minute	V	= volt
RS	= Reinforcing stimulus	vol.	= volume
RT	= Reaction time	VTE	= Vicarious trial and error
S	= Stimulus	WHO	= World Health Organization

ACKNOWLEDGEMENTS

It is possible to mention only a few of those who have contributed to the making of this Encyclopedia. Special thanks are due to Professor O. Köhler of Verlag Herder and Freiburg University, and to Herr F. Novak of Würzburg University. In production Mr D. Cahill's proofreading and the advice and help of Frau G. Pallat, Herr A. Zimmermann and Mr J. Gibbons were invaluable. The translations into English were made by J. Cumming, D. Geoghegan, V. Green, J. Griffiths, J. F. Hargreaves, W. Hargreaves, D. Livingstone, J. Maxwell and H. Repton.   *J.C.*

Phasopathy. A reversible endogenous-episodic overemphasis of a psychic-mental developmental phase which can last for weeks or years but then disappear again; resulting difficulties in upbringing, at school and work or disturbances of social adaptation can have a pathological effect as an abnormal partial condition during the course of some psychic process. Phasopathy must be distinguished diagnostically from an inherited mental handicap, character impairments acquired from harmful environmental influences, and irreversible personal divergences toward abnormality of unmistakably somatic origin, or resulting from a post-sickness condition.

Bibliography: Engels, H. J.: La psychologie, science auxiliaire. Revue de Neuropsychiatrie infantile et d'Hygiène mentale de l'enfance, 1964, *12*, 747–54.

H.J.E.

Phenomenal field. The whole area of that which is experienced simultaneously; it may be divided into the phenomenal ego and the environing phenomenal field or location. The concept of field (q.v.), which gestalt theory borrowed from physics, indicates that states and processes at different positions in this area are dynamically connected and mutually determined.   *P.Th.*

Phenomenal motion. An obsolescent term for any perception of movement that cannot be explained by mechanico-biological data alone (e.g.: we perceive the movement of a stone when it is thrown, although the image on the retina remains constant).   *V.M.*

Phenomenology (Ger. *Phänomenologie*). The theory of *phenomena*, or *appearances*. The phenomenological approach is to examine an object from the standpoint of its appearance. This may be appearance in the external world of the senses, apprehensibility in the experiential sphere, or even the symbolic visual representation of mental structures or processes. The word "phenomenology" is used in a narrow and in a wide sense. In the narrow sense, the word stands for a philosophico-psychological method initiated by Edmund Husserl (1859–1938) that has spread significantly in philosophy and science.

1. *The "pure phenomenology" of Husserl.* For Husserl (1913) this means obtaining an immediate "*Anschauung*" (direct intuition or perception) of the bases of cognition. His appeal "back to things" meant: we must banish all preconceived theory of knowledge (q.v.) and of cognition, and obtain a *pure view of the reality of subjective experience*. From experience of direct "seeing", the phenomenologist obtains an essential, general content ("categorial perception"). The merely empirical givenness of the individual instance is stripped down to an "ideating abstraction".

Cognition, like other sense experiences, cannot be explained by means of psychologico-anatomistic analysis: like the others, it is a sensory whole. Husserl called the attempt to derive mental phenomena psychologically "psychologism" (q.v.), and showed that it was mistaken. He was convinced that only the phenomenological method could disclose the requisite basic concepts of psychology as a science. Fundamental notions cannot be proved, but only indicated. Husserl's phenomenology is grounded upon the psychology of his teacher Brentano (q.v.), according to whom the essential characteristic of consciousness is *intentionality* ("consciousness is always *consciousness of. . .*"). See *Act psychology*.

2. *Anthropological phenomenology.* Max Scheler (1874–1928), who was not a pupil of Husserl's but had similar ideas, developed a phenomenology of the "value-qualities of being", and of the vital principles of the human personality. Scheler's work was fundamental for the psychology of the "feelings", or emotion (q.v.). "Intentionality" was the central concept of his theory of the person: the person forms the center of acts and by his very nature cannot become an object. According to

Scheler's famous formulation (1916), man and animal have a fundamentally different relationship to the world: the animal has environment (*Umwelt*), man has world (*Welt*).

Martin Heidegger (1889–) found Husserl's ideas most fruitful. French existentialism also developed from Husserl and Heidegger; Merleau-Ponty (1966) developed a phenomenological anthropology.

3. *Psychological phenomenology.* A. Pfänder's (1870–1941) *Phänomenologie des Wollens* (1960), a study of the "phenomenology of volition", may be described as the classical work of psychological phenomenology, which uses an emphatic form of categorial intuition and a rigorous descriptive style.

4. *The phenomenological approach in psychological methodology.* "Categorial intuition", according to Husserl, is the means of obtaining basic psychological concepts for psychology. Such concepts as perception, volition or emotion are so postulated as to allow that which is essentially perceptual or volitional, etc., to emerge from the particular event or process as an ideating abstraction. Classification into concepts of this kind does not take place, as with categorical or area concepts, on the basis of an *either-or*, but (as with type concepts) by means of a *more-or-less*. Round about the pure case which has been seen to be the center, are grouped those processes which have been encountered as more or less according with that pure case. The individual occurrence is measured against the abstracted pure case. Binswanger (1922) has shown how important phenomenology can be for psychological methodology. Phenomenological conceptual perception is directed to meaningful wholes. A connection with the individual findings obtained by means of natural-scientific analysis is possible only if a primacy of meaningful wholes is recognized. Buytendijk's work (1953) attempts this kind of synthesis. Straus (1956) also deserves mention in this connection. See *Ganzheit; Existence analysis.*

Bibliography: Binswanger, L.: Einführung in die Probleme der allgemeinen Psychologie. Berlin, 1922. Id.: The case of Ellen West. In: May, R. *et al.* (Eds.): Existence: a new dimension in psychiatry and psychology. New York, 1958, 237–64. Buytendijk, F. J. J.: Die Frau, Natur, Erscheinung, Dasein. Cologne, 1953. Id.: Pain: its modes and functions. Chicago, 1962. Farber, M.: The foundation of phenomenology: Edmund Husserl and the quest for a rigorous science of philosophy. Cambridge, Mass., 1940. Graumann, C. F.: Grundlagen einer Phänomenologie und Psychologie der Perspektivität. Berlin, 1960. Husserl, E.: Logische Untersuchungen. Halle, 1900–01 (Eng. trans.: Logical investigations. London, 1970). Id.: Ideen zu einer reinen Phänomenologie und phänomenologischen Philosophie. Halle, 1913. Kaam, A. van: Existential foundations of psychology. Pittsburgh, 1966. Lersch, P.: The levels of the mind. In: David, H. P. & Bracken, H. von: (Eds.): Perspectives in personality theory. New York, 1957, 218–41. Id.: Aufbau der Person. Munich, [10]1966. May, R. (Ed.): Existential psychology. New York, 1961. Merleau-Ponty, M.: Phenomenology of perception. London, 1962. Id.: The structure of behavior. Boston, 1963. Id.: Les sciences de l'homme et la phénoménologie, Bull. de Psychol., 1964, *18*, 141–70. Pfänder, A.: Der Formalismus in der Ethik und die materiale Wertethik. Halle, 1916. Raneurello, A. C.: A study of Franz Brentano: his psychological standpoint and his significance in the history of psychology. New York, 1968. Sartre, J.-P.: Existentialism. New York, 1947. Id.: The psychology of imagination. New York, 1948. Id.: The emotions: outline of a theory. New York, 1948. Id.: Being and nothingness. New York, 1956. Scheler, M.: Der Formalismus in der Ethik und die materiale Wertethik. Halle, 1916. Id.: The nature of sympathy. London, 1970. Spiegelberg, H.: The phenomenological movement. A historical introduction. The Hague, 1960. Straus, E.: Vom Sinne der Sinne. Berlin, 1956. *J. Rudert*

Phenothiazines. A chemical subgroup of the neuroleptics (q.v.). They are divided, according to chemical criteria, into promethazine and propylamine derivatives (promazine, chlorpromazine, trifluopromazine), propylpiperazine derivatives (perazine, prochlorperazine, fluphenazine, perphenazine, homofenazine) and alkylpiperidyl derivatives (mepazine, thioridazine). Phenothiazines have a broad spectrum of effect due to multiple impact points in the central (among others, the reticular formation (q.v.), hypothalamic regulating centers) and peripheral nervous system (adrenolytic, antichlolinergic, antihistaminic), with a varying combination and degree of intensity of effects for the individual derivatives. The clinically significant neuroleptic effect is quite varied in strength and duration (e.g. weak with promazine, strong with fluphenazine). Phenothiazines have an antiemetic effect, increase appetite and lower the temperature (chiefly in the sense of deficient compensation; in large doses they produce extrapyramidal symptoms (also after chronic applications), and predispose to narcosis (q.v.). The effect of small doses in healthy persons is unstable, depending on the situation and person (see *Differential psychopharmacology*); in comparison with tranquilizers (q.v.), sedative effects appear quite early. Tranquilizing effects also appear after first application, but, clinically, therapeutic effects appear fully only after several applications.

Bibliography: **Gordon, M.:** Phenothiazines. In: **Gordon, M.** (Ed.): Psychopharmacological agents, Vol. 2. New York, 1967. **Herminger, G., DiMascio, A. & Klerman, G. L.:** Personality factors in variability of response to phenothiazines. Amer. J. Psychiat., 1965, *121*, 1011–94. *G.D.*

Phenotype. The visible type of an individual: i.e. the sum of all actually developed characteristics (see *Genotype*). Individuals with the same phenotype are not (necessarily) the same genetically: e.g. a black guinea-pig may be homozygotically or heterozygotically black with the allele (q.v.) for black dominating that for white (dominant-recessive inheritance).
H.Sch.

Phenylalanine. An essential amino-acid, which decomposes into tyrosine (q.v.) in the organism. In certain individuals this process is disturbed because an enzyme is absent; the result is phenylketonuria (q.v.), which produces serious intelligence and personality defects if not treated during the first months of life.

Bibliography: **Grüter, W.:** Angeborene Stoffwechselstörungen und Schwachsinn am Beispiel der Phenylketonurie. Stuttgart, 1963. **Lyman, F. L.:** Phenylketonuria. Springfield, 1963.   *W.J.*

Phenylketonuria. A recessive (q.v.) hereditary metabolic anomaly in which the conversion of phenylalanine into tyrosine (i.e. the oxidization of phenylalamines) is disturbed owing to an enzymatic deficiency. The disorder presents as a phenylpyruvic oligophrenia, or various degrees of mental defect (q.v.) and a tendency to convulsions early in life. A cure is possible only with a very early diagnosis and a phenylalanine-reduced diet beginning before three years of age.   *E.D.*

Pheromones. Chemical substances which promote communication within a species. In special scent glands the female silk-moth produces a substance to which the males are extraordinarily sensitive. The exaltolides (musk-like substances) are claimed to produce similar sex-specific reactions in man.   *V.Pr.*

Phi coefficient. A parametric technique for calculating the degree of interaction between two alternative variables, according to the formula

$$r_\Phi = \frac{ad - bc}{\sqrt{(a + b)(c + d)(a + c)(b + d)}},$$

in which ad and bc indicate the products of the two diagonal values in a fourfold table. *G.Mi.*

Philosophy and psychology. At the beginning of this century psychology prided itself on its newfound self-realization as a *natural science*. Today the literature would seem to be aware of the philosophical tradition of psychology as no more than an historical phenomenon.

The major question in the general discussion

of the future orientation of psychology at the time of its separation from philosophy was the problem of the "subjectivism" of self-observation (introspection or self-knowledge). Research was concerned with the processes of *consciousness* (q.v.), the *directly* experienced quality of which was available only to individual self-observation. Analysis was carried out by means of *description* and *comparison*. An attempt was made, but with the aid of *abstraction*, to formulate general laws. The result of this procedure was a *phenomenal* determination of the general nature of psychological processes (e.g. the four axioms formulated by K. Bühler for the psychology of *association* (q.v.), and *constructs* concerning the relationship of processes (e.g. the laws of association).

The *phenomenalistic* approach—a product of the prevailing "psychologism" (q.v.) (J. Locke, J. S. Mill, G. T. Fechner, W. Dilthey, *et al.*) could not, using the modes proper to philosophy, *objectify* the principle of the "subjectivism" of individual experience, as attempted in cognition theory, e.g. in Husserl's "transcendental reduction" or Hegel's "self-reflection of the thinking subject" (idealism). No philosophically satisfying future could be forecast for psychology, whereas the introduction of the category of quantity enabled scientific justice to be done to psychological phenomena.

Admittedly, the *source* of psychic events remained the *experiencing subject*. But measurement and calculation made individuals comparable according to definite criteria. In this way, a basis was created for intersubjectivity, which made it possible to think in terms of experimental-psychological arrangements. Of course these experiments were largely determined by criteria of formal logic, the various interpretations of which led to violent controversy (e.g. between W. Wundt and K. Bühler).

In psychophysics (q.v.) (E. H. Weber, G. T. Fechner) previous assertions about the nature of psychic phenomena became practically meaningless, and were supplanted by *inductively* obtained statements about general *formal* relationships of quantifiable, observed data (e.g. the intensity of physical stimuli, or experienced sensations). This was another step on the way from the psychology of consciousness to scientific psychology. If the quality of experiences was now only a fictitiously determined criterion of order, the immediacy of the experience could be dispensed with too. At this stage, European psychology began to accord with "reflexology" (I. P. Pavlov) and "behaviorism" (J. B. Watson), which replaced *self-observation* by the *observation of others*, and widened the methodological principle of intersubjectivity by the *externalization* (instrumentalization) of observational data. The determination of the general nature of psychological phenomena by analysis and abstraction was replaced by *operational definition* (q.v.) (see Nagel *et al.*, 1971; Bradley, 1971).

Psychology as a natural science now obeys the rule "*savoir pour prévoir*", and seeks to predict, plan, control; in short, to *manipulate* the processes of nature. The subjectivism of the experiencing individual would now seem (at least as a methodological problem) to have been banished from psychology.

However, the individual as the "container" or "bearer" of facts, i.e. as the *object* of psychological research, cannot be ignored, even by an extremely mechanistic psychology (Eysenck, 1972). But, together with the method, the object of psychology has undergone a conceptual transformation.

The subjective processes of the individual, his contents (i.e. his qualities) have been *reified* as *facts* related to one another by causal function. The distinctive nature of the individual at any given time can no longer be thought of on the basis of *a priori* determinations of "substance" (q.v.), of "entelechial personal development" and of "totality", but is divided into individual "parts" with random frequency and random degrees of intensity.

At this point the scientific and theoretical problem of subjectivism becomes *the* question of the theory of knowledge, which asks: Can the object "individual" still be sufficiently grasped in its reality by the rational and purposive conceptual models of a scientific psychology, or does an understanding of this object necessarily lead back to the individual as *subject* of cognition? For it *is* the individual who carries out this research into himself, and in this act devises the process of research and the categories of his own knowledge of himself. This problem of psychology is not yet wholly elucidated.

True, in modern psychology the "former" individual, with his *a priori* assumptions, is either implicitly or explicitly the subject of examination—rather as if determining fundamental nature and a purposive and rational supposition could be taken as one and the same thing. But the "totality" of psychic phenomena or their "entelechial inner laws" cannot be empirically verified; they can only be grounded on the philosophical explanation of the essence of a thing.

For example, many authors' developmental psychology presupposes a meaningful totality of the individual and a development following its inner laws, for without these postulates psychology can have no laws governing the association of facts in time: i.e. no process of development subject to any laws at all (Piaget, 1953, 1965). True, the causal relationship of component processes can be explained by means of functional models in regard to conditions defined at any particular time, but there is no causal explanation for, e.g., the sequence of definite qualities of thought (q.v.) in the development of an individual. The process of thought as development can be indicated only on the plane of *mind* conforming to law and therefore necessary. The "if" of time is not a condition for this process, is not a fact, and cannot be postulated.

A similar problem arises when examining *attitudes* (q.v.) which are objectified, i.e.

typologized, by a concept of items derived from their process of development. Conditions for degrees of intensity, and positive or negative valences of attitudes, can be asserted, but the "semantic" space (see *Semantics*) of attitudes and attitude change is determined not only by conditions but by *meaning*. When an attitude originates as a meaningful relation, this cannot be explained from conditions, i.e. from facts, because it is not the facts themselves but individuals who make the connection. Freud's attempt to interpret psychological events as meaningful contexts (relationships) in depth psychology (q.v.) still deserves full consideration as a conceptual model. In this connection, the "critical theory" (q.v.) of the Frankfurt School (Horkheimer, Adorno, Marcuse, Habermas) conceives Freud's *psychoanalysis* (q.v.) as a form of "systematically generalized self-reflection" (Habermas, 1972), only to show that "this dimension (of self-reflection) is again shattered on the plane of positivism". A "legitimate path" would lead us back from "conventional theory"; such a path would be the approach of Pierce and Dilthey: i.e. "a methodology that depends upon the attitude proper to the theory of knowledge". Freud's concept of psychoanalysis as a (natural) science is seen as a "pseudo-scientific self-delusion", thus enabling the still unexplained position of psychoanalytic interpretation between hermeneutics and causal-functional thought to be explicated as "the logic of general interpretation". There is still no answer to the question of how this generalization can be legitimized, for the treatment of psychoanalysis as a form of self-reflection is a matter not only of abstractive generalization, but of grounding. This does not occur in the natural-scientific approach, nor—as self-reflection—with "critical theory" (cf. Horkheimer & Adorno, 1972).

Psychology is most akin still to philosophy when investigating psychological acts that are not of a purposive-rational nature, such as those manifestations of subjective experience which, as human *culture*, we call games and dances, and such creative phenomena as art, language and cognitive thinking. The fact that these phenomena cannot be adequately explained by modern psychology shows most clearly that the fiction of the object of psychology as a functional model has become the "as if" of the reality of an individual whose creative acts are neither predictable nor manipulable (cf. Berlinger, 1969; 1970).

When reduced to a fact, the subject of psychology is in the paradoxical situation of having deprived himself of his power of self-reflection in favor of an objectivistic methodology. Facts can say nothing about themselves or about their relationships with other facts; facts are not a subject but an object. Here psychologism becomes redundant, and here the exploration of the creative acts of the individual can go no further.

This state of affairs is not altered by an *instrumentalist formulation* of research processes and concepts. The instruments of research do become increasingly differentiated and measure more and more accurately; but instruments do not *know* what they are measuring. The object is defined by the instrument, but the instrument is designed by the still subjective individual, who, for example, selects items according to his prescientific understanding of the object. Recourse to representative sampling allows representation only in regard to the distribution of facts in the population, but not in regard to the basic factual question about the "what" of the object (e.g., in the case of intelligence tests, about the "what" of intelligence). What is *intelligence* as man understands himself in any particular epoch? A selection instrument of a certain social class, or a construct defined by its purpose and by conditions proper to specific times, and hence limited operationally? The same problems arise for concepts such as "adapted-unadapted", "neurotic-healthy", and so on. If they are taken as unproblematic facts, they become subject to arbitrary evalua-tion and can serve the ends of manipulation (q.v.). The situation is different if they are limited by condition and purpose.

The individual runs the risk of falling into the hands of purposive-rational manipulation, if he succumbs to a functional explanation of psychic processes (Chomsky, 1971; Horkheimer & Adorno, 1972).

But of course he remains a *subject:* the subject is not determined by facts, by a superficial concept of empiricism; instead the subject draws up the categories which determine facts. Through *consciousness* he is always involved in a relationship to himself and to the object; he not only reacts out of his involvement, but possesses the power of *conceiving* himself in this relatedness. Only on the basis of this concept of self is it possible to discern the nature not only of the conditions but of the meaning for man of purposive-rational determinations.

Bibliography: Anscombe, G. E. M.: An introduction to Wittgenstein's Tractatus. London, [3]1967. **Ayer, A. J.:** The problem of knowledge. London, 1956. **Berlinger, R.:** Demiurgie als Ermächtigung zum Werk. Philosophische Perspektiven, 1969, *1*, 52–65. **Id.:** Der musikalische Weltentwurf. Philosophische Perspektiven, 1970, 2, 305–16. **Bradley, J.:** Mach's philosophy of science. London, 1971. **Chomsky, N.:** Problems of knowledge and freedom. New York, 1971; London 1972. **Eysenck, H. J.:** Psychology is about people. Harmondsworth & New York, 1972. **Habermas, J.:** Knowledge and interest. London & New York, 1972. **Horkheimer, M. & Adorno, T.:** Dialectic of enlightenment. New York, 1972. **Jaspers, K.:** The perennial scope of philosophy. New York, 1949. **Nagel, E., Bromberger, S. & Grunbaum, A.:** Observation and theory in science. Baltimore, Ud. & London, 1971. **Piaget, J.:** Logic and psychology. Manchester & New York, 1953. **Id.:** Psychology and philosophy. In: **Wolman, B. B. & Nagel, E.** (Eds.): Scientific psychology: principles and approaches. New York, 1965, 28–43. **Sartre, J.-P.:** Transcendence of the ego. New York, 1960. **Watson, J. B.:** Behaviorism. New York, 1925. **Wellek, A.:** Mathematics and intuition: the relationship between psychology and philosophy reconsidered. Acta psychologica, 1964, *22*, 413–29. **Winch, P.:** The idea of a social science and its relation to philosophy. London, [3]1963.

P. Braun

Phimosis. Narrowing of the opening of the penile prepuce (foreskin) preventing it being drawn back over the glans. *Phimosis vaginalis:* narrowness of the vagina.   *G.D.W.*

Phi-phenomenon. A phenomenon *sui generis* (M. Wertheimer). Denotes the optical impression of motion (apparent motion) generated when objectively stationary, relatively similar objects are presented one after the other at a certain distance in time.

Bibliography: Wertheimer, M.: Expt. Studien über das Sehen von Bewegung. Z. f. Psychol., 1912, 61.
                                                                            I.M.D.

Phlegmatic. The phlegmatic person is one of the four types of temperament according to Hippocrates; that variant of personality in which water predominates. The phlegmatic character is said to be calm, constant, sluggish, not easily upset and fixed in his habits. *W.Se.*

Phobia. An abnormal fear which is either: (*a*) a fear of an object or situation which is not generally considered to be frightening, e.g. lifts, domestic animals, and so on; or (*b*) an abnormally intense fear of an object or situation which normally arouses some degree of fear in most people, e.g. surgery, dentistry, etc.

Such phobias used to be classified by adding the appropriate Greek prefix, e.g. agoraphobia, claustrophobia, zoophobia, etc. Modern classifications divide phobias into those arising from specific objects, e.g. dog phobia, cat phobia, etc., or situations, e.g. school phobia, party phobia, etc., or reactions to them such as blushing phobia, fainting phobia or vomiting phobia. Phobias can be associated with almost any psychiatric condition but are most often associated with anxiety states. Phobias associated with obsessional states can show bizarre features leading to queer compulsive behavior rituals to overcome them. See *Anxiety; Paranoia; Schizophrenia.* *P.Le.*

Phoneme. 1. An hallucinatory voice. This symptom is commonest in schizophrenia. The patient hears voices usually talking to him often abusing him, giving him instructions or commenting on his actions. **2.** Closely related vocal sounds using the same or a similar symbol. *R.H.*

Phonemics (syn. *Phonology; Phonematics*). The study of the smallest categories of sound symbols—phonemes—which can be distinguished in any particular (spoken) language. In contrast, (articulatory) phonetics deals with the so to speak still more elementary structures which can be analyzed independently of speech: sounds which can be distinguished according to the places and the special manner in which they are produced: in the larynx, the mouth or the nose. Acoustic phonetics describes, partly with the aid of depictive, technical methods (visible speech, sonagrams) the physical characteristics of sounds and sound sequences. (Linguistic) questions concerning phonemics touch partly on psychological problems (see *Language; Psycholinguistics; Speech*). In determining phonological *units* (phonemes), invariant, distinguishing characteristics have to be found which belong to whole classes of sound pictures, notwithstanding the variability caused by individual and regional peculiarities or by emotional color. The Prague School (Trubetzkoy, 1935) developed operational methods for this purpose. Differences between phonemes are described in terms of distinctive features (Jakobson & Halle, 1956), so that a phoneme always appears as a group of such features. Distinguishing phonemes and neglecting some differences of sound pictures in perception involves psychological problems (Hörmann, 1970).

Two stages are distinguished in the *acquisition of sounds and phonemes.* When he can only babble, the individual is able to produce all the sounds which can conceivably be articulated, but even then accent and intonation patterns exclusive to a specific language are making their appearance (Weir, 1966). After that the child gradually acquires in communication the stock of phonemes used in his native language. In the word "papa", for example, the universal basic pattern of syllable construction (consonant/vowel, closed/open) operates. The basic stock of consonants is then further differentiated in regard to the features oral/nasal, labial/dental. The stock of vowels is similarly built up. A morbid deterioration in the ability to use language (aphasia, q.v.) takes place in the reverse order.

Under what conditions and by what means individual sound structures come to have a semantic function (see *Semantics*), a connotative or denotative meaning, is open to argument. Onomatopoeic interjections (e.g. *brr, hui, pst*) are suggestive of sound symbolism. Experimental psychophonetics deals with these questions with the aid of an "impression differential": more or less elementary sound structures are rated by testees on standard scales according to "general qualities" and then related to one another and to other semantic units by the use of the Osgood three-dimensional system of general semantic "basic" components: evaluation, activity, potency (see *Semantic differential*). Diverse attempts have been made to explain the immediate semantic efficiency of more or less elementary sound structures. One starts from the (universal) covariations existing between the sound behavior of perceptible objects and certain other features (in general, large objects have a deep sound, small objects a high one), and supposes that appropriately generalizable associative connections are learnt between the feature of size and certain dimensions of sound (Brown, 1958). Another is based on covariations between sound structures and meanings as they have been formed specifically and more by chance as the individual language developed (Taylor & Taylor, 1965). In contrast to these theories based on association, the "general qualities" of sound structures (Ertel, 1969) described in the semantic differential system are traced back to the unconditioned, innate response tendencies of the autonomic nervous system, a method which recalls the interpretations of gestalt psychology (see *Ganzheit*).

Bibliography: Brown, R. W.: Words and things. Glencoe, Ill., 1958. Ertel, S.: Psychophonetik. Göttingen, 1969. Hörmann, H.: Psychologie der Sprache. Berlin, ²1970. Jacobson, R. & Halle, M.: Fundamentals of language. The Hague, 1956. Taylor, K. & Taylor, M.: Another look at phonetic symbolism. Psychol. Bull., 1965, *64*, 413–27. Trubetzkoy, N. S.: Anleitung zur phonologischen Beschreibung. Prague, 1935. Weir, R. H.: Some questions on the child's learning of phonology. In: Smith, F. & Miller, G. A. (Eds.): The genesis of language. Cambridge, Mass., 1966, 153–72.   *B. Insam*

Phonism. A phonism is an auditory sensation produced by something other than sound, e.g. an internally produced buzzing or ringing in the ears.   *C.D.F.*

Phonognomics. A term which has won a certain currency since the beginning of the nineteenth century as a designation for a subdivision of the psychology of *expression* (q.v.): i.e. the part played by expression in spoken pronouncements in general, and—in a narrower sense—the part played by speech in expression ("speech analysis", etc.).

Bibliography: Davitz, J. R. (Ed.): The communication of emotional meaning. New York, 1964.   *D.G.*

Photometer. An optical instrument for measuring the intensity of light (luminance or candlepower).

Photometry. A way of determining color by measurement, limited to measuring the light intensity emitted, reflected and transmitted by some object.   *G.Ka.*

Photoreceptors. *Light receptors* of the eye; *cones* (q.v.) are elements of the retina (q.v.) which are sensitive to light and can perceive color; *rods* (q.v.) are insensitive to color and can only register degrees of brightness (appraise grey). The human eye possesses on average 6×10^6 cones (situated foveally and perifoveally) and 120×10^6 rods (none in the fovea, increasing towards the periphery). See *Retina.*   *K.H.P.*

Phrenology. F. J. Gall and G. Spurzheim assumed that mental and emotional characteristics could be found in specific areas of the brain; that they could be detected from the external shape of the skull; and that the development of brain areas indicated the development of corresponding psychological features. See *Localization.*   *H.H.*

Phylogenesis. *History of the evolution of species.* The present forms of organisms on the earth have arisen as a result of a continuous change of hereditary characteristics (see *Mutation*) and division of species from organisms which usually had a simpler structure: e.g. man's ancestors about 400 million years ago were fish-like creatures living in water and breathing through gills.   *H.Sch.*

Physicalism. A term advanced by R. Carnap in 1931 and adopted by the Vienna Circle (Carnap, Neurath, Hempel, etc.: see *Logical positivism; Positivism*). It designates a thesis according to which all the sciences, and especially the human sciences, can and should be expressed in the language of the physical sciences, in order to *unify the sciences* (O. Neurath) by means of a language which is universal, homogeneous and free from any metaphysical implication, and includes only empirically manipulable propositions, i.e. those which designate observable properties of things (see *Protocol sentences*). After having explained the rules of formation and transformation so that any proposition in various sciences can be expressed in them, it is possible (by transforming the qualitative into the quantitative) to *reduce* the total number of disciplines to a small number of deductive systems, and ultimately to one such system. "The application of physicalism to psychology is the logical basis for the method of behaviorism" (Carnap).

Bibliography: Jorgensen, J.: The development of logical empiricism. In: Encyclopedia of unified science, Vol. 2 (9). Chicago, 1951, 77. Morris, C. W.: Logical positivism, pragmatism, and scientific empiricism. Paris, 1937.   *M.-J.B.*

Physiognomic test. A general term for a test which draws conclusions about the underlying personality (q.v.) of some individual with the aid of his physiognomy (q.v.). Such tests are based on the theory that everything in the "psyche" leaves its mark on the *physiognomy*. See *Expression; Graphology; Traits.*   *H.J.A.*

Physiognomy. The human face as a vehicle of expression when at rest (free from mimicry). The nature of the expression is determined by the body's structure and the imprint left by traces of habitual mimic innervation. (See *Habit.*) Physiognomic research (physiognomics as the theory of facial expression) makes use of photographs, sketches (Brunswik), average likenesses, and learning experiments. Results so far have shown that the validity of judgments based on the impression (q.v.) given by the physiognomy is slight (coefficient between 0.00 and 0.50); nevertheless, certain systematic tendencies dependent on various factors appear in judgments.   *F.Ki.*

Physiological psychology. In its most general form, the theory of the relations between physical and mental (psychic) processes, including all attempts to reveal such relationships. It has as its object the scientific investigation of the mechanisms by which the 12^9 nerve cells of the human brain with their almost incalculably numerous links between one another can produce and control the behavioral variety of a living creature, which is also "infinitely" great. Physiological psychology derives from psychology; the questions it deals with rely chiefly on physiological methods for their answers. The basic problem is to elucidate behavior by the analysis of causes, behavior in this case meaning every kind of activity directed to the environment or communication with it for the purpose of exchanging information. Physiological psychology thus requires contributions from almost all subdivisions of physiology (q.v.) and a sophisticated knowledge of it requires thorough familiarity with methods and problems. *Physiopsychology* is a synonym, while *neuropsychology* (q.v.), or *neurophysiology* and *psychophysiology* (q.v.), are concerned with somewhat more narrowly defined fields, although the boundaries are often not absolute. In the English literature there has been a tendency to group "experimental psychology" and physiological psychology together; this approximation should be avoided. Physiological psychology uses methods taken from both "chemical" and "physical" physiology: the action of hormones and behavior changes resulting from them are examples related to chemistry, while the development of micro-electrode techniques has made electrophysiology the most successful branch of the subject in recent years. Hence, although not a separate science, physiological psychology acts as a bridge between psychology and physiology, and is one of the most active and fruitful branches of the two parent disciplines. See *Hormones; Neuroanatomy; Neuropsychology; Psychopharmacology.*

Bibliography: Fearing, F.: Reflex action. A study in the history of physiological psychology. Cambridge, Mass., ²1969. **Glickman, S. E. & Milner, P. M.** (Eds.): The neurological basis of motivation. New York, 1969. **Gross, C. G. & Zeigler, H. P.:** Readings in physiological psychology. New York & London, 1968–9. **Isaacson, R. L.** (Ed.): A primer of physiological psychology. New York, 1971. **Milner, P. M.:** Physiological psychology. New York, 1971. **Stellar, E. & Sprague, J. M.** (Eds): Progress in physiological psychology. New York, 1967 (Vol. 1); 1968 (Vol. 2); 1970 (Vol. 3). **Thompson, R. F.:** Foundations of physiological psychology. New York & London, 1967.

K. H. Plattig

Physiological clock. A mechanism which is still largely unexplained, but is presumably controlled from the brainstem, and is responsible for the primitive estimation of time demonstrated by organisms. It is presumably based on the rhythmic or periodical operations of the organic functions or of metabolism. External environmental influences such as the alternation of light and dark, temperature, dampness, etc., can affect the physiological clock just as much as interventions which accelerate or retard the metabolism.   *H.Ro.*

Physiologism. A term for the tendency of certain research workers to claim that all psychic processes can be explained *physiologically*. See *Psychologism.*   *H.J.A.*

Physiology includes the scientific description of the life processes in cells and organisms, and causal analysis. In research methodology, chemical physiology (biochemistry) is usually separate. *General physiology* deals with the general bases of vital processes; *special physiology* takes a special field such as animal, plant or cell physiology. In general, and for practical (medical and psychological) reasons "physiology" simply means *human physiology*, which is sub-divided into normal and pathological physiology.

Historically, physiology has developed from anatomy, from which the corresponding academic institutions split off. In teaching, largely for anatomical and functional considerations, *vegetative* is distinguished from *animal* physiology. The former deals with the life processes which take place in a comparable manner both in the stationary plant world and the animal world, and embraces "metabolism" and "reproduction", including all auxiliary nutritional and supply mechanisms (blood, heart and circulation, breathing, metabolism and energy supply, nutrition, digestion and elimination—externally by way of the intestines and kidneys/water supply, and the theory of hormones dealing with internal secretion, to which may be added reproduction, and developmental physiology). *Animal physiology*, on the other hand, embraces all the processes by which the animal is distinguished from the stationary plant, that is to say, everything which has to do, directly or indirectly, with locomotion. This comprises all such systems as the muscles, peripheral nerves, sense organs, and includes the physiology of information and regulation, and the central nervous system with the central and peripheral autonomic nervous systems, as well as the "physiology of behavior". Together with psychology and anatomy, physiology makes possible a convergent view of the human organism, which ultimately supplies a total picture within the framework of *biology;* the physiology of behavior is a link between physiology and psychology. See *Behaviorism*.

Bibliography: American Physiological Society (J. Field, Ed.): Handbook of Physiology. Washington, since 1954.   *K. H. Plattig*

Physiology of behavior. The "physiology of behavior" (*Verhaltensphysiologie*) is a form of comparative physiology closely associated with Erich von Holst. It combines a number of biological disciplines (e.g. sensory, movement, nervous and hormonal physiology) with ethology (q.v.) to allow analysis of animal and human behavior in accordance with natural-scientific principles. The essential concern is: "What physiological processes within an organism are responsible for a given behavior pattern and are directly expressed in it?"

(Hassenstein, 1966). Typical procedure consists, first, of the quantitative measurement of certain behavior patterns under systematically "varied test conditions" and, second, of the "logical and mathematical interpretation of measurements obtained", frequently by using models (Holst, 1969). Investigations are so conducted as to leave the organism (or at least the behavior-directive system under examination) as intact as possible. Important basic data are, e.g.: the existence of innate movement sequences (inherited coordinations); the spontaneity of numerous behavior patterns not caused by external stimuli; innate stimulus selection (see *Innate releasing mechanism* = IRM; Lorenz, Tinbergen); and the inherited disposition to diverse forms of evaluation of learnable associations between forms of behavioral readiness and external stimuli (e.g. "following" imprinting, sexual imprinting, learning by experience to complete instinctive behavior sequences; see *Imprinting*). Among the main tasks of the Max Planck Institute in this field (at Seewiesen, Starnberg, Germany) are system analyses in humans and animals: e.g. the reafference principle (q.v.), constancy phenomena in optical perception, relative coordination, analyses of instinct and motivation in uninfluenced experimental animals (or in those undergoing hormone administration or cerebro-physiological stimulation), and analyses of social behavior in animals. The synthesis of behavior-determinative physiological processes in living systems according to the known laws of their association is predominantly of value to the psychology of learning and perception. See *Comparative psychology; Instinct; Animal psychology*.

Bibliography: Eibl-Eibesfeldt, I.: Grundriss der vergleichenden Verhaltensforschung. Munich, ²1969. Id.: Love and hate. London, 1972. Hassenstein, B.: Kybernetik und biologische Forschung. Frankfurt, 1966. Hinde, R. A.: Animal behavior. New York & London, ²1969. Holst, E. von: Zur Verhaltens-physiologie bei Tieren und Menschen. Gesammelte Abhandlungen, Vols. 1, 2. Munich, 1969–70. Id. & Saint Paul, U. von: On the functional organization of drives. Anim. Behav., 1963, *11*, 1–20. **Lorenz, K.:** Evolution and modification of behavior. Chicago & London, 1965. **Id.:** Studies in animal and human behaviour, Vols 1, 2. London, 1970–1. **Tinbergen, N.:** Animal behavior. New York, 1965. **Id.:** The study of instinct. London, ²1969.   *K.E.G.*

Physostigmine (syn. *Physostigmine salicylate; Eserine*). An alkaloid which excites the parasympathetic system by inhibiting cholinesterase (see *Cholinesterase inhibitors*). Obtained from the Calabar bean. Effects last for many hours. Little used in medicine because of its undesirable effects. Most important physiological effects: miosis, promotes peristaltic action, bradycardia, increased blood pressure and perspiration. The psychic effects of physostigmine are obscure. In animal experiments small doses are credited with improved learning. With small doses there is a corresponding desynchronization of electrical activity in the EEG. See *Psychopharmacology of the ANS*.

Bibliography: see *Cholinesterase Inhibitors.*   *W.J.*

Piaget, Jean. B. 9/8/1896 at Neuchâtel, Switzerland. Piaget was awarded his doctorate at the University of Neuchâtel in 1918, for a dissertation on a zoological subject. He then worked with H. Lipps and E. Bleuler, at the Sorbonne, and with A. Binet. From 1921, at the prompting of E. Claparède, he began to teach and research at the Institut J. J. Rousseau in Geneva. In 1925 he was offered a chair of philosophy in Neuchâtel, and in 1929 a professorship of scientific thought at Geneva. In addition, in 1929 Piaget became director of the Bureau International Office de l'Education, and deputy director of the Institut J. J. Rousseau, becoming its co-director (together with T. Bovet and E. Claparède) in 1932. From 1936 he was also lecturing at the university of Lausanne; in 1940 he became director of the psychological laboratory at the University of Geneva, and editor (with A. Rey and

M. Lambercier) of the *Archives de psychologie*. Piaget was then elected the first president of the recently founded Swiss Society for Psychology, and edited (together with Morgenthaler) its journal *Revue Suisse de Psychologie*. In 1955 he founded the "Centre International d'Epistémologie Génétique" in Geneva, with a grant from the Rockefeller Foundation.

Piaget ranks as one of the most important developmental psychologists. His contribution to the subject is unique, both in the originality of theory and method and the variety and scope of his investigations. He is chiefly interested in the theoretical and experimental investigation of the qualitative changes in the cognitive structure occurring in the course of development, and in their description in mathematico-logical terms. As well as studying the development of intelligence, Piaget has worked (genetically) on the following subjects: perception, causality, language, moral judgment, object, space, number, time, quantity, motion, speed, geometry, logic, genetic epistemology, etc. In Piaget's theory of *intelligence* (q.v.), a distinction may be made between a general theory of cognitive function independent of any stages, and a theory of the development of intelligence linked to special stages. In his non-phasic theory of intelligence Piaget tries to derive the genesis of intelligence organically from lower forms of behavior. He starts from the assumption that all behavior, no matter whether it is an external action or an internal one in the form of a thought, represents an adaptation. *Adaptation* he considers to be a *fluid state of balance* between the *assimilation* of the environment to the individual and the *accommodation* of the individual to the environment. Whereas during biological adaptation the transfers are of a material kind, psychic life begins with the appearance of functional interaction. Piaget understands *cognitive development* to be a process of increasing equilibrium between assimilatory and the accommodatory transfers, and an accompanying generalization, differentiation and coordination of the cognitive schemata created by them. These develop from a state which was originally global and which is characterized by an imbalance between the reciprocal transfers (rhythms, e.g. in reflexes and instincts), passing through a limited state of balance ("adjustments", e.g. in perception and sensorimotor intelligence) to a form of organization possessing a mobile balance and characterized by mobility, permanence and stability of cognitive structures ("operational groupings" in logical thought). See *Development*.

In his theory of *the development of intelligence in stages*, Piaget distinguishes four different periods of development relative to the form of organization of cognitive structures, and passing organically into one another: the periods of (*a*) *sensorimotor intelligence*, (*b*) preoperational representation, (*c*) concrete operations and (*d*) formal operations. The period of sensorimotor intelligence embraces the time when development is taking place from the first reflex-like forms of behavior shortly after birth, passing through the first motor habits, the connecting of means and ends, and active experimentation, and finally reaching the stage of spontaneous invention and the internalization of what until then were sensorimotor schemata, at the age of 1½ to 2 years. The most important addition in the following period of *preoperational representation* (2 to 7 years) consists of the acquisition of the symbolic function as the product of an inward imitation of the outward world, and as a requirement for the mastery of speech. Characteristics of preoperational thinking are egocentricity, centralization, immobility, realism, irreversibility, and transductive formation of conclusions and "preconcepts". At about the age of 7, thinking loses its egocentric and unilaterally centered character and, at the stage of "concrete operations" (7–11 years), reaches a mobile state of balance marked by a system of now reversible coordinated transformations. But, whereas

operations at this stage are still bound up with concrete activity, at the last stage of the development of intelligence, the period of *formal operations* (11 to 15 years), they become independent of the concrete object, and the individual acquires the capacity to draw purely formal conclusions from hypothetical assumptions.

Main works: The language and thought of the child. New York & London, 1926 Judgment and reasoning in the child. New York & London, 1928. The child's conception of the world. New York & London, 1929. The child's conception of physical causality. New York & London, 1930. The moral judgment of the child. New York & London, 1932. The psychology of intelligence. New York & London, 1950. Play, dreams and imitation in childhood. New York & London, 1951. The origins of intelligence in children. New York & London, 1952. Jean Piaget. In: Boring, E. G., *et al.* (Eds.): A history of psychology in autobiography, Vol. 4. Worcester, Mass., 1952, 237–56. The child's conception of number. New York & London, 1952. Logic and psychology. Manchester & New York, 1953. The construction of reality in the child. New York & London, 1954. Le développement de la perception de l'enfant à l'adulte, Bull. Psychol., 1954–5, *8*. The child's conception of space. New York & London, 1956 (with B. Inhelder). Les "préinférences" perceptives et leurs relations avec les schèmes sensori-moteurs et opératories. In: Etudes d'épistemologie génétique. Paris, 1958, *6* (with A. Morf). The growth of logical thinking. London & New York, 1958 (with B. Inhelder). The child's conception of geometry. London & New York, 1960 (with A. Szemiska). The early growth of logic in the child. London & New York, 1964 (with B. Inhelder). The mechanisms of perception. London & New York, 1969. Structuralism. New York & London, 1971.

Bibliography: Ausubel, D. P.: A critique of Piaget's theory of the ontogenesis of motor behavior,

J. Genet. Psychol., 1966, *109*, 119–22. **Baldwin, A. L.**: Theories of child development. London, 1967. **Brearley, M. & Hitchfield, E.**: A teacher's guide to reading Piaget. London, 1966. **Flavell, J. H.**: The developmental psychology of Jean Piaget. New York & London, 1963.   *W.W.*

Pia mater. A term for the soft membrane covering the brain.

Pick's disease; Pick's syndrome. See *Dementia, presenile*.

Picrotoxin. A psychopharmaceutical agent with a highly stimulating effect on the central nervous system. Even in very small doses it causes convulsions and poisoning. The mechanism of picrotoxin is probably a blocking of inhibiting substances. It has an opposite effect to GABA, which raises the convulsion threshold. Picrotoxin is a strong circulatory analeptic. In animal experiments, subconvulsive doses of picrotoxin increased retention performance in maze problems.

Bibliography: **McGaugh, J.**: Drug facilitation of memory and learning. In: **Efron, D. H.** (Ed.): Psychopharmacology 1957–1967. Washington, 1968.
                                                    W.J.

Picture arrangement test. Any test in which S. has to put pictures in an order, usually according to "content".   *H.J.A.*

Picture completion test. Any test in which incomplete pictures have to be completed by S. The missing elements can either be inserted or identified.   *H.J.A.*

Picture Frustration Test (*PF Test*). The PF test was developed by L. Rosenzweig as a projective (q.v.) technique (on the basis of frustration-aggression theories) for individual differences in reacting to frustration (q.v.) situations. S's reaction to problem situations

drawn in cartoon form is intended to show whether he tends to reply *extrapunitively*, *impunitively* or *intropunitively* to frustrations. The *validity* of the adults' version is unsatisfactory, whereas that for children is better.

Bibliography: **Rosenzweig, S.**: An outline of frustration theory. In: **Hunt, J. McV.** (Ed.): Personality and the behavior disorders. New York, 1944.   *G.L.*

Picture Story Test. A thematic apperception method published by Symonds (1948), which in its basic theoretical assumptions and material equipment may be compared to the Thematic Apperception Test (q.v.). The test is designed for young people between the ages of twelve and eighteen. There are twenty pictures (of a rather gloomy nature) of juveniles in situations typical of their age. For evaluation the author has proposed counting the frequency of the themes as well as making the quality of the contents a criterion. He gives frequencies resembling norms for the themes. Few estimates of validity and reliability are available.

Bibliography: **Symonds, P. M.**: Symonds' Picture Story Test. New York, 1948.   *D.P.*

Piéron, Henri. B. 18/7/1881 in Paris; d. 6/11/1964 in Paris. Piéron was a French experimental psychologist who began as Janet's assistant in La Salpêtrière. In 1912 he succeeded Binet as Director of the Laboratory for Physiological Psychology at the Sorbonne. From 1923 he held simultaneously a professorial chair for the sensory physiology of the senses at the Collège de France which had been specially created for him. He was one of the founders of the Institut Français d'Anthropologie and of the Institut d'Etude de Travail et d'Orientation Professionnelle. In 1940 he became president of the Association Française pour L'Avancement des Sciences. He received international recognition as president of the International Congress for Psychology held in Paris in 1937, and as president of the International Union for Scientific Psychology. From 1913 until his death he was editor of the journal *L'Année Psychologique*.

Piéron's wide interests and range of research activity were remarkable, included about five hundred publications, and covered four main fields: general experimental psychology, animal psychology, psychophysiology and psychopathology. The physiology of the senses was one of his main interests for more than fifty years. He was also one of the most important representatives of applied psychology (q.v.) in France and a champion of French "psychotechnology", evidence of which is given by the foundation of the Institut d'Etude du Travail and the publication in seven volumes of the *Traité de Psychologie Appliquée* (1949) and *Examens et Docimologie* (1963). Piéron is generally considered to be the initiator of the French "psychologie du comportement", which was akin to American behaviorism in declaring the study of behavior (in contrast to that of the "contents of consciousness") to be the goal of psychology, and seeking to explain matters psychological from physiological foundations without recourse to any process of consciousness.

Main works: Le cerveau et la pensée. Paris, 1923. Psychologie expérimentale. Paris, 1927. Henri Piéron. In: Boring, E. G. *et al.* (Eds.): A history of psychology in autobiography, Vol. 4. Worcester, Mass., 1952, 257–78. Aux sources de la connaissance: la sensation, guide de vie. Paris, ³1955 (Eng. trans. of 1st ed. of 1945: The sensations, their functions, processes and mechanisms. New Haven, Conn., 1952). Les échelles subjectives. Peuvent-elles fournir la base d'une nouvelle loi psychophysique? L'Année Psychologique, 1959, *59*, 1–34. Vocabulaire de la psychologie. Paris, 1957. De l'actinie à l'homme, Vols. 1, 2. Paris, 1958.   *W.W.*

Pigment color mixture. A summative color mixture is obtained with the color op; the subtractive color mixture is produced by mixing colored powders or liquids by double absorption. The color resulting when a yellow pigment is mixed with a blue pigment is green, and not grey as would be expected according to the laws of summative color mixing. The pigments act in this case as a filter: the yellow pigment blocks blue and purple and lets red, green and yellow through; the second pigment only lets blue, purple (which however are kept back by the first pigment) and green through. In consequence the only radiations to pass the two filters are those corresponding to the color green.   *G.Ka.*

Pilocarpine. A cholinergic substance which greatly increases secretion (saliva, tears, sweat, water from the anterior chamber of the eye). Other physiological effects: increased blood pressure, tachycardia. Small doses lead to excitation of the reticular formation, which is blocked by atropine. Arecoline (q.v.) and muscarine (q.v.) are related to pilocarpine.   *W.J.*

Pilot study. A preliminary study carried out before a full or main study (of which it is a simplified form) in order to collect information which will help in, or even provide a decisive basis for, the main study. See *Pretest*.   *H.-J.S.*

Pintner-Patterson Scale of Performance Tests. This test, devised in nineteen-seventeen, was one of the first great attempts to develop standardized series of action tests with general norms. The complete series consisted of fifteen tests of which ten were made into a shortened form. Compared with former tests it is outstanding, especially for the wide range of tasks, the standardization of the procedure and the size of the sample.   *F.G.*

Piston effect. The piston effect is similar to the *tunnel effect* (q.v.) and is an example of a *kinetic screen* effect. Rectangular objects move back and forth in a slit at one end of which is a screen. With appropriate timing, one object going behind the screen followed by a second object coming from behind the screen will appear as a single object moving like a piston. *C.D.F.*

Pituitary dwarfism (syn. *Hypophyseal dwarfism; Nanosomia; Microsomia*). Underdevelopment consisting of a failure of normal growth in stature as a result of an insufficiency or an absence (very seldom isolated) of pituitary growth hormone (see *Somatotropic hormone*) conditioning delayed growth after the second to the third year of life (in untreated cases stature is 100 to 140 cm). Pituitary dwarfism usually occurs together with an inborn disturbance of pituitary gonadotrophin production, which (in addition to inadequate growth or dwarfism) evokes a sexual infantilism (secondary hypogonadism; hyper-, hypogonadism), although there are also pituitary dwarfs whose sexual development is normal. Another combination is pituitary dwarfism with hypothyroidism (secondary hypothyreosis) as a result of simultaneous insufficiency of thyreotropic pituitary hormone.

A distinction is generally made between two main forms of pituitary dwarfism: 1. The tumor form, in which tumors have destroyed the adenohypophysis (or anterior lobe of the hypophysis, q.v.) or may be localized in the hypothalamus (q.v.) = hypothalamo-hypophyseal dwarfism), and is clinically often associated with headaches, disturbed vision, vomiting, disturbances of optical field, etc. 2. The idiopathic form, the causes of which are still largely unknown but are thought to be malformations in the hypothalamo-hypophyseal area; among a small group of individuals it is a family malady. For the most part, boys are affected.

Clinically and psychopathologically, an important feature is the differential diagnostic determination of pituitary dwarfism-with-hypothyroidism as distinct from other forms, and particularly that without hypothyroidism.

Psychologically and psychopathologically, intellectual performance in non-hypothyreotic pituitary dwarfism is normal to above-average; compensatory mechanisms often help adjustment to inadequate stature and associated psycho-social stresses. It is especially burdensome if insufficient gonadotrophin production leads to delayed sexual maturation. Inadequate motivation is a marked feature of hypothyreotic dwarfism.

Prognosis and therapy: Apart from the tumor forms, the outlook is physically good, but somewhat problematic psychically. Combined medical and psychological treatment (hormone therapy, psychotherapy, q.v., and sex counseling) is advisable.

Bibliography: Gardner, L. J. (Ed.): Endocrine and genetic diseases of childhood. Philadelphia, 1967. **Jores, A. & Nowakowski, H.:** Praktische Endokrinologie. Stuttgart, 1964. **Martin, M. M. & Wilkins, L.:** Pituitary dwarfism: Diagnosis and treatment. J. clin. Endocr., 1958, *18*, 679. **Money, J.** (Ed.): Sex research: new developments. Chicago, 1968. **Wilkins, L.:** The diagnosis and treatment of endocrine disorders in childhood and adolescence. Springfield, Ill., 1965. *H. Maisch*

Placebo. Strictly speaking, a substance administered in drug tests as a biologically inactive control which resembles in perceptible qualities (form, taste, smell) the preparation under examination. In a broader sense, biologically *active* substances also are referred to as "placebos" when they have certain side-effects in common with the particular substance, but not with the principal effects under investigation (*active placebo*). Neither the subject nor the experimenter should know that a placebo is being administered (double blind test): this is an essential control in psychopharmacological and pharmacopsychiatric investigations, because the mere fact of administering a preparation usually produces unmistakable suggestive changes in almost all the dependent variables. The degree and mode of placebo action depend on many variables. Where the effects are considerable, it is more difficult to determine the significant action of the preparation.

Bibliography: Haas, H., Fink, H. & Härtfelder, G.: Das Placebo-problem. In: Jucker, E. (Ed.): Fortschritte der Arzneimittelforsch., 1959, *1*, 279–454. Kissel, P. & Barrucand, D.: Placebos et effet placebo en médecine. Paris, 1964. Lienert, G. A.: Die Bedeutung der Suggestion in pharmakopsychologischen Untersuchungen. Zschr. exp. angew. Psychol., 1955, *3*, 418–38. Ross, S., *et al.*: Drugs and placebos: a model design. Psychol. Rep., 1962, *10*, 383–92. Schindel, L.: Placebo und Placebo-Effekte in Klinik und Forschung. Arzneimittel-Forsch., 1967, *17*, 892–918.   *W.J.*

Placebo reactors. Individuals who react to the administration of placebos as to a biologically active substance. According to the test situation and the nature of the dependent variables, twenty to forty percent of subjects in unselected samples react to placebos. It is often supposed that such reactors are characterized by specific personality traits. Correlation studies have shown that, in comparison with non-reactors, placebo reactors register a higher score with respect to the following variables: neuroticism (q.v.), primary suggestibility (q.v.), telling lies, submission, acquiescence. Despite these correlations, there is no proof that there are placebo reactors who will habitually and generally react to a placebo. Different studies suggest that certain individuals react strongly or not at all, according to the situation, and that correlations with personality variables are specific to the situation. See *Traits; Type.*

Bibliography: Fischer, S.: The placebo reactor. Dis. nerv. syst., 1967, *28*, 510–515. Honigfeld, G.: Nonspecific factors in treatment: 1. Review of placebo-reactors and placebo reactions. 1964, *25*, 145–56. Steinbook, R. M. & Jones, M. B.: Suggestibility and the placebo response. J. nerv. ment. Dis., 1965, *140*, 87–91.   *W.J.*

Planned experiments. Experiments constructed according to a factorial experimental plan and evaluated by variance analysis. According to the number of independent variables considered, a distinction is drawn between simple planned experiments (two independent variables) and those which are complex (three or more independent variables).   *G.Mi.*

Plasticity. 1. The *ability* of organisms during development and in concrete situations to *respond adaptively and adequately* to new environmental conditions (in the sense of relative freedom from genetic determination, educability, flexibility, and changeability). **2.** The *capacity of the organism to assume a new* form genetically. **3.** A *thought or intelligence factor* in the sense of the ability to undergo restructuring; embraces agility in thinking, readapting, discovering and deducing the essentials from stable structures. **4.** *Ability of other parts of the organism to act as substitutes* and take over functions where there has been partial failure. **5.** *Influence* which eidetic (q.v.) images may be subject to from antecedent conditions.   *H.H.*

Plateau; plateau formation. See *Learning curves.*

Plateau phase. According to Masters & Johnson (1966) the second of four phases in the sexual reaction cycle, occurring after the excitement phase (q.v.) and before the orgasmic and the resolution phase. Characteristic of both sexes in the plateau phase are muscular tension, increased heart rate and blood pressure; the woman also experiences, e.g., swelling of the breasts, sex flush in the face and the upper part of the body, opening of the labia majora, and swelling and coloring of the labia minora, swelling of the outer third of the vagina, secretion of lubricating fluid; in the man there is a contraction of the anal muscle, a complete erection and an increase in testicular volume, a small increase in the diameter of the penis, and a slight secretion from Cowper's glands.

Bibliography: Masters, W. H. & Johnson, V. E.: Human sexual response. Boston & London, 1966.

J.Fr.

Play. During the child's earliest years most of his time is occupied by play, which may be defined as a joyful bodily or mental activity, which is sufficient to itself and does not seek any ulterior goal (Rüssel, 1959). The child has an urge to express himself and to play: this might be called a "play drive". Among various "theories of play", most support has been given to the ideas of K. Groos (1898), who held that play was a way of practicing important activities and acquiring skills. C. Bühler (1967) distinguishes (by content) between functional, fictional, receptive and constructive play. Developmental psychology puts functional play in the first place. It begins in the first year, and its purpose is the formation and practice of a function or skill (e.g. moving the limbs, arranging and disarranging playthings); it is characterized by a desire to acquire a function or skill.

In the middle of the second year come fictional, "pretend" or acting games. Here the child gives himself or the thing he is playing with a rôle (q.v.), and the basis of the game is a fantasy (feeding the doll and putting it to bed). Imitation (q.v.) of things seen and of one's own experiences is basic to this play form. At about the same time come the *receptive* games (looking at pictures, listening to fairy stories, etc.). The constructive games (building with bricks, drawing, playing with sand or clay) also occur in the second year. At nursery-school age, a child is ready for *games with rules.* Their distinguishing characteristic is that they are bound by strict rules ("it", "hide and seek", and ball games). Play reaches a high point in about the seventh year, when

various sorts of games go through phases of popularity at different times.

Bibliography: Beach, F. A.: Current concepts of play in animals. Am. Nat., 1945, *79*, 523–41. **Berlyne, D. E.:** Conflict, arousal and curiosity. New York, 1960. **Bühler, C.:** From birth to maturity. London, 1935. **Id.:** Kindheit und Jugend. Göttingen, 1967. **Devore, I.** (Ed.): Primate behavior. New York, 1965. **Lehmann, H. C. & Witty, P. A.:** The psychology of play activities. Cranbury, N. J., 1927. **Millar, S.:** The psychology of play. Harmondsworth & New York, 1968. **O'Connor, N. & Franks, C. M.:** Childhood upbringing and other environmental factors. In: **Eysenck, H. J.** (Ed.): Handbook of abnormal psychology. London, ²1971. **Piaget, J.:** Play, dreams and imitation in childhood. New York & London, 1951. **Rüssel, A.:** Spiel und Arbeit in der menschlichen Entwicklung. In: **Thomae, H.** (Ed.): Handbuch der Psychologie, Vol. 3. Göttingen, ²1959, 502 ff. **Schlosberg, H.:** The concept of play. Psychol. Rev., 1947, *54*, 229–31.

M.Sa.

Playing dead. An innate behavior pattern which serves to mislead a predator. Young animals—predominantly birds leaving the nest and mammals—cease movement when danger threatens or their parents give a warning call, and use their coloring to "merge" optically with the background so that the predator can fixate them only with difficulty. Beetles draw their legs in when disturbed, and fall to the ground, where they can scarcely be detected.

V.P.

Pleasure. Enjoyment; gratification. The positive affect associated with fulfilment of needs and desires, and the attainment of goals.

G.D.W.

Pleasure principle. According to Freud, the "pleasure principle" is opposed to the "reality principle" (q.v.); it controls the "primary psychic processes", which include primitive need states and associated images said to dominate in dream, in fantasy, in psychotic conditions, in a more adequately controlled form in art, in the empathic understanding of others, and even in religious experience or mass behavior. If the reality principle predominates, e.g. in a state of self-absorption, "secondary psychic processes", the ego (q.v.) and the actual environment of the individual are more to the fore.

Bibliography: Freud, S.: Beyond the pleasure principle. London, ²1959.   *W.T.*

Plethoric type. A term used by the Italian de Giovanni in 1877 for a person with a broad, plump physique.   *W.Se.*

Plethysmograph. An instrument for recording changes in volume of some part of the body (usually due to variations in blood supply); e.g. *penile plethysmograph:* for measuring penis volume, which is sometimes used as an indicator of sexual arousal.   *G.D.W.*

Plexus. A term in neuroanatomy (q.v.) for macroscopic or microscopic networks of nerve pathways or fibers. The brachial plexus is formed from the nerves C5–T1 of the spinal cord. From this emerge the nerves for the arm and the shoulder. The lumbosacral plexus contains the nerve fibers for the pelvis and the lower limbs. There are many other networks in the autonomic nervous system. The arteries are surrounded by delicate networks of the sympathetic system (q.v.). In the wall of the gastro-intestinal canal there are the intramural plexuses of the autonomic nervous system.
                                                            G.A.

Pneumatic chamber. Used in experiments requiring different atmospheric pressures (high-, low-pressure chamber); particularly important for research in occupational psychology and medicine, but used also for special studies of aptitude and in training courses (e.g. astronauts, pilots, divers, submarine crews).
                                                        G.R.W.M.

Pneumograph. An instrument for recording respiration.

Poetzl's phenomenon. Poetzl observed that briefly presented perceptual material which does not appear in the conscious memory may nevertheless later become part of dream content.   *C.D.F.*

Poggendorff illusion. One of the geometric illusions. The diagonal line is continuous, but appears bent as it passes behind the uprights.

                                                            C.D.F.

Point-biserial correlation. A parametric procedure to determine the extent of the correlation between a quantitive, normally distributed (i.e. continuous) variable and a dichotomous or alternative feature. (See *Correlational techniques.*)   *G.Mi.*

Point Scale of Performance Tests. A non-verbal series (consisting of eight different tests) by Arthur (1930). Used for assessing practical and concrete intelligence (q.v.) between the ages of five and sixteen years.

Bibliography: Arthur, G.: Point Scale of Performance Tests. New York, 1930.   *H.J.A.*

Poisson distribution. A highly asymmetrical distribution: the random distribution of very rare events. The Poisson distribution is a marginal case of the binomial distribution (q.v.): it occurs when N is high and when the elementary probability approximates to zero.
                                                            G.Mi.

Polarity. A relationship between features or traits which are antithetical pairs.   *K.P.*

Polarity profile. See *Semantic differential.*

Police psychology. The purpose of police psychology in the broad sense is to advise the police in their practical work. This counseling (e.g. in regard to riot control) draws upon most branches of psychology, but particularly criminal and social psychology. In the narrower sense, police psychology is concerned with the assessment of policemen, their character, attitudes (q.v.) and relationships, and with selection techniques. At present a great deal of research into police psychology is being done in West Germany. The following are only three of a number of completed Anglo-American studies: Marshall (1966) established that, by comparison with law and social welfare students, police recruits had a statistically significant more unyielding, i.e. harsher, attitude to punishment (q.v.), i.e. they more often advocated harsher punishment for criminals. It was not established whether this fiercer attitude was the result of a process of self-selection in those choosing a police career, selection by the authorities, or adaptation to a role (q.v.). Police recruits showed *greater rigidity*, one of the principal characteristics of the authoritarian personality (q.v.). Of the 282 policemen studied by Skolnick (1967), approximately 70% were concerned about their social standing, 66% considered themselves middle class, and 51% regarded it as "most important" to own a house. 250 out of 700 policemen (35%) gave other policemen as their friends. Several American criminologists already describe this remarkable social phenomenon as a "sub-culture". Most policemen believe they are able to distinguish between guilt and innocence, and do not attach much weight to the findings of the court. Cicourel (1968) showed that lay theories of the causes of delinquency form the basis of judgments made by the police. The police "know what they know", and the problem of legal proof does not arise for them in their daily routine. The North

American police favor upper-class delinquent youths from "important families". Middle-class delinquent youths were not seen as actually dangerous to authority; they merely had "psychological problems". The lower-class youth, on the other hand, comes up against the full force of "law and order", particularly if he denies his delinquent behavior and belongs to a racial minority. Nevertheless, one may doubt whether so small a survey is representative of the whole US police force. The results of pertinent West German researches are still awaited. See *Abnormal psychology; Criminality; Forensic psychology; Guilt; Mental defect; Psychopathy; Social psychology.*

Bibliography: Cicourel, A. V.: The social organization of juvenile justice. New York & London, 1968. **Marshall, J.:** Law and psychology in conflict. Indianapolis & New York, 1966. **Skolnick, J. H.:** Justice without trial. Law enforcement in democratic society. New York & London, 1967. **The President's Commission on Law Enforcement and Administration of Justice:** Task force report: the police. Washington, D.C., 1967.   *H. J. Schneider*

Poliomyelitis (*Infantile paralysis*). An inflammatory disease of the grey substance of the spinal cord (anterior horns), its extension, and possibly also of the brain; it is caused by a virus which occurs in three forms. As a result the Nissl bodies in the plasma of the nerve cells are destroyed. The pathological symptoms, chiefly muscular paralysis, are only partly reversible, so that frequently there is permanent paralysis of single muscles or groups of muscles, and atrophy from non-use. This disease appears sporadically, but it can assume epidemic proportions—usually in the summer months; it is carried in contaminated water and enters the blood stream through the intestines. There is also an abortive form, i.e. one in which there are no paralytic symptoms. Since oral vaccination with non-virulent live viruses was introduced, the disease has practically disappeared.   *E.D.*

Political psychology. The study of the *personal aspect of political processes*. Various methods are used. The subject comprises: 1. Research into *techniques:* emotional means of exerting influence, forms of indoctrination, and rules for civic cognitive learning processes and socialization methods as well as processes for reaching political decisions. These techniques are governed by success criteria and their results have only a limited predictability. 2. Understanding given *uniformities* of political behavior which occur in spite of, or because of, motivational homogeneity and heterogeneity: e.g. investigations of election and electoral behavior. 3. Interpretations, especially neopsychoanalytical, monobiographical or typological aspects of political élites, basic personalities or exponents of political systems. For the most part these take as their starting point research into antidemocratic syndromes (see *Authoritarian personality*). 4. Enlightenment: i.e. making known the aspects mentioned under 1 to 4 to participants in political processes. 5. Finally, as an applied science, political psychology considers aids to orientation in the instrumental political use of knowledge. All this can be handled as by an objectively unprejudiced or a politically committed researcher.

Political psychology in its present form derives from cultural-anthropological origins. In early "culture-and-personality research", interpretations of self-perpetuating and stabilizing aspects of a culture predominated. The effect of primary institutions (children's education) is considered in neo-psychoanalysis as an irreversible form of imprinting. The corresponding social structure satisfies social expectations and fears contained in this education (see *Socialization*); it corresponds to the sociocultural needs and social perspectives of the typical personality belonging to these institutions. Between the social institutions and members—with regard to their *basic personality structure* but not to their *biographical development*—there exists a kind of "prestabilized

harmony". This *stabilization hypothesis*—which is not accepted by all researchers into culture and personality—served as a starting-point for further empirical lines of research.

The object of investigation was the personality type which supports or produces fascist systems—the "authoritarian personality". This led on to research into terrorism, which may be extended to include certain aspects of group dynamics, and studies the findings of the psychology of mass observation and certain manipulative forms of language and communication (Baeyer-Katte, 1971).

Research into the political personality must begin with the *power-hungry figure* seen as a type exhibiting the exaggerated dynamic urge that so interested Alfred Adler (q.v.). But Lasswell (1950) has already begun to see interpersonal patterns of behavior (forms of influence) in which power is wielded and accepted, as typical examples of situations where power has been seized against a background of certain general sociocultural conditions.

The interpretation put forward by totalitarian systems, according to which a united political will and a consenting public opinion act in compliance with the behavioral pattern of the whole population, at first gave rise to the impression that the monolithic state had come into being voluntarily. But the real motive seemed to be less the prevailing ideology—whether with a scientific gloss or an emotional appeal—than a need for obedience and conformity (q.v.). The supposition that the family system (Horkheimer, 1936) supplied the culture-specific conditions was examined empirically in the investigations of authoritarianism (q.v.), rigidity and fascism by the Californian School and the political psychology of Eysenck (1954). The methods used were taken from the general development of empirical psychology. The pioneering work of T. W. Adorno, E. Frenkel-Brunswik, J. D. Levinson and R. N. Sandford (*The Authoritarian Personality*. New York, 1950) was based on the results of research into prejudice (Murphy & Likert, 1938) on the one hand and Fromm's hypotheses (1941) on the other. Apart from many studies in the same mold, critics have examined the method of scaling (q.v.), the special questionnaire technique and a lack of tolerance concerning the ambiguities and contradictions (a scale criterion of the F scale) to be found in the last analysis in the investigators themselves (Christie & Jahoda, 1954; Bass, 1955; K. Eyferth, 1963). The last major survey of the follow-up research pertaining to the Adorno *et al.* model was undertaken by Kirscht & Dillehay (1967). The authoritarian syndrome required a scientific basis for a typology valid for the Nazi era; it partly maintained its position after some corrections had been made (Chapman & Campbell, 1957). Roghmann (1966) provides a comprehensive critical study of these investigations.

Investigations which take the subject further follow on the one hand the Dogmatism Scale (Rokeach, 1948; 1960), on the other, the criteria, elaborated by H. J. Eysenck, of toughmindedness and tendermindedness as well as radicalism versus conservatism. Eysenck points especially to the fact that Fascists and Communists show the same authoritarian values. It is precisely this result which indicates the problems inherent in such definitions of political matters obtained from behavioral patterns. It is surely evident that, under a Fascist regime, supporters of the governing party and the Communist party will not behave alike but (politically) quite differently. The political essence of political behavior has therefore to be established functionally—in agreement or disagreement with the given social order.

If one looks back and uses the concepts of systematic theories which have in the meantime become widespread in political psychology, it may be said that three basic forms of political behavior have been dealt with: behavioral patterns which are stabilizing, conducive to change, and directed against the system (dysfunctional). Of course, like all such simplifications, this division does some violence to the whole picture. But it does show a course of development which can be recognized and substantiated in broad outline (Easton, 1965).

Change conforming to the system—the possibility of internal reform and historical development—is the way in which complicated social systems work. In the nineteen sixties Parsons (1964) and his collaborators developed the concepts which enable political psychology to group its partial findings as a plan of research into political behavior. The key concept of Parsons in this respect is the definition of the evolutionary universals in a society. It states that social systems have to be regarded as living systems: they are always developing new structures and complexes of structures by means of which they can better "adapt" to the challenge of their political environment—that is to say, deal more actively with them and assert themselves by appropriate systematic processes. *Democracy* (q.v.) is such an "invention" of political culture. Since Parsons' concept is linked to the idea of historical development, he considers democracy (representative democracy based on the right to vote) as a social universal. In different ways, but with the same function (the optimization of the political process), this discovery is made in its own time in every social order or taken over by cultural diffusion. Among other things, this means that the personal system of the democrat must correspond to the structural system of democracy. The transformation is effected by participation. The agencies of socialization possessed by democracy as a system of opinions and values are not just parents, but the whole of society without any time limit. The "political structure" of a society thus establishes the political behavior appropriate to it, and this behavior for its part supports the culture. It is a case of self-regulating processes whose political aspect is represented by institutionalized "political behavior", and not a case of an intervening control procedure outside the regular processes. Political behavior may thus be quantified, e.g. in the use of the vote, party membership, the assumption of political elective offices and the measurable state of information; in numerous studies it has been taken as evidence for the state of democratization (Kaase, 1971). Lazarsfeld, Berelson & Gaudet (1948) and Berelson, Lazarsfeld & McPhee (1954), in their studies of elections, indicate methods which can be useful, on the one hand, in election psychology and, on the other, in the connection there between elections and electoral behavior (Schenck & Wildenmann, 1963). Simultaneously, with the breakthrough in small-group research initiated by Homans (1950), the significance of the pioneer study by Levin & Lippitt (1938) increases inasmuch as it sees leadership styles as political control processes for solving problems in small groups. This approach, which is taken further by Verba (1961), lays proper emphasis on the aspect of a political control system—in addition to the studies of self-regulation which were chiefly prevalent in the school of civic cultural research. Of course, control procedures are also found in relation to political processes, but by no means only, in group leadership behavior. They always happen when there is input into the political process (Deutsch, 1969). The theoretical foundation for civic culture research in which political behavior thus receives the value of a resolution to participate after a prepolitical stage of socialization, is given by Almond in his article "Comparative political systems" (1956). *Political behavior* is not exclusively the *behavior of politicians* but includes the behavioral patterns of all men as protagonists inside the working rules of democracy. By comparing systems it is hoped to understand the requirements for participation—or, on the other hand, the conditions for apathy and loss of interest in

politics. The theory that political rôles should be learnt through practice is prominent (Allport, 1945). But this is soon joined by extensive concepts based on learning theory (q.v.) and by the concept of internalization, which goes back to neo-psychoanalysis and is under modification by T. Parsons. Almond & Verba (1963) have found in empirical studies, and by comparison of cultures, a positive correlation between the standard of scholastic education, political knowledge and political participation. The conclusion was therefore quickly drawn that further scholastic education also advances democratization, especially in underdeveloped countries (see Pye, 1963). The move "into politics", that is, the crossing of a threshold by which social behavior becomes political, appears at the outset as a form of awareness of subjective competence with its roots in family participation patterns: in the assumption of responsibility in non-political social affairs. Nevertheless, a large number of studies yielded widely varying results regarding the efficiency of the individual factors in *education for citizenship*. Dennis compiled a comprehensive bibliography for the Council of Civic Education (1968). Variables such as great political interest shown by parents (Converse, 1954), the dominance of the mother or the father (who may also belong to two different parties), did reveal significant relationships, but a detailed interpretation reveals complex, multi-causal possibilities. The position is the same concerning the influence of the type of school. There is disagreement not only on the age at which instruction in politics is given (Adelson & O'Neil, 1966). The comprehensive investigations of Langton & Jennings (1968), taking eight variables into account, show only very slight relations between civics taught in school, political orientation and commitment. As long as political socialization is measured by external participation criteria, the results will always remain bogged down in formal correlation analysis. These lines are followed, too, by the two major German studies

(Masermas *et al.*, 1967; Jaide, 1970). The institutionalized agencies of socialization are not even a guarantee of loyalty to democracy (Langton, 1969). Criticism of the hypothesis of automatic processes of political socialization changes the problem of stability more and more into one of equilibrium, or into the observation of processes seeking some balance within social adaptation and integration. As early as 1969, Hyman (who offers a summary of the empirical results of political socialization as they were in 1959) criticized the relative lack of results in all quantitative assessments. This points to a difference between the unreflecting behavior of political participation, and critically reflective control behavior in the presence of this system. Political behavior of this second, higher order would consist in counter-control endeavors (as Ebert, 1970, for example, shows), or in counter-control against counter-control, i.e. in those political forms of behavior which try to make dysfunctional movements functional. Only investigations of the strategies necessary for this and the requisite degree of cognitive separation of rôles within the performance of political rôles would allow political psychology to come into its own (Johnson, 1971). Here it has much in common with the questions currently posed in conflict and peace research: namely, the effects of behavior patterns which conform or are hostile to the system, and accord systems based on threats (Boulding, 1967) or on confidence (Lukmann, 1968), and the effects of non-systematic rôle innovations.

A collection of important contributions to the sociological aspects of political behavior is offered by Allardt & Rokkan (1970). Three series appearing periodically deal with special questions in the field: the *Yearbook of Political Behavior Research* edited by H. Eulau (from 1961), *Politische Psychologie* (from 1963, containing a comprehensive subject catalog, by W. Jacobsen). The most recent effort is *Studies in Behavioral Political Science*, edited by Presthus (from 1969).

Bibliography: Adelson, J. & O'Neil, R.: The growth of political ideas in adolescence: The sense of community. J. of Pers. and Soc. Psychol., 1966, *4*, 295–306. Adorno, T. W., et al.: The authoritarian personality. New York, 1950. Allardt, E. & Rokkan, S.: Mass politics. Studies in political sociology. New York, 1970. Allport, G. W.: The psychology of participation. Psychol. Rev., 1945, *53*, 117–32. Almond, G. A.: Comparative political systems. J. of Politics, 1956, *18*, 391–409. Id. & S. Verba: The civic culture. Political attitudes and democracy in five nations. Princeton, 1963. Auwin, K., Baeyer-Katte, W. v., Jacobsen, W., Jaide, W. & Wiesbrock, H. (Eds.): Politische Psychologie. Eine Schriftenreihe, Vols. 1–8. Frankfurt, 1963–69. Baeyer-Katte, W. v.: Terror. In: Soviet system and democratic society. New York & London, 1972 (in press). Berelson, B. R., Lazarsfeld, P. F. & McPhee, W. N.: Voting. Chicago, 1954. Boulding, K.: Die Parameter der Politik. Atomzeitalter, 1967, *7/8*, 362–74. Chapman, L. J. & Campbell, D. T.: Response set in the F-scale. J. abn. soc. Psychol., 1957, *55*. Christie, R. & Jahoda, M. (Eds.): Studies in the scope and method of "The Authoritarian Personality". Glencoe, Ill., 1954. Coleman, J. S. (Ed.): Education and political development. Princeton, 1965. Converse, E. T.: The nature of belief systems in mass publics. In: Apter, D. (Ed.): Ideology and discontent. New York, 1964. Dennis, J.: Major problems of political socialisation. Midwest J. of Political Science 1968, *12*, 85–114. Deutsch, K. W.: Politische Kybernetik. Modelle und Perspektiven. Freiburg i.Br., 1969. Easton, D.: A systems analysis of political life. New York, 1965. Ebert, T.: Gewaltfreier Aufstand – Alternative zum Bürgerkrieg. Frankfurt, 1970. Eyferth, K.: Typologische Aspekte des Problems der autoritären Persönlichkeit. In: Autoritarismus – Nationalismus – ein deutsches Problem? Pol. Psychol., Frankfurt, 1963, 67–74. Eysenck, H. J.: The psychology of politics. London, 1954. Fromm, E.: Escape from freedom. New York, 1941. Habermas, J., *et al.*: Student und Politik. Eine soziologische Untersuchung zum politischen Bewusstsein Frankfurter Studenten. Neuwied, ²1967. Homans, G.: The human group. New York, 1950. Horkheimer, M. (Ed.): Studien über Autorität und Familie. Paris, 1936. Hyman, H. H.: Political socialization. A study in the psychol. of political behavior. New York, 1969. Jaide, W.: Jugend und Demokratie. Politische Einstellung der westdeutschen Jugend. Munich, 1970. Kaase, M.: Demokratische Einstellung in der BRD. Sozialwiss. Jahrbuch für Politik, 1971, *II*, 119–316. Kirscht, J. P. & Dillehay, R. C.: Dimensions of authoritarianism: a view of research and theory. Lexington, 1967. Langton, K. P. & Jennings, M. K.: Formal environment: The school. In: Langton, K. P. (Ed.): Political socialization. New York, 1969. Lasswell, H. D. & Kaplan, A.: Power and society. A framework of political inquiry. New Haven, 1950. Lasswell, H.D.: Power and personality, New York, 1946. Lazarsfeld, P. F., Berelson, B. R. & Gandet, H.: The people's choice. New York, 1948. Lewin, K. & Lippitt, R.: An experimental approach to the study of democracy and aristocracy: A preliminary note. Sociometry, 1938, *1*, 292–300. Lipset, S. M.: Political men. New York, 1960. Luhmann, N.: Vertrauen: ein Mechanismus der Reduktion sozialer Komplexität. Stuttgart, 1968. Milbrath, L. W.: Political participation. Chicago, 1965. Murphy, G. & Likert, R.: Public opinions and the individual. New York, 1938. Parsons, T.: Evolutionary universals in society. American sociological Rev., 1964, *29*, 339–57. Id.: The political aspect of social structure and process. In: Easton, D. (Ed.): Varieties of political theory. Englewood Cliffs, 1966. Pye, L. W. (Ed.): Communications and political development. Princeton, 1963. Roghmann, K.: Dogmatismus und Autoritarismus. Kritik der theoretischen Ansätze und Ergebnisse dreier westdeutscher Untersuchungen. Kölner Beiträge, Vol. 1, 1966; Rokeach, M.: Generalized mental rigidity as a factor in ethnocentrism. J. of Abn. and Soc. Psychol., 1948, *43*, 299–78. Id.: The open and closed mind. New York, 1960. Scheuch, E. K. & Wildenmann, R.: Zur Soziologie der Wahl. Cologne, 1963. Verba, S.: Small groups and political behavior: A study of leadership. Princeton, 1961.

W. von Baeyer-Katte

Pollution. Defilement. Non-scientifically used to refer to the discharge of semen other than during sexual intercourse. See *Masturbation*.

G.D.W.

Poltergeist. (From German, meaning "noisy spirit"). Disturbance characterized by bizarre physical effects of assumed paranormal origin suggesting mischievous or destructive intent. As opposed to a haunt (q.v.), the poltergeist phenomenon seems to depend upon the presence of a particular individual = the "poltergeist focus", usually, but not always, a child or adolescent. W. G. Roll has introduced the more neutral expression RSPK (= recurrent spontaneous psychokinesis). See *Psychokinesis*.

J.B.

Polyandry. Union of one woman with several men. It was found particularly in Ceylon and among Indian mountain tribes, but also among American Indians, where the husbands held in common had as a rule to be brothers.

W.Sch.

Polygamy. Union in marriage of more than two partners (see *Monogamy*); in the past it was much more widespread as polygyny (q.v.) than as polyandry (q.v.).

W.Sch.

Polygraph. A multipoint recorder. Used in psychology, psychophysiology (q.v.) and medicine for the simultaneous recording of several signals. According to the requirements of the task, the polygraph provides a record of: (*a*) *biosignals*, i.e. EEG (q.v.), ECG (q.v.), cardiac activity, arterial blood pressure, breathing, and gas metabolism, skin temperature and skin resistance (q.v.), body movements, electromyograms, etc.; (*b*) *stimulus values*, i.e. frequency and intensity of motor and logomotor behavioral patterns, test performances, etc.; (*c*) *general experimental conditions*, i.e. time intervals, air conditioning, acoustic level, etc. Polygraphs are widely used in medicine as electrocardiographs and electroencephalographs, in criminology as lie detectors (q.v.), and in psychophysiology for recording the physiological components of changes in *arousal* (q.v.), occurring, e.g. during periods of emotion, stress (q.v.), sleep (q.v.) and dream (q.v.).

By contrast with the old smoked and paper kymographs, or simple "event" recorders, polygraphs today are complicated electronic devices with possibly as many as thirty pre-amplifiers and monitoring systems. Each of the machines of up to sixteen final amplifiers drives a writing system whose pointer visualizes the signal pattern on a recording tape by the usual carbon paper method, or by a thermal or ink recording method. Usually there are several feed rates ranging from about 0.01 to 250 mm per second. Signals with a maximum frequency of about 200 c/s can be recorded with sufficient accuracy in this way. A polygraph is equipped with electrodes, probes and transducers for recording primary signals. The technical characteristics of these recorders and the amplifiers and writing systems have a specific influence on the quality of the signal recording.

Since the evaluation of recordings is usually very tedious, automatic data processing of bio-signals has been introduced in recent years. See *Psychophysics*.

Bibliography: Brown, C. C. (Ed.): Methods in psychophysiology. Baltimore, 1967. **Mackenzie, J.:** The ink polygraph. British Med. J., 1908, *1*, 1411. **Schönpflug, W.** (Ed.): Methoden der Aktivierungs-forschung. Berne, 1969. **Venables, P. H. & Martin, I.** (Eds): A manual of psychophysiological methods. Amsterdam, 1967.   *J.F.*

Polygyny. Union, resembling marriage, of one man with several women; widespread in Africa, Asia and Australia among primitive peoples and in highly civilized societies. But there is no justification for concluding purely on the basis of this ethnological material that some genetically determined "polygamous factor" exists in man (the predominance of monogamy has been established).   *W.Sch.*

Polyopia. Multiple vision, monocular diplopia. Several images of an object are seen with one eye, e.g. where there is astigmatism (q.v.).
                                                  R.R.

Polymorphous perversity. A psychoanalytic concept referring to the wide range of stimuli and activities which have erotic value to the infant, and serve as sexual outlets, but which would be considered perversions in adulthood. See *Perversion*.   *G.D.W.*

Pons. A part of the occipital brain containing in part or completely the nuclei (q.v.) of the fifth, sixth, seventh, and eighth cerebral nerves. The fibers of the important pyramidal tract, into which the action potentials for voluntary movement are led, run through the pons.

Bibliography: Sidmann, R. L., Sidmann, M. & Arnold, G.: Neuroanatomy. Ein Lehrbuch in program-mierter Form, Vol. 1. Berlin & New York, 1971.
                                                  G.A.

Ponzo's illusion. One of the geometric illusions. The upper horizontal line appears longer than the lower although they are objectively equal. A common explanation of this illusion is that the two diagonals are seen as receding parallel lines and hence size *constancy* (q.v.) is mis-applied to the two horizontal lines, the upper being seen as further away.

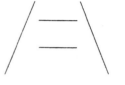

                                                  C.D.F.

Pooling. Term for combining values into classes when establishing frequency distribu-tions (q.v.). Chance fluctuations are usually evened out by pooling. In variance analysis (q.v.) pooling is the combination of variance components the equality of which has been statistically verified.   *G.Mi.*

Population. 1. The totality or number of all the possible realizations of a random variable. Characteristic statistical values of the popula-tion are known as parameters (q.v.); they are quite exact. According to the number of possible realizations, populations can be finite or infinite in extent.   *G.Mi.*

2. In statistics "population" denotes a finite or infinite number of individuals (events). The area to which population applies can be laid down at will by defining its elements. For example, all the people, all the motorists, all the houses (in a town for example) constitute the population of the people, the motorists or the houses of a town.

A typical problem of inferential statistics is to give an optimal estimation of the values of a population distribution (parameter) from the values of a sample (q.v.) of that population. See *Statistics*.   *W.H.B.*

Poriomania. A desire to wander which occurs without any motivation and ranges from aimlessly running away and ranging about to traveling about in a manner outwardly inconspicuous and wholly adapted to a given situation. The crucial factor is the stressful cause responsible for setting off.   *A.Hi.*

Pornography. Originally the depiction of harlotry; now generalized to the expression of lewdness and obscenity of any kind, particularly through books, post-cards, films, etc. Both "obscenity" and "pornography" are to a large extent socially (and usually also legally) defined, for what violates the accepted conventions of one time and place is often regarded as completely innocuous in another.

Bibliography: Abelson, H. *et al.*: Public attitudes toward and experience with erotic materials. Technical reports of the Commission on Obscenity and Pornography (C.O.P.), Vol. 6. Washington, 1970. Amoroso, D. M. *et al.*: An investigation of behavioral, psychological and physiological reactions to pornographic stimuli. C.O.P., Vol. 6, Washington, 1970. Bender, P.: The definition of "obscene" under existing law. C.O.P., Vol. 2. Washington, 1970. Ben-Veniste, R.: Pornography and sex crime: the Danish experience. C.O.P., Vol. 7. Washington, 1970. Berger, A. S. *et al.*: Pornography: high school and college years. C.O.P., Vol. 9. Washington, 1970. Burgess, A.: What is pornography? in: Hughes, D. A. (Ed.): Perspectives on pornography. New York, 1970. Byrne, D. & Lamberth, J.: The effect of erotic stimuli on sex arousal evaluative responses, and subsequent behavior. C.O.P., Vol. 8. Washington, 1970. Cairns, R. B.: Psychological assumptions in sex censorship. C.O.P., Vol. 1. Washington, 1970. Clor, H.:

Obscenity and public morality. Chicago, 1969. Eliasberg, W. G. & Stuart, I. R.: Authoritarian personality and the obscenity threshold. J. soc. psychol., 1961, *55*, 143–51. Goldstein, M. J. *et al.*: Exposure to pornography and sexual behavior in deviant and normal groups. C.O.P., Vol. 7. Washington, 1970. Howard, J. L. *et al.*: Effects of exposure to pornography. C.O.P., Vol. 8. Washington, 1970. Money, J.: The positive and constructive approach to pornography in general sex education, in the home and in sexological counseling. C.O.P., Vol. 10. Washington, 1970.   *G.D.W.*

Porteus Labyrinth Test (syn. *Porteus Maze*). The testee has to find his way out of different labyrinths graded in order of difficulty. Used as a battery test with children to test intelligence and development, and also in diagnostics when there is no recourse to speech.

Bibliography: Porteus, S.: The Porteus Maze Test and intelligence. Palo Alto, 1950.   *V.H.S.*

Positionality. The central concept of the recent theory of expression (see *Expression*) for which Frijda (1953) and Kirchhoff (1957) are chiefly responsible. Frijda defines positionality as "that structure of relations which a particular person establishes or seeks to establish at any given time with his environment. The activity structure in which and with which these relations are achieved is indivisibly linked with positionality" (1965). Kirchhoff defines the positionality of a living thing as "the (psychophysically neutral) manner in which that being exists at any moment; this manner is defined with varying degrees of completeness and differentiation for fellow beings through the phenomenality of the subject and for the latter through his own experience" (1957). According to Kirchhoff, *pathognomic* expression is "positionality in its phenomenality". Proceeding from Kirchhoff's concept of positionality, Holzkamp proposes that Frijda's concept should be used to denote the *nature of an individual's relations* (1965).

Bibliography: Frijda, N. H.: The understanding of facial expression of emotion. Acta Psychol., *9*, 1953. **Id.**: Mimik und Pantomimik. In: **Kirchhoff, R.** (Ed.): Handbuch der Psychol., Vol. 5. Göttingen, 1965. **Holzkamp, K.**: Zur Geschichte und Systematik der Ausdruckstheorie. In: **Kirchhoff, R.** (Ed.): Handbuch der Psychol., Vol. 5. Göttingen, 1965. **Kirchhoff, R.**: Allgemeine Ausdruckslehre. Göttingen, 1957.

J.Mi.

Positivism. In the narrower sense, positivism is the doctrine associated with A. Comte (1798–1857), according to which one knows only facts, the validity of this knowledge being assured by experimental science. This notion characterizes the most advanced "state" in the history of human societies (the "positive state"). In the wider sense, positivism is any theory of knowledge (epistemology; cognition theory, q.v.) which takes into account only given data determined by a particular science, and excludes the possibility of any metaphysical apprehension of the profound nature of things (J. S. Mill, H. Spencer). *Logical positivism* (q.v.) (neo-positivism, logical empiricism) sees knowledge as consisting of "protocol sentences" (q.v.) derived from the observation of facts, and of a proficiently shaped formal and tautological language which coordinates these facts. See *Physicalism; Behaviorism.*   *M.-J.B.*

Posodynics. A central concept in the characterology of Bahnsen (1867). A man's capacity for enduring pain (q.v.). Two types are distinguished: the *eucolic* with a great capacity for suffering, and the *dyscolic* who can scarcely endure any pain.   *P.S.*

Postdormitium. The period of time before waking up, which may be characterized by vivid imagery.   *W.Sch.*

Posthypnotic. After hypnosis (q.v.); pertaining to phenomena which last after the subject has awakened from hypnosis or which only begin to take effect then: for example, the carrying out of "posthypnotic instructions".

H.-N.G.

Posthypnotic amnesia. See *Hypnosis.*

Posthypnotic state. Some suggestion given during hypnosis (q.v.) is carried out after the hypnotic state, i.e. in the posthypnotic state. The time elapsing between the end of the hypnosis and the performance of the suggested action can also be fixed during hypnosis by suggestion. During this time no specific physiological and emotional changes can be observed in subjects. Shortly before the suggestion is put into effect, individuals have a vague notion that they must do something important. The desired action takes place automatically. The reality of the suggestion is correspondingly reshaped hallucinatively. When the suggested action concluding the posthypnotic state has been performed, there usually occur subsequent rationalizations of the preceding action. It is extremely improbable that any criminal behavior will occur during the posthypnotic state.

Bibliography: Gill, M. M. & Brenman, M.: Hypnosis and related states. New York, 1959. **Kleitman, N.**: Sleep and awakefulness. Chicago & London, 1963.

D.Va.

Posthypnotic time suggestion. A suggestion to be carried out at a fixed time after the hypnosis (q.v.) (e.g. a suggested waking time for treatment of a nocturnal enuresis, q.v.). The date suggested can, under certain circumstances, be even a year later—sometimes a significant therapeutic advantage.   *H.-N.G.*

Postremity theory (E. R. Guthrie). A theory of learning (q.v.) based on the postulate that a stimulus situation which has occurred with two or more irreconcilable responses, or has preceded these, becomes a conditioned situation only for the last response to be given.

Bibliography: Guthrie, E. R.: The psychology of learning. New York, 1952.   *H.Ha.*

Postulate. An assumed, indemonstrable proposition fundamental to a deductive system. Euclid uses it on the one hand as a *request* (to the reader) to accept the existence of an object and of a specific, simple and easily grasped property pertaining to it, and on the other hand for the possibility of certain construction processes necessary to the development of the system, even though the content of that which is requested may not enjoy the same degree of evident universality as the axiom (q.v.). The content of a postulate is always specific to a given science. In the experimental sciences "postulate" is synonymous with "heuristic hypothesis". In systems theory (since the criteria of evidence and universality no longer apply), the notion of the postulate is replaced by that of the axiom. Finally, by extension, "postulate" designates any proposition admitted, whether implicitly or no, as essential for a coherent presentation. For Kant, the postulates of practical reason are metaphysical theses, which are theoretically indemonstrable though necessary to lend meaning to moral life.   *M.-J.B.*

Potency. 1. Power, particularly high power; latent or potential power.

2. Ability to complete coitus (q.v.). In the case of a man this can be disturbed in particular by the diminution or the loss of erection (see *Impotence*) or by the premature ejaculation of semen when the penis is inserted into the vagina (*ejaculatio praecox*), and in the case of a woman when there are organic malformations or vaginal contraction (see *Vaginism*). This type of potency is related to the "normal working of an organic function" or to the presence or absence of frigidity (Giese, 1968, 136).

3. In general the ability to procreate or to produce a child. In the case of the man the power to produce fully developed sperm cells (begins with puberty and remains until advanced old age), in the case of the woman the ability to form fully developed ova and to carry a child for the full term (fertility); this capacity declines as the ovarian function is slowly lost (between the ages of forty-five and fifty-five). A disturbance of this type of potency (infertility) is not related to the intactness of the first type (q.v.), nor is it a generally valid norm for forming a union.

4. The ability or power to experience coitus or other sexual activities as sexually pleasurable or satisfying. This type of potency, especially in the case of women, depends in large measure on psychological and biographical factors; it is related primarily to individual behavior and psychosexual experience during coitus, and not to functional intactness (see 1 above), e.g. in men. There are men as well as women who remain sexually unsatisfied in spite of an orgasm (q.v.) or an ejaculation, and this type of potency can fail to occur especially where there are sexual perversions. See *Sexuality*.   *H.M.*

Power drive (syn. *Will to power*). According to Adler (q.v.) this drive occurs as a reaction to the experience of powerlessness and inferiority of the child in its original family. To compensate this condition the individual attempts as a child (and still more as an adult) to secure his position and gain power and control over others. If the child's experience of his own powerlessness and inferiority is lessened or avoided altogether through his environment, the power drive becomes a social and community interest. If the experience of powerlessness and inferiority is particularly strong, the drive may be overcompensated and become pathological.   *W.T.*

Power test. A performance test which differentiates those taking it by the varying order of difficulty of its items. The increase in difficulty from item to item should be as uniform as possible and not be too great. The principle of the power test cannot be applied to personality (q.v.) tests. Here, instead of the difficulty gradient, use is made of the graded degree to which the personality dimensions being assessed are found to be present. *P.S.*

Practical psychology. See *Applied psychology.*

Practice usually refers to repeating the same or similar overt responses, but includes single occurrences and the covert (silent rehearsal), and is nearly equivalent in scientific psychology to *experience* as a cause of behavior modification. It means much the same as in common usage: *acting, doing,* but without the connotation of preliminary try-out.

1. *Significance.* Practice is used to study molar behavior and physiological and sensory processes, and test theory. It is not a separate topic and is indexed under many labels: *theory, conditioning, learning, memory, transfer of training, rest, work, inhibition, adaptation,* and *extinction.* Repetitions change response value (error, size, rate, persistence), and all prediction takes into account existing practice-rest conditions, and amount and recency of past experience. The "nature-nurture" issue shows essentially all behavior considered in terms of dependence on practice.

Practice has high priority in theory and the psychology of learning: learning is defined by lasting behavior changes related to practice; and behaviorism bases critical distinctions between theories on the conception of practice's role in learning (Tolman, Guthrie, Hull, Estes). Components and loci of temporary effects of repetition—on drive, fatigue, adaptation—are also important, but psychology gives little attention to muscle-strengthening.

Rest is an inevitable complication, variable, and test of activity. Rest and repetition can have opposite effects on a given behavior, but theory relates them by the same constructs: accrual vs. decay of reactive inhibition; *other* learning as interference, to explain forgetting.

2. *History and methodology.* Practice has been prominent for eighty to ninety years. Its importance grew as psychology shifted from human mind to human and animal behavior; from introspection to methods that brought in practice by requiring overt action; and as learning became theory's chief issue. Repeated response has the same history as behavioral psychology: Ebbinghaus (1885), Cattell, and Functionalism, en route from Wundt to Watson (1912) and behaviorism, this century's dominant psychology; ideas, methods, tasks (Pavlov, Yerkes, Thorndike, Skinner), and inputs from mathematics, encouraged objectivity and exact statement. Task and theoretical diversity put methodological care on within-trial events; Hull made isolating and describing practice's learning and performance effects a primary research goal, and gave formal status to negative factors in repetition.

Laboratory psychology meters practice out in structured environments for a given number of units, or to a criterion response level on standard tasks that present stimuli, provide for response and scoring, and minimize unwanted stimuli and responses. Practice alternates with rest in *trial* units, defined as stimulation with opportunity to respond, constant in duration or in number of stimulations. Measured strength of the behavior studied (frequency, speed, size, e.g. to discrete, rate to continued stimuli) is related to graded values of an *experimental variable* (amount of practice or different values for groups of human or animal subjects in, e.g. stimuli, inter-trial rest, subjects' physical state); and neurophysiological variables and changes are also under study.

Behavior is related to practice variables: directly and immediately, while a difference in practice conditions obtains; directly, but later, in memory tests for change in practice residuals over time; or indirectly, in transfer of practice residuals to new tasks or practice conditions.

3. *Research*. Relating amount, duration, and direction of behavior change to what response is repeated (simple-complex, new-old), to what cues, how (ignored, rewarded, punished), and how often, is a major task. Practice has diverse effects, dependent on both positive and negative factors (adaptation, failure to reward, work inhibition, lowered drive), and much of psychology is directed to practice: repeated responding makes and breaks habits; changes vary from fleeting to permanent; temporary loss can mask lasting gain; rest causes forgetting or recovery from decrement; practicing one task helps or harms remembering, learning, or performing others.

Repetition changes reflex and already acquired behavior, but most research uses new, learning, tasks: conditioning methods analyze basic strengthening and weakening processes with simple stimulus-response tendencies; discrimination and choice add intra-task transfer of learning and inhibition; skill and serial tasks bring in timing and chaining. Task category is important, since an observed behavior, by speed or other index, depends both on the tendency to make the response on cue and on competing tendencies that can block it.

(*a*) *Assuring practice*. A trial provides opportunity; practice requires responding. The organism must be capable of the action (cats tug strings, but do not bark) and it must occur: (i) spontaneously—as operant methods take advantage of an act likely to occur (people talk, pigeons peck), or similar ones for gradual shaping to standard, and vary factors that change its probability; or (ii) by stimulation— e.g. the US in classical conditioning (food, shock). Incentive, instruction, pre-training, drive, physical restriction, and other techniques to assure stimulation, limit interference, or arouse activity, shape and steer the subject to the behavior to be practiced.

(*b*) *Learning*. Subjects practicing new tasks under certain conditions typically show gradual improvement. Error declines, amplitude and speed increase, usually as a simple exponential function of trials (for habit competition and probability indices, an ogive). The conditions vary somewhat with task category. *Conditioning* requires (i) drive, e.g. hunger, (ii) a cue-response sequence, e.g. bell-salivation, followed by (iii) a reinforcing stimulus, e.g. food, contingent on behavior (instrumental) or a US independent of response (classical). *Complex human learning* relies on social motives not always specified, and feedback follows cue-response sequences. If the conditions are not met, performance stays the same or worsens—or the response fails to occur. Extinction, memory, and transfer tests verify that the behavior trends reflect learning, and relate degree of learning to number of trials. Other variables (intra-trial stimulus and response events and temporal relations; meaningfulness in rote verbal learning; intermittent reinforcement, e.g.), influencing acquisition, retention, resistance to extinction, are a main part of the study of learning.

(*c*) *Habit breaking*. The basic procedure to weaken conditioned response by practice is *extinction:* cue, response opportunity, no reinforcement. Extinction is gradual for animal subjects, abrupt for human. But behavior recovers over rest, and can be persistent —e.g. if based on anxiety, after partial reinforcement, if instructions imply a response is expected. *Punishment* weakens if it exceeds reward, or if it—or added cues—evokes strong competing behavior e.g., but augments behavior based on aversion. *Counter-training*, combining extinction with reinforcing new responses, is an effective method, especially when it follows gradual stages in altered environments to make new behavior more, and old less, likely on return to the original situation.

(*d*) *Distribution of practice*. Continued perceptual-motor tasks (e.g. tracking) are stressed as trial/rest spacing has little effect with low work loading (e.g. verbal learning, conditioning). Output falls off with all-out work at a well-learned task and recovers with rest. Habit increments usually exceed inhibitory in new tasks and practice yields net trial-to-trial gain, but the limit of present performance grows with trial/rest spacing (in longer rest between trials or shorter trial duration). Transfer tests for lasting decrement from massed practice find behavior shift with shift to new spacing: massed practice conceals, not retards, learning. Single-rest designs vary length of rest or pre-rest practice and infer the course of accrual and dissipation of inhibition from improvement from pre- to post-rest score. Forgetting can override rest benefits or appear in warm-up decrement, despite improved performance after a rest.

4. *Comment*. Practice is evaluated with all experimental psychology in its analytic approach and use of theory to integrate varied phenomena under general principles; it is as general a term as *response*, and includes its problems of definition, elicitation, measurement, and interpretation. College texts in basic psychology (Hilgard & Atkinson, 1967; Kendler, 1968) introduce both scientific method and practice. Science's case (Nagel, 1961; in psychology, Hyman, 1964; Marx, 1963), design and experimental methods (Sidowsky; Underwood, 1966), and practice methodology and data (Deese & Hulse, 1967; Hall, 1966; Kimble, 1961; Marx, 1969; Melton, 1964) are further elaborated in other readings.

Bibliography: Corso, J. F.: The experimental psychology of sensory behavior. New York, 1967. Deese, J. & Hulse, S. H.: The psychology of learning. New York, ³1967. Floyd, W. F. & Welford, A. T. (Eds.): Symposium on fatigue. London, 1953. Hall, J. F.: The psychology of learning. Philadelphia, 1966. Hilgard, E. R. & Atkinson, R. C.: Introduction to psychology. New York, ⁴1967. Holding, D. H.: Principles of training. London, 1965. Hyman, R.: The nature of scientific inquiry. Englewood Cliffs, N.J., 1964. Kendler, H. H.: Basic psychology. New York, ²1968. Kimble, G. A.: Hilgard and Marquis' conditioning and learning. New York, ²1961. Marx, M. H. (Ed.): Theories in contemporary psychology. London, 1963. Id.: Learning processes. London, 1969. Melton, A. W. (Ed.): Categories of human

learning. New York, 1964. Nagel, E.: The structure of science. New York, 1961. Sidowski, J. B. (Ed.): Experimental methods and instrumentation in psychology. New York, 1966. Underwood, B. J.: Experimental psychology. New York, ²1966.

Ina McD. Bilodeau

Practice, immanent. See *Learning, latent.*

Practice period. The term *practice* refers to the repeated performance of some activity with a view to its improvement. Practice may be *massed* into one long, continuous period, or it may be *distributed* into a series of shorter periods (trials) which are interspersed with periods of rest. The latter condition is usually found to be more favorable to learning. A period of practice is used in some learning experiments in order to equate subjects for previous experience on the task, or at least to reduce this differential.   *G.D.W.*

Practice therapy. An (organismic) psychotherapeutic procedure involving the use of autosuggestion (q.v.) and suggestion (q.v.), including techniques to induce increased performance, or training of the will (see *Autogenic training*), and even art therapy and psychodrama (q.v.).   *F.Ma.*

Pragmatism. 1. An epistemological movement which would have the truth of any assertion reside in the consequences which it may have in our lives. There are two main varieties: (*a*) that in which the notion of truth is wholly coincident with that of individual interest (Callicles: cf. Plato's *Gorgias*); (*b*) that in which truth corresponds to the exaltation of a group (class, religious, or national truth).

2. The doctrine associated mainly with C. S. Peirce, W. James (q.v.), and J. Dewey (q.v.): "In order to ascertain the meaning of an intellectual conception one should consider what practical consequences might conceivably result by necessity from the truth of that conception; and the sum of these consequences will constitute the entire meaning of the conception." (Peirce.) "Truth lives . . . for the most part on a credit system. Our thoughts and beliefs 'pass', so long as nothing challenges them, just as bank-notes pass so long as nobody refuses them. But this all points to direct face-to-face verifications somewhere, without which the fabric of truth collapses like a financial system with no cash-basis whatever." (James.)

Bibliography: Dewey, J.: How we think. New York, 1910. James, W.: Pragmatism. London, 1907. Peirce, C. S.: Collected papers (Ed. C. Hartshorne & P. Weiss). New York, 1931–5. *F.B.*

Praise and blame. Expressions of approval and disapproval respectively, of a person or his behavior. Considered jointly in psychology as methods of manipulating human behavior (see *Reinforcement*), especially with children. *G.D.W.*

Precocity. Abnormally early development of physical and mental capacities. The term is often applied to the existence of sexual experience appropriate to a later stage of development. *K.E.P.*

Precognition. A form of ESP (q.v.) in which the target (q.v.) is some future event. Precognitive hit (q.v.) = hit with forward temporal displacement. Foreknowledge that does not depend on inference. *J.B.*

Preconscious. The system comprising all those psychic processes which can be activated at any time and without the inner resistance of the individual. See *Subconscious; Unconscious; Psi-system.* *W.T.*

Preconscious memory. A term introduced by Frank (1969) into information psychology

(q.v.) and cybernetic education (q.v.) to characterize the second "temporal channel" of a *psycho-structural model* (q.v.). In this model, short-term storage (i.e. memory), as the first "temporal channel", precedes preconscious memory. In short-term storage, information becomes conscious. The information proceeds from short-term storage to preconscious memory, the latter being conceived as consisting of short- and long-term memory. Information can be recalled from the preconscious memory into the short-term store, i.e. data can become conscious memories. The term does not indicate any connection with Freud's notional pre- and un-conscious.

Bibliography: Frank, K.: Kybernetische Grundlagen der Pädagogik. Baden-Baden, ²1969. *D.Vo.*

Prediction (syn. *Prognosis*). 1. *Definition and Methods.* Psychological prediction, strictly speaking, means forecasting the probability of future courses of action on the basis of present and past behavior. This behavior is influenced by environmental, innate and personality factors and can be consciously or unconsciously motivated. In a broader sense, *individual prediction* has its place in all fields of psychology and involves not only the personality at the time of the test but the shape it will take in the future. A distinction is drawn between *clinical, typological and statistical* predictions according to the method adopted. Statistical individual prediction makes use of prediction tables which have been compiled on the basis of a fairly wide range of experience. These tables are simply aids in the hands of an experienced psychologist when he is objectifying prediction decisions. They must not be applied mechanically or automatically. Clinical individual prediction does *not consciously* use any statistical prediction tables. However, as a preparation for deciding on some prediction, it carefully studies the life history and the family circumstances of the individual, makes a purposeful exploration (q.v.) and applies psychodiagnostic test methods. Improper forms of clinical prediction are based upon the intuition, speculation, subjectivism (prejudice) of the researcher; they cannot provide a sufficient foundation for psychological decision. Either the statistical or clinical method may be the type used for the individual prediction (this may consist of a typological application of factorial groups taken from statistics), or may be made on the basis of clinical experience.

2. *Criminal Prediction.* The most important field in which individual prediction is applied is in criminal psychology. The prognostic judgment relating to the lawbreaker is divided into two parts—its purpose and its aim. This division is partly linked to an examination at different points of the causes leading to the crime and the remedial measures to be taken. In broad outline prediction can be said to fall into the stages of *predelinquency, possibility of recidivism* and *prediction of treatment.* The last two stages refer only to those who are *already guilty of some criminal offense.* Criminal prediction dealing with predelinquency tries to detect children and juveniles who as yet have committed no criminal offense but who possess personality *traits* (q.v.) which make it highly likely that they will tend to become persistent criminals, as they are particularly susceptible to criminal influences.

3. *Historical survey.* Criminological prediction research began in the USA in 1923. Since then it has dealt chiefly with the problem of forecasting success (non-relapse) and the failure (relapse) during the period of parole in the case of adult convicts and occasionally also in that of juvenile convicts, but in individual cases it has also studied how to forecast success or failure when the probation system is used. Research into ways of forecasting criminal behavior at the stage of predelinquency only began relatively late, in 1940. The first useful *prediction table* was compiled by E. W. Burgess. He analyzed the files of three thousand convicts who had been placed on pro-

bation and obtained twenty-one factors on the basis of the correlation of his factors obtained from the files with the criteria of success (no relapse) and failure (relapse). S. & E. Glueck, a married couple who work together, began their prediction research in 1925, almost contemporaneously with E. W. Burgess. After carrying out comprehensive empirical investigations by the longitudinal method (q.v.) for many years, and others by the cross-sectional method since 1940, the Gluecks compiled about fifty different personality tables of all kinds. Their Social Prediction Table is the most popular table dealing with criminal prediction. Like most of their prediction tables, it consists of *five important factors:* upbringing of the boy by the father, maternal control of the boy, paternal affection for the boy, maternal affection for the boy, and closeness of the family unit. Studies of the reliability and retrospective and prospective validity of the Social Prediction Table have so far proved negative. As a result of this, a table for criminal prediction was drawn up with the following three social factors: mother's control of the boy, boy's upbringing by the mother, and closeness as a unit of the family. The first German criminal prediction table was developed by R. Schiedt. An inquiry showed that statistical methods of criminal prediction are used in only a few states in the USA (e.g. in Illinois, Ohio, California, Colorado). In Japan the tables compiled by the Gluecks have met with much approval. In the Federal German Republic and the other West European states, statistical methods of criminal prediction are only occasionally made use of. In Eastern Europe and other parts of the world research into criminal prediction is as good as unknown.

4. *Present state of research and most important results.* In essence only three methods for making criminal prediction tables were known until a short time ago: (*a*) the compilation of special stimuli configurations—mostly by using test methods devised already for other

purposes—with the aim of making a criminal prediction (such methods employ parts of tests, test profiles and batteries); (b) the summation of factors likely to lead to a relapse, all of which are given the same weighting (Burgess method); (c) the combination of a few selected personality characteristics with different ratings in a table (Glueck method).

The *main weakness* of these methods of criminal prediction, astonishingly enough, remained hidden until a few years ago; it is that they completely neglect the *interdependence and interdependence correlations of their individual factors with one another and with their criteria of success or failure*. This weakness is overcome by *structural prediction tables* which have very recently been developed afresh everywhere in North America. The classification method developed by W. T. Williams and J. M. Lambert from plant ecology was adopted and developed further by L. T. Wilkins and MacNaughton-Smith into a new and promising method for constructing criminal prediction tables. This procedure is based on the following *methodological principles:* it starts from the assumption that there is a high degree of reciprocal action which as yet has not been discovered and cannot even be studied yet with the present research methods used by criminal psychology between prediction factors and a considerable variation spread of individual dissimilarity among the criminal population. In consequence it attempts to classify the empirical data according to the presence or absence of certain characteristics and to subdivide hierarchically the heterogeneous criminal population into relatively homogeneous risk groups differing structurally from one another according to the presence or absence of characteristics which are related in different degrees to the criteria of success or failure. The personality characteristics, chiefly objective external factors, are combined for each risk group, so that something like a typology of risk groups is created. Well-known structural tables for

criminal prediction have been devised quite recently by D. Glaser, K. B. Ballard and D. M. Gottfredson and T. Grygier. The first investigations of their validity have produced favorable results.

5. *Criminal prediction studied scientifically.* The method used at present is first to look especially for external factors which differentiate sharply, are accurate and can be ascertained objectively and concerning which items of information can be obtained relatively easily and then to combine them factorially in the sense of structural prediction tables. The criticism of principle made by dogmatic penologists and theoretical sociologists against the application of criminal prediction tables can be traced back to misconceptions and insufficient knowledge of the ways in which they can be applied. Important are doubts about the harmful retroactive effects of criminal prediction decisions in socio-psychological matters. For there is a serious danger that children exposed to criminal dangers will be "stigmatized", that they will commit criminal actions in a spirit of defiance, and that they will be actually forced into a delinquent rôle by unreasonable parents, siblings, teachers and school friends. The concept of "social progression" is used in this connection to denote a dynamic force which exerts on the members of some socially deviant, nonadapted group a pressure which drives them continuously to more serious social deviation (the pressure of social nonconformity). Such a negative progressive effect can be found in children and juveniles who have been the subject of an unfavorable criminal prediction, especially because as yet no new and effective methods of treatment have been devised which are suitable for preventing early criminality; the same may be said with some modifications for the prediction of recidivism. A recidivist who is unfavorably criticized runs the risk of finally giving up. Because he is being regularly sent to prison or is obliged to remain there to serve the whole of his outstanding sentence,

the team responsible for treating him can as a result of the unfavorable decision be all too easily inclined in such cases entirely to lose its educational enthusiasm. See *Conscience; Criminality; Personality; Traits; Type.*

Bibliography: Höbbel, D.: Bewährung des statistischen Prognoseverfahrens im Jugendstrafrecht. Göttingen, 1968. **Mehl, P. E.:** Clinical vs. statistical prediction. Minneapolis, 1954. **Mey, H. G.:** Prognostische Beurteilung des Rechtsbrechers. Die deutsche Forschung. In: Undeutsch, U. (Ed.): Handbuch der Psychologie, Vol. 11. Göttingen, 1967, 511–64. **Ohlin, L. E.:** Selection for parole. A manual of parole prediction. New York, 1951. **Schneider, H. J.:** Prognostische Beurteilung des Rechtsbrechers: Die ausländische Forschung. In: Undeutsch, U. (Ed.): Handbuch der Psychologie, Vol. 11. Göttingen, 1967, 397–510.

H. J. Schneider

Predictive validity, coefficient of. A special kind of validation (q.v.) of a test. If a test, e.g., is to make it possible to predict later performances, validation must be carried out in such a way that the agreement between the predicted and the observed value can be quantified. See *Test theory.* *W.H.B.*

Predormitium. Period of time before deep sleep. The concepts of pre- and post-dormitium (q.v.), which were defined phenomenologically, are now being added to by the more precise formulations of neurophysiological research into sleep (q.v.). *W.Sch.*

Pre-ejaculatory secretion. Under sexual stimulation some drops of a transparent secretion may be emitted from the orifice of the male urethra. The slightly alkaline secretion comes from the Cowper glands and neutralizes acidic traces of urine before ejaculation (q.v.). It may contain actively mobile spermatozoa. As pre-ejaculatory secretion can make the glans penis move more easily, it is also thought of as a lubricant (q.v.). *V.S.*

Pre-encephalon. See *Cerebrum.*

Preformation theory. A theory about the development of the organism prevalent until the middle of the eighteenth century. It was supposed that the embryo was not formed afresh from the protoplasm (epigenesis) but was contained in it and was already formed in all its parts. The logical consequence is the theory which states that every species was created as a pair already containing all its progeny "fitted one into the other". Growth was interpreted by preformation theory as being simply increase in size, and its origin was considered to be either in the ovum (ovulist) or the spermatozoon (animalculist). Darwinism (q.v.) demolished preformation theory; modern genetics (q.v.) has shown that, whereas the "ground plan" of the organism is already present in the hereditary factor, its development can in no way be equated with increase in size. *W.Sch.*

Pregenital stage. This phase comprises the period until the successful conclusion of the Oedipal problem (see *Oedipus complex*) at about the age of four to six years; the subsequent primacy of the genitals signifies not only a purely physical development, but psychosocially the possibility of turning toward the object, another person and experiencing feelings of pleasure. The three or four parts of the pregenital stage, according to Freud, are the oral (q.v.), the anal-sadistic (q.v.) and the phallic (q.v.). Freud discovered these phases or expressions of sexual partial instincts (q.v.) retrospectively, while analyzing his patients and by analogy from the sexual perversions (q.v.). Analytical therapeutical experience shows that neuroses (q.v.) and other psychic disturbances whose origin can be traced to a pregenital phase (autochtonous or regressive) are much more serious and more difficult to treat than disturbances which occur later. Erikson's modification of the theory of a pregenital stage emphasizes the psychosocial aspect more; he distinguishes the *zonal* (body zones), *modal* (typical forms of behavior, e.g.

embodying, retaining-eliminating, and penetrating) and the aspect of modality, "the readiness to experience exclusively the zonal and modal aspect" (to receive, take, retain, make, i.e. to show initiative).   *W.Sch.*

Pregnance; pregnance, tendency to. *Pregnance* denotes clarity, an optimal state of structuring, a stage of consciousness which emphasizes the essential. A tendency to pregnance (W. Wertheimer, W. Köhler) is a tendency toward a "good gestalt" (configuration), a force resulting in the dynamic arrangement of a field or system which will produce the completeness, regularity, etc., of something perceived or will lead to the solution of a problem by "centering" or changing the functions of the parts in the whole. See *Ganzheit*; *Lewin*.   *J.M.D.*

Prejudice. 1. *Definition.* The term has a similar derivation in several European languages (*préjugé, Vorurteil, prejudizio, perjudicado*). It refers to "preconceived opinion, bias (*against, in favour of*, person or thing)" (The Concise Oxford Dictionary). However, in social psychology it applies mainly to hostile attitudes towards one or more social groups (for example, racial, national, ethnic, religious). Allport (1954), for instance, defined prejudice as "an antipathy based upon a faulty and inflexible generalization. It may be felt or expressed. It may be directed toward a group as a whole, or towards an individual because he is a member of that group" (p. 9).

Prejudice is an attitude. It must be distinguished from *discrimination*, which in this context can be defined as inequitable treatment of individuals because of their membership of a particular group. Prejudice may or may not express itself in discrimination. Discrimination may or may not be caused by prejudice.

2. *The social and the individual approaches.* The distinction between prejudice and discrimination corresponds roughly to different emphases given to their study by social scientists interested mainly in social processes and those interested mainly in psychological processes. The former seek to relate the social characteristics of an intergroup situation (such as competition for resources, power and status differentials, and so on) to the social effects (such as discrimination) that these conditions may have. The latter are more interested in the genesis of prejudice in an individual, in the analysis of its various aspects, and in the relations that obtain between prejudice and the individual's overt social behavior. There is considerable overlap between these two types of interest. The traditional psychological viewpoint is exemplified by Berkowitz (1962) who stresses "the importance of individualistic considerations in the field of group relations. Dealings between groups ultimately become problems for the psychology of the individual" (p. 167). The interaction of social and cultural factors (such as social norms) with the psychological determinants of prejudice has, however, also been stressed by many social psychologists (e.g., Pettigrew, 1958).

3. *Psychological theories of prejudice.* Prejudice can be considered in terms of its motivational, cognitive and behavioral components. These approaches are complementary rather than mutually exclusive. The motivational roots of prejudice have been sought in the human response to frustration with its important derivative of displaced hostility. A synthesis of Freudian ideas and of concepts from learning theory was attempted by Dollard *et al.* (1939). The theory assumes that interference with goal-directed behavior which constitutes a frustration creates hostile impulses which, if they cannot be directed at the frustrating agent, will be displaced towards other objects. Therefore hostility and aggression following upon frustration encountered in the social environment will tend to focus on selected outgroups which provide relatively easy targets. This hostility will be accompanied

by projections and rationalizations whose function it is to "justify" to the individual his choice of substitute targets.

The frustration-aggression hypothesis was also combined with assumptions about generalization of aggression based on concepts deriving from Hullian learning theory. A recent critical analysis based on experimental research can be found in Berkowitz (1962).

An important advance in the understanding of prejudice from the point of view of its role in personality organization has been made by Adorno *et al.* (1950). They considered prejudice as a symptom which should be viewed against the background of emotional needs characteristic of individuals who display the syndrome of "authoritarian personality". Prejudice is not an isolated attitude; it is inherent "in the type of approach and outlook a subject is likely to have in a great variety of areas ranging from the most intimate features of family and sex adjustment through relationships to other people in general, to religion and to social and political philosophy" (p. 971). The background of this syndrome is to be found in the emotional problems arising in the course of early socialization.

Methodological and theoretical criticisms followed the statement of the theory and of its related assumptions about an "ethnocentric personality" characterized by a generalized hostile attitude towards outgroups. These criticisms were mainly concerned with the validity of the measures employed (e.g. Christie and Jahoda, 1954), the possibility of wider theoretical formulations (e.g. Rokeach, 1960), and the role of situational variables in the genesis of prejudice (e.g. Pettigrew, 1958; Banton, 1967).

The interest in the cognitive aspects of prejudice was first represented by studies of stereotypes: that is, the attribution of common characteristics to a group with a corresponding neglect of individual differences. Through the influence of Allport (1954) and others, this interest widened to an analysis of stereotypes

as a part of the general tendency to categorize the social environment in order to be able to cope cognitively with its complexities. Hostile stereotypes have been found to be resistant to change in direct relation to the intensity of prejudice which they reflect. Social consensus in the use of stereotypes was extensively studied by Manz (1968). The system of beliefs which underlies the formation of stereotypes was considered by Tajfel (1969) in relation to an individual's attempts to understand the processes of social change by which he is affected, and to the consequences that this may have for his social behavior.

Various aspects of prejudice have been studied with a diversity of methods ranging from experiments testing some of the specific hypotheses, through attitude scales, questionnaires and surveys, to clinical depth interviews, field studies and developmental studies.

4. *Prejudice and behavior.* The relations between prejudice and behavior are complex and no simple generalizations are possible. Outstanding for their combination of attitudinal, behavioral and situational variables have been the studies of Sherif (1966) in which he related intergroup conflict and competition to the formation of intergroup attitudes and to consequent behavior. In this, perhaps Sherif's work represents an indication of future developments. The study of prejudice in its relation to social behavior, and of the conditions leading to its increase or reduction, will have to include an analysis of psychological processes carefully set against the social and cultural background of intergroup relations.

Bibliography: Adorno, T. W., *et al.*: The authoritarian personality. New York, 1950. **Allport, G. W.:** The nature of prejudice. Cambridge, Mass., 1954. **Banton, M.:** Race relations. London, 1967. **Berkowitz, L.:** Aggression: a social psychological analysis. New York, 1962. **Christie, R. & Jahoda, M.** (Eds.): Studies in the scope and method of the "authoritarian personality". Glencoe, Ill., 1954. **Dollard, G.,** *et al.*: Frustration and aggression. New Haven, 1939. **Manz, W.:** Das Stereotyp. Zur Operationalisierung eines sozialwissenschaftlichen Begriffs. Meisenheim a. G., 1968. **Pettigrew, T. F.**: Personality and socio-cultural factors in intergroup attitudes: a cross, national comparison. J. Confl. Resol., 1958, *2*, 29–42. **Rokeach, M.**: The open and closed mind. New York, 1960. **Sherif, M.**: In common predicament: social psychology of intergroup conflict and cooperation. Boston, 1966. **Tajfel, H.**: Cognitive aspects of prejudice. J. Biosocial. Sci., 1969, *1*, Suppl. No. 1: Biosocial aspects of race, 173–191. *H. Tajfel*

Premenstrual syndrome. A set of physiological and psychological symptoms occurring in the three or four days previous to menstruation, differing from woman to woman but characteristically involving depression and/or irritatibility. Also called *premenstrual tension*, and *premenstrual molimina*. *G.D.W.*

Prepuberty. (syn. *Pre-adolescence*). A stage of development lasting approximately a year and immediately preceding the beginning of puberty (q.v.). It features a non-specific emotional and behavioral lability, increased interest in intellectual matters and a sudden intensification of vertical growth (the pre-puberal spurt). To this extent, prepuberty may be considered a special developmental "phase". Many specific aspects of prepuberty are conditioned not, as was once supposed, by maturation but by culture, i.e. experience. See *Adolescence; Child psychology; Development; Youth.* *H.-J.K.*

Presbyacusis. After the age of forty to fifty years, hearing can be expected to become less acute, the symptom being an increasing lowering of the upper acoustic level. At c^6 as a very crude approximation, an average deterioration in the faculty of hearing can be found amounting to about 10 to 15 db for every decade of life. Deviations admittedly lie between 4 and 25 db, so that it is scarcely possible to give exact norms for this decline due to age (presbyacoustic law). *M.Sp.*

Presbyophrenia. The loss of mental powers (in particular the ability to perceive and to remember) occurring in old age due to senile atrophy of the brain. See *Aging; Gerontology.* *C.Sch.*

Presbyopia. Owing to physical processes taking place in the lens (q.v.) as age increases, the eye loses its power of *accommodation*. Till the age of forty-five approximately, these processes often remain unnoticed, then it is suddenly realized that it has become impossible to read at the normal reading distance. Near vision, in particular, is affected. In this respect presbyopia resembles hyperopia (q.v.) but it is not a pathological process. It can be corrected by the use of convex lenses of up to 3+ diopters. *R.R.*

Pre-school age. The kindergarten or nursery-school age; the years immediately preceding entry to the infant (i.e. primary) school. The term is used largely in connection with pre-school education, but is not tied to a precise age group, since the age of entry to schooling varies from country to country, and some have more or less extensive nursery school provisions. See *Education, pre-school.* *R.O.*

Presentation, method of. A formal aspect of the psychological experiment which determines the manner in which an individual will be confronted with a stimulus or a constellation of stimuli. The main variables of the stimulus are: modality, quality, intensity, duration, etc. There are also variables such as mode of instruction, society, objects, etc. *P.S. & R.S.*

Presenting (sexual). Showing the genital zone can have a soothing effect, be a greeting ceremony or indicate a rank inside a hierarchy. Sexual presenting need not necessarily be intended for someone of the opposite sex.

Male baboons of an inferior rank adopt female presenting behavior in front of a superior male. Strong males of the same species present their genitals when watching over the troop. Very probably this is the origin of the phallic cult (q.v.) of many primitive tribes.

V.P.

Pressure balance. An appliance invented by W. Wundt for measuring sensitivity to pressure.

Pressure points. Parts of the body surface which are sensitive to pressure. The receptors for pressure (Merkel's disks, Meissner's corpuscles, free nerve endings) are shaped like points and are of varying density; they are distributed over the whole surface of the body. There are about 720,000 of them, and some 80,000 are distinguished from the rest by special sensitivity (the greatest density is at the tip of the tongue, the least is at the back).

P.S.

Pressure, sense of. The sense of pressure or touch belongs, together with the sensations of pain or temperature, among the skin senses (see *Haptics*). The sensation of pressure arises from a mechanical deformation of the skin. The receptor organs for the sense of pressure are: nerve endings on the hair follicles, Meissner's corpuscles, Merkel's disks, Pacini's corpuscles (in deeper layers) and free nerve endings.

P.S.

Pressure, sensitivity to. Excitability of the sense of pressure (q.v.), which can be determined quantitatively. It depends on the nature and the density of the pressure receptors.

P.S.

Prestige. Social esteem in which a person is held due to the application of certain criteria (which actually or only supposedly exist).

The criteria applied (e.g. income, influence, social origin, behavior), the extent to which there is general agreement with the manner of application (value consensus), and the form in which prestige is built up, may differ with individual groups, classes or societies, and influence group dynamics (q.v.) in different ways.

C.B.

Prestige, susceptibility to (*Prestige suggestibility*). An individual tendency to change one's judgments, opinions or attitudes (q.v.), even though conditions are otherwise the same, when the *source* of the particular communication (originator or communicator) is given a positive value (esteem, influence, prestige, q.v.; indicated by professional respect, expertise, title, public service or general sympathy). The stability and situational dependence of a personality trait of susceptibility to prestige or social influence are not authenticated; in this it contrasts with an ideomotor quasi-hypnotic, susceptibility to influence (which H. J. Eysenck calls *primary suggestibility*); prestige suggestibility tends to be classified as *secondary suggestibility*.

H.D.S.

Pretest. 1. Syn. for pilot study (q.v.). **2.** A practice run-through of a test: used to familiarize Ss. and personnel with test procedure. **3.** A preliminary test carried out in order to determine, e.g., the anticipated direction of a trend, or how great the sample range of the main test should be, or some standard for the main test.

Priapism. 1. Lewdness, licentiousness. **2.** Persistent, abnormal erection of the penis, particularly when resulting from organic disease rather than sexual desire. **3.** Sometimes used as a synonym for *satyriasis*.

G.D.W.

Primacy-recency effect. Diametrically opposed phenomenal forms in acts involving learning or judging; it takes the form of emphasizing the stored *initial* (primacy) or *final* (recency) information in a learning or information series presented successively. *Primacy effect* (*primary law*): the first informative items in a series are learnt or retained better than those which follow (see *First impression*). *Recency effect* (*recency law*): items of information are learnt more proficiently the later they are acquired in a series. The primary effect needs to be observed when at the end of the series a judgment of the whole or a reproduction (q.v.) has to be attempted, the recency effect when each item of information in succession is used in making some judgment (e.g. judgment of personality). See *Rating*.   *F.-C.S.*

Primary colors. The three colors sufficient to produce every other color when the necessary changes in intensity (mixture) have taken place. Numerous combinations are possible. Optimal results are obtained with three frequency bands of approximately 650, 530 and 460 m., corresponding to red-orange, yellow-green and purple-blue.   *G.Ka.*

Primary drives. Term for a class of dynamic factors which are considered to have a physiological foundation and to be conditioned by heredity. The concept is based on a hypothetical distinction between motives which are *inherited* and others which are the *result of learning processes*. More recent research has, however, shown that it is doubtful whether there are any needs whatsoever which are related to some object or directed to some end, yet are not grounded in experience. Affects activated by certain stimuli are thought to be more probable than components of drive systems conditioned by heredity. See *Drive; Instinct; Need; Motivation*.   *H.-J.K.*

Primary factors. Factors of the first order, i.e., factors which are obtained from factor analysis (q.v.) of the intercorrelations of tests.

Ant.: factors of the second (third) order, which are extracted from factor analysis of the intercorrelations of factors (rotated at an oblique angle) of the first (second) order.

K.Pa.

Primary Mental Ability Tests (PMA). Batteries of tests to assess intelligence (q.v.) in the age groups 5–7, 7–11 and 11–17 years. PMAs were constructed by Thurstone (1948, 1949, 1953) on the basis of his *multiple factor theory* of intelligence. According to his theory each of the three batteries of tests embraces five group factors of intelligence—of course, the same factors will not be found in all of the three batteries. Reliability figures for the different sub-tests of the PMA fluctuate between $r = 0.63$ and $r = 0.98$.

Bibliography: Thurstone, L. L. & Thelma, G.: SRA Primary Mental Abilities—Elementary—Ages 7 to 11: Examiner Manual. Chicago, 1948; **Id.**: SRA Primary Mental Abilities—Primary—Ages 5 to 7: Examiner Manual. Chicago, 1953.   *P.S.*

Primary processes. According to Freud (q.v.) the *primary process* belongs to the unconscious (q.v.) whereas the *secondary process* characterizes the relation between the preconscious and the conscious (q.v.). In the primary process, psychic energy flows freely from one notion to another in conformity with the well-known mechanisms of condensation (q.v.), repression (q.v.), etc., with a tendency to return. In psychic processes, libido (q.v.) endeavors to gratify every desire. In contrast to this, in the secondary processes the ego endeavors to steer its libidinal energy into a somewhat more objective and moderated path. The division between primary and secondary processes is taken to be two different forms of circulation of psychic energy, one of which is *free*, the other tied (or, also, compelled). It is also possible to speak of an opposition between the pleasure principle (q.v.) and the reality principle (q.v.). See *Depth psychology*.

J.L.I.

Primitive reaction type. Characteristic: "The experience enters the mind and immediately makes its exit in the form of a response". "A person to whom impression and expression come easily but whose memory is not good". In psychopathic states the primitive reaction type is among the "explosives" and the "unstable". *W.K.*

Principal colors. See *Fundamental colors.*

Principal-component method, a factor-analysis method introduced by H. Hotelling, widely used by psychologists. Although the calculations involved take longer, it is regarded as more accurate than the somewhat cruder centroid method. The term "principal component" (or "principal axis") was chosen so as to avoid confusion with "factor" (e.g. of a product) already current in mathematics. See *Factor analysis.* *W.H.B.*

Prismatic spectacles. Spectacles which distort the visual world (e.g. by inverting the retinal image), as used in studies of perceptual-motor adaptation. See *Stratton's experiment.*
G.D.W.

Prism effect. See *Stratton's experiment.*

Prison psychosis. The term covers a wide variety of psychopathological symptoms and syndromes closely bound up psychologically with imprisonment, i.e. psychogenic reactions (responses to abnormal experience). The clinical picture varies with the personality of the prisoner and includes depression (q.v.), anxiety (q.v.), psychogenic semiconsciousness, agitated states. Simulation psychoses are simulated mental disorders (Ganser's syndrome, q.v., pseudodementia, clowning and attitudinizing, childish behavior, etc.). Especi-

ally characteristic are psychogenic delusions such as that of innocence or of the imminence of reprieve. After prolonged imprisonment, persecution mania and similar disorders may occur, accompanied sometimes by hallucinations, and sometimes by quarrelsomeness. See *Psychoses, functional.* *C.Sch.*

Prison psychology. The branch of psychology concerned chiefly with the psychological effects of the loss of liberty. In addition it seeks to develop methods of treatment to overcome the negative psychic effects and to prevent recidivism after discharge from prison. Such psychology differentiates corrective systems according to the different methods of therapy used. One or several classification institutions have the task of seeing that each convicted person is assigned to that corrective institution or that block inside the institution which is most likely to meet the requirements for his treatment. For this purpose classification institutions use diagnostic and prognostic methods which have been worked out by criminal psychologists. Psychologists specializing in this field are employed as therapeutic experts in prisons. Recently, methods of diagnosis and treatment have begun to be devised for sentences served outside prison. The "Community Treatment Project" in Sacramento and Stockton (California) may be quoted as an example. See *Criminality.* *H.J.S.*

Probabilism. Primarily those moral doctrines which assert that it is sufficient to act in conformity with *probable rules* (plausible rules) as (they would be) approved by respectable individuals (authority) or convention. A second use of the term is for those doctrines which affirm that it is impossible to know, not any truth, but absolute truths, and which acknowledge only *probable judgments*, mainly at the level of empirical knowledge. A "probable judgment" would then refer to the *degree* *of credibility* to be given the future occurrence of a fact; or to that which may be given hypotheses regarding past events from which facts known in reality have ensued; or, finally, to the laws which govern such known facts (induction, q.v.), or allow others to be inferred from them (prediction, q.v.) (A. Cournot, 1801–1877). *M.-J.B.*

Probabilistic psychology. In a famous article, E. Brunswik (1943) showed that in regard to the conditions that release a behavior, *and* in regard to its effects, *probabilisms* must replace the unequivocal physical schemata of the determinists.

Bibliography: Brunswik, E.: Organismic achievement and environmental probability. Psychol. Rev., 1943, *50*, 255–72. *P.M.*

Probability theory. Questions of probability were first studied seriously in the seventeenth and eighteenth centuries; they arose primarily in relation to games of chance. Many of the great European mathematicians, notably Pascal, Fermat, Laplace, de Moivre, Bernouilli and Bayes, were concerned with probability. Textbooks on the subject have been written in many languages.

There is considerable difference of opinion, even amongst experts, about the nature of probability theory. This is due in part to the different types of situation in which the word "probability" has traditionally been used. Let us take just three examples:

1. On the day of the Grand National, a man may consider the chances—or probability—of a particular horse winning, and may express his "degree of belief" by giving the horse odds of say 9 to 1: that is, a probability of 0.9 of winning.

2. A coin is tossed 100 times and gives heads 55 times. Here we may consider the likelihood of some hypothesis, for instance that the coin is unbiased, and express this in terms of a probability statement. This procedure is common in simple tests of significance.

3. We may wish to determine the relative frequencies with which the six faces of a dice occur when it is rolled a large number of times. The relative frequencies are then referred to as probabilities.

One school of thought (of which Savage, 1962, following de Finetti, is a leading proponent) believes that a theory of probability can most satisfactorily be founded on the idea of "degrees of belief", or subjective probabilities (see example 1). Another school of thought, following Fisher, maintains that statements of probability truly refer to statements about the likelihood of hypotheses: that is, of propositions about which there is uncertainty (see example 2). Although these two points of view should be kept in mind, it is the case that the term "probability theory" is most widely taken to mean the application of mathematics to the description of random events (see example 3) for which, in a long series of observations, the relative frequencies of the possible outcomes tend to stable limits.

Bibliography: Arthurs, A. M.: Probability theory. London, 1965. Gnedenko, B. V. & Khintchine, A. Y.: An elementary introduction to the theory of probability. London, 1961. Lindley, D. V.: Introduction to probability and statistics. Cambridge, 1965. Parzen, E.: Modern probability theory and its applications. New York, 1962. Savage, L. J.: The foundations of statistical inference. London & New York, 1962.

A. E. Maxwell

Probable error (abb. PE; syn. *Probable deviation; Probable discrepancy*). An index of the variability of a measure, and an index of dispersion with a limited range of applicability. Defined as equal to 0.6745 of the standard error, and used for certain purposes (e.g. test construction) because of its distinctness. In the normal distribution about half of the values (deviations from the mean) are within the range of that mean $\pm$PE.

H.J.S.

Proband. See *Testee*.

Problem box. A cage which presents a problem to the animal, which must be solved in order to gain some reward, particularly escape: e.g. Thorndike puzzle-box; Skinner box (q.v.).

G.D.W.

Problem children. A collective term with no standardized meaning for a number of behavioral disturbances found in children and juveniles and calling for special therapy. The use of the term "problem children" lays emphasis on the fact that the child is the cause of difficulties and not that it has difficulties itself. Reasons why there are problem children are, for example, education, conflict (q.v.), handicaps of various kinds (criminality, q.v.), neurosis (q.v.), neglect, psychopathy (q.v.). See *Child psychology; Criminality*.

H.M.

Problem solving. The process requisite to reach a desired goal starting from a set of initial (cognitive) conditions. By introspection (q.v.), or by the observation of behavior in solving problems, the psychology of thinking attempts to obtain information about the structure, phenomenology and course of thinking processes. Certain classes of problems (e.g. the Tower of Hanoi) can be more or less easily split up into their individual components, which on the one hand facilitates a phasic study of the underlying processes and on the other hand makes it possible to simulate the processes (within certain limits).

Bibliography: Maier, N. R. S.: Problem solving and creativity in individuals. Belmont, 1970. *R.Hä.*

Process form (Ger. *Verlaufsgestalt*). A gestalt-psychological term (see *Ganzheit*), allowing for consideration of the time factor: i.e. structural alterations in time are viewed as "form" (e.g. melody). In a wider sense, the term has a "dynamic" implication, as when (especially in modern German psychology as represented by Heiss and Thomae) emphasis is laid on the "processual" aspect of the individual, when "process form" would be the kind and mode of development (q.v.) and the permanently changing existential reference of personality (q.v.).

Bibliography: Koffka, K.: Principles of gestalt psychology. New York, 1935. Thomae, H.: Persönlichkeit. Bonn, 1955. *K.E.P.*

Production principle of identification (syn. *Compensation principle of identification*). (N. Ach). This may be observed in the phenomenon that man assigns meaning to words: a verbal symbol does not simply represent the object but represents it in apprehension and itself becomes part of the object seen as idea. Ach chanced upon this fusion of *thing* and *name* when investigating concept formation and the attribution of meaning. See *Concept; Ach-Vygotsky method*.

H.W.

Production procedure. A psychophysical method for determining subjective equality or some other perceived relationship. The subject is given control of the variable stimulus, which he adjusts until he judges it to be in a given relationship (e.g. equal) to the standard stimulus. Syn. *Adjustment procedure; Method of reproduction*.

G.D.W.

Productive thinking. Term for creative thinking which leads to something new for humanity or for the individual, even if in certain cases it was new only at the time when the thinking occurred. There are different definitions of "thinking", e.g. as a dynamic process caused by forces which effect some arrangement or restructuring inside the system, possibly of the inquiry being undertaken, of items of information, notions, etc., and which render it possible to "solve problems". See *Creativity; Thinking*.

I.M.D.

Productivity. 1. *In psychology:* a wealth of ideas, creative thinking or acting, often synonymous with *creativity* (q.v.). **2.** *In industrial theory:* the relation between expenditure and returns. An *increase in productivity* is made possible by various measures (e.g. technology, work study, marketing); it is not always the same as maximization of profit (see *Industrial psychology*).   *G.R.W.M.*

Product-moment correlation. A parametric method for determining the extent of the reciprocal relationship between two quantitative variables. It is calculated as the mean standardized deviation product (standardized covariance). See *Correlational techniques*.
    G.Mi.

Product sum. The sum of the products of the homologous measurements of a bivariate (q.v.) distribution. The product sum forms a link in the calculation formulae of various statistical kinds of measurement, as, for example, in the raw value formula for determining the product-moment correlation (q.v.).
    G.Mi.

Profile. A graphic representation of the results of a test battery in order to show clearly and simultaneously the relative height of the various results of an individual. The arrangements of the test may be linear or circular. In the latter case the setting of the tests may to some extent correspond to their degree of similarity, which is not the case with linear profiles. Profiles were first used by G. J. Rossolimo (1911) for an intelligence test and later by R. Meili and D. Wechsler, etc., for interests and emotional tendencies.   *R.M.*

Progesterone. Gonadotrophic hormone (q.v.). Progesterone is secreted, particularly in the second half of the cycle, from the corpus luteum; and there are large amounts during pregnancy. A single exogenous administration of progesterone has only very temporary effects (lasting a few hours). Performance is reduced and there are other deleterious subjective results. Experiments with animals tend to show that progesterone reduces the quantity of catecholamines (q.v.) in the central nervous system, and this has led to speculations about the etiology of depression (q.v.) during pregnancy. In male subjects the administration of progesterone decreases the intensity of the action of LSD. There are many natural and synthetic substances related to progesterone. See *Ovulation inhibitors*.

Bibliography: Zuckermann, S.: The ovary. Vols 1, 2. New York, 1962.   *W.J.*

Program. 1. In general: plan, purpose, timetable (e.g. of research, study). **2.** In electronic data processing (EDP): instructions for a computer (q.v.), indicating the sequence in which certain operations are to be carried out; for this, special programming languages (q.v.) (e.g. Fortran, Algol, Cobol) are used by programmers.   *G.R.W.M.*

Program language. Programs (q.v.) formulated with the elements of a program language can be automatically processed by a computer. A distinction is made between a *machine code* or *machine language* and a *problem-oriented program* language; the latter enables instructions to the computer (q.v.) to be formulated in the notation used in that problem area. For example, Algol uses algebraic "language" in combination with logical conditions. Computers translate automatically into the machine code. In addition to Algol, there is Fortran, which is used mainly where mathematics is required. Cobol in economics, PL 1 and Algol 68 are recent developments.
    K.-D.G.

Programmed instruction. Programmed instruction is a learning process objectified and split up into *steps* (q.v.); the individual is expected to become personally active by making an outward response. This determines, at least in part, the time when the next teaching step will begin. The steps *either* are very short, containing little information, and the response expected at any particular place is easy, *or* the individual receives some comment on his response after a very brief space of time (at least while actually working); this comment determines, at least in part, what the selection and sequence of further steps will be. See *Instructional technology*. H.F.

Bibliography: Coulson, J. E. (Ed.): Programmed learning and computer-based instruction. New York, 1962. Green, E. J.: The learning process and programmed instruction. New York, 1962. Lange, P. C. (Ed.): Programmed instruction. 66th Yearbook, Part II, NSSE. Chicago, 1967. Lysaught, J. P. & Williams, C. M.: A guide to programmed instruction. New York, 1963. Mager, R. F.: Preparing instructional objectives. Palo Alto, Cal., 1962. Markle, S. M.: Good frames and bad: a grammar of frame writing. New York, 1964. Ofeish, G. D.: Programmed instruction: a guide for management. New York, 1965. Entelek-Northwester U. Programmed instruction guide. Boston, 1967. Joint Committee on Programmed Instruction and Teaching Machines: Recommendations for reporting the effectiveness of programmed instruction materials. Washington, D.C., 1966. Smallwood, R. D.: A decision structure for teaching machines. Cambridge, Mass., 1962. Stolurow, L. M.: Teaching by machine. Washington, D.C., 1961. Taber, J. I., Glaser, R., & Schaefer, H. H.: Learning and programmed instruction. Reading, Mass., 1965. Thomas, C. A. et al.: Programmed learning in perspective: a guide to programme writing. Barking, 1963. R.G.

Programming. The setting up of a program (q.v.), i.e., fixing the order of the stages, actions and processes leading to certain goals. In education, programming denotes the development of teaching programs (q.v.). In electronic data processing, programming denotes the translation of a computer schedule of algorithms (q.v.) into a program language (q.v.). K.W.

Progressive Matrices Test. A matrices test (q.v.) (standardized by Raven, 1960, for English conditions) to determine intellectual ability. According to Raven, the method allows assessment of clear thinking and perceptual reasoning. The text exists in two versions: the standard form with matrices printed in black and white, and a colored form designed for children under eleven and for persons over sixty-five. The standard form is normalized for the age group 6–65; for the colored matrices there are norms from $5\frac{1}{2}$ to 11 and from 65 to 85. Calculations of retest reliability gave values for both forms ranging between $r = 0.63$ and $r = 0.98$.

Bibliography: Raven, J. C.: Guide to the Standard Progressive Matrices. London, 1960. Id.: Guide to using the Coloured Progressive Matrices. London, 1965. P.S.

Progressive paralysis. A syphilitic inflammation of the brain tissue, which may supervene eight to ten years after infection and which occurs chiefly in the area of the frontal lobes. Chronic syphilitic encephalitis causes atrophy of the nerve cells, and as a result progressive dementia, and sometimes psychotic images, e.g. euphoria (q.v.), paranoia (q.v.), depression (q.v.), delusions (q.v.), hallucinations and impairment of reasoning. A neurological examination reveals pupillary disturbances and occasionally other morbid symptoms. The diagnosis is confirmed by blood tests. Therapy (penicillin) at an approximate stage can usually arrest the process, but cannot restore deficits. C.Sch.

Projection. An (inner) defense (q.v.) mechanism in which a personal motive that is forbidden or can no longer be gratified is perceived by the person concerned as a motive of one or several *other* persons. This (erroneous) perception usually contributes to diminishing anxiety about increased possibilities of gratification of the motive which can no longer be gratified or is forbidden, or to making a more effective renunciation of the gratification of this personal motive than would be possible without projection. It is not always possible to make a clear distinction between projection on the one hand and the perception or interpretation of the motives of other people on the other hand. The more outside observers agree with the affected individual about his perception of motives in another person, the more improbable it is that the case is one of projection. Working partly along the same lines as Freud, Dollard & Miller (1950), two experts on learning theory, point to the complexity of this learning mechanism. Even a child discovers that members of a community behave alike, that certain forms of behavior (e.g. friendly approach or aggression) can easily lead to similar behavior in others and that the punishment is less severe if someone else was the leading spirit, i.e. if the motive responsible for the punishment was someone else's. Prejudices, certain untried opinions and superstitions are frequently based on projections. Serious projections, i.e. such as completely ignore reality, occur in psychoses (q.v.), especially in paranoia (q.v.), depression (q.v.) and schizophrenia (q.v.). Freud's concept of projection as a defense mechanism came in for several modifications, especially during the development of projective (q.v.) methods, where its function as anxiety preventing mechanism, for example, was often disputed (H. A. Murray).

Bibliography: Miller, N. E. & Dollard, J.: Personality and psychotherapy. New York, 1950. **Toman, W.:** Psychoanalytic theory of motivation. London & New York, 1960.   *W. Toman*

Projection, eccentric. The introspective observation that sensory experiences are usually localized outside the body at the same position as the stimulus object, particularly as regards the visual and auditory sense modalities. Thus the blue is seen as on the sky rather than in the retina, and the sound of a radio receiver is perceived as being at its source rather than in the ears. (A rather pointless piece of philosophy associated with Helmholtz.)   *G.D.W.*

Projection fibers. The projection tracts are composed of projection fibers. They join parts of the brain together and to the spinal cord. Such fibers conduct the flow of action only in one direction, either from the center in the direction of the periphery or vice versa. Projection fields are areas of the cortex at which projection fibers begin or end. Examples: anterior and posterior central convolution (q.v.), motor pathways (q.v.), gyrus (q.v.).

Bibliography: Gardner, E.: Fundamentals of neurology. Philadelphia & London, 1968.   *G.A.*

Projective interest test. Any interest test in which the interests of the individual are ascertained by a projective technique. *H.J.A.*

Projective techniques. Projective techniques are a group of psychological techniques and procedures that claim to disclose the basic (underlying, hidden) personality structure and motivations of a subject by having him organize, respond to, or deal with materials or stimuli in a free, unlimited way without reference to a preconceived system of correct or incorrect answers.

Projective is derived from *projection*; these terms frequently refer to techniques developed for representing three-dimensional surfaces on two-dimensional planes, as in the practical fields of cartography and map-making (for instance, Mercator projections). By the end of the sixteenth century, projection not only denoted the *action* of projection, that is, in throwing or casting forth or forward, but the less tangible mental process, as in the construction of mental projects, scheming, and planning. Actual references to projective techniques were not found until some time in the twentieth century; but around 1900, *projection* was already being used to mean "the tendency to ascribe to another person feelings, thoughts, or attitudes present in oneself, or to regard external reality as embodying such feelings, etc., in some way" (see: Random House Dictionary of the English Language, 1966).

Projection as a defense mechanism differs somewhat from projection as used in projective techniques. The former concept is generally attributed to Freud, who used it as early as 1896 (see: Freud, 1950). In this sense, projection is a defensive system or process in which impulses, wishes, and ideas are externalized because their conscious recognition would be too painful to the ego. But, as Murray (1951) and others have indicated, projections as elicited by a projective technique can actually be unrepressed, conscious, acceptable, or even admirable, and need not include defensive or anxiety-avoidant components.

For a detailed and specific account of the use of inkblots and various other projective stimuli in human affairs (inkblots, for example, were used by Leonardo da Vinci in the fifteenth century to stimulate the imagination [da Vinci, 1882]) the reader is referred to Zubin, Eron & Schumer (1965). From the beginning of recorded history, the evidence suggests that amorphous and ambiguous stimuli, for example, clouds, entrails of animals, and so on, were used for divination, reaching decisions, omens, predictions of things to come, and various sacrificial purposes. Bypassing such early use of ambiguous stimuli, we note that the majority of techniques and stimuli currently described in the literature on projective techniques have had a long history of use and study in the laboratory. Inkblots were used before Hermann Rorschach's time in experiments on imagination and in the investigation of intelligence. In the early decades of this century, Stern (see: Stern, 1938) and others employed pictures of a somewhat ambiguous nature in the investiga-

tion of testimony (*Aussage*) and Binet and Simon (1905) used them for measuring intelligence; Ebbinghaus (1897) and Ziehen (1923) employed incomplete sentences to measure intelligence, and picture completion methods were also used in this connection. Laboratory explorations of will and imagination often employed word association methods.

Historically, projective techniques arose as a protest by "dynamically" oriented clinical psychologists against what they regarded as the inability of objective methods to meet the demands of personality diagnosis. The development of these procedures, with its accompanying revolt against the rigorous framework demanded by workers in the field of intelligence and achievement testing, seemed to be based on new principles. For example, the scoring of responses as "correct" or "incorrect" was abandoned; freedom and choice in performance were introduced into the instructions; scoring procedures became more complex, as did interpretation of the responses of S; and the style and manner of S's performance began to assume importance. Some critics point out that, as a result of these more "liberal" attitudes, many scientific and psychometric standards were sacrificed.

Details of the development of projective instruments will not be presented here. Three major influences on the nature of projective techniques should be noted, however: although Hermann Rorschach's classic monograph was not published until shortly before his death in 1922 (see: third ed., 1942), he conducted his "experiments" with inkblots before World War I; Morgan & Murray published a note on the Thematic Apperception Test (TAT) about two decades later (1935); a few years later, Frank (1939) proposed his projective hypothesis and was generally credited with the labeling of projective methods as such.

In describing projective methods, Frank (1939) offered a celebrated classificatory scheme: constitutive, constructive, interpretative, cathartic, and refractive methods. Actually, many classificatory schemes have been described, so that even these can be classified into, say, those that stress the nature of the materials, the manner of interpretation, or the type of behavior or response that is required of S.

In any event, the wide variety, scope, and range of projective procedures and methods can only be indicated, not specified, because of space limitations. (For detailed references, summaries, and descriptions of a large number of projective methods, see: Rabin [1968], Schneidman [1965], Zubin, Eron, & Schumer [1965], and especially Buros [1965].) Besides the Rorschach and Thematic Apperception Technique (TAT)—the two most frequently used instruments—there are various derivatives and modifications of pictorial methods, such as the Blacky Pictures and Children's Apperception Test, many adaptations of drawing procedures, such as the House-Tree-Person technique, a wide variety of sentence completion and story-telling methods, various play kits and materials, filmed puppet materials (e.g., Rock-A-Bye, Baby), etc. Additional techniques include: the Howard Inkblot Test, Kahn Test of Symbol Arrangement, Levy Movement Blots, Lowenfeld Mosaic Test, Schneidman Make A Picture Story (MAPS) Test, Rosenzweig Picture-Frustration Study, the Holtzman Inkblot Technique, and many others.

It is virtually impossible to describe the heterogeneity, methodologically speaking, of the extant techniques. They differ in terms of normative samples, amount of reliability and validity data, objectivity of scoring, scope and content of personality variables the technique is purportedly reflecting, and theoretical bias of the constructs on which the procedure seems to be based. The diversity and range of quality and quantity in this field are impressive. Even the *raison d'être* for different techniques varies: some techniques were developed because of dissatisfaction with available instruments, and were offered as "better" and more effective substitutes; other techniques were "custom-made" for specific experimental investigations (see: Lesser [1961] for a discussion of such instruments); others were introduced because they seemed to possess clinical "richness" and utility. Critical appraisal of the different methods also covers a wide range. Several reviewers are quite impressed with the clinical depth and effectiveness of some techniques (for example, the Blacky Pictures); other reviewers are more skeptical, wondering why some techniques were even put before the professional public when knowledge about them was so meager.

In general, the promise of projective techniques, according to many reviewers and critics, has not been fulfilled. Even their extensive use in cross-cultural research (Henry, 1955; Lindzey, 1961; and Zubin, Eron & Schumer, 1965) has been severely criticized. Yet some of the clinicians who question the scientific status of many of these instruments use them clinically, claiming that their use yields abundant rewards, especially in experienced hands. Nevertheless, the researcher is hard put to demonstrate this clinical effectiveness, no matter how ingenious and inventive he is in simulating the clinical situation. Moreover, the years of training required to become expert in the use of many projective methods, and the time involved in their administration, scoring, and interpretation, raise issues in regard to their efficiency and economy, especially since some psychologists feel that such techniques are often used to elicit information more readily available through other methods, such as standardized interviews or observations.

The methodological problems inherent in many of these techniques are not easily solved. Some of them have to do with the current status of personality theory, diagnosis, and the thorny issues relating to the criteria to which one presumably looks to validate projective instruments. Psychiatric diagnosis, definitions of mental health and illness, and questions concerning prediction and outcome are criterion problems filled with considerations concerning their own reliability and validity, independent of equally complex considerations concerning the instruments themselves (Zubin & Endicott [1969] summarize some of these issues).

Although projective methods are characterized by some of the most difficult problems in the psychometric field, needless to say, not all methods are thus plagued to an equal degree. Yet, ironically, the most frequently used techniques, such as the Rorschach and TAT, seem to be beset with more complex problems than many of the other instruments (Zubin, Eron, & Schumer [1965] present an exposition of some of these problems, especially with regard to considerations of reliability and validity). These include, in addition to questions of reliability, problems in connection with sampling considerations, base rates, item validity, overall validity of interpretations, cross-validation of findings, and so on. Further, to understand the projective response, the variables which have been shown to influence it must be carefully examined. For many instruments, these include not only the entire reinforcement history of S but also the parameters of the stimulus situation itself. Thus, among the variables related to the S's response are: S's verbal-expressive skills; his productivity (frequently a reflection of intellectual and socio-cultural variables); the interaction between E and S and various other examiner effects; the nature of the test situation; the manner in which S assigns cognitive and verbal meaning to perceptual events (as in the Rorschach); the set and attitude toward testing that S brings to the situation; and the nature of the stimulus materials presented to S. Needless to say, not all of the foregoing have been sufficiently studied or understood. The picture is not entirely bleak, however, and there are new developments. Some researchers, for example, are trying to solve some of the foregoing problems by constructing newer, more refined techniques (for example, the Holtzman Inkblot Technique [1961, 1968]).

Perhaps the severest criticism that can be made of the current projective techniques is the lack of a specified scientific model for their structure which can give rise to testable hypotheses for probing the tenability of both hypotheses and model. Consequently, most research is of the ad hoc variety. When such models become available it will become possible to integrate the results of projective technique investigations with the rest of the science of psychology. That these techniques have persisted despite scientific evidence of their validity is proof of the need to answer the questions they are tackling. Whether they are suitable for the task remains to be seen.

Bibliography: Binet, A. & Simon, T.: Application des méthodes nouvelles au diagnostic du niveau primaire. Année psych., 1905, *11*, 245–336. **Buros, O. K.:** The sixth mental measurements yearbook. Highland Park, N.J., 1965, 409–540. **Ebbinghaus, H.:** Über eine neue Methode zur Prüfung geistiger Fähigkeiten und ihre Anwendung bei Schulkindern. Z. Psychol., Physiol., 1897, *13*, 401–59. **Frank, L. K.:** Projective methods for the study of personality. J. Psychol., 1939, *8*, 389–413. **Henry, J.:** Symposium: projective testing in ethnography. Amer. Anthrop., 1955, *57*, 245–70. **Holtzman, W. H.:** Holtzman inkblot technique. In: **Rabin, A.** (Ed.): Projective techniques in personality assessment. New York, 1968, 136–70. **Holtzman, W. H.,** *et al.*: Inkblot perception and personality—Holtzman inkblot technique. Austin, 1961. **Lesser, G. S.:** Custom-making projective tests for research. J. proj. Tech., 1961, *25*, 21–35. **Morgan, C. D. & Murray, H. A.:** A method for investigating fantasies: the thematic apperception test. Arch. Neurol. Psychiat., 1935, *34*, 289–306. **Murray, H. A.:** Foreword. In: **Anderson, H. M. & Anderson, G. L.** (Eds.): An introduction to projective techniques. Englewood Cliffs, N.J., 1951, 11–14. **Rabin, A. I.** (Ed.): Projective techniques in personality assessment. New York, 1968. **Random House** dictionary of the English language. The unabridged edition. New York, 1966. **Rorschach, H.:** Psychodiagnostics. Berne, 1942. **Schneidman, E. S.:** Projective techniques. In: **Wolman, B. B.** (Ed.): Handbook of clinical psychology. New York, 1965,

408–521. **Stern, W.**: General psychology from the personalistic point of view. New York, 1938. **Ziehen, T.**: Die Prinzipien und Methoden der Begabungs-, insbesondere der Intelligenzprüfung bei Gesunden und Kranken. Berlin, 1923. **Zubin, J. & Endicott, J.**: From milestone to millstone to tombstone (Review of: Rapaport, D., Gill, M. M. & R. Schafer: Diagnostic psychological testing). Contem. Psychol., 1969, *14*, 280–83; **Zubin, J., Eron, L. D. & Schumer, F.**: An experimental approach to projective techniques. New York, 1965.   *F. Schumer & J. Zubin*

Prolepsy. A normal speech variant found in very young children which is due to the psychic conditions of a lively attentiveness outrunning the ability to speak. Word images occur more quickly than sound formations with the result that a sound belonging to a subsequent syllable breaks through before the act of speech has reached it. This phenomenon is described as *proleptic* or *anticipatory* assimilation. Example: *gugar* for *sugar*.   *M.Sa.*

Promiscuity. A prescientific concept which is vague, ambiguous and often used to express a moral judgment; it refers to hetero- or homosexual intercourse with "a variety of partners". Sexual freedom, the frequent change of partners and premarital sexuality do not constitute promiscuity; they are rather attitudes and forms of behavior in the context of psychosexual learning processes necessary to obtain personal and sexual experience of hetero- or homosexual partnership. Promiscuity might possibly be defined (following Giese's argument) as apersonal (non-binding) sexual activity involving or directed at anonymous partners which does not go beyond the "purely sexual" and is largely ephemeral in character. In this sense, promiscuity is an aspect or principal feature of genuine perversions. See *Perversion; Sexuality.*   *H.M.*

Prompting. (Prompts = learning aids.) Prompting denotes the *offering of learning aids* during a learning process. The method is used especially for learning paired associates (q.v.). The prompts are offered in the form of a complete or partial presentation of the response (q.v.) which has to be learnt immediately *before* the opportunity for an overt response arrives (proffered stimulus). In programmed instruction (q.v.) very frequent use is made of prompting: the context of the learning step, the sentence structure, correlative words, opposites or examples (connotative prompting) point to the correct response; or the response appears directly and is highlighted by the type of print; or it appears in fragmentary form (denotative prompting). Investigations indicate that prompting can be more important than reinforcement (q.v.) by confirmation of the answer. But at the same time there is also the danger of over-prompting: the irrelevant syntax is learned instead of the substance. See *Instructional technology.*

Bibliography: Glaser, R.: Teaching machines and programmed learning. Washington, 1965.   *H.I.*

Propaganda. The concept came into general use in 1622 with the institution of the Vatican *Congregatio de Propaganda Fide* (Congregation for the Propagation of the Faith); today it is frequently thought of as a variety of publicity. Propaganda is the systematic attempt to influence the attitudes of individuals or groups by spreading deliberately chosen items of information, irrespective of whether these items are true, true in part, or untrue. As distinct from education, propaganda—strictly speaking—is defined as an intentional attempt to change usual standards. In general, propaganda makes use of available patterns of thinking, feeling and acting and these are mobilized as a frame of reference, the object of propaganda being represented as if it were perceived as part of this system; other systems of reference contradicting this tendency *are not mentioned* and are avoided. The process consists of deliberately intensifying the relation between the individual and the extraneous group and thus creating prejudices and a system of stereotypes with persuasive and formalized phrases and slogans (appraisal and decision patterns). If propaganda is to be effective, the following are the most important considerations: (*a*) trustworthiness of the communicator; (*b*) absence of interfering attitudes; (*c*) coincidence with individual experience; and (*d*) absence of counter-propaganda (e.g. where there is a monopoly in totalitarian states). See *Attitude; Prejudice; Manipulation; Stereotype.*

Bibliography: Albig, W.: Modern public opinion. New York, 1956. Katz, D. *et al.* (Eds.): Public opinion and propaganda. New York, 1956.   *W.N.*

Proportion. The numerical relation of two mathematical quantities to one another. The relative (q.v.) frequency of classes (q.v.) of values is sometimes referred to as proportional frequency.   *G.Mi.*

Proprioceptive; proprioceptive reflex. Reflexes are divided topographically (according to where the receptor is located in the organism) into *extero-, intero-* and *proprioceptive* reflexes. Proprioceptive reflexes (known also as personal reflexes) may be regarded as special forms of interoreceptive reflexes involved in the position of the body in general, or of individual limbs. The pressure and stretching receptors in the muscles, tendons and ligaments as well as the receptors of the labyrinth (q.v.) mediate such proprioceptive reflexes. These are important for coordinating and controlling movement. See *Motor skills.*
     H.R.

Proprium. A term used by Allport to denote the personal central area; it replaces such expressions as *ego* (q.v.), *self* (q.v.), etc.,

which, according to Allport, were given too specific a meaning. Even the aspect of the individual and his knowledge of himself was referred to as "self", hence Allport proposes that the "term 'proprium' should be used to denote the self as 'object' of 'knowing and feeling' ". Proprium embraces seven aspects: 1. sense of the corporal self; 2. sense of continuing self-identity; 3. self-respect, pride; 4. extension of the self; 5. self-image; 6. self as someone capable of rational action; 7. propriate striving.   *H.J.A.*

Prosencephalon. See *Forebrain.*

Prostitution. The relatively indiscriminate granting of sexual favors for payment or material reward. Prostitution is not confined to one sex; in almost every society there is hetero- (female) and homo- (male) prostitution. Official and unofficial attitudes towards prostitution vary from its rejection as a "manifestation of social disease" (Società Italiana di Medicina, Rome, 1950), its banning by law (e.g. in parts of the USA), to prostitution as a legally authorized form of economic activity (e.g. in Japan). There are just as many variations in the forms taken by heterosexual prostitution: religious prostitution, temple prostitution which does not have the character of prostitution as understood in Europe, and the ancient Greek system of *hetaerae*, Roman *bonae* (low-class prostitutes), Japanese geisha girls, brothel prostitution (the "stews") from the Middle Ages to the twentieth century, street prostitution, occasional prostitution, public and clandestine prostitution, etc. There are also numerous theories about the origin of prostitution: the main lines are those of the biologico-psychological, economic and environmental theories (Bernsdorf, 1968).

1. *Heterosexual prostitution:* its structure and extent in every society are chiefly

determined by two factors: (*a*) tolerance of premarital sexuality results in young men having less intercourse with prostitutes; (*b*) the less unmarried men there are of any age, the less frequent are contacts with prostitutes. Hence, in the nineteenth and even in the twentieth century, heterosexual prostitution was a safety valve for tabooed premarital sexuality, a mechanism which bourgeois society saw as an evil necessary to preserve the "ideal of virtuous feminine purity".

2. *Homosexual prostitution* differs in certain fundamental respects from female prostitution: (*a*) homosexual prostitution is chiefly occasional; (*b*) female prostitution offers the heterosexual world a deviant sexual alternative, homosexual male prostitution provides a deviant sub-culture with a deviant form of sexual contact; (*c*) a female prostitute receives payment because her client has an orgasm (q.v.), the male prostitute is almost always paid for his own orgasm; for this reason alone, male prostitution is more infrequent than female. Furthermore, contrary to general belief, male prostitutes are mostly heterosexual and usually remain so. See *Homosexuality*.

Bibliography: Bernsdorf, W.: Soziologie der Prostitution. In: Giese, H. (Ed.): Die Sexualität des Menschen. Stuttgart, 1968. Esselstyn, T. C.: Prostitution in the United States. Annals of the American Academy of Political and Social Science, 1968, *375*, 133.   *H.M.*

Protanopia. Form of color blindness (q.v.) in which the first receptor pigment of the cones which is sensitive to red is completely absent, whereas in protanomaly it has a diminished effect. See *Color vision*.   *K.H.P.*

Protean behavior. Used to distract the attention of the enemy from its prey. If a lizard is seized, it frequently sheds its tail, which then writhes violently, thereby attracting attention and enabling the threatened animal to make good its escape. Many birds—chiefly those which nest on the ground—pretend that a wing has been injured when a predator comes near the nest and so entice it away. Among higher mammals a certain number of artifices reminiscent of "human" behavior and designed to deceive an enemy are known.

V.P.

Protective inhibition. In Pavlov's behaviorism protective inhibition is the diminished effectiveness of a stimulus when its intensity has exceeded a certain level. Pavlov derives the phenomenon from an inhibition process said to prevent excessive functional deterioration of cortical cells. More recent findings in brain physiology, however, tend not to support this interpretation of the phenomenon; corresponding modifications have been made in Pavlovian theory (cf. Pickenhain, 1959). Protective inhibition is conceived as a form of *unconditioned inhibition* (q.v.).

Bibliography: Pavlov, I. P.: Lectures on conditioned reflexes. Vols. 1 & 2. New York & London, 1928/41.

Protocol sentences (syn. *Basic sentences*). Carnap (1932/33) uses the term for sentences which the original protocol contains and which form the basis of an empirical system of scientific concepts ("system language"). Such sentences transcribe a *direct and actual event*, a factual being (factual stage), the elementary experience of a single individual in his unity and complex and concrete totality (sophism), "thus", "here", "now". Although they may belong to the protocol language, whose atomistic sentences they are, they are nevertheless intelligible in their *intersubjectivity*. They need no further verification and are used to check the sentences of the *system language*, or as a basis for all remaining basic sentences of a science.

Bibliography: Carnap, R.: Über Protokollsätze. Erkenntnis, 1932/33, *3*, 215–28. Neurath, O.: Protokollsätze. Erkenntnis, 1932/33, *3*, 204–14.

M.J.B.

Protopathic sensibility. A collective concept for sensations of pain and temperature as well as for crude sensations of pressure and contact. It is conducted along anterior nerve pathways (q.v.) in the spinal cord. By contrast, epicritic (q.v.) (gnostic) sensitivity is conducted in the phylogenically recent posterior pathways. *G.A.*

Pseudodebility. Slight feeble-mindedness affecting only a few functions and remediable given special etiological conditions (such as illness, sensory or speech defects, environmental but not hereditary factors) and the right methods of treatment and education. See *Mental defect.* *M.A.*

Pseudo-hallucination. A hallucination which lacks the quality of objectivity. Hence one may see things which have no basis in reality, but one is nevertheless aware of their unreality. Pseudo-hallucinations are particularly a feature of states produced by drugs. *C.D.F.*

Pseudo-isochromatic charts. Charts designed for the diagnosis of anomalous color vision, such as those in the *Ishihara tests* (q.v.). They are composed of various colored dots arranged so that a normal person perceives a meaningful pattern (e.g. a number or letter) whereas color-blind individuals perceive either a different pattern or none at all. The principle upon which they are based is that certain pairs of hues (especially red and green) are not distinguishable to the color-blind person, who is then forced to make his response in terms of other cues such as relative brightness, or else can make no response at all. *G.D.W.*

Pseudolism (Latin: *pseudolus* = habitual liar). A certain psychological or psychopathological phenomenon; orgiastic experience of imagined or fanciful sexual acts, usually in full knowledge of their pseudo-nature, the fictitiousness of the act—even where it is built into a real sexual incident (Giese, 1965, 12). The pseudolist uses language in a most abnormal way in the form of writing (e.g. obscene letters), speaking, reading (sexual gossip), listening (to himself or other persons) in which the fictitious sexual actions or roles are lived through in a kind of sexual waking dream in an attempt to get rid of the reality and its demands. Giese has shown the psychopathological relations between pseudolism and perversion (q.v.) on the one hand and between pseudolism and "obscene" literature on the other. See *Pornography.*

Bibliography: **Giese, H.:** Psychopathologie der Sexualität. Stuttgart, 1962. **Id.:** Das obszöne Buch. Beitr. z. Sexualforsch., 1965, *35.* *H.M.*

Pseudoneurosis. Frankl used the term to denote those diseases which occur with neurotic symptoms but are of somatic origin. Thus agoraphobia (fear of open spaces), for example, may be the manifestation of a disguised hyperthyreosis, the objective symptom of which is too great activity. There is much dispute about this concept of pseudoneurosis. In normal medical terminology it is used to denote cases in which a neurosis has been wrongly diagnosed but where in reality there is some somatic disease. A patient whose blood pressure is too high may have, for example, a bad headache, palpitations of the heart, and little power of concentration, but all this may be due to hypertonia (q.v.). In many cases there is a common term to describe disorders which have organic or neurotic causes; thus tachycardia can be the expression used for both heart damage and a heart neurosis. *J.L.I.*

Pseudo-pregnancy. Physical symptoms of pregnancy (missing the period, swelling of the body) without the actual state occurring.

A classic example of a psychosomatic connection (see *Psychosomatics*) which has already been described in animals (e.g. dogs).

W.Sch.

Pseudoscope. A device which reverses the normal optical relationships so that the image which normally falls on the left retina is presented to the right eye, and vice versa. Used in the investigation of retinal disparity as an important basis of the perception of visual depth; distance relations tend to be reversed so that convex surfaces appear concave, and so on.

G.D.W.

Psi. Abbreviation of "parapsychical" (= paranormal) usually used in hyphenated expressions: for example, "psi-ability", "psi-process", etc. Introduced by J. B. Rhine as a non-committal term for the critical component in parapsychological phenomena.   *J.B.*

Psi Gamma ($\psi\gamma$). Paranormal cognition. A term introduced by R. H. Thouless as more non-committal than extrasensory perception (q.v.).

J.B.

Psi Kappa ($\psi\kappa$). Paranormal action (= psychokinesis, q.v.). A term introduced by R. H. Thouless to correspond to his psi gamma (q.v.).

J.B.

Psilocybin. An alkaloid of the Mexican narcotic mushroom "teonanacatl". Its narcotic effects are qualitatively similar to those of LSD and mescalin; disturbances of perception, thinking and affect are experienced (see *Psychotomimetics*). It differs from the other substances mentioned in the time it takes to act (psilocybin begins to act most quickly—after about thirty minutes, and its effects wear off quite rapidly—after two to four hours).

Bibliography: Hollister, L. E. & Hartmann, A. M.: Mescalin, lysergic acid diethylamide and psilocybin: comparison of clinical syndromes, effects on color perception and biochemical measures. Comp. Psychiat., 1962, *3*, 235–41. **Wolbach, A. B.** *et al.*: Comparison of psilocin with psilocybin, mescalin and LSD-25. Psychopharmacologia, 1962, *3*, 219–23.   *G.E.*

Psi missing. Score in a parapsychological experiment which is significantly below chance-expectation, suggesting a paranormal avoidance of the target (q.v.).   *J.B.*

Psi-systems. According to Freud's first version of the topological structure of the psyche these are the *preconscious* system and the *unconscious* system. Both are censored by the conscious system; as a result thoughts and desires can pass from the preconscious without any internal resistance, whereas those from the unconscious cannot immediately become conscious, or can only do so in the face of internal resistance. See *Freud.*   *W.T.*

Psychagogy. A term for "minor" or "clinically active" psychotherapy (Schultz, 1963), designed to develop in neurotics and persons with crisis-like disorders self-confidence and an understanding of their own worth; this it does by showing the patient some goal fitted to his personality and by supervising his progress. Hence it may be extremely useful when behaviorally disturbed children or seriously ego-disturbed patients (e.g. psychotics) are in need of treatment. Its object is to use prophylaxis to eliminate incipient wrong attitudes, to control unstable behavior by clear information and, when the principal psychotherapeutic work has been concluded, to guide the patient to the *discovery of his own personality* along the lines of "Achieve what is in you". Thus the psychagogue is in part doctor, teacher and priest—according to H. Schultz-Henche he is a teacher trained in depth psychology. Schultz situates psychagogy between psychotherapy of the mind and the organism, whereas other writers (Kurth, 1960) lay greater emphasis on the pedagogic aspect (therapeutic education). The principal method of psychagogy is counseling in its various forms. Important supportive methods in current use are *logotherapy* (q.v.), *autogenic training* (q.v.), with graded exercises in active hypnosis (E. Kretschmer), and *rational psychotherapeutic* breathing (L. Heyer). "Bibliotherapy" is widely used in Anglo-Saxon countries; the aim here is for the patient to understand himself by special reading assignments. More ambitious is music therapy (q.v.) (Pontvik), which uses mainly Bach's organ music (possibly interspersed with jazz) to arouse the patient and induce a *cathartic* action. Therapeutic education, in which psychagogy has only an advisory function is, together with the educative special treatment of a defect, "exemplary counselling and guidance in the Socratic sense" (Kurth, 1960).

Bibliography: **Kurth, W.**: Psychotherapie. Munich, 1960. **Schultz, J. H.**: Die seelische Krankenbehandlung. Stuttgart, [8]1963. **Zulliger, H.**: Gespräche über Erziehung. Berne, 1960. *E.U.*

Psychalgia. Every pain is accompanied by some emotional change. Pain could thus be considered as a sensation of feeling. When pain actually occurs without any physical connection, it is described as "psychalgia" ("psychic pain"). In most cases it is interpreted as a symptom of some transformation and its psychogenesis is looked for. But in reality psychalgia should be regarded as a depressive or thymopathic equivalent; examples are headaches or pain in the arm and also precordial pain. They appear as symptoms of what is actually nothing but a disguised depression. See *Psychosomatics*. *J.L.I.*

Psychasthenia. The term was introduced by Janet and denotes a general lowering of the psychic level. Psychasthenics have great difficulty in adapting to their environment and accepting reality: anxiety states, obsessions (q.v.), etc., also occur. Nowadays the word "psychasthenia" is rarely used. Janet's patients suffered chiefly from *anxiety* states, *phobias* (q.v.), and occasionally feelings of depersonalization; hence Janet wished to contrast neurasthenia (q.v.) and hysteria (q.v.). Modern psychology sometimes speaks of *asthenic psychopaths*; characteristic symptoms are a very pronounced tendency to become fatigued and hypochondriac personality traits. *J.L.I.*

Psyche. For the Greeks, the personification of the vital principle: *life, soul*. A designation for the soul in the most general sense, in contrast to the material body, or *soma*. In the narrowest sense, the term represents the totality of mental acts, or psychic functions and determinants of behavior (Wundt). In psychoanalysis (q.v.) it is the totality of conscious and unconscious: *subjectivity* as opposed to that which is wholly organic. In depth psychology (q.v.) the term is used to avoid the religious and spiritualistic implications of the words "soul" and "spirit". The notion of "psyche" suggests (but does not necessarily imply) a dualism. *M.R.*

Psychesthetic proportion. Scales of temperament found in the schizothymic (q.v.) and schizoid (q.v.) constitution when the criterion of sensitivity is applied. Degrees of stimulability can occur in one individual or, one degree can decide permanently the individual style of response (E. Kretschmer). Psychesthetic proportions of the schizothymic constitution are: (*a*) sensitive (nervous), (*b*) dry, (*c*) hypesthetic (severe, cool); of the schizoid constitution: (*a*) hyperesthetic (oversensitive), (*b*) anesthetic (cold, apathetic). See *Traits*. *W.K.*

Psychiatric Screening Test. Known also as the Saslow Screening Test. An inventory used to elucidate the question of how far a patient has the tendency to transform affective experiences into somatic reactions. There are two forms depending on the intellectual level of the individual. See *Psychosomatics*.

Bibliography: Saslow, G., Counts, R. & Dubois, P. H.: Evaluation of a new Psychiatric Screening Test. Psychosomatic Medicine, 1951, *13*, 242–53.   *H.J.A.*

Psychiatry. That branch of medicine which is concerned with mental disorder and mental illness.   *R.H.*

Psychical research. The original term for parapsychology (q.v.), still widely current in England. Ex.: "Society for Psychical Research".   *J.B.*

Psychic energy. A metaphor for the dynamic aspect of behavior. Inasmuch as it refers to diverse significations of "energy" in physical theory, the term implies a particular answer to the mind-body problem (q.v.). It also stands for a Freudian model of the various forms of libido (q.v.). See *Energy, psychic or psychical* for an account of Freud's notion.   *P.M.*

Psychic epidemic. An expression formerly used to characterize behavioral phenomena which spread rapidly in some population, e.g. suicide "epidemics", a general fear of certain diseases. The inclination to imitate certain critical ways of behaving seems to be greater in periods of crisis, possibly because the ground has already been prepared by more general forms of uncertainty.   *H.D.S.*

Psychic functions. When a symptom, either physical or psychological, is found to offer some secondary benefit or provide emotional comfort of some kind to the patient, then it is said to have a psychic function. (Used in this sense the term *psychic* is synonymous with *psychological*, and is usually avoided in scientific psychology because of its connection with spiritualism.) Symptoms with psychic functions, e.g. *psychic blindness* and *psychic pain*, may or may not have a simple physiological basis, so long as they serve a psychological function, and are thus distinguished from *psychogenic* symptoms, which are presumed to have no physical origin.   *G.D.W.*

Psychic photography. The paranormal production of images on a light-sensitive film. Also known as "thoughtography".   *J.B.*

Psychic saturation. See *Saturation*.

Psychic tempo. See *Tempo, personal*.

Psychic treatment. Out-of-date term for psychotherapy (q.v.).

Psychoacoustics. The physics of sound as relating to audition and to the physiology and psychology of sound reception.

Psychoanalysis. Its founder, Freud, defined this as a scientific discipline consisting (*a*) of a method of research the object of which is to bring to light the unconscious meaning of words, actions and mental images; (*b*) of a psychotherapeutic method based on this research and employing specific means of intervention such as the interpretation of secret wishes and the resistance which seeks to prevent their free expression; and (*c*) of a system of psychological and psychopathological theories constructed on the data supplied by the method of interpretation or emerging during the treatment of patients. It may be said with good reason that psychoanalysis is the work of a single researcher, its founder.

As the starting-point for his psychodynamic theories Freud (q.v.) used the work of the French school. In 1885 he learned from J. M. Charcot, the great clinician at the Salpêtrière, that certain symptoms of illness which have apparently been caused by nerve damage are in reality related to psychic factors that may influence them; cases of hysterical paralysis which can be successfully treated by hypnosis (q.v.) are an example. A short time afterwards (1889) Freud went to Nancy where H. Bernheim was carrying out experiments with so-called post-hypnotic suggestion (see *Hypnosis*). As he reflected on the automatic mechanism at work in the actions performed as a result of instructions received during hypnosis coupled with the order completely to forget these instructions, Freud became convinced that there are psychic factors capable of determining a series of behavioral acts while remaining hidden from the person concerned. From there it was possible to go on to investigate what further actions of everyday occurrence and what further symptoms might be determined by such mysterious psychic factors with an *unconscious* and yet *very strong dynamic* action. It began to occur to Freud that many cases of so-called parapraxis (q.v.) are in reality not casual actions, the result of fatigue or absentmindedness. In fact these actions prove to be due to those very same *unconscious* factors which operate in the carrying out of post-hypnotic instructions; moreover these actions always have some meaning which the person performing them is least able to recognize. Not only is this so, but this person often shows that he has no wish to recognize this fact whereas everybody else who saw what he did knows the significance of his action, and he angrily rejects their interpretation (1901).

Having reached this point, Freud was able to establish that the unconscious facts which had been observed belong to a world shut in by a barrier making it impossible for them to get out freely. They are shut up in this world by reason of a process which Freud called "repression", and are firmly held back there by a psychic censorship; this exclusion from the consciousness is responsible for a particular form of illness. Words, actions and mental images cannot in fact be kept out of the consciousness without resulting in an impoverishment of the personality. The great discovery made by Freud concerning these facts was that everything related to the unconscious has a pulsating dynamic character and is always trying to come into the light (consciousness); and since the barrier formed by censorship does not allow it to do this, it resorts to circumventive measures.

Inside the psyche a play of forces and counter-forces thus becomes stabilized and there is a latent and lasting conflict (q.v.): when the energy on either side is quantitatively feeble, as is the case in normal psychic life, the conflict is not disturbing and a breaking of the unconscious through the censorship is accepted casually and with profound inward relief, as happens in "humor" (q.v.) and in emotional participation in works of art (see *Literature, psychology of; Sublimation*). But if, instead, the conflict becomes really intense as a result of the excessive amount of energy, a compromise is arrived at between the unconscious drive and the defense opposing it, and symptoms of illness, psychoneurotic symptoms, appear.

The concept of the dynamic unconscious therefore leads on to the notion of repression, censorship, impoverishment of the personality and its being weighed down by dynamic compromises. It is also linked to the concept of desire for the repressed elements: to the extent that they manage to break through to the surface, they determine the behavior, appetites and needs of the subject, and, correlatively, the fear and destruction of such desires result in the total extinction of all vital desire.

To uncover the unconscious motivation of normal and psychopathological behavior, to mitigate the intensity of any conflict and to enrich the personality by the recovery of those energies hitherto denied it, is a program which corresponds to the first of the three aspects with which psychoanalysis has to deal, as Freud realized.

1. *Therapeutic technique.* Considered from a therapeutic angle, psychoanalysis is derived as a new method from the abovementioned postulates; when psychic life in its neurotic forms is more or less seriously disturbed by conflicts between drives and defense, and when in its psychotic forms it may be shattered because a drive has become too strong (or a defense too weak), so that there is now a direct link between the unconscious and reality, the impulse behind the drive loses, when there is accurate interpretation, the violent and pragmatic character which it possesses from its origin in a primitive psychic world. *Interpretation* is above all a question of *understanding*, and in order to make the unconscious intelligible, Freud accomplished a major task in his major work *The Interpretation of Dreams* (1900). Dreams (q.v.) appeared immediately to Freud as a royal road to the unconscious, and it is quite clear why: the physiological relaxation of the censorship occurring during sleep allows impulses to come to the surface which either remain shut up in the unconscious or else become only indirectly visible through compromises, i.e. in parapraxis or psychoneurotic symptoms. Through long reflection on his own dreams and those of his patients Freud managed to decipher the language of dreams, to define the laws governing the dynamic activity of the unconscious world and to make available a masterly storehouse of information—which has never been bettered—for further interpretation.

Interpretation is not concerned exclusively or even to any great extent with the account the patient gives of his dreams and the circumstances of his life, but it also looks closely into all that he conceals, forgets or repeats; in addition it concentrates on his behavior, especially with regard to the psychoanalyst from whom he is receiving treatment, and on his contradictions, repetitions or anything which is strange. To help in such an analysis the patient must to the best of his ability conform to the fundamental rule of psychoanalysis, which requires him to express in words everything that occurs to him and not to be deterred by useless, improper or absurd thoughts. In this way the conversation based on "free association" that is characteristic of psychoanalysis develops and enables the analyst to interpret two basic aspects of the unconscious: what is repressed, by directly deciphering the contents expressed in words, and the repressive forces; while he is doing this, he must watch with the utmost care how the patient defends himself and endeavors to evade the obligation imposed upon him by the fundamental rule. Interpretation, it must be remembered, is a method that must be applied in stages: not when the psychoanalyst has understood, but when the patient is able to respond, and shows by his dreams, his remarks and his behavior that he is already on the point of understanding what the interpretation is bringing to the light of consciousness.

To judge the suitable moment for the interpretation, the psychoanalyst needs to have clinical sensitivity and experience and a good training; if he does not possess this, it is quite possible that the repressive forces of the material interpreted at an inappropriate moment will be intensified. The result is that *resistance* builds up and makes therapeutic work more difficult. There may in any event be strong resistance due to traits of character from the beginning of the analytical work, so that the analysis of what is repressed has to be neglected in order to enable these traits to be dealt with by character-analysis according to the teaching of W. Reich (1950). Apart from its function and its usefulness as a source of information, interpretation gives rise to a process the knowledge of which is due entirely to psychoanalysis: transference (q.v.). By that is meant the strong emotional relationship of devoted submission or bitter hostility which develops between the analyst and the subject being analyzed and which, as Freud showed, is a recrudescence of the affective links between the patient and the persons who were most important to him in the world of his earliest childhood: mother, father or substitutes for them.

Transference has to be interpreted and the patient to be shown which person is really the object of his affect; it is only by such an analysis that the patient can overcome the affect and make the transference into an instrument for achieving considerable progress toward an adult way of life. But if the patient does not analyze the affect, because he refuses to accept the interpretation that his love or his hate are directed not toward the analyst but toward other persons, then the transfer produces such violent resistance to treatment that the analysis cannot be completed (1937) and has therefore to be interrupted. The manipulation of transference is one of the difficulties of analytical technique; the analyst can fail in his task if he succumbs to the belief that the feelings which the patient expresses about him do really refer to him. This attitude, known as "counter-transference", can ruin psychoanalysis; and so that it may be avoided, it is essential that everybody intending to become a psychoanalyst should submit to a long "didactic psychoanalysis".

2. *Psychological and psychopathological theory*. The theoretical concept is based on clinical practice and experience gained from innumerable patients, on knowledge of the normal working of the psyche which was acquired in didactic psychoanalysis, on the observation of young children and for some time now on psychological experiments as well. To Freud more than to anyone else belongs the credit for having recognized that the prime cause of repression is to be found in wrongly handling (denying) the drive-impulses, the libidinous desires in early childhood. It is impossible for repressed drives to grow, that is to say, they remain primitive, and as they have a dynamic character they nevertheless have a permanent influence on the behavior of the subject who, although biologically an adult, remains infantile with respect to those drives which were repressed in childhood.

Freud described the different stages from the first to the sixth year of life through which the libido (q.v.) passes in its development (1905), and found in neurotic adults—almost in a crystallized form—the immature forms of libido development (1908, 1931). He then showed that immaturity of the libido is always bound up with a condition of "narcissism" (q.v.), i.e. with self-love which acts as a barrier to the free display of the subject's feelings towards others; only when the libido has detached itself from excessive interest in its own body and can concentrate on interpersonal relationships, does it reach maturity; this takes place as the result of a long process lasting from the sixth year of life until adolescence and terminates with it. At the end of this stage, manhood or womanhood as the case may be is reached completely, there are no neurotic or psychotic symptoms, and narcissism has been outgrown. Freud had assimilated the libido (q.v.) to eros (q.v.), the life-drive, and later (1926) he set beside the libido a further fundamental energy, aggression (q.v.), assimilating it to the death instinct (q.v.).

This last-named step did not meet with the approval of all psychoanalysts, especially from the point of view that "life serves death", however, the principle has found increasing recognition that from the earliest months of life aggression (q.v.) is an active basic energy of psychic life. The English school of psychoanalysis founded by Melanie Klein has studied these ideas in detail (1955).

Hence *libido* and *aggression* form the two poles between which the dialectic of the emotional life is conducted, and they are the material of that unconscious psychic and instinctive process, strained to the point of discharge, which Freud called the "id" (q.v.), thereby substituting this concept for the "unconscious" which preceded it. Against the "id" Freud set the "ego" as a force derived from the "id" with the object of assessing reality and calculating the suitable moment for giving effect to its impulses. And finally Freud recognized a third psychic force, the "super-ego", which in the subject represents society with its taboos, and its conventional standard of conformist perfection (1923).

Quite recently, and especially in the USA., many psychoanalysts have postulated the existence of an "ego" which is not derived from the "id" but has always been autonomous, is not bound up with conflict, and interacts with the three forces enumerated by Freud. This "ego" is credited with operating the intellectual mechanisms (H. Hartmann, 1939) which enable optimal adaptation and the synthesis of reality to take place, in other words, creativity (q.v.) and the higher operations of thought (E. Kris, 1950), which in Freud's original scheme were performed instead by sublimation (q.v.) of the instincts (Freud, 1917). But modern psychoanalysis agrees with Freud in ascribing to the "ego" the formation of those systems of alarm and protection known as defense (q.v.) mechanisms (Anna Freud, 1937). In this connection the "ego" has a double function: as a force assessing internal and external reality the "ego" notices any possible threat and mobilizes anxiety; as a force releasing responses the 'ego" determines what is the best possible defense mechanism to deal with any situation, and primarily that known as repression (1926). In English psychoanalysis, major significance is attached not to repression but to projection (q.v.) and introjection (q.v.), a mechanism which (because it appears in early childhood, pervades the whole of behavior, and has important consequences) has

proved to be the factor determining the normal or pathological nature of mental functioning (M. Klein, 1955).

So, on the anthropological and psychological levels, psychoanalysis is a method by means of which it is thought by some to be possible to approach the unresolved problems of man's innermost life; the taming of primitive energies which it involves leads in fact to the removal of defenses which no longer have any reason to exist, and the subject experiences a sense of renewal and enrichment which he has never known before. His illness is said to be cured, his unconscious is gradually made conscious and his emotive personality, formerly infantile, becomes adult; the neurotic symptoms disappear, and the general orientation of the personality shifts from egocentricity to authentic, life-giving altruism. While the psychoanalysis which studies the "id" highlights above all the infrastructure of the psyche and suggests a new approach to the whole subject of human life, psychoanalysis which is directly concerned with the dynamic of the "ego" approximates increasingly to the dynamics of social life, as may be seen in E. Erikson's thought (1950–1964); it also leads to the conceptual model of ego-development in classical psychology and offers the possibility of direct experimental control. Nevertheless, the claims of psychoanalysis are contested by nearly all schools of modern scientific psychology as unproven. See *Behavior therapy; Behaviorism; Conditioning; Drive; Instinct; Need; Child psychology.*

Bibliography: Abraham, K.: Clinical papers and essays on psychoanalysis. London, 1955. **Ancona, L.:** La psicoanalisi. Brescia, 1963. **Bowlby, J.:** Attachment and loss, Vols 1, 2. London, 1969–71. **Erikson, E.:** Childhood and society. New York, 1950. **Id.:** Insight and responsibility. New York, 1964. **Eysenck, H. J.:** What is wrong with psychoanalysis? In: Uses and abuses of psychology. Harmondsworth, 1953, 221–41. **Fliess, R.** (Ed.): The psycho-analytic reader: an anthology of essential papers with critical introductions. London, 1950. **Freud, A.:** The ego and mechanisms of defence. London, 1937. **Freud, S.:** Standard edition of the complete works of Sigmund Freud, London & New York, 1953–: especially: The interpretation of dreams (Vols. 4–5); Psychopathology of everyday life (Vol. 6); Three essays on the theory of sexuality (Vol. 7); Character and anal eroticism (Vol. 9); A general introduction to psychoanalysis (Vol. 16); Beyond the pleasure principle (Vol. 18); Psychoanalysis and libido theory (Vol. 19); The ego and the id (Vol. 19); Inhibition, symptoms and anxiety (Vol. 20); Humour (Vol. 21); Libidinal types (Vol. 21); Analysis terminable and interminable (Vol. 23). **Hartmann, H.:** Ego psychology and the problem of adaptation. New York & London, 1959. **Klein, M.:** New directions in psychoanalysis. London, 1955. **Reich, W.:** Character analysis. New York & London, 1950. **Rycroft, C.:** Reich. London, 1971.

L. Ancona

Psychocatharsis. See *Cathartic method.*

Psychodiagnostics. The identification of the psychological characteristics of an individual with the aid of special methods. In the past the concept was more widely understood in the sense of *human knowledge*, that is the understanding of a person's psychological features, and the notion of "characterology" coined by J. Bahnsen in 1867 could be equated with it. Psychodiagnostics in the simply defined, narrow sense is theoretically based on Galton's (q.v.) work (1883) and its practical origin was in the diagnosis of intelligence defects by C. Rieger, a Würzburg psychiatrist (1885). This was followed by the work of E. H. Münsterberg (1891) and A. Kraepelin (1895). In the sphere of education a beginning was made by J. McK. Cattell in the USA (1888) and by A. Binet and V. Henri (1895) in France. These names are given as the initiators of the tests as well as of differential psychology, and psychodiagnostics consists in the combination of these two efforts.

1. *Fields of application.* The comprehension of a total personality in all its aspects, as befits its origin in characterology, has up to the present been widely understood by the word "psychodiagnostics" (see *Personality*). It was applied to a wide range of methods, e.g.

graphology, or the form-interpretation of H. Rorschach (see *Rorschach test*), which was published under the title "Psychodiagnostics". But psychodiagnostics has quite specific functions from its origin in psychiatry and in methods of testing. The application of psychological methods in psychiatric diagnosis is of foremost importance. It is used most frequently in connection with brain damage of an endogenous or traumatic form and it has further related functions in the determination of the success of therapy in psychosomatic illnesses and in criminology (see *Prediction*). In the above function the psychologist's diagnosis complements the diagnosis of the doctor. Psychodiagnostics is also applied in educational and vocational guidance and in the determination of particular aptitudes, as for instance of pilots or in the diagnosis of exposure to the danger of accidents (see *Accident research*). This list indicates a certain difference between psychodiagnostics and medical diagnostics. In the case of the latter it is predominantly a question of the determination of a temporary condition, while psychodiagnostics on the whole ascertain lasting characteristics. Psychodiagnostics is not, therefore, for the most part diagnosis but prognosis (q.v.). Naturally the boundaries are fluid since the psychologist can also, for example, ascertain the seriousness of amnesia caused by accidents or the temporary effect of psychopharmacology. Many methodological and theoretical difficulties stem from the predominantly predictive orientation of psychodiagnostics. Psychodiagnostics relies on tests in all their forms more and more exclusively, but with a varying selection according to the questions posed at present. For problems of aptitude in school, work, the army and sport, ability tests (q.v.) (intelligence tests, concentration tests, educational-maturity tests, etc.) play a substantial part. But they are generally supplemented by personality tests (see *Projective techniques; Traits; Questionnaires*), which differ greatly according to whether the field is criminological, clinical or vocational guidance. The following are the three main classification groups by which the tests are distinguished: (*a*) the so-called *projective techniques* (q.v.) which give information regarding above all the affective and motivational aspects; (*b*) the questionnaire (q.v.), with evaluation and observation procedures by which information is given to an appropriate third party on habits, behavioral tendencies and inclinations but also simply on personality traits. Inclination and interest tests are generally employed for the purpose of vocational guidance, the Minnesota Multiphasic Personality Inventory (q.v.) for clinical diagnostics and the Multiphasic Personality Inventory (q.v.) and the Minnesota Multiphasic Questionnaire (q.v.) for determining neurotic tendencies and the extraversion-introversion dimension (q.v.). (*c*) *Objective personality tests* are still used relatively seldom but are likely to predominate in the future. In these tests, behavior, reactions and abilities that can be objectively recorded and estimated in strictly controlled situations offer the bases for a diagnosis. E. Kraepelin's experiment in measurement, which was developed in respect of psychodiagnostics by R. Pauli (1938–1951), may be regarded as a forerunner of such tests (see *Pauli test*). Methods like graphology (q.v.) and physiognomics (q.v.) cannot easily be included in these three groups, nor can behavior observation, the interview (see *Exploration*) and anamnesis. The last three are gradually becoming more reliable in terms of evaluative procedures and are being made more accessible to scientific revision. If such conditions are fulfilled, these methods will form a very valuable part of the psychodiagnostic repertoire.

2. *Method.* The problems of psychodiagnostics stem from the fact that on the basis of scanty objective data and few test results—that is, relatively small samples of behavior—which have been obtained in a very short time and under very special conditions, assertions have to be made about behavior in quite different situations, in which a person is occupied in an entirely different way and has perhaps later experienced certain changes in development. From this it will be clear that the value of psychodiagnostics and its application depends upon data obtained by different means and also upon the means employed, in fact on the *reliability* (q.v.) and *validity* (q.v.) of the tests. There are two types of procedure in psychodiagnostics. One may be described as statistical or psychometric, the other clinical or intuitive. Also the twin concepts of nomothetic (q.v.) and idiographic (q.v.), which were employed by W. Windelband in the identification of two scientific types, describe the same difference. Using statistical methods and the most abundant data, that group of persons is defined to which the individual under examination most probably belongs. Test-norms, clinical syndromes or other data obtained from thousands of cases are used as criteria. This procedure is most clearly represented by the Minnesota Multiphasic Personality Inventory (q.v.) in regard to clinical diagnosis, and by the Strong Vocational Interest Test. A somewhat modified form of this method consists in the discovery of *syndromes* that are characteristic of certain forms of illness, personality, type, etc. These are carried out on the basis of the results of H. Rorschach's method of shape interpretation, for example, or of Wechsler's intelligence test (q.v.). Examination results must necessarily be available for the statistical method. These results define the degree of relationship between each score and a diagnosed trait. In borderline cases the diagnosis can be undertaken with the aid of the computer (q.v.), which is of course needed for aspects of medical diagnostics. Among the complexities of psychological studies the greatest deficiency is the lack of an adequate amount of reliable information and a personality theory on which psychodiagnostics might build. In the clinical or intuitive method the psychologist combines the results that have been obtained,

his observations, and his information based on psychological insight and knowledge and on his personal experience; whereas in the statistical method correct interpretation depends on the reliability and integrity of the definitions of dependence, and stands or falls, as in the clinical method, on the psychological insight and the experience of the psychologist. Objectivity and reliability of diagnosis in clinical procedure are negatively influenced principally by so-called "systematic tendencies" in personality judgments (Cohen, 1969), such as the primacy-recency effect (q.v.), leniency effect (q.v.), social desirability. A comparison would therefore necessarily favor the statistical method if the empirical basis were always reliable, and if it included all the very numerous and sometimes also fortuitous individual variations. On the basis of a great number of experiments, Meehl (1954) established that both methods lead to approximately the same number of correct results. In practice a combined method is very often applied and with advantage. In fact the clinical method in no way excludes the application of objective tests (q.v.), questionnaires, etc., nor a consultation of the research results in conjunction with the applied tests. It is desirable that psychodiagnostics should find ever wider empirically verified principles, and that the psychologist should control the diagnosis based on them and eventually correct and amplify them with individual variations which are not yet statistically classified and sometimes only occur in very rare cases. It might be said that the psychologist must work idiographically on the basis of the most nomothetic knowledge available.

3. *Results.* Nothing is more difficult than to judge whether the psychodiagnostic conclusions made about a person are correct. Here it is a question of the so-called *validity problem* (control of the verification of a diagnosis). The accuracy of the psychodiagnostic conclusions depends, on the one hand, upon the validity of the methods used (see *Test theory; Construct validity*), and, on the other hand, upon the control of verification in the various fields of psychodiagnostic practice. In the case of aptitude tests, the results of such experiments are often satisfactory, while in regard to the value of psychodiagnostics in the field of total personality the results of controlled research are quite contradictory. It may be said with certainty that the value of a conclusion which relies only on a test is generally low, but that a judgment in regard on some psychological aspects of a person, when based on scientifically sure methods, (the use of several tests) is more certain than without the application of such methods. The effectiveness of these techniques has long been overestimated, but today their field of application is better known, and certainty in the interpretation of results and an ability to differentiate are growing with the increasing extent of scientific research.

Bibliography: Anastasi, A.: Psychological testing. New York, 1954. **Brengelmann, J. C.:** Psychologische Methodik und Psychiatrie. In: **H. W. Gruble** *et al.* (Ed.): Psychiatrie der Gegenwart, Vol. 1. Berlin, 1963, 134–77. **Cattell, J. McK.:** Mental tests and measurements. Mind, 1890, *15*, 373–80. **Cattell, R. B.:** Objective personality motivation tests. Chicago, 1967. **Cohen, R.:** Systematische Tendenzen bei Persönlichkeitsbeurteilungen. Berne, 1969. **Cronbach, L. J.:** Essentials of psychological testing. New York, ²1954. **Drenth, P. J. D.:** Der psychologische Test. Munich, 1969. **Freedman, F. S.:** Theory and practice of psychological testing. New York, 1951. **Galton, F.:** Inquiries into human faculty and its development. London, 1883. **Heiss, R.** (Ed.): Handbuch der Psychologie, Vol. 6. Göttingen, 1963. **Jenkins, J. J. & Paterson, D. G.** (Eds.): Studies in individual differences. London, 1961. **Meehl, P. E.:** Clinical vs. statistical prediction. Minneapolis, 1954. **Meili, R.:** Lehrbuch der psychol. Diagnostik. Berne, 1961. **Rapaport, D., Gill, M. M. & Schafer, R.:** Diagnostic psychological testing. New York, 1968. **Stern, E.:** Die Tests in der klinischen Psychologie. Zürich, Vol. 1, 1954; Vol. 2, 1955. **Thorndike, L. & Hagen, E.:** Measurement and evaluation in psychology and education. New York, 1961. *R. Meili*

Psychodrama. The dramatic presentation of personal or general conflict (q.v.) or crisis situations for diagnostic and therapeutic purposes, together with the practice of unaccustomed modes of behavior. The distinguishing factor in the psychodramatic event is temporary adoption of a certain role (q.v.), within which more or less determined situation the players have a great deal of freedom of action. Psychodrama is used particularly as a contribution to group therapy (q.v.), but also as a method of dealing with other social psychological problems (e.g. research into opinions, training of personnel). J. R. Moreno (1914; 1959) invented psychodrama as a specific practice in group therapy. However, the therapeutic effect of acting out conflicts in the sense of an "action catharsis" has always been known. This shows that man's need to act out a rôle relieving him of his emotional tensions ("abreaction") is rooted in his nature (e.g. children's games, carnival, early theatrical forms; see *Play*). Moreno's conception of psychodrama differed sharply from Freud's psychoanalysis (q.v.), which was more concerned with words and the individual. Moreno began with the idea that spontaneity and creativity were distinguishing marks of the self realized personality. Independently of this ideology, psychodrama began to be used as a method in the most varied forms of psychotherapy. In order to illustrate and demonstrate the various theories of the time, e.g. the psychoanalytic school, the cathartic method, theories of learning, (q.v.), behavior therapy (q.v.), psychogogic (q.v.) and pedagogics, many different techniques of psychodrama were developed. In most groups, for example, they were distinguished in form and content by the type of play (patient- or theme-centered; in group problems one speaks of *sociodrama*), and by the way it was acted (monologue, exchange of parts, mirroring methods, the activating technique of Ploeger, 1968, 69), in the modes of expression (verbal, mime, use of puppets or masks), the form of intervention of the director (advising or not), etc. Psychodramatic therapy is best practiced in conjunction with other forms of individual or group therapy. (See *Group dynamics*.)

Bibliography: **Blatner, H.**: Psychodrama, rôle playing and action methods. Thetford, 1970. **Corsini, R. Shaw, M. E. & Blake, R. R.**: Rôle playing in business and industry, New York, 1961. Le psychodrame: Bulletin psychologique, *285*. Paris, 1970. **Moreno, J. L.**: Who shall survive? New York, 1963. **Ploeger, A.**: Die Stellung des Psychodrama in der Psychotherapie. Möglichkeit und Grenzen der Therapie mit dem Psychodrama, in **Batagey, R.** (Ed.): Gruppenpsychotherapie und Gruppendynamik, Vols. 2 & 3. Göttingen, 1968. See also the journal Folia Psychodramatica (Louvain, Belgium). *B. Schmidt*

Psychogalvanic reflex (Abb. PGR). See *Skin resistance*.

Psychogenic disorders. Usually applied to both behavioral and physical disorders which are thought to have a psychological rather than a physiological origin. *R.H.*

Psychogenic vomiting. Vomiting of psychological origin. Also called *nervous vomiting*, and *hysterical vomiting*. This symptom is apparently most common in young women, and is supposed by psychoanalysts to be a symbolic expression of the desire to reject a hated idea or person. *G.D.W.*

Psychogram. A description of the psyche (q.v.); a full comprehensive record of all psychological data (anamnesis, remarks on behavior, tests) on a person, together with an interpretation thereof. Rules for making out a psychogram are given in the Rorschach manual. *D.Ba.*

Psychoid. 1. As a noun: a reality analogous to "being with a soul." For Driesch, it is synonymous with "entelechy" (q.v.). Bleuler used the word (in 1925) to characterize the organizing principle of lower organisms all the way down to the Protozoa. **2.** As an adjective: quasi-psychic, quasi-mental; like the psychic or mental.   *P.M.*

Psychokinesis (abb. PK). Paranormal action. Physical process assumed to be of paranormal causation. In experimental parapsychology the term PK was introduced by J. B. Rhine to refer to the influence of the subject's volitions on a falling dice or similar random process. Power of mind over matter. Also called "telekinesis" (obsolete).   *J.B.*

Psycholinguistics. The term is now used almost universally as a synonym for "psychology of language" (see *Language*). It first came into general use in about 1950 (Osgood & Sebeok, 1965). It comprises some very heterogeneous, interdisciplinary interests in language problems (e.g. in linguistics, communications research, information theory, psychology, and cultural anthropology), with an emphasis on the methods of experimental psychology. Traditional linguistic psychology was more descriptive and comparative, speculative and theoretical. Despite the wide variety of questions proper to psycholinguistics, it is being developed more against the background of consistent, empirically referent theories, giving rise to two partly complementary and partly opposed basic approaches (Dixon & Horton, 1968). The behaviorist S-R theory begins mainly with learning processes and results (see *Learning theory*), as detectable in significant elementary units; the cognitive approach, on the other hand, owes its stimulus more to modern linguistics, and starts from the processes of the comprehension and generation of sentences (see *Grammar; Speech*). Some psycholinguistic *research* areas, which are less well integrated theoretically, are concerned with the linguistic aspects of peripheral processes of reception and production, and the interactions between linguistic processes and

diverse conditions (i.e. emotion; Davitz, 1964), thought processes (see *Inner speech*), social context (see *Language barrier; Sociolinguistics;* Ervin-Tripp, 1969; Herrmann & Stäcker, 1969; Miller & McNeill, 1969; Moscovici, 1967; Wiener & Mehrabian, 1968), and personality (q.v.) variables. Important problems and contributions arise also in various applied fields: diverse speech defects and appropriate therapies afford useful knowledge (Rieber & Brubacker, 1966), e.g. the treatment of impaired articulation, of mutism (e.g. by verbal conditioning: see *Verbal behavior, establishment and modification of;* Salzinger, 1969), etc. (see *Aphasia*). The acquisition of reading and writing, of vocabulary (in the mother tongue as well as in other languages (see *Bilingualism*), and of grammar, offer a number of problems (Crothers & Suppes, 1967; Osgood & Sebeok, 1965; Rosenberg & Koplin, 1968; Scherer & Wertheimer, 1964). Much preliminary theoretical work has been done in the field of computerized language translation.

The behavioristic variety of psycholinguistics favors simple, easily manipulable S-R systems, such as (natural or constructed) words and syllables, and to this extent recalls the older memory research. Language is conceived as "verbal behavior", which consists essentially of (open or hidden) "verbal responses" (Dixon & Horton, 1968; Mowrer, 1960; Salzinger & Salzinger, 1967; Skinner, 1957; Staats, 1968). The associative actualization of verbal responses from any stimuli and the acquisition or modification (paired or serial) of associations (verbal learning) are the fundamental processes for method and theory (Deese, 1965). More or less directly (e.g. by generalization, q.v., and transfer, q.v.) detectable associations of linguistic stimuli and responses (with one another, or with other forms of stimulus and response) are interpreted as denotative or connotative meaning (Creelman, 1966; Rommetveit, 1968) (see *Semantics*), in part by recourse to "mediating" elements (mediation theory: Dixon & Horton, 1968). Linguistic activity is apprehended as a Markoff process (q.v.), which leads to difficulties in the case of rules of syntax (Chomsky, 1968; Hörmann, 1970).

The more mentalist and cognitive form of psycholinguistics follows Chomsky in opining that the behaviorist and associationist approach must have untenable consequences (Miller & McNeill, 1969). The observable extent of interpretative and productive language competence would be explicable only in terms of the effects of grammatical rule systems (see *Grammar*), which are ontogenetically constructed as competence in a many-layered canon of comprehension and production strategies. The methodological foundation of such constructs corresponds in part to the linguistic analysis and evaluation of free utterances. An increasing number of experimental investigations (Hörmann, 1970; Jakubowicz, 1970; Miller & McNeill, 1969) are being carried out into assumptions about units of linguistic competence and their reciprocal relations. Experimental problems include, e.g., sentence structure, the psychological relevance of linguistically defined transformations, the increasing complexity of sentences, and the implications of the use of negatives. See *Communication*.

Bibliography: Brown, R. (Ed.): Psycholinguistics. Selected papers. New York, 1970. **Chomsky, K.:** Cartesian linguistics. New York, 1966. **Id.:** Language and mind. New York, 1968. **Creelman, M. B.:** The experimental investigation of meaning. New York, 1966. **Crothers, E. & Suppes, P.:** Experiments in second-language learning. New York, 1967. **Davitz, J. R.:** The communication of emotional meaning. New York, 1964. **Deese, J.:** The structure of associations in language and thought. Baltimore, 1965. **Dixon, T. R. & Horton, D. L.** (Eds.): Verbal behavior and general behavior theory. Englewood Cliffs, 1968. **Ervin-Tripp, S.:** Sociolinguistics. In: **Berkowitz, L,** (Ed.): Advances in experimental social psychology. Vol. 4. New York, 1969, 91–165. **Herrmann, T. & Stäcker, K. H.:** Sprachpsychologische Beiträge zur Sozialpsychologie. In: **Graumann, C. F.** (Ed.): Handbuch der Psychologie, Vol. 7. Göttingen, 1969, 398–474. **Hörmann, H.:** Psychologie der Sprache. Berlin, 1967. **Jakubowicz, C.:** Recherches récentes en psycholinguistique. L'année psychol., 1970, *70*, 247–93. **Miller, G. A. & McNeill, D.:** Psycholinguistics. In: **Lindzey, G. & Aronson, E.** (Eds.): Handbook of social psychology, Vol. 3. Reading, Mass., 1969, 666–794. **Lyons, J.:** An introduction to theoretical linguistics. Cambridge, 1968. **Moscovici, S.:** Communication processes and the properties of language. In: **Berkowitz, L.** (Ed.): Advances in experimental social psychology, Vol. 3. New York, 1967, 225–70. **Mowrer, O. H.:** Learning theory and the symbolic processes. New York, 1960. **Osgood, C. E. & Sebeok, T. A.** (Eds.): Psycholinguistics. Bloomington, 1965. **Rieber, R. W. & Brubaker, R. S.** (Eds.): Speech pathology. Amsterdam, 1966. **Robins, R. H.:** General linguistics: an introductory survey. London, ²1970. **Rochford, G. & Williams, M.:** The measurement of language disorders. Speech Path. Ther., 1964, *7*, 3. **Rommetveit, R.:** Words, meanings, and messages. New York, 1968; **Rosenberg, S. & Koplin, J. H.:** Developments in applied psycholinguistic research. New York, 1968. **Salzinger, K.:** The place of operant conditioning of verbal behavior in psychotherapy. In: **Franks, C.** (Ed.): Behavior therapy: appraisal and status. New York, 1969, 375–95. **Salzinger, K. & Salzinger, S.** (Eds.): Research in verbal behavior and some neurophysiological implications. New York, 1967. **Saporta, S.** (Ed.): Psycholinguistics. New York, 1961. **Scherer, G. A. C. & Wertheimer, M.:** A psycholinguistic experiment in foreign-language teaching. New York, 1964. **Skinner, B. F.:** Verbal behavior. New York, 1957. **Slobin, D. I.:** Psycholinguistics: basic psychological concepts. New York, 1971. **Staats, A. W.:** Learning, language, and cognition. New York, 1968. **Wiener, M. & Mehrabian, A.:** Language within language. New York, 1968.

G. Kaminski

Psychological moment. A term stemming from the hypothesis that incoming information is perceived in discrete units approximately 1/6 seconds long. Within such a psychological moment all the information taken in is lumped together, so that any temporal sequence in it cannot be perceived. The length of these moments is thought to be affected by drugs and other abnormal states, and hence is related to *time sense*.   *C.D.F.*

Psychologism. An attitude that wants the "psychological point of view" to dominate the specific viewpoints of other human sciences (e.g. logic, philosophy, sociology, etc.). Psychologism is therefore a variant of empiricism (Locke, Hume, J. S. Mill. Its representatives in Germany in the nineteenth century were Fries, Beneke and Sigwart). But, whether the suggested method is introspection (considered as the unique instrument of logical or philosophical knowledge), or modern experimental method, the term is mainly used *polemically* (and pejoratively) by the opponents (e.g. the Neo-Kantians, Husserl, R. Carnap, Piaget) of the view it characterizes, who assert that it is necessary to make a distinction between *normative* and *factual* problems (to assert the independence of values from psychological experience), or between the objective validity of knowledge and the actual behavior of an individual. *M.-J.B.*

Psychologists. People who, in the exercise of their profession, deal with psychic experience and behavior and with the multifarious ways in which it is expressed as well as with the causes and conditions of what is psychic. The *work of the practicing psychologist* in the most diverse fields of applied psychology can be classified into three kinds of activity, i.e. *psychodiagnostics* (q.v.) (recognition of individual peculiarities including the conditions responsible for the actualization of such characteristics; psychological reports); *counseling* (vocational guidance, q.v., educational guidance, q.v., etc.); and *psychotherapy* (treatment, changing individuals either by means of psychological influence on them or on the environmental influences to which they are subjected). *W.Se.*

Psychology as a science. There was a very strong movement in Germany at the beginning of this century which set up psychology in its own right as opposed to natural sciences such as physics or biology, without, however, denying it the rigor and objective control

constitutive of any science. Erismann asserted that the natural sciences were concerned with *explanation* (*Erklären*), whereas psychology, when attempting to grasp central phenomena of the mental life, had recourse to comprehension, or *understanding* (*Verstehen*). *P.M.*

Psychology, empirical. Known also as *scientific psychology* as distinguished from speculative, academic (armchair) psychology (q.v.). It deals with actual experience and sets out to study this experimentally with exact methods. *H.J.A.*

Psychology, functional. A trend in psychology which regards psychic processes and forms of behavior more as active processes than as structures or items of consciousness. As a rule it lays special emphasis on the usefulness of such activities for the individual's survival and adaptation and in so doing is akin to biology (q.v.). In cultural anthropology (q.v.), too, there is a functional school which is concerned chiefly with the adaptive character of the cultures under investigation. The American social sciences in particular have been very strongly influenced by functionalism, the chief proponents in the history of psychology being J. R. Angell, J. M. Baldwin, J. Mc. K. Cattell, S. T. Hall and W. James.
Bibliography: **Boring, E. G.** *et al.*: Foundations of psychology. New York & London, 1948. *W.Sch.*

Psychology without a soul. This paradoxical term ("psychology" means "science of the soul") was used by F. A. Lange (q.v.) in his *History of Materialism* (1866) to describe scientific psychology in its first stirrings. As a science it ignored the soul as an explanatory principle, and attempted to describe "mental facts" on the basis of their elements (see *Elementarism*). The term has now lost its polemical bite and is only of historical interest. *P.M.*

Psychometrics. The application of measurement and mathematics to psychology in general and particularly mental testing and the analysis of experimental results.   *G.D.W.*

Psychometry. In parapsychology: a form of ESP (q.v.) involving the use of a token-object (q.v.). Also known as "token-object reading".
                                                                      J.B.

Psychomotor reactions. See *Motor skills.*

Psychomotor tempo. See *Tempo, personal.*

Psychoneuroendocrinology. This new discipline is concerned with the neuroendocrine control of behavior, in which hormone-physiological and neurophysiological methods are employed in combination, such as the implantation of hormones (q.v.) in certain areas of the brain, and the division of action potentials under the influence of hormones, etc.   *K.Fi.*

Psychoneurosis. In his earliest works Freud spoke of "actual neuroses" and "psychoneuroses" or "transfer neuroses". Among the actual neuroses he placed neurasthenia and the anxiety neuroses, tracing their origin to the damming-up of sexual secretions as a result of sexual abstinence or certain anomalies in sexual behavior. The psychoneuroses or transfer neuroses he divided into three groups: hysteria (q.v.), the phobias (q.v.), and the obsessional neuroses (q.v.). Later he added other types such as the narcissistic and character neuroses, in which the dynamic force was basically psychological and not somatic. Psychiatry, too, has distinguished the psychoneuroses from the *organic neuroses.* The latter belong to the group which today are brought together under the concept of "psychosomatic disorders". The former, on the contrary, embrace neuroses which have psychic and not

internal-organic symptoms. (See *Neuroses; Psychoses, functional.*)   *J.L.I.*

Psychopathia sexualis. Sexual psychopathology. Emotional illness characterized by sexual perversions. Term introduced as the title of a book by the German sexologist R. von Krafft-Ebing (1840–1903); rare in Anglo-American psychiatry.   *G.D.W.*

Psychopathology. The systematic study of the etiology, symptomatology and process of mental disorders. It is that part of abnormal psychology which is concerned with illness, disease or maladjustment.   *R.H.*

Psychopathology, psychoanalytic schema of. The schema, according to S. Freud (q.v.), K. Abraham and O. Fenichel, in cases of psychic illness whose cause is not organic, bacterial or some injury, results from a regression (q.v.) to those psychic phases of development in which fixation took place. The model arranges psychic illnesses of varying degrees of gravity according to (*a*) the fixation phase, (*b*) the elementary direction of the interests involved, (*c*) the elementary aspects of the personal relationships, and (*d*) the dominant anxieties of the patient, but also of the child as he passes normally through a particular phase at a particular time (see table).

The schema is in part the subject of controversy, but in principle it can be tested empirically, and has been tested in part. Among such tests are investigations of the relative frequency with which psychic illnesses of the same group occur together in the course of a single life, and also among members of the same family, in addition the relative frequency with which any mental disorders occur in the family; then investigations of the coincidences in time of traumatic environmental conditions (e.g. parental role conflicts whether emergent

6

Fixation stage	Elementary interests	Relations to individuals	Most primitive anxieties	Psychological disorder
Early oral stage	Oral and tactile stimulation; also stimulation of other sensory areas	No object person	Total panic; end of existence	Schizophrenia
Late oral stage	Oral, oral-aggressive, tactile and kinesthetic manipulation and stimulation	Unconditionally caring, "almighty", mother	To be lost; to "disintegrate"	Mania, depression, impulsive neuroses, organ neuroses, hypochondria
Early anal stage	Body manipulation and primitive manipulation of material including (involuntary) destruction of material; primitive manipulation of excretory function	Powerful, supportive parents; oscillation between own omnipotence and impotence	Destruction or serious mutilation	Paranoia, tics, stuttering, masochism
Late anal stage	Refined body and material manipulation; shaping of material; control of excretion	More or less just, "giving and taking", parents; realization of finer nuances of one's own power	Destruction, less serious mutilation	Compulsive neuroses, tics, stuttering, sadism
Early genital stage	Genital manipulation and stimulation; interest in all aspects of relations between men and women	Sex-specific parents; acceptance of own sex	Genital mutilation	Hysteria (anxiety or conversion hysteria); homosexuality; other deviations

or becoming manifest, the early loss of some person(s): see *Family; Family constellation*) among mental disorders of the same type, but also among all mental disorders in comparison with the average population; and finally, investigations of correlations between deteriorations of the actual life situation of the patients and actual forms of sickness, as well as transitions to other forms of illness which would have to be cured. The greater the actual deterioration of a life situation, the lower in its group and the more pronounced a particular manifestation of a mental disorder is. Improvements in the actual life situation would result in transitions in the reverse direction (toward higher, i.e. milder psychic illnesses). *W. Toman*

Psychopathy. Although the term psychopathy has been used in a variety of contexts (see: Craft, 1965), there is a growing tendency among behavioral scientists to restrict its use to a relatively specific clinical and behavioral disorder (Albert, Brigante & Chase, 1959). The disorder has been extensively described by Cleckley (1964) and Karpman (1961), and, in a broad sense, is covered by the American Psychiatric Association (1952) category: sociopathic personality disturbance—antisocial reaction.

Briefly, the psychopath (or sociopath) is an impulsive, irresponsible, hedonistic, "two-dimensional" person who lacks the ability to experience the normal emotional components of interpersonal behavior, including guilt, remorse, empathy, affection, and genuine concern for the welfare of others. Although he is often able to mimic normal emotions and to simulate affectional attachments, his social and sexual relations with others remain superficial and demanding. His judgment is poor, and he seems unable to delay the gratification of his momentary needs no matter what the consequences to himself and to others. As a result, he is frequently in trouble; in attempting to extricate himself from difficulty he often produces an intricate and contradictory web of lies and rationalizations, coupled with theatrical and sometimes convincing explanations, expressions of remorse, and promises to change. Many psychopaths are very callously predatory and aggressive; others are more typically parasitic or passively manipulative, relying upon a glib sophistication, superficial charm, and the appearance of being helpless to obtain what they want.

Although many psychopathic individuals are constantly in trouble with the law, many others manage to avoid imprisonment for long periods of time, even though their behavior may be grossly antisocial (see: Robins, 1966). They may be protected by family and friends, or operate in a sector of society that condones or tolerates their behavior. In some cases they may be charming and intelligent enough to carry out unethical and unscrupulous practices in a legal or quasi-legal manner, or to talk their way out of prosecution and conviction.

Psychopathy can be distinguished from other forms of antisocial and aggressive behavior that are more symptomatic of some basic emotional disturbance (neurotic delinquency or "psychopathy"), or that reflect socialization in a deviant subculture (subcultural delinquency or dysocial "psychopathy"). Unlike psychopaths, neurotic and subcultural delinquents are quite able to experience guilt and remorse for their behavior and to form warm affectional relationships with others. The clinical distinction between psychopathic, neurotic, and subcultural forms of antisocial behavior is supported by statistical studies of case history data, behavior ratings, and responses to questionnaires (e.g. Jenkins, 1966; Quay, 1964).

Although the general literature on psychopathy is very extensive (see bibliography by Hare & Hare, 1967), it is just beginning to receive the attention it deserves from the behavioral and biological sciences. The relevant research and theory are summarized below, with more extensive discussions being available elsewhere (Craft, 1965; Hare, 1970; McCord & McCord, 1964).

1. *Physiological studies.* A considerable number of studies has made use of electro-encephalographic (EEG) recordings to determine whether psychopathy is associated with abnormalities of the brain. Although many of these studies can be criticized on methodological and conceptual grounds, their results are relatively consistent. It appears that the incidence of EEG or brain-wave abnormalities among psychopathic individuals is unusually high, the most common abnormality being the presence of an excessive amount of slow-wave (4–7 cps) activity, either widespread or, in the case of severely impulsive and aggressive psychopaths, localized in the temporal areas of the brain (e.g. Hill, 1952). Some investigators, noting that the slow-wave activity of psychopaths bears some resemblance to the EEG patterns usually found in children, have suggested that psychopathy is associated with structural or functional immaturity of the brain. A second hypothesis, based upon the presence of localized EEG abnormalities, is that psychopathy is related to some defect or malfunction of brain mechanisms concerned with emotional activity and the regulation of behavior.

The functioning of the psychopath's autonomic nervous system has attracted the interest of several investigators. The results of this line of research (reviewed by Hare, 1968a, 1970) have been somewhat equivocal. In general, however, they tend to support the hypothesis that psychopaths fall at the lower end of a dimension of autonomic arousal and lability. They are also consistent with clinical statements about the psychopath's lack of anxiety and guilt, and about his failure to respond appropriately in situations usually considered to have emotional significance for normal individuals.

2. *Psychopathy and arousal* (q.v.). In any given situation there appears to be a level of cortical arousal that is optimal for peak behavioral efficiency, hedonic tone, and awareness of the environment. However, the conditions that permit normal persons to enjoy an optimal level of arousal tend to produce a state of arousal in psychopaths that is below what for them would be an optimal level (Eysenck, 1967; Hare, 1968a; Quay, 1965). Since one of the most important determinants of arousal is stimulation, psychopaths tend to become quickly bored and restless in situations that are dull and tedious or otherwise lacking in stimulation. At the same time they appear to have an inordinate need for stimulation, particularly stimulation that is novel, varied and unpredictable (e.g. Skrzypek, 1969), or that is associated with activities that others would consider dangerous, foolhardy or frightening, but which psychopaths find exciting (e.g. Lykken, 1957). There is also some evidence that psychopaths are less attentive to weak stimulation (Hare, 1968a, 1968b) and more tolerant of strong stimulation (Thorvaldson, 1969) than are normal individuals.

3. *Learning.* There have been several attempts to account for psychopathic behavior in terms of an inability to learn the modes of behavior necessary for adequate social functioning. Eysenck (1967), for example, considers the psychopath to be an extravert, and therefore generally inferior in the acquisition of responses associated with the process of socialization. Other investigators (e.g. Lykken, 1957) have suggested that the psychopath's learning-deficit may be more specific than this, being largely confined to fear-conditioning and avoidance learning. Concerning the former, the evidence clearly indicates that psychopaths develop classically conditioned fear responses less readily than do normal persons (Lykken, 1957; Quinn, 1969). Moreover, psychopaths appear to exhibit an unusually steep "temporal gradient" of fear arousal (Hare, 1965a, 1965b; Schalling & Levander, 1967). That is, compared with normal persons, they show little fear arousal

in the interval prior to impending pain or punishment. In effect, aversive events expected in the future have no immediate emotional impact on the psychopath, a finding that has important implications for his apparent inability to stay out of trouble. Learning to inhibit behavior likely to have unpleasant consequences, for example, may be viewed as a two-stage process (Mowrer, 1947) involving the conditioning of fear to cues associated with punishment, and the subsequent reinforcement (by fear-reduction) of behavior that removes the individual from the fear-producing cues. The psychopath's apparent disregard for the future consequences of his behavior may therefore be seen as a failure of cues (verbal, symbolic, kinesthetic, visual, and so on) associated with punishment to elicit sufficient anticipatory fear for the instigation and subsequent reinforcement of avoidance responses. There is some empirical support for this position. Lykken (1957), using an ingenious "mental maze," found that psychopaths learned a sequence of rewarded responses but failed to learn to avoid responses punished with electric shock. Similar findings have been obtained by several other investigators, including Schachter & Latané (1964). An additional finding by these latter investigators was that an injection of adrenalin greatly enhanced the ability of the psychopathic subjects to avoid shocked responses. Presumably adrenalin, which increases the activity of the sympathetic nervous system, augmented the psychopaths' capacity for experiencing anticipatory fear.

Apart from fear conditioning and avoidance learning, there is little evidence that the learning ability of psychopaths differs from that of normal persons, particularly where appropriate attempts are made to motivate them to perform well (see review by Hare, 1970).

4. *Socialization.* Broken homes and disturbed family relationships, especially parental loss and rejection, have been used to account for almost every form of abnormal and antisocial behavior, including psychopathy (McCord & McCord, 1964; Wiggens, 1968). It is difficult, therefore, to determine in what ways the background of psychopaths might differ from that of other disorders. One reason for this unhappy situation is that the majority of studies made use of a retroactive approach to the problem: that is, they relied upon interviews with adult subjects to determine what took place many years before.

An extensive study by Robins (1966) largely overcame this limitation by studying the adult social and psychiatric status of persons who had been referred to a guidance clinic some thirty years earlier, and for whom a great deal of information on family background, social behavior, and so on was available. Briefly, Robins found that the childhood predictors of adult psychopathy included truancy, theft, lying, lack of guilt, refusal to obey parents, and sexual misbehavior. Although most psychopaths came from broken homes, this fact was less important than having a father who was himself psychopathic or alcoholic, a finding that is consistent with other evidence that maternal rejection and behavior have less to do with the development of antisocial behavior than do the personality and behavior of the father (e.g. Andry, 1960).

On a more theoretical level, Gough (1948) has suggested that the psychopath is pathologically unable to role-play. As a result, he is unable to see himself as a social object and to foresee the consequences of his own behavior. And because he cannot judge his own behavior from another's point of view, he is unable to experience embarrassment, loyalty, contrition, or group identification. Nor can he understand the reasons for societies' objections to his behavior.

The psychopath's low resistance to temptation and his lack of guilt have been interpreted as the result of the delayed and inconsistent administration of punishment for transgressions (Hare, 1970). Similarly, his impulsivity and inability to delay gratification have been related to a family background in which impulse-control training was generally poor, and in which parental models displayed little control over their own behavior (Arieti, 1967).

Buss (1966) has suggested that psychopathy reflects the modeling of parental behavior characterized by coldness, remoteness and the inconsistent administration of affection, rewards, and punishments.

As a final point, it is worth noting that most socialization theories, including those concerned with psychopathy, tend to view the child as a more or less passive member of the socialization process. It may be more appropriate to view the parent-child relationship as an interactive one in which the behavior and socialization techniques of the parents are partly determined by the characteristics of the child. It is possible that some of these characteristics (e.g. assertiveness, social responsiveness) are influenced by genetic and constitutional factors (Bell, 1968; Eysenck, 1967).

5. *Modification of psychopathic behavior.* The traditional psychological and biological therapeutic techniques have proved to be almost totally ineffective in the modification of psychopathic behavior. There are several reasons for this situation, including the well-known limitations of the techniques themselves. For one thing, the psychopath neither suffers from personal distress nor sees anything wrong with his behavior, and he is therefore not motivated to change. For another, his way of life can be very rewarding, at least in the short run; being periodically punished, usually well after the act, does little to offset the immediate gratification obtained. As a result, his behavior is well established, and from his own egocentric point of view, quite sensible.

It is likely that any significant modification of the psychopath's behavior would require a major restructuring of his social and psychological environment. It may be necessary, for example, to set up an intensive, long-term program, patterned after the therapeutic community concept for improving interpersonal relations (e.g. Craft, 1965; McCord & McCord, 1964; Stürup, 1964), but including attempts to increase the motivating influence of fear and anxiety and to make social reinforcements more effective.

Bibliography: Albert, R., Brigante, T. & Chase, M.: The psychopathic personality: A content analysis of the concept. J. Gen. Psychol., 1959, 60, 17–28. American Psychiatric Association: Diagnostic and statistical manual: Mental disorders. Washington, 1952. Andry, R.: Delinquency and parental pathology. London, 1960. Arieti, S.: The intrapsychic self. New York, 1967. Bell, R.: A reinterpretation of the direction of effects in studies of socialization. Psychol. Rev., 1968, 75, 81–95. Buss, A.: Psychopathology. New York, 1966. Cleckley, H.: The mask of sanity. St. Louis, Mo., ⁴1964. Craft, M.: Ten studies in psychopathic personality, Bristol, 1965. Eysenck, H. J.: The biological basis of personality. Springfield, Ill., 1967. Gough, H.: A sociological theory of psychopathy. Amer. J. Sociol., 1948, 53, 359–66. Hare, R.: A conflict and learning theory analysis of psychopathic behavior. J. res. Crime Delinq., 1965 (a), 2, 12–19; Id.: Temporal gradient of fear arousal in psychopaths. J. abnorm. Psychol., 1965 (b), 70, 442–45. Id.: Psychopathy, autonomic functioning, and the orienting response. J. abnorm. Psychol., 1968 (a), 73, Monogr. Supp.; Id.: Detection threshold for electric shock in psychopaths. J. abnorm. Psychol., 1968 (b), 73, 268–72. Id.: Psychopathy: theory and research. New York, 1970. Id. & Hare, A.: Psychopathic behavior: a bibliography. Excerpta Criminologica, 1967, 7, 365–86. Hill, D.: EEG in episodic psychotic and psychopathic behavior: A classification of data. EEG clin. Neurophysiol., 1952, 4, 419–42. Jenkins, R.: Psychiatric syndromes in children and their relation to family background. Amer. J. Orthopsychiat., 1966, 36, 450–57. Karpman, B.: The structure of neurosis: With special differentials between neurosis, psychosis, homosexuality, alcoholism, psychopathy, and criminality. Arch. Crim. Psychodyn., 1961, 4, 599–646. Lykken, D.: A study of anxiety in the sociopathic personality. J. abnorm. soc. Psychol., 1957, 55, 6–10. McCord, W. & McCord, J.: The psychopath: An essay on the criminal mind. Princeton (N.J.), 1964. Mowrer, O.: On the dual nature of learning – a reinterpretation of "conditioning" and "problem-solving". Harvard educ. Rev., 1947, 17, 102–48. Quay, H.: Personality dimensions in delinquent males as inferred from the factor analysis of behavior ratings. J. res. Crime Delinq., 1964, 1, 33–37 Id.: Psychopathic personality as pathological stimulation seeking. Amer. J. Psychiatr., 1965, 122, 180–83

Quinn, M.: Psychopathy and the conditioning of autonomic responses. Unpublished diss., University of British Columbia, 1969. Robins, L.: Deviant children grown up. Baltimore, 1966. Schachter, S. & Latane, B.: Crime, cognition, and the autonomic nervous system. M. Jones (Ed.): Nebraska symposium on motivation. Lincoln, 1964, 221–75. Schalling, D. & Levander, S.: Ratings of anxiety proneness and responses to electrical stimulation. Scand. J. Psychol., 1964, 5, 1–9. Skrzypek, G.: The effects of perceptual isolation and arousal on anxiety, complexity preference, and novelty preference in psychopathic and neurotic criminals. J. abnorm. Psychol., 1969, 74, 321–29. Stürup, G.: The treatment of chronic criminals. Bull. Menninger Clin., 1964, 28, 229–43. Throvaldson, S.: Detection threshold and tolerance level for electric shock in psychopaths. Unpublished M.A. thesis, University of British Columbia, 1969. Wiggens, J.: Inconsistent socialization. Psychol. Reports, 1968, 23, 303–36.   R. D. Hare

Psychopharmacology. 1. *Definition, demarcation and development of psychopharmacology.* This, strictly speaking, is a sub-field of psychology, which investigates psychic and correlative physiological effects of natural and synthetic chemical substances (chiefly psychopharmaceuticals) after these have been introduced into the organism—whether a "healthy" human individual, or an animal. To classify psychopharmacology among the usual fields of psychology does not seem possible. In so far as it is regarded as complementary to pharmacotherapy (q.v.), it is thought of as applied or clinical psychology (q.v.). If it is considered as a discipline dealing with the physiological bases of behavior, it is general or physiological psychology. No sharp demarcation of psychopharmacology from other disciplines (such as pharmacology, pharmacopsychiatry or pharmacotherapy) dealing with psychotropic (q.v.) substances is possible.

Although psychopharmaceuticals have been known for centuries, psychopharmacology as a science is less than a century old. The psychiatrist E. Kraepelin (1856–1926) is considered to be its founder and it was under him that, from the end of the nineteenth century, numerous investigations were conducted into the effect of stimulants (q.v.) and sedatives (q.v.), etc., on a series of arithmetical performances, memory and learning processes and processes requiring attention. In spite of isolated studies on a larger scale which dealt in particular with the effect of narcotics (q.v.), stimulants (q.v.), opiates (q.v.) and gonadotropic hormones (q.v.), the researches on which Kraepelin had embarked did not subsequently lead to the foundation of any systematic partial discipline of psychology. But when completely new types of preparation were developed which proved effective (see *Pharmacotherapy*) in cases of psychosis (see *Neuroleptics*) and neurosis (see *Tranquilizers*), interest in psychopharmacological research grew extremely rapidly. Whereas in pharmacopsychiatry interest is concentrated on the therapeutic efficacy of the new substances, especially in cases of schizophrenia (q.v.), as well as on hypotheses concerning the biochemistry of mental disorders (Wooley & Shaw, 1955), psychopharmacology attempts to explain inter- and intraindividual variation in reaction when tranquilizers are used. The considerable variability of effect found with these preparations in comparison with those known hitherto led to numerous studies of the relationship between reaction to pharmaceuticals and personality factors (Eysenck, Kornetsky, Dimascio, Janke—cf. bibliography) as well as situational factors (see *Differential psychology*).

Practical work to be done in assessing the action of psychotropic substances in healthy individuals may be grouped under the following headings: 1. Classification of new substances, of tranquilizers (q.v.), stimulants (q.v.), antidepressives (q.v.), sedatives (q.v.) and soporifics on the basis of their relative action. 2. Development of hypotheses concerning possible therapeutical indications. 3. Analysis of psychic side-effects of pharmaceuticals used in the treatment of somatic diseases. Analgesics (q.v.), antihistamines (q.v.), antihypertonics (q.v.), remedies for colds and many other medicines do not merely remove the target symptoms but also frequently induce fairly pronounced psychic changes the exact understanding of which is very important, e.g. in deciding whether a person is fit to drive. 4. Relatively healthy individuals constitute a considerable proportion of consumers of tranquilizers, stimulants and other medicines. Pharmacopsychological studies make it possible by suitably planned multifactorial experiments to give considered recommendations for certain situations and persons when disturbances are to be expected in particular circumstances. It is very important to analyze the effects of soporifics (q.v.) (aftereffects), tranquilizers (q.v.) and alcohol on fitness to drive.

2. *Psychopharmacology and psychological research.* For all partial disciplines of non-applied psychology, psychopharmacology is a basic discipline pursued under special aspects and to be considered in conjunction with physiological psychology (q.v.). In principle every pharmacopsychological study makes a contribution to the question of the inter- and intraindividual variability of psychic processes. Pharmaceuticals (biochemical variations derived from them) are regarded as a special class of stimuli (independent variables) which may be fundamentally compared to all other stimuli in psychology. A systematic understanding of the relations between drug-induced "biochemical lesions" (Russell, 1966) and behavior is, however, at the present moment in its earliest stages because the influence of psychopharmaceuticals on biochemical processes is largely unknown in detail. *Human* psychopharmacology in particular is chiefly dependent on speculation and analogies with animal psychopharmacology. Nevertheless, above all other fields of psychology, it provides the opportunity to use in its interpretations the biochemical processes that take place between the stimulus (drug) and the response

(behavior). The importance of psychopharmacology as a basic psychological discipline will increase in proportion as biochemical correlates of behavior are found in animal experiments, because as a rule in human beings biochemical processes can be varied only indirectly and as a result of administering pharmaceuticals. The following lines of research in modern psychopharmacology are examples of the use of psychotropic substances as "tools" of psychological basic research:

(*a*) Psychopharmaceutical agents, biochemical "lesions" and behavior: present research is concentrated mainly on the relations between variations of the substances found in the body such as acetylcholine (q.v.), serotonin (including those which are similar, e.g. tryptophan, q.v., tryptamine) and noradrenalin (q.v.) (including those which are similar, e.g. dopa, q.v., dopamine, q.v.) and variations of behavior. Substances most commonly used in experiments are cholinesterase (q.v.) inhibitors and cholinergic (q.v.) substances for the manipulation of acetylcholine in the central and autonomic nervous systems. Monoaminooxydase (q.v.) inhibitors for varying noradrenalin and serotonin concentrations and reserpine (q.v.) and LSD for manipulating serotonin. Learning and memory (acetylcholin, serotonin) moods and affects (noradrenalin, serotonin) and experimentally induced "psychotic" behavior (serotonin) are used as major psychological variables.

(*b*) Psychopharmaceuticals and covariations of physical and psychic processes: numerous psychophysiological models (e.g. activation theory), as well as the consequent diagnostic applications, are based on the correlations between physiological and psychological variables which have been obtained under normal conditions. Investigations with psychopharmaceuticals can make a contribution to the adequacy of such models. Several investigations show that under the influence of certain preparations correlations are found quite different to those under normal conditions. With a large number of preparations (e.g. anticholinergics, q.v., barbiturates, q.v.), there occur dissociations between behavior and physiological processes (see EEG; *Skin resistance*; *Pulse rate*; etc.) as well as dissociations inside different physiological systems.

(*c*) Psychopharmaceuticals and learning. Main points of research in this field are; (i) Relations between learning and memory and ribonucleic acid (RNA), substances inhibiting and promoting the synthesis of RNA (see *Antibiotics*); (ii) Pharmaceuticals and consolidation: whereas certain substances (e.g. strychnine, picrotoxin, pentetrazol) which stimulate the central nervous system seem to improve retention when administered immediately after some learning process, hypnotics and narcotics (e.g. ether) given in large doses cause retention to deteriorate. The analysis of the relation "learning and time when preparation was administered" can provide fresh knowledge about the consolidation or perseveration theory of memory. Because of their selective action, psychopharmaceuticals are undoubtedly superior to other stimuli (e.g. electric shocks, hypothermia, anoxia).

(*c*) State-dependent learning: behavior learnt under the influence of pharmaceuticals is reproduced less well in conditions where pharmaceuticals are not used than when the experimental conditions are kept constant. It is evident that an organismic condition induced by pharmaceuticals has to be regarded as a conditioned stimulus. So far, however, no results of experiments with human beings are available.

(*d*) Psychopharmaceutical agents and personality: psychological personality models should make it possible to predict individual differences in reaction to psychopharmaceuticals. The best-known personality model which has made use of such differences is that of H. J. Eysenck.

(*e*) Psychopharmaceuticals and emotion: the most important fields of research deal with the question of how far psychotropic substances can induce emotional variations of specific emotional qualities going beyond a general heightening or lowering of arousal. The possibility of specific changes results from the fact that many preparations have a relatively specific action on hypothalamic, thalamic or limbic structures. Special importance is attached to studies in which pharmaceuticals acting on the autonomic nervous system are used to change autonomic reaction patterns whereas cognitive-situational factors are kept constant or varied (Schachter, 1966). As different pharmaceuticals have different periphero-physiological action patterns, physiological (James-Lange theory) and physiologico-cognitive (Schachter, 1966) emotion theories can be tested by psychopharmacological studies (see *Emotions*). Other investigations are concerned with the question whether depressions are to be studied in connection with the central serotonin and catecholamine metabolism.

(*f*) Psychopharmaceuticals and motivation: the central topic of psychopharmacological research into motivation is how the action of the pharmaceutical agent administered is processed by the individual in accordance with the habitual or temporary motivational situation. Pharmaceuticals may be considered as stimuli which disturb the normal adaptation level, i.e. the optimal activation (q.v.) level. As differential psychopharmacology (q.v.) has shown, many individuals under certain situational conditions respond to such disturbances with paradoxical reactions (e.g. excitation in the case of tranquilizers, q.v., or heightened performance in the case of sedatives, q.v., and narcotics, q.v.). Paradoxical reactions are the result of complex interactions between situational conditions, personality characteristics and the nature and dose of the preparation. In this research pharmaceuticals are seen as tools for studying motivational processes. A further range of problems dealt with by psychopharmacological research into motivation is how pharmaceuticals influence central "reward" and "punishment" systems. The autostimulation rate, following a technique devised by L. Olds, can be modified by numerous drugs.

3. *Planning and execution of psychopharmacological investigations* of the only slight constancy of intra- and interindividual action of psychotropic substances, psychopharmacological investigations yield results that can be interpreted and reproduced only when numerous factors have been eliminated or checked. The following table shows the most important of these factors as well as some methods for eliminating and checking them:

Factors	Control or elimination method
1. Spontaneous changes and changes conditioned by learning and practice	Comparison with placebo substance: if possible, comparison with standard preparations (especially in clinical tests)
2. Suggestion	
(a) Knowledge that some substance has been administered	Comparison with placebo; comparison with the action of preparation when administered without subject's knowledge
(b) Uncertainty whether a placebo or an active substance has been administered	Standardization, by disclosure ("instruction"), of the subjective probability that a placebo or an active substance will be received
(c) General awareness of the mode of action of psychoactive substances	Interindividual standardization by disclosure of the degree of information
(d) Awareness of the way in which the substance is expected to act	(a) Disclosure, but not of the specific action (e.g. "mode of operation so far unknown") (b) Specific instruction (e.g. "the preparation has a sedative effect")
(e) Expectation of psychic action on account of fairly strong somatic side-effects	Comparison with "active" placebo, i.e. a substance with the somatic side-effects but not the main psychic effects
3. Subjects' characteristics	
(a) Age, sex, weight, habitual personality traits, etc.	Homogenization of the sample by selection (e.g. only "neuroticism"); parallelization with independent groups, factorial experimental designs
(b) Health characteristics	Elimination of testees with certain diseases (e.g. liver or gastro-intestinal diseases)
(c) Voluntary cooperation of testees	Check on personality traits of volunteer testees

Factors	Control or elimination method
(d) Initial individual disposition	Elimination of diverse initial dispositions by adaptation (test cycle before administration of the preparation), habituation (practice tests) or standardization (e.g. standard meals). Subsequent correction by regression methods (e.g. covariance analysis) in order to take initial disposition into account
(e) Experiences with psychopharmaceuticals and psychopharmacological investigations, attitudes, expectations	Standardization by instruction. Elimination of testees with "considerable experience"
(f) Antecedent activities	Standardization. Inquiry into particularities. Possible elimination of testees
4. Situational conditions	
(a) Experimenter's knowledge (as under 2)	As for 2
(b) Sex and behavior of experimenter	Homogenization (elimination) or control by factorial experimental designs
(c) Social conditions	Standardization: group or individual experiments
(d) Spatial conditions	Standardization: same space for testees, freedom from interruption
(e) Time conditions (day, week, year)	Restriction to short periods, compensation, factorial test designs
5. Dosage: characteristic effects	Use of minimum of three doses
6. Time: characteristic effects	Several measurements during an investigation
7. Characteristic effects in comparison with other substances	Use of standard preparations
8. Test instruments	
(a) Selective effects of psychopharmaceuticals	Abstention from "global measurements, multivariant test batteries in the areas of experience, behavior and physiological processes
(b) Ambiguity of effects	Use of tests that are factorially as simple as possible. Control of complex tests by factorially simple tests
(c) Varying sensitivity of tests with different types of preparation, e.g. insensitivity of speed tests with sedatives	Use of different batteries according to mode of effect; in speed tests, control of motivational factors by scaling techniques
(d) "Unreliability" of certain tests against a placebo	(a) Control of ceiling effects by "no preparation" conditions (b) No use of tests with high incidence of placebo effect
(e) Reinforcement effects by using several tests	Use of batteries with least possible correlation

Bibliography: (1) *Journals and lit.:* Psychopharmacologia. Berlin, from 1960. International Pharmacopsychiatry. Basle, from 1968; Pharmakopsychiatrie—Neuropsychopharmakologie. Stuttgart, from 1968. Psychopharmacological Abstracts. Bethesda, from 1961. Neuro-Psycho-Pharmacology. Amsterdam, from 1958. **Caldwell, A. E.:** Psychopharmaca. A bibliography of psychopharmacology. Washington, 1958. **Kobayashi, T.:** International bibliography on psychopharmacology, Vol. 1. Tokio, 1968. **Wortis, J.** (Ed.): Recent advances in biological psychiatry. New York, from 1960. (2) *General introductions:* **Black, P.:** Drugs and the brain. Baltimore, 1969. **Clark, W. G. & del Guidice, J.** (Eds.): Principles of psychopharmacology. New York, 1970. **Dews, P. B.:** Psychopharmacology. In: **Bachrach, A. J.** (Ed.): Experimental foundations of clinical psychology. New York, 1962. **Efron, D. H.** (Ed.): Psychopharmacology. A review of progress 1957–67. Washington, 1968. **Elkes, J.:** Behavioral pharmacology in relation to psychiatry. In: **Gruhle, H. W.** *et al.* (Eds.): Psychiatrie der Gegenwart in Forschung und Praxis, Vol. I/1. Berlin, 1967. **Eysenck, H. J.** (Ed.): Experiments with drugs. Oxford, 1963. **Goodman, L. S. & Gilman, A.** (Eds.): The pharmacological basis of therapeutics. New York, 1965. **Joyce, C. R. B.** (Ed.): Psychopharmacology—Dimensions and perspectives. London, 1968. **Lippert, H.:** Einführung in die Pharmakopsychologie. Bern, 1959. **Nordine, J. H. & Siegler, P. E.:** Animal and clinical pharmacological techniques in drug evaluation, Vol. 1. Chicago, 1964. **Ross, S. & Cole, J. O.:** Psychopharmacology. Ann. Rev. Psychol., 1960, *11*, 415–38. **Russell, R. W.:** Psychopharmacology. Ann. Rev. Psychol., 1964, *15*, 87–114. **Siegler, P. E. & Moyer, J. H.:** Animal and clinical pharmacologic techniques in drug evaluations, Vol. 2. Chicago, 1967. **Solomon, P.:** Psychiatric drugs. New York, 1966. **Steinberg, H.** (Ed.): Animal behavior and drug action. London, 1964. **Thompson, T. & Schuster, C. R.:** Behavioral pharmacology. New York, 1968; **Uhr, L. & Miller, J. G.:** Drugs and behavior. New York, 1960. (3) *Drugs, biochemistry and behavior:* **Deutsch, S. A.:** The physiological basis of memory. Ann. Rev. Psychol., 1969, *20*, 85–104. **Domagk, G. F. & Zippel, H. P.:** Biochemie der Gedächtnisspeicherung. Naturwissensch., 1970, 57, 152–62. **Eiduson, S.** *et al.*: Biochemistry and behavior. Princeton, 1964. **Freedman, D. X.:** Aspects of the biochemical pharmacology of psychotropic drugs. In: **Solomon, P.** (Ed.): Psychiatric drugs. New York, 1966. **Mandell, A. S. & Mandell, M. P.** (Eds.): Psychochemical research in man. New York, 1969. **Young, R. D.:** Developmental psychopharmacology: a beginning. Psychol. Bull., 1967, *67*, 73–86. **Russell, R. W.:** Effects of "biochemical lesions" on behavior. Acta Psychol., 1958, *14*, 281–94. **Russell, R. W.:** Biochemical substrats of behavior. In: **Russell, R. W.** (Ed.): Frontiers in physiological psychology. New York, 1966. **Weiss, B. & Laties, V. G.:** Behavioral pharmacology and toxicology. Ann. Rev. Pharmacol., 1969, *9*, 297–326. (4) *Special topics:* **Baker, R. R.:** The effects of psychotropic drugs on psychological testing. Psychol. Bull., 1968, *69*, 377–89. **Corning, W. C. & Ratner, S. C.:** Chemistry of learning. New York, 1967; **Düker, H.:** Über reaktive Anspannungssteigerung. Zschr. exp. angew. Psychol., 1963, *10*, 46–72. **Gaito, J.:** Molecular psychobiology. Springfield, 1966. **Kimble, D. P.** (Ed.): The anatomy of memory. Palo Alto, 1965. **Janke, W.:** Experimentelle Untersuchungen zur Abhängigkeit der Wirkung psychotroper Substanzen von Persönlichkeitsmerkmalen. Frankfurt, 1964. **Janke, W. & Debus, G.:** Experimental studies on anti-anxiety drugs with normal subjects: methodological considerations and review of the main effects. In: **Efron, D. H.** (Ed.): Psychopharmacology 1957–67. Washington, 1968. **Janke, W.:** Methoden der Induktion von Aktiviertheit. In: **Schönpflug, W.** (Ed.): Methoden der Aktivierungsforschung. Berne, 1969. **Lennard, H. L.:** A proposed program of research in sociopharmacology. In: **Leiderman, P. H. & Shapiro, D.** (Eds.): Psychobiological aspects to social behavior. London, 1965. **McGaugh & Petrinovich, L. F.:** Effects of drugs on learning and memory. Int. Rev. Neurobiol., 1965, *8*, 139–96. **Mikhel'son, M. Y. & Longo, V. G.:** Pharmacology of conditioning, learning and retention. Oxford, 1965. **Miller, N. E. & Barry, H.:** Motivational effects of drugs. Psychopharmacologia, 1960, *1*, 169–99. **Overton, D.:** Dissociated learning in drug states (state-dependent learning). In: **Efron, D. H.** (Ed.): Psychopharmacology 1957–67. Washington, 1968. **Schachter, S.:** The interaction of cognitive and physiological determinants of emotional state. In: **Spielberger C.** (Ed.): Anxiety and behavior. New York, 1966. **Stein, L.:** Chemistry of reward and punishment. In: **Efron, D. H.** (Ed.): Psychopharmacology 1957–67. Washington, 1968. **Trouton, D. T. & Eysenck, H. J.:** The effects of drugs on behavior. In **Eysenck, H. J.** (Ed.): Handbook of abnormal psychology. London & New York, ²1971.

W. Janke

Psychopharmacology of the ANS. ANS drugs, i.e. pharmaceuticals, are substances which lead to alterations of the activity of the *autonomic nervous system* (q.v.). Most ANS drugs also affect the CNS, and many influence the endocrine system. A distinction is made between

ANS drugs which take effect primarily in the central autonomic regulation centers (hypothalamus, q.v.; limbic system), and those which take effect primarily in the peripheral autonomic neuron(e)s. This division is, however, only conditionally useful, since many ANS drugs take effect both centrally and peripherally, and of course a wholly straightforward separation of the peripheral and central ANS is not possible. Other possibilities of division of ANS drugs correspond to the separation of the ANS into the *sympathetic* and *parasympathetic* divisions. Sympathetic-stimulant substances are known as *sympathicomimetic* (q.v.), sympathetic-inhibiting substances as *sympathicolytic* (q.v.). By analogy, within the parasympathetic system, *parasympathicomimetic* are differentiated from *parasympathicolytic* substances. The tables below list a selection of ANS substances.

The effective mechanism of ANS drugs may be described (in somewhat simplified terms) as the influencing of the natural body transmitter substances acetylcholine (parasympathetic ganglia, preganglionic fibers of the sympathetic division, neuromuscular connections) and noradrenalin(e) (postganglionic fibers of the sympathetic division). The effect on the natural-body acetylcholine and noradrenalin(e) action may be *direct* or *indirect*.

Examples of drugs with pronounced effects on the sympathetic system

Direct effect:

Many substances (app. 500), e.g.:
adrenalin(e) (epinephrine)
noradrenalin(e) (norepinephrine)
isopropylnoradrenalin(e) (isoprenalin(e))
phenylephrin(e)
synephrin(e)
angiotensin
vasopressin
LSD
psilocybin

Alpha receptor blockers:
dibenamine
ergot alkaloids (e.g. ergotamine)
phentolamine
tolazolanine
yohimbine
                      (sympathicolytic)
phenoxybenzamine

Beta receptor blockers:
dichlorisopropylnoradrenalin(e) (dichlorisoprenaline)
propanolol
pronethanol

Cholinergics:
acetylcholine (ACh)
methacholine (mecholyl)
carbachol
bethanechol
muscarine
pilocarpine
arecoline
tremorine

Anticholinergics:
atropine, scopalamine, homatropine, and numerous related substances

Inhibit acetylcholine at muscle end plates:
curare
D-tubocurarine
gallamine
toxiferine

Indirect effect:
(sympathicomimetic)
phenylethylamine
tyramine
tryptamine
amphetamine, methamphetamine
metaraminol, mephentermine
cocaine

Inhibit enzymatic breakdown:
monoaminooxidase inhibitors
    e.g. isoproniazid (antidepressive)
    e.g. tranylcypromine
ephedrine
o-methyl-transferase-inhibitors
    (e.g. pyrrogallol)

Inhibit enzymatic build-up:
alpha-methyldopa
alpha-methyltyrosine

Inhibit storage:
reserpine
guanethidine
bretylium

False transmitter formation:
alpha-methyldopa

Anticholinesterase, cholinesterase inhibitors:
neostigmine (Prostigmine)
edrophonium (Tensilon)
physostigmine (Eserine)
pyridostigmine
diisopropylfluorophosphate (DFP)
various nerve poisons (e.g. tabune)
parathione (E 605) and many pesticides

Promote enzymatic build-up:
dimethylaminoethanol
deanol

Promote enzymatic breakdown:
cholinesterase-related substances

The most important mechanisms are: (*a*) drugs work in principle in a manner similar to that of transmitter substances; (*b*) drugs intensify the effect of transmitter substances by inhibition of their enzymatic breakdown; (*c*) drugs weaken the action of transmitter substances (i) by blocking them in the post-ganglionic fibers or at the receptors, (ii) by inhibition of their enzymatic build-up, or (iii) by promoting their breakdown; (*d*) drugs intensify or weaken the action of transmitter substances by influencing their suitability for storage; (*e*) drugs replace the natural trans-mitters by 'false" transmitters; (*f*) blockade of acetylcholine action at the muscle end plates. The effects of ANS drugs differ considerably according to their effective mechanisms and modes of action (central or periph-eral). They are used therapeutically, e.g., as: antidepressives (q.v.), antihypertonics (q.v.), hypertonics (q.v.), antihistamines (q.v.), circu-lation regulators, spasmolytics (q.v.), muscle relaxants (q.v.), stimulants (q.v.), or neuro-leptics (q.v.). It is psychologically significant that the diverse ANS substances induce different autonomic patterns and combinations of autonomic and central-psychic variations, making it possible to use them as "tools" in emotion research (see *Psychopharmacology*), e.g. to block autonomic feedback in stress experiments. See *Emotions; Stress.*

Bibliography: Fawaz, G.: Cardiovascular pharma-cology. Ann. Rev. Pharmacol., 1963, *3*, 57–90. **Koelle, G. B.:** Cholinesterases and anticholinesterase agents. Handbuch expt. Pharmakol., 15, Berlin, 1963. **Langemann, H.:** Pharmakologie des VNS. In: Akt. Fragen Psychiatr., 1966, *3*, 74–105. **Marley, E.:** The adrenergic system and sympathicomimetic amines. Advanc. Pharmacol., 1964, *3*, 167–266. **Volle, R. L.:** Pharmacology of the autonomic nervous system. Ann. Rev. Pharmacol., 1963, *3*, 129–52. **Zaimis, E.:** Pharmacology of the autonomic system. Ann. Rev. Pharmacol., 1964, *4*, 365–400. **Nickerson, M.:** The pharmacology of adrenergic blockade. Pharmacol. Rev., 1949, *1*, 27–101.   *W. Janke*

Psychophysical law. See *Weber-Fechner law.*

Psychophysics. Psychophysics concerns the manner in which living organisms respond to the energetic configurations of the environ-ment. Stimulus energy in many forms affects the organisms through one or another of its specialized sensory receptors. Therefore many of the problems of psychophysics relate to the operation and behavior of sensory systems. A central problem is to determine the quanti-tative relation between stimulus input and response output—the so-called operating characteristic of the sensory system. Efforts to determine the functional relation between perceptual experience and the physical stimu-lus that produces it have given rise to a variety of psychophysical methods, many of which have found uses in other fields, ranging from the scaling of preferences to the measurement of the public consensus concerning the serious-ness of various crimes.

1. *History*. In an early attempt at psycho-physical scaling (about 150 B.C.), Hipparchus proposed that a useful measurement of stellar magnitude could be based on the apparent brightness of the stars. The brightest star was assigned to the first magnitude and the dim-mest to the sixth. The distance between those limits was then partitioned in such a way that the apparent distances from one star magni-tude to the next appeared equal. This scale of equal appearing intervals, based on six cate-gories of apparent brightness, served astron-omy for many centuries. When the develop-ment of photometry finally produced physical measurements of the light intensity, each of the steps on the visual scale of stellar magnitude turned out to be approximately four decibels, a value that represents a constant distance on a logarithmic scale. The logarithmic scale of stellar magnitude was hailed by Fechner as an important confirmation of the psychophysical law that bears his name. Only in recent decades has it become clear that the scale obtained by partitioning stellar magnitudes into categories is not an adequate test of Fechner's law.

In 1860 G. T. Fechner published his monumental *Elements of Psychophysics*. Although he argued that a direct measurement of sensation remains impossible, Fechner saw the possibility of an indirect approach. Instead of measuring sensation, he proposed to measure just noticeable differences, JND, which increase, as E. H. Weber had shown, in proportion to stimulus intensity. Fechner assumed that there is a fixed increment in sensation, corresponding to each JND in the stimulus. Hence, when the stimulus ϕ increased by constant ratios, the sensation ψ would increase by constant differences, and the result would be a logarithmic relation

$$\psi = k \log \phi$$

In the absence of any serious alternative, Fechner's logarithmic relation became the accepted psychophysical law. Alternatives had been suggested, however, for the relation between percept and stimulus has long engaged man's attention. In 1728, for example, the mathematician Gabriel Cramer conjectured that the perceived value of money, often called "utility", may grow as the square root of the number of, say, dollars. This early suggestion of a power function was followed in the 1850s by a similar conjecture when J. A. F. Plateau proposed that the apparent lightness of a surface grows as a power function of the reflectance. Plateau reasoned that, since the apparent relation among different shades of gray remains essentially the same when the level of the illumination changes, the *ratios*, not the *differences* (as Fechner argued), among the sensations produced by the shades of gray must remain constant. If the ratios remain fixed, then sensation must follow a power law. But Plateau eventually abandoned his conjecture when further experiments seemed not to bear him out.

A major procedural advance was made by J. Merkel when he undertook in 1888 to determine the stimulus that would appear to be double a given standard stimulus. That method was the forerunner of what is now called ratio production, and it was a method that could have settled the matter of the psychophysical law if it had been fully exploited. But Merkel's work had little effect on the course of psychophysics.

It was not until the 1930s that Merkel's procedures were re-invented and used with other procedures to determine a loudness scale. Many workers in acoustics had become aware that Fechner's logarithmic law was defective, because Fechner's law would predict that the decibel scale could serve as a loudness scale. In particular, Fechner's law predicts that 100 decibels should sound twice as loud as 50 decibels. Actually, 100 decibels sounds about twice as loud as 90 decibels.

2. *The power law*. Definitive evidence for the power law emerged in 1953 when S. S. Stevens employed the methods of equisection, ratio production, and magnitude estimation to demonstrate that the sensations of both loudness and brightness obey a power law. Following that demonstration, Stevens undertook to explore the other sense modalities and to devise additional experimental procedures with which to validate the power law. As a result of that undertaking, together with the work of many other laboratories, the psychophysical power law now stands as the most pervasive and perhaps the best-supported quantitative generalization in psychology. There appears to be no exception to the rule that on all prothetic continua the subjective magnitude ψ grows as the stimulus magnitude ϕ raised to a power. Hence the formula may be written

$$\psi = k\phi^{\alpha}$$

where α is the exponent. Conveniently, in double logarithmic coordinates, this equation becomes a line whose slope corresponds to the exponent.

Each sense modality tends to have its characteristic exponent, ranging from 0·33 for apparent brightness to 3·5 for the sensation produced by electric current through the fingers. The exact value of the exponent may depend on various parameters, such as the duration of the stimulus, the state of sensory adaptation, the presence of inhibiting stimuli (contrast), and so on. The exponent is also affected by the method of measurement, and an unbiased measure of the exponent can be approximated only with the aid of multiple experiments in counterbalanced designs. The

apparent inclination. Prothetic continua include, but are not limited to, those continua on which discrimination is mediated by an additive process at the physiological level. Increasing loudness, for example, involves the addition of excitation to excitation. Increasing pitch, however, involves a metathetic process in which new excitation is substituted for old, thereby changing the locus of the excitation.

Measured exponents and their possible fractional values for power functions relating subjective magnitude to stimulus magnitude

Continuum	Measured Exponent	Possible Fraction	Stimulus Condition
Loudness	0·67	2/3	3000 Hertz tone
Brightness	0·33	1/3	5° target in dark
Brightness	0·5	1/2	very brief flash
Smell	0·6	2/3	heptane
Taste	1·3	3/2	sucrose
Taste	1·4	3/2	salt
Temperature	1·0	1	cold on arm
Temperature	1·5	3/2	warmth on arm
Vibration	0·95	1	60 Hertz on finger
Vibration	0·6	2/3	250 Hertz on finger
Duration	1·1	1	white noise stimuli
Finger span	1·3	3/2	thickness of blocks
Pressure on palm	1·1	1	static force on skin
Heaviness	1·45	3/2	lifted weights
Force of handgrip	1·7	5/3	hand dynamometer
Vocal effort	1·1	1	vocal sound pressure
Electric shock	3·5	3	current through fingers
Tactual roughness	1·5	3/2	feeling emery cloths
Tactual hardness	0·8	4/5	squeezing rubber
Visual length	1·0	1	projected line
Visual area	0·7	2/3	projected square

Table above gives representative values of the exponents thus far obtained for a variety of perceptual continua.

In addition to the measured values of the exponents, an attempt has been made in the Table to suggest the rational fraction that would correspond to the exponent under ideal conditions. Many of the measured values have been obtained by the method of magnitude estimation, which, because of a regression effect, tends to underestimate the exponent.

3. *Two kinds of continua.* Most continua, including those in the Table, belong to the class called prothetic. They concern the question *how much* (quantity) as opposed to *what kind* or *where* (quality). Only a few continua belong to the class called metathetic. Examples are pitch, apparent azimuth, and

The main difference between the two kinds of continua resides in the functional relations observed among the three principal kinds of scaling measures. On metathetic continua a linear relation may be obtained among all the measures. On prothetic continua the three types of measures are non-linearly related.

4. *Three kinds of measure.* Most of the measures that have been used for scaling perceptual continua fall into one or another of three classes.

(a) *Magnitude scales.* Ratio scales of apparent magnitude have been erected by several methods. The most direct method is the matching of values on a perceptual continuum to values on some standard or reference continuum, such as length or number. For example, ten observers adjusted the length of a line of light projected on a wall in order to make its length appear proportional to five different loudnesses presented in random order. The geometric means of the lengths produced were found to be related to the sound pressures of the stimuli by a power function with an exponent of 0·69, a value very close to the exponent for loudness listed in the table.

A more convenient procedure is to ask the observer to match numbers to a series of stimuli. He then assigns numbers proportional to the apparent magnitude of the stimuli presented by the experimenter. This matching procedure is called *magnitude estimation*. In a reverse procedure, called *magnitude production*, the experimenter assigns a set of numbers in irregular order and the observer adjusts the stimuli to produce what he judges to be a sensation proportional to each number. Because all matching procedures are characterized by a regression effect, or centering tendency, the exponent obtained by magnitude estimation is smaller than that obtained by magnitude production.

Magnitude scales may also be constructed by Merkel's method of ratio production, which he called the method of doubled stimulus. In fact, there are many variations on the procedures that can be used to determine apparent or subjective ratios. Fractionation is a name applied to some of them.

Cross-modality matching may be used to validate the scaling of various continua. Thus, if numbers have been matched to two continua, say, loudness and brightness, the two resulting power functions can be used to predict what observers will do when they match loudness to brightness directly. The exponent of the predicted matching function is given by the ratio of the two exponents obtained with number matching. The results of many such cross-modality comparisons show that the power functions meet the test of transitivity: the exponents of two such functions can be used to predict a third.

Cross-modality matching uses the procedures that have long been used within a single modality, for instance, for determining equal loudness contours, photometric matches, and heterochromatic equations.

(*b*) *Partition scales.* As noted above, stellar magnitudes and the lightness of grays were scaled by dividing a continuum into finite segments. On metathetic continua, observers can make such partitions without a systematic bias, but on prothetic continua the partition scale gives a smaller exponent than the magnitude scale; that is, relative to the magnitude scale, the partition scale is curved. The degree of non-linearity in the partition scale depends very much on the methods used. Under favorable conditions, the observer may bisect the distance between two fixed values with only a small net bias. But even there, the results depend on the order of presentation, with the result that a strong hysteresis effect is observed: the bisection point is set higher in ascending than in descending order.

In the most common form of the partition scale, the category rating scale, the observer assigns one of a finite set of numbers or adjectives to each stimulus, for example, the numbers 1 to 7, or the adjectives, small, medium, and large. The resulting category scale is usually highly curved relative to the magnitude scale, except, of course, on metathetic continua. Limiting the observer's response to a finite set of numbers forces him to partition the continuum. He is thereby prevented from making a proportional number assignment in a way that would preserve ratios. On prothetic continua, the restriction to a finite set of numbers or categories produces a dramatic curvature in the scale.

(*c*) *Confusion scales.* This class includes such scales as JND, discrimination, paired comparisons, and successive intervals. The common feature of these scales is that some measure of variability or confusion is taken as the unit. Fechner's JND, which became the unit of his scale, is essentially a measure of variability or "noise". If there were no noise or confusion in human judgments, the JND would become infinitely small. Similar to the JND scales are the scales that L. L. Thurstone built on the method of paired comparisons, which make use of the dispersions among the observer's judgments in order to derive a unit for the scale.

On metathetic continua, the confusion scale may be linearly related to the magnitude scale. For example, the JND for pitch is a constant size when measured in mels, the subjective unit of pitch. On prothetic continua, however, the confusion scale approximates a logarithmic function of the magnitude scale. In numerous experiments by G. Ekman, this logarithmic relation has been shown to hold not only for sensory scales, but for scales involving attitudes, preferences, esthetic judgments, and so on.

5. *Other problems.* Although scaling has always been the central problem of psychophysics, other topics have commanded interest. Among the important topics are the measurement of thresholds and the so-called neural quantum, the application of information theory to the channel capacity of sensory systems, the application of decision theory to the study of signal detectability, and the use of proximity analysis in the development of multidimensional scaling. These and other branches of psychophysics have become major subjects in their own right, and the methods of psychophysics have found important uses in many applied areas.

Bibliography: d'Amato, M. R.: Experimental psychology: methodology, psychophysics, and learning. New York, 1970. Ekman, G. & Sjöberg, G.: Scaling. Annual Rev. Psychol., 1965, *16*, 451–74. Fechner, G. T.: Elemente der Psychophysik, 1860 (Eng. trans. Elements of psychophysics. New York, 1966). Stevens, S. S.: On the brightness of lights and the loudness of sounds. Science, 1953, *118*, 576. Stevens, S. S.: On the psychophysical law. Psychol. Rev., 1957, *64*, 153–81. Stevens, S. S.: Psychophysics of sensory function. In: Rosenblith, W. A. (Ed.): Sensory communication. Cambridge, Mass., 1961, 1–33. Stevens, S. S.: Ratio scales of opinion. In: Whitla, D. K. (Ed.): Handbook of measurement and assessment in behavioral sciences. Reading, Mass., 1968, 171–99. Stevens, S. S.: Le quantitatif et la perception. Bull. de Psychol., 1968–69, *22*, 696–715.   *S. S. Stevens*

Psychophysiological methods. A combination of psychological and physiological methods the purpose of which is to be able to give a valid description of psychophysiological phenomena. Under conditions which can be described psychologically, e.g. anxiety, physiological processes (e.g. secretion of catecholamine) are measured, or under conditions which can be described physiologically, e.g. muscular work on the ergometer, psychological data (e.g. calculation of internal tension) are collected. Only by looking at it from these dual aspects is a complete picture of the states and responses of organisms and their constitutional relationships obtained (see *Psychophysiology*).

Whereas practically all psychological methods, including observations of behavior, tests and introspection, can be used for certain psychophysiological inquiries, there are in the case of physiological methods several limitations that apply especially to some of the methods which are reliable technically as measurements. Since psychophysiological investigations are usually carried out on people free as far as possible from disabilities and in as natural a situation as possible, painful or complicated methods, e.g. direct measurement of arterial blood flow and determination of blood volume per heart beat, measurement of blood-flow through the muscles, catheters and probes, are generally all unsuitable because they may give rise to considerable psychophysiological sideeffects.

Most biosignals can be recorded with a well-equipped polygraph (q.v.), others require additional devices.

A second category of variables consists of clinical and chemical laboratory methods: differential blood picture and drop in blood pressure, electrolyte and pH value of the body

Psychophysiological Methods

Biosignal	Abbreviation	Recording device	Most important parameters
Cortical potentials, spontaneous or evoked (electroencephalogram)	EEG, EVP	Electrodes	Frequency band (α, β, δ, ϑ), DC components, change of frequency, e.g. alpha-block, SW complex, other patterns
Cardiac potentials (electrocardiogram, cardiotachogram)	EKG (ECG)	Electrodes	Pulse rate, irregularity of pulse, and other parameters
Blood pressure, arterial		Indirect: microphone Direct: sphygmomanometer (pressure cuff)	Systolic and diastolic blood pressure; blood pressure amplitude
Pulse waves (pulse pressure), e.g. radial and femoral pulse (sphygmogram, oscillogram)		Sphygmograph, or photoelectric device	Pulse frequency, systolic and diastolic phases, pulse wave speed
Pulse volume (rating of blood flow) (finger plethysmogram, as volume-, rheo-, or photo-plethysmogram)		Sphygmograph, impedance meter or photoelectric device	Pulse volume change
Respiration, respiration-conditioned thoracic movements (pneumogram)		Thermistor, pneumograph, thoracic recorder	Respiratory frequency, duration of inspiration and expiration
Respiration speed (pneumotachogram)		Breathing (oxygen) mask and differential pressure variator	Respiration speed
Respiratory volume, metabolism (spirogram)	RQ	Breathing mask, spirometer and gas analysis apparatus	Breathing volume, minute volume of air, respiratory quotient (CO_2/O_2)
Blood gases	pO_2 pCO_2 pH	Special-purpose electrodes	gas partial-pressures, pH value (hydrogen-ion concentration)
Body temperature, Skin and body cavities		Resistance thermometer, thermoelement, thermistor	Absolute value and local temperature differences
Skin resistance, skin conductance, psychogalvanic reactions (galvanic skin response) (electrodermatogram)	SR, SC, GSR (PGR)	Electrodes	Skin conductance, GSR latency, amplitude and frequency
Skin potential, skin potential reactions	SP, SPR	Electrodes	Latency, amplitude and frequency of SPR
Body movements, tremor (actiogram, mechanogram, tremogram)		Movement and acceleration recording devices, tremograph	Frequency and amplitude
Muscle action potentials Electromyogram	EMG	Skin or needle electrodes Electromyograph	Frequency and amplitude, Amplitude frequency product, electromyointegral
Eyelid reflex		Electrodes or photoelectric recorder	Frequency
Eye movements (electrooculogram, electronystagmogram)	EOG, ENG	Electrodes	Amplitude, direction Frequency
Pupillary reflex (pupillogram)		Photographic techniques or photoelectric recording	Size of pupil
Gastro-intestinal motility (electrogastrogram)	EGG	Magnetic detectors, electrodes or radio probes	
Gastro-intestinal-pH-value		Radio probes	pH value (hydrogen-ion concentration as expression of acidity or alkalinity)

fluids: blood serum, urine, saliva; biochemical parameters such as creatinin, uric acid, albumen, lipids, blood sugar, cholinesterase and other enzymes. Particular attention must be given to work in determining enzymes and hormones which will become more important as further progress is made in chemical laboratory methods. Finally those methods of vegetative-endocrinal and neuromuscular diagnostics are still available which, in order to test some dynamic function, apply a stress to the body by sensory stimuli, change of position, muscular effort or some drug, and then attempt to determine individual control quality (vegetative (q.v.) lability or stability) from counter-regulation.

The physiological methods mentioned above differ very considerably from one another with respect to reliability and definition. There is still no methodical line of discussion in this field comparable to test theory (q.v.) and test construction in psychology. Of course, checking methods is made more difficult by several problems:

1. Marked functional fluctuation depending on the time of day, season, weather, nutrition, nicotine, so that the classical reliability concept of parallel or repeated measurements can scarcely be employed.

2. Major difficulties of standardization, since the investigations should be conducted in rooms shielded from electro-magnetic forces (so-called Faraday cage), and which are sound and fire-proof and air-conditioned; a watch must be kept for effects due to habituation and situation.

3. Relatively large errors of measurement due to methods concerning biochemical quantities, e.g. in determining hormones.

4. Absence of absolute comparability—at most it is intraindividual—of precisely those methods which are frequently used because they are sensitive to psychologically induced changes in condition: the recording of skin resistance and the finger plethysmogram.

5. Phasic time-lags due to varying latencies of the effector organs or to the time needed to collect urine.

6. Quite excessive number of polygraph recordings required to cover fully the wealth of information.

7. Possibility of response patterns specific to the individual and the stimulus.

8. Dependence of an interpretation on the initial values of the function in question and on the other system parameters, as a change in value represents the displacement of a multiple dynamic balance.

9. Necessity for a multivariate strategy and non-linear models if counter-regulating, compensatory processes are to be described at all appropriately.

In many psychophysiological investigations there is a somewhat superficial and uncritical analysis of biosignals, whose conditions, measurement and implications have to be regarded as most doubtful from a physiological standpoint. In addition there exists a manifest uncertainty whether certain characteristics are sufficient (just what can a change of skin resistance, q.v., tell us?) or whether individual physiological values can rank as more or less valid indicators of dimensions of latent states (arousal, activation, q.v., stress, q.v., etc.), or of lasting dimensions of characteristics (vegetative lability, q.v.; sympathicotony, q.v., etc.). The theoretical interpretations and the practical consequences (e.g. a validity check on such "indicators") have not yet become sufficiently clear. To suppose that there is one uniform activating dimension seems in any case out-of-date idea. The dimensional approach is also open to question, for physiological values represent functional patterns (synergisms) adapted to changing demands which arise because of more or less complex integration achievements on higher or lower planes of the central nervous system. The study of these integrative achievements, their coordination or dissociation, promises to give better results than the superficial inspection of pulse, and GSR.

A standard combination of physiological techniques is impossible. In each inquiry criteria such as repeatability, reasonableness, economy and physiological meaningfulness will call for a different selection: during inner tension and emotional excitation as well as during a multiplicity of tasks many writers are agreed that—largely independently of the quality of the emotions—a relatively distinct covariation of the following physiological values may be observed: pulse rate, breathing, systolic blood pressure (automatic recording difficult), skin resistance and peripheral blood flow (standardization problems), body movements (recording problems), frequency change in brain potential fluctuations (accurate EEG analysis difficult), corticosteroid and catecholamine secretion (rather less reliability, and in the case of urine values only as the mean value of the collecting period).

How many-sided psychophysiological methods are can only be sketched here: in addition to the above methods there are also those dependent on the type of constitution, inventories to list physical infirmities or the momentary state of physical activation, methods for conditioning (q.v.) autonomic and motor responses (e.g. eyelid movement) methods for determining sensory thresholds or orientation response (see *Orientation reflex*) and habituation, as well as many special procedures which have proved their worth in this field bordering on various disciplines. Psychophysiological methods also depend on technological progress: the construction of new measuring instruments, the development of biotelemetric systems for recording biosignals in everyday situations, the use of laboratory computers for the more rapid and exhaustive processing of biosignals and the automatic control of experiments.

The special problems of psychophysiological methods must not be underestimated, but a steadily increasing application of these combined methods can be expected; they

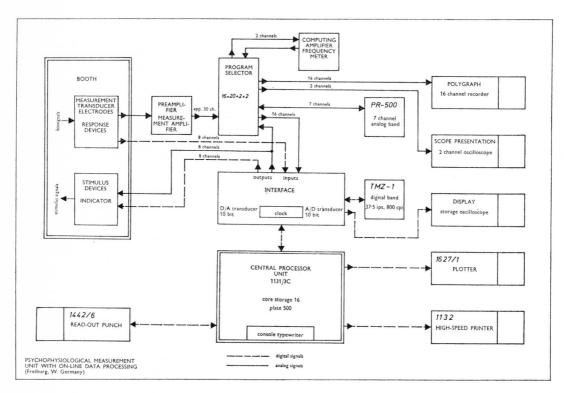

PSYCHOPHYSIOLOGICAL MEASUREMENT UNIT WITH ON-LINE DATA PROCESSING
(Freiburg, W. Germany)

have great theoretical merit and can be used in many practical ways.

Bibliography: Brown, C. C. (Ed.): Methods in psychophysiology. Baltimore, 1967. **Fahrenberg, J.:** Psychophysiologische Persönlichkeitsforschung. Göttingen, 1967. **Mackay, R. S.:** Biomedical telemetry. New York, ²1970. **Tompson, P. N. & Yarbrongh, R. B.:** The shielding of electroencephalographic laboratories. Psychophysiology, 1967, *4*, 244–8. **Venables, P. H. & Martin, I.** (Eds.): Manual of psychophysiological methods. Amsterdam, 1967. *Journals:* Computer Programs in Biomedicine, Amsterdam. Das Ärztliche Laboratorium, Berlin. GIT Fachschrift für das Laboratorium, Darmstadt. EDV in Medizin und Biologie, Stuttgart. Elektromedizin, Berlin (from 1971: Biomedical Engineering). Psychophysiology, Baltimore.   *J. Fahrenberg*

Psychophysiology is concerned with psychophysical processes, i.e. those life processes which are susceptible to psychological, physiological and biological methods. In this field which borders on various traditional disciplines, theories are still at variance. Other areas have partly impinged upon the territory of the old concept of physiological psychology and relieved it of certain fields of research: the physiology of the brain and psychophysics, psychosomatics, the physiology of behavior, psycho-endocrinology, psychomorphology, the study of constitutional types, neuro-psychology and psychophysiology in the narrower sense. Common to these already partly independent disciplines is the question of the physiological and biological bases of experience (state of health and consciousness) and of behavior. Differences exist in regard to the quantity and kind of permissible variables (central nervous, peripheral, vegetative-endocrine and motor functions, observation of behavior, psychological tests), in regard to selection and general applicability of experimental situations (from the anesthetized uterus in labor to telemetrical studies on a person in an everyday situation), and consideration of individual differences, and in regard to the question of whether types of behavior and experience can be explained physiologically. Extreme "physiologism": that is, the reduction of psychologically definable models to neurophysiological terms, is certainly seldom encountered today.

The distinguishing mark of psychophysiology is psychological-physiological double interpretation. This dualism in the method of definition emerges from the peculiar position (peculiar historically and in relation to the theory of perception) of the methods of both techniques, especially if the methods of experiential psychology and the style of interpretation proper to a commentator on the arts are accepted as psychological methods. However, the use of such means of definition which differ in their terms of reference conveys nothing in respect of the duality or identity of the observed life processes (bodily functions, behavior, q.v., experienced subjectivity). The different systems of classification are looked upon as complementary forms which are equally necessary to the description of the higher life processes.

A theory of the organism relating to the psychophysical individuality of a person is only possible by the mutual supplementation of psychological and physiological methods and if it is based on a synopsis of different areas of data.

Themes of *general psychophysiology* are—apart from the mind-body problem and the theory of the organism—general methodology and the bases of a psychophysiological double interpretation and systems analysis.

The chief functions of *specialized* psychophysiology are the definition and classification of psychophysical phenomena such as orientation reaction (q.v.), perception of pain, anxiety (q.v.), hunger, trauma (q.v.), exhaustion, nervousness. Many authors have sought to classify the extraordinary diversity of psychophysical phenomena within certain concepts: activation (q.v.), arousal, stress (q.v.), ergotropy-trophotropy, psychovegetative lability, and other concepts of dimension.

These notions are useful indeed, yet on the one hand they are still held in too general a sense to be employed without qualification, and on the other hand, from the psychological or physiological point of view, they are too one-sided in meaning. Multivariate analyses have hitherto hardly been tried; because of the special problems of psychological method they are additionally complicated. Therefore the formulated questions of psychophysiology are still often determined from single phenomena and from certain functions which seem specially interesting, for example, secretion of catecholamine, EEG (encephalography, q.v.), or even only from very special classification techniques, e.g. skin resistance to electrical impulses (PGR) (q.v.) and evoked potentials. On the other hand, a number of significant studies have been published which demonstrate the theoretical value and the practical possibilities of application. The present position of research is represented by many catch-words: emotion impact (q.v.), activation (q.v.), fatigue (q.v.), hormone research (q.v.), noise research (q.v.), psychosomatic medicine (q.v.), sleep and dream research (q.v.), stress research (q.v.). Specific physiological patterns of certain emotions could hitherto—contrary to the interpretation of many representatives of psychosomatic medicine—not be established with certainty, also the concept of a dimension of psycho-vegetative lability (nervousness, neuroticism, q.v.), as well as the question of a co-variation of central nervous (EEG) arousal and peripheral ergotropic inversion of function, are still debated. Clearly more progress must first be made in the simple definition of psychophysical correlates before, as the second step, more differentiated theoretical concepts can be developed: e.g. a clearer analysis of dimension, and before taxonomy can be undertaken.

Practical applications will follow chiefly in clinical psychophysiology in relation to psychosomatic medicine, then first on the basis of broadly-planned and fundamental longitudinal (q.v.) (time series) studies of psychophysical correlates the success of a certain therapy might be judged: psychoanalysis of psychosomatic disorders, classical and operant conditioning (q.v.) of vegetative and motor forms of behavior, influence through autogenic training (q.v.), hypnosis (q.v.), psychopharmacology, methods of physical medicine, investigation into subjective observation of disturbances in bodily function, and also studies in response correlation or self-control of biorhythm.

All in all, psychophysiology can be regarded as a basic discipline of psychosomatic medicine and of all biologically orientated personality research.

Bibliography: Ax, A. F.: Goals and methods of psychophysiology. Psychophysiology, 1964, *1*, 8–25. Black, P.: (Ed.): Physiological correlates of emotion. New York, 1970. Cattell, R. B.: A brief survey of present knowledge and hypotheses on psychophysiological state dimensions. In: Cattell, R. B. (Ed.): Handbook of multivariate experimental psychology. Chicago, 1966. Delius, L. & Fahrenberg, J.: Psycho-vegetative Syndrome. Stuttgart, 1966. Eysenck, H. J.: The biological basis of personality. Springfield, Ill., 1967. Fahrenberg, J.: Psychophysiologische Persönlichkeitsforschung. Göttingen, 1967. Hess, W. R.: Psychologie in biologischen Sicht. Stuttgart, ²1968. Jung, R.: Neurophysiologie und Psychiatrie. In: H. W. Gruhle *et al.* (Eds.): Psychiatrie der Gegenwart, Vol. 1, Pt. 1 A. Berlin, 1967. Levi, L. (Ed.): Emotional stress. Basle, 1967. Martin, I.: Somatic reactivity. In: Eysenck, A. J. (Ed.): Handbook of abnormal psychology. London, ²1971; Rothschuh, K. E.: Theorie des Organismus. München, ²1963. Royce, J. R.: Concepts generated in comparative and physiological observations. In: Cattell, R. B. (Ed.): Handbook of multivariate experimental psychology. Chicago, 1966. Schönpflug, W. (Ed.): Methoden der Aktivierungsforschung. Berne, 1969. Sternbach, R. A.: Principles of psychophysiology. New York, 1966.

J. Fahrenberg

Psychoprophylaxis. Prevention of mental disturbances (psychohygiene, q.v.) by appropriate measures; it always corresponds to a particular theory of *neurosis* (q.v.) and is an important aim of educational counselling (q.v.).   *W.Sch.*

Psychoreflexology. Also known as *objective psychology.* Developed by W. Bekhterev and J. P. Pavlov. According to this theory, all mental disorders are to be explained as neuro-psychological; they all originate in physical causes and are to be classified as such. Fundamental concept of the method: the object of scientific psychology can be observed, classified and measured only in its physical aspects.   *H.W.*

Psychoses, functional. *Psychopathology* may be described as the branch of psychological science concerned with the systematic investigation of deviant behavior. It involves the application of the principles of learning, perception, motivation and physiological psychology in order to understand the abnormal. Some of the usual criteria of deviancy are personal distress, disabling behavioral tendencies and disturbances of motor behavior, mood and thinking. The disturbances that reflect greater deviancy, severity and disorganization of the personality are called *psychoses.* When the individual fails to take care of himself or seems likely to injure himself or others, society puts him in hospital or locks him up. Hence the fact of institutionalization also constitutes a definition of the psychotic condition.

Classification of the psychotic disorders is based primarily on the symptom syndromes exhibited, and secondarily on life history data such as type of onset, duration, age, sex and number of recurrences. Attempts at classification based on the concept of physical disease have so far proved unsatisfactory because no organism has been implicated, no lesions have been demonstrated, and no consistent central nervous system changes have been identified. Although there are several biochemical theories regarding causal agents, and there is some evidence of genetic determinants, on the whole there is no systematic basis for regarding the psychoses as physical diseases. The 18th International Classification of Diseases (ICD-8) recognizes the present status of the psychoses as disorders without any known organic etiology.

1. *The elementary syndromes.* The standard psychiatric nomenclature is widely regarded as comparatively unsatisfactory for decision making or as a schema for research. One important defect is poor agreement among classifiers through non-objective criteria for category membership. A related defect is the absence of decision rules for combining multiple indicators in a diagnostic decision. In addition, there are questions whether some of the categories overlap too much, some are too broad, and others are invalid. Finally there is the complaint that most of the diagnostic classes are of little or no value for prognosis or for treatment selection.

The defects in nomenclature have produced a wide variety of strategies for solving them. Investigators have sought to objectify the vague terms by use of rating scales, and to make the diagnostic procedure uniform by structured interviews. Another approach has been to establish existing categories more firmly by providing more objective definitions of terms and by establishing consensual validation for the accepted psychiatric classes. Finally, some investigators have sought to establish a descriptive system on the basis of currently discernible symptoms, by using modern multivariate statistical procedure; this consists of interviewing patients before treatment and rating them immediately afterwards on observable behaviors defined in a standardized rating schedule. The relations among the behaviors and symptoms are rated and then analyzed to isolate all independent syndromes (symptom clusters) to be found.

Twelve psychotic syndromes have been identified in numerous independent studies of hospitalized U.S. patients (Lorr, Klett & McNair, 1963). The equivalence of the syndromes observed in U.S. samples to those found in patients observed in six countries

(England, France, Germany, Italy, Japan and Sweden) have recently been established (Lorr & Klett, 1969). The same symptom groupings may be found in women as well as in men.

Brief descriptions of each of the twelve psychotic syndromes or dimensions are given below. Each variable is regarded as present in all patients to some degree. A low score on a syndrome implies a mild, and a high score a severe, disturbance. For additional details and for description of the scales the reader is referred to Lorr & Klett (1966).

(a) *Excitement*. Speech is hurried, loud and difficult to stop. The level of mood and self-esteem is elevated. Emotional expression tends to be unrestrained and histrionic. (b) *Hostile belligerence*. Expressions of complaints, hostility and resentment concerning others are common. Difficulties and failures are blamed on others. (c) *Paranoid projection*. There is evidence of unwarranted fixed beliefs that attribute a hostile, persecutory or controlling intent to persons around the patient. (d) *Grandiosity*. An attitude of superiority is associated with unwarranted beliefs of possessing unusual powers. Divine missions may also be reported. (e) *Perceptual distortions*. There are reports of false perceptions in the form of voices that threaten, accuse or demand. (f) *Obsessional-phobic*. Uncontrollable acts and rituals, recurrent unwanted thoughts, specific fears, and ideas of personal change and unreality are reported. (g) *Anxious-depression*. Vague anxiety as well as specific concerns are reported. The mood is dysphoric and the attitudes towards the self are derogatory. In addition, feelings of guilt and remorse for real and imagined faults are evident. (h) *Functional impairment*. There are complaints of inability to concentrate, work or to make decisions. Interest in people, sex and social activity is much reduced or lacking. (i) *Retardation*. Speech, ideation and motor activity are slowed or blocked. There are also apathy and disinterest in the future. (j) *Dis-orientation*. There is a functional disorientation with respect to time, place and season. There may be failure to recognize persons the patient should know well. (k) *Motor disturbances*. Bizarre postures are assumed and maintained. Peculiar and manneristic facial and body movements are manifested repeatedly. (l) *Conceptual disorganization*. Speech is rambling, incoherent, or unrelated to the question asked. The same words or phrases are repeated in a stereotyped fashion. New words (neologisms) may be invented and incorporated in speech.

An important characteristic of this descriptive system is that all patients are uniformly assessed for all behaviors and symptoms. Conventional procedures are unsystematic in that each case is examined with respect to a slightly different set of symptoms. Furthermore, since life-history events are excluded from definition of the syndromes there is no confounding of data sources as in conventional diagnoses. This means that it is possible to evaluate the independent contribution of each towards the prediction of some specified outcome. The procedure also provides the psychiatrist with a distinctive profile or configuration of scores on the twelve syndromes.

2. *The major syndromes*. The elementary syndromes are by no means completely independent of one another. They combine in meaningful ways into more inclusive dimensions. For example, anxious depression is often associated with functional impairment and retardation. Recent efforts (Lorr *et al.*, 1967; Overall *et al.*, 1967) to define the major psychotic disorders or syndromes in terms of disturbances of thinking mood and behavior have converged. When the correlations among the scores defining the elementary syndromes are analyzed by multivariate statistical procedures, five more inclusive behavioral dimensions emerge. The same patterns have been isolated in U.S. data, and in ratings obtained in cross-national studies. Sex differences are negligible with respect to the nature of these

disorders, although men and women may differ in severity (Lorr & Klett, 1968).

Each of the major syndromes will be characterized in terms of the elementary symptom clusters. Of course, in practice, the elementary syndrome scores defining each disorder are weighted and then summed to yield a measure of severity.

(a) *Schizophrenic disorganization.* This disorder is characterized by psychomotor retardation and apathy, functional disorientation and motor disturbances. Conceptual disorganization is also present but to a lesser degree. (b) *Paranoid process.* Characterized by the joint presence of paranoid projection, perceptual distortion (hallucinations), grandiosity and obsessive thinking. (c) *Hostile paranoia.* Somewhat narrower than the previous two described. It is defined by hostile belligerence and paranoid projection. (d) *Psychotic depression.* Characterized by anxious depression, functional impairment and by obsessional and phobic symptoms. (e) *Disorganized hyperactivity.* Primarily characterized by excitement, conceptual disorganization and motor disturbances. Grandiosity may also be evident but not uniformly.

3. *Conventional diagnostic classes.* The major psychoses not attributed to physical conditions, as listed in ICD-8, include Schizophrenia, the Affective disorders, the Paranoid states and a miscellaneous category. These groupings are typically defined by a combination of current symptoms and life-history events. Included are such differentia as type of onset, premorbid personality, duration of the disturbance, age, and number of episodes. Each major disorder and the subtypes subsumed under it will be described briefly and then compared with the syndromes delineated earlier.

Schizophrenia is characterized as a thought disorder. Disturbances in thinking are reflected in delusions and hallucinations. The mood is ambivalent, constricted or marked by apathy. Behavior is withdrawn and sometimes

bizarre. Typically, there is a loss of empathy with others. The withdrawn subtypes are called simple, hebephrenic, catatonic (withdrawn) and schizo-affective (depressed). The excited subtypes are called acute, catatonic (excited) and schizo-affective (excited). The paranoid subtype is recognized as being differentiable into the hostile, the grandiose and the hallucinatory.

The simple subtype is recognizable symptomatically only by the lack of interests or attachments, and by apathy and indifference. The hebephrenic is characterized by disorganized thinking, inappropriate affect and manneristic movements. The catatonic exhibits stupor, mutism, negativism, and occasionally a resistance to movement called "waxy flexibility". The symptoms of these withdrawn and apathetic subtypes appear to correspond to what was identified earlier as schizophrenic disorganization.

The paranoid subtypes are characterized primarily by delusions of persecution and grandiosity associated with hallucinations, and occasionally by excessive religiosity. The syndrome previously described as Paranoid Process appears to include the symptom pattern included here under the paranoid subtype. The paranoid schizophrenics are commonly differentiated from the non-paranoid because this separation is useful for prognosis, for treatment, and for sound theoretical reasons. The paranoid subtypes and the withdrawn subtypes correspond well to this separation. However, the allocation of the excited subtypes is presently in doubt although it is possible to regard these as transient states.

The *Affective psychoses* represent the second major grouping of disorders. This group is characterized by deviation in mood, in the form of elation or depression, unrelated apparently to any precipitating life event. Included here are involutional melancholia and manic-depressive illness, depressed type. Both are described as exhibiting depressed mood with retardation or agitation, and thus may be differentiated only on the basis of age or the presence or absence of previous episodes. The manic subtype is characterized by excessive motor activity. There is also a circular or bipolar subtype which involves both a depressive episode and a manic episode. The major syndrome (identified statistically) corresponding to the excited subtype is disorganized hyperactivity. This syndrome, however, is also defined by motor disturbances and thus represents both the excited catatonic and the so-called manic-depressive, manic subtype. On the depressive side the subtype symptomatology is seen in psychotic depression.

The third major grouping of psychotic disorders is called *paranoid states*; these include paranoia and Involutional paranoid state. These are disorders in which a persecutory or grandiose delusion is primary. Disturbances in mood, behavior, perception and thinking are said to derive from these delusions. The diagnostic manual acknowledges that many authorities question whether the paranoid states are truly distinct or merely variants of schizophrenia or paranoid personality. It does seem that the evidence for this set of disorders is quite shaky.

In summary, it can be said that there is a rough correspondence between the major syndromes of psychotic behavior (statistically determined) and the major psychotic disorders (clinically established). Yet it is important that the elementary and major syndromes constitute a dimensional rather than a typological conception of the psychotic disorders. The psychiatric subtypes are presumably homogeneous subgroups of individuals, characterized by a common set of symptoms and behaviors. Classification of a fresh case in a diagnostic subtype is done on an all-or-none basis; that is, the individual either belongs or does not belong to the category. The process is similar to diagnosing a disease such as pneumonia; either one has or does not have

pneumonia. In contradistinction, the dimensional approach is quantitative in character. Every person receives a score on each syndrome, and thus has a "profile" or set of scores.

4. *Emerging models*. The modern model of the behavior disorders is both dimensional and typological. Most of the symptoms and behaviors defining the psychoses are not qualitative and discrete but quantitative and continuous in character. Therefore a behavior disorder and those changes resulting in it from natural causes or treatment should be assessed by quantitative and continuous variables. The dimensional approach offers an objectively defined minimal set of non-overlapping descriptors (syndromes) to represent the domain of deviant behavior. It also provides a more useful and objective basis for evaluating changes in a disorder.

In the typological approach individuals are described on all the syndromes of behavior deviation. They are then grouped together into mutually exclusive subgroups on the basis of similarity of syndrome score profile. Each subgroup is thus objectively defined in terms of possession of a common score profile. There have been investigations concerned with the development of such psychotic typologies, but none has as yet been tested sufficiently to warrant description here. It should be noted that members of two diagnostic classes may differ in their life history antecedents and yet be quite similar symptomatically. For example, involutional melancholia and the depressive subtype of manic-depressive psychosis appear to have similar syndrome score patterns even though they differ with respect to age and number of previous episodes of disturbance.

Bibliography: Lorr, M. & Klett, C. J.: Cross-cultural comparison of psychotic syndromes. J. Abnorm. Psychol., 1969, *74*, 531–43. **Id.:** Major psychotic disorders. Arch. Gen. Psychiat., 1968, *19*, 652–8. **Id.:** Inpatient multidimensional psychiatric scale. Manual. Palo Alto, Calif., 1966. **Id.:** Higher level psychotic syndromes. J. Abnorm. Psychol., 1967, *72*, 74–7. **Lorr, M., Klett, C. J. & McNair, D. M.:** Syndromes of psychosis. Oxford, 1963. **Overall, J. E., Hollister, L. E. & Pichot, P.**: Major psychiatric disorders. Arch. Gen. Psychiat., 1967, *16*, 146–51.   *M. Lorr*

Psychosis of association. If a person who has hitherto been of sound mind becomes deranged under the influence of a deranged person with whom he is closely associated (*paranoid schizophrenia*), and if he himself experiences the same hallucinations and changes in mood as the first subject, the latter (inducent) is said to have "induced" the second subject (induced person). A study of psychoses has shown that only psychoses of delusion are transmitted in this way (Scharfetter, 1970). Because of their hereditary disposition, the induced persons are liable to the psychoreactive development of schizophrenic psychoses under differing psychodynamic conditions. See *Paranoia; Schizophrenia.*   *C.S.*

Psychosomatics. 1. *Definition.* The term psychosomatics is used with different meanings. The commonest and narrowest use is to signify a limited number of diseases which have certain characteristics. Less commonly it means a holistic philosophy of medicine, which regards disease as a relation between the individual and his environment, both considered as integrations of the psychological and material aspects. Its practical application is seen in the approach of the physician to the treatment and management of the patient, whatever the disorder. An outcome of this, and perhaps a third meaning, underlines the recent researches which regard disease as an ecological problem. Different schools of psychology agree with the general definition, i.e. the range of the subject, although they concentrate on different aspects, e.g. psychoanalysis is concerned with unconscious dynamics, and learning theory studies the conditioning of the autonomic nervous system.

2. *Psychosomatic disorders.* The characteristics of these disorders are:

(*a*) They show disturbances of function together with damage in the organs of the body. In this they differ from mental disorders. (*b*) Emotional disturbances play an essential part in them, in precipitating the onset, recurrence or exacerbation of symptoms. This distinguishes them from purely "organic" disorders. (*c*) They are chronic disorders with a phasic course. (*d*) They tend to be associated with other psychosomatic disorders. This may occur in the family or at different periods of life in one patient. (*e*) They show a great difference in the incidence between the sexes. Thus, asthma is twice as common in boys as in girls, before puberty; after, it is less common in men than in women. Duodenal ulcer is much more common in men and thyrotoxicosis is commoner in women.

There is no universal agreement as to which conditions should be included as being psychosomatic, but the following brief list (in systems) is generally accepted.

Respiratory: asthma, vasomotor rhinitis. *Gastro-intestinal:* peptic ulcer, colonic disorders. *Cardio-vascular:* hypertension, coronary disease, migraine. *Skin:* urticaria, rosacea, neurodermatitis (atopic eczema). *Endocrine:* thyrotoxicosis, diabetes mellitus, menstrual disturbances. *Other:* rheumatoid arthritis. There is much debate whether pulmonary tuberculosis and ulcerative colitis should be included. There is some evidence that emotional factors play a part in the onset and course of the former (Kissen, 1958), but it is doubtful if this is true of the latter.

3. *Physiology of the emotions.* It is an empirical fact that emotional disturbances are associated with the onset of psychosomatic disorders and exacerbations of their symptoms; there is also good evidence that such disturbances play a part in the etiology. The philosophical problem of how mental changes can produce damage to bodily organs can be evaded by taking into account the fact that emotional changes are always accompanied by bodily changes. The emotional reactions

and bodily changes can be therefore regarded as different aspects of the reaction of the individual to stresses; it remains only to consider how the bodily changes can give rise to lesions in the organs.

The function of the internal organs is controlled by the autonomic nervous system (ANS). Most of the organs have a double supply, consisting of adrenergic and cholinergic fibers with opposing actions. Under normal conditions the two act together; thus, when the heart accelerates it can be shown that there is an increased activity in its sympathetic (adrenergic) supply and a decreased activity of its parasympathetic (cholinergic) supply.

Some of the simpler reflexes which affect the activity of the internal organs are mediated by those parts of the ANS which lie outside the central nervous system (CNS), e.g. peristalsis of the intestine. Most of the others involve the spinal cord. The low level reflexes are integrated in hierarchical systems at higher levels of the CNS, in order to maintain internal conditions at an optimum level. With exposure to stress, e.g. extremes of temperature, asphyxia, pain, or situations of danger, a wide discharge of impulses occurs through the whole of the ANS, and the changes produced can be seen to be those associated with fear or rage. The Cannon-Bard theory of the emotions regards such changes as an adjustment of the individual to an emergency. The center which organizes this discharge is the hypothalamus, and it is linked through the amygdaloid nucleus, hippocampus and anterior nucleus of the thalamus to the cingulate gyrus of the cerebral cortex. These higher nuclei form the "limbic system" which links the organization of emotional responses to the activities of the rest of the CNS.

The discharge through the ANS is accompanied by activity in a parallel system: the endocrine glands. Stimulation of the autonomic supply to the medulla of the adrenal gland produces a release of adrenalin and noradrenalin into the circulation and these hormones produce in each organ the same effect as direct stimulation of the autonomic nervous supply. In addition, the hypothalamus controls the activity of the pituitary gland, which releases hormones which stimulate other endocrine glands, especially, from the present viewpoint, the adrenal cortex and the thyroid. The former plays an essential part in the reaction of tissues to damage and the latter increases metabolism and potentiates the effect of adrenalin.

The response to stress can be divided into three stages:

(a) An immediate response (taking about a second) via the ANS, (b) A delayed response (of the order of a minute) via the secretions of the adrenal medulla. (c) A long-term reaction to chronic stress via the adrenal cortex and thyroid.

These emergency reactions can be directly related to the manifestations of the psychosomatic disorders. Stimulation of the parasympathetic supply to the bronchioles causes contraction of the muscle fibers and narrowing of the lumen of the bronchioles, and this is the first stage of an attack of asthma. Stimulation of the autonomic supply to the stomach leads to engorgement of the gastric mucous membrane, which becomes friable and easily injured. Such injuries do not heal unless the membrane returns to normal. Wolff & Wolf (1947) demonstrated in the human subject that these phenomena occurred in states of anxiety and anger. One of the hormones of the adrenal cortex, cortisone, is now used therapeutically, and two well-known complications of its use are the development of peptic ulcer and the flare-up of pulmonary tuberculosis.

4. *Specificity.* Not all individuals develop psychosomatic disturbances in response to (psychological) stress and, furthermore, they suffer from different disorders. Much research and theorizing has been devoted to the problems of "specificity" and, considering only the psychological aspects, this may be viewed in

terms of the predisposing personality, the nature of precipitating stress and specific aspects of the intermediate mechanisms.

Many of the earlier researches were based on the theory that certain types of personality were particularly liable to develop specific psychosomatic disorders. Various "personality profiles" were described, but it became clear in time that the resemblances between the profiles were much greater than the differences. Most of these types of personality were variations of the "obsessional" or "anancastic" personality. Since most of the original work lacked adequate controls, or even any at all, and since the obsessional personality is a common normal type, it is not surprising that subsequent work largely discounted the earlier findings. In some cases it would appear that the personality of the patient is better regarded as the result of the illness rather than the cause, for example, in ulcerative colitis. Despite much criticism, some of the research findings have been confirmed, but they are not specific, for example, sufferers from duodenal ulcer tend to be of an anxious disposition. Much the same may be said of the studies on the nature of the psychological stresses which precipitate illness.

Much research has been devoted to the mechanism by which emotional disturbances can effect the activity of an organ. In summary, there are very few functions which are not under the control of the CNS, either through the ANS or the hypothalamus-pituitary endocrine system. Earlier researches demonstrated easily that the response to stress showed a different pattern between individuals. It was also shown that different stresses, evoking fear or resentment, had different patterns of response. Attempts were made to show that the pattern was fixed for each individual, but even if this is true, it is not important. The autonomic response is not only related to ongoing activity but also to the (voluntary) patterns of behavior evoked. The ANS is easily conditioned, and therefore its response will depend also on the history of the individual. Not only is this true of classical conditioning (q.v.), but also of operant conditioning and the latter implies that modification of the ANS plays a part, not only in the development of psychosomatic disorders, but in their recurrence and recovery.

Psychological mechanisms have been studied from the psychoanalytical point of view. The unconscious mechanisms described do not differ essentially from those which underlie the neuroses and personality disorders; this is to be expected, since the response of an individual to stress is based on the totality of his life-experiences. Psychotherapy must be based on his individuality. As controlled trials of psychotherapy are extremely difficult to carry out, the evidence that such treatment plays a significant role in the recovery of the patient is still tenuous.

5. *Recent developments.* The most important aspect of new work is the increasing rigor of research techniques: for instance, comparison with appropriate control groups and the use of psychometric methods for assessment of personality. Scales have even been devised to measure life-stresses. New techniques for continuous recording of physiological changes, including multiple recording and telemetering, have given much more detailed information about the response to stress. Intensive research on operant conditioning of autonomic function has not only illuminated problems of mechanism, but has opened up important possibilities for treatment (Miller, 1969).

Epidemiological studies have investigated the role of genetic and environmental factors and have attempted to identify vulnerable groups. Whole populations have been studied intensively (Essen-Moller, 1956) and followed up for a considerable period (Hagnell, 1966). A special development is based on an ecological approach. An early paper is that of Hinckle & Wolff (1958). They demonstrated the existence of a group of disease-susceptible individuals. With an increasing number of illnesses, type, variety (including mental illnesses), and severity increase. Although each individual has a fairly steady rate of illness, there are episodes of increased rate which occur when the individual feels he is threatened, when life is unsatisfying and full of conflict, and no satisfactory solution is possible. This work has been extended by Holmes Rahe (1967), who quantified life change by means of a schedule of recent experiences. They were able to show that a significant increase of life changes preceded a clustering of severe illnesses. It also succeeded a cluster (Rahe & Arthur, 1965). This work has given specific content to the holistic notion that disease is a reaction to environmental changes, and that the difference between somatic and mental disease is less than current tradition maintains. The study of psychosomatic disorders is entering a new and interesting period.

Bibliography: Essen-Moller, E.: Individual traits and morbidity in Swedish rural population. Acta Psychiat. et neurol. Scand., 1956, Suppl., 100. **Hagnell, O.:** A prospective study of the incidence of mental disorders. Stockholm, 1966. **Hamilton, M.:** Psychosomatics. London, 1955. **Hinckle, L. E. & Wolff, H. G.:** Ecologic investigations of the relationship between illness, life experiences and the social environment. Ann. intern. Med., 1958, 49, 1373–88. **Holmes, T. H. & Rahe, R. H.:** The social readjustment rating scale. J. psychosom. Res., 1967, 11, 213–8. **Kissen, D. M.:** Emotional factors in pulmonary tuberculosis. London, 1958. **Leigh, D. & Marley, E. M.:** Bronchial asthma Oxford, 1967. **Miller, N. E.:** Learning of visceral and glandular responses. Science, 1969, 163, 434–45. **Rahe, R. H. & Arthur, R. J.:** Life-change patterns surrounding illness experience. J. psychosom. Res., 1968, 11, 341–5. **Wolff, H. G. & Wolf, S.:** An experimental study of changes in gastric function in response to varying life experiences. Rev. Gastroenteral., 1947, 14, 419–34. **Wretmark, G.:** Peptic ulcer individual: study in heredity, physique, and personality. Acta psychiat. et neurol. Scand., 1953, Suppl., 84.

M. Hamilton

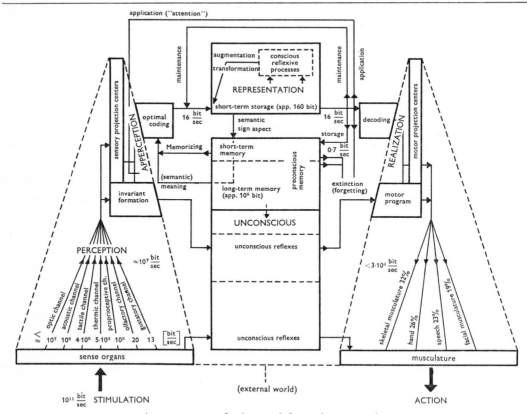

An organogram for human information processing

Psychosomimetics. See *Psychotomimetic drugs*.

Psychostructural model. Every physical model of a mental phenomenon realized through a means of communication, and every model that can be programmed mathematically for a computer is a "psychostructural" model. The starting-point of the psychostructural model within cybernetic education is the "organogram" of information psychology (q.v.). From this, in itself very rough, concept of a model, different more or less far-reaching simplifications were simulated on a computer and applied as the basis for the production of instructional algorithms (Frank, 1966). The most complex psychostructural model at present in existence underlies the formal didactics of Cogendi (q.v.). Here optimal coding was simulated through a deterministic automaton representing informational accommodation; short-term storage was simulated through a probabilistic coordinator, and short-term memory through a probabilistic automaton. (See diagram on previous page.)

Bibliography: Frank, H.: Ansätze zum algorithmischen Lehralgorithmieren. Lehrmaschinen, 1966, *4*, 70–112. **Riedel, H.:** Psychostruktur. Quickborn, 1967. *H.F.*

Psychosyndrome, endocrine (M. Bleuler). Mental disturbances occurring in different endocrine (internal secretion) malfunctioning show the same range of symptoms (and are similar to the so-called local psychosyndrome of the brain). They are recognized by disturbances in the *control of impulses* (excitatory-inhibitory), of *affect* (anxious, manic, depressive, irritable, liable to outbursts of temper), of *individual urges* (increase or inhibition of the need to move, of hunger, thirst and sexuality). Intellectual functions, however, are not impaired.   *C.S.*

Psychosyndrome, organic (E. Bleuler). *Amnesic syndrome* (q.v.); *Korsakov's syndrome* (q.v.).

Psychosynthesis. Form of psychotherapy (q.v.) regarded as the complement of a psychoanalysis (q.v.). It aims above all at the reconstruction of the personality after defense mechanisms and resistances have been corrected by analytical methods. Regarded as superfluous by S. Freud, who asserted that psychosynthesis took place automatically as soon as neurotic conflicts were resolved, but emphasized by C. G. Jung and authors of similar views (A. Maeder, P. Tournier, H. Trueb). The causes of psychiatric illness are not greatly clarified when seen from the aspect of development possibilities and the self-discovery of the patient. Appellative methods supplement the therapy. (See *Psychagogy*.)
                                                                                              W.Sch.

Psychotechnics. A theory introduced to psychology in 1903 by Stern for the classification of the terms of reference of applied psychology (q.v.) necessary to psychological judgment (psychognostics), i.e. for the provision of aids in psychological treatment (psychotechnics). For Münsterberg (1912), who attempted to define the field of psychotechnics, it is "the science of the practical application of psychology in the service of cultural problems. It should be a kind of psychological technique which helps people to achieve all the cultural aims they aspire to (for example in the industrial, social, educational, scientific, medical and legal fields) by the control of the mental mechanism." As in the course of time the application of the psychotechnics theory and related psychology gained acceptance, O. Lipmann condemned them (without lasting success) using the concept of *technopsychology* (also known as *psychotechnology*). The latter was intended to make the pure application of psychological perceptions more intelligible in practice. Giese in 1925 distinguished between *subject psychotechnics*, i.e. "adaptation of environment to the character of the human mental life" (e.g. arrangement of place of work, shape of tools, organization of work, etc.). The theory of psychotechnics has today lost its significance and therefore also its problems. It is now often equated with applied psychology or used as a special expression for practical industrial and vocational psychology (q.v.).   *A. Thomas*

Psychotherapy, literally "treatment of the mind", refers to any of a variety of psychological means used to modify mental, emotional, and behavior disorders. This may occur in individual interviews where therapist and patient verbally explore the patient's conflicts, feelings, memories and fantasies in order to attain insight into the causes of the presenting problems, or it may be conducted in small groups of six to twelve patients, or, in the case of children, may take the form of play between child and therapist during which the child expresses feelings and learns new behavior patterns through his relationship with the therapist.

Psychotherapy is distinguished from medical techniques such as chemotherapy (q.v.) or electroconvulsive therapy (q.v.), which are often employed in treating mental disorders, particularly in the more severe forms found among patients in mental hospitals.

1. *History.* Psychological methods of influence have been employed in primitive forms for thousands of years to remedy psychological disorders. These methods include witchcraft, religious healing, and diverse forms of punishment. In the late nineteenth century scientific systems of intervention were devised, based in part upon the pioneering efforts of psychiatrists such as Philippe Pinel in France, who argued that insanity resulted from social and psychological stresses. Early systems focused upon the importance of a therapeutic social influence created by the physician, and upon various forms of persuasion and suggestion, including hypnosis, which was applied as a therapeutic technique by eminent physicians such as Jean Charcot in France and Josef Breuer in Austria.

This nineteenth-century work culminated in the development between 1895 and 1939 of *psychoanalysis* (q.v.) by Sigmund Freud, who had worked with both Charcot and Breuer. Freud, however, gave up hypnosis and turned to the key techniques of *free association* (q.v.) by the patient, *interpretation* by the therapist, and formation of a *transference relationship* between patient and therapist. Psychoanalysis may be considered to be the first and most elaborate *system* of psychotherapy. Freud's method gradually gave way to numerous variants of his technique espoused by his pupils, such as Carl Jung, Otto Rank, and Alfred Adler. Other approaches, such as those devised by Karen Horney, Harry Stack Sullivan, Franz Alexander, and so on, were greatly influenced by his writings. Even those who depart considerably from Freud's assumptions regarding the *unconscious* (q.v.), *psychic structure*, free association, and so on, such as Carl Rogers, Albert Ellis, and Viktor Frankl, still employ as their chief mode of intervention the verbal self-exploration interview format which Freud invented.

2. *Current therapies.* Several dozen systems of therapy are now in vogue in addition to those which derive more directly from the Freudian traditions. These range widely from *existential therapy* (q.v.), which focuses upon philosophical and religious issues such as values, meaning, and purpose in life, to *behavior therapies* which utilize conditioning techniques, and are far more specific and mechanistic in style (see *Behaviorism*). In addition, a wide variety of group methods has emerged which range from the verbal self-exploratory psychoanalytic type to more active *encounter groups* in which confrontation, touching and other actions are common, and in which the goals include intensive experiencing of strong feelings as opposed to insights *per se*.

Therapists affiliated with differing positions divide on a number of important issues. Some are interested in making unconscious experience conscious, and in probing the early history of the patient's life, whereas others are more concerned with modifying conscious attitudes or overt behaviors in the present. Some, such as *client-centered therapists* (q.v.), believe that if the therapist provides a warm and understanding relationship for the patient this will suffice to stimulate positive personality change. Many others agree that such a relationship is necessary but that it is not sufficient for change; technical interventions such as interpretation and advice are necessary. Behavior therapists believe that such techniques as reinforcement, desensitization or aversive conditioning are most important, and that the "ideal" therapeutic relationship is neither necessary nor sufficient. Others argue that the results of all (including behavioral) therapies are due to non-specific influences such as the aura which surrounds the treatment techniques and settings of prestigious practitioners publicly identified as "healers". Advocates of this "placebo" effect oppose those who believe in specific effects of specific techniques. (See *Behaviour therapy*.)

Another controversy is whether overt symptomatic behavior such as that involved in phobias and sexual disorders can be changed directly by re-conditioning without full self-exploration and insight, and without thereby harming the patient. A related point of debate focuses upon divergent models of pathology, with psychoanalysts arguing that an underlying, unconscious conflict produces symptoms, and behaviorists positing that symptoms are learned behaviors which follow ordinary laws of reinforcement and conditioning. This contention often centers on the issue of whether intrapsychic private events or external behavioral ones predominate in the control of behavior. Theorists and practitioners also divide in their emphasis upon the biological determinants of disturbed behavior, with environmentalists advocating the primacy of social and psychological factors in the patient's history, and the more genetically and biochemically oriented arguing for the predomi-

nance of biological predispositions, defects, and temporary chemical imbalances. The latter more frequently use some combination of psychotherapy and chemotherapy.

Classifying the divergent range of techniques and systems is difficult, but they may be arranged crudely in terms of the extent to which they focus respectively upon: (*a*) conceptual restructuring (attitude change or insight), (*b*) changing emotional states or emotional responsiveness and sensitivity, or (*c*) modifying behavior. Although all therapies touch upon each of these domains, different ones are known for their emphasis on a particular area. For example, psychoanalysis is noted for its emphasis upon insight, client-centered therapy for its focus upon feeling states, and behavior therapy for its attention to behavior modification.

Historically, the divergent approaches have competed and contended for primacy and influence, each one claiming to be helpful for a wide range of disorders; but in recent years there has been a more concentrated effort to isolate from these broad-gauged techniques or systems the specific ingredients, agents or influences which are most efficacious in relation to specific patient syndromes. Therefore, instead of asking which system is best, inquiry increasingly focuses upon which specific influences have what effects upon which symptoms under what conditions. This development is similar to the advances made in medical therapy when it became possible to make precise chemical analyses of various potions and remedies in common use. Results of that line of investigation revealed that nineteenth-century medical compounds were composed of largely inert, useless or harmful agents and a small number of truly therapeutic chemicals.

Although psychological therapies are inherently more complex than drug treatment, similar investigations in psychotherapy have begun to yield an analogous picture, and modern therapies are beginning to emerge which have specific potency in relation to given pathologies. For example, *systematic desensitization* has become a popular method for treating phobias; although it was devised by behavior therapists, it is being increasingly endorsed by adherents of opposing schools such as psychoanalysis and client-centered therapy. Such actions, unthinkable in the past, mark the growing maturity and scientific commitment of the field. School affiliations and clinical "wisdom" are gradually being retired as arbiters of therapist behavior in favor of a more empirical basis for devising and selecting techniques.

3. *Psychotherapy research.* In 1952, psychotherapists were stunned by H. J. Eysenck's analysis of statistical studies of therapy, in which he concluded that there was no evidence that psychotherapy had any unique effect upon patients beyond that attributable to nonspecific everyday-life influences. At about the same time, Carl Rogers and his students had been conducting pioneering research studies on the therapeutic process and were calling for a more rigorous empirical approach to treatment. These and similar influences stimulated an outpouring of research studies which attempted to bring psychological treatment more fully within the framework of science by demonstrating therapy's specific effects and objectifying the processes leading to its outcomes.

Outcome research has revealed that the average cross-section of therapy as normally practiced has only modest effects when compared to the spontaneous changes occurring among untreated control group cases; however, this conclusion is based upon data averaged across heterogeneous samples of patients and therapists. When these samples are subdivided according to various criteria, interesting results emerge. For example, patients seen by more warm and empathic therapists show a higher than average improvement rate, whereas those seen by less warm and empathic therapists show lower

than average improvement. Similar differences in outcomes appear between cases whose therapists differ in degree of personal adjustment and in amount of professional experience. It has also been found that outcomes vary considerably across patient types and across techniques. For example, more severely disturbed patients respond less well than the moderately disturbed, and behavioral desensitization techniques appear to be more effective with specific phobias than relationship and insight oriented techniques. It is currently more evident than before that outcome is a complex function of patient characteristics, therapist characteristics, and technique. The measurement of therapeutic effects in research studies is therefore entering a stage of specificity in which more homogeneous samples of therapists are treating more homogeneous sets of patients with more precisely defined procedures and, in each case, with respect to a previously selected specific criterion.

Process research examines the "live" or recorded interaction of therapist and patient in order to discover the precise types of interactions, influences, and responses which produce change. To illustrate, it has been found that therapists who have personal conflicts in areas such as dependency or hostility tend to avoid discussion of these topics and thus impede exploration of them by their patients. On the other hand, less anxious therapists are better at encouraging self-exploration, which leads to personality change. It has also been found that when therapists probe too deeply in sensitive areas patients defend themselves by silence or by changing to a different topic.

Therapist research evaluates therapist characteristics which are related to both process and outcome, for example, the role of therapist adjustment levels or conflict areas as noted above. The evaluation of therapist traits includes studies revealing that those treating schizophrenics have varying success rates which are discriminable by their scores on the *Strong Vocational Interest Blank*, and studies showing that therapist values tend to shape the direction of value changes in patients over the course of therapy.

Patient research has established that responsiveness to therapeutic interventions is a function of longstanding traits and presenting symptoms. These include: motivation for change; severity of disturbance, symptom complexity and duration; degree of psychological and environmental resources; cultural, educational, economic status; openness to emotional experience; and so on.

Analogue research explores therapy phenomena by recreating elements of clinical situations under experimental control, so that causes and consequences can be more firmly established. Frequently, this involves isolating a procedure from its context to determine whether it has certain predicted consequences. Behavior therapy researchers have used this method particularly well, for example, by testing which ingredients of desensitization do the work of producing change such as relaxation induction, hierarchy item presentation, and personal contact with the therapist. They have also pioneered in setting-up analogues of treatment based directly upon bodies of pure experimental work which then lead toward the invention of entirely new techniques. Some scholars argue that this will be the primary mode of therapy research in the future. New methods will come from laboratories in learning, personality, social psychology, and so on, rather than from the clinic itself.

4. *Psychotherapy, psychology, and society.* Psychotherapy is an applied area of psychology and as such influenced by the methods and principles of the field in general. It in turn has had a fertilizing effect upon thought and inquiry in nearly every basic field of psychology. The problem of measuring personality change has stretched the boundaries of the measurement field; analyses of psychodynamics have stimulated interest in the effect of

motives on perceptions; case history material has posed hypotheses for developmental psychology; and the concept of therapeutic change as re-education has in part prompted developments in learning, such as renewed interests in social learning and mediational processes, and so on.

On the other hand, psychotherapy is criticized by modernists as being far too limited in scope to resolve the increasingly frequent pathologies rooted in social decay, changing mores, international conflicts, inflexible institutions, and harmful community structures. Those moving toward *community psychology*, in which intervention occurs in the community and often at the level of social structure, consider psychotherapy to be a miniscule influence in the backwash of a time of turbulent upheaval and social crises. Theirs is an ecological model rather than one focusing upon individual change.

However history may deal with the social significance of psychotherapy, it is unlikely that its contribution to an understanding of the mechanisms of personality change will be erased. The fact that social and political influences preoccupy many minds today does not obscure the fact that powerful psychological processes transpire between pairs of individuals, in families, and in small groups.

Bibliography: Bandura, A.: Principles of behavior modification. New York & London, 1969. Bergin, A. E. & Garfield, S. L.: Handbook of psychotherapy and behavior change. New York & London, 1970. Eysenck, H. J.: The effects of psychotherapy. New York, 1966. Ford, D. H. & Urban, H. B.: Systems of psychotherapy. New York & London, 1963. London, P.: The modes and morals of psychotherapy. New York & London, 1964. Rogers, C. R.: Client-centered therapy. Boston, 1964. Strupp, H. H.: Psychotherapy and the modification of abnormal behavior: an introduction to theory and research. New York & London, 1970. Strupp, H. H. & Bergin, A. E.: Some empirical and conceptual bases for coordinated research in psychotherapy. International Journal of Psychiatry, 1969, 7, no. 2, 18–90; no. 3, 116–68. Strupp, H. H. & Bergin, A. E.: Research in individual psychotherapy: a bibliography. (National Clearing

House for Mental Health Information, National Institute of Mental Health.) Washington, D.C., 1969. **Truax, C. B. & Carkhuff, R. R.:** Toward effective counseling and psychotherapy. Chicago, 1967. **Wolberg, L. R.:** The techniques of psychotherapy, 2 Vols. New York, 1967.   *A. E. Bergin*

Psychoticism. A factor evolved by Eysenck (1971) through an analysis of criteria, which distinguishes three groups of normal, schizophrenic and manic-depressives Ss. from each other (with scores increasing in that order). Psychoticism tests are, for instance, judgment of spatial distance, reading speed, level of proficiency in mirror drawing, and adding rows of numbers. See *Traits; Type.*

Bibliography: **Eysenck, H. J.:** Classification and the problem of diagnosis. In: **Eysenck, H. J.** (Ed.): Handbook of abnormal psychology. London, ²1971.
M.A.

Psychotomimetic drugs. Psychotropic drugs (q.v.) which can produce temporary conditions similar to psychosis. They are also known as *psychosomimetic drugs, hallucinogenic, fantastic, eidetic, psychotogenic, psychodysleptic* and *psychedelic* drugs. *Chemically* they are classified under *indolalkaloids* (derivates of lysergine, dimethyltryptamine, bufotenin, psilocybin, ibogaine, harmine), derivates of *phenylethylamine* (mescalin), derivates of *piperidine* (belladonna-alkaloids, q.v., and other anticholinergic substances, phencyclidine) and *tetracannabinols* (which produce the effect of cannabis, q.v.). In connection with *psychotomimetic effects*, LSD (q.v.), mescalin (q.v.) and psilocybin have hitherto been studied at greatest depth. The patterns of effect of these are similar. Differences occur mainly in the duration of the effect, (psilocybin—peak effect after about 30 minutes, duration of effect 2–4 hours; LSD—peak effect after 1–1½ hours, duration of effect 5–6 hours; mescalin—peak effect 2–2½ hours, duration of effect 8 hours and longer). With chronic use, tolerance and cross-tolerance can be developed to these substances. The psychological changes affect perception, and cognitive and affective functions. Possible disturbances of perception are hallucination, illusion (mainly in the visual field), intensification of the perception of colour, synesthesia, changes in form and space perception, disturbances of physical patterns, etc. In the cognitive field, depersonalization phenomena, loss of control over thoughts, etc., can occur. The affective changes can, according to the subject's original state of health, consist of euphoria (q.v.), dysphoria or extreme variations of mood. Before mental changes begin, dizziness, feelings of weakness, nausea, tremor, sleepiness or other somatic symptoms can occur. Observable autonomic effects are, on the whole, however, relatively few (dilation of pupils, increased muscular tension, and so on). EEG research indicates a slight increase of alpha-rhythm or the desynchronization pattern. The similarity of mental changes provoked by these substances with schizophrenic psychosis inspired the hope that some light might be thrown on the origins of schizophrenia (q.v.) by the pattern of effect of these drugs (see *Psychopharmacology*). This hope has not been fulfilled up to the present. The view commonly held today is that the conditions induced by these drugs differ from schizophrenia even in their symptoms.

Bibliography: **Downing, D. F.:** Psychotomimetic compounds. In: **Gordon, M.** (Ed.): Psychopharmacological agents, Vol. 1. New York & London, 1964. **Efron, D. H.** (Ed.): Psychopharmacology: a review of progress 1957–67. Washington, 1968. **Hollister, L. E.:** Chemical psychoses. Springfield, 1968. **Leuner, H.:** Die experimentelle Psychose. Berlin & Göttingen, 1962. **Levine, J.:** LSD – a clinical overview. In: **Black, P.** (Ed.): Drugs and the brain. Baltimore, 1969.
G.E.

Psychotomimetic effect. The result of psychotropic drugs (q.v.) which consists in the creation of a psychosis-type (see *Psychoses*) condition. Substances whose main effect is psychotomimetic are known as psychotomimetic drugs (q.v.). As a consequence of overdosage when taken chronically, psycho-tomimetic effects can persist in the case of many psychotropic drugs.   *G.E.*

Psychotonic drugs. Synonym for *stimulants* (q.v.).

Psychotonolytic drugs. Synonym for *tran-quilizers* (q.v.).

Psychotropic drugs. Chemically differing, natural and synthetic substances, whose principal effects are psychotropic, i.e., they induce in the nervous system behavioral and experiential changes which are at present mainly reversible. Their effect is for the most part neurophysiologically selective in various regions of the central nervous system (for example the limbic system, reticular system, thalamus, cortex) and they interact with different neurohumeral substances (see *Transmitter substances* and *Biogenic amines*). Psychologically, the motivational and emotional learning, retention and integration aspects of behavior are affected most of all. They are usually classified under hypnotics (q.v.), stimulants (q.v.), neuroleptics (q.v.), anti-depressives (q.v.), tranquilizers (q.v.) and psychotomimetic drugs (q.v.) (cf. table). *Substances* with psychotropic sideeffects which are not included under psychotropic drugs are: analgesics (q.v.), antiallergics, antibiotics (q.v.), antiemetics (q.v.), anti-epileptics, antihistamine (q.v.), antihyper-tensives (q.v.), anticonvulsives (q.v.), anti-Parkinson drugs, antipyretics, antitussives, aphrodisiacs (q.v.), hormones (q.v.), muscle-relaxants (q.v.), narcotics (q.v.), spasmolytics (q.v.), autonomic drugs, vitamins (q.v.). In the absence of a strict division, centrally induced effects are often hardly distinguishable from indirect effects of the afferent input of peripherally induced changes, e.g. in the autonomic nervous system. The general, rough classification of psychotropic drugs takes into account dosage, situation, actual and habitual personality traits (see Differential psychopharmacology), and such major clinical-therapeutic characteristics as symptoms treated, therapeutic dose, side-effects, and addiction. The classification which is generally used in the application of drug therapy with reference to its effect on animals gives species-specific differences. Forecasts of the effects in patients are more successful in tests on more highly developed organisms, and of behavior under model experimental conditions (for example, aggressive behavior, active and passive evasive reaction, resistance to stress). Classification according to chemical similarity admits rough partial subdivisions into families of substances, but allows no specific forecast of effects. New psychotropic drugs are discovered partly by chance observation but developed mainly with regard to optimal therapy of specific target symptoms through systematic variation of the chemical composition of known drugs. Possibilities of applying and studying psychotropic drugs exist in various practical and scientific disciplines. (See *Pharmacopsychiatry*; *Pharmacotherapy;* *Psychopharmacology;* *Pharmacopsychology;* *Neuropharmacology*). The identification of psychotropic drugs usually follows the international chemical abbreviation (as in this encyclopedia) or one or more trade-names, according to whether the substance is commercially obtainable.

Bibliography: Black, P.: Drugs and the brain. Baltimore, 1969. **Burger, A.** (Ed.): Drugs affecting the central nervous system. Medical Research, Vol. 2. New York, 1968. **Clark, W. G. & del Giudice, J.**(Eds.): Principles of psychopharmacology. Ch. 4: Structure and metabolism of psychotropic drugs. New York, 1970. **Dietsch, P.:** Versuchssituation und Tranquilizerwirkung. Arzneimittel-Forsch., 1969, *19*, 472–4. **Elkes, J.:** Behavioral pharmacology in relation to psychiatry. In: **Gruhle, H. W.** *et al.* (Eds.): Psychiatrie der Gegenwart I/1A. Berlin, 1967. **Ippen, H.:**

A selection of psychotropic drugs, mainly from those which are of significance in pharmacotherapy (q.v.). The shortened, non-proprietary names are listed, together with a sample "trade" name, and letters indicating class and (if the drug appears in a separate encyclopedia entry) the family of substances. Abbreviations: H = hypnotics; N = neuroleptics; T = tranquilizers; S = stimulants; A = antidepressives; P = psychotomimetic drugs; Mo = monoaminooxidase inhibitors; Ba = barbiturates; Ph = phenothiazines; Ra = rauwolfia alkaloids; Bu = butyrophenones; Am = amphetamines.

Shortened, non-proprietary name	Trade name	Class	Shortened, non-proprietary name	Trade name	Class
Allobarbital	Dial	H-Ba	Mepazine	Pacatal	N-Ph
Amitriptyline	Elavil	A	Meperone		N-Bu
Amobarbital	Amytal	H-Ba	Mephenesin	Tolserol	T
Amphetamine	Benzedrine	S-Am	Meprobamat	Miltown	T
Azacyclonol	Frenquel	T	Mescaline		P
Barbital	Veronal	H-Ba	Methamphetamine	Desoxyn	S-Am
Benactyzine	Suavitil	T	Methohexital	Brevital	H-Ba
Benperidol		N-Bu	Methotrimeprazine	Levoprome	N-Ph
Bromisovalum	Bromural	H	Methylphenidate	Ritalin	S
Butabarbital	Butisol	H	Methyprylon	Noludar	H
Caffeine		S	Nialamide	Niamid	A-Mo
Captodiamine	Suvren	T	Nitrazepam	Mogadon	T/H
Carbromal	Adalin	H	Nortriptyline	Aventyl	A
Carisoprodol	Soma	T	Opipramol	Ensidon	A
Chloral hydrate		H	Oxazepam	Serax	T
Chlordiazepoxide	Librium	T	Paraldehyde		H
Chlorpromazine	Thorazine	N-Ph	Pentobarbital	Nembutal	H-Ba
Chlorprothixene	Taractan	N	Perphenazine	Trilafon	N-Ph
Cocaine		P	Phenaglycodol	Ultran	T
Cyclobarbital	Phanodorn	H-Ba	Phencyclidin	Sernyl	P
Deserpine	Harmonyl	N-Ra	Phenmetrazin	Preludin	S
Desipramine	Pertofrane	A	Phenobarbital	Luminal	H-Ba
Dextroamphetamine	Dexedrine	S-Am	Pipradol	Meratran	S
Diacetylmorphine	(Heroin)	P	Prochlorperazine	Compazine	N-Ph
Diazepam	Valium	T	Promazine	Sparine	N-Ph
Dibenzepin		A	Promethazine	Phenergan	N-Ph
Droperidol	Inapsine	N-Bu	Psilocin		P
Emylcamate	Striatron	T	Psilocybin		P
Ethinamate	Valmid	H	Rescinnamine	Moderil	N-Ra
Ethyl-iso-butrazine	Ditran	N-Ph	Reserpine	Reserpoid	N-Ra
Fluphenazine	Prolixin	N-Ph	Secobarbital	Seconal	H-Ba
Glutethimide	Doriden	H	Tetrahydrocannabinol		P
Haloperidol	Haldol	N-Bu	Thalidomide	Distaval	H
Heptabarbital	Medomin	H-Ba	Thioridazine	Mellaril	N-Ph
Hexobarbital	Sombucaps	H-Ba	Thiothixene	Navane	N
Hydroxyzine	Atarax	T	Triflupromazine	Vesprin	N-Ph
Imipramine	Tofranil	A	Trifluoperazine	Stelazine	N-Ph
Iproniazid	Marsilid	A-A-Mo	Trifluperidol	Triperidol	N-Ph
Isocarboxazid	Marplan	A-Mo	Trimipramine	Surmontil	A
Lysergide (LSD -αS)	Pacatal	P	Tybamat	Solacen	T

Index Psychopharmacorum. Stuttgart, 1968. **Janke, W.**: Verwendungsmöglichkeiten einiger multivariater statistischer Verfahren für die Klassifikation von Psychopharmaka. Arzneimittel-Forsch., 1964, *14*, 582–4. **Pöldinger, W. & Schmidlin, P.**: Index psychopharmacorum 1966. Berne, 1966. **Wandrey, D. & Leutner, V.**: Neuro-Psychopharmaca in Klinik und Praxis. Stuttgart, 1965.   *G. Debus*

P technique. When measurements are made concerning a single individual at S different points in time (or under S different conditions) in respect of m variables where S is greater than m, and the variables in the situation correlate and factorize, this technique is known as a P technique. The factors evolved in a P technique are state factors. In the same factor, weighted variables show similar profiles. (See *Factor analysis*.)   *G. M.*

Pubertas praecox. Precocious puberty.—Abnormally rapid maturation in children, manifested in the premature development of the secondary sex characteristics and onset of functioning of the primary sex organs, usually with accompanying sex interest. May occur as a result of *pituitary gland* malfunction.

                    G.D.W.

Puberty. A second independent stage, which at first takes a negative form, introduces the age of puberty. It is an age of uncertainty of direction together with introversion in defence against outside influences. Eventually new values begin to be stabilized. The latter stage is announced by more extraverted tendencies, such as joining youth groups and forming friendships with the opposite sex. The goal of puberty is independence and adaptation to adult life. These changes cause "inner turmoils" (S. Freud), that is to say strong conflicts of the child with himself. The working out of these conflicts often causes difficulties, which lead to aggression (q.v.) directed against the self, as in disturbances of bodily and sexual development. One symptom of such conflicts is the puberty slimming craze. It is most common in girls and its symptoms are: psychologically determined refusal of food, loss of weight usually accompanied by constipation and amenorrhea. See *Child psychology; Youth.*   *M. Sa.*

Publicity. In its psychological aspect, publicity ("advertising" in the larger sense) is concerned to *inform* and to *"motivate"*. It offers information about the existence of a commodity, and sometimes about its purpose, but in competitive situations about the "unique" or special nature of the "product", in which case non-thematic information is very important. In consumer motivation there are at least three conceptually and formally distinct possibilities: (*a*) motivation by increasing the "appeal" of the product (e.g. by emphasizing the degree of its "reality"); (*b*) by adapting the "image" to the consumer; (*c*) by adapting the consumer to the "image"—largely by manipulation of his attitudes (the "standardization of needs" effect); (*b*) and (*c*) represent a diminution of "semantic distance" (see *Semantics*) between image and consumers. Each of the three measures leads to a steeper gradient of appeal.

The psychology of publicity (a division of marketing or consumer psychology) is concerned with the psychological "laws" of publicity. In principle it may be considered as a branch of applied social psychology. It developed from a not wholly psychotechnically oriented and autonomous aspect of advertising (consumer) psychology into a part aspect of marketing psychology (q.v.). It became more exact as the findings of general psychology found increasing acceptance. Psychologists in the service of (or concerned scientifically to examine) publicity, study its media in terms of the findings of communications (information) and motivation research into the psychological structure of (the) consumers (in question).

Bibliography: **Britt, S. H.** (Ed.): Psychological experiments in consumer behavior. New York, 1971. **Brückner, P.**: Die informierende Funktion der Wirtschaftswerbung. Berlin, 1967. **Dichter, E.**: Motivating human behavior. New York & London, 1971. **Ehrenberg, A. S. C. & Pugh, F. C.**: Consumer behavior. Harmondsworth, 1971. **Horkheimer, M. & Adorno, T.**: Dialectic of enlightenment. New York, 1972. **Perloff, R.**: Consumer analysis. Ann. Rev. Psychol., 1968, *19*, 437–66. See also *Marketing*.

B.Sp.

Public opinion. "Opinion publique" (J. J. Rousseau, 1750), closely related to the English "climate of opinion" (Glanville, 1661), "law of opinion" (J. Locke, 1671). All three concepts were formulated in (pre)revolutionary periods, i.e. in times when the government and the popular will were at odds. Its limitation to political matters (Lippmann, 1922; Hennis, 1956; Habermas, 1962) is more recent; in the eighteenth and nineteenth centuries public opinion was recognized as a social force (exerting an influence both on an individual member of society and on the rulers in order to compel action in conformity with prevailing views (F. v. Holtzendorff, 1879). The reciprocal integrating effect was forgotten when E. A. Ross (1896) introduced the concept of *social control* for the pressure which public opinion brings to bear on the individual (Noelle, 1966).

At the moment there is no generally accepted definition of public opinion (Schmidtchen, 1959, 236; W. P. Davison: International Encyclopaedia of the Social Sciences, vol. 13, 1969, 188), but it is hardly likely that the proposal to do away with the concept (H. Schelsky, 1967, and others) will be achieved now that demoscopy (q.v.) has come into being. Results of opinion polls (q.v.) are not yet a reflection of public opinion. The existence or development of a prevailing opinion, the conviction that this opinion is shared by a majority (cf. also Hofstätter, 1949, 53 ff.), the conviction that the prevailing demands may be achieved, and expectations that developments are moving in the direction of these demands—the conjunction of these factors which may be measured by opinion polls leads to a sociopsychological dynamism, the perception of which probably led in the beginning to the formation of the concept.

Bibliography: Habermas, J.: Strukturwandel der Öffentlichkeit. Neuwied, 1962, ⁵1969. Hennis, W.: Meinungsforschung und repräsentative Demokratie. Tübungen, 1957. Hofstätter, P. R.: Die Psychologie der öffentlichen Meinung. New York, 1922; Munich, 1964. Noelle, E.: Offentliche Meinung und Soziale Kontrolle. Tübingen, 1966.   E.N.-N.

Public relations. (Abb. PR). **1.** Leading public relations experts define public relations as "the conscious, planned and permanent striving to build and maintain mutual understanding and trust in public activities". Public relations work is the dialogue which each group (q.v.) in society or each individual must hold in social intercourse. Public relations work is the effort of social groups with different opinions to reach some form of agreement. It cannot solve conflicts, but can free them from misunderstandings so that their factual solution becomes possible. Daily discussion shows how many emotional obstacles there are to understanding and how

important public relations are to the solution of problems by a proper formulation of them. The task and aim of public relations is thus the reassurance of social groups through recognition and trust.

In contrast to advertising, whose purpose is to maximize sales, the work of public relations is to win social acceptance for the group or firm. Hence information which is an aid to understanding in socio-political life is part of public relations, whereas information which helps to sell the goods is proper to publicity (q.v.). In its preliminary analysis of the situation and subsequent attempts to deal with it, public relations uses the methods of empirical social research, from the depth psychology interview (q.v.) to broad field studies.

2. The exchange of communication between organizations, such as firms, businesses, groups and so forth, and the public, and in particular the attitudes (q.v.) and opinions of the public concerning these organizations. Public relations in the active sense aims to maintain and create favorable relations with the public. It seeks through publicity, activities, services, etc. to win interest, sympathy, regard and trust for the organization.   *B.Sp.*

Puerilism. 1. A state of childishness: that stage which follows infancy and precedes puberty. **2.** An abnormal state in an adult when the mind appears to revert to its childhood state.   *J.P.*

Puerperal psychosis. A term used loosely to refer to psychic disturbance in a woman after childbirth. It does not characterize any specific condition.

Pulfrich effect (*C. Pulfrich*, 1858–1927). An object oscillating in the frontal plane viewed binocularly seems to describe a horizontal ellipse if one eye is partially covered by a grey or colored filter. The stereoscopic effect is explained as follows. Different time intervals occur between stimulus and perception (perception times) for the right and left eye according to the varying light intensities. The resulting disparity of diagonals leads to a perception of depth.   *W.P.*

Pulse. The number of arterial fluctuations of blood-pressure produced by the heart per minute. It is normally 70 a minute, but in extreme cases of trained athletes at rest it can fall to 50 a minute and with extreme excitement and certain circulatory diseases it can rise to 200 a minute. The pulse can be felt in the superficial arteries synchronously with the frequency of the heart-beat. In the past it was much more important evidence than today in the diagnosis of circulation. The characteristic deviations from the norm were therefore given special names like *pulsus frequens* or *rarus* (frequency), *regularis* or *irregularis*, *celer* or *tardus* (rising fast or slowly), *altus* or *parvus* (large or small pressure fluctuations), *durus* or *mollis* (high or low blood pressure).
                                                                    E.D.

Punishment. Punishment is the presentation of an aversive event contingent upon a response. In practice, most studies of punishment employ events that are unquestionably aversive. Electric shock has been used in a large majority of studies of punishment of animal subjects, since its physical characteristics are easily measured and controlled. The withdrawal of a positive reinforcement contingent upon a response has also been used as an aversive event.

Punishment may also be defined as the presentation of an event contingent upon a response that reduces the probability of that response. This, of course, parallels the familiar functional definition of a positive reinforcement.

Although several theories of punishment emphasize a symmetrical opposition between punishment and positive reinforcement, the term "negative reinforcement" is no longer used as a synonym for punishment. This term is now used to describe the withdrawal of an aversive stimulus contingent upon a response (that is, the escape operation).

The technical uses of the word "punishment" in psychology are closely related to the general use of the word, but several differences should be noted. The aversive event need not be administered by an animate agent, and there is no implication of retribution.

Although the relationship between a response and an aversive event is central to all contemporary definitions of punishment, some definitions emphasize the contiguity between a response and an aversive event rather than the contingency between the response and the aversive event.

1. *History*. Punishment has been used for two major purposes: to facilitate the acquisition of new responses, and to suppress the performance of established responses. The early research on discrimination learning of rats demonstrated that punishment of erroneous responses facilitates learning. In addition, punishment can also suppress ongoing responses. Such suppression is particularly rapid when an alternative response is rewarded. Some concern has been expressed about undesirable sideeffects of punishment, particularly in child rearing.

2. *Severity*. The severity of a punishment may be specified in terms of its intensity, duration, and frequency. If the punishment is extremely mild (for example, an external inhibitor) response suppression may be temporary and complete recovery may follow, but if the punishment is severe, the effects of punishment are permanent.

3. *Relationship between response and aversive event*. An aversive event that is contingent upon a response (punishment) has a greater effect on that response than an aversive event that is independent of a response. In

addition, contiguity is important. The shorter the temporal interval between the response and the aversive event the greater the effect of the punishment upon the response (the delay-of-punishment gradient). In contrast, there is some evidence that various measures of emotional upset (ulcers, interference with learned discriminations, and so on) may be greater when the aversive event is unpredictable and uncontrollable.

4. *Paradoxical effects of punishment.* Under some conditions punishment may paradoxically increase the response it was designed to suppress. For example, mild punishment of the correct (rewarded) response in a relatively difficult two-choice discrimination can facilitate the learning of the discrimination. Punishment of an escape or avoidance response can also result in facilitation of the response, and if positive reinforcement is associated with punishment an animal may appear to be masochistic. To resolve such paradoxes it is necessary to recognize that a punishing event has varied effects (it serves as a discriminative stimulus, a fear-arousing stimulus, it elicits competing motor responses, and so on).

5. *Applications in behavior therapy.* Basic research on the principles of punishment and the conditioned emotional response has had important applications in the development of effective behavior therapy (q.v.). Prominent among behavior therapies are punishment procedures designed to suppress maladaptive instrumental acts. Numerous case studies have been reported in which punishment has led to a marked alleviation of such problems as stuttering, writer's cramp, head-banging, and sexual fetishes. See *Aversion therapy.*

Bibliography: Azrin, N. H. & Holz, W. C.: Punishment. In: Honig, W. K. (Ed.): operant behavior: Areas of research and application. New York, 1966, 380–447. Bandura, A.: Principles of behavior modification. New York, 1969. Boe, E. E. & Church, R. M.: Punishment: issues and experiments. New York, 1969. Brush, F. R.: Aversive conditioning and learning. New York, 1970. Campbell, B. A. & Church, R. M.: Punishment and aversive behavior. New York, 1969. Church, R. M.: The varied effects of punishment on behavior. Psychol. Rev., 1963, 70, 369–402.

R. M. Church

Pupillary reflex. The width of the pupils (central aperture in the iris, q.v.) is regulated by the fluctuation of the muscles *dilator* (enlargement, innervated by the sympathetic nerve) and *sphincter* (contraction, innervated by the parasympathetic nerve) *pupillae.* When a strong light strikes only one eye the width of of the pupil is immediately reduced (see *Miosis*), and not only of the eye on which the light falls (direct reaction to light) but also of the eye that has not been exposed to the light (consensual reaction to light). This purely reflexive, unconscious, unexposed reaction is a pupillary reflex. This is to be distinguished from *pupil reaction* in convergence (q.v.) In accommodation (q.v.), which leads to a convergent movement of both eyes, it comes about by the linked innervation of the parasympathetic component of the *nervus oculomotorius* at the same time as a contraction of the pupils of both eyes. In this way the amount of light entering the eye is reduced (near objects are brighter) and depth of focus increased (by the dimming of marginal rays, spherical aberration).   *R.R.*

Purkinje figure; Purkinje (-Sanson) image; Purkinje phenomenon (effect). Three materially different things which are named after J. E. Purkinje (1787–1869). **1.** *Figure:* by entoptic observation an observer can make the blood vessels of his retina visible. Entoptic observation can be undertaken with the help of a diaphanoscope (sclera illuminator) or a small lamp moved near the sclera or with a perforated screen moved backwards and forwards near to the eyeball in front of the aperture of the pupil. A movement of the light or of the perforated screen is needed to counteract the adaptation of the receptors (see *Stabilized retinal image*). The entoptic image perceived by the observer of the blood vessels of his retina is the Purkinje figure.

2. *Image:* also known as Purkinje–Sanson image. Reflexions of a light are made by the cornea and lens which are observable when a suitable light shines on someone else's eye. (Painters often depict this image as the characteristic light of the eye.) Generally only three images are observable: one reflected by the anterior surface of the cornea and two by the lens surface. The image reflected by the posterior surface of the cornea is very weak and only visible in optimal conditions. Of the four images three are upright, the image from the posterior surface of the lens being upside-down. This image is used to determine the curvature of the lens in accommodation (q.v.).

3. *Phenomenon:* the function of spectral sensitivity to light is dependent upon the eye's adaptability. Accordingly the sensitivity maximum fluctuates with adaptation to the dark from the wavelength range 555 NM to 505 NM. To demonstrate Purkinje's phenomenon two colors are chosen, one orange-red, the second blue-green (or simply red and blue), so that in bright illumination the orange-red is brighter than the blue-green, and when the light is gradually dimmed the blue-green seems brighter to the observer. (See *Duplicity theory*).   *A.H.*

Puromycin. An antibiotic (q.v.).

Purposivism. An active animal's purposive behaviour is decisive; it learns to anticipate the result of its actions.

Bibliography: Tolman, E. C.: Purposive behaviour in animals and man. New York & London, 1932.
                                                        K.Fi.

Pursuit-rotor. A more or less large spot moving in a circle must be followed by a pointer so that the pointer does not leave the spot. The method was developed in the U.S.A. during research into motor learning.

Bibliography: Cronbach, L. J.: Essentials of psychological testing. New York, ²1960.   *K.M.*

Puzzle box. A box used by Thorndike (q.v.) to investigate the behavior (learning) of animals. The box is fitted with a mechanism which opens a door when actuated. Animals, e.g. cats, are put in the box so that their attempts to leave it can be observed. At first the exit mechanism is set off by chance, but its operation is then learnt (over several trials), and finally occurs systematically. The puzzle box was a forerunner of the Skinner box (q.v.).

Bibliography: Thorndike, E. L.: Animal intelligence. Psychol. Rev. Monogr. Suppl., 1898, No. 8 (reprinted in *Animal intelligence*, New York, 1911).   *R.Hä.*

Pyknic (type). One of the classifications of human *body build* (q.v.) described by E. Kretschmer. It is characterized by a medium-sized, squat figure, a soft, broad face on a short, massive neck. The deep, barrel chest expands below into a portly paunch. The face is soft and broad, presenting from the front a flat pentagon. The nose is broad with a fleshy to thick snub end. The pyknic type is especially often observed among patients with manic-depressive psychosis. Among normal people the pyknic body structure is often correlated with a cyclothymic (q.v.) temperament. See *Traits; Type.*   *W.Se.*

Pyknolepsy. Petit-mal epilepsy (q.v.).

Pyknomorphy. One of the typical forms of body structure described by K. Conrad, which is to be traced back to a primary growth tendency toward thickness to the detriment of length. Primary growth tendency to length at the expense of thickness causes its opposite, leptomorphy. K. Conrad explains the primary variants of the leptomorphic and pyknomorphic bodybuilds by the development of temperament, dependent on genes, by a propulsive or conservative growth tendency. According to this, pyknomorphy occurs as a result of a conservative development which comes to a halt on the threshold of harmonization after the first but before the second change of shape. The appearance of pyknomorphy conforms to a large extent with the pyknic body structure described by E. Kretschmer. See *Traits; Type.* *W.Se.*

Pyramidal tract. Formerly (Holms & May, 1909) the suggestion that fiber paths exclusively from the large pyramid-shaped Betz cells of area IV of the brain were responsible for the voluntary motor system was connected with the "pyramidal tract" concept. After overlapping on the opposite side of the body in the "pyramids" (so called after their outward shape) above the *medulla oblongata*, the paths extend to the motor cells of the anterior horn. These pathways of voluntary movement were contrasted with the so-called *extra-pyramidal system* (see *Parkinsonism*). Today we know that only 30 per cent of the fibers of the pyramidal tract originate in the large Betz cells. A great proportion of the fibers do not cross to the opposite side; even ascending fibers are found in this tract. The opposition of involuntary movements (see *Extrapyramidal system*) and voluntary motor (pyramidal) movement is pointless. Voluntary movement sequences are explained today neurophysiologically by control systems which go beyond the bounds of the earlier theory. *M.A.*

Q

Q correlation. A correlation in which n individuals are correlated in regard to m characteristics where m is greater than n. This kind of correlational technique, which statistically is no different from the usual R correlation (q.v.), derives from W. Stephenson. It is used especially in clinical psychology (q.v.). *G.Mi.*

Q sorting. A rating technique (q.v.) in which a large number of statements are sorted into a series of categories so that the resulting frequency distribution (q.v.) corresponds to a defined distribution. The advantage of Q sorting is that it guards against faulty use of the rating scale. Originally (in investigations by W. Stephenson) a testee sorted some 100 statements written on cards (e.g. dealing with traits) according to their accuracy or their correctness with reference to different concepts (e.g. self-concept); he then went on to calculate the results with the Q technique (q.v.). (See *Scaling*.)

Bibliography: **Stephenson, W.:** The study of behavior. Chicago, 1953. *G.Mi.*

Q technique. Synonymous with Q analysis. A factor analysis (q.v.) which starts from Q correlations (q.v.). Individuals are factorized and the extracted factors can be interpreted as types. The factor matrix of a Q technique thus contains the factor loadings of the individual persons in the type factors. There is reciprocity between R and Q techniques in so far as the factor matrix of R technique (q.v.) is equivalent to the factor-value matrix of Q technique, and *vice versa.* *G.Mi.*

Qualitative characteristics. Those characteristics which can be exclusively grouped into categories differing in content and between which there are numerical relations. Qualitative characteristics can only be classified by means of nominal scales (q.v.). According to the number of possible classes a distinction is made between alternative (q.v.) (e.g. sex) and multiple-class characteristics (eye color, employment). Qualitative characteristics are discrete (q.v.) or discontinuous variables.

G.Mi.

Quality. 1. In general: kind, nature, goodness; as opposed to quantity (q.v.), it cannot be measured and can be quantified only to a limited degree.

2. In the psychology of perception a characteristic of sensory perception together with intensity and duration. Whereas the last two largely depend directly on the stimulus, quality depends on the sensation felt by the receptor, the sensory cell which has been excited.

3. In psychodiagnostics (q.v.) the quality and quantity of a performance in conjunction with time are the predominant criteria for evaluation. The quality of a performance includes both the latter's merit and its degree of difficulty (complexity), whereas quantity includes speed of performance, or the number of answers (solutions) in a certain time.

H.J.A.

Quality of gestalt (Ger. *Gestaltqualität*). The essential character or form of a whole when apprehended as a configuration of parts. See *Ganzheit.*

Quantification. A term used for the grouping of numbers into characteristics. If the characteristics are qualitative (q.v.), quantification is possible only by enumeration, i.e. by determining the class frequencies. Where the characteristics are quantitative (q.v.), quantification is synonymous with measurement (q.v.).   *G.Mi.*

Quantitative characteristics. The characteristics which vary in their degree of distinctness and are therefore (fundamentally) capable of being measured. It is assumed that they are continuous, even when the methods of measurement employed enable only discrete values to be obtained (e.g. memory: the number of elements noticed). According to the nature of the possible quantification, a distinction is made between ordinal (q.v.), interval (q.v.), and proportional (q.v.) variables. (See *Scaling; Methods of psychology.*)   *G.Mi.*

Quantity. In general: amount, size, number. As opposed to quality (q.v.), the characteristic of a phenomenon which permits it to be measured or counted. In psychodiagnostics (q.v.), a quantity in performance is a score, i.e. the speed of the performance (time as measure), or the number of tasks solved (answers) in a given period of time.   *H.J.A.*

Quantization. The splitting up of a complex or a quantity into elements which in the given

connection may be considered the maximum possible. Signal transformation (q.v.) of *continuous signals* into *discrete* signals and in the coding (q.v.) of a news item with a multidimensional signal function so that it can be transmitted over a one-dimensional channel. Example: two-dimensional copies of pictures are reduced at the transmitting end to lines and then to image-dots (information quanta) and subsequently reconverted at the receiving end into a two-dimensional complex.   *H.R.*

Quartile. The three points by which a frequency distribution (q.v.) can be divided into equal quarters are known as quartiles. The first quartile of a distribution therefore contains 25% of all the cases, the second, the median, contains 50%, and the third, 75%. The first and third quartiles are known as the lower and upper quartiles.   *G.Mi.*

Quartimax methods. Analytical, *orthogonal* rotation methods of rotating the factor matrix. See *Factor analysis.*   *G.Mi.*

Quasi-experiment. An experiment, the results of which are invalid on account of a defective experimental design. A quasi-experiment allows no conclusions to be drawn regarding the connection between dependent and independent variables, since the independent variables were inadequately conceived and controlled.

Bibliography: Campbell, D. T. & Stanley, J. C.: Experimental and quasi-experimental designs for research in teaching. In: Gage, N. L. (Ed.): Handbook of research on teaching. Chicago, 1963.   *F.Ma.*

Quasi-need. A distinction was made by Lewin (1926) between quasi-needs and "real" needs. The former are "intended acts" or "purposive thoughts", and depend on "real" needs. The latter can be traced back to instincts (q.v.) or "central desires". Zeigarnik is of the opinion that quasi-needs are aftereffects of unaccomplished acts.   *H.M.*

Questioning. The first phase of questioning occurs around the second year when a child wants to know the names of things, the questions being related to the designating function of language (K. Bühler). The second phase (questioning proper, i.e. questions prefaced by "why") starts during the third year and represents the child's attempt to classify the world around him.

Bibliography: **Bühler, K.:** Die geistige Entwicklung des Kindes. Jena, ³1922. **Stern, C. & Stern, W.:** Kindersprache. Leipzig, ²1920.   *S.Kr.*

Questionnaires. "Questionnaire" describes a variety of instruments and techniques. Often it consists of a printed form containing a structured set of questions, all of which the subject is required to answer—usually in writing, but sometimes orally, as in public opinion surveys and market research. Form, method of administration and subject matter may all vary widely. The content areas in psychology found most suitable to questionnaire methods have been: biographical data, opinions, attitudes, values, and personality traits. Some cognitive tests might be classed as questionnaires, but the term is rarely applied to them.

An important distinction is between open-ended and objectively scored items. To the first type the subject phrases his response with little constraint from the experimenter, and analysis of the results will be to some extent subjective. In the second type the questionnaire constructor will pre-determine a few response categories and require the respondent to endorse one or other. This restricts variety of response, but facilitates objective coding and analysis.

1. *Item construction.* Constructing good items is not simple and is more art than

science, objective principles being few and dependence upon experience considerable. Evaluation and scaling of items can, however, more readily be reduced to a set of rules. Common faults found in questionnaire items are bias, ambiguity, over-elaboration and lack of discriminative power. Crude bias may be obvious; for example, questions like the Latin words *nonne* and *num*, may pre-dispose the subject in the direction of "Yes" or "No". This may occur also in subtle forms, so that whether a question is slanted is not easily detectable.

Ambiguity is also a matter of degree. It is worth noting that the following words often require careful placement to make quite clear what they qualify: "always", "only", "often", "sometimes", "usually", "many", "most", and so on. Moser (1958) quotes another instance of faulty question construction. In one survey women were asked, "Is your work made more difficult because you are expecting a baby?", irrespective of whether they *were* expecting a baby. The answer "No" would then be ambiguous because it might mean either "not expecting a baby" or "work not made more difficult". Over-elaborate syntax and phrasing should be avoided; items should be as plain and spare as is consistent with lucidity. An especially undesirable form of elaboration results in double-barrelled statements: for example, "Are you satisfied with the service and prices in this restaurant?" Many people may be satisfied with service but not with prices, or *vice versa*. These and other dangers apply to all questionnaire construction; when the questionnaire is to be administered to a cross-section of a national population or to any unselected sample of subjects, special care should be taken to make the questions clear, simple and unambiguous.

Many writers (for instance, Jahoda, Cook & Deutsch, 1951) have made useful distinctions between different kinds of information to be elicited. According to type of information, modifications in questionnaire design may well be necessary, as between those designed to tap facts and those concerned with, e.g. beliefs, feelings, standards of action, reasons for beliefs.

2. *Opinion questionnaires.* Innumerable opinion and attitude questionnaires have been constructed, particularly in the USA. "Opinion" and "attitude" have become almost synonymous in this context. Three main attitude-scaling techniques are available, devised by Thurstone, Likert and Guttman respectively. Each of these has its merits, and the first two methods have been very widely used. The technique of equal-appearing intervals (Thurstone & Chave, 1929) extends methods already used in psychophysical studies of perception and sensation. It enables the questionnaire constructor to assign a "scale value" to each item and to place each respondent on the required attitude continuum according to the median scale value of the items he endorses. The Likert technique is similar to those used in constructing ability tests, but a distinctive feature is that the respondent is presented with five alternative degrees of endorsement of each item. The Guttman scaling technique (Stouffer, 1950) produces short, highly homogeneous scales.

3. *Personality questionnaires.* These have been developed on different lines from those concerned with attitudes and are of considerable theoretical importance. They vary even more widely in type, being essentially means of classifying people according to the personality theory of the constructor, which may be based on clinical syndromes, on ideal types, or on traits and dimensions. The best known instrument of the first type is the Minnesota Multiphasic Personality Inventory, a huge amalgam from which less general instruments have been developed; for example, the Taylor Manifest Anxiety Test.

Classification of personality by discrete types is open to criticism; consequently, few questionnaires are based on this approach. An interesting exception is the Myers-Briggs inventory, based on the two-by-four Jungian typology of "introvert" and "extravert", and the cross-classification into "sensation", "perception", "intuition" and "feeling" types.

Many personality questionnaires are based on the dimensional approach, and attempt to assess the most important general traits, in the sense of accounting for maximum variance in an unselected sample of people. Identifying such traits has depended largely upon the technique of factor analysis (q.v.). The most important measures of this kind are those of Cattell, Eysenck and Guilford, particularly the two former. All these are derived from factor-analytical studies, but with different presuppositions. Cattell's questionnaire for adults assesses sixteen dimensions, Eysenck's only two. Each approach has some advantages: Cattell provides a more detailed profile, but Eysenck gives factors that are probably more reliable and pervasive (Eysenck & Eysenck, 1969).

4. *Criteria of good questionnaires.* The requirements for good single items have been discussed in an earlier section; in addition, questionnaires employed as psychological tests should satisfy the usual criteria of reliability and validity. If they are carefully constructed and item-analyzed, adequate reliability should be assured. Validity, however, whether of attitude or of personality questionnaires, is difficult to evaluate, since there will typically be no simple real-life criterion with which to compare the test score. The evaluator is therefore more dependent on construct validity and on a network of indirect inferences. As stated, many questionnaires in this area are valuable exploratory instruments, but their validity should never be taken for granted, least of all by non-psychologists. (See *Objective tests.*)

Bibliography: Eysenck, H. J. & Eysenck, S. B. G.: Personality structure and measurement. London, 1969. Jahoda, M., Cook, S. W. & Deutsch, M.: Research methods in social relations. New York, 1951. Moser, C. A.: Survey methods in social investigation. London, 1958. Stouffer, S. A.: Measurement and prediction. Princeton, 1950. **Thurstone, L. L. & Chave, E. J.**: The measurement of attitude. Chicago, 1929.   *H. J. Butcher*

Quotidian cycle. In order to give a clear picture of how individual behavioral items are distributed and change during the first year of life, Bühler (1967) introduced the "quotidian cycle". In a cycle corresponding to the twenty-four-hour day, individual forms of behavior, such as sleep, feeding, state of semi-consciousness and wakefulness, are divided into sectors according to the percentage of time they occupy. Such cycles show that sleep, which at birth takes up more than three-quarters of the total cycle, has by the end of the first year fallen to barely one half, reflecting the increasing alertness of the young infant.

Bibliography: Bühler, C.: Kindheit und Jugend. Göttingen, 1967.   *M.Sa.*

R

Race. A group of individuals of a species who, while they are distinguished from one another by individual hereditary characteristics (e.g. skin color), can nevertheless produce fertile young. For a long time the significance of race for human psychology has been exaggerated, partly for ideological reasons (anti-Semitism, q.v., in Europe, prejudice, q.v., against negroes in the USA). In the opinion of many modern anthropologists, typical racial characteristics can be shown to exist only in the field of physical anthropology, while in psychological matters the genetically determined "racial traits" can scarcely be distinguished from cultural influences. This seems to confirm the complete assimilation of a new culture in a few generations (for instance by American immigrants). See *Abilities; Differential psychology.* *W.Sch.*

Radiatio optica. L.-P. Gratiolet (1958) described this part of the optic tract (q.v.) of which it constitutes the fourth neurone, passing from the *corpus geniculatum laterale* to the *area striata* of the occipital lobe, which represents primary cortical field V1. *K.H.P.*

Radio. One of the mass media of communication (q.v.), important for the direct transmission of the latest information. Although it is now much less used owing to the competition of audio-visual media (especially where light entertainment is concerned), radio retains its pre-eminence for "live" broadcasts, news, and "background" music. Given equal conditions, information communicated by radio makes less impact and is remembered less well than where communication is personal and audio-visual, but it is more effective than purely visual communication (e.g. by the printed word). *A.D.S.*

Ragoni-Scina contrast. Two black squares, each on white backgrounds, are viewed simultaneously one through a sheet of colored glass and the other by reflection from the surface of the same sheet. This is by having the squares in planes at right-angles to each other and the glass in between them at 45 degrees to each. The square viewed by reflection appears the same colour as the glass sheet while the square viewed through the sheet appears in its complementary color. *C.D.F.*

Randomizer. A device used in electronic data processing to produce random numbers and simulate stochastic processes. *F.M.*

Random sample. A random sample occurs when every element of the population has an equal chance of being included in the sample. *H.-J.S.*

Range. The interval between the highest and the lowest observed value in a sample. As the size of the sample increases, it supplies less and less information about the details of the range. Lord tests (q.v.) use range instead of standard deviation.   *A.R.*

Rank order. A quantitative classification of a continuous variable the interval magnitudes of which are unlike or unknown. Rank orders are used with variables which vary with respect to their degree of distinctness but for the measurement of which there are no exact methods, so that only "greater or smaller" judgments are possible.   *G.Mi.*

Rank-order correlation. A non-parametric correlational technique the use of which postulates ordinal variables (q.v.). Rank-order correlations were developed by Spearman and Kendall. (See *Correlational techniques*.)
                                            G.Mi.

Rapport. A (verbal) relationship existing in the state of restricted consciousness between the hypnotist and the hypnotized individual; it represents a particular kind of inward dependence and a willingness to carry out any suggestions (q.v.) which may have been made. See *Hypnosis*.   *H.N.G.*

Rate tests. Techniques for determining empirically the subjective information (q.v.) of news by finding the expectancy probability of the signs (news elements). In a Shannon rate test, a test is predicted sign by sign and replaced by the sequence of the rate tests necessary for each sign, and from it an upper and lower limit for the subjective information can be derived. By using branching models to fix the prediction strategy, Weltner (1970) has extended and defined arbitrary sign repertoires and also indicated important simplified

methods for practical use. F. Attneave has applied rate tests to pictures and graphic representations.

Bibliography: Weltner, K.: Informationstheorie und Erziehungswissenschaft. Schnelle, Quickborn, 1970.
                                            H.F.

Rating. 1. A term for a subjective assessment made on an established scale. It enables rough information to be obtained about the degree to which continuous characteristics exist for the comprehension of which no exact methods are available. Ratings are the bases of direct scaling methods. Data obtained by ratings have the character of ordinal scales (q.v.) but can be converted by suitable scaling techniques into scales with higher values. See *Scaling*.   *G.Mi.*
2. The result of a statistical rating technique.
                                            A.R.

Rating scale. A multi-stage scale on which degrees of a characteristic are arranged subjectively by a rater. Such scales usually have five, six or seven stages which can be formulated verbally or shown by numbers; they are used, for example, in Q sorting (q.v.) and polarity profiles (q.v.). They have the standard of ordinal scales (q.v.) and form the starting point for direct scaling techniques (see *Successive intervals*) by means of which they can be converted into scales with higher values. See *Scaling*.   *A.R.*

Rating techniques. Methods for rating parameters on the basis of statistics calculated from samples (q.v.). The best known rating techniques of mathematical statistics are the maximum likelihood and the minimum chi-square methods. The former, using normally distributed scores, leads on to the method of smallest squares.   *A.R.*

Rationalism. In general this term designates those systems which, being grounded in reason, hold to its primacy over faith, feeling (sentiment) or experience, and conceive understanding as the establishment of coherent and necessary connections. More specifically, in regard to the value of knowledge, rationalism postulates the intelligibility of everything (everything has its *"raison d'être"* or "reason for being"), or the capacity of human intelligence to know the truth because the laws of being are not distinct from the laws of thought. In regard to the origin of knowledge, the term denotes the existence of systematic and normative (forms of) knowledge *within* the (absolute or human) mind (spirit). In the theory of voluntary behavior, rationalism is opposed to any irrational impulsion of the will. *M.-J.B.*

Rationalization. 1. The process of interpreting the reasons why certain events took place. In psychoanalysis (q.v.): a defense (q.v.) mechanism in which apparent reasons tolerated by the superego take the place of real reasons which are not admitted.

2. The process of systematic improvement of business structures. In economics and in industrial psychology (q.v.): the optimization of the relation between performance and necessary expenditure. Essential measures in rationalization are *specialization* (reducing the range of work by the division of labor), standardization (establishing norms for work processes), and mechanization or automation (the transfer of human functions to substitute technical devices). Special problems of industrial psychology arise from changes in work requirements due to rationalization (more attention must be given to construction, servicing, controlling and supervising), and in consequence a special study must be made of educational programs and stress factors (increase of psychic as compared with physical stress). *J.N.*

Ratio scale. A ratio scale represents the most complete form of metric classification. As in the interval scale (q.v.), its units of measurement are constant; it has an absolute zero point, at which the measured variable is in fact zero. Therefore statements such as "A is twice as big as B" are also possible. A weighing scale is a ratio scale. *G.Mi.*

Rauwolfia alkaloids. Alkaloids (numbering about a hundred) deriving from the plant *Rauwolfia Serpentina*, indigenous to India and used for centuries as a folk medicine (see *Reserpine*). Since the isolation in 1952 of reserpine as a psychotropic drug with emotional and motor inhibitory effects, hydrogen-oxygen compounds from these alkaloids have formed a chemical subdivision of neuroleptics (q.v.). Neurochemically, the reserpine-type alkaloids increase central storage capacity (mainly indicated in the area of the hypothalamus, q.v.) for noradrenaline (q.v.) (also for noradrenaline in the peripheral sympathetic nerves) and serotonin. In higher doses, rauwolfia alkaloids induce extrapyramidal arousal (pseudo-Parkinson effect: see *Parkinson's disease*), and a considerable drop in blood pressure (hence they are used as anti-hypertonics), but not narcosis. Action commences slowly and is long-lasting (up to twenty hours).

Bibliography: Schlittler, E. & Plummer, A. J.: Tranquilizing drugs from rauwolfia. In Gordon, M. (Ed.): Psychopharmacological agents. Vol. 1. New York, 1964. *G.D.*

Raw scores. Quantitative values which originally obtained in a measurement and not converted algebraically. The magnitude of the statistical values of raw scores is determined by these alone and is not subject to any external convention, as is the case, e.g., with standard scores. *G.Mi.*

R correlation. In the R technique of factor analysis (q.v.) an intercorrelation matrix is factorized whose coefficients have been calculated by correlation of m characteristics to n individuals where n is greater than m. It represents the most general kind of correlation or factor-analytic technique, and is reciprocal to Q technique in so far as its factor matrix corresponds to the factorial value matrix of the Q technique. The factors extracted by the use of an R correlation are interpreted as *characteristic factors*.   *G.Mi.*

Reaction formation. An internal defense mechanism in which a no longer gratifiable motive (or one gratifiable only under threat of punishment) is replaced by a motive at the other end of the existing continuum. Primitive manipulation wishes (e.g. daubing) no longer satisfiable as formerly are released through violent desire for contact (which occurs much more often because of its minimal satisfaction value), prodigality through thrift, obscenity through extreme politeness, disappointed love through malevolent pursuit of the beloved. Characteristics of reaction formation are the lack of ordinary, average forms of motive satisfaction and the inability to take advantage of the many possibilities of satisfaction as circumstances change, except by rigid adherence to extreme forms of gratification.   *W.T.*

Reaction time. The amount of time taken by a subject in responding to a stimulus. In the classical experiment, the subject makes a predetermined response (usually lifting his finger off a telegraph key) as quickly as possible upon receiving a pre-arranged signal (e.g. the onset of a light). The interval between stimulus and response is measured by some kind of chronometer, today usually an electronic timer.

Simple reaction time involves only one stimulus and one prescribed response. Of the various forms of *complex reaction time*, *discrimination R.T.* involves alternative stimuli, response being made to some of them but

not others, and *choice R.T.* refers to a situation of alternative responses as well as stimuli. Subjects may be classified in terms of *reaction types* depending upon the characteristic direction of their attention; the *motor type* concentrates on the response that is to be made, giving faster R.T.s, but a greater number of false reactions, whereas the *sensory type* is set to appraise the stimulus. An important variable in determining the speed of R.T. is the *preparatory interval*, i.e. the amount of time elapsing between warning the subject to be ready and the actual occurrence of the stimulus.

An early application of the reaction time experiment was in the rough calculation of the speed of nerve transmission by estimating the total distance that the message and command would have to travel between receptors and muscles. The early hypothesis that R.T. might constitute a very fundamental measure of intelligence has not been supported, and it is even doubtful that laboratory-measured R.T. has any validity in predicting adaptive responses in real-life situations, e.g. stopping an automobile in an emergency.   *G.D.W.*

Reaction timers. Instruments for testing the behavioral reactions of the subject to a given stimulus. There are very many reaction timers with the help of which the time between stimulus and response in the case of simple reactions, and choice and simple reaction can be measured. The reaction timer developed by Mierke (also known as the "*Kieler determination instrument*") and, similar to this, the "*Vienna determination instrument*" are used to ascertain time-related reaction capacities. The task of the subject consists in responding with a specific reaction inside a fixed length of time to a variable number of optimal stimuli (for example different colored stimuli, or stimuli consisting of different geometric patterns) and acoustic stimuli (higher and deeper sound). The number of signals given and the speed of the signal sequence can be varied in this way. The number of correct responses within a test series serves as a criterion of capacity. In traffic psychology (q.v.), industrial psychology (q.v.) and psychopharmacology (q.v.), reaction timers or determination instruments are used to establish certainty and exactitude in the performance of multiple reaction, in the level and load capacity of individual efficiency, in individual behavior under risk and stress circumstances, and all the psychological factors of work behavior, e.g., fatigue, distraction, attention, etc.

Bibliography: Mierke, K.: Wille und Leistung. Göttingen, 1955. Müller, A. & Uslar, D. von: Ergebnisse mit dem Determinationsgerät nach Mierke bei Fahrtauglichkeitsuntersuchungen. Diagnostica, 1963, 9, 156–70.   *A. Thomas*

Reaction types. Traits relating to speed, strength, fluidity, economy, harmony, etc. of reaction (e.g. Ewald types: see *Biotonns*). The concept of reaction types is also related to mental processes: hysterical (q.v.), primitive (q.v.), sensitive (q.v.), anancastic (q.v.), etc.
                                                          W.K.

Reactive inhibition. The tendency (postulated by Hull in 1943 in his hypothetico-deductive theory of learning, q.v.) of every reaction to engender in the organism a (fatigue-like) state opposed to the recurrence of that reaction. Reactive inhibition is defined as a negative impulse; i.e. its reduction (through the conclusion of existing activity) has an intensifying effect and can become part of the foundation of the learning process (see *Conditioned inhibition*).

Bibliography: Hull, C. L.: Principles of behavior. New York, 1943.   *L.B.*

Readiness. A physiological condition, also variously defined as "tendency", "urge", "impulse", as a result of which certain actions are carried out in preference to all others. The causes, as yet scarcely analyzed, lie in the activity of certain brain structures, in concentrations of hormones and transmitter substances, etc. (See *Action-specific energy*.) Readiness is subject to hypertrophy and atrophy. It is rare for an instinctive action to be motivated by only one manifestation of readiness; the motivation is for the most part multiple. See *Arousal; Drive; Instinct; Vigilance*.

Bibliography: Hinde, R. A.: Animal behavior. A synthesis of ethology and comparative psychology. New York & London, ²1970.   *K.Fi.*

Reading is the optical (in the case of Braille, tactile) perception of written symbols and their arrangement as specific meaningful content. Reading disorders consist of an inability to apprehend signs as configurations and/or inadequate association of signs and meaningful contents. Methods of learning how to read are usually either *synthetic* (based on the letters) or *analytic* (based on whole words, sentences, or meaningful wholes). Tinker (1965) summarizes research into the psychological factors fundamental to proficient reading, including the *appearance* of the reading material (type, light, color, etc.).

Bibliography: Carter, H. L. J. & McGinnis, D. J.: Diagnosis and treatment of the disabled reader. New York & London, 1970. Deboer, J. J. & Dallman, M.: The teaching of reading. New York & London, ³1970. Dechant, E.: Diagnosis and remediation of reading disability. New York & London, 1969. Roswell, F. G. & Natchez, G.: Reading disability: diagnosis and treatment. New York & London, ²1971. Smith, F.: Understanding reading. A psycholinguistic analysis of reading and learning to read. New York & London, 1971. Tinker, M. A.: Bases for effective reading. Minneapolis, 1965.   *H.Sch.*

Reafference principle. Overall connection system of the organism which at every level of efferent synaptic information processing collates the issue of instructions and their execution, and in the case of a discrepancy makes possible a retransmission for correction at the higher centers. As orders (the results of action potential) go out from a superordinate central nervous center (for example the pyramidal pathways) by way of synapses to an effector (e.g. a muscle), a temporarily delayed stimulus (efference engram) is detached from the efferent signal sequence at the connection point and collated with the retransmission concerning the execution of orders by the effector (*reafference*). When the efference engram and reafference disagree, a message (*exafference*) is sent back to the superordinate centers and corrects the original efference. At the most the retransmissions can ascend partly as far as the central nervous system and there cause a *conscious correction-decision*. A clear example of the reafference principle is eye movement and the coordination of the eye-hand system.

Bibliography: Holst, E.v. & Mittelstaedt, H.: Das Reafferenzprinzip. Naturwiss., 1950, **37**, 256–72.

M.S.

Real anxiety (syn. *Actual anxiety*). Freud (q.v.) distinguishes real from neurotic *anxiety* (q.v.). The neurotic variety derives from inner releasers, whereas the "real" kind is the product of external phenomena. According to Freud, civilized man has to be educated to a condition of real anxiety. No child exhibits it initially. He sees children's real anxiety in the face of parental punishment as a predecessor of the later anxiety of *conscience* (q.v.). Real anxiety as an isolated phenomenon is problematical in view of the differential probability and intensity of avoidance reactions to similar objects or situations offered on diverse occasions by different individuals.   *U.H.S.*

Reality, denial of. Ignoring the relevance of essential part-aspects of one's own physical, psychic and/or social environment; effectively similar to repression and isolation. Examples:

a soldier under fire who suddenly behaves as if he were on a dance floor, or a political detainee who makes light of his captor's threats. Denial of reality often occurs in psychoses, especially in mania (q.v.), depression (q.v.), and schizophrenia (q.v.).   *W.T.*

Realization (Ger. *Realisierung*). A scientific method founded by O. Külpe. The real is recognized as, or postulated as, true. Perception (q.v.) is enunciated as a basic principle of experience. Thought mediates the structures and laws of that which is perceived. See *Würzburg school*.   *H.W.*

Reality. The world independent of consciousness. In the broader sense the term also embraces the *experienced world;* as subjective reality it is contrasted with objective reality. The term often serves to distinguish certain parts of the experienced world from others: e.g. the indirectly encountered from the merely visualized.   *P.T.*

Reality principle. According to Freud (q.v.), opposed to the pleasure principle (q.v.). It controls the secondary psychological processes. Under its influence (and through experience and learning; according to Freud, through object cathexis and object anti-cathexis), the primary processes are modified and made adaptable. While the primary psychological processes are attributed to the id (q.v.), the secondary processes belong, according to Freud, to the *ego* (q.v.). In waking life these latter rule over dream and sleep conditions, in adult life over childhood, in a refreshed condition over fatigue, in a state of health over conditions of mental illness. The development of the individual may be defined as a continuous transition to an ever higher share of the secondary processes in the whole life of the mind and to a growing dominance of the reality principle over the pleasure principle.   *W.T.*

Reason (Lat. *ratio;* Fre. *raison;* Ger. *Vernunft*). **1.** A philosophical term, synonymous with understanding (q.v.), or insight. It denotes intellectual ability as a whole in contrast to sensory capacity. In psychology, "reason" is often opposed to intuition (q.v.), instinct (q.v.) or emotion (q.v.). **2.** The power to proceed from premises to consequences. **3.** Clarity of mind, of thinking. **4.** A cause, ground or principle; an efficient cause; a final cause. **5.** (Kant) That mental faculty which transcends conditions of possible experience, and not including understanding (*Verstand*) or sensibility (sense experience).

H.J.A. & J.M.

Receptors. In earlier literature on the subject the term "receptors" often has the same meaning as organs of the brain or parts of the brain's organs. Receptors were postulated in regard to different parts of the brain (i.e. organs for the perception of stimuli which could be invested with certain subjective qualities). In the physiology of the brain, especially "objective" physiology, the concept of "receptor" is understood broadly as to extent and narrowly in respect of capacity. A sensory organ, i.e. an organ perceptive of signals or stimuli, is also called a receptor when no phenomenal (perceptive) experiences result from its activity (see Hensel, 1966). Pavlov described receptors as the analyzers of *primary* signal systems, and defined these as points of contact between the environment and mental activity. In the general use of the term, the influence of cybernetic and communications models is increasingly influential. In this view, the receptor is less an organ, or part of an organ, and more a biological, cybernetic (or biocybernetic) function.

As a rule, however, such receptor functions clearly also correspond to specialized organs

(see *Psychophysics*). The receptor is an information transformer: a function of transformation, which transforms a signal, a stimulus or physically measurable event into a specific stimulus for the nervous system, or is in a position to transform the former into the latter.

The receptors may be classified as follows: (*a*) *exteroceptors:* information transformers for exterior stimuli. (*b*) *interoceptors:* information transformers for interior stimuli as, for example, *proprioceptors* for stress conditions, changes of muscle tension, sinew tension, changes of position and arrangement of joints; *visceroceptors* which transfer signals through inner organs, such as blood vessels, the heart, etc. Much more difficult and at the same time more problematic is the coordination of specific receptors with qualities of experience (e.g., in the case of skin receptors).

Bibliography: Hensel, H.: Allgemeine Sinnesphysiologie: Hautsinne. Geschmack, Geruch. Berlin & New York, 1966. **Field, J., Magoun, H. W. & Hall, V. E.** (Eds.): Handbook of Physiology. Vol. 1: Neurophysiology. Baltimore, 1959.   *A.Ha.*

Recessive. Those features are recessive which cannot be distinctly marked as heterozygous since they are suppressed by dominant genes (q.v.). Many hereditary diseases are recessive: e.g. albinism, diseases of the blood, and sickle-cell anemia. They first become manifest when they appear as homozygous.   *K.Fi.*

Recidivism. The repetition of an offense by someone already punished for it. Criminal psychology (q.v.) investigates the conditions for recidivism. See *Criminality; Punishment.*

Bibliography: Glueck, S. & E. T.: Ventures in criminology. London, 1964.

Reciprocal innervation (Sherrington). Involuntary stimulation of the motor neurons of a spinal segment activates the muscular agents and inhibits their antagonists in the innervated extremity: contraction of the flexor muscles with simultaneous repose of the extensor, and *vice versa.*   K.-H.P.

Reciprocal inhibition. Wolpe (1958) developed the theory and psychotherapeutic method of reciprocal inhibition (which accords with Sherrington's neurophysiological concept of mutual inhibition, q.v., of reflexes, 1906) as a possibility of forgetting inadequate modes of behavior. At the moment of appearance of a desired reaction, another reaction is caused which is basically incompatible with the desired mode of behavior (e.g. relaxation with reaction to anxiety), and therefore checks it. With frequent association, the reaction to be eliminated will be increasingly weakened and finally disappear. The method has been mainly applied during recent years in the psychotherapy (q.v.) of phobias (q.v.), but also in the treatment of many other behavioral disturbances. (See *Aversion therapy; Behavior therapy.*)

Bibliography: Sherrington, C. S.: Integrative action of the nervous system. New Haven, 1906. **Wolpe, J.:** Psychotherapy by reciprocal inhibition. Stanford, 1958.   *L.B.*

Recognition. The ability to judge a datum according to whether it is identical with one perceived on an earlier occasion. It might be said to require less effort than remembering proper. See *Memory; Reminiscence.*

Recollection, part(ial). A memory image which offers only part of the event remembered, and whose full significance cannot be immediately recognized. Recollections from early childhood are mostly partial in character. They are isolated, but when the event is reconstructed (possibly by "psychoanalyzing" what a person knows or thinks), the connection with that person's relevant interests can often be recognized. In a certain sense, contemporary (and perhaps all) recollections are really partial. The significant aspect can usually be made more easily conscious than is the case when the recollection is very early or, if later, very isolated. In general, reminiscences represent the beginning, the end, or the resumption of an interrupted series of events. See *Memory; Reminiscence.*

Bibliography: Adler, A.: Erste Kindheitserinnerungen. Internat. Z.f. Individual-Psychol., 1933, **11. Freud, S.:** Introductory lectures on psycho-analysis. London, [2]1929. **Toman, W.:** Das Erinnerungsbild und seine motivationstheoretische Bedeutung. Z.f.exp. und angew. Psychol., 1963, **10,** 125–39.   *W.T.*

Reconstruction method. A memory research technique to test how well structures are remembered. Items previously learned in a certain sequence are given to the testee as a disordered series; he is required to restore them to the original sequence. The number of correct ascriptions is a measure of the memory performance.   *E.H.*

Recreation. Leisure activity engaged in for its own sake. Refreshment, relaxation, pastime, sport, holiday, amusement. To indulge in these activities is said to *recreate* one (as in popular usage. (See *Vacation.*)

Recreational therapy (J. E. Davis): Recreation "prescribed by a medical authority as an adjuvant in treatment" (includes drama, music, dancing, painting, excursions, discussion groups, athletic games, and so on).

G.D.W.

Rectangular distribution. A distribution in which (*a*) the density for a defined sphere of a continuous characteristic is uniform, and (*b*) the values of the function (e.g. frequencies) are uniform for a defined number of classes of a discrete variable. E.g. every distribution transformed according to a percentile rank scale is a rectangular distribution.　　*W.H.B.*

Rectangular frequency polygon. A graphic representation of rectangular frequencies. Rectangular frequencies are incorporated in intervals since it is assumed that observations are distributed equally over an interval.　*A.R.*

Red-green blindness. Color blindness in which red and green are confused; usually associated with protanopia (q.v.) but less frequently with deuteranopia (q.v.).　　　　*K.H.P.*

Redirection activity. An ethological concept referring to behavior elicited by two different stimulus situations but directed toward only one. For instance, some male birds will defend their territory against intruders only after they have acquired a mate. Hence two conditions are necessary to evoke this aggressive behavior: the intrusion of a rival, and the presence of a mate, although the behavior is directed only toward the rival.　　　*G.D.W.*

Reductionism. The term denotes a viewpoint which, in the sciences or in philosophy, accounts for the superior by means of the inferior, or postulates a causal link between levels of reality which, in their very specificity, ought to depend only on the mode of explanation proper to them. That type of materialism which reduces mind to matter is a form of reductionism, as are the empiricism and psychologism which would reduce problems of validity to questions of fact. The same is true of those theories which try to account for mental phenomena in terms of biological control systems, or physico-chemical mechanisms (reflexes); or of those which see human societies as extensions of the "natural state" of animal societies, or which explain the diversity of the same as derived from conditions of the physical environment.　*M.-J.B.*

Redundancy. A term from information theory which describes quantitively the possible abbreviation of a sequence of symbols when using an optimal coding, and of the same repertoire of symbols. The redundancy of a code allows transmission of information to take place without disturbance. Without redundancy, an error in the transmission of code elements always leads to the coding of another symbol and consequently cannot be discovered. Redundancy can be used to discover, locate and even correct errors. The redundancy of human speech, which is relatively secure against disturbance, stands at 0.7–0.8. The disadvantage of redundancy in the discovery and correction of errors is that the length of the code words increases with the degree of redundancy and safety from disturbance.

P.-B.H.

Reference, association of. See *Association, laws of.*

Reference group. See *Group.*

Referral and reports. Only those expressions of opinion which satisfy the following conditions usually come under the heading of psychological reports: (*a*) the judgments are made after intensive preliminary studies; (*b*) the preliminary studies make use of the most recent findings of psychological research in the field of the report, and of empirical studies specially made to support the judgments; (*c*) the judgments should furnish an answer to an actual question.

The questions asked in a psychological report can relate to individuals and to their environment; hence a distinction is made between individual diagnostic reports and those dealing with the environment.

1. *Individual diagnostic reports.* In almost all fields of applied psychology (q.v.), psychologists are concerned with the diagnostic

judgment of people, either in vocational selection, school counseling, educational guidance (q.v.), clinical psychology (q.v.), military psychology (q.v.), forensic psychology (q.v.) (e.g. law relating to guardians and children, determining legal maturity and responsibility, judging the credibility, q.v., of witnesses), and traffic psychology (q.v.).

According to the specific purpose the psychologist has in mind, Heiss (1964) distinguishes three forms of report: (*a*) a report as a *representation* and picture of a personality; (*b*) a report as expressing an attitude and a judgment; (*c*) a report giving advice. A description of the personality as an aim in itself is, in practice, rare. The report expressing attitude and judgment demands from the psychologist that he should compare the findings on some individual with a more or less *clearly defined standard value*, e.g. in the case of a report on juvenile responsibility with a developmental norm; hence it comes about that many reports expressing some attitude make an interindividual comparison.

The counseling report (e.g. dealing with school, education, life, marriage) has a strong individual reference. It is not oriented toward an objective norm independent of the individual concerned, but deals with the individual himself, with *intraindividual* matters. It must take into account all those factors in the environment and personal relationships which can be seen to have caused a behavior, to be influencing the course it is taking, and whose influence is expected to continue. Such reports give some individual advice which ought to include predictions (q.v.) about constancy and change of behavior as time and situation vary.

Of the three purpose-based forms of applied diagnostics according to Cronbach (1964) "selection" is a case of the report expressing an attitude and a judgment, "deciding on suitable therapy" a case of advice giving; the third form, according to Cronbach (namely, diagnostics as "classification"), can precede both the expression of an attitude and a decision about treatment.

In practice, the different purpose-based forms do not occur independently but together. However, according to the case, one or the other purpose will be more prominent. There are also always special problems which basic psychological research has not yet been able to solve satisfactorily, and which go beyond purely diagnostic psychology. The necessity for empirically devised personality criteria for selection and classification, for statements of job requirements, for vocational profiles and for factors concerning ability and credibility of witnesses is an urgent matter, because they would lead to more efficient diagnostic reporting. (See *Personality; Traits; Type.*)

The problem of the counseling report is the decision as to how the present diagnostic state of the person in question can be transformed into a future desirable state (the object of treatment). An explicit and detailed behavioral theory seems necessary from which a suitable form of treatment could be logically derived. The hypothetical constructions used by the diagnostician must allow description of changes in a person: e.g. attitude change (q.v.), clarified habits, ideas, roles, skills, etc. Hence the diagnostician needs a consistent, proficiently researched, experience-based theory dealing with all such processes of change in an individual.

Unfortunately, there is scarcely any guidance for practical psychological diagnosis. Two groups stand out among the diverse practical methods of procedure: *one is more inductive and the other more deductive.* Someone drawing up a report inductively bases all the detailed pronouncements on the traits and behavior of an individual exclusively (or at any rate largely) on individual diagnostic data which have been collected empirically. Where the method is more deductive, some findings are based on diagnostic observation (the starting point is thus inductive), but after that, further characteristics of the individual not noticed during the investigation are derived from relevant personality theories.

The method used in preparing the report depends very much on the writer's attitude to personality theory. There are various possible ways of observing behavior, but (according to Heiss, 1964) the report should deal with (*a*) the interpretation as a characteristic of the behavioral form observed during diagnosis, (*b*) the question of what conditioned the behavior, (*c*) a causal analysis of the behavior, (*d*) a genetic interpretation of the behavior, (*e*) summary consideration of the behavior. Another important standpoint is a record of the specific form of behavior that it is thought will appear under certain conditions. Seitz (1971) has attempted to produce as comprehensive a classification as possible based on personality theory.

A special problem of individual diagnostic reporting is the fact that so far diagnostic investigation methods are still hardly suitable for checking by a systematic comparison the manifestation of a characteristic where environmental conditions vary, or the same characteristic exists on different behavioral planes (see *Psychodiagnostics*). Hence diagnostic psychology needs to refine its existing psychological methods or construct new and more differentiated ones based on a comprehensive though precise personality theory. Of course, reports on an individual diagnosis can *never express more than probability*. The degree of probability the report possesses is determined by the reliability (q.v.) and the specific validity (q.v.) of the investigation techniques employed. The report should mention the degree of probability; no certainty should be falsely claimed for it.

2. *Reports on the individual's environment.* Environment here always refers to its *effect on* the individual. What is important is not the objective description and recording of the environment but its psychological relevance. If so far a comprehensive behavioral theory

has been demanded as the basis for making an effective report, what is now required from this behavioral theory is that it should also embrace the complex interaction of the individual with his varied environment. The possible subjects of a psychological report on the environment could be arranged according to a classification of all the possible environmental factors, but this can only be one of emphasis. Sells (1963) mentions the following main aspects of the total stimulus situation, which are involved in behavioral variance, and whose action in forming behavior can therefore also be considered: (*a*) natural aspects of the environment (e.g. reports on the effect of weather, geographical, nutritional conditions on the behavior of individuals); (*b*) aspects of the environment due to man (e.g. reports on the influence of group membership, the influence of education, politics, art and literature on the formation of personality); (*c*) problems, situations and circumstances in which they occur (e.g. reports on accidents and their causes); (*d*) external reference characteristics of the individual (e.g. reports on the dependence of behavior on biologically defined factors such as age, sex; on socially defined factors such as family's importance, social status, etc.); (*e*) behavior of the individual in relation to others (e.g. reports on the effect of varying techniques of group leadership on the well-being of the individual in the group).

Such reports may be provided by private and public authorities (e.g. employers, school authorities, transport ministry). They serve partly to criticize conditions already in existence, especially where unsatisfactory (e.g. analysis of why accidents happen), but also afford a basis for a purposeful planning and shaping of the environment (e.g. design of traffic signs, development of new housing patterns).

The basic difficulties in this area of report compilation are the same as those found with individual diagnostic reports, especially the attempts to note and record general psychological facts and considerations without checking them sufficiently with regard to their applicability to any object of the report that is limited to certain conditions. Without this specific synchronization, a report loses its effectiveness. This depends also on the degree to which theoretical or empirical preliminary studies enable the writer to make judgments representing a decision rather than a measurement. Of course, certain decisions will never be possible in psychology, but there will be those with a higher or lower degree of probability and where the degree of probability can also be calculated; the difficulty will be greater where complex psychological considerations determine the attitude to be taken in the report. Since, in practice, recording and processing of data will usually be restricted for economic reasons, a complex process of judgment will remain a judgment of measurement to a certain degree (in relation to the clarity and validity of existing norms, theories, knowledge, etc., and to the methods used in drawing up the report).

Bibliography: Anastasi, A.: Psychological testing. New York, 1961. **Cronbach, L. J.:** Essentials of psychological testing. New York & London, ³1971. **Hörmann, H.,** et al.: Symposion 111: Die Beziehungen zwischen psychologischer Diagnostik und Grundlagenforschung. In: **Merz, F.** (Ed.): Bericht uber den 25. Kongress der Deutschen Gesellschaft für Psychologie in Münster, 1966. Göttingen, 1967. **Heiss, R.:** Über den Begriff des Verhaltens und das Modell der Persönlichkeit in der diagnostischen Psychologie. In: **Heiss, R.** (Ed.): Handbuch der Psychologie, Vol. 6, Psychologische Diagnostik. Göttingen, 1964. **Johnson, D. E. & Vestermark, M. J.:** Barriers and hazards in counseling. New York & London, 1971. **Rapaport, D.** et al.: Diagnostic psychological testing. New York & London, ²1971. **Sells, S. B.:** Dimensions of stimulus situations which account for behavior variance. In: **Sells, S. B.** (Ed.): Stimulus determinants of behavior. New York, 1963. **Tredgold, R. F. & Wolff H. H.:** U. C. H. notes on psychiatry. London, 1970.

W. Seitz

Reflective psychology. For Karl Bühler the various aspects of psychology were: psycho-

logy of experience, psychology of conduct, and psychology of works. The method of the first of these must be one of the modes of reflection, which gives access to that which is lived and elucidates the conditions of possibility. This approach is related to *Geisteswissenschaftliche Psychologie* (q.v.), phenomenology (q.v.) and existentialist psychology (q.v.).   *P.M.*

Reflex. An involuntary automatic response to an environmental change acting as a stimulus to the organism. This response is mainly of a motor type, and manifests itself in a *reflex movement* of a muscle or limb. The nervous excitation runs along a well-defined track down the *reflex* arc whose entry is represented by the sensory receptor transmitting the stimulus from the environment into nervous arousal. By way of afferent centripetal nerves, the stimulus reaches the reflex center which, according to the kind of reflex, consists of a simple synapse or a complicated system of nerve cells containing many synapses and connective neurons. By way of efferent centrifugal fibers, the stimulus arrives at the organ. See *Conditioning, classical and operant.*   *E.D.*

Reflex inhibition occurs with the activation of neurones which inhibit other nerve cells or gradually compensate their activity. See *Arousal; Inhibition.*   *U.H.S.*

Refraction. The normal-sighted (emmetropic) individual possesses a refraction strength of 58 diopters, which result from the surface shape and refraction indices of the refractory media (see *Cornea; Aqueous humour; Lens; Vitreous humour*). With these 58 diopters and with a normal eyeball length of 24 millimeters, the eye is capable of forming on the retina (q.v.) a clear image of an object at more than 4 meters from the eye; rays of light from the object strike the eye (to all intents and purposes) parallel with the axis. Through accommodation (q.v.) by means of the lens, an eye can increase its refractive strength by 14 to 72 diopters. *R.R.*

Refractory phase. The *non-arousable period* of the activity phase of an excitable cell. It serves the replenishment of exhausted energy reserves and varies widely in duration according to the speed of the metabolism. While nerve and skeletal muscles are refractory for only a few milliseconds after stimulation commences, the heart muscle is refractory for the whole period of its action, and even *absolutely refractory* during its *contraction*, and *relatively* during repose. In this relative reflex the heart is excitable only by supranormally large stimuli, a circumstance which leads to extrasystoles. *E.D.*

Refractory period. According to Masters & Johnson (1966), an observable part of the resolution phase of the male sexual excitement cycle. The refractory period begins after ejaculation and ends with the decline of sexual excitement. It is characterized by the relaxation of the penis and diminished psychophysiological sexual arousability. In women, however, a new plateau phase is linked to the orgasmic phase throughout which, given adequate sexual stimulation, they are capable of further orgasms.

Bibliography: Masters, W. H. & Johnson, V. E.: Human sexual response. Boston, 1966. *J.F.*

Regio olactoria. An area in the region of the upper part of the nasal cavity in which the olfactory epithelium and olfactory cells are situated. The olfactory epithelium is surrounded by a static layer of air. Odors normally reach the regio olfactoria by diffusion of normal breath into this layer of air. If olfactory sensitivity is intensified, the air is moved about ("sniffing"). *R.R.*

Regression. 1. An inner defense (q.v.) mechanism which usually appears when others do not suffice to achieve and sustain renunciation of satisfaction necessitated by the real or psychologically induced environment. It consists in the return of the person to earlier phases of motive development. According to Freud (q.v.) and his disciples, mental disorders such as regression derive from earlier phases of mental or motive development, and sometimes those phases succeeded by traumatizations, though remedies could be found (substitution satisfaction), or those phases which directly preceded the traumatic phases. All states of extreme deprivation or frustration (q.v.) in which defense mechanisms are (even though not completely) established, represent states of temporary regression (Toman, 1954, 1968). Anxiety (q.v.) and aggression (q.v.) are to be interpreted for the course of their duration as states of regression. Also states of fatigue, of physical weakness caused by illness bring about regression states of motive satisfaction; after a long day's work, for example, one can sustain only the lighter type of conversation. Regression has been described by Freud and Kris (1952) as a part of the creative process. Scientists and artists have often adopted primitive attitudes towards new advances within their own professional fields. They temporarily abandon conventional and established ways of thinking to pursue unexpected ideas and summarily reject current notions. But after this regression (or incubation, q.v.) phase, those concerned rediscover the path to the full and complex reality of their sphere of activity. Regression as part of the creative process may be described as "regression in the service of the ego" (Kris, 1952). Regression also serves the ego (q.v.) as part of a psychopathological process. Indeed its consequences cannot easily be erased, and it affects the ego itself for a long period.

Bibliography: Freud, S.: The ego and the id. London, ²1962. Id.: Introductory lectures on psychoanalysis. London, ²1929. Kris, E.: Psychoanalytic explorations in art. New York, 1952. **Toman, W.**: Dynamik der Motive. Vienna & Frankfurt, 1954. **Id.**: Introduction to psychoanalytic theory of motivation. London & New York, 1960.   *W. Toman*

2. *In statistics* regression represents the fact that the estimated or predicted standard values of a dependent variable are nearer the sample mean than the corresponding standard values of the independent variable. The term "regression" was introduced by Galton (q.v.) ("*law of filial regression*").   *G. Mikula*

Regression analysis. Statistical analysis of the functional dependence of an incidental variable on one or several independent variables. Regression analysis permits the prediction of the unknown values of dependent variables on the basis of knowledge of the corresponding values of independent variables. Both dependent and independent variables must be measured on an interval scale (q.v.). Simple and multiple regression are distinguished according to the number of independent variables, and linear and curvilinear (nonlinear) regression according to the equation of the line of regression (q.v.).   *G.Mi.*

Regression, atavistic. See *Atavistic regression.*

Regression coefficients are the two coefficients *a* and *b* of the regression line (q.v.), although the term is usually applied only to *b*. In the case of linear regression (q.v.), *a* represents the distance of the point of intersection of the straight line of regression with the ordinate from the origin of the coordinates, and *b* represents the rise of the straight line of regression.   *G.Mi.*

Regression equation. The regression equation of the line of regression permits the prediction of the value of the dependent variables on the

basis of an arbitrary (also unobserved intermediate) value of the independent variables.
                              G.Mi.

Regression lines. In the case of simple *regression* (q.v.), those lines are regression lines which, according to the *method of least squares* (q.v.) are so disposed that the sum of deviations of the empirical values from it is minimal. In linear regression it is a straight line. The angle formed by both regression lines of a bivariate distribution designates the level of correlation existing between both variables. In a correlation $r = \pm 1$, both regression lines occur together.   *G.Mi.*

Regulation. Setting, maintaining or changing the conditions of a system by external determination of the input values without feedback. Examples are the regulation of a computer (q.v.) by a program (q.v.), and regulation of learning by a film or broadcast lecture. See *Feedback system.*   *K.-D.G.*

Rehabilitation. The prevention, removal or reduction of a physical, mental or social disability, development of remaining potentialities, and attempt to put a person into a position where he can dispose fully of his physical and mental faculties to achieve his own aims and contribute to the needs of society or (if this is not possible, or only with extreme discomfort) to live with whatever help is necessary. The following are associated with rehabilitation: recovery or substitution of the physical and mental faculties necessary to everyday life; balanced training for the particular handicap, (pre-) school and vocational education; acquisition and retention of a proper place of work, living quarters, car, etc.; foundation and continuation of satisfactory social contact; where necessary financial assistance and care. Rehabilitation is proposed when a person is disabled, i.e. in the case of an illness or injury which means a break in social life and necessitates the building of a new career or, in the case of congenital damage, a special way of life. Rehabilitation is the care of disabled in all respects and is therefore planned and carried out with the cooperation of all the appropriate specialists, certainly with a medical specialist, a psychologist and if possible a sociologist, along with others according to the circumstances of the case: a specialist in the training of handicapped people, a special schoolteacher, careers adviser, a social worker, an accountant, a technical teacher, an occupational therapist, a physiotherapist and a physical educationist. The practical tasks of the psychologist in rehabilitation are educational, vocational and marriage guidance, the removal of psychosocial factors that tend to hinder rehabilitation and that promote activation in the disabled, investigation of his social environment, individual and group discussion with the disabled and his dependents, other psychagogic procedures (see *Psychagogy*), behavior therapy (q.v.), and psychotherapy (q.v.), communication and companionship. The scientific psychology of rehabilitation inquires into the mental determinants of the success of rehabilitation and their interaction with physical and social factors. It is concerned with the creation of procedures for the diagnosis of these determinants, and for the prognosis and improvement of successful rehabilitation. Outstanding work is being done especially in the USA, yet there is a lack of integrated and comprehensive research.

H.D.L.

Reid's movement illusion. A kinesthetic illusion corresponding to the *horizontal-vertical illusion*. A person is asked to move a stick from left to right a certain distance and then through the same distance at right-angles. The former distance is underestimated in comparison to the latter.

C.D.F.

Reincarnation. A form of survival (q.v.) in which the individual is supposed to recommence a new life cycle after death by being reborn. A rebirth.

J.B.

Reinforcement may be viewed either as a procedure or as a process. As a procedure, reinforcement is an event which either naturally in the environment or artificially by experimental arrangement is contingent upon the occurrence of some specified response, and which then maintains the performance of that response. In this arrangement there is a two-way interaction between the individual and its environment. The response operates upon the environment, and the environment in turn supplies the reinforcement event which maintains the behavior. The resulting behavior is said to be operant, because it operates upon the environment, or instrumental, because it alone produces the reinforcing event. What kind of event will be reinforcing in a given instance may have to be determined. Here it may be easy to maintain some behavior in a dog or a small boy with a pat on the head, but difficult to get the same reinforcing effect in a rat or a grown man.

Procedurally, we may distinguish two kinds of reinforcers: positive reinforcers, e.g. food, are those whose presentation maintains behavior, whereas negative reinforcers, e.g. painful stimulation, are those whose removal has the same effect. The two kinds of reinforcers have other effects upon behavior, of course, which are quite different. Negative reinforcement should be, but often is not, carefully distinguished from punishment. The latter is, procedurally, making the onset of an aversive stimulus contingent upon some response, and, in terms of process, what weakens the response with this procedure.

Conceptually, at least, we may distinguish between primary and secondary (acquired, or conditioned) reinforcers, according to whether the reinforcing effect of an event requires no prior experience with it, or whether some prior learning is necessary. Food is said to be a primary reinforcer for the hungry rat, but some kind of experience in the situation, with deprivation, or with the particular food, may be necessary in this instance. Smiling is said to be an acquired reinforcer for humans, the acquisition supposedly being based upon the prior association of smiling with primary reinforcement, but it seems more likely that the reinforcing effect of a smile can be demonstrated in infants prior to any appropriate learning. The distinction between primary and secondary reinforcement may only have merit when a previously neutral stimulus is established as a reinforcer within the context of a particular experiment. Even in this case it is possible that the critical stimulus may have associative or informational effects in addition to, or instead of, a reinforcement effect. Experimental studies have left considerable uncertainty both as to how the secondary reinforcers are established, and as to how they function.

Some psychologists, most notably the followers of B. F. Skinner, argue that the well-known reinforcement principles used in maintaining behavior are now sufficiently well understood and sufficiently effective that little else need be considered in predicting and regulating behavior. The two main principles involved in reinforcement are (a) differential reinforcement, i.e. a routine for ensuring that reinforcement is given only when the desired response occurs in the presence of a particular stimulus configuration, and (b) a schedule of reinforcement, i.e. a routine for reinforcing the desired response only on certain occasions, such as every tenth time it occurs. Armed with these principles, a number of psychologists of Skinnerian persuasion have recently made dramatic inroads into the behavior problems presented by autism and retardation, speech defects, neurosis, and psychosis (Ullman & Krasner, 1965). Although reinforcement can be used to explain the acquisition of new

responses, often the response in question is already in the individual's repertoire, but occurs inappropriately. Hence the emphasis in practice upon differential reinforcement, and upon maintaining an appropriate rate of response.

Other psychologists, while not denying the practical effectiveness of reinforcement in regulating behavior, consider its effect to be cognitive rather than directly on performance. The individual is said to know that his behavior produces reinforcement; and if the reinforcement is needed or desired, then the individual will perform the response to obtain it. Thus reinforcement can be viewed as a utilitarian reward for appropriate behavior.

Most psychologists assume that reinforcement is more than a procedure. They regard it as a process, something which happens in the individual's nervous system to make learning occur when a response is followed by reinforcement. It is said to be a mechanism which, somehow, connects a particular response to particular stimuli. Current accounts of reinforcement derive from Thorndike's (1911) law of effect, which states that a response will or will not be learned depending upon the pleasant or unpleasant effect of the response. There have been specific theories of the reinforcement process. The most famous theory is Hull's (1943) hypothesis that reinforcement is necessary and sufficient for the acquisition of instrumental behavior. Hull proposed, in addition, that reinforcement invariably involved drive reduction. Reinforcing events were those, like food, which reduced the individual's hunger drive, or termination of shock, which reduced the pain and fear drives. Hull's theory fails to explain many experimental findings, such as learning based upon saccharin (which is non-nutritive, and cannot reduce hunger), sexual excitation, exploration, or brain stimulation. Such evidence has led Miller (1963) and others to suggest that reinforcement may consist of a sudden increase in excitation (q.v.). Hope of finding the physiological basis of reinforcement followed Olds' (1961) work on the apparent reinforcing effect of electrical stimulation in certain parts of the septal area of the brain. This hope may ultimately be realized.

It may be noted that even the most thorough-going reinforcement theorists, for example, Hull and Skinner, admit that there are other mechanisms of learning which do not require reinforcement; classical or Pavlovian conditioning is one instance.

Bibliography: **Hull, C. L.**: Principles of behavior. New York, 1943. **Miller, N. E.**: Some reflections on the law of effect produce a new alternative to drive reduction. In: **Jones, M. R.** (Ed.): Nebraska symposium on motivation. Lincoln, 1963. **Olds, J.**: Hypothalamic substrates of reward. Physiol. Rev., 1962, *42*, 554–604. **Thorndike, E. L.**: Animal intelligence. New York, 1911. **Ullman, L. P. & Krasner, L.**: Case studies in behavior modification. New York, 1965.   *R. C. Bolles*

Rejection. (Social) rejection is a somewhat ambiguous term used sometimes in social psychology and personality study to characterize the negative pole of a continuum between rejection and acceptance (when the word "rejectance" is occasionally used for emphasis). M. Rokeach's studies of dogmatism see readiness to reject experiences, objects, individuals or groups (e.g. ethnic minorities) as a sign of a consciousness operating as a closed system (closed mind; closedness) as opposed to an open system (open mind; openness), the latter then being identical with acceptance. The term is also used to describe social relations within a family (E. H. Erikson), and a person's attitude to himself (self-rejection, A. H. Maslow). Repression (q.v.) is often invoked by analytic theorists to explain the phenomenon.

W.D.F.

Relation theory. The perception of a gestalt depends on the apprehension of relations rather than the component parts between which the relations occur. Thus a tune is recognized as the same in many different keys. See *Ganzheit; Structure.*   *C.D.F.*

Relative frequencies. The class frequencies of a frequency distribution (q.v.) related to the full extent of the sample. Column (q.v.) or sector diagrams are used to show relative frequencies.   *G.Mi.*

Relative frequency, cumulative. The summated relative frequencies of a distribution which are calculated by the successive addition of class frequencies of an entire random sample; these classes are the successive classes of a distribution. Cumulative relative frequency is used for determining the percentile rank of a value.   *G.Mi.*

Relativity, principle of; relativism. The principle that any aspect of behavior or experience can only be understood within its context (background stimuli, antecedent conditions, etc.). *Gestalt theory* and *adaptation level theory* (H. Helson) in the areas of perception and psychophysics are examples of approaches which acknowledge the importance of relativity. The *Weber-Fechner law* has sometimes been referred to as the *principle of relativity*, although it is a very special case. *Cultural relativism:* the view that human behavior generally, and concepts such as *morality* and *deviance* in particular, are very much dependent upon the nature of the society in question.   *G.D.W.*

Relaxants. Non-specific and inexact term for tension-reductive pharmaceuticals. See *Tranquilizers.*

Relaxation. In cybernetic terms, the return of a system to the normal state due to

135 RELIABILITY

trophotropic adjustment after ergotropic actuation. The effect of relaxation pauses diminishes with the pause length with negative acceleration. To counter fatigue, especially in intensely fatiguing activities, several short pauses (to eliminate fatigue peaks, favourable motivation effect) are preferable to a greater number of long pauses (see *Fatigue*). *J.N.*

Relaxation therapy. 1. Psychotherapeutic methods the object of which is to reduce intrapsychic tensions and physical cramps. In addition to hypnosis (q.v.), treatment consists of the relaxation exercises of *autogenic training* (q.v.) as well as other (auto-) suggestive techniques. **2.** Physiotherapeutic methods are predominantly those designed to relax the muscles: e.g. active exercises or passive gymnastics for the sick.

Bibliography: Stokvis, B. & Wiesenhütter, E.: Der Mensch in der Entspannung. Lehrbuch autosuggestiver und übender Verfahren in der Psychotherapie und Psychosomatik. Stuttgart, ²1963. *H.N.G.*

Releaser. J. von Uexküll (1909) was of the opinion that an animal's whole environment is stored in its brain as nerve models in the shape of simplified images. K. Lorenz (1935) regarded as an "innate releaser" the "receptor correlate", i.e. the ability to respond to a certain code combination. N. Tinbergen (1942) translated "innate releaser" as "innate releasing mechanism". By "releasing mechanism" (R.M.), Schleidt (1962) understands an agency which directly triggers off a certain response and can accomplish the following performances: selectivity for certain stimuli, integration of various stimuli, linkage of stimulus and response, dependence of moods, coupling of learning mechanisms. The innate releasing mechanism (IRM) has been selected by phylogenetic adaptation and is thus present at birth. An acquired releasing mechanism (ARM) is developed ontogenetically by the individual. An IRM modified by

experience (IRME) is an IRM completed by habit and learning. If an experienced animal reacts to simple traps (q.v.), that is a case of IRM, if it reacts selectively, IRME suggests itself, and this probably is usually the case with vertebrates. A releasing mechanism as a neurosensory device has yet to be localized.

Bibliography: Schleidt, W.: Die historische Entwicklung der Begriffe "Angeborenes auslösendes Schema" und "Angeborener Auslösemechanismus". Zeitschrift für Tierpsychologie. 1962, *19*, 697–722. Tembrock, G.: Grundriss der Verhaltenswissenschaften. Grundbegriffe der modernen Biologie, Vol. 3. Stuttgart, 1968. Tinbergen, N.: The study of instinct. Oxford, ²1971. *K. Fi.*

Releasing factors. Neurohormones (see *Hormones*) detected in the hypothalamus (q.v.); chemical polypeptides which contribute to the excretion of glandotropic hormones (q.v.). The chemical structures and function of RFs are not as yet wholly clear. They probably provoke the synthesis of glandotropic hormones.

Bibliography: Bajusz, E. & Jasmin, E. (Eds.): Major problems in neuroendocrinology. Basle, 1964. *W.J.*

Reliability. 1. In the measurement of variables, that part of the result derivable from systematic and non-erroneous effects. Total variance therefore consists of permissible (true) variance and erroneous variance. The term is used mainly in factor analysis (q.v.) and test construction. See *Test theory*. *H.-J.S.*
2. The accuracy with which a measurement technique measures a characteristic. Reliability is expressed by the relation between error variance (q.v.) and total variance of the measurement scores. Different aspects of reliability can be distinguished, and these are also shown in the methods used for determining reliability: (*a*) *the stability of a measurement technique;* this is determined by the test or test-repetition method; (*b*) *the parallel test reliability* which is determined

on the basis of the correlation of the measurement results with two equivalent methods of measuring; (c) the *internal consistency* (q.v.) which is determined by the split-half method (q.v.) and consistency analysis (see *Kuder-Richardson* formula 20). (See *Test theory*.)

Bibliography: Guilford, J. P.: Psychometric methods. New York, 1954.   *G.Mi.*

Religion, psychology of. I. 1. *Concept.* The psychology of religion investigates the psychological laws governing religious attitudes; its object is not the truth about the divine (theology), but the human reality in which belief in a divine revelation comes into being. According to its particular function, the psychology of religion may form part of the comparative study of religions, of the phenomenology of religion, of theology (theological anthropology, pastoral psychology), or generally of psychology in the context of the human sciences.

As *pastoral psychology*, the psychology of religion may be of service—though from a critical standpoint—to the church and religion in its pastoral ministry to society and individuals. The founders of modern pastoral psychology include A. T. Boisen, S. Hiltner, C. A. Wise, P. E. Johnson, O. Pfister and W. Gruehn.

2. *History.* Interest in psychology, and with it in the psychology of religion, originated in observation of and reflection on the self, which was the result of a growth in awareness of the complexity of consciousness (q.v.) and the consequent development of perception of the psychic as a separate element in human existence. Hence the psychology of religion is as old as the idea of the "soul" (q.v.).

An interest in the psychology of religion may be found in early Christian writing, in, e.g., Paul (Epistles, c. 49–56), Tertullian (*De anima*, c. 210–211), Gregory of Nyssa (*Dialogue with Macrina on the Soul and Resurrection*, c. 380) and Augustine (*Confessions*, c. 400). In particular, the mystics of

various periods may be regarded as predecessors of the psychology of religion in the modern sense, although there was at first no sense of the psychology of religion as a study distinct from theology, and empirical and metaphysical statements are found side by side. This can be seen particularly in Luther, whose observations on the psychology of religion always have for him also a theological and anthropological significance: "*Sicut de Deo cogitas, sic ipse.*" A direct line leads from Luther to Kierkegaard (*Either–or*, 1843; *the Concept of Dread*, 1844) and *also* to, among others, Feuerbach (*the Essence of Christianity*, 1841; *The Essence of Religion*, 1851). Luther's fellow reformer, Melanchthon, also wrote "on the soul" (*De anima*, 1540). Relevant also are Pascal's *Pensées* (1670) and Schleiermacher's *Reden über die Religion* (1799). Nietzsche must also be included among the predecessors of the modern psychology of religion.

The psychology of religion as a separate discipline in the modern sense begins with the "race" psychology of W. Wundt (q.v.) (1832–1920). Wundt put forward the hypothesis of four stages in the development of religion (from the primitive stage, through totemism, to the cult of heroes and gods, and that of humanity). Related to the ethnologico-genetic approach are the theories on the history of religion of N. Söderblom (*Das Werden des Gottesglaubens*, 1915), F. Heiler (*Das Gebet*, 1918), R. Otto (*The Idea of the Holy*, 1917), T. Andrae (*Die letzten Dinge*, 1940), and others.

The USA produced an empirical and experimental psychology of religion, whose main representatives are G. S. Hall (1881), Starbuck (1903), G. A. Coe (*The Spiritual Life*, 1900; *The Psychology of Religion*, 1916), James (1902), E. S. Ames (*The Psychology of Religious Experience*, 1910) and J. H. Leuba (*A Psychological Study of Religion*, 1912). J. B. Pratt's *The Religious Consciousness*, like James's *Varieties*, is one of the classics

of modern psychology of religion. In Europe, the experimental psychology of religion became known through the work of the Würzburg school (q.v.): O. Külpe, K. Bühler, K. Marbe, W. Stählin, K. Girgensohn, W. Gruehn. This school made especial use of questionnaires (q.v.) and interviews (q.v.), diaries and other autobiographical material; the objects of investigation were at first striking religious phenomena, such as conversion and mysticism, but later included more ordinary phenomena. Independent of the Würzburg school was the work of Durkheim (1912), Beth (1926ff), Dehm (1923), W. Frühauf and E. Eichele. Many investigations in the USA and in Europe have studied religion among children and young people. In this field a close connection can be seen between the psychology of religion and the psychology of *development* (q.v.): see the works of, among others, Piaget (q.v.) and Goldman (1964).

The contribution of depth psychology (q.v.) to the psychology of religion has generally received too little recognition. The work of Sigmund Freud (q.v.) and his school (Pfister, 1944, etc.), and the later works of Fromm (1965) and E. H. Erikson, are of great importance for the psychology of religion, as are the investigations of C. G. Jung (q.v.) and authors influenced by him (e.g. Schär, 1950; Rudin, 1960). The individual psychology (q.v.) developed by A. Adler (q.v.) has also influenced contemporary thinking in the psychology of religion (especially through the work of Künkel, 1957).

3. *Methods.* On the basic assumption that the phenomenon of religion in all its forms, collective, ethnological and individual, is something that can be empirically described and analyzed, any particular branch of research can call on all the modern methods of the human sciences. Due correlation and interdependence in this field of medical, sociological, ethnological, historical-genetic and psychological approaches are important.

Only through cooperation between the whole range of anthropological methods is an adequate psychology of religion possible, just as the psychology of religion itself can only be properly understood as an aspect of or factor in the wider field of anthropology. Whether there are any methods specific to the psychology of religion may be doubted, although a psychology which takes account of the hermeneutical circle (W. Dilthey, E. Spranger) will be more suitable for the investigation of religion than an experimental psychology which isolates individual facts and phenomena; nevertheless, the value of the latter as an auxiliary discipline should not be underestimated. No less important than the concepts of depth psychology are the findings of social psychology (q.v.), especially group dynamics (q.v.), and of medicine. Efforts are being made to find out how the empirically accessible aspect of religion may be determined and changed by a person's social relationships, and to understand its psychosomatic role as both cause and effect of chemo-physiological and other processes (cf. the current problem of hallucinogenic drugs).

In the past, interest was concentrated on genetic problems. Investigations have been made into the origin of religion in human history (W. Wundt, q.v., S. Freud, q.v., historians of religion), and in the life of the individual, and especially of the child ("genetic" psychology of religion: H. Clavier, 1913; Goldman, 1964; Piaget, 1945); while it is true that all stages have to be taken into account, religious awareness in man nevertheless clearly shows age-specific characteristics in every stage of life. Investigations related to particular occupations (Dehn, 1923; Demal, 1953; Piechowski, 1927; Rudin, 1966; Rey, 1969, etc.), to particular denominations (the affinity of Catholicism with oral sexuality and of Protestantism with anal sexuality would be an interesting study), or to sex (Hainz, 1932, etc.) should all provide valuable information.

In this field, the psychology of religion must work closely with sociology (sociology of religion). Since the individual's religious attitude cannot be considered in isolation from his environment, representative results are more likely to be produced by social psychology and depth psychology than by the experimental (associative) methods of the Würzburg school. In this connection it should be remembered that in a pluralistic society very different stages of religious development may exist side by side, from primitive animism through the institutional forms of the so-called higher religions to an assertion of individual autonomy which regards itself as "beyond all religion"; from observance of taboos and magical attitudes, through a religious morality, to liberal outlooks among groups of some intellectual distinction. This means that at the same time and in the same society, or even within the same denomination, one may find every stage and form known to the history of religions. The same is true of "styles" in religion, the sensuousness of a thoroughly magical worship of images, and the bleak austerity of iconoclastic asceticism, pietism, liberalism, orthodoxy, etc. These are expressions of religious group norms (see also *Meditation*) which recur in all religions, and obviously correspond to some basic structures or human needs.

4. *Research.* One of the most important tasks of the psychology of religion is the criticism of religion. This may be regarded as a special case of the criticism of ideology, which in its turn may be regarded as a secularized criticism of religion. Today the psychology of religion must concern itself with the secular forms of human religious awareness, such as mass hysteria in politics, the manipulation of opinion and uncritical adulation of idols, unthinking acceptance of authority, all the forms of unconscious dependence, etc. Critical attention should also be devoted to the political use of religion, e.g. by means of the concept of "psychological defense" or by

the exploitation of primitive stages of religious feeling, e.g. in courts (crucifix, oath), or in other circumstances in which obligations or restrictions are to be imposed. The psychology of religion might be said to have political responsibilities. The results of the historical psychology of religion are relevant here; this is concerned with investigating the psychological background of crusades, wars of religion, the persecution of witches, forced conversions, etc., but reveals structures which are still effective.

Among these structures are the role of religion as projection and wish-fulfilment and the rationalizing function of the—usually unconscious—interests of the corresponding theologies at various periods, in which individual and collective needs motivate the community. Other structures in this category are taboo (q.v.), prejudice (q.v.) and dogma, and all defense mechanisms, which are found in many forms in religions as means of overcoming anxiety (q.v.). This makes the basic phenomenon of fear an important object of research in the psychology of religion. In this connection one should also mention anthropological phenomena which occur in the context of religion, such as fanaticism, tolerance and intolerance, missionary activity, asceticism, monasticism, hedonism, forms of sublimation (Jesus the beloved, Marian mysticism, devotion to the saints), conversion (which as an object of research marked the beginning of the modern psychology of religion), voices and visions, castration (q.v.) and prostitution (q.v.) performed for religious motives, martyrdom and sadomasochism (q.v.), inspired dreams in sanctuaries, ecstasy, religious devotion to the sexual organs, ancestor-worship, etc. Tendencies to monistic or dualistic ways of thought may also be investigated by psychological techniques.

In connection with the phenomena of dogmatism and ideologically oriented security tendencies, the categories of law and gospel

(Paul, Luther) are of interest, as are individual dogmatic propositions and their background and content in relation to collective mythology (e.g. virgin birth, the Resurrection, the dogma of the Trinity). So also are changes in the meaning of dogmas and their function in the psychological system of individual believers, e.g. "great" theologians, whose lives cannot be viewed in isolation from their theology (and *vice versa*). Examples are the doctrine of justification in the context of Luther's life and its different function in the case of Melanchthon or Osiander, or in the case of the "orthodox" Lutherans of Karl Barth. Other topics are the categories of obedience and maturity, the role of women in Christian tradition (including the question of their eligibility for the ministry), the therapeutic function of confession and absolution for individuals and groups, the investigation by psychology of religion and comparative religious studies of the relation of the individual to the collective (and *vice versa*) in the categories of guilt, sin (separation), conscience, morality, and so on.

Finally apocalyptics—the relationship of which to the ideas of schizophrenics (see *Schizophrenia*) was pointed out in particular by Boisen (1936), is an important area of investigation for the psychology of religion, as is Christian and non-Christian eschatology, including the secularized forms of Marxism, and the meaning of goal projections and "real utopias" (E. Bloch, 1970) for individual life styles. The psychology of religion also investigates the way in which religious experiences are objectified—e.g. mythological and poetical statements, religious art, dogmas, messiahs, sacred texts, persons and objects, metaphysics or attempts to avoid it, and of course all ritual or cultic expressions of "religious" experience, sacred meals, washings, ceremonies, etc. Office-holders in religions also have to be studied, and the expectations associated with them by believers (father-figures: "Father" as a title for

priests, obligatory wearing of beards, celibacy; archetypes (q.v.) and "representatives" of deities; religious communities of men and women ("brothers" and "sisters"); father-and mother-goddesses, religious groups as "families", etc.).

The psychology of religion also studies the function of animals and animal symbols. Lastly, it must also investigate the basic experience of the human search for meaning, which, like fear, is—in psychological terms— at the root of religious feeling. Nor can psychology of religion ignore the fact that all men have some sort of idea of transcendence, some sort of "faith", and that their health depends on the form of their religion, which is a particular way of coping with conflict (q.v.), and it must be aware of the influence which religions exercise on the relations between human groups, including whole nations (wars of religion, alliances, etc.). It is possible that certain dogmas which impose restrictions on aggression (q.v.), in fact have exactly the opposite effect to their apparent intention of establishing peace, but no conclusive evidence is yet available. This is another example of the political responsibilities of the psychology of religion.

5. *Future possibilities.* The psychology of religion is in its early stages as an independent scientific discipline and there is immense scope for development. Teaching posts in the subject are rare. In the form of analytical pastoral psychology with a critical attitude to the churches, the psychology of religion can make an important contribution to overcoming the churches' identity crises, and even those of religions, by revealing the unconscious roots of the crises and finding new methods of communication. The psychology of religion can help to stimulate freedom and creativity where authoritarianism and legalism, conservatism and dogmatism have restricted thought and feeling.

The psychology of religion may be able to offer the ecumenical movement a way of breaking down denominational barriers by increasing each denomination's awareness of its historical identity. A similar approach may also have an effect on the barriers between the higher religions, and even between religions at different stages of historical development. In this way, the psychology of religion will be at the service, not of a destructive positivistic critique of religion, but of a testing of spirits whose aim is human emancipation.

Bibliography: Archiv für Religions-psychologie founded by W. Stählin, 1914 ff. **Berggrav, E.:** Religionens terskel. 1924 (Ger. trans.: Der Durchbruch der Religion im menschlichen Seelenleben. 1929). **Berguer, G.:** Traité de la Psychologie de la Religion. Geneva, 1946. **Bernet, W.:** Inhalt und Grenzen der religiösen Erfahrung, 1955. **Beth, K.** (Ed.): Zeitschrift f. R., 1926 ff. **Birk, K.:** Sigmund Freud und die Religion. Münsterschwarzach, 1970. **Bloch, E.:** Philosophy of the future. New York, 1970. **Boisen, A. T.:** The exploration of the inner world. Chicago, 1936. **Id.:** Religion in crisis and custom. New York, 1955. **Id.:** Out of the depths. New York, 1960. **Canziani, W.:** Religion als empirische Wissenschaft. In: Der Psychologe, Vol. 2. (1959), 409–80. **Clark, W. H.:** The psychology of religion. New York, 1958. **Deconchy, J. P.:** Structure génétique de l'idée de Dieu chez des catholiques francais. Garçons et filles de 8 à 16 ans. Brussels, 1967. **Dehn, G.:** Die religiöse Gedankenwelt der Proletarierjugend. Leipzig, 1923. **Demal, W.:** Praktische Pastoralpsychologie. Vienna, ²1953. **Durkheim, E.:** The elementary forms of the religious life. London, 1915. **Freud, S.:** Totem and taboo. London & New York, 1950. **Id.:** Moses and monotheism. London, 1939. **Fromm, E.:** Das Christus-Dogma und andere Essays. Munich, 1965. **Id.:** Psychoanalysis and religion. New York & London, 1950. **Girgensohn, K.:** Der seelische Aufbau des religiösen Erlebens. Gütersloh, 1921. **Glasenapp, H. von,** Die fünf grossen Religionen, 2 vols. Düsseldorf, ²1954. **Goldman, R.:** Religious thinking from childhood to adolescence. London, 1964. **Grensted, L. W.:** The psychology of religion. 1952. **Griesl, G.:** Pastoralpsychologische Studien. Innsbruck, 1966. **Gronbaek, V.:** Religionspsykologi. Copenhagen, 1958. **Id.:** Seelsorge an alten Menschen. Göttingen, 1969. **Id.: Gruehn, W.:** Werterlebnis. Gütersloh, 1924. **Id.:** Religionspsychologie. Breslau, 1926. **Id.:** Die Frömmigkeit der Gegenwart. Münster, 1956. **Hainz, J.:** Das religiöse Erleben der weiblichen Jugend. Düsseldorf, 1932. **Harsch, H.:** Das Schuldproblem in Theologie und Tiefenpsychologie. Heidelberg, 1965. **Hellpach, W.:** Grundriss der Religionspsychologie. 1951. **Hermann, W.:** Zur Frage des religionspsychol. Experiments. In: Beiträge zur Förderung Christlicher Theologie, 1922, 26, 5. **Hiltner, S.:** Religion and health. New York, 1943. **Hollweg, A.:** Theologie und Empirie. Stuttgart, 1971. **Hostie, R.:** C. G. Jung und die Religion. Freiburg, 1957. **Johnson, P. E.:** Psychology of religion. New York, 1945. **Jung, C. G.:** Psychology and religion: west and east. London & New York, 1951. **Keilbach, W.:** Die Problematik der Religionen. Paderborn, 1936. **Kietzig, O.:** Religiös, kirchlich, gläubig. Göttingen, 1934. **Kretschmer, W.:** Psychologische Weisheit der Bibel. München, 1955. **Künkel, F.:** Die Schöpfung geht weiter. Eine psychologische Auslegung des Matthäus-Evangelium. Evangeliums. 1957. **Langeveld, M. J.:** Das Kind und der Glaube. Braunschweig, 1959. **van der Leeuw, G.:** Phänomenologie der Religion. Tübingen, 1933. **Leitner, H.:** Psychologie jugendlicher Religiosität innerhalb des deutschen Methodismus. Munich, 1930. **McKenzie, J. G.:** Souls in the making. New York, 1929. **Meng, H. & Frued, E. L.** (Eds.): Psychoanalysis and faith: The letters of Sigmund Freud and Oskar Pfister. London, 1963. **Mensching, G.:** Die Religion. Stuttgart, 1959. **Müller-Freienfels, R.:** Psychologie der Religion, 2 Vols. 1920. **Oates, W. E.:** The religious dimensions of personality. New York, 1957. **Pfister, O.:** Das Christentum und die Angst. Zürich, 1944. **Piaget, J.:** La formation du symbole chez l'enfant. Neuchâtel & Paris, 1945. **Id.:** Le jugement et le raisonnement chez l'enfant. Neuchâtel & Paris, 1947. **Piechowski, P.:** Protestantischer Glaube. Berlin, 1927. **Pöll, W.:** Religionspsychologie. Münich, 1965. **Potempa, R.:** Persönlichkeit und Religiosität. 1958. **Pratt, J. B.:** The religious consciousness. New York, 1920. **Preuss, H. G.:** Illusion und Wirklichkeit. Stuttgart, 1971. **Pruyser, P. W.:** A dynamic psychology of religion. New York, 1968. **Rey, K. G.:** Das Mutterbild des Priesters. Zürich, 1969. **Richter, L.:** Zum Situationsbewusstsein der gegenwärtigen Religionspsychologie. In: ThLZ, 1960, 85, 333–42. **Rudin, J.:** Psychotherapie und Religion. Olten, 1960. **Id.:** Fanatismus. Olten, 1961. **Schär, H.:** Erlösungsvorstellungen und ihre psychol. Aspekte. Zürich, 1950. **Id.:** Religion und Seele in der Psychol. C. G. Jungs. Zürich, 1956. **Id.:** Was ist Wahrheit? Zürich, 1970. **Scharfenberg, J.:** Sigmund Freud und seine Religionskritik als Herausforderung für den christlichen Glauben. Göttingen, 1968. **Schmid, L.:** Religiöses Erleben unserer Jugend. Zollikon, 1960. **Spinks, G. S.:** Psychology and religion. London, 1963. **Spranger, E.:** Die Magie der Seele. Gotha, 1947. **Starbuck, E. D.:** The psychology of religion. New York, ²1903. **Stewart, C. W.:** Adolescent religion.

New York, 1966. **Stollberg, D.**: Therapeutische Seelsorge. München, 1969. **Id.**: "Religionspsychologie pädagogisch". In: Pädagogisches Lexikon. Stuttgart, ⁵1971. **Sundén, H.**: Die Religion und die Rollen. Berlin, 1966. **Thouless, R. H.**: An introduction to the psychology of religion. Cambridge, 1923. **Thun, T.**: Die Religion des Kindes. Stuttgart, 1959. **Id.**: Die religiöse Entscheidung der Jugend. Stuttgart, 1963. **Id.**: Das religiöse Schicksal des alten Menschen. Stuttgart, 1969. **Trillhaas, W.**: Die innere Welt. Munich, 1946. **Vergote, A.**: Psychologie religieuse. Brussels, 1966. **Wiemann, H. N. & R. W.**: Normative psychology of religion. New York, 1935. **Wise, C. A.**: Religion in illness and health. New York, 1942. **Wobbermin, G.**: Systematische Theologie nach religionspsychol. Methode, 2 Vols. Leipzig, 1921/22. **Wunderle, G.**: Das religiöse Erleben. 1922.

D. Stollberg

II. *Origins of religious experience.* Religion is a universal phenomenon prompted by motivations as common to men at all cultural levels as is sex. Religion existed for hundreds of thousands of years before any of the great religions came into existence, hence religion is motivated by the same psychological functions as mankind. There is no instinct or emotion exclusively peculiar to the religious nature. Psychologists, to explain the nature of religion, must be acquainted with comparative religion. The great religions of the world— Hinduism, Buddhism, Confucianism, Christianity, Islam—have their roots in the religions of prehistory. In spite of esthetic differences, all religions subscribe to certain basic beliefs such as a Supernatural Being(s), immortal souls, moral codes, and after death, an assessment of the individual's life. Religion, therefore, has everywhere a common psychological nature. Some of the most stimulating studies in the psychology of religion derive from Sigmund Freud and C. G. Jung, though their views of religion are diametrically opposed. Various authors: William James (*Varieties of Religious Experience*, 1902) was an important American psychologist writing on religion before Freud and Jung. J. H. Leuba (*A Psychological Study of Religion*, 1912) collected forty-eight different definitions of religion. J. Bissett Pratt (*The Religious*

Consciousness, 1930) argued that religion is not one department of psychic life but involves the whole man. L. W. Grensted (*The Psychology of Religion*, 1952) said that "The material for the psychologist lies not in the existence of God. . . . Our beliefs and worship lie open to the inspection of the psychologist, but God does not" (p. 16). According to Freud (*Totem and Taboo*, 1913), the Oedipus complex is closely associated with the origins of religion, but Ian Suttie (*Origins of Love and Hate*, 1939) suggested that the Oedipus complex is not, as Freud said, universal. The matriarchal preceded the patriarchal forms of religion. Bronislaw Malinowski (*Sex and Repression in Savage Society*, 1937) asserted that in matrilineal societies the Oedipus complex is not present in the same forms as in patrilineal societies. All religions have their female and male psychological aspects.

Worship is objective when performed only in order to gratify (the) God(s). On the other hand, subjective worship exists for the benefit of the worshipper rather than for the gratification of deities. Prayer, psychologically, promotes human personality; it is beyond autosuggestion. If it passes over into worship, and from worship into communion, the Divine is viewed psychologically as the satisfaction of a being whose profoundest need is completeness. See: F. Heiler, *Prayer, a Study in the History and Psychology of Religion*, 1932.

The technique most productive of religious experience is contemplation. A crucifix for Christian contemplatives, the use of the *mandala* for Buddhist contemplatives and of the *yantra* for Hindu and oriental yogi, are means by which the mind of the experient is detached from the phenomenal world and brought to spiritual focus. Psychologically, contemplation is the means by which the phenomena of daily life arouse a sense of the mystery of being. See: R. C. Zaehner, *Mysticism—Sacred and Profane*, 1957 (see *Meditation*).

The concept of archetypes (q.v.) is one of Jung's most important contributions to the psychology of religion. According to Jung, the archetypes, which are primitive, non-personal and common to mankind and time, are the means by which the significant contents of dogmas and doctrines are most satisfactorily expressed. The instinct-emotion associations most active in religion, produce sentiments which are more unconsciously instinctual than consciously intellectual, and help us to understand psychologically that religion is in many ways a matter of feeling rather than of reason, though reason is not incompatible with it. See *Emotion; Instinct*.

Bibliography: **Eliade, M.**: Patterns in comparative religion. London, 1958. **Freud, S.**: Totem and taboo. London, 1938. **Id.**: Moses and monotheism. London, 1939. **Fromm, E.**: Psycho-analysis and religion. London, 1950. **James, W.**: The varieties of religious experience. London & New York, 1902. **Jung, C. G.**: Modern man in search of a soul. London, 1936. **Id.**: Psychology and religion: west and east. London, 1958. **Id.**: Memories, dreams, reflections. London, 1963. **Pratt, J. B.**: The religious consciousness. London, 1930. **Spinks, G. S.**: Psychology and religion. London, 1963; Boston, 1965; Utrecht, 1966; Tokyo, 1969.   *G. S. Spinks*

III. As a form of methodical scientific enquiry into religious experience the psychology of religion began towards the end of the nineteenth century. It was the result of the growth of the science of comparative religion and of the ever deeper probings of the psychology of experience. In order to clarify the psychic significance of the religious experience, the psychology of religion makes use of the methods of empirical psychology.

The following stages may be distinguished in the development of *method*. W. Wundt (1832–1920), in accordance with current evolutionary theories, employed the "anthropological" method. It did not attempt to describe the course of religious experience in the present but was chiefly concerned with the historical origins of religious images and the accompanying forms of religious rites.

Wundt's law of four stages (religion of primitive man, totemism, gods and heroes, the development of humanism) is not the result of his research but a preliminary schema for it. In America, E. D. Starbuck (1866–1947) and W. James (1842–1910) won popularity for the psychology of religion, firstly by their method of questioning its basis and their research into the phenomenon of conversion, secondly by their description of so-called ideal cases and biographical details of conversions. The interpretation of religious material was still under the tutelage of philosophy; immanentist, biologistic and pragmatist tendencies were not admissible. In French Switzerland, T. Flournoy (1854–1920) attempted a purely observational approach, but observed chiefly sick and eccentric people. His positivistic and patho-logistic approach led him to regard mysticism as a cousin of epilepsy (q.v.) and hysteria (q.v.). He was more interested in parapsychical phenomena than in natural and spontaneous religious experiences. Evangelical theology tried to describe systematic theology in terms of the psychology of religion, and even to justify it, e.g. G. Wobbermin (1869–1943). The expression "transcendental religion" shows that this method owes more to philosophy than to empirical research. In accordance with the findings of O. Külpe (q.v.) on the specific nature of religious experience, K. Girgensohn (1875–1925) and W. Gruehn (1887–1961) studied its empirical foundations. They agree that there is no such thing as an elementary religous feeling, that to be precise, religious experience is a complex structure, a process in which an *intellectual moment* is of paramount importance and involves a relationship to totality (ego-function). The validity of this theory has been questioned on numerous counts and the emotional side of religious experience accorded more significance than the intellectual. It must be assumed that religious feeling is not to be equated with any one basic emotion.

Others who have contributed to the study of piety as a psychic phenomenon are S. Freud (q.v.) through psychoanalysis (q.v.), A. Adler (q.v.) through his individual psychology (q.v.), and C. G. Jung (q.v.) through his analytic or complex psychology (q.v.). Their researches ran into difficulties because they did not clearly distinguish the empirical and therapeutic aspects from the a-priori and metaphysical aspects of religion. Freud saw religion as a temporary "human compulsive neurosis". Adler tried to explain God as exclusively immanent in human instinct. Jung described religion and God as purely functional archetypes, or constructs of the psyche. V. E. Frankl's logotherapy (q.v.) or existential analysis (q.v.) sees its therapeutic task as a theoretical confrontation with the spiritual problems of the patient, seeking to arouse his willingness to take responsibility without making the decision for him.

Recent work in the psychology of religion seeks to establish it upon a broad methodological basis and to experiment with new methods of research, which have been tried in other branches of experimental psychology. Work is being done at present particularly in social psychology (q.v.) and personality research (q.v.). (See also *Attitude; Role; Group dynamics; Prejudice; Authoritarian personality.*)

Research is particularly interested in the genuineness of religious experience, with special reference to the current popularity of hallucinogenic drugs, and also in the problem of the manipulation (q.v.) of people through religion.

Bibliography: Berguer, G.: Traité de la Psychologie de la Religion. Geneva, 1946. Clark, W. H.: The psychology of religion. New York, ⁵1963. Frankl, V. E.: Ärztliche Seelsorge. Vienna, ⁶1952. Girgensohn, K.: Der seelische Aufbau des religiösen Erlebens. Gütersloh, ²1930. Griesl, G.: Pastoralpsychologische Studien. Innsbruck, 1966. Gruehn, W.: Die Frömmigkeit der Gegenwart. Constance, ²1960. Hostie, R.: C. G. Jung und die Religion. Freiburg, 1957. James, W.: The varieties of religious experience. London & New York, 1902. Johnson, P. E.: Psychology of religion. New York, 1959. Keilbach, W.: Die Problematik der Religionen. Paderborn, 1936. Leuner, H.: Die toxische Ekstase. Bibl. psychiat. neurol. 1968, *134*, 73–114. Pöll, W.: Religionspsychologie. Munich, 1965. Pruyser, P. W.: A dynamic psychology of religion. New York, 1968. Rudin, J.: Psychotherapie und Religion. Olten-Freiburg, 1960. Starbuck, E. D.: The psychology of religion. London, 1899; New York, ²1903. Sunden, H.: Die Religion und die Rollen. Berlin, 1966. Thun, T.: Die Religion des Kindes. Stuttgart, 1959. Id.: Die religiöse Entscheidung der Jugend. Stuttgart, 1963. Id.: Das religiöse Schicksal des alten Menschen. Stuttgart, 1969. Trillhaas, W.: Die innere Welt. München, ²1953. Vergote, A.: Psychologie religieuse. Bruxelles, 1966. Journal: Psychologie religieuse. Brussels, from 1957.

W. Keilbach

IV. *The genetic psychology of religion.* The first specific researches into the psychology of religion in children (H. Clavier, 1913) were concerned with the genesis of the idea of God: material anthropomorphism (6–7 years), mixed anthropomorphism (8–11 years), and spiritualization (from 12 years) were later established as the distinguishing factors in the child's idea of God (influence of Piaget, q.v.).

According to R. Goldman, the development of the idea of God passes from the *intuitive* (up to 7–8 years), via the *concrete* (from 7–8 till 13–14 years) to the *formal* (after 13–14 years). J. P. Deconchy, as a result of his free-association researches, differentiates between phases of *attribution* (9–10 years), *personalization* (12–13 years), and *internalization* (15–16 years).

The Louvain center for the psychology of religion conducted researches into the connection between the child's image of God and that of his parents, and has established: the specificity of the symbolic father-and-mother image, the comprehensive nature of the God image, a difference between various groups. Research based on Piaget's work has been carried out into the connection between the growth of moral consciousness (see *Conscience*) and belief in God (Caruso,

Havighurst, Jahoda, A. Godin). Research has been carried out in Louvain into the perception of the symbolic communication of religious attitudes in religious rites between the ages of six and twelve (J. M. Dumoulin, J. M. Jaspard).

Four fields of current psychological research into the genetic psychology of religion may be distinguished: (*a*) Research into different situations, perceptions and experiences which can be seen and expressed in terms of specific elements of religious language (e.g. God who reveals himself as witness, judge, merciful, protective . . .). For each of these experiences and categories the implicit psychological processes must be analyzed (see *Motivation; Symbolization; Identification*, etc.). (*b*) The connection of religious behavior with a specific image of God and the recognized attributes of the parental image, throws light on the structure of religious behavior and the recurrence of the Oedipus complex. (*c*) By means of semantic scales (see *Semantic differential*) the connotations of religious language are compared with those of profane language. This can reveal the agreements and conflicts between human and religious realities, and provide useful data for clinical psychology (q.v.) (see *Depth psychology; Psychoanalysis*). (*d*) The connection between types of religious behavior and personality structures (q.v.), has been the subject of various works of research, particularly in clinical and social psychology, e.g. the contrast between a "authoritarian" or "dogmatic" religion and "liberal" or "humanistic" forms (Allport, Rokeach, Siegman). Only a few works have appeared to date on the varieties of religious and atheistic behavior in relation to different personality traits.

Bibliography: Deconchy, J. P.: Structure génétique de l'idée de Dieu chez des catholiques français. Garçons et filles de 8 à 16 ans. Brussels, 1967. **Goldman, R.:** Religious thinking from childhood to adolescence. London, 1964. **Vergote, A.:** Psychologie religieuse, Brussels, 1966.

A. Vergote & J. M. Jaspard

Religious type. One of the ideal types, which E. Spranger describes in his "forms of life" (q.v.). It is characterized by striving for the highest spiritual values. People of the religious type are chiefly intent upon ethical aims and seek for knowledge. They regard economic affairs as of secondary importance and tend to shun the use of force.   *W.K.*

Reminiscence. Reminiscence may be defined as an improvement, attributable to rest, in the performance of a partially learned act. The basic experimental design for studying reminiscence is:

Experimental Group	Practice	Rest	Recall
Control Group	Practice	No Rest	Recall

If the experimental group performs better than the control group in recall, reminiscence has occurred.

It will be recognized that reminiscence is a special and limiting case of a phenomenon that has long been known. Very often, performance is better under conditions of distributed than under conditions of massed practice. The benefits of distributed practice result from the interpolation of a *series* of rests, while reminiscence is defined in terms of the effects of a *single* rest. Because it is the simple, limiting case of a range of phenomena, considerable theoretical importance has attached to the explanation of reminiscence.

Reminiscence, as distinct from the phenomena of distributed practice, was not identified until Ballard's (1913) study of the memorization of poetry by children. Careful studies of reminiscence in the verbal learning situation, such as those by Ward (1937) and Hovland (1938), reveal small reminiscence gains over rest periods that may not be longer than a few minutes. Although the reminiscence effect tends to be small and transitory in verbal learning situations, large reminiscence benefits are found in motor learning situations (Bell, 1942) and these gains have been shown to occur over rest periods of up to two years in length (Koonce, Chambliss, & Irion, 1964).

Reminiscence is a function of a number of variables and conditions:

1. Length of rest interval: Amount of reminiscence increases to a maximum and then decreases as length of rest increases (Ward, 1937; Ammons, 1947). Optimum length of rest is much longer in motor learning than in verbal learning situations.

2. Amount of pre-rest practice: As amount of pre-rest practice increases, amount of reminiscence at first increases and then decreases (Ammons, 1947; Irion, 1949). The decrease with large amounts of pre-rest practice may reflect the fact that a performance asymptote is being approached.

3. Previous distribution of practice: Much more reminiscence is obtained following massed pre-rest practice than following distributed pre-rest practice (Hovland, 1938). If pre-rest practice were to be very widely distributed, it is probable that the introduction of a single additional rest would have no effect at all.

4. Chronological and mental age: Reminiscence appears to increase and then to decrease as a function of increasing chronological age. For the chronological ages that yield most reminiscence (early adulthood), amount of reminiscence appears to be an increasing function of mental age (Thumin, 1962).

Early explanations of distribution and reminiscence gains centered upon various forms of two theories, the fatigue theory and the perseveration theory. In simplest form, the fatigue theory holds that the learner becomes tired during practice. Rest allows him to recover from fatigue, then his performance improves. The perseveration theory was first advanced by Müller and Pilzecker (1900). It holds that, after the termination of formal practice, some kind of learning process continues to operate which, in effect, gives additional, unintended practice to the learner. Rehearsal might be one example of such a perseverative process, but it is not necessary to the theory that the perseveration be intentional or that the learner be able to report that it is occurring. To these two general theoretical approaches can be added the differential forgetting theory in which it is held that, during practice, the learner acquires two sets of habits: correct ones and a set of competing and incorrect ones. It is further held that, during a rest, all habits lose strength through forgetting, but that weak habits are forgotten at a *faster rate* than strong habits. Since training situations are usually arranged so that correct habits will be stronger than incorrect ones, a rest period should weaken the interfering habits more than the correct ones, and this differential forgetting should result in less interference and better performance following a rest. (See *Habit*.)

In more recent times, Hull's theory has had a strong influence on interpretations of reminiscence. Hull (1943) introduced two inhibitory constructs: *reactive inhibition* and *conditioned inhibition*. Reactive inhibition has the property of increasing as a function of the amount of work performed during practice and of dissipating spontaneously during rest periods. Therefore, although reactive inhibition is defined more precisely than fatigue, it possesses properties similar to those that are intuitively ascribed to fatigue. Performance is degraded in proportion to the amount of reactive inhibition that has accumulated. Conditioned inhibition also acts to degrade performance, but conditioned inhibition is held to be more permanent than reactive inhibition. Since conditioned inhibition does not dissipate spontaneously in time, an accumulation of it should be associated with a failure of reminiscence to occur.

A number of studies pertinent to Hull's

theory have appeared. Kimble and Horenstein (1948) measured the growth of reminiscence in time and fitted these data to Hull's theoretical formula for the decay of reactive inhibition. Moreover, an experiment by Adams and Reynolds (1954) demonstrated that very nearly *all* of the reminiscence gains in a motor learning situation could be accounted for in terms of the decay of a *single* inhibitory factor (such as reactive inhibition). This finding has been confirmed by several investigators.

However, some of the other theoretical explanations of reminiscence retain their attractiveness—partly because of their reasonableness, partly because of supporting data obtained in special situations, and partly because the theoretical ideas seem to have validity in other contexts (as witness the usefuless of the idea of perseveration or consolidation in contemporary treatments of short-term memory). Eysenck (1965) has advanced a three-factor theory of reminiscence that employs the concepts of perseveration, reactive inhibition, and conditioned inhibition. Very possibly, some such complex explanation of the phenomena of reminiscence will be required when all the learning situations in which reminiscence has been studied are taken into account. Perhaps, for example, reactive inhibition will account for most of reminiscence gains in motor learning situations while perseveration might play a more prominent role in the explanation of reminiscence in verbal memorization situations.

Further material and extensive lists of references may be found in Bilodeau & Bilodeau (1961), Irion (1966), and McGeoch & Irion (1952). See *Memory*.

Bibliography: Adams, J. A. & Reynolds, B.: Effect of shift in distribution of practice conditions following interpolated rest. J. Exp. Psychol., 1954, *47*, 32–6. **Ammons, R. B.:** Acquisition of motor skill: II. Rotary pursuit performance with continuous practice before and after a single rest. J. exp. Psychol., 1947, *37*, 393–411. **Ballard, P. B.:** Obliviscence and reminiscence. Brit. J. Psychol., Monogr. Suppl, 1913, *1*, No. 2. **Bell, H. M.:** Rest pauses in motor learning as related to Snoddy's hypothesis of mental growth. Psychol. Monogr., 1942, *54*, No. 1, No. 243. **Bilodeau, E. A. & I. McD.:** Motor-skills learning. Ann. Rev. Psychol., 1961, *12*, 243–80. **Eysenck, H. J.:** A three-factor theory of reminiscence. Brit. J. Psychol., 1965, *56*, 163–81. **Hovland, C. I.:** Experimental studies in rote-learning theory. I. Reminiscence following learning by massed and distributed practice. J. exp. Psychol., 1938, *22*, 201–24. **Hull, C. L.:** Principles of behavior. New York, 1943. **Irion, A. L.:** Reminiscence in pursuit-rotor learning as a function of length of rest and of amount of pre-rest practice. J. exp. Psychol., 1949, *39*, 492–9. **Irion, A. L.:** A brief history of research on the acquisition of skill. In: **Bilodeau, E. A.** (Ed.): Acquisition of skill. New York, 1966. **Kimble, G. A. & Horenstein, B. R.:** Reminiscence in motor learning as a function of length of interpolated rest. J. Exp. Psychol., 1948, *38*, 239–44. **Koonce, J. M., Chambliss, D. J. & Irion, A. L.:** Long-term reminiscence in the pursuit-rotor habit. J. exp. Psychol., 1964, *67*, 498–500. **McGeoch, J. A. & Irion, A. L.:** The psychology of human learning. New York, ²1952. **Müller, G. E. & Pilzecker, A.:** Experimentelle Beiträge zur Lehre vom Gedächtnis. Z. Psychol., 1900, *1*, 1–300. **Thumin, F. J.:** Reminiscence as a function of chronological and mental age. J. Geront., 1962, *17*, 392–6. **Ward, L. B.:** Reminiscence and rote learning. Psychol. Monogr., 1937, *49*, whole No. 220.

A. L. Irion

REM phase. See *Dream; Sleep.*

Repellants. Chemical substances emitted as a warning to members of the same or other species of an enemy, or in order to make the latter's prey uninviting for the future. Minnows when injured secrete a repellant to warn other fish. Many species of beetle squirt foul-smelling liquid from their extremities or spit out a corrosive gastric fluid which makes them inedible as prey.   *V.P.*

Repercussion. The effect of emotional occurrences on vegetative activities (e.g. profuse sweating, dilatation of the blood vessels). (See *Emotion; Stress.*)   *H.W.*

Repertoire (syn *Repertory*). In information theory (q.v.) the quantity of well-defined, reliable signals within a code (q.v.), or a number of events which, broadly speaking, are incompatible as pairs.

If a repertoire has only a finite number of elements, it is *finite*. A repertoire *in some order* is an alphabet.

Before a code (q.v.) is drawn up or the information (q.v.) calculated, the repertoire must be determined, e.g. the repertoire of letters, words, sounds or perceptual elements.

P.-B.H.

Repetition compulsion (syn. *Compulsive repetition*). According to Freud, the more or less irresistible tendency of an individual to repeat unpleasurable, even partly painful and traumatic experiences. Repetition compulsion is said to control the death instinct (q.v.). Freud "explained" the phenomena of recurrent nightmares or anxiety dreams, neurotic symptoms and transference as the effects of compulsive repetition. It has been claimed that it is possible to show that anxiety dreams derive from "libidinous" pleasurable motives (see *Libido*) that could not be fully gratified in reality. The nightmare itself is the answer to, and defense of, this libidinous motive produced by the dreamer from the introjected punishment (q.v.) tendencies of the environment. It seems possible to demonstrate the gratification value of symptomatic behaviors even in neurotic symptoms. The symptomatic actions partly gratify, in a minimal form, even the forbidden or no longer gratifiable motive. Toman has indicated repetitions of all primary drive and motive gratifications, and has explained phenomena characterized as "repetition compulsions"as emphatic repetitions of more primitive and aggressive motive gratifications. See *Obsession*.

Bibliography: **Toman, W.**: Repetition and repetition compulsion. Internat. Journ. Psychoanalysis, 1956, *37*, 347–50. **Id.**: Introduction to psychoanalytic theory of motivation. London & New York, 1960.

W.T.

Representation, principle of. Klages' term for a thesis conceived within graphology (q.v.), and at first related only to handwriting but later generalized only in regard to human expression: man's urge toward representation, which is rooted in his experience of the world he perceives, follows a personal (unconscious) guiding image: "Man's every voluntary movement is partly determined by his personal guiding image" (Klages).   *B.K.*

Representative. Samples (q.v.) are representative if their composition corresponds to the population from which they were taken. To obtain representative samples, random techniques (random samples, q.v., random numbers) or controlled techniques (see *Organized sample*) may be used. Conclusions about the population can only be drawn on the basis of the results of samples when the latter are representative of the population. (See *Sampling techniques; Opinion polls*.)   *G.Mi.*

Representative conclusion. A conclusion which concerns the basic population and which is drawn on the basis of a representative sample (q.v.). Thus, for example, on the basis of a statistic, a conclusion is drawn about the size of the corresponding parameter (q.v.) of the population.   *G.Mi.*

Representative poll/sampling. The use of a partial sample which in its essential structural characteristics corresponds to the population from which it was drawn. The results of the sampling as embodied in the *representational poll* are held to be valid for the population. The elements (people interrogated) of the sample (q.v.) are either selected by *random control* (e.g. by lot) or by random control (e.g. *quota technique*) from the population. See *Opinion polls*.   *A.H.*

Repression. In psychoanalytic theory: an inner defense (q.v.) mechanism by means of which a motive that is no longer gratifiable (or gratifiable only in the case of subsequent punishment) is replaced by similar gratifiable motives. The removal of a motive from the continuum of related motives accelerates the gratification sequences of still gratifiable motives. This state is experienced psychically as an *anxiety-aggression state*; it can become aggression if there is still a prospect of gratifying the blocked motive, and anxiety if environmental conditions seem insurmountable. This anxiety-aggression state may be equated with a transient *regression* (q.v.), which, like the anxiety-aggression state itself, comes to an end when a new pattern of gratifications of the persistent motives becomes fixed. Renunciation of the non-gratifiable motive would then be assessed as provisionally successful. A successful renunciation enables the individual in question automatically to resist opportunities of weaker and average intensity for gratification of the original motive. Finally he no longer perceives them as such opportunities. Only opportunities of above-average intensity for gratification of the repressed motive (those stronger than all opportunities since to gratify the repressed motive since repression) are experienced as recent temptation situations. In this case, subsequent repressions, additional repression work, and additional substitute gratifications are needed to maintain renunciation, and to avoid future temptation by even these more intense opportunities for gratification of the repressed motive. Should such a motive be gratified, the individal experiences guilt feelings, and introjected punishment motives occur. Examples of repression are weaning a baby, bereavement, or giving up cigarettes. Repression is successful and the state of unrest (provided by the accelerated gratification sequences of related motives) ceases, when the child no longer experiences the need to suck even when the breast is directly presented; when the thought or memory of the lost person no longer evokes any feeling of mourning or regret; when the former smoker can smoke a cigarette (maximal temptation situation) and it no longer appeals to him. Cases of repression in everyday life, e.g. "Freudian slips" (q.v.), are relatively transient and can be relatively slight phenomena. They are secondary repressions, which are codetermined by older, primary repressions. See *Depth psychology; Psychoanalysis.*

Bibliography: Freud, A.: The ego and the mechanisms of defence. London, 1937. **Freud, S.:** Inhibitions, symptoms and anxiety. London, ²1936. **Toman, W.:** Introduction to psychoanalytic theory of motivation. London & New York, 1960. *W. Toman*

Reproduction. Voluntary reminiscence (q.v.). A term for the recall of items of information which have been noted at some earlier time and stored in the memory (material of experience and learning). Reproduction must be distinguished from recognition (q.v.). (See *Memory.*) *F.-C.S.*

Reproduction methods. A broad term for a series of methods in the psychology of memory in which, as opposed to recognition methods, a free reactivation of retention is required. The retention performance is determined according to the amount of freely reproduced material previously learned. *E.H.*

Reserpine. The best-known member of the rauwolfia alkaloids (q.v.), a chemical subgroup of the neuroleptics (see *Psychopharmaceuticals*). Its importance as a therapeutic agent has decreased today because of possible massive side-effects (extra-pyramidal excitation, depression, q.v., circulatory strain). Because of its action on the central storage of catecholamines (q.v.) and serotonin, as well as its antagonism to LSD, reserpine has been used experimentally in numerous investigations. In healthy persons reserpine (1–2 mg) remained active for a long time (up to 12 hours) and caused no impairment of function but enhanced sensitivity to afterimages (q.v.); after about three hours the period of sleep was prolonged (paradoxical sleep). When the dose was increased to 5 mg there was a deterioration of performance and subjective sedation.

Bibliography: **Brown, J. W., DiMascio, A. & Klerman, G. L.:** Exploratory study on the effects of phrenotropic drugs on competitive paired-associate learning. Psychol. Rep., 1958, *4*, 583–9. **Hartmann, E.:** Reserpine: its effect on the sleep-dream cycle in man. Psychopharmacologia, 1966, *9*, 242–7. **Lehmann, H. E. & Csank, J.:** Differential screening of phenotropic agents in man: psychophysiological test data. J. clin. exp. Psychopath., 1957, *18*, 225–35.   *G.D.*

Residuum. 1. An *engram* or *trace* which—according to the psychology of association and the classical psychology of memory—every experience leaves and which forms the substratum for the reproduction (q.v.) of this experience. (See *Engram; Reminiscence; Memory*.)

2. *Factor analysis:* the correlation left over when factors have been extracted.   *F.-C.S.*

Resistance in the psychological sense is an individual's refusal to acknowledge as such unconscious motives which tend to affect his behavior and (in hidden form) his subjective experience. All defense (q.v.) mechanisms specific to a person can be diminished or removed only in the face of his own involuntary psychic resistance. In psychotherapy the patient is helped by a slow process intended to remove his defense mechanisms. Whereas Freud (q.v.) and his disciples were inclined (in the first years of psychoanalysis, q.v.) to confront patients initially and directly with the "contents" of their most repressed motives, afterwards care was taken to ensure a *gradual* cancellation of the client's inner defenses. Too intense confrontations with unconscious motives can so increase a

patient's resistance, and frighten or tax him, that he insists on abandoning the therapy.

Bibliography: **Toman, W.:** Introduction to psychoanalytic theory of motivation. London & New York, 1960.   *W.T.*

Resolution. The final part of an act of will which is followed directly by a readiness to act. It presupposes deliberation and consideration of the aspects relevant to the decision and implies knowledge of the personal responsibility for this decision. To that extent resolution needs to be distinguished from a *spontaneous* decision resulting from an emotional situation.
P.S.

Resolution phase. The term given by Masters and Johnson (1966) to the fourth and last phase in the sexual reaction cycle, coming after the excitation phase (q.v.), the plateau phase (q.v.), and the orgasmic phase (q.v.). Characteristics of this phase common to both sexes are a return to a normal blood pressure and a normal heart rate. In addition there are in the woman, the following: disappearance of the sex flush, shrinking of the nipple area; diminution of the labia minora, return to original position of the labia majora, the clitoris and the uterus, shrinking of the orgasmic platform in the vagina; in the man there are: shrinking of the penis in two stages, reduction of testicles and return to normal position (see *Refractory period*).

Bibliography: **Masters, W. H. & Johnson, V. E.:** Human sexual response. Boston, 1966.   *J.F.*

Resonance technique. A global method of perceiving expressive phenomena. The technique is characterized by a somewhat "intuitive" procedure based on impressions.
D.G.

Resonance, theory of. The supposition, first expressed by H. von Helmholtz, that in the hearing process a tone is split up into its components because the fibers of the basilar membrane together with the liquid surrounding them behave like a set of resonators. According to this theory the resonance frequency of the fibers decreases from the base to the top of the basilar membrane as the length of the fibers and the strain from the column of liquid becomes greater towards the top and the tension of the fibers decreases. This theory of resonance was criticized by G. von Békésy and O. F. Ranke and replaced by the so-called *dispersion* or *hydrodynamic theory*. (See *Sense organs: the ear.*) *W.P.*

Resonator. A hollow object (e.g. cylinder or box), open at one end, which is used to magnify the loudness of a tone in accordance with its natural frequency. *G.D.W.*

Respiration. Synonymous with breathing, this represents the process whereby O_2 is inhaled and CO_2 exhaled by the respiratory system. By means of the different muscles of respiration (see *Respiratory organs*) pressure is alternately decreased (*inspiration, drawing in of breath*) and increased (*expiration, expelling of air*), and as a result fresh air is taken in and spent air is breathed out. The volume of air breathed is controlled by means of the CO_2 regulating cycle through the respiratory center in the wall of the fourth ventricle in the medulla oblongata. Sensory vagus fibers of the lung make it possible to control the kind and depth of breathing and offer the possibility of influencing subjectively (voluntarily) the autonomic nervous system. *E.D.*

Respiratory system. All those organs which together are responsible for external respiration. They consist of a series of air passages including nasal chambers, mouth, throat, pharynx, larynx with epiglottis, trachea, bronchi and bronchioles and the pulmonary vesicles which constitute the major part of the lung. This system is contained in the thoracic cavity which by expanding and contracting produces the increase and decrease in pressure necessary for the movement of air which is breathed (see *Respiration*). The muscles which accomplish this are transverse and can be innervated at will. In the main they are the intercostal muscles and the diaphragm, which in warm-blooded animals also serves to separate the abdomen from the thoracic cavity. *E.D.*

Response set. Any of those influences which, as specific answer tendencies of the testee, falsify the intended dimensions of a test. Two basic forms are distinguished: *formal* response sets include all those conditioned by the particular form of the question (see *Acquiescence tendency*); *content* response sets are those which evoke a false answer by reason of the specific content of an item or test. The most important sets of this kind are: simulation and dissimulation, defensive attitudes, lying.

The influence of response sets can constitute a considerable part of the variance of a test procedure and therefore has to be taken into account in test construction. A variety of scales have been developed to guard against the content form: e.g. in the MMPI, or A. L. Edwards' "Social Desirability Scale".

Bibliography: Adams, G. S.: Techniques de minimisation ou d'exploitation des tendences de réponse dans les inventaires structurés d'auto-évaluation. Res. de Psychol. appl., 1961, *11*, 233–62; 303–41. *P.Z.*

Responsibility. The ability to commit a (punishable) offense, insofar as that action is dependent on the mental state of the individual in question. Responsibility (see *Guilt*) in this sense is a legal construction but unknown in psychopathology; its varieties can be defined only in relation to an actual legal code.

Legal norms usually rely on the assumption of the existence of *freedom* of human decision, and of responsibility for such decision. According to Knobloch (1965), the most frequent causes of lack of responsibility are: (*a*) mental sickness in the sense of a mental disturbance of fairly long duration, characterized by more or less typical onset, course and possible cessation; (*b*) chronic mental sickness without a specific beginning, course and progression (this category includes developmental disorders and retardations, psychopathies, oligophrenias, and some cases of deaf-muteness); (*c*) short-term mental disturbances (these are most often pathic affects or intoxications, severe cases of disturbed consciousness, episodic disturbances in the course of chronic nervous illnesses, mental disturbances after brain concussion, etc. See *Alcoholism; Child psychology; Criminality; Deficiency, mental; Mental defect; Psychopathy; Schizophrenia; Traits; Type.*

Bibliography: Blau, G. & Müller-Luckman, E.: Gerichtliche Psychologie. Neuwied, 1962. Ehrhardt, H. & Villinger, W.: Forensische und administrative Psychiatrie. In: Psychiatrie der Gegenwart, Vol. 2. Berne, 1961. Knobloch, F. & J.: Soudní psychiatrie pro právníky a lékare. Prague, 1965. Thomae, H. & Schmidt, E.: Psychologische Aspekte der Schuldfähigkeit. In: Undeutsch, U. (Ed.): Handbuch der Psychologie, Vol. 11. Göttingen, 1967.   *O.T.*

Restitution of psychological functions (*higher cortical*). The restitution of functions after brain damage (see *Brain pathology*) is one of the major problems of *neuropsychology* (q.v.). Traditional conceptions, according to which mental processes are functions of isolated sectors of the brain, led to the conclusion that since damaged nerve-cells of the cortex do not regenerate themselves, functions disturbed because of multiple brain damage are lost for ever and cannot be recovered (see *Localization*).

Clinical practice has shown, however, that functions disturbed because of brain damage can be restored or can redevelop. This phenomenon required an explanation, which was given by a series of papers in neurology and neuropathology during the last century. Multiple brain damage can lead to two main types of functional disturbance: the pathological center can put the cellular tissue in a temporary state of inactivity or disturb it irrevocably.

In the first case, the pathological condition leads to disturbance of the synaptic conductability of a stimulus; this disturbance is induced by biochemical changes, above all by a reduced secretion of acetylcholine (q.v.), which ensures the transmission of the stimulus to the synapse (see *Nervous system*); possibly a mechanism of the reflector inhibition (or inhibition caused by irradiation, q.v.) of functions in the damaged nervous tissue is also involved. Such a temporary inhibition can occur both in the cortical sectors which border directly on the center of the damage, and in the cortical areas situated well away from but connected to the center by the nervous system (for example the areas which are situated symmetrically with the center), or in the deeper subcortical formations. This temporary type of inhibition has been described as "diaschisis" by K. Monakov. To restore the temporarily inhibited function the synaptic connectability of the cells which exist in the condition of diaschisis must be restored. To this end substances can be used which overcome acetylcholine antagonists (cholinesterase, q.v.) and restore the active effect of acetylcholine. Such substances are eserine, prostigmine and galantamine, etc. Wartime experience has shown that the introduction of these substances into the bloodstream leads to the disinhibition of temporarily inhibited functions (e.g. of movement), while it has no influence on the functions disturbed by damage to the nerve cells. In the event of a unilateral hemiplegia, for example, produced because of an injury to the cortical motor area of the arm, the introduction of these substances restores the temporarily impaired motor functions of the leg but not of the arm. An essential role in the removal of inhibitory states is also played by the *exercise* of corresponding functions. This contributes to the reactivation of the uninjured but temporarily inhibited cells. In all these cases the disturbed function is restored to its earlier form.

The second kind of functional disturbance takes place because of destruction of the corresponding nervous apparatus (or area of the cerebral cortex). In these cases also, however, the disturbed functions can be restored. This is explained by the fact that the highest cortical functions (perception, behavior, speech, writing, calculation, etc.), are never a function of one isolated, limited sector of the brain (see *Localization*). Accordingly, diffuse brain damage disturbs only one of the conditions necessary for the normal working of the whole functional system (e.g. the synthesis of stimuli in one whole simultaneous or successive structure, spatial and temporary analysis and synthesis, the entire tone of the cortex, etc.) and yet leads secondarily to the failure of the whole system. Such an explanation of a disturbance to the highest cortical functions in the event of local damage of the brain shows why the disturbed functions can be restored and allows a means of restoration. In this sense a restoration of the disturbed functions can be achieved only through the functional reconstruction of the system, in other words the disturbed member of the functional system must be replaced by one of the uninjured members. Training for the restoration of psychological functions of patients with diffuse brain injuries is based on this principle.

The restoration of speech or writing ability to a patient with damage to the cortical area (see *Broca's area*) serves as an example of such training. Here the disturbed speech—(phonematic) hearing is replaced by *visual* or *kinesthetic analysis* of perceived speech. A further example would be the restoration of spatial orientation, disturbed because of injury to the parietal-occipital sector of the cortex, by successive verbal-logical analysis of spatial relations.

The training, whose object is to restore functions lost because of injuries to different parts of the brain, must be differentiated and backed up by a special program, which begins with a neuropsychological analysis of the disturbance.

Bibliography: Bethe, A.: Plastizität und Zentrumlehre. In: **Bethe, A.** (Ed.): Handbuch der normalen und pathologischen Physiologie. Vol. 15. Berlin, 1931. **Monakow, C. von:** Lokalization im Grosshirn und der Abbau der Funktionen durch lokale Herde. Wiesbaden, 1914. **Goldstein, K.:** Aftereffects of brain injuries in war. New York, 1942. **Luria, A. R.:** Restoration of functions after brain trauma. Oxford, 1963. **Id.** *et al.* Restoration of higher cortical functions following brain damage. In: **Vinken, P. J. & Bruyn, G. W.** (Eds.): Handbook of clinical neurology. Amsterdam, Vol. 3. 368–433. *A. R. Luria*

Restorff effect. If the data of a learning series differ materially, those items which contrast categorically with the majority of others, are retained better than those which resemble categorically most of the others.

Bibliography: Restorff, H. Von: Analyse von Vorgängen im Spurenfeld: 1. Uber die Wirkung von Bereichsbildung im Spurenfeld. Psychol. Forsch., 1933, *18*, 299–342. *E.H.*

Resultant. The sum of adjusted quantities or vectors (q.v.).

Resumption of interrupted actions. A phenomenon studied by M. Ovsiankina (1928), a pupil of Lewin's, and traced to a "quasineed", characterizable in dynamic terms as a *tension system* (q.v.). The intensity of the need to resume depends, *inter alia*, on the structure of the behavior, on the stage in which it is broken off, and on the attitudes of the subject.

See *Lewin; Need; Attitude; Achievement level.* *J.M.D.*

Retardation. Delayed development. "Retardation" is mainly applied to measuring the differences between intellectual ability and the statistical age-norm (see *Intelligence*). Some authors also assess temporary "developmental inhibitions" and disharmonious lapses in the physical sphere as "retardation". The concept implies nothing concerning the origins of retardation: for example emotional disturbances, conditions of upbringing, cultural deprivation, sensory and motor handicaps, illnesses, inherited factors, damage to parts of the brain. See *Autism; Deficiency, Mental; Mental defect.*

Bibliography: **Heber, R.:** Manual of terminology and classification in mental retardation. Amer. J. ment. Defic. Monograph. Suppl., 1959, *64,* No. 2. **Zigler, E.:** Mental retardation: Current issues and approaches. In: **Hoffman, M. L. & L. W.:** Child development research, Vol. 2. New York, 1966, 107–68. *H.M.*

Retention. In contrast to forgetting, "what remains in the memory". Retention, according to R. S. Woodworth and H. Schlosberg, is one form of the four processes of memory: memorizing, retention, recall, and recognition. A distinction is also made between immediate retention (for seconds or at most minutes) and memory (q.v.) (for hours and years). (See *Memory; Reminiscence*).
H.-J.A.

Retention curve. A graphic representation of retention (see *Learning; Memory; Reminiscence*): e.g. the relative frequency of correct reproductions of learned items after variously long intervals from the point of attainment of the learning criterion. Retention R at any point in time T is usually expressed by an exponential function ($R = a \cdot e^{-bt}$ for $t > 0$). The intensity of the falling off b is dependent

on the learning process investigated (verbal, motor), on the kind of retention measurement (e.g. reproduction, recognition), and the kind of learning assignment (meaningful, nonsense) and the learning conditions (Bahrick, 1964). In conditioned learning, the drop in the intensity of learned response with time is characterized not as forgetting but as extinction. The speed of extinction depends on the number of unconditioned (or unrewarded) rehearsals after the attainment of the learning criterion or on the length of the interval of time in which there was no further response (latent extinction). A learned behavior can often be elicited after its extinction. (See *Conditioning, classical and operant*). Forgetting is mainly explained in that old and new associations suppress the learned associations (interference theory; see *Memory; Inhibition*).

Bibliography: **Bahrick, H. P.:** Retention curves: facts or artifacts? Psychol. Bull., 1964, *61,* 188–94. **Kintsch, W.:** Learning, memory, and conceptual processes. New York, 1970. *M. Hofer*

Reticular activating system (abb. RAS). A term introduced in 1958 by W. H. Magoun (USA) and G. Maruzzi (Italy) for the *formatio reticularis* or reticular formation (q.v.). Magoun and Maruzzi discovered its arousal function: sensory nerve bundles from parts of the body supply the cortex (q.v.) directly, but also send branches to the formation which, when there is excitation, selectively dispatch signals to the cortex. The signals reaching the cortex from the formation have an "arousal function"; they produce the activation of the brain which does not take place by direct excitation of the cortex. The formation continues to maintain the aroused state (attention) of the cortex. Different results show that it is probable that the RAS plays some part in mental disturbances. The RAS inhibits and promotes not only sensory but motor impulses, it modifies voluntary and reflex movements which—when regulated by the cortex alone—are jerky and convulsive. See *Arousal.*   *H.W.*

Retina. The inner layer of the eye's wall. The non-percipient portion (*pars caeca retinae*) in the area of the ciliary body (see *Lens*); it is clearly divided from the remaining, far bigger percipient area (*pars optica retinae*) by a jagged line (*ora serrata*). The retina is normally located apart from the pigment epithelium and is close to the vitreous humour. The retina is fixed only at the blind spot (q.v.) (the optic nerve papilla) and at the *ora serrata*. The pale reddish colour of the retina is caused by visual purple (rhodopsin). Near the posterior ocular pole lie the blind spot (q.v.) and the *macula lutea* (or yellow spot) whose centers are about 4 mm. from each other.

Anatomically, the retina has ten layers. But it is more practical to give the distribution according to function: (*a*) pigment epithelium; (*b*) rods and cones; (first neuron); (*c*) bipolar ganglionic cells (second neuron), or *ganglion retinae*; (*d*) large ganglionic cells (third neuron) or *ganglion fasciculi optici* (working from the outer to the inner layers). Between these extends the glia membrane (supporting membrane). The light must first penetrate a part of the retinal layers until it reaches the light-sensitive rods and cones. The retina originates developmentally from a protrusion of the brain.

In the retina, stimuli (light is a physiological stimulus) are changed by chemical reaction into nervous impulses, which are then conducted in the *fasciculus opticus* to the optic centers. The retina exhibits an electronic potential, which in the healthy eye can be detected as an electroretinogram.

With the aid of an ophthalmoscope (H. von Helmholtz) the vessels of the retina (arteries and veins) may be clearly distinguished from the *macula lutea* (q.v.), the blind spot and the rest of the retina, and pathological variations

from the physiological image. The size of the retinal image depends on the type of ophthalmoscope. An upright and inverted representation can be obtained.   *R.R.*

Retroactive inhibition. See *Memory.*

Retrocognition. A form of ESP (q.v.) in which the target (q.v.) is some past event. Retrocognitive hit (q.v.) = hit with backward temporal displacement. Knowledge about the past that does not depend on either memory or inference.   *J.B.*

Retrograde amnesia. Amnesia for memories of events which occurred before the cause of that amnesia. For example retrograde amnesia can occur for events which led up to an accident involving head injury, one of the results of which is the amnesia.   *R.H.*

Reversibility; reversible figures. A class of figures for which there is more than one perceptual interpretation. In these circumstances, rather than all interpretations being seen simultaneously, a single interpretation is seen which abruptly gives way to some other. These changes in interpretation are called reversals. One class of reversible figures includes the *Necker cube* (q.v.) and the *Schröder staircase* (q.v.) for which there are two three-dimensional interpretations of two-dimensional representations. Another class of reversible figure includes *Rubin's figure* (q.v.) in which reversal involves an alteration in which part is seen as *figure* and part is seen as *ground.*   *C.D.F.*

Reversible lenses. See *Stratton's experiment.*

Reversion. An inner defense (q.v.) mechanism in which, apparently because of the impossibility, or fear of a specific form, of motive satisfaction, its opposite is sought. Insofar as reversion is not reaction formation, it is considered as more vaguely defined and less worthy of interpretation than other defense mechanisms. *W.T.*

Reward. In behaviorism, reward and reinforcement (q.v.) are frequently used as synonyms. A *reward* has a motivating function. In human individuals it increases in addition the feeling of self-esteem and social status. Its efficacy depends on its size, its frequency, the time lapse between it and previous behavior as well as on various personality variables. See *Punishment.*

Bibliography: Skinner, B. F.: Science and human behavior. New York, 1958. *B.L.*

Rhathymia. A dimension of temperament developed by Guilford (1959) based on factor analysis and represented by the Rhathymia scale of the Guilford-Zimmerman temperament survey (1947). Rhathymia manifests itself in an unconcerned, carefree merry attitude; antipole: prudent seriousness and conscientiousness. Rhathymia correlates closely with Eysenck's extraversion/introversion dimension. See *Traits; Type.*

Bibliography: Guilford, J. P.: Personality. New York, 1959. *H.H.*

Rheobase and chronaxie. Units of measurement in testing peripheral nerve functions. Electrode stimuli are applied over the nervous regions or put right into the nerve and the latter is stimulated by electrical rectangular impulses of varying duration (0·01–8 msec.) and intensity. For the stimulus threshold (the smallest stimulus that produces any excitement, e.g. a movement of the appropriate muscle) the Nernst rule applies: $I . t =$ constant. This relation is called the stimulus time span curve and is different for every individual nerve. To describe this function the smallest impulse current strength to have an effect over the desired rectangular impulse duration is referred to as *rheobase* and the smallest rectangular stimulus duration to effect a stimulus at double rheobase is referred to as "chronaxie". *E.D.*

Rhine, Joseph Banks. B. 29/9/1895 in Tuniata, Pennsylvania. Director of the "Foundation for Research on the Nature of Man" (Durham, N.C.). 1928: instructor in philosophy and psychology; 1930: assistant Professor; 1934: associate Professor; 1937 to 1950: full Professor and director of the parapsychology laboratory at Duke University. In 1937 founded (with W. McDougall's support) the *Journal of Parapsychology.*

Rhine has carried out research into the most varied areas of parapsychology. In 1928 he began, under McDougall's direction, to investigate the hypothesis of life after death, and until 1940 was principally concerned with the investigation of clairvoyance (q.v.). Subsequently he intensified his interest in questions of precognition (foreknowledge) and psychokinesis (q.v.) and (from 1945) problems of telepathy (q.v.). In order to explain paranormal phenomena, Rhine postulates a psychic(al) function (psi-function, q.v.), which is supposed to operate outside physical laws proper, and whose mode of operation he has tried to investigate, with—since 1950—animal experiments.

Main works: Extra-sensory perception. Boston, 1934. Extra-sensory perception after 60 years. Boston, 1940; New York, [2]1960 (with others). The reach of the mind. New York, 1947. Parapsychology: from Duke to FRNM. New York, 1965. Parapsychology today. New York, 1968 (with others). *W.W.*

Rhodopsin. Also known as erythropsin or visual purple. Red-violet coloring material of the rods (q.v.) which above all determines the red colour of the back of the eye. This substance is a chromoproteid, i.e., the combination of the protein (albumin) "opsin" with the (added non-protein) group "neoretinal b". Neoretinal b is chemically "11 cis retinal" which derives stereoisomerically from "all-trans-retinal", the vitamin A aldehyde. Opsin only induces retinal in cis-form to combine and to form rhodopsin with it. When this combination is exposed to the light then c-trans-configuration of the retina takes place; the resulting trans-retinal is released from the opsin; stereo-configuration, dependent on the quantities of light, and the separation have the following effect: (a) membrane depolarization together with stimulus of the rods, (b) the visual purple pales to visual white. Lack of vitamin A prejudices regeneration in rhodopsin and consequently leads to hemeralopia (q.v.).
K.H.P.

Rhombencephalon. A general term which embraces the *metencephalon* and *myelencephalon*. The metencephalon consists of the pons (q.v.) and cerebellum (q.v.). Higher up, the rhombencephalon adjoins the mesencephalon and lower down, the spinal cord. The term indicates an evolutionary process. Initially, at the cerebral end of the neural duct, there are two main sections, the prosencephalon and the rhombencephalon, which then become more differentiated.
Bibliography: Clara, M.: Entwicklungsgeschichte des Menschen. Leipzig, 1966.   *G.A.*

Rhythm. 1. In general the time structure of a series where there is change. **2.** In biological systems especially the natural (autonomous) time structure of some functional operation (e.g. bioelectrical processes in the conduction of excitation, pulse frequency, rate of breathing, body movements, menstruation cycle,

fluctuations of attention). Biological rhythms can be partly explained by the adaptation which is necessary for life of the biological functional operations to rhythmic processes in the physical environment (inter alia fluctuations of ultra-violet irradiation during the year, change of light intensities during the day and—especially for man—also in the social environment (certain time conventions); in part they represent the homeostatically regulated utilization of organ capacities within their natural limits, i.e. in general the constant alternation of work and rest, of *ergotropic* and *trophotropic* functional proclivities. Rhythmic processes form the basis of performances with a time orientation (sense of time, "biological clock"; time indicator, time consciousness; (see *Time*). For arranging work it is especially advisable to take into account the fluctuations in daily rhythm of the "physiological readiness for work" (O. Graf, circadian rhythms). Rhythm disturbances and desynchronization of different internal and external rhythms represent an important area in diagnostic activity.   *J.N.*

Ribonucleic acid(s). I. (RNA) Found in nucleic protein substances as an important component of chromosomes (q.v.) and acts as a carrier of inherited characteristics to the amino acid sequences of specific proteins. Like desoxyribonucleic acid (DNA) it consists of a nucleic acid, a sugar (ribosis), phosphoric acid and one of the four nucleic bases: *adenin, guanin, cytosin* or *uracil*. (See *Desoxyribonucleic acid*.)   *E.D.*

II. High molecular substances (nucleic acids) present in all cells (mainly cytoplasm), also in viruses and bacteria. Ribonucleic acid is of fundamental importance for protein synthesis. At least three kinds are to be distinguished: *ribosomal* RNA (rRNA) which represents about 80–90% of cell RNA, *messenger* RNA (mRNA) and *transfer* RNA (tRNA). The three RNAs form different substances in protein synthesis. mRNA forms the first substance in which it supplies to rRNA the information deposited in desoxyribonucleic acid (DNA) for proteinsynthesis. tRNA places the specific amino acid requested at disposal for the formation of protein. Since McConnell's experiments with planaria, RNA has occupied a central position in biochemical research. RNA extracted from the brains of conditioned animals and injected into the brain of an unsophisticated animal leads to behavior which corresponds to that of the trained animal, (see *Psychopharmacology*). Transfers of brain extracts have been carried out on many other animals besides planaria (goldfish, rats, mice, etc.). Many of these experiments have proved negative, but those which took place under carefully controlled conditions were largely positive. Experiments with the supply of yeast RNA produced varying results. RNA was used by Hyden as a dependent variable, especially through the working group. From these experiments it emerged that learning (q.v.) leads to increased RNA synthesis (see *Memory*). Disturbance of RNA synthesis by antibiotics (q.v.) prevents the retention of learning material. It has not hitherto been made clear which of the following hypotheses regarding the meaning of RNA is to be accepted: (*a*) RNA has a special significance beyond the normal protein synthesis in respect of learning and its retention; (*b*) RNA has a special significance in respect of learning and its retention only as a link; (*c*) RNA has a special role only in learning and not in retention; (*d*) RNA has no special role in learning or its retention.

Bibliography: Cantoni, G. L. & Davies, D. R.: Procedures in nucleic acid research. New York, 1966. **Corning, W. C. & Ratner, S. C.:** Chemistry of learning. New York, 1967. **Domagk, G. F. & Zippel, H. P.:** Biochemie der Gedächtnisspeicherung. Naturwiss., 1970, *57*, 152–62. **Gaito, J.:** Molecular psychobiology. Springfield, 1966. **Gaito, J. M.:** Macromolecules and learning. In: **Bourne, J. H.** (Ed.): The structure and function of nervous tissues. New York, 1969. **Glassman, E.:** The biochemistry of learning: an evaluation of the role of RNA and protein. Ann. Rev. Biochem., 1969, *38*, 605–46. **Id.:** The biochemistry of learning: an evaluation of the role of RNA and protein. Ann. Rev. Biochem., 1969, *38*, 605–46. **Walas, O.** (Ed.): Molecular basis of some aspects of mental academy. London, 1966.   *W.J.*

Ribot's law. Formulated by the French psychologist Ribot (1839–1916) (q.v.): the loss of memorized material which occurs in old age, or when there are organic or traumatic disturbances of memory (q.v.), takes place in an order inverse to that in which it was accumulated: material memorized at a later date, such as experiences, kinds of behavior, learning material, is the first to be lost, and the last is material acquired at an (ontogenetically) early date (e.g. childhood memories) and primitive emotions.

Bibliography: Ribot, T.: Les maladies de la mémoire. Paris, 1881.   *F.C.S.*

Ribot, Théodule. B. 18/12/1839 in Guingamp; d. 9/12/1916 in Paris. From 1889, professor of experimental psychology at the Collège de France in Paris. Ribot is considered to be the founder of French psychology. He was the first scholar in France who endeavored to detach psychology from philosophy and to introduce the principles of experimental psychology. In his two early monographs *La psychologie anglaise contemporaine* (1870) and *La psychologie allemande contemporaine* (1879) (Eng. trans.: English psychology. London, 1873. German psychology of today. New York & London, 1886), he brought to the notice of his fellow countrymen English associationism and German experimental psychology as it was at the time of Wundt (q.v.). Among those who studied under him were Pierre Janet (q.v.), his successor at the Collége de France, and Georges Dumas.

Although Ribot introduced experimental psychology into France, he was not an experimental psychologist in the same sense as Wundt. He was fundamentally a pure theorist who neither had a psychological laboratory nor supported his theories with experimental investigations. Even his publications in his main field of work, psychopathology, were scarcely based on clinical experience, so that he had to admit to Janet that he had taught psychopathology without having seen the patient (Misiak & Sexton, 1966).

His works dealt on the one hand with pathological disorders of memory (q.v.) (*Les maladies de la mémoire*, 1881), of volition (*Les maladies de la volonté*, 1883), and of personality (q.v.) (*Les maladies de la personnalité*, 1885). Ribot sought to show that these abnormalities were due to disturbances of cerebral function. In his later publications he was more concerned with the psychology of affective and emotional states (*Psychologie des sentiments*, 1896. *La logique des sentiments*, 1905. *Essai sur les passions*, 1907. *Problèmes de psychologie affective*, 1910).

Bibliography: **Misiak, H. & Sexton, U. S.:** History of psychology: an overview. New York, 1966. *W.W.*

Riemann(ian) space. After the mathematician B. Riemann (1826–66): the curved space of Riemannian geometry (see *Linear space*). The concept of n-dimensional, Riemannian space occupies a central position in the binocular vision theory of R. K. Luneburg (1903–49). Luneberg's theory concerns the prerequisites for scaling of subjectively perceived spatial relations (see *Space perception*). For this purpose, he distinguishes between a physical space (with a Euclidian geometrical structure) and a visual space (with a Riemannian geometrical structure). On the basis of this theory a better explanation is possible of some phenomena in the perception of spatial relations (e.g. Hillebrand's alley, q.v.).

Bibliography: **Luneburg, R. K.:** Mathematical analysis of binocular vision. Princeton, 1947. **Raschewski, P. K.:** Riemannsche Geometrie und Tensoranalysis. *F.Ma.*

Right associates procedure (syn. *Paired associates; Retained members method*). A method for testing the retention of material presented in pairs during the learning phase. One item (e.g. a word) acts as stimulus, the other as response. S. has to give the right response on re-presentation of the stimulus item. See *Memory; Reminiscence.* *E.H.*

Rigidity. Inappropriate adherence to a habit, set, or action when objective conditions demand change. The word is ambiguous, and research has revealed different types of rigidity. For example, Cattell and Tiner (1949), with seventeen tests from past studies, found two factors: dispositional rigidity (persistence of a response through inability to shift to another), and ideational inertia (inability to give up perceptual or thought habits). Dispositional rigidity is identified with perseveration (mental inertia), a term introduced by Neisser (1894) and also called "secondary factor" (Wiersma, 1906). Guilford (1957) distinguishes adaptive flexibility (ability to alter a set with changing problems) from spontaneous flexibility (diversity of ideas in unstructured situations). In brain injury, Goldstein (1943) differentiates primary rigidity (inability to change set) from secondary rigidity (in a too difficult task S. sticks to a previous task). Rokeach (1960) distinguishes dogmatic thinking (resistance to changing single beliefs) from rigid thinking (resistance to change of a system of beliefs or set).

Tests of rigidity include Einstellung water jar problems (Zener & Duncker, 1920; Luchins, 1942); fluctuations of Necker cube (McDougall, 1929); Gottschaldt's embedded figures; card sorting; and pencil and paper tests (e.g. Gough-Sanford scale, 1952). Performances on such tests and tasks may provide operational definitions of rigidity. The Californian authoritarianism scale (F-scale) has been used as a measure of personality rigidity. Both semantic and empirical problems in this field are numerous.

Bibliography: Cattell, R. B. & Tiner, L. G.: The varieties of structural rigidity. J. Personal. 1949, *17*, 321–41. Chown, S. M.: Rigidity—a flexible concept. Psychol. Bull. 1959, *56:3*, 195–223. Rokeach, M.: The open and closed mind. New York, 1960.

P. McKellar

Rigor. Increase of muscular tonus; "wax-like" stiffness. It persists from the beginning to the end of the examination when movement is passive. It is a symptom of diseases of the extrapyramidal system, especially in Parkinsonism (q.v.) and Parkinson's disease (q.v.).   *H.W.*

Ring sector illusion. An illusion produced by color contrast. A ring of uniform grey lies on a field which is half red and half green. If the boundary between red and green is covered by a thin strip then the two halves of the ring appear to be different shades because of contrast with the surrounding colours.

C.D.F.

Risk taking. Despite the extensive research on risk-taking behavior carried out over approximately the past fifteen years, the construct itself is quite elusive and, in fact, defies explicit definition. Indeed, Kogan and Wallach (1967) describe risk-taking behavior on the basis of the kinds of situations in which it is likely to be elicited. For those authors, behavior reflective of risk-taking dispositions occurs in "situations where there is a desirable goal and a lack of certainty that it can be attained. The situation may take the form of requiring a choice between more and less desirable goals, with the former having a lower probability of attainment than the latter. A further possible, but not necessary, characteristic of such situations is the threat of negative consequences for failure so that the individual at the postdecisional stage might find himself worse off than he was before he made the decision" (p. 115). The following sections consider the various kinds of influences impinging upon the risk-taking domain. These include task and situational factors, personal characteristics, and influences deriving from group interaction.

1. *Task and Situational Influences.* Decision-making situations vary in the degree to which their outcomes involve aspects of chance and skill.

Where tasks of a chance nature are concerned—gambling decisions in this case—the most sophisticated work has been carried out by Slovic and his associates. On the basis of several empirical studies, Slovic & Lichtenstein (1968) reinterpret the findings on gambling choices in terms of two fundamental processes: (*a*) the relative importance that subjects assign to the various probability and pay-off components of a bet, and (*b*) limitations on information-processing capacities which lead the decision-maker to focus on particular components of a bet to the exclusion of other components.

Comparisons of decision making in chance and skill contexts has been a major concern of the British psychologist John Cohen (e.g. 1960). In decision-making situations offering equiprobable chance vs. skill alternatives, subjects tend to prefer the latter. Presumably, equal objective probabilities are not subjectively equal, subjects apparently biasing probabilities upward when they believe they have control over outcomes.

Unlike bets in which all the necessary information is available to the subject, much decision making involves the accumulation of additional information. The amount of information sought will be a function of the gravity of the decision (i.e. the nature of the positive or negative outcomes contingent upon it), the cost of obtaining the information, and the consistency of the information being gathered (Irwin & Smith, 1957). Studies of this kind are highly relevant to risk taking, for individuals must decide when a decision is most optimal in the face of progressively increasing costs and decreasing value of the incentive. Wide individual variation reflective of differences in risk-taking dispositions seems to be a common feature of information-seeking activity (e.g. Lanzetta & Kanareff, 1962).

A central issue in the study of risk taking concerns the relative predominance of gain maximization and loss minimization in arriving at decisions. Rettig & Rawson (1963), working with hypothetical ethical dilemmas, have shown that severity of censure—if apprehended in an unethical act—has greater influence than potential gain in the prediction and actual occurrence of unethical ("risky") behavior. Comparable findings in other decision contexts, some involving monetary gain and loss (e.g., Atthowe, 1960), reinforce the conclusion that university students tend toward conservatism in decision making.

In regard to the issue of prior gains and losses on subsequent decisions, contrary to Edwards' (1962) claim that previous outcomes have negligible impact, investigators working in both naturalistic and laboratory contexts have obtained sequential effects. McGlothlin (1956) in a study of race-track betting found that prior losses facilitated risk taking, whereas prior winnings enhanced conservatism. Kogan and Wallach (1964) obtained similar results in the laboratory.

Comparisons of risk taking in naturalistic and laboratory contexts point to higher risk levels in the former. Differences can be traced to competitive elements in the naturalistic situation, for the introduction of competition in the laboratory (Preston & Baratta, 1948) yields risk levels highly similar to those obtained in field settings.

2. *Effect of Personal Characteristics.* Sex, age and social-class differences in risk taking have been reported. Sex differences indicative of greater risk taking in males have been found for children (e.g. Kass, 1964), but such differences appear to be attenuated in adulthood (Kogan & Wallach, 1964). Less is known about age differences, for psychologists have

not studied risk taking across the entire life span. Wallach & Kogan (1961) obtained higher risk levels in university students relative to a gerontological sample of comparable education. Comparisons of subjects differing in social class—university students vs. enlisted military personnel—have indicated stronger risk-taking dispositions in the latter group (Scodel, Ratoosh & Minas, 1959).

The bulk of research on personality and motivational correlates of risk taking has been focused on the achievement motive (e.g. Atkinson, 1957). It must be noted that this work concerns the development of a theory of achievement motivation (q.v.), not a theory of risk taking as such, and accordingly will not be treated here.

Central to the psychology of risk taking is the issue of its generality vs. specificity. An initial empirical attack on this "convergent validation" issue by Slovic (1962) revealed little generality across risk-taking measures. A subsequent large-scale study devoted to the same issue by Kogan & Wallach (1964) also failed to show much generality. The latter authors, however, by resorting to a moderator variable analysis, were able to demonstrate generality for some individuals and specificity for others. Generality was most typical of those "motivationally disturbed" subjects who were highly test anxious and defensive. In contrast, subjects low in test anxiety and defensiveness manifested a high degree of specificity, in the sense that risk-taking levels were not constant across different decision situations. The Kogan-Wallach research also offers evidence for maladaptive irrationality in the subgroup strongest in "motivational disturbance"—for example, adhering to a risky strategy despite a high rate of failure.

3. *Risk Taking and Interaction in Groups.* A stable and oft-cited social-psychological phenomenon—the "risky-shift effect"—has generated a great deal of research and theoretical controversy over the past decade. The effect states that group interaction has a

risk-enhancing influence on prior individual decisions. This shift toward risk in groups has now been demonstrated in a variety of decision contexts and in numerous countries, though it should be noted that cautious shifts sometimes occur.

Various interpretations of the "risky-shift effect" have been advanced: (a) diffusion of responsibility: group influenced decisions are more risky because the blame for failure of a risky choice will not fall upon a single person but rather will be diffused across the members of a group (e.g. Wallach & Kogan, 1965); (b) the risk-taker as group leader—groups become more risky because leaders are more inclined to take risks and they persuade the other group members to follow that course (e.g. Hoyt & Stoner, 1968); (c) the familiarization explanation—thorough individual study of the decision situations produces shifts toward risk, and hence the risky-shift effect is not truly a group phenomenon (e.g. Bateson, 1966); (d) risk as a cultural value—individuals in Western society value risk more highly than caution and believe that they are no less risky than their peers, but discover in the group context that some of their peers are more risky, thereby offering a rationale for shifts toward greater risk.

The final interpretation listed above, first advanced by Brown (1965), has gained the greatest acceptance in part because it has been able to account for both risky and cautious shifts in groups (e.g., Stoner, 1968). A review of the "risky-shift" literature is contained in Kogan & Wallach (1967), and a more up-to-date review in Dion, Baron, & Miller (1971).

Bibliography: Atkinson, J. W.: Motivational determinants of risk-taking behavior. Psychol. Rev., 1957, *64*, 359–72. Atthowe, J. M.: Types of conflict and their resolution: A reinterpretation. J. exp. Psychol., 1960, *59*, 1–9. Bateson, N.: Familiarization, group discussion, and risk taking. J. exp. soc. Psychol., 1966, *2*, 119–29. Brown, R.: Social psychology. New York, 1965. Cohen, J.: Chance, skill, and luck. Baltimore, 1960. Dion, K. L.. Baron, R. S. & Miller, N.: Why do groups make riskier decisions than individuals? In: Berkowitz, L. (Ed.): Advances in experimental social psychology, Vol. 5. New York & London, 1971. Edwards, W.: Subjective probabilities inferred from decisions. Psychol. Rev., 1962, *69*, 109–35. Hoyt, G. C. & Stoner, J. A. F.: Leadership and group decisions involving risk. J. exp. soc. Psychol., 1968, *4*, 275–84. Irwin, F. W. & Smith, W. A. S.: Value, cost, and information as determiners of decision. J. exp. Psychol., 1957, *54*, 229–32. Kass, N.: Risk in decision-making as a function of age, sex, and probability preference. Child Develpm., 1964, *35*, 577–82. Kogan, N. & Wallach, M. A.: Risk taking: A study in cognition and personality. New York, 1964. Id.: Risk taking as a function of the situation, the person, and the group. In: New directions in psychology, III. New York 1967, 111–278. Lanzetta, J. T. & Kanareff, V. T.: Information cost, amount of payoff, and level of aspiration as determinants of information seeking in decision making. Behav. Sci., 1962, *7*, 459–73. McGlothlin, W. H.: Stability of choices among uncertain alternatives. Amer. J. Psychol., 1956, *69*, 604–15. Preston, M. G. & Baratta, P.: An experimental study of the auction-value of an uncertain outcome. Amer. J. Psychol., 1948, *61*, 183–93. Rettig, S. & Rawson, H. E.: The risk hypothesis in predictive judgments of unethical behavior. J. abnorm. soc. Psychol., 1963, *66*, 243–8. Scodel, A., Ratoosh, P. & Minas, J. S.: Some personality correlates of decision making under conditions of risk. Behav. Sci., 1959, *4*, 19–28. Slovic, P.: Convergent validation of risk taking measures. J. abnorm. soc. Psychol., 1962, *65*, 68–71. Slovic, P. & Lichtenstein, S.: Relative importance of probabilities and payoffs in risk taking. J. exp. Psychol. Monogr., 1968, *78*, (No. 3, Part 2). Stoner, J. A. F.: Risky and cautious shifts in group decisions:The influence of widely held values. J. exp. soc. Psychol., 1968, *4*, 442–59. Wallach, M. A. & Kogan, N.: Aspects of judgment and decision-making: Interrelationships and changes with age. Behav. Sci., 1961, *6*, 23–36. Id.: The roles of information, discussion, and consensus in group risk taking. J. exp. soc. Psychol., 1965, *1*, 1–19.   *N. Kogan*

Ritualization (The formalization of instinctual acts.) The term was first used by Huxley to designate every change in a kind of behavior intended to improve signalling function. There are many possible causes: change of external stimuli, of motivation, of orientation components, of movement sequence, of co-ordination, intensity and rapidity of movements; striking characteristics of shape and color, etc. are formed. Wickler (1967) suggests the term *"semanticization"*. Semanticization *on the part of the sender* is the clarification of a signal, *on the part of the receiver* it is the improvement of sense-organs, releasing devices and learning mechanisms. When semanticization is positive, there is an improvement, when it is negative, there is a deterioration of communication until desemanticization takes place. There is both ontogenetic and phylogenetic semanticization. Ritualization in the old sense is phylogenetic semanticization on the part of the sender.

Bibliography: Tinbergen, N.: "Derived" activities, their causation, biological significance, origin and emancipation during evolution. Quart. Rev. Biol., 1952, *27*, 1–32. **Wickler, W.:** Vergleichende Verhaltensforschung und Phylogenetik. In: **Heberer, G.** (Ed.): Die Evolution der Organismen. Stuttgart, ³1967, 420–508.   *K.Fi.*

Roborants. A rarely used synonym for *stimulants* (q.v.) or neurodynamic substances (q.v.).

Rods. Elongated elements in the retina (q.v.), sensitive to light but not to color (see *Photoreceptors*), about 60μ long, with a diameter of about $1–2\mu$. They consist of an outer and an inner member, and can scarcely change their shape or their position (in the primates almost not at all). The rod fiber, with its nuclear swelling, is attached to the rod on the inside of the eyeball; together they form the rod cell, of which there are estimated to be approximately 120 million arranged round, not in, the *fovea centralis* (q.v.) in each eye; they increase in relative density toward the periphery of the retina. That their spatial breakdown power does not increase concurrently is connected with the fact that a larger number of rods are attached to a single nerve fiber at the periphery of the retina. Rods contain the light-sensitive pigmented material *rhodopsin* (q.v.) which helps to transform grey values (intensity degrees of

brightness) into membrane depolarizations of the rod cell analogous to stimulus intensity. In this process, approximately 10^3 stimulus intensity units (e.g. apostilb or lux) can be transmitted out of the total number of rods. The sensitivity of the rods is greater and their threshold is lower than those of the color-sensitive *cones*. When they are not functioning properly, e.g. because of a vitamin A deficiency, night blindness (see *Hemeralopia*) develops; physiologically, this is "central scotoma" (failure of the central field of vision), which always occurs when the light densities in the surrounding field necessary for stimulation of the rods are not reached, since the *fovea centralis* (q.v.) contains only cones (q.v.) but no rods. (See *Sense organs: the eye*.)

K.H.P.

Role. A term used mainly in social psychology, where it occurs in its principal sense of "social role". It has to do with the very essence of this area of psychology, which is in fact the meeting place of sociology and psychology, since it implies both socially determined individual behaviors and social models defined and practiced by actual individuals. Its acceptations are linked with the origin of the term and its historical development.

1. *Origin of the term.* Etymologically, the term "role", derived from the medieval Latin word *"rotulus"* (Latin *"rota"* = wheel), signifies on the one hand a rolled-up script, and on the other hand the lines an actor recites in a theater. From the eleventh century, the term *"rôle"* has been used in French in the sense of "social function", or "profession".

Here we already have the model (and interpretation of a model) of individual behavior and social function, but current usage adds other derived meanings: role as a —usually inauthentic—individual attitude ("mere role-playing!"), and rôle as the major aspect of an individual in a social context ("he plays a political rôle"). These different meanings of the term (dramatic, personal, social) reappear in small in its acceptations in social psychology; hence their diversity and complexity.

2. *History.* Before appearing under the actual term "role", the concept itself occurred intermittently in the human sciences, under various titles, in the USA and in France and Germany. In psychology, the notion was emphasized when man was considered as an individual in relation to another or the group. Often the "dramatic" aspect of the human individual, the distance between "being" and "appearance", or the importance of the other in the determination of self is underlined. Sociologists arrive at the concept from the basis of the function and task of the individual in the social group.

After this first stage, the term "role" was used systematically by G. H. Mead, who studied the processes of communication and founded them on "role-taking", i.e. on mental substitution for one's partner, and adoption of his attitude. Role-taking allows a forecast of another's actions so that one's attitude can adapt to them, but it can also reveal self as self appears to the other. The personality (q.v.) is formed in the course of a whole series of "role-takings", which allow a gradual integration of the roles presented by those surrounding the child. All those mental activities which depend on an inward flexion (such as reflection, introspection, and so on) are founded on such "role-taking". Role, as defined thus by G. H. Mead, is close to attitude (q.v.), and is located in an essentially horizontal and interpersonal dimension.

Linton studied roles in relation not only to other individuals but to the group. For Linton, the concept of role is connected with that of *status*, of social position within a particular system. Role is the actualization or dynamic aspect of status, or the conduct prescribed for individuals on the basis of their status.

Whereas Linton associates role with sociological concepts such as status, T. M. Newcomb locates it more exactly in the sociological sphere. For him the term ought strictly to denote the theoretical model which actual individuals translate more or less faithfully into their role behavior. If these models, associated with social positions, represent constraint for the individual, that is due to the agreement, or consensus, of individuals in the group who expect a specific behavior from all those with a given status.

J. L. Moreno considers role not only as a constraining model, but as deriving from the very spontaneity of the individual who creates and grounds it: in Moreno's work it appears with all its personal, dramatic and social implications, and in the perpetual melée of action.

Among the foremost theoreticians of role one might cite Parsons, who analyzes the notion in the social system (relations between individuals are structured by roles), and in the personality system (which can interiorize various roles).

3. *Definition.* The notion of role has been taken up by many authors, but their definitions are not unambiguous; they diverge significantly in regard to the following: (*a*) the aspect of psychosocial reality to which they apply, which is either the individual or the group, or the interaction itself; (*b*) their range: sometimes they comprise a very limited area (in one of his definitions, Linton suggests the practice of the rights and duties associated with status), and sometimes they designate all socially determined behaviors; (*c*) their level of abstraction: for some, role is a theoretical model directing from without the actual behaviors of an individual; for others, it is the observable actions themselves.

An additional difficulty is met in regard to the dramatic (or, more exactly, the psychological) connotations of the word. Among the diverse definitions available, certain general examples use "role" as an organized model of behaviors, relative to a certain position of the individual in an interactional whole. Several specific cases may be envisaged on this basis.

Social role: position becomes status; the model of behavior is defined by the consensus of group members and has a functional value for the group. *Dramatic role:* the position is provided by the play's theme: the model defining the actor's performance was created by the dramatist. *Personal role:* the individual determines his own position in relation to others, and acts in accordance with his own model of behavior—which he uses as a standard for intersubjective relations.

4. *Position of the concept.* The marginal position of this concept, located as it is between psychology and sociology, raises a number of problems. Is role a social function or the character assumed by the individual? What is the relation between social and personal role? between prescribed and actual role? between role and status? . . .

It seems useful to distinguish several perspectives in the study of the notion: the *sociological* standpoint of the model and of theoretical role; that of *interaction*, where social and personal determining factors influence role behavior; and the *psychological* perspectives of the personality which perceives and interprets roles, and can even interiorize them.

At present "role theory" comes increasingly under discussion; the term stands for more than one concept, and in fact a number of interconnected notions (such as *norm, model, status, consensus*) are grouped round about the concept of role. There have been some interesting attempts to apply a mathematical model to the theory. The notion of role offers the main link between anthropologists' and sociologists' analyses of group behavior and psychologists' and psychiatrists' analyses of individual motivation (Kluckhohn & Murray): this makes it a conceptual tool of value throughout the human sciences (anthropology, sociology and psychology).

Bibliography: Banton, M.: Roles: an introduction to the study of social relations. London, 1965. **Biddle, B. J.**: Role theory: concepts and research. New York, 1966. **Dahrendorf, R.**: Homo sociologicus: Ein Versuch zur Geschichte, Bedeutung und Kritik der Kategorie der sozialen Rolle. Kölner Z. Soziol. Soz.-psychol., 1958, *2*, 178–208; *3*, 345–78. **Gross, N., Mason, W. S. & McEachern, A. W.**: Explorations in role analysis. New York, 1958. **Linton, R.**: The cultural background of personality. New York, 1945. **Mead, G. H.**: Mind, self and society. Chicago, 1934. **Moreno, J. L.**: Who shall survive? A new approach to the problem of human interrelations. Washington, 1934. **Newcomb, T. M.**: Social psychology. New York, 1950. **Parsons, T.**: Essays in sociological theory, pure and applied. Glencoe, Ill., 1954. **Rocheblave-Spenlé, A. M.**: La notion de rôle en psychologie sociale. Paris, 1962. **Sader, M.**: Rollentheorie. In: **Graumann, C. F.** (Ed.): Handbuch der Psychol., Vol. 7, Göttingen, 1969, 204–31. **Sarbin, T. R.**: Role theory. In: **Lindzey, G.** (Ed.): Handbook of social psychology. New York, 1954, 223–66. *A. M. R-S*

Role conflict. Occurs when a person is faced, occasionally or constantly, with mutually contradictory and competing role expectations (q.v.) which result from his membership of several different groups, and make it difficult for him to behave in conformity with individual role expectations. *A.S.-M.*

Role expectations. Certain notions concerning the behavior of an individual occupying a *formally* or *informally* defined position in a group. A distinction is made between expectations involving (*a*) *prescribed* and (*b*) *predicted* role behavior. Hence role expectations reflect (*a*) norms and aims of the group (q.v.) and describe how the occupant of a role (q.v.) has to behave in certain situations; and (*b*) refer to the probability that a role bearer will actually behave in a certain way in certain situations. Both kinds of role expectations refer both to expectations in respect to the behavior of other individuals in the group, and also to those in respect to the individual's own behavior in the group.

Bibliography: Thibaut, J. W. & Kelley, H. H.: The social psychology of groups. New York, 1959.

A.S.-M.

Role playing. 1. Adoption by an individual of any social *role* (q.v.). **2.** A form of children's play in which different social roles (q.v.) are imitated by the child, either in groups (e.g. cops and robbers) or individually. It is an important element in the socialization process of a society with a differentiated structure. Moreno uses role playing (1959) in psychodrama (q.v.) for psychotherapeutic purposes; by changing roles, the patient learns to recognize the motivation of the other actors, and abreacts his emotions cathartically.   *W.Sch.*

Role theory. Sarbin (1954) considers role theory to be an interdisciplinary theory involving cultural anthropology, sociology and psychology. Its aim is to examine human behavior or social interactions on a relatively complex level, and it consists of pronouncements about the combination of the concepts of "role" (q.v.) "position" as a system of role expectations with and "self". A survey of the work so far done in the field of social interaction which uses role concepts shows, however, that there is no system of postulates, which might satisfy the conditions for a theory (Sader, 1969).

Bibliography: Sarbin, T. R.: Role theory. In: **Lindzey, G.** (Ed.): Handbook of social psychology. Vol. 1. Cambridge, Mass., 1954, 223–58.   *A.S.-M.*

Romberg's sign. If an individual can stand still with his feet close together and his eyes open, but starts to sway when he closes his eyes, then he is said to exhibit Romberg's sign. It is a sign of *tabes dorsalis*, but may be seen also in other disorders of the posterior columns and in hysteria.   *J.P.*

Rorschach test. A technique developed by H. Rorschach (1922) which consists of ten plates or cards containing ink-blots, five of which are in black and white and the other five in colors; the subject has to interpret them freely. The interpretations are encoded with the aid of a system of signs according to localization, determination by form, color, movement, etc., frequency and content; they are then evaluated with a projection hypothesis to obtain a personality assessment (see *Projective techniques*). There are a number of parallel forms (q.v.) and modifications by S. Behn, C. Drey-Fuchs, H. Zulliger, M. R. Harrower & M. E. Steiner, W. H. Holtzman, etc.

Bibliography: Klopfer, B. *et al.*: Developments in the Rorschach technique, Vols. 1 & 2. Yonkers on Hudson, 1954/1956. **Rorschach, H.**: Psychodiagnostics. Berne, 1942. **Spitznagel, A. & Vogel, H.**: Formdeuteverfahren. In: Heiss, R. (Ed.): Handbuch der Psychologie, Vol. 6. Göttingen, ³1966, 556–634.   *H.H.*

Rotation. A term for the analytical or graphic transformation of a factor matrix with the object of interpreting the content of the extracted factors. The rotation criterion most commonly used is that of L. L. Thurstone's simple structure. It requires the factors to be rotated so that on or near them are the greatest possible number of end-points of characteristic vectors. In graphic (visual) rotation this is done by subjective evaluation of the factor structure, in analytical rotation by the mathematical definition of maximum or minimum optimal values. Rotation methods can be subdivided, according to the angle made by the factors with one another, into orthogonal and oblique. See *Factor analysis*.   *G.Mi.*

Rotation tachistoscope. A device for momentary presentation of visual stimuli. In contrast to the tachistoscope (q.v.) proper, a perforated rotating disc is used in this version in order to elicit multiple visual impressions at predetermined intervals.   *F.Ma.*

R-p diagram. Traxel's graphic presentation of the findings of threshold tests in psychophysics (q.v.). The diagram represents the distribution of categories of judgment (e.g. perceived/not perceived). The stimuli values (Ger. *Reiz* = stimulus = R) appear on the abscissa, and the frequencies of judgments (p values) on the ordinate. The diagram allows the compensation of random deviations and enables one to estimate the relative frequency of judgments for all other stimulus intensities between the presented stages.

F.Ma.

R-R relation. An association between two response (reaction) events such that the first response represents one of the conditions for the second response.

Rubin's figure. Rubin constructed many figures which showed ambiguity as to which part of the diagram was figure and which part ground. He used these figures to investigate the factors which allow us to differentiate figure from ground in the things we normally perceive.

For diagram see *Figure-ground* in Vol. 1.

C.D.F.

Ruleg ("Rule" + "e.g."). A term used for the rule-example technique, a didactic programing strategy evolved by Evans, Glaser & Homme, which divides subject matter into rules and examples for instructional purposes. Incomplete examples and rules which have to be completed by the pupil himself, and others which are expressed negatively, are formula-ted. Each learning step contains either one element (a rule or example), or a combination of two or three elements. See *Instructional technology.*

Bibliography: Evans, J. L., Glaser, R. & Homme, L.: The RULEG system for the construction of programmed verbal learning sequences. J. Educ. Res., 1962, *55*, 515–20. **Glaser, R.:** Teaching machines and programmed learning, Vol. II. Washington, 1965.

H.I.

Rutz typology. A typology of expression, based on body build, carriage and muscle tension, alleged to be applicable to artistic modes of representation, including speech: (*a*) the *spherical type:* a Caesarean type, sturdy frame, "easily excitable, hot-blooded, inconstant", compliant, mutable, dependent on outside influences; (*b*) the *parabolic type:* small, slim, "persevering and single-minded", not easily influenced, rational and orderly; (*c*) the *pyramidal type:* hard, "jerky, inflexible", cool, forcible; markedly narrow loins and angular waist.

Bibliography: Rutz, O.: Neue Wege zur Menschenkenntnis. Kampen, 1935. *W.K.*

Rybakoff's figures. Irregular geometrical figures that have to be divided in two so that the two segments can be formed into a square. Originally suggested by the Russian psychiatrist T. Rybakoff (1911) and developed further by various authors.

Bibliography: Meili, R.: Lehrbuch der psychologischen Diagnostik. Berne, [5]1965. **Id.:** Figuren von Rybakoff. Berne, 1956. *R.M.*

S

S. Abbreviation for *subject*.

Sadism. A sexual anomaly in which sexual satisfaction is achieved by inflicting pain. The intensity of the anomaly varies from those who are sexually aroused by pained facial expressions to those who achieve organismic relief only from blood, pain, torture and even death. Loosely, the term sadism is used also for pleasure in cruelty without obvious sexual arousal or satisfaction. The word originated from the eighteenth-century French Marquis de Sade who in his debauched life and writings presented examples of sadism as well as many other perversions (q.v.).

Followers of Freud find sadism to be normally associated with the second, or anal, (hence anal-sadistic) stage of infantile sexual development, when the cutting of teeth and strengthening of muscles allows the child to feel power and the ability to hurt others. This sadism can be destructive or possessive. It is said to be normally a "polymorphous perverse" phase that is superseded by the genital phase of sexual development.

Anne Broadhurst

Sadomasochism. A term used in sexual science, introduced by von Krafft-Ebing in 1907 and derived from the work of the Marquis de Sade (1740–1814) and the Austrian short-story writer Ritter von Sacher-Masoch (1836–95). Sadomasochism denotes in the first instance sexually deviant forms of behavior which occur relatively infrequently (e.g. by comparison with homosexuality, q.v.), incur relatively weak social sanctions and do not lead to the formation of sexual subcultures (Simon & Gagnon, 1970). Sadomasochism is reflected in pornography (films, photographs, sadomasochistic appliances and devices), and to some extent in art. The general meaning of the term can be defined through its two components: (*a*) sadism: sexual excitement and satisfaction obtained by a person who inflicts pain, maltreatment and humiliation on a partner. In a wider sense: obtaining pleasure by tormenting and humiliating others. Etiology: defense against (unconscious) fears of castration (q.v.); (*b*) masochism (q.v.): sexual excitement and satisfaction by experiencing and tolerating pain, torment and humiliation. In the wider sense: all pleasure obtained through pain, setbacks, disappointment or humiliation.

The characteristic component of these sexually deviant behavior patterns is the general process of sadistic, masochistic and usually sadomasochistic interaction; Freud (1924) and more recently Schorsch (1971) have drawn attention to the "play" aspect of this behavior. Phenomenologically the psychopathology of the sadomasochistic arrangement is characterized by the following typical features of the partners' roles: behavior resembles a game with specific rules and parts (e.g. master and slave) which are completely artificial (the roles can be adopted or abandoned at any time; there is no personal commitment and the "punishment" is administered without emotional involvement); the artificial aspect of the "role playing" always remains conscious. "The decisive factor is the fiction of complete submission or domination; the administration or suffering of physical pain is not an essential feature" (Schorsch, 1971). The decisive importance of fantasy (q.v.) in sadomasochism, sadism and masochism was recognized at an early date but different explanations have been given: psychiatrists and sexual scientists have sought an explanation in the "artificial character of these games" (Schorsch, 1971), while psychoanalysts have referred to the psychogenesis and psychodynamics of the personality. The importance of masochistic masturbation fantasies has also been highlighted, above all as a defense against the feelings of guilt and anxiety which block the "ultimate pleasure" (Fenichel, 1960, 358–65).

From the criminological angle, sadomasochism is a very rare phenomenon. The extensive surveys of sexual delinquents conducted by the Kinsey Institute have not shown a single "modern Sade" (Gebhard *et al.*, 1965, 134). Sadomasochism in the narrower sense, as the interdependence and interaction of sadists and masochists in an artificial game situation, is a sexual deviation which cannot generally be equated with sexual aggression, brutality in crimes of indecent assault or sadistic killing. Murder as an integrative component of sexual satisfaction (e.g. murder of a child) is estimated to be very rare (one in one million) by sexual scientists (Gebhard, 1965, 134). Sadistic or masochistic masturbation fantasies are most common—by comparison with other groups of sexual delinquents—in delinquents who commit their offenses with menace or violence (9–17%) (Gebhard *et al.*, 1965, 504).

Etiology: Freud considered sadism and masochism to be sexual perversions resulting from a fixation—conditioned by guilt feelings or fear of castration—on an originally normal, active or passive attitude to sexual experience and the sexual object, which is then exaggerated and becomes the sole center of interest. He assumed to begin with that masochism developed out of sadomasochism—through regression from the object to one's own ego and to pregenital stages of sexual development in early childhood—and not simply "an extension of sadism turned against the individual's own person, which takes the place of the sexual object". Freud subsequently revised his theory and differentiated between three main forms of masochism with complex hypotheses: (*a*) erogenous masochism = pleasure experienced through pain = a component of the residual "death wish" in the organism which has libidinal connotations and persists through all phases of libido development; erogenous masochism is the basis of the two other forms; (*b*) feminine masochism = expression of a "situation which is characteristic of femininity" and of the feminine "nature" (= "being castrated, used as the object of copulation or bearing children"); (*c*) moral masochism (the most important form) = satisfaction of an unconscious guilt feeling or need for punishment of the ego; moral masochism is generally subconscious and the relationship with sexuality (q.v.) is blurred; pain, humiliation, debasement or self-punishment become the important factor, regardless of whether they are inflicted by a loved person, by an individual toward whom the "victim" is indifferent, or by anonymous powers (affinity with asceticism). In severe cases of moral masochism in which no connection with sexuality is demonstrable and the person concerned torments himself unconsciously, there can be no question of sexual perversion (Fenichel, 1960).

The etiological concept of sadism, masochism and sadomasochism is closely related to the psychoanalytical theory of infantile sexuality, and the psychoanalytical concept of neurosis (summarized by Fenichel, 1960). In spite of the psychoanalytical theories, knowledge of the origins of sadism, masochism and sadomasochism is still very scanty.

Bibliography: Fenichel, O.: The psychoanalytical theory of neuroses. London, 1960. Gebhard, P. G., et al.: Sex offenders. London, 1965. Giese, H.: Psychopathologie der Sexualität. Stuttgart, 1962. Schorsch, E.: Sexualstraftäter. Stuttgart, 1971.

H. Maisch

Salivary reflex. A congenital physiological mechanism necessary for the digestion of food. Stimulation of the mucous membrane of the mouth or the nose leads to the direct (unconditioned) secretion of saliva. Indirect (conditioned) triggering of the salivary reflex can come about by the perception (real or imagined) of food, its signs or symbols. The salivary reflex became famous in the psychology of learning because it was the means whereby the Russian physiologist Pavlov (q.v.) discovered and studied the process of classical conditioning.   *H.Ro.*

Salpêtrière School. Its founder, J. M. Charcot the neurologist, was particularly interested for administrative reasons in bringing all patients suffering from convulsions together to be cared for in a special department. Most patients were epileptics (see *Epilepsy*) and hysterics. The study of hysteric syndromes had engaged the attention of French medicine for many years. Charcot described four phases in an attack of hysteria and thus established a certain analogy with an attack of epilepsy. But he also insisted that hysteria (q.v.) is not just a woman's illness but can occur equally in men. The therapy he used was hypnosis (q.v.) and other suggestive methods. The Salpêtrière was a large hospital which, in addition to medical patients, had formerly admitted prostitutes, criminals and other kinds of asocial cases. Later, when

Pinel was the principal, it was converted into a psychiatric clinic.   *J.L.I.*

Sample. If G is a number of articles of the same kind, the population (q.v.), a sample is a part of this number selected from the population according to certain criteria. The number of elements in this selected part are called N (the sample size). In statistics (q.v.) one looks at random samples because it is only in these that the sampling error can be found. When planning experiments, a distinction is made between independent and dependent (q.v.) samples. In the case of dependent (correlating) samples, these or approximately identical objects according to some control characteristic are examined in order to decrease the sampling error. Sampling methods (q.v.) are used in order to obtain samples (see *Opinion polls*).   *A.R.*

Sampling. The selection for study of a small group of people, animals, or items from a larger group (the *population*) in such a way that it is *representative* of that larger group, i.e. that conclusions based on the sample can be generalized to the population from which the sample was drawn. *Sampling theory*, which is a part of *statistics* (q.v.) and the mathematics of *probability* (q.v.), is concerned with ensuring that the sample is selected in such a way that valid *inferences* can be made about the nature of the population from an examination of the sample. In *random sampling* every item in the population has an equal chance of being drawn. *Quota sampling* implies randomness within the restriction that certain sub-groups of the population (e.g. male and female; social class categories) are proportionately represented.   *G.D.W.*

Sampling error (syn. *Sample bias*). The extent to which the sample bias of a parameter constructed on the basis of a sample deviates from the true value. The sampling error can be systematic or random. The random sampling error decreases as the size of the sample increases. It can be estimated by the standard error (q.v.). In variance analysis (q.v.) the variance between the groups is the sampling error. *A.R.*

Sampling techniques. The sampling technique determines the extent to which measurements made of the sample hold good for the population as a whole. Greater accuracy can always be achieved by increasing the size of the random sample. However, to obtain twice the degree of accuracy it is necessary to quadruple the size of the sample; choice of the sampling technique is therefore determined to some extent by cost. A distinction can be made between sampling techniques based on the principle of random sampling (probability sampling) and those based on non-random (non-probability) sampling. Non-random samples are generally chosen by experts using their own judgment while in the case of random samples there is a known probability of each element of the population being included in the sample. Although it is conceivable that more accurate results may be obtained by non-random sampling, this is not generally confirmed by practical experience; the decisive factor, however, is that an indication on the accuracy of results can only be given in the case of random selection.

The random methods can be divided into simple, limited and multi-stage categories. In the simple method, every element of the population has the same likelihood of being included in the sample. The choice can be made by drawing lots or by simulation with random numbers. Simple random samples are also sometimes taken to include systematic selection in which individuals are selected at given intervals from a list of all the population elements. The most important techniques

using limited random selection are the stratified sample and cluster sample.

In the stratified sample, the basic population is divided into strata which must be as homogeneous as possible; selection is then effected on a strictly random basis within the individual strata. The number of individuals selected from each stratum must not correspond to the share accounted for by this stratum in the basic population; if it does correspond to that share we speak of a proportional sample. In a cluster sample we refer to groupings already present in the population (e.g. school classes, houses, towns) which must be as non-homogeneous as possible. Random clusters are then chosen and used as the sample. By comparison with pure random samples, stratified samples result in an increase in accuracy which is all the more substantial the more homogeneous the strata are and the more clearly they are separated from each other. On the other hand the cluster method is less accurate than the purely random procedure. The reduction in accuracy is smaller the greater the lack of homogeneity in the composition of the clusters and the smaller the differences between individual clusters. The cluster method is characterized by low sampling costs. Multi-stage sampling generally takes the form of a sequence of cluster selections, e.g. villages may be selected first and individual houses then chosen at random in the villages. The stratified and cluster methods may also be combined. In non-random sampling the quota method plays an important part, since it is successfully used by opinion research institutes. Each interviewer is required to question a number (quota) of individuals having characteristics selected with a given code, e.g. a specific number of persons of a particular sex with a specific income level and political attitudes, etc. The quotas are determined proportionately to the structure of the population as a whole, to the extent that this is known. The quota method therefore has some similaritiy to the stratified sampling technique, with the important difference that within the quotas selection is left to the skill of the interviewer. Common errors are: e.g. that more intelligent persons tend to be consulted because they can be expected to answer the questions more quickly, and that telephone subscribers tend to be chosen because it is easier to contact them in advance and so avoid any loss of time, etc. Because of these distortions, quota sampling cannot be classified as a random method. A further type of non-random sampling is frequently used for preliminary studies where a sample may be taken simply because it is easily accessible, e.g. students at an institute of psychology may be used as subjects. This method is known as opportunity sampling. It is not really possible to generalize from the results achieved.

A special sampling technique is the sequential method, which is particularly advantageous if the study of an individual entails very high costs or is only rarely possible (e.g. in medicine).

Bibliography: Cochran, W. G.: Sampling techniques. New York, 1953.   *A. Rausche*

Sander's parallelogram illusion. One of the geometric illusions. The diagonal AB appears shorter than BC although they are objectively equal.

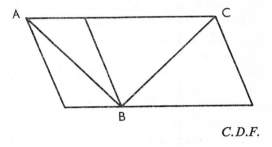

                                        C.D.F.

Sanguine temperament. A concept of temperament which goes back to Galen but was presumably defined as a psychological term only in modern times: hasty temperament (q.v.), impressionable, unstable. The word "sanguine" has been in common use since the sixteenth century. See *Type.*   *W.K.*

Sapphism. Lesbianism (q.v.). Female homosexuality. (After the Ancient Greek poetess Sappho, queen of the island of Lesbos).
                                        G.D.W.

Satiation. Psychic satiation denotes a state of affect-colored aversion from an action which is performed repeatedly or a monotonous situation which has been lasting a long time. It must be distinguished from fatigue (q.v.), which does not primarily cause psychic satiation although it may appear as an accompanying phenomenon during the process of satiation (Lewis, 1928; Karsten, 1928). Even a behavior which initially has an element of pleasure does not by any means always produce a greater fixation of pleasure when it is repeated several times, but causes unpleasure. Instead of satisfaction and an inclination to repeat the act, psychic satiation makes its appearance, the positive challenging character disappears and is replaced by a negative challenging character. In experiments with simple repetition exercises the following observations were made as satiation began to develop (Karsten, 1928): variation in execution, execution as a subsidiary act, arrangement of the exercise into subdivisions, digression, physical fatigue, worsening of performance, structural disintegration, sense of futility, the feeling of marking time, emotional outbursts and finally discontinuance. The increasing emotional tension spreads to acts belonging to adjacent areas (associated satiation); the aversion turns not only against drawing lines but against drawing in general.

To the extent to which the challenging character of the task becomes negative, other, extremely "contrary tasks" take on a positive challenging character. Or the psychic satiation is removed when the task is embedded in a new meaningful context and is given a new target (earning money, competitive struggle), in which case the work which had previously caused satiation is taken up with renewed zest.

Bibliography: Karsten, A.: Psychische Sättigung. Psychol. Forsch., 1928, *10*, 142–254. **Lewin, K.:** Bedeutung der psychischen Sättigung für einige Probleme der Psychotechnik. Psychotechn. Z., 1928, *3*, 182–8. **Kounin, J. S.:** Experimental studies of rigidity. Character and Pers., 1941, *9*, 251–82. **Rivera, J. de** (Ed.): Gestalt. Contributions to the dynamics of behavior. New York, 1970.

A. Karsten

Saturation. In colors: the state of fulness of hue or color. It can range from a very slight degree of intensity where a certain color can only just be recognized as such and is not easily distinguishable from grey up to a maximum where this color has its full strength and life. In this sense the *degree of saturation* of a color can also be defined as its "distance" from grey, i.e. from the absence of color in a restricted sense. Saturation is in proportion to the composition of the spectrum of the stimulus: the greater the purity of the radiation, the more intense is the phenomenal saturation.

G.Ka.

Satyriasis; satyromania. Abnormally strong heterosexual desire in a male. Cf. *nymphomania* (female equivalent). Personal noun: *satyromaniac.* *G.D.W.*

Scales, major and minor. In the Western tradition, the usual systems of succession of notes in an octave. These scales can begin at any pitch and are characterized by definite changes of interval which, however, are distributed differently. *B.S.*

Scaling. In psychology, the term "scaling" denotes the theory and practice of associating numbers with objects. Since the characteristics of psychological objects (e.g. relative willingness to cooperate) are in the great majority of cases not fixed with reference to time and place, scaling is the basis of any comparative psychological statement. A strict definition of scaling must be based on measurement theory.

Measurement of a characteristic implies mapping a set of objects onto a subset of real numbers; the relationship between the associated numbers must correspond to the relationship between the characteristics of the objects which are being studied. Let M be a set of objects and R a relationship with M; (M, R) is then known as an empirical, relational system (Tarski, 1954). Example: let M be a class of pupils and R designate the characteristic "more cooperative than". If M is a subset of real numbers we speak of a numerically relational system.

Measurement consists in transforming an empirical system onto a numerically relational system. A one-to-one mapping f of a relational system (M, R) onto another (N, S) is known as an isomorphism if aRb applies only when $f(a)Sf(b)$ is also realized, i.e. if both systems have identical structures. If $x = (M, R)$ is an empirical relational system $y = (N, S)$ a numerically relational system while f is an isomorphism of on, then (, f) is a scale. Scaling consists in preparing a scale.

In preparing a scale, the existence and validity of the transform f must be demontrated. For this purpose we set out from a relational system in which the required conditions (axioms) are considered to be met. Conclusions regarding existence and validity are drawn from the axioms. This is a theoretical task which has to be carried out once only. For practical scaling purposes we must examine whether the axioms for the investigated empirical relational system are met and follow scaling instructions which associate scale values with the objects.

Example: Thurstone (1927) postulated that on repeated presentation each stimulus from a set of stimuli to be scaled assumed a position which oscillated on the continuum of sensations. The probability density of the position corresponded to a standard distribution. The dispersions for the stimuli under examination were identical. It follows that the frequency with which stimulus *a* is given a higher ranking than stimulus *b* in relation to a particular characteristic, corresponds to the subjective distance between *a* and *b* (law of comparative judgment). If the standard distribution and a number of additional axioms are assumed to be accurate for the stimulus scaling, by comparing the order of magnitude of pairs, we obtain with the Thurstone scale, a scale of relative subjective distances between the evaluated objects.

From the scale level it is possible to conclude which statements concerning scale values are meaningful. A statement is said to be meaningful if its validity remains constant with the permissible transformations; otherwise it is said to be meaningless. In certain circumstances, rank relationships are sufficient for measurement at interval scale level. Suppes & Winet (1955) showed that an interval scale may be based on rank orders of differences (higher ordered metric scales).

The BTL system (Bradley-Terry-Luce) of scaling, based on Luce's selection axiom (1963) is particularly important. The BTL scaling leads on to the theory of signal detection and to developments in the sphere of probabilistic learning models.

Further variants of scaling methods may be classified as follows: stimulus-centered scaling only considers the differences between objects to be evaluated, whereas reaction-centered scaling covers both judging individuals and their judgments. The first group (e.g. application of Thurstone's law of comparative judgment, 1927) originates primarily from psychophysics, while the latter (e.g. Guttman scales) has been primarily determined by social psychology. Direct scaling differs from the indirect version in that it requires the judgment to be given directly in numerical terms. No satisfactory measurement models are available for these methods (e.g. categorial

and magnitude scales) while the indirect methods, which are generally based on judgment frequencies, sometimes have an axiomatic basis. Deterministic scaling attempts to convert the empirical system directly into its numerical equivalent, while probabilistic scaling introduces probability functions as an intermediate stage. The distinction between one-dimensional and multidimensional methods of scaling is significant; in the former instance a single, subjective judgment continuum is postulated to distinguish between objects while in the latter several independent distinguishing features are assumed. The problem of defining axioms for multidimensional scaling has not yet been completely solved. Torgerson (1958) suggested a generalization of Thurstone's model for multidimensional scaling, which does, however, contain certain inherent contradictions. Shepard (1966) developed the principles of a multi-dimensional scaling based solely on rank judgments, but nevertheless arrived at a presentation at interval level. Further development then led to conjoint measurement (Luce and Tukey) which has tried more recently to determine simultaneously the effect of several parameters involved. See *Test theory*.

Bibliography: Coombs, C. H.: A theory of data. New York, 1964. **Luce, R. D.** *et al.* (Eds.): Handbook of mathematical psychology, Vol. 1. New York, 1963. **Pfanzagl, J.:** Theory of measurement. Würzburg & Vienna, 1968. **Shepard, R. N.:** Metric structures in ordinal data. Journal of Mathematical Psychol., 1966, *3*, 280–315. **Sixtl, F.:** Messmethoden der Psychologie. Weinheim, 1967. **Suppes, P. & Winet, M.:** An axiomalization of utility based on the notion of utility differences. Management Science, 1955, *1*, 259–70. **Tarski, A.:** Contributions to the theory of models. Indagationes Mathematicae, 1954, *16*, 572–81. **Torgerson, W. S.:** Theory and methods of scaling. New York, 1958. **Thurstone, L. L.:** A law of comparative judgment. Psychol. Review, 1927, *34*, 273–86.

K. Eyfuth

Scalogram analysis. A method for constructing an attitude scale from items in accumulated form (according to L. A. Guttman) with the object of the *unidimensionality of the scale*. This object is obtained when to each individual item (q.v.) from a person with a more extreme attitude (q.v.) a response is given which is more extreme (or at least equally decided) than that of a person with a less extreme attitude. Thus the degree of the attitude to be measured is expressed in the response to each individual item; ideally, too, the constellation of the responses is reproducible from each attitude scale score (total score). The Guttman scale appears all the more problematic, the more complex in regard to material the attitudes to be measured appear.   *H.D.S.*

Scanning. A method of research and exploration used in electronics, data processing and video-technique by which measurements and calculations are processed to obtain information (q.v.) from definite information carriers.

Picture material, for example, chiefly in screen plates which include different grey values, is analyzed by mechanical symbol recognition in a way similar to the working method of the retina. If there are complex structures they are explored by a point of light produced by a cathode ray tube according to an exploration program and arranged as both black and white values.   *B.R.*

Scatter. The appearance of different test results, observations, abilities, qualities, etc., generally understood as the deviation from the mean value. Also a synonym for standard deviation (q.v.).   *A.R.*

Sceno test. Developed by the child psychotherapist G. von Staab in 1939. According to the depth-psychology conception of the test, the construction of figures by means of the child's projections and identifications (q.v.) evokes a representation of his (unconscious) conflicts. The child builds something with

plasticene figures (potential representations of real persons) and with animals, plants, bricks, etc. The course of the building and the final result, which the child comments on, are recorded. Non-standardized evaluation and interpretation follow with reference to matter and quality.

Bibliography: Staab, G. von: Sceno-test. Berne, 1964.   *P.G.*

Schafer-Murphy effect. The effect whereby reward can determine the perception of an ambiguous figure. Whereas normally the two aspects of an ambiguous figure may be seen equally often, if one of them is associated with a reward then that aspect of the figure will later be seen more often.   *C.D.F.*

Schicksal analysis (*Analysis of destiny; Analysis of the past*). Szondi (1948) introduced this term for a method which tries to find the secrets of destiny in the personality, and to locate, in addition to the personal unconscious, the "family unconscious" and the circumstances connected with it (choice of career, choice of friends, etc.) which influence every person's life. The main method used, in addition to family research, is the Szondi test (q.v.). Schicksal analysis in general and the Szondi test are based on the thesis that two persons whose hereditary endowment includes concealed analogous, recurrent inherited factors will attract one another.

Bibliography: Szondi, L.: Experimentelle Triebdiagnostik. Berne, 1947. **Id.:** Schicksalsanalyse. Basle, ²1948. **Id.:** Schicksalsanalytische Theorie. Berne, 1963.   *J.L.I.*

Schizoid. According to Bleuler (1922), the schizoid "retains his independence of his social surroundings . . . and endeavors to withdraw from the effective influences of the living and dead environment and to pursue his own goals". "Because he does not respect reality and the existing order, he is led on the one hand to endeavor to change it and on the other to turn it upon himself". According to Kretschmer (1970), the term indicates an extreme type of temperament located in psychesthetic proportion (q.v.) which frequently correlates with the leptosomic (q.v.) and asthenic body build.

Bibliography: Bleuler, E.: Die Probleme der Schizoidie und der Syntonie. Zeitschrift neurologischer Psychiatrie, 1922, *78*, 375. **Kretschmer, E. & Kretschmer, W.:** Medizinische Psychologie. Stuttgart, [13]1970.   *W.K.*

Schizophrenia. This term covers a group of severe, common and often incapacitating mental illnesses, which although manifest in a wide variety of psychological symptoms and abnormal behavior, are thought to have enough in common to justify their being grouped together. More patients are in hospital with schizophrenia than with any other medical or surgical condition, and since its maximum incidence is around 30 years of age it must be regarded as one of the major incapacitating illnesses of mankind; the world total of schizophrenics is probably about 9,000,000.

1. *History.* The term schizophrenia was introduced by E. Bleuler in 1911, but under "*dementia praecox*" Kraepelin had previously brought together Morel's "*démence précoce*", Kahlbaum's "catatonia" and Hecker's "hebephrenia" (Kraepelin, 1899). Kraepelin showed that this group of conditions could be differentiated from manic-depressive insanity by its special symptoms and its worse prognosis. In general, the majority of manic-depressives recover completely from or between their illnesses, in contrast to most schizophrenics, who show residual symptoms such as emotional blunting and loss of drive and initiative. This differentiation is still the basis of the present international classification of psychoses and other mental disorders (WHO., 1965).

2. *Clinical features.* (The descriptions given here are based upon the British glossary to the 8th Revision of the I.C.D. (WHO., 1965) and are probably close to current German and Scandinavian usage.) The disturbance that is thought to underlie the various types of schizophrenia shows itself as an utterly unfamiliar experience, in clear consciousness, whereby the person's innermost thoughts, feelings or acts seem to be known to, shared with or caused by others. This experience is often accompanied or followed by delusions that individuals, organizations, or natural or unnatural forces (e.g. television, hypnosis, witchcraft) are responsible. Hallucinations are common, particularly auditory, as voices in the third person or commenting upon the patient's thoughts and actions. Thought processes may be disturbed, so that thinking becomes vague, with unusual logic and idiosyncratic use of words or association of ideas. There may be sudden breaks in the flow of thought or speech, which may become incomprehensible. Perception may be disturbed so that normally irrelevant features of a percept become important, and may lead to delusions of reference in which the patient believes that everyday objects and situations (e.g. statements on television or in the press) possess a special, usually sinister, meaning intended specially for him. The emotional state may become capricious and inappropriate, and there may be extreme abnormalities of motor behavior, such as stupor or over-activity. A wide variety of other symptoms of less diagnostic importance may occur, and may be all that can be detected at any one time (e.g. delusions of persecution, grandiose and religious delusions; hallucinations of smell, taste and touch; sensations of bodily change, sexual change or interference; depersonalization; changed perception of the surroundings).

3. *Classification.* The symptoms may change during one illness, or from one illness to another, but many clinicians still traditionally follow Kraepelin and divide schizophrenia

descriptively into several sub-types, the commonest being *paranoid*, in which delusions (frequently of persecution) and hallucinations dominate the clinical picture. In the *hebephrenic* form, thought disorder and capricious affect, such as silly giggling, predominate. The *catatonic* type is characterized mainly by psychomotor manifestations such as hyperkinesis, stupor, repetitive movements, or automatic obedience. Other varieties such as *simple*, *latent* and *residual* have been described, but their usefulness has been questioned. The term "schizo-affective" is used to describe a small minority of patients showing typical symptoms of both schizophrenia and manic-depressive psychosis. *Paraphrenia* is a term introduced by Kraepelin (1899) to designate patients intermediate between his categories of dementia praecox and paranoia; the predominantly delusional illness develops later and produces less social deterioration than in *dementia praecox*, but the presence of auditory hallucinations eliminates the use of the term paranoia. More recently, the term has been used loosely to be almost synonymous with paranoid schizophrenia, particularly in elderly patients. Kraepelin considered dementia praecox, paraphrenia and paranoia to be separate disease entities, but this was not supported by later work on their outcome and hereditary basis. The historical development of the concept of schizophrenia has always been closely linked with that of paranoia (Lewis, 1970).

Kleist & Leonhart (1961) have developed complicated classifications of schizophrenia into subgroups according to detailed symptoms. The disorder is believed to be basically physical, affecting different parts of the nervous system, singly or in various combinations. This work has not found supporters outside Germany, with the exception of Fish (1962). Langfeld (1956) has proposed a much simpler and more widely accepted division into a "nuclear" group having typical symptoms and a poor prognosis, contrasted with a "schizophreniform" group with less typical symptoms and a much better prognosis.

4. *Diagnosis.* Kurt Schneider has been particularly influential in Europe with his view that diagnosis should rest upon simple description of the above symptoms (Schneider, 1958), in contrast to Bleuler who proposed that diagnosis should depend upon the presence of four inferred primary processes underlying the observed symptoms. These are: (i) loosening of thought associations; (ii) disturbances of affect; (iii) autistic thinking; (iv) ambivalence (Bleuler, 1950). These concepts have never been clearly defined, and followers of Bleuler tend to develop a wide concept of schizophrenia, particularly when also influenced by prominent American teachers such as A. Meyer and H. S. Sullivan, who regarded schizophrenia as the end result of a gradually developing reaction to life experiences and interpersonal relationships.

The diagnosis of schizophrenia still relies entirely upon descriptions of the patient's history, mental state and behavior, since the neurophysiological or biochemical mechanisms responsible for schizophrenia remain uncertain and no structural abnormality of the brain has ever been reliably demonstrated. This lack of reliable, quantifiable data has allowed different concepts of the nature of schizophrenia to arise, so that diagnosis between psychiatrists can be unreliable unless precautions are taken to ensure uniformity of interviewing and consistent use of descriptive terms. Most European psychiatrists use diagnostic criteria similar to those described here, but in North America the use of much broader concepts often results in the diagnosis of schizophrenia being given to patients who have any type of delusion or hallucination, or marked difficulties with interpersonal relationships and self-expression. In Europe, such patients would probably receive a diagnosis of atypical affective illness or personality disorder (Kendell *et al.*, 1971). Any figures quoted in the following sections must be viewed in the light of the underlying diagnostic uncertainties.

5. *Epidemiology*. By European statistics, the annual incidence of new cases is about 150 per 100,000 population, and just under one per cent of the population will receive this diagnosis at some time in their lives. The peak incidence is between 25 and 35 years. Schizophrenia is common in all races and cultures (Mischler & Scott, 1963), and is commonest in the lower socio-economic groups in dilapidated areas of large cities. A downward social drift due to incapacitating residual symptoms is the probable explanation of this (Goldberg & Morrison, 1963).

6. *Etiology and mechanisms*. No single general cause of schizophrenia is known. Both environmental stress and genetic predisposition seem to play a part in many patients, but in others neither of these influences is evident: *Genetic predisposition:* The near relatives of schizophrenics have a much greater incidence (about 12% in siblings) than the general population, and monozygotic twins have a greater concordance rate (about 60%) for the illness than dizygotic twins. Selection bias makes the interpretation of surveys of twins difficult (Rosenthal, 1962) but an important genetic component in schizophrenia is generally accepted, probably with a polygenic mode of inheritance (Shields, 1967). A monogenic theory involving partial penetrance has also been proposed (Slater, 1958). Since schizophrenia results in the genetic loss of so many fertile individuals, carriers of the predisposition who do not manifest the illness should have some compensatory advantage, but this has not yet been identified.

Family and environment: Much recent work from the USA is based upon the assumption that schizophrenia is caused by parents who submit the child to conflicting emotional relationships and illogical confusing habits of verbal and non-verbal communication. This work remains theoretical, since the suggested abnormal styles of communication have not been shown to be specific to schizophrenia (Mischler & Waxler, 1965). In adults, objective evidence has at last been obtained to confirm the simple but important observation that schizophrenic illnesses may be precipitated by stressful events (Brown & Birley, 1968).

Biochemical: Some hereditary conditions are known to be associated with metabolic abnormalities arising from the lack of dysfunction of specific enzymes, but widespread and enthusiastic biochemical investigations of schizophrenic patients have up to now produced only theories. Much attention has been given to the metabolic pathways of noradrenaline, an important substance found in all parts of the nervous system, since it bears a tantalizing resemblance to mescaline and other compounds which can cause hallucinations and delusions. The skin pigment melanin, the amino-acid methionine, and transmethylation reactions, have all been of recent interest. Unfortunately, the negative conclusions expressed in Kety's review of 1959 still hold.

Psycho-physiological: Slowness is characteristic of many chronic schizophrenics, and this has led to the investigation of their reaction time and state of arousal by means of skin potential levels, and fusion thresholds of auditory and visual stimuli. Strong evidence has emerged that, contrary to expectation, social withdrawal is associated with excessive cortical arousal (Kornetsky & Mursky, 1966; Venables, 1968). This could mean that chronic schizophrenics are either quick to develop or slow to dissipate reactive inhibition, but this and other interpretation of these findings can only be tentative since the concepts of arousal and inhibition are complex and debatable, and chronic schizophrenics are unlikely to be a homogeneous group. This line of inquiry seems likely to be rewarding.

Cognitive disorder: Early descriptive studies of schizophrenic thought disorder suggested an inability to form abstract concepts ("concrete thinking"), plus an inability to preserve conceptual boundaries ("over-inclusive thinking"; Cameron, 1954). Subsequently Payne developed a theory of schizophrenic thought disorder involving over-inclusiveness and slowness (Payne, 1960), but the discrimination of schizophrenics from other psychiatric patients by Payne's battery of tests has not been confirmed by others. A more recent but more complex approach has been Bannister's utilization of Kelly's Repertory Grid, a sorting test in which the relationships between conceptual categories are measured statistically (Bannister, 1965). Cognitive disorders on all these measures are associated with the hebephrenic type of schizophrenia, and are usually absent in patients with systematized delusions. As in the psychophysiological studies, concepts of arousal, attention and distractability are brought into discussions of the test results. These tests have not yet proved to be of much value in clinical diagnosis, but they are important in the investigation and understanding of some of the symptoms of schizophrenia viewed as disorders of short-term handling and retrieval of information.

7. *Other theories of schizophrenia.* Psycho-analytic concepts have not proved helpful in either the understanding or treatment of schizophrenia. In psychoanalytic terms schizophrenia is regarded as a disturbance of ego organization and object relations, arising from abnormal early interaction between mother and child. There is regression back to the very early narcissistic level at which the self is not differentiated from the environment. Paranoid delusions are regarded as a repressed form of homosexual wishes. Federn (1952) and Klein (1952) have produced modern variations of psychoanalytic theories, but even convinced psychoanalysts usually accept that interpretative psychotherapy is of no use with schizophrenic patients, a view confirmed by a large-scale clinical investigation (May, 1968). Jung's use of his "word-association test" in schizophrenia is historically important as an early

example of clinical experimental psychology, and he did a great deal of descriptive work on the relationship between the symbolism of schizophrenic symptoms and mythology. His belief that schizophrenia is due to emergence of the unconscious due to weakening of the will had no special impact. Kretschmer (1925) proposed a constitutional theory of mental illness, in which schizophrenia is one extreme of a continuum, the other end being normality; schizoid personality disorder occupies an intermediate position between. Body type is said to vary in the same way, the tall thin (asthenic) type being associated with schizophrenia. Kretschmer's theories have influenced the thinking of many clinicians, but reliable evidence for the importance of these fairly weak correlations has not been produced. Existential theories and therapy have recently arisen in Germany but are not widely accepted or used (Binswanger, 1958).

8. *Treatment of schizophrenia.* The modern treatment of schizophrenia that has evolved over the last fifteen years is empirical, and consists of phenothiazine drugs for the acute phases (commonly chlorpromazine or trifluorperazine), followed by a planned program of social stimulation and work training or re-training, often aimed at achieving a less ambitious level than before the acute illness. Ideally, a system of in-patient units, day hospitals, assessment and training workshops, supervised hostels and sheltered employment facilities should be available, which together with long-term psychiatric follow-up form a comprehensive system aimed at keeping the patient as much in contact with normal community life as possible. Positive contact with the patient needs to be maintained, to avoid a drift into an isolated, vagrant or institutionalized existence. This concept of community care has greatly improved the prognosis of all forms of schizophrenia, and even with the limited facilities usually available, only a small proportion of patients now remain in hospital for more than two years, the majority being

discharged within six months; this often remains so even when re-admissions are necessary. It is easy to overestimate the role of phenothiazines in this improved prognosis, and there are good grounds for believing that improvement in daily social care and living conditions in mental hospitals has been just as important (Hoenig, 1967; Wing & Birley, 1970).

Electroconvulsive therapy is effective in the acute catatonic forms of schizophrenia, but its use in other forms is debatable. Insulin coma and leucotomy are no longer widely used. The rise and fall in popularity of insulin coma treatment, which was the treatment of choice all over the world for about twenty years between 1935 and 1955, is one of the most striking recent examples of how a non-specific treatment effect can be universally accepted by clinicians in spite of the lack of objective and controlled evidence of its efficacy (Ackner, 1952).

The recent development of therapy based upon modern learning theories has resulted in the successful application of operant conditioning techniques and token economies to both verbal and social behavior of chronic schizophrenics (e.g. Allyon, T. & Azrin, N., 1968). Surprisingly encouraging results have often been obtained but adequate control of the ward environment is often difficult to achieve, and the major problem is how to obtain generalization of the response to other environments. This appears to be a promising area for further research.

9. *Future developments*. It is likely that new drugs and more refined techniques of physiological and biochemical investigation will allow the identification of subgroups of patients with different underlying etiology or mechanisms of symptom production. These sub-divisions will presumably reflect disturbances in the biochemical reactions and inter-neuronal connections which determine how the brain stores, retrieves and integrates information.

Bibliography: Ackner, B. & Oldham, A. J.: Insulin treatment of schizophrenia, Lancet (i), 1962, 504–506. Allyon, T. & Azrin, N.: The token economy: a motivational system for therapy and rehabilitation. New York, 1968. Bannister, D.: The genesis of schizophrenic thought disorder, Brit. J. Psychiat., 1965, *111*, 377. Binswanger, L.: Schizophrenie. Pfüllingen, 1958. Bleuler, E. P.: Dementia praecox and the group of schizophrenias. New York, 1950. Brown, G. W. & Birley, J. L. T.: Crises and life changes and the onset of schizophrenia. J. of Health & Social Behavior, 1968, *9*, 203. Cameron, N.: Experimental analysis of schizophrenic thinking. In: Kasanin (Ed.): Language and thought in schizophrenia. California, 1944. Federn, P.: Ego psychology and the psychoses. London, 1952. Fish, F.: Schizophrenia. Bristol, 1962. Goldberg, E. M. & Morrison, S. L.: Schizophrenia & social class. Brit. J. Psychiat, 1963, *109*, 785–802. Hoenig, J.: The prognosis of schizophrenia. In: Recent developments in schizophrenia. Brit. J. Psychiat. Special Publ. No. 1, 1967. Kendell, R. E., Cooper, J. E., Gourlay, A. J., Copeland, J. R. M., Sharpe, L. & Gurland, B. J.: The diagnostic criteria of American and British psychiatrists. Archiv. Gen. Psychiat, 1971 Kety, S. S.: Biochemical theories of schizophrenia. Science, 1959, *129*, 1528–96. Klein, M., Heimann, P., Isaacs, S. & Riviere, J.: Developments in psychoanalysis. London, 1952. Kleist, K.: Schizophrenic symptoms and cerebral pathology. J. Ment. Sci., 1960, *106*, 246. Kornetsky, C. & Mursky, A. F.: On certain psychopharmacological and physiological differences between schizophrenic and normal persons. Psychopharmacologia (Berl.), 1966, *8*, 309–18. Kraepelin, E.: Lehrbuch der Psychiatrie. Leipzig, [8]1899. Kretschmer, E.: Physique and character, trans. Sprott, W. J. H., London, 1925. Langfelt, G.: The prognosis in schizophrenia. Acta Psychiat. Scand. Suppl., 1956, *110*. Leonhard, K. Cycloid psychoses—endogenous psychoses which are neither schizophrenic or manic depressive. J. Ment. Sci., 1961, *107*, 633. Lewis, A. J.: Paranoia and paranoid—a historical perspective. Psychological Medicine, 1970, *1*, 2–12. May, P. R. A.: Treatment of schizophrenia—a comparative study of five treatment methods. New York, 1968. McGhie, A.: Studies of cognitive disorder in schizophrenia. In: Recent developments in schizophrenia. Brit. J. Psychiat. Special Publ. No. 1, 1967. Mischler, E. G. & Scotch, N. A.: Sociocultural factors in the epidemiology of schizophrenia. Psychiatry, 1953, *26*, 315. Mischler, E. G. & Waxler, N. E.: Family interaction process and schizophrenia—a review of current theories. Merrill-Palmer Quart., 1965, *II*, 269. Payne, R. W.: Cognitive abnormalities.

In: **Eysenck, H. J.** (Ed.): Handbook of abnormal psychology. London, 1960, 193–261. **Rosenthal, D.:** Problems of sampling and diagnosis in the major twin studies of schizophrenia. Psychiat. Res., 1962, *I*, 116–134. **Roth, M.:** The natural history of mental disorder in old age. J. Ment. Sci., 1955, *101*, 281–301. **Schneider K.:** Clinical psychopathology (trans. **Hamilton, M.**). New York, 1958. **Shields, J.:** The genetics of schizophrenia in historical context. In: Recent developments in schizophrenia. Brit. J. Psychiat. Special Publ. No. 1, 1967. **Slater, E. T. O.:** The monogenic theory of schizophrenia. Acta genet. (Basle), 1958, *8*, 50–56. **Smythies, J. R.:** Recent advances in the biochemistry of schizophrenia. In: Recent developments in schizophrenia. Brit. J. Psychiat. Special Publ. No. 1, 1967. **Venables, P. H.:** Experimental psychological studies of chronic schizophrenia. In: **Shepherd & Davies** (Eds.): Studies in psychiatry. London, 1968. **W.H.O.:** International statistical classification of diseases (section V), 8th Revision, W.H.O., Geneva, 1965. **Wing, J. K. & Brown, G. W.:** Institutionalism and schizophrenia. Cambridge, 1970. **Yates, A. J :** Behavior therapy. New York, 1970. Ch. 14.   *J. E. Cooper*

Schizothyme. A constitutional temperament having some affinity with the leptosomic (q.v.), asthenic type and in which introversion (q.v.) and psychesthetic proportion (q.v.) are strongly marked. The schizothyme is characterized by a "very sharply defined individual zone", "a conscious contrast between the ego and the outside world", "a touchy or indifferent withdrawal from the mass of his fellow men", the predominance of "dreams, ideas or principles".   *W.K.*

School counselor. A person who gives advice to all those concerned with the education of young people at school and to the pupils themselves. He assists the parents and teachers when important decisions concerning school admission and school course have to be taken; he helps also to remove difficulties at school and to solve educational problems. The student is given advice commensurate with his specific abilities in the choice of subjects, in deciding on a career and in coping with difficulties which appear as work progresses and his personality develops. The duties which a school counselor is required to perform are so extensive that anybody taking up this work should have had some training in psychology, educational theory and practical teaching. See *Vocational guidance.*

H.S.

School neurosis. The term indicates a neurotic weakness of behavior which shows up in the area covered by school or is triggered by it. Occasionally the forms this behavioral disorder takes can only be seen when the individual is at school (school mutism, cramp, phobia, aphasia), but usually they appear both in and out of school (separation anxiety, performance anxiety, difficulties with learning, weakness of concentration, social difficulty). To cure the behavior due to school neurosis is one of the tasks of the school psychologist (q.v.) and the school counselor (q.v.). See *Neurosis; Educational psychology.*   *H.S.*

School psychologist. As a rule this officer is assigned to an educational authority or to a large school; his duties are to decide the suitability of a child for school (see *School readiness*), to determine the reason for failure at school and to show what are the specific areas in which the pupils are gifted (q.v.) or possess ability (q.v.). In addition to these tasks, which are primarily diagnostic, the school psychologist has also chiefly to look ahead (advice on school career) and to counsel. See *Vocational guidance.*   *H.S.*

School readiness. The term should not—as the concept of readiness might suggest—be understood as being relatively independent of the environment in the sense of biologistico-automatic growth models. School readiness is rather *that state of development necessary for a certain rudimentary instruction* which is more the result of learning than of maturation processes.

School readiness has to be considered as a relational concept which is determined partly by the demands of society (teaching aims and methods, school organization), which the latter makes on the school beginner, and partly by the particular state of the child's development. Three more or less prognostic groups of school readiness criteria are specified for the school system at present in existence:

1. *Somatic criteria:* the general state of health (nutritional standard, functional efficiency of the organs and senses), change of structure (Zeller criteria), growth of second teeth.

2. *Psychic criteria:* ability to arrange, to think, language capacity, learning motivation. It is believed that these criteria can be determined with the tests of school readiness in use nowadays.

3. *Sociological criteria:* family situation, school education and occupation of the parents, number of children, attendance at nursery school, social behavior.

There are no established criteria for predicting success in the first school year. School readiness tests in general only possess validity coefficients of up to $v = 0.60$. No decision about keeping any individual child down can be taken with such tests. But in proficiently organized primary schools there is no definite need for selection procedures but only for recommending certain treatment. See *Educational psychology.*   *H.Ma.*

Schroeder's staircase. A *reversible figure* which appears alternately as the top of a staircase seen from above or the underneath of a staircase seen from below.   *C.D.F.*

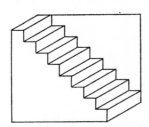

Scientific management. A system of the American engineer F. W. Taylor (1856–1915) according to a scientifically based method of industrial management for the purpose of rationalization and increasing productivity. Taylor believed that maximization of gain and harmonious cooperation could be achieved for both social partners, if each worker had a definite task ("pensum") which had to be fulfilled in a standard time ("normal time") and in a standard way ("the one best way"), (substituted for individually obtained "rules of thumb"). His study of the loading of unwrought iron (1899) is famous. *Criticism:* treatment of men as extension of the machine with disregard of physiological (see *Fatigue,* etc.), psychological (individual differences) and social factors (see *Hawthorne experiment*). See *Industrial psychology.*   *W.F.N.*

Sclera. The outer layer of the eye (q.v.). Its thickness varies locally and ranges between 0.3 mm and 1.5 mm. About 15 circular degrees nasally from the posterior pole of the eye it is traversed by the optic nerve and joins on to the cornea with a circular boundary line (limbus corneae). Adhesive fibers in the sclerotic wall form a dense fibrous network comparable to the fibrous network of a balloon. That is why the sclera possesses such an extraordinarily tough elasticity; together with the intraocular pressure it fixes the shape of the eyeball.   *R.R.*

Scopolamine (synonym for hyoscine). An anticholinergic substance with strong central and psychological effects, occurring in solanacene and one of the belladonna alkaloids (q.v.). Scopolamine is comparable to *atropine* (q.v.) in many of its effects (e.g. dilatation of the pupils, storage reduction, reduction of the EEG—arousal under stimulation, slow EEG waves). Psychological effects are, however, to some extent different: its effects in humans, in contrast to those of atropine, are to induce fatigue and inhibit the faculties (especially extended concentration, reduction of vigilance). Altogether, the peripheral physiological effects of the two substances are comparable, but psychologically the effect of scopolamine is stronger. The effects persist for several hours (more than five). With higher doses, scopolamine has psychosomatic effects. The amnesic effects often attributed to it are not sufficiently attested. In animal research, surprisingly, no sedative effects have been discovered. Many experiments (in rats) show an increase in activity. Faculties are usually impeded. Scopolamine in animal experiments leads to delay in habituation to new stimuli; it is often applied for therapeutic purposes, e.g. in conditions of excitation (usually in combination with other sedatives).

Bibliography: Colquhoun, W. P.: Effects of hyoscine and meclozine on vigilance and short term memory. Brit. J. Industr. Med., 1962, *19*, 287–96. Helmann, H.: Die Scopolaminwirkung. Basle, 1952. Longo, V. G.: Behavioral and electroencephalographic effects of related compounds. Pharmacol. Rev. 1966, *18*, 965–96. Ostfeld, A. M. & Aruguete, A.: Central nervous system effects of hyoscine in man. J. Pharmacol. exp. Therapeut., 1969, *137*, 133–9. Parkes, M. W.: An examination of central actions characteristic of scopolamine: comparison of central and peripheral activity in scopolamine, atropine and some synthetic basic esters. Psychopharmaciologia, 1965, 1–19.

W.J.

Score. Number (generally a total of points) assigned to an individual on the basis of an objective measurement (e.g. a test) or a subjective judgment (see *Rating; Scaling*).

A.R.

Scotoma. An area in the visual field which is blind or partially blind. All people have one blind spot, since the region where the optic nerve leaves the retina has no receptors. Scotomata can result from damage to the retina or to the brain. *C.D.F.*

Scotopia (*Twilight vision*). Twilight vision has different properties from day vision since it is mediated by the *rods* rather than the *cones*. The existence of these two systems is indicated by the discontinuity in the dark adaptation curve. With twilight vision a person is insensitive to color and his periperhal vision is better for fine detail than his central vision, since there are no rods in the fovea. *C.D.F.*

Screen effect. 1. *Static screen effect.* An effect whereby we strongly perceive the continuation of objects behind screens although there is no immediate or objective evidence for the particular continuation we perceive.

2. *Kinetic screen effect.* This is the same effect concerning the way we perceive the continuation of moving objects behind a screen. The *piston effect* (q.v.) and the *tunnel effect* (q.v.) are examples of kinetic screen effects. *C.D.F.*

Scribbling stage. The first stage in the development of drawing in a child. Normally it occurs at the age of 2 or 3, but there can be considerable variations in time, since an essential role is played by perception, sensory motor activity, imagination, memory, motivation and intelligence in acquiring the ability to draw.

Séance. Meeting at which a medium (q.v.) officiates. Also called "sitting" or "session". *J.B.*

Sea sickness. A kinetosis released by the movement of the ship (movement sickness), which manifests itself in giddiness, nausea (indisposition), vomiting and other vegetative disturbances like perspiration, weakness and palor. It is caused by strong excitation of the vestibular (q.v.) apparatus. Its effects are increased by lack of optical information concerning the movement, e.g. in the interior of the ship. It can however be regarded as a defense mechanism toward adverse environmental conditions, especially in the case of discrepancy of mental impressions comparable to the automatic reflexes of dead insects.

E.D.

Seashore test. See *Music, psychology of.*

Secondary drives. Motive forces in human behavior which are not innate (*primary drives*) but learnt. The psychology of learning explains their origin as follows: situations which often occur together with a condition of reduction of primary drives can eventually occur on their own and are then striven for by the organism on their own account. There is also the explanation of "vicarious reinforcement" in the process of the creation of secondary drives, or *introjection*. This helps the transmission of ethical and esthetic values in the process of nurture. (See *Drive.*)   *A.Ro.*

Secondary, primary function. In behavior accompanying attention we note two opposite processes. Fluctuation or distraction (oscillation) is a "primary function" and perseverance (q.v.) is a "secondary function". (K. Gross, G. Heymans.)   *H.W.*

Secondary processes. According to S. Freud these are set against the *primary processes* (q.v.), motives (q.v.), opinions of a man which accord with his reality and can be striven for or satisfied in real situations. They are controlled by the "reality principle" (q.v.).

W.T.

Second sight (syn. *Deuteroscopy*). Form of precognition (q.v.) in which the sensitive (q.v.) sees a person's double situated alongside that person. This is taken to portend his imminent demise. Associated with Scottish folklore.   *J.B.*

Secrecy, obligation of. For the psychologist this is largely covered by a professional code of ethics. In some countries, a breach of the vow of secrecy on the part of a psychologist can result in proceedings in a court of civil or criminal law.   *H.J.S.*

Secretion. Discharge or emission of products of the glands. A distinction is made between *external secretions* of the exocrine glands such as the salivary, digestive, tear and sweat glands and the *internal secretions* of the endocrine (q.v.) or hormone glands.   *E.D.*

Security. A general human need for stability in existence; it is a matter of contention whether it is a vital need (such as hunger or thirst motivation), or socio-cultural in nature (see *Drive; Need; Motivation*). Cantril's (1965) list of human hopes and fears based on questionnaires (twenty thousand individuals from thirteen countries) begins with (*a*) gratification of those needs oriented toward survival; (*b*) securing of what has been achieved hitherto; and (*c*) aspiration to order and certainty in one's own life, and to the calculability of existence. Concern for the satisfaction of survival needs is an experience which draws on all the energies and thoughts of those under such pressure. The need for security in all areas of life leads men to devise various methods to anticipate regulation of danger and disorder: in industrial societies we have, e.g., "social security" and "insurance" and "assurance" (economic security), and "industrial security" or "industrial safety". See *Anxiety; Accident proneness; Accident research.*

Bibliography: Cantril, H.: The pattern of human concerns. New Brunswick, N.Y., 1965. **Thomae, H.:** Das Individuum und seine Welt. Göttingen, 1968.

G.R.W.M.

Sedation threshold. A pharmacopsychological test introduced by Shagass (1957) for diagnosis and prognosis. The barbiturate (q.v.) amobarbital natricum (sodium amytal r) is administered intravenously with a speed of 0.5 mg/kg body weight per 40 sec. During the injection an EEG is taken frontally. The sedation threshold is defined as the amobarbital quantity (in mg/kg bodyweight) experienced during the fast wave in the region of 17–25 Hz, a strong increase of amplitudes. The occurrence of slurred speech correlates roughly with it. Repetition reliability and objectivity of the procedure is high. The sedation threshold correlates *inter alia* with manifest anxiety (q.v.), it is higher in reactive than endogenous depressions (q.v.) and lower in hysterical (see *Hysteria*) than in dysthymic (see *Dysthymia*) subjects (in H. J. Eysenck's interpretation).

Bibliography: Shagass, C.: A neurophysiological test for psychiatric diagnosis: results in 750 patients. Amer. J. Psychiatr., 1957, *114*, 1002–10. **Id.:** Sedation threshold: technique and concept. In: **Brill, H.** (Ed.): Proceed. 5. Intern. Congr. Neuro-Psycho-Pharmacology. Amsterdam, 1967. *W.J.*

Sedatives. Substances which are applied therapeutically in higher doses as hypnotics (q.v.), in lower doses for the purpose of affective and motor inhibition. They have been used much less since the development of tranquilizers (q.v.), because of their frequent tendency to induce fatigue and hinder faculties. However they have more in common pharmacologically with tranquilizers than with neuroleptics. *E.L.*

Segmental innervation. The whole surface of the human body can be divided into skin areas (dermatome, Read's zones) each of which is sensorily innervated by one and the same *segment of the spinal cord*. The internal organs also can be associated with segments of the spinal cord so that when painful diseases of an organ occur, it happens not infrequently that corresponding dermatomes are also irritated and cause pain. *E.D.*

Segment illusion. Of two identical segments of circles placed one above the other, the upper will appear larger. In addition, if monocularly fixated, the lower one will appear nearer. The trapezium illusion is identical except that the segments are replaced by trapezia. *C.D.F.*

Selection (syn. *Natural selection*). A term used in genetics. Selection, together with mutation, plays a decisive part in the evolution of species. Selection takes place because creatures that are more fitted to survive in their environment have more offspring than those not so well fitted to survive. Selection is used to refer not only to the choice of genetic types in breeding but to the singling out of specific *personality traits* in the development of the individual. See *Traits*. *W.L.*

Selective perception. Because of the volume and complexity of stimulation with which a person is continually bombarded, all perception is selective, but in some circumstances it can become abnormally so. A person will selectively perceive those aspects of his experience that he has found most important in the past. Hence the attaching of extreme importance to various aspects of the world through stress, psychiatric disturbance, poverty or even a strong expectation induced by experimental manipulation can result in selective perception of an extreme kind. People see only what they want to see or what they expect. *C.D.F.*

Selectivity. The ability of a test item to differentiate between testees in whom a given feature is emphasized to a greater or lesser extent. Selectivity is often defined as the correlation between a test item and the total point value. There is a clear relationship between difficulty and selectivity. See *Test theory*. *A.R.*

Self. The individual, as subject to his own contemplation or action. According to Hegel: "Consciousness first finds itself in self-consciousness—the notion of mind—its turning-point, where it leaves the particolored show of the sensuous immediate, passes from the dark void of the transcendent and remote super-sensuous, and steps into the spiritual daylight of the present." (*Phenomenology of Spirit.*) Williams James makes a distinction between the self as known, or the *me*, the empirical ego, and the self as knower, or the *I*, the pure ego: "Whatever I may be thinking of, I am always at the same time more or less aware of myself, of my personal existence. At the same time it is I who am aware; so that the total self of me, being as it were duplex, partly known and partly knower, partly object and partly subject, must have two aspects discriminated in it, of which for shortness we may call one the *Me* and the other the *I*". (*Textbook of Psychology.*) But Wittgenstein observes: ". . . James' introspection showed, not the meaning of the word 'self' (so far as it means something like 'person', 'human being', 'he himself', 'I myself'), nor any analysis of such a thing, but the state of a philospher's attention when he says the word 'self' to himself and tries to analyze its meaning. (And a good deal could be learned from this.)" (*Philosophical Investigations.*)   *J.M.*

Self concept. The totality of attitudes (q.v.), judgments, and values of an individual relating to his behavior, abilities (q.v.) and qualities. "Self concept" embraces the awareness of these variables and their evaluation. Self concept has been investigated by the use of the Q sorting method (q.v.), which distinguishes between first *the real self-description* and second the discrepancy between this and an *ideal self-description*.

Among theories of the self and the self concept we may mention that of C. Rogers, whose client-centered psychotherapy (non-prescriptive psychotherapy) is founded upon his theories of the self. These theories elicited numerous empirical studies on the self concept which show, for example, that parental behavior during upbringing has a strong influence on the appearance of the self concept and that the measure of ego-ideal discrepancy is closely connected with the measure of failure in adjustment. (See *Ego.*)

Bibliography: Byrne, D.: An introduction to personality. A research approach. Englewood Cliffs, N.J., 1966.   *D.B.*

Self-knowledge. I. Kant considered self-knowledge to be the beginning of all human wisdom, yet the academic psychology of the nineteen-seventies does not include the term among its basic concepts and it does not appear in contemporary dictionaries of psychology. The main concern of psychology is the attempt to apprehend others psychologically. Only the various branches of depth psychology (q.v.) still insist that anyone who seeks to analyze others must first undergo a training analysis. It would seem reasonable that the assessment of others should be preceded by self-assessment.

According to Hector (1971), self-knowledge is one of the two pillars of psychology. Self-knowledge begins with a survey of one's own life, taking into account outward stages and inner conditions, and enabling one to reach an understanding of one's personal development and a critical judgment of one's spiritual and intellectual existence. Any theoretical scientific question about the truth and error of self-knowledge can produce only flexible answers. Of course it is possible to arrive at an essentially erroneous self-image (self-deception). However, the probability of such deception drops when the process is psychologically controlled.   *H. Hector*

II. "Self-knowledge" is found as an entry in dictionaries of philosophy, where it is defined as the knowledge of the ego (q.v.), of the self, of the dispositions (see *Anlagen*), abilities, errors and weaknesses, suasions and response patterns of one's own person (q.v.). Hector (1971) believes that any judgment of an other ought to be preceded by self-knowledge in the form of one's own case history (q.v.). Such a life history (q.v.) can certainly help one toward self-knowledge, but hardly resolves the complex problem of self-knowledge posed by the requirement "Know thyself!" (inscription above the temple of Apollo at Delphi) and the "*individuum ineffabile*" thesis. For the psychology of the twentieth century—when it became clear that there could be no self-knowledge without self-deception—"self-knowledge" became (if reflected upon at all) a pre-scientific (lay) term for more precisely conceived (and operationally definable) psychological concepts such as: self-judgment, self-assessment, self-image, and self-concept. Self-concept research has shown that what each individual knows about himself and how he sees himself, derives from the way in which he has been and is considered by others (role, q.v., role expectations, mirror-image). If one's own self is falsely assessed, this leads to difficulties and conflicts with one's fellows and the environment (see *Conflict*). The therapeutic effect of the psychological (analytic, exploratory) interview, of psychoanalysis (q.v.) and, above all, of non-directive therapy (q.v.) resides ultimately in the fact that clients correct their erroneous self-image in the course of psychotherapy, and thus attain once more to personal and social harmony. See *Abilities; Differential psychology; Personality; Philosophy and psychology; Traits; Type; Meditation.*

Bibliography: Hector, H.: Selbsterkenntnis als fehlender Psychologie-Begriff. Praktische Psychol., 1971, *25*, 97–8. Kierkegaard, S.: Either/or. Princeton, N.J., 1944. *F. Novak*

Semantic differential. A method developed by C. E. Osgood (1952, 1957) and P. R. Hofstätter (1957) to allow rating of an idea, concept or object on a series of scales. A series of dimensions (e.g. soft-hard, strong-weak) is divided into stages (usually seven). A subject's ratings of a concept may be represented as a "polarity profile". The average values of a concept assigned a position by a number of subjects reflect a group idea or opinion (see *Stereotype*). Well-known "stereotypes" of this kind are e.g., sex roles and national characters. The degree of similarity of two concepts may be determined by correlational techniques (e.g. "love" and "red," $r = +0.89$). According to Hofstätter, the matrices of similarity correlations of a number of assigned concepts from the sphere of personality yield factors, which he interprets thus: $F_1 = positive$ outward orientation; $F_2 = negative$ outward orientation; $F_3 = inward$ orientation. Osgood's three basic dimensions, or factors, reduced from a large number of scales, are: *potency*, (strong-weak, etc.), *activity* (fast-slow, etc.), *evaluation* (good-bad, etc.). See *Attitude; Psycholinguistics.*

Bibliography: Hofstätter, P. R.: Psychologie. Frankfurt, 1957. Osgood, C. E.: The nature and measurement of meaning. Psychol. Bull., 1952, *49*, 197–237. Id., Suci, G. J. & Tannenbaum, P. H.: The measurement of meaning. Urbana, Ill., 1957. *P.G.*

Semantization (syn. *Ritualization*). The development of a behavior pattern into a pure signal. Even human greeting ceremonies are thought to have developed from combat rituals. Raising one's hat derives from removing a helmet, and a military salute from raising one's visor. Both gestures indicate trust. *V.P.*

Semantics. The noun "semantics", derived from the Greek adjective σημαντικόγ ("significant"), in the sense of science of meaning or of signification, is a modern creation. It is used by different authors within a wide range of connotations. Many use it as synonymous with "semiotic", the general study of signs, in particular of linguistic signs, others as denoting only that subfield of semiotic which deals with such relations of signs to things other than signs as denotation, connotation, reference, designation, and the like, with "pragmatics" reserved for the subfield that deals with the relations of signs to their users, while "syntax" deals with the relations of signs among themselves. Synonyms for "semantics" in its narrow linguistic use are "semology", "semasiology", and "semantology", but these terms are rarely used.

In logical semantics, one often distinguishes, with Mill, between denotation and connotation, or with Frege and Quine, between denotation and sense, or with Carnap, between extension and intension. Carnap also distinguishes between descriptive semantics, the empirical study of meaning in natural languages, and pure semantics, the analytical study of meaning in constructed language-systems. Whereas descriptive semantics is the result of an abstraction from descriptive pragmatics, the psychological, sociological, and ethnological study of actual speech behavior, pure semantics is independent of pragmatics, though the choice of rules for the semantic systems to be investigated may be guided by pragmatic facts, and is so in general for those systems that are meant to stand in "close correspondence" with natural languages.

In linguistics, the development of theoretical semantics is only in its beginnings. It was long hampered by certain philosophical and, in particular, ontological preconceptions, from which many linguists thought to escape by retreating into the study of meaning change and etymology, subjects still often identified with semantics in general. But there still exists little unanimity on even the most basic issues in theoretical semantics such as whether words (or morphemes) are to be regarded as the fundamental carriers of meaning so that the meaning of larger units (up to sentences) is to be treated as resulting from the meanings of their component words by some combinatory rules (sometimes called rules of projection), or whether sentences should be regarded as the fundamental meaning carriers, with the meanings of their component words considered to be some function of the meanings of the sentences in which they may occur.

Componential meaning analysis works reasonably well in some simple cases, and there seems little wrong in looking at the meanings of "father", "mother", "son", and "daughter" as simple conjuncts of the meanings of "parent" and "male", "parent" and "female", "child" and "male", and "child" and "female", respectively. How far this kind of analysis can be usefully driven and how universal it is, are questions under active discussion. It seems that the treatment of semantic fields, in the sense of Trier-Weisgerber, requires not only componential rules, but also rules of quite different kinds, of various degrees of universality, such as the rules that "parent-of" and "child-of" denote converse relations, as do "greater-than" and "smaller-than", "sells-to" and "buys-from", or the rules that "male" and "female" are antonyms, that "father-of" and "parent-of" are hyponyms, and of many other much more complex kinds.

The meaning of metaphorical and idiomatic expressions are clear instances of cases which cannot be handled by simple combinatorial-componential techniques exclusively. Other phenomena, that sometimes create difficulties in communication, are semantic ambiguity, whether of the accidental type—homonymy—or of the more essential one—polysemy—, and vagueness. How these difficulties are overcome, through utilization of linguistic context or of extra-linguistic, situational context, is still little understood.

Insufficiently understood is also so far the functioning of indexical (cotext- and context-dependent) expressions, whether of the deictic type ("I", "you", "now", "here", etc.), of the anaphoric type (pro-elements of various kinds, pro-nouns, pro-verbs, pro-adjectives, pro-sentences, etc.), or of still other types. Their treatment transcends semantics and belongs rather to pragmatics, since for understanding their role in communication the cotexts and contexts of their utterances have to be taken into account.

In standard modern generative-transformational linguistic theory (originating with Chomsky), the semantic component of the total grammar of a language is considered to operate on certain structures generated by the syntactic component, sometimes called deep structures, interpretatively, providing them with one or more semantic representations (or readings), while the phonological component provides other structures generated by the syntactic component, sometimes called surface structures, with their phonological representations.

In another version of this theory, the semantic component itself is supposed to directly generate semantic representations. It should be noted that in this version these representations are often modelled along norms provided by logical systems developed independently by modern symbolic logicians for mathematical and philosophical, but not necessarily for linguistic, reasons. These developments throw new light on the problem of the precise relationship between semantics and logic and may support attempts made (e.g., by Bar-Hillel) to identify logic with universal (or transcendental) semantics.

Since all these theories are still in active development, the last word on the relations between deep structure, semantic representation, and cognitive content has not yet been said.

A recent subfield of applied semantics is computational semantics, in which the use of computers for the determination of the semantic representation(s) of sentences of natural languages, as well as of constructed languages, is investigated.

Due to the lack of adequate semantic theories, the field of psychosemantics, that brand of psycholinguistics which deals with the psychological aspects of meaning, is still in its very first beginnings. Experimental studies in this field, using quantitative techniques, have not yet gone beyond studying the strengths of meaning association of various expressions, usually of single verbs or small phrases (Osgood's "semantic differential").

Various measures of the meaning content, or of the semantic information, carried by declarative sentences of natural or constructed languages, defined on the basis of absolute and conditional logical probability measures of these sentences (not to be confused with the statistical probabilities of the utterances of these sentences) have been proposed (e.g. by Carnap and Bar-Hillel), but so far the applications have been rather restricted.

Bibliography: Bar-Hillell Y.: Language and information. Reading, Mass. & Jerusalem, 1964. Id.: Aspects of language. Amsterdam & Jerusalem, 1970. Carnap, R.: Replies and expositions, III. In: Schilpp, P. A. (Ed.): The philosophy of Rudolf Carnap. La Salle (Ill.), 889–944. Chomsky, N.: Aspects of the theory of syntax. Cambridge, Mass., 1965. Cohen, L. J.: The diversity of meaning. London, 1962. Creelman, M. B.: The experimental investigation of meaning. New York, 1966. Katz, J. J.: The philosophy of language. New York & London, 1966. Lakoff, G.: Generative semantics. New York, 1971. Lorenz, K.: Elemente der Sprachkritik. Frankfurt a/M, 1970. Lyons, J.: Introduction to theoretical linguistics. Cambridge, 1968. Quinel, W. V. O.: Word and object. New York & London, 1970. Schaff, A.: Introduction to semantics. Oxford & Warsaw, 1962. Ullman, S.: The principles of semantics. Glasgow, ²1957. Weinreichl, U.: Explorations in semantic theory. In: Sebeok, T. A. et al. (Eds.): Current trends in linguistics, III. The Hague, 1966, 395–477. Ziff, P.: Semantic analysis. Ithaca, N.Y., 1960. Y. Bar-Hillel

Semicircular canals are filled with liquid, stand vertically one on top of the other, lie at any given time in a spatial plane, and serve as part of the organ of balance for the reception of acceleration. Inside the canal on both sides are movable tufts of hair in a colloid mass (*cupulae*) which during accelerations are turned outwards by the liquid flowing into the arcades and which impart a mechanical stimulus to the sensory cells situated at their lower end.   *M.S.*

Semiotic(s). The general theory of signs, which can derive from *natural* and *artificial* languages. Three aspects are usually distinguished:

Syntax is concerned with the relations between signs and other signs or series of signs. The syntactic rules of a language enable the permissible associations of basic elements to develop into more complex structures (sentences). See *Grammar*.

Semantics (q.v.) studies the connection between signs and their meanings.

Pragmatics is concerned with the relation between linguistic signs and their users, the human transmitters and receivers of information. According to K. Bühler's model of language, the signal and symptom functions are the main objects of pragmatic investigation. The factor of evaluation disclosed by the semantic differential (q.v.) technique (good-bad, beautiful-ugly, etc.) also lies in this area.
                                                       B.R.

Senility (syn. *Decrepitude*). Terms for the physical and mental decline of performance which usually occurs in old age. This aging process of the mind and body is accompanied by an enfeeblement of vitality and activity, and the psychic tempo slows down. Attention (q.v.) and initiative are usually reduced, and the capacity for self-control is partly lost. An old person's powers of observation suffer (see *Memory*), especially with regard to new impressions, and frequently there are impaired powers of judgment and comprehension. (See *Aging; Gerontology*.)   *M.Sa.*

Sensation. "Sensation is a psychic phenomenon incapable of further division and is produced by external stimuli acting on the sensory organs; in its intensity it depends on the strength of the stimuli, and in its quality on the nature of the sensory organs." That is how H. Rohracher paraphrased the concept of sensation in the classical sense, and he distinguished sensation from perception (q.v.) as follows: "Perception is a complex psychic phenomenon consisting of sensory sensations and *components of experience*, the cause or content of which is located in space and so leads to the apprehension of objects belonging to the outside world." Of course, this separation of sensation and perception is scarcely feasible in practice, and the boundary between the two concepts in the literature is becoming increasingly obscure (cf. S. H. Bartley).

After Heraclitus and Protagoras had spoken of sensation and the communication of knowledge by means of sensation as early as the fifth century B.C., the problem of sensation in the eighteenth century became urgent for classical science because of empiricism.

The physiologists Bell (1811) and F. Magendie (1822) showed that the afferent (q.v.) nerves transmitting sensation are different from the motor nerves; the former reach the spinal cord by way of the posterior roots, the latter leave it by way of the anterior roots. W. Wundt (1874) had begun to distinguish between sensations and perceptions: sensation is an element, perception is composed of complexes of these elements (see *Psychology of Elements*). He said that in sensation there is intensity and quality, but in perception space and time. Thus Wundt agrees with the psychology of association in opposition to gestalt psychology, in which sensation is understood as a part of perception or is completely absorbed by it (while in physiological psychology sensation has absorbed perception) (cf. E. G. Boring). Finally behaviorism examines the sensations of humans and animals through their "distinctive behavior", and therefore uses "discriminating reaction" as an expression of sensation. The psychology of information (q.v.) uses the possibilities created by information theory (q.v.) to interpret the information content of sensations mathematically.

The senses as conveyors of sensations. Using the word in its strict physiological meaning it may be said that sensation is the primary direct psychic correlate of an excitation of the senses by stimuli and contains information (q.v.) about the quality and quantity of these stimuli. Aristotle had been the first to state without the help of any apparatus that there were five senses, namely, sight, hearing, smell, taste and touch. Subsequent detailed study with improved apparatus subdivided the main sense of touch into the sense of pressure and contact (somesthetics), the sense of heat and the sense of pain; to these were added the sense of position and movement (kinesthetics) as a special form of somesthetics, and the sense of balance (see *Sense organs*). The senses are characterized by the following psychological and physiological criteria: (*a*) their excitation leads to a single class of experience with mostly different qualities of sensation. (*b*) Their adequate excitation is only possible if there is an amount of energy exceeding a certain minimum (threshold value). For an inadequate excitation even far greater amounts of energy are required. (*c*) The single senses or sensory channels have specific intakes (sensory cells, sensory receptor cells, neuro-epithelium). (*d*) From these specific sensory receptors a direct neuron path leads by way of synapses to certain areas of the cerebral cortex which are known as primary projection fields (q.v.) and in the direct vicinity of which there lie secondary projection fields (short and long term storage).

If the dimensions of experience and memory (q.v.) which in classical definitions of sensation are associated with perception are excluded, one must then say that sensations occur when these primary projection fields are excited, and that it does not matter whether they are excited adequately by way of the specific and relevant sensory channel or inadequately, i.e., by some direct electrical stimulus. The so-called "reflection theory" of Soviet writers could therefore be valid only if one ignored that cortical projection fields are excited inadequately, i.e., after by-passing the sensory cells (see *Hallucination*).—Cf. Lenin, quoted according to B. G. Ananiev, p. 5: "Sensation is an image of matter in motion."

The physiological mechanism of sensation. A stimulus (q.v.) (a physico-chemical state with an energy content) impinges—usually after passing through an organ that carries stimuli (eyeball, external auditory channel and middle ear, nasal passages, derma and subcutaneous fatty tissue)—on a specific sensory receptor cell which becomes excited if the energy of the stimulus is above the threshold. Sechenov was probably the first to state that sensations represent some kind of transformation of external energy in the sensory organs and finally in the brain (q.v.) itself. Continuing from there, Pavlov called the sensory organs the "transformers of external energy" and recognized correctly that each functional act of these organs, which he classified as "peripheral ends of the analysators", represents a transformation of external energy into a process of nervous "excitement". The excitement expresses itself in physico-chemical changes in the cell membrane which lead to a change of the "membrane potential" and hence to the creation of a receptor potential (= generator potential) which is necessarily dependent on stimulus intensity (intensity functions, according to E. H. Weber, q.v., G. T. Fechner, q.v., S. S. Stevens, W. D. Keidel). The generator potential releases a salvo of neuro-action potentials (NAP) on the adjoining efferent nerve fiber, the frequency being proportional to the amplitude of the generator potential (coding of the stimulus intensity "continuous-analogous" in the amplitude of the generator potential and "discrete analogous" in the frequency of the

NAP). Several further synapses are passed in which there is each time a reduction of the NAP frequency (Keidel speaks of the reductive behavior of the synapses) by way of the necessary recoding (discrete-analogous into continuous-analogous and finally at the postsynaptic axon once more discrete-analogous). The excitation of the cortical projection fields can be directly demonstrated in the electro-corticogram (electric potential lead direct from the exposed cerebral cortex) as an "evoked potential" with a latency of approximately 10 m sec after the sensory cell excitation. This can also be proved indirectly by an EEG message from the intact, unopened scalp. The amplitudes of these evoked cerebral potentials are proportional to the degree of the receptor cells, which of course are subject to influences of adaptation, contrast, etc., and can therefore not give any simple "reflection" of the environment. In addition, these amplitudes are altered by central nervous, psychic

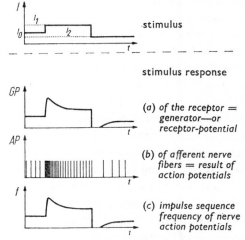

Schematic representation of connections between stimulus and physiological stimulus responses. Abscissa: time (standardized for all four axes). Ordinates: I: stimulus intensity; GP: amplitude of generator potential; AP: amplitude of action potentials measured on nerve fibers for a typical time sequence; f: frequency, number of action potentials passing over a point on the afferent nerve fibers in the set time unit. Upward movement of stimulus from I_0 to I_1, then downward from I_1 to I_2, so that I_2 (as here) is less than I_0. (Plattig, 1968.)

influences such as attention (q.v.), vigilance (q.v.), expectation, etc. Altogether, however, they represent a sufficiently accurate and objective correlate of sensation (W. D. Keitel, M. Spreng, K. H. Plattig, G. Guttmann). But how a sensation becomes conscious remains a complete mystery.

Bibliography: Ananiev, B. G.: Psychologie der sinnlichen Erkenntnis. Berlin, 1963. **Boring, E. G.:** Sensation and perception in the history of experimental psychology. New York, 1942. **Keidel, W. D. & Spreng, M.:** Elektronisch gemittelte langsame Rindenpotentiale des Menschen bei akustischer Reizung. Acta Oto-Laryngologica, Stockholm, 1963, *56*, 318–28. **Plattig, K. H.:** Über den elektrischen Geschmack. Reizstärkeabhängige evozierte Hirnpotential nach elektrischer Reizung der Zunge des Menschen. Z. Biol. 1969, *116*, 161–211. **Rohracher, H.:** Einführung in die Psychologie. Vienna & Innsbruck, ⁹1965. *K. H. Plattig*

Sensation function. According to C. G. Jung one of the four basic functions of the psyche. Together with intuition (q.v.) it is one of the irrational functions because it bypasses reason and transmits facts only without their meaning or value.   *W.L.*

Sensation type. A functional type (q.v.) corresponding to the leading "irrational" psychic "basic function" of sensation ("conscious perception") which is linked "concretely" to sensory impression or "abstractly" to subjective "esthetic" evaluation. Hence it appears extraverted as naïve realism or introverted as an experience of the profoundly "portentous" and of the "significant".   *W.K.*

Sense organs. The universe contains atoms and molecules which cause vibrations and radiation by means of regular movements; in so far as they affect the sense organs, they are called *stimuli*. The sense organs contain specifically reactive receptors (q.v.) (selection of stimuli) in which (adequate) stimuli evoke a potential which expands within the receptor. If it exceeds a critical value, it brings about total depolarization and action potentials in the nerve fibers. By analogy with communications technology a stimulus may be conceived as information encoded by means of a frequency code and broadcast over the nerves. The quantity of information depends on impulse frequency and the number of receptors.

1. *The eye.* The eye (q.v.) mediates most information concerning the environment. It produces an image of the environment on its light-sensitive layer, the retina (q.v.). Since the eye is a living structure, in addition to the physically conditioned faults, errors occur which distort the image. Physiological *contrast* (q.v.) (cf. Fig. 1) serves to correct the

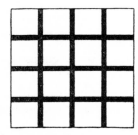

Fig. 1. Lattice contrast (L. Hermann). Bright spots appear at the points where the black lines intersect.

image: the retinal elements on which the light stimulus falls produce a contrasting effect (*inhibition*) in their environment; hence the difference between the object and its environment is enlarged; contrast largely compensates for dioptric imperfections, and thus affords the prerequisite for the proficient operation of the eye.

The eye's sense of space comes from its ability to perceive two separate points (see *Corresponding retinal points*). Its power of analysis, or *visual activity*, is greatest in the *fovea centralis* (q.v.). The limit of visual activity is reached when two cones are excited which are separated by an element excited by about twenty-five per cent less. Since recent anatomical research suggests that the diameter

of a cone is smaller than had earlier been assumed, J. J. Oppel conjectures that the individual cone is not linked to the center by a separate fiber, but that several cones unite as an aggregate which is possibly sensitive to different colors. Hence visual activity is independent of the color of the test sign.

In the focused eye visual activity is measured at a distance of 5 m., since the light-sensitive layer of cones has a thickness that allows a shifting of the object within limits. Moreover, the dispersion circles at 5 m. are still too small to cause any substantial disturbance to physiological correction through contrast. The eye's power of analysis is still the same even at a shorter distance, if the experimental conditions are constantly maintained. It is optimal if illumination exceeds 1000 lx (König).

In the periphery of the retina, visual activity decreases quickly (to one-third at a distance from the center of the retina of 5°, and to one fifth at 10°). The decrease is smaller if presentation time is reduced, because a counter-effect sets in with the stimulus: this causes the threshold to give way (local adaptation). The influence of presentation time is evident also in foveal vision; the product of the angle of vision and presentation time is constant (photo-chemical principle: R. Bunsen & H. E. Roscoe). Processes take place in the eye that are similar to those on a photographic plate. When an object moves in a horizontal direction in relation to the observer, visual activity at first increases, but then decreases considerably (fast traffic). With a circular movement of the object (radar set) it decreases more slowly; there is a regular connection between it and the number of rotations.

If an object approaches the observer (<5 m.), its image on the retina will quickly be so indistinct that contrast no longer suffices for compensation. Alteration of the distance between lens and retina is possible only in lower animals (cuttlefish). In mammals and young humans, the lens (q.v.) is soft and elastic; under the influence of colloidal forces, it can approximate a globular shape, if a bundle of fibers attached to its equator slackens (see *Accommodation*).

The radius of curvature of the (less elastic) anterior surface of the lens decreases in the process by about one half (from 10 mm. to 5.33 mm.), and that of the posterior surface by only 0.67 mm. However, this does not mean that the posterior surface is not involved in the accommodation process. Since the volume of the lens cannot change, its anterior surface can become flatter under distance adjustment of the eye, only if the mass of the lens can give way against the (more elastic) posterior surface. Therefore the posterior surface is already dilated with distance adjustment. According to Gullstrand, the change in the shape of the lens is insufficient to explain the entire increase in refractive powers of the young eye; he attributes a third of it to a displacement of more strongly refractive masses within the lens from the periphery back to the center (intracapsular accommodation mechanism).

The suspensory ligament is slackened when ciliary muscle contracts on excitation of the oculomotor nerve (*nervous oculomotorius*), which belongs to the parasympathetic nervous system. Von Helmholtz thought it improbable that contraction of the radial fibers in the ciliary muscle restored distance adjustment of the eye. Recently, however, the presence of sympathetic nerve fibers between the small muscle cells of the ciliary muscle has been reported. The influence of the sympathetic was investigated in experiments by Meesmann, Monjé, Siebeck and others, and may now be taken as established. Therefore adjustment of the eye to ∞ should not be described as loss of accommodation, but as near and distance accommodation.

When at rest, the eye adjusts to a finite distance, as in short sight (see *Myopia*), e.g., in fog, and in darkness, when there is no cue for fixation (empty space or night myopia). Since the lens grows constantly throughout life, like the hair and nails, but cannot get rid of the old substance, the substance of the lens thickens to form the inelastic lenticular nucleus, which increases with age and makes the lens progressively less elastic. The ability to adjust the eye to near objects therefore constantly decreases, and the range of accommodation is reduced: in the young it is ten to fourteen diopters, but at sixty drops to one diopter.

Two further processes are linked to that of accommodation: the *convergence* movement of the eyes and the *contraction of the pupils*. Just to see with both eyes an object situated close at hand, it is necessary to bring it into the *foveae centrales* so that images can be formed bilaterally. The axes of vision of both eyes must be directed to the object; the eyes must carry out a convergence movement (see *Convergence*). If they do not, double images occur. Whether the convergence movement or the accommodation adjustment is the first process, is not yet clear. The extent of convergence (in contrast to accommodation width) is practically independent of age; the near point in convergence is ten cm. away from the eye. Variation of pupil width (see *Pupillary reflex*) is linked with convergence. The pupil is formed from the iris; its pigment is responsible for the particular color of the eye. It "screens off" marginal rays and reduces the effect of lens errors. It contracts when the eyes converge and are adjusted to close surroundings, and thus assists near accommodation. Depth of focus increases when the pupil is contracted; at a pupil width of two mm. at reading distance it amounts to three cm.; with near work no change of eye focus is necessary. The width of the pupil is also influenced by the incidence of light (on the second eye too) and by age. Since its width constantly fluctuates, it is natural to regard pupillary movement as the result of an automatic control circuit, and not as a reflex in response to the stimulus of light. The retina serves as an antenna, the pupillary center as a regulator. The diameter of the pupil fluctuates between eight and two mm., and the incidence of light in the ratio of 16:1. In very strong light the pupils can contract violently and cause the pain of dazzle or glare (q.v.). The maximal pupillary diameter diminishes with age. The contraction of the pupil after the incidence of light lasts 4″, widening 16″. Widening is the first stage of dark adaptation (q.v.).

The totality of objects that can be perceived simultaneously by the unmoving eye is the *field of vision*, or *visual field*. The field of vision is limited by the orbital roof, the bridge of the nose and the cheeks. The periphery is color-blind; then comes a zone in which blue and yellow are discerned; farthest towards the center are the limits for red and green. The limits of the field of vision, especially those for color, are dependent on the luminance of the test signs, their size and saturation. The point at which the nerve fibers leave the eye (*papilla nervi optici*) is blind. It is situated in the field of vision between 10° and 20° away from the middle of the retina. Even in the case of unilateral vision, the blind spot (q.v.) is not noticed, since its environment is of too little importance. Outside the limits of the field of vision, sensitivity at individual points of the retina can be measured by the method of light perception perimetry (see *Perimeter*). Refraction anomalies can be easily adjusted in this way. Deficiencies of the visual field help doctors to locate, e.g., tumors.

Twilight and night vision. Print on white paper appears black even when the letters in the midday sun throw back into our eyes three times as much light as the paper at dawn. The reason is the accommodation of the eye to the different proportions of light. The sensitivity of the eye (see *Dark adaptation*) increases with diminishing light. If the eye was previously adapted to daylight, after a longer period in complete darkness its increase can exceed 10,000 times. The curve is appropriately represented as a logarithmic scale. It is dependent on the area of the retina in question.

The greatest increase in sensitivity is found in an area 10° to 20° away from the middle of the retina, and the least at the very center. The increase is further dependent on the color of the light stimulus (least in the case of red, most in the case of green), on the size of the test sign (number of elements) and on the age of the subject. Adaptation to darkness decreases with increasing age, as is the case with near accommodation, after age fifty. It is greater binocularly than monocularly, yet the adaptation of the one eye does not influence that of the other. Adaptation to darkness starts with the widening of the pupil; in the following phase of five to ten minutes the aftereffect of the previous light adaptation must first be overcome (it has nothing to do with the transition from cones-vision to rod-vision). After forty-five minutes, the eye has practically adapted to the darkness; in the case of a longer period the sensitivity increase is only smaller. The speed of the adaptation process allows no conclusions regarding the degree of sensitivity achieved after complete adaptation. It is clear that speed of adaptation and the terminal condition are two different and independent processes. The sensitivity in different adaptation conditions is studied by perimetry.

The discovery of visual purple by L. Kühne in the nineteenth century seemed to afford an explanation of dark adaptation. *Rhodopsin* (q.v.) occurs mainly in the rods of the retina; therefore the adaptation capacity of the middle of the retina is also small. It is assumed today that only a part of the adaptation process (not perhaps the largest) takes place because of visual purple.

In the human retina there are two kinds of light-sensitive receptors: *cones* (q.v.) and *rods* (q.v.). This finding grounded the theory of the double function of the retina, "duplicity theory" (q.v.), which states that the rods mediate night vision, and the cones day (and color) vision. Many observations, which were previously interpreted in the sense of the duplicity theory, can be explained in other ways. Therefore it is now thought that the duplicity theory is to be understood less crudely. Cones and rods work together so that information is conducted to the brain by a minimum of conduction pathways.

Electric potentials are discharged from every living tissue. From the potential difference between retina and cornea, a resting current is created in which, during exposure to light, an action current, the *electroretinogram* (ERG; see *Electroretinography*) is set up. The ERG has a complicated course caused by different processes. Hopes of being able to associate one of these processes with the cones and another with the rods remain unfulfilled. It has not yet proved possible even to derive the action potential from human brain cells. ERG plays a special part in medical diagnosis.

Sensitivity to light. Between the incidence of a stimulus on the eye and the occurrence of sensitivity there is a time-lapse of at least 0.035 seconds (*Sensitivity time*, Fröhlich, 1929). Its duration is dependent on the course of the light stimulus, its duration and strength, the adaptation condition of the observer and his attention, and it can increase to above two seconds. As a part of reaction time it is important for the car driver and in rapid flight. Fig. 2 shows that the abovementioned factors also influence the duration of sensitivity and its course in time. Maximum sensitivity does not occur at the beginning of sensitivity; the position of maximum sensitivity and the duration of sensitivity play a part in the fusion of two stimuli, which changes with the logarithm of the intensity of the light stimulus. In daylight the fusion frequency amounts to sixty; even in twilight, twenty stimuli fuse per second. The luminance corresponds to the sum of the luminances of the fused stimuli (Talbot-Plateau law).

For the peculiarities and theories of *sensitivity to color*, see *Color perception; Color vision; Color blindness.*

Eye movements. By virtue of its globular shape, the eye can (without any movement of the head) turn to an object incident in the periphery of the retina (peripheral vision, q.v.). The totality of objects that can be included (without any head movement) in direct vision is called the *field of vision*, or visual field. Eye movement depends on three

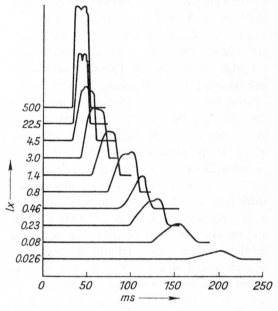

Fig. 2. Temporal sequence of visual sensation process as dependent on stimulus intensity. The abscissas give the time in msec, the ordinates show intensity of light.

pairs of muscles. The eyes can revolve about 50–60° outwards and 70–80° inward. The power of movement continuously diminishes with age; only inward and downward movement increases up to the thirtieth year of life, and remains constant from then on. Generally only 18° of possible movement are used; the field of vision is extended by the additional movement of the head. Rotation of the eye on its axis is also possible by means of the oblique eye muscles. The same position of the eye, however, always accords with a definite position of the line of vision (Donders' *law of constant orientation*). Listing's law (q.v.) gives us some information about this position. In studying eye movements, it is necessary to distinguish the voluntary from the involuntary. Those movements made during the observation of an object show no relationship with the object, except in following contours, when the movements are interrupted by occasional pauses and backward "leaps" (saccades). Similar eye movements occur in reading; a line of 12 cm. is explored in five leaps at reading distance. Only half is seen sharply (foveal vision). The letters seen indistinctly are "made up"; hence misprints are easily overlooked. Regular eye movements (possible up to 30°) are unusual under physiological conditions. During pauses, the eye adapts very quickly to the different light intensities (local adaptation). Rhythmic movements are brought into relationship with innervation of the eye muscles. Similar movements are to be observed during the mere imagination of objects and during dreams (q.v.). An (initially, at least) voluntary movement leads to fixation of an object. Fixation is performed by a central area of the fovea of about 100 mm. By backward movements, which last about 20 msec., and often occur in groups, the eye avoids having to travel through slow deviations. Fixation point and the beginning of rough correction movements depend on the appearance of the object. Fixation movements are related to rhythmic head movements. Involuntary movements occur when the eye is no longer in a position to keep in view the object under observation. It then makes a backward movement (nystagmus), and seeks a new viewing point. Nystagmus is influenced by optical and psychological factors (psycho-optic reflex). It is used in the objective study of dark adaptation and visual acuity. Similar eye movements can be caused independently of the optic stimulus of the vestibular apparatus. During sleep (q.v.) the eyes move outward and upward (Bell's phenomenon), and are thus protected from the incidence of light; the pressure of the eyelids on the eye is also reduced.

The localization of static objects is effected by means of the retinal point. As this changes,

the perception of an object movement occurs. Although a similar movement of the image on the retina can be caused by eye movements, both can be easily distinguished one from the other. Errors are rare, since image fluctuation on the retina follows either an impulse current from the center (efference), which then adjusts the return message resulting from the movement (reafference), or this adjustment fails and the return message reaches the center. In the first case the eye has moved, in the second the object.

Eye movements control one's ability to estimate the height and width of an object. The precision with which one can assess the parallelism of two lines is well-known. Eye movements can, however, lead to "illusions". Undivided lines, surfaces or angles can be thought to be smaller when subdivided. According to Fröhlich (1929), even the Müller-Lyer illusion (q.v.) is due to eye movements. Other "illusions" (see *Kundt's illusion* and *Münsterberg's illusion*) can be explained by different width values of the retinal halves. Similarly with the subjective vertical (set up in the dark with the help of a line of light), which diverges outward about 1° with its upper end in the middle. All illusions of this kind can be interpreted on the basis of physiological conditions (see *Geometrical-optical illusions*).

An object is seen singly with both eyes when portrayed at "identical" points. Objects do not form at *identical points of the retina* (q.v.) if they are seen double. Objects which deviate from one another on the horizontal only up to 9 minutes of arc are an exception. Transversely disparate deviations within these limits do not as a rule lead to double images, but are given a new meaning in a spatial impression. Diversity of image in binocular vision is (according to C. Wheatstone) the origin of *depth perception* (q.v.). Since this theory cannot explain the dependence of depth of focus on time and many other observations, M. Monjé assumes that eye movements or their intention are the real reason for depth of vision, in which case transverse disparation may be the ruling factor. Looking corresponds in the optical field to "exploration" in the tactile field (dynamic theory of sight). According to this theory the eye does not have a special position; it functions according to the same principle as other sense organs (taste, touch). See *Visual perception*.

2. *The ear*. The ear communicates information in the same way as the eye. The origin of the information is in the environment. Like the eye, the ear is an exteroceptor. Its main task is the mediation of speech, which is impossible without constant supervision by the ear (see *Deaf mutism*). The adequate stimuli are longitudinal vibrations in which the air is displaced by sound sources. The human larynx is also one of these sound sources. The real organ of hearing is situated in *the labyrinth*, which is hollowed out of the hard substance of the petrosal bone and filled with fluid (perilymph). Since the perilymph's resistance to sound waves is about 3500 times greater than that of air, the air waves must be adjusted closely to the proportion of the perilymph. Via the external ear, sound reaches the external auditory canal, which is closed at the end by the tympanic membrane (characteristic sound 2000 Hz). The tympanic membrane vibrates as a rigid mass about an axis situated on its upper edge. It transfers its vibrations to an angular lever formed by the three *auditory ossicles*. The long shaft of the *hammer* is attached to the tympanic membrane. It is situated on the extension of the incus, which transfers the vibration to the foot of the stapes (stirrup) in the ratio of 1.3:1. Since the active part of the tympanic membrane is in the ratio of 17:1 to the surface of the foot of the stapes, strength is increased up to twenty-two times, and movement amplitude declines simultaneously. The characteristic frequency of the whole system is between 1200 and 1400 Hz; the system is well muffled and especially suitable for the transmission of low frequencies

in the field of human speech (80–600 Hz). Since the tympanic membrane stops reacting entirely at 2000 Hz, the transmission of energy at this frequency rapidly declines; bone conduction replaces air conduction. The tension of the tympanic membrane is not changed by the muscles of the middle ear but the chain of auditory ossicles is stiffened, and its vibration muffled. That part of the labyrinth which assists hearing is called the *cochlea* because of its shape. Around the bony bar of the axis the *scala vestibuli* ascends from the oval window (the foot of the stapes) to the end of the cochlea, and changes into the *scala tympani*. Both are divided by a sac containing viscous endolymph; the foundation of this sac is formed by the basilar membrane, which bears the sense cells. The basilar membrane is 33.5 mm. long; its width is 0.5 mm. at its end, but this declines to 0.04 mm. in the area of the foot of the stapes. No principle of frequency analysis except that of resonance was known at the time of Helmholtz, he therefore believed that it also applied to the basilar membrane of the ear. Ranke and Békésy were the first to realize that the inner ear is full of fluid. Since the canal depth near the foot of the stapes is small in comparison with the sound wavelengths, these are transmitted proportionately at first; very soon the canal depth is equal to the shortest wave length. When an added force occurs perpendicularly to the direction of locomotion, vertices are formed; the smaller the frequency, the later this phenomenon—it is latest when the frequency near the end of the cochlea is deepest. Moreover the basilar membrane is narrowest (and therefore hardest) in the area of the oval window, and becomes softer as its width increases. But its flexibility increases at the same time, and the frequency of the conducted waves is again dependent on flexibility. Since energy cannot be lost, it induces a maximal bend in the basilar membrane and at the same time a maximal stimulus to the associated hair cells. The measurement at the maximal point of maxism in the ear of a corpse shows an approximate logarithmic dependence on the amount of vibrations from the stimulus, i.e., the increase of a sound at a certain percentage rate signifies a definite distance of the new stimulus from the original one, at 2.6 mm. an octave. Since the basilar membrane is 30 mm. long, according to the hearing distance, it can take 11.5 octaves.

When the waves occur up to 800 Hz, the whole head vibrates. Compression waves are created by the rhythmic compression of the

attributed to the inner hair cells. They may be compared to the cones of the eye. The hair cells are not distributed regularly over the basilar membrane, and their number is at its greatest in the middle area, corresponding to selectivity of frequency.

The intensity threshold and the possibility of variation difference in volume must be distinguished from the possibility of variation in sounds of different frequency and selectivity. The absolute threshold for different sounds is dependent on frequency. At 18 Hz a pressure

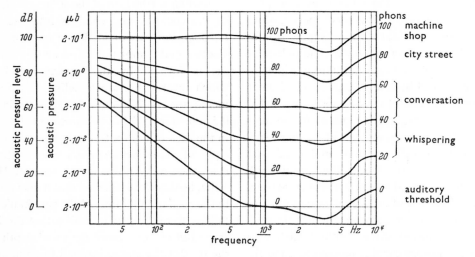

Fig. 3. Curves of equal loudness. The loudness of a sound in phons corresponds to the decibel value of a 1000 Hz sound ("normal noise") that sounds equally loud (E. Schütz).

labyrinth walls. These waves (like those caused by the foot of the stapes) lead to a bulging of the basilar membrane (bone conduction). The origin of this is the difference in the volumes of both scales and their elasticity.

The adequate stimulus for the excitation of sense cells is their curvature. The inner hair cells are situated in a row on the bony ledge and have an isolated connection with the auditory center. A row of external hair cells corresponds to each cell. A nerve fiber links cells over 1–2 mm. of the basilar membrane. Neighboring areas overlap. They are more sensitive than the inner hair cells, but can communicate only a rough location; however, the continuous linkage with the center is

of 1 dyn/cm.^{2} is necessary to cause sound sensitivity. The pressure which is necessary to reach threshold falls with increasing frequency, at 1000 Hz to 2.10^{-4} dyn/cm.^{2}. This value corresponds to a sound intensity of 10^{-16} Watts, (see Fig. 4). Since the auditory field at 1000 Hz contains 10^{13} divisions of energy it is advantageous to choose a logarithmic system of comparison. The "bell" (after A. G. Bell) serves as a unit. By this is understood the logarithmic proportion of sound power in relation to the absolute threshold at 1000 hz (1 decibel [db] = 1/10 bell). The upper frequency limit for the young is 22,000 Hz; the upper limit declines constantly with increasing age (down to one octave), and finally (at the age of 70) is 10,000–12,000 Hz. Selectivity is at its greatest in the vocal field when the duration of sound and its intervals is limited to 1″. In the area from 500–2000 Hz it is optimal (0.3%) and fluctuates up and down. As the maximum for the basilar membrane is very wide, this selectivity can be achieved only by a physiological process (contrast). 1500 individual sounds can be distinguished. The variation threshold for two sounds of equal frequency amounts to approximately 10% (= 1 db). The upper limit of the auditory field is actually not an auditory limit but one of *pain* (q.v.). The whole auditory field contains 340,000 sounds. The "loudness" (q.v.) of a sound sensation is measured in *phons*. The phon scale differs from the decibel scale, in that the latter is independent of the frequency of its zero point at a sound pressure of 2.10^{-4} dyn/cm.^{2}, whereas the phon scale is dependent on frequency; its zero position corresponds at every sound to the absolute threshold (see Fig. 4). At 1000 Hz the scales agree. The loudness of whispering amounts to 20, of conversation to 40–60 phons; a car horn at a distance of 1 m. is 90 phons. In the case of a steady load of 65 phons, the natural protective mechanisms of the ear are already overtaxed; If 95 phons is exceeded, protective measures are necessary (see *Noise level*). The ear can adapt to a sound lasting a longer time. *Adaptation* is not to be confused with fatigue (q.v.). Rather the alternation of stimulus material in *adaptation* is arranged so that the intensity threshold is at its greatest in the given conditions. The extent of adaptation in the ear is substantially less than in the eye.

The *sensation time*, the period between the incidence of a stimulus and the occurrence of sensation, is in the same dimension as in the eye; dependent on sound intensity, it is between 35 and 150 msec. Since the motor constituent of a reaction is not influenced by the sensory stimulus, the reaction time must also occur under comparable conditions within the same order of magnitude. But,

whereas in the eye not only the initial but the maximum sensation time follows a logarithmic regularity (see Fig. 2), in the ear only the sensation time follows such a system, and the maximum is reached for all magnitudes of stimulus after 180 msec. (Monjé, 1926).

Using one ear, the *direction* from which the sound comes is established by gauging the

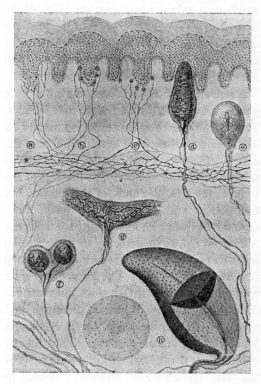

Fig. 4. The sense organs of the skin (Kahn). (*a*) free nerve endings (pain); (*b*) cells of epidermis; (*c*) cells in hypodermis; (*d*) tactile apparatus (pressure sensation); (*e*) Krause end bulbs (cold?); (*f*) Golgi-Mazzoni terminal corpuscles (itching?); (*g*) Ruffini's brushes (heat?); (*h*) lamellar corpuscle left, cross-section right.

sound source. In both ears, a sound not emanating from the median plane is distinguished by its *intensity and the time of incidence*. Since the sensation time does not play a part in both ears, Monjé (1935) attributes localization to the fluctuation of sensation maxima. The distance of a sound wave can be known with considerable certainty independently of its intensity by the diversity of the frequency spectrum. The speed of the flow of air is perceptible with near sound waves but not with distant waves. The ear, therefore, reacts more to quality than to quantity. See *Auditory perception*.

3. *Skin senses* (*a*) *Touch*. The "skin senses", or "cutaneous senses", include several senses which as a rule act together, (see Fig. 4). In feeling an object, an *excitation* of the *pressure and touch receptors* of the *organs of the sense of temperature* and eventually those also of the sense of *pain* (q.v.) occurs simultaneously. The sensation of touch is communicated by a plexus of nerves in the area of the hair follicles. The Meissner corpuscles are found mainly on hairless parts of the skin in the papillae of the derma. They are particularly numerous at the extremities of the body, at the end of the tongue, the lips, the ends of the fingers, but sparse, e.g., on the skin of the back. Their number declines with age. As the spatial sense is empowered by its capacity to perceive two separate points, it must be especially equipped at the ends of the body. The sense of pressure communicates a great deal of information concerning the environment. Pressure and touch are further mediated by Merkel's and Vater's or Pacini's corpuscles, and possibly by independent nerve endings in hairless parts of the skin. The absolute threshold amounts to 0.03 erg, and the variation threshold to 3%; hence the former is very small in comparison with other sense organs, and the latter comes between those of the eye and the ear. The time necessary for the creation of sensation in respect of rapid (electric) skin stimulus is in the same proportion as with the eye and the ear; it is inversely proportional to the logarithm of stimulus intensity (Fröhlich, 1929).

Besides its contributions to spatial sensation, the sense of touch carries a large quantity of information concerning the condition of the body. In this regard, deformation of the skin provides the major stimulus. The organism can adapt itself very quickly to a continuous stimulus. The sensation of touch is especially affected by adaptation; electrophysiological tests show that the thin nerve fibers which communicate pressure sensation go on firing after initial adaptation.

Rhythmic stimuli induce a particular sensation, "prickling" (vibration sensation). A stimulus somewhat in excess of threshold travelling over the skin causes the tickling sensation (especially on the lips, the palms of the hands and the soles of the feet).

Perception of depth is communicated by the Vater–Pacini particles, the Golgi apparatus, and the receptors which branch out with their non-myelinated, tree-like ramifications in muscular sheaths, and wind around the tendons. The position of limbs is not communicated by muscle sense, but mainly by the sense organs of the skin and the Pacini corpuscles.

(*b*) *Pain* (q.v.). A shift of metabolic into pathological processes, whether caused by damage to the skin or by chemical substances, leads to the sensation of pain through depolarization in fine nerve fibers situated in the upper layers of the epithelium. Pain (q.v.) is not communicated by special sense organs; hence there is no *specific* stimulus (as with light in the case of the eye). The release of pain sensation requires much greater energy; there is also no summation and no adaptation to pain; its sensation time is long.

Two kinds of pain are distinguished: *superficial* and *deep pain*. The former is conducted by medullated nerve fibers at a mean speed of 20–30 msec., and the deep pain is conveyed by thin non-myelinated, slow-conducting fibers. Superficial pain can be more easily located than deep pain, because the density of the nerve fibers is less in deep pain than in superficial, and therefore the possibility of contrast formation is smaller. The sensations within the body are not so delicate as on the skin. They inhibit above all the voluntary motor system and therefore bring about relaxation or protection of a diseased organ. The fluctuation of vegetative tonus is substantial;

dominance of sympathetic tonus occurs (see *Autonomic nervous system*) together with rising blood pressure and heart beat, increased clarity of consciousness, and defense and flight readiness. The temporal course of the stimulus plays an important part in deep pain. The stomach, the intestine and bladder are, e.g., insensitive to a cut, but react violently to stretching, spasms and lack of oxygen.

If pain nerves are destroyed, reduced pain sensitivity is produced (hypesthesia), and is often linked with increased painfulness (*hyperpathy*); then, with regeneration, there is a stage of altered sensitivity (*paresthesia*).

No special organ has hitherto been found for the sensation of *itching*. One hypothesis is a combination of weak pain stimuli and touch stimuli. Its origin is also related to protopathic pain, or attributed to a still undiscovered "mediator substance", formed by means of an axon reflex, which only then effects a change in tissue chemistry. In spite of considerable similarity, there is a big difference between pain and itching; pain induces defense, itching causes tickling. Morphine relieves pain but promotes itching; on the other hand heat causes pain but prevents itching.

Sense of temperature. The cold (*Krause's end bulb*) and heat receptors (*Ruffini's corpuscles*) are sense organs (the former situated at a depth of 0.1 mm in the skin, the latter at 9.5 mm.) which ensure a constant body temperature. Today it is assumed that, instead of the end particles, independent nerve endings operate as receptors (H. Hensel). Cold stimuli, since they are not situated so deep down in the skin, are easier to locate. Their contribution to the representation of the environment is greater than that of the heat receptors. The heat receptors react in temperatures above the mean and the cold ones in those below it. Sudden changes lead to an excessive reaction which then declines to a constant value (adaptation). "Burning heat" and "biting cold" are not pure temperature sensations but mixed sensations on the edge

of the temperature scales. The sensation of variation is dependent on surface (spatial summation) and on the speed of the change (temporal summation). Therefore wood feels warmer than metal at the same temperature, and water seems colder than air at the same temperature. (When small cutaneous areas cool down because of a draught, the counteraction of the body can fail, and encourage a cold.) Internal parts of the body seem to be insensitive to temperature.

4. *Taste.* The spectrum of taste sensation consists of four fundamental qualities: *sweet* (the end of the tongue), *salty* and *sour* (the edge of the tongue), and *bitter* (the base of the tongue). Further sensations are formed from a combination of these tastes. Smell and the co-stimuli of touch-, temperature-, and pain-receptors make a further contribution to taste. The taste buds are embedded in the papillae of the tongue. There are approximately twenty sense cells grouped in a bud and each one of these bears an easily broken peg which projects into a small hole. To be able to reach these holes, the matter to be tasted must be water-soluble and diffusible. However, it is still impossible to understand all the basic sensations from their physical and chemical properties. The sour sensation is linked with the presence of H-ions, and the salty sensation tastes of sodium chloride. Other salts, e.g., magnesium sulphate, cause a salty sensation at the end of the tongue but a bitter sensation at its base. The bitter sensation alone is induced by quinine. The sweet sensation can be caused by inorganic (diluted lead solution) and quite different organic compounds (cane sugar, saccharine). Levorotatory aminoacids taste sweet, dextrorotatory bitter, or they are tasteless. It has therefore been thought that the sweet taste occurs when neighboring hydroxide groups possess excessive cohesive forces which, because of the geometrical structure of the molecule, cannot be neutralized and react to the atom groups in the nerve ends of the taste buds (R. S. Schallenberger). The

term "contrast" is sometimes used in connection with taste, as is "aftertaste" or "change" (e.g., by means of 2% sulphuric acid) and "insensitivity". The individual parts of the tongue are supplied by different nerves; according to recent findings, excitation in respect of salty, sour and bitter is conducted via different nerves, and on a quantitatively different scale. The individual reaction is greatest for sweetness; the sensory nerves of the soft palate also participate in this reaction. It is concluded from the evidence of electrophysiological tests that receptors with a narrow field and a wide field must be distinguished. The significance of areas of taste for the composition of saliva must also be noted.

5. *Smell.* Although in the history of development the sense of smell is to be reckoned among the oldest functions of the senses, hitherto it has not been possible to explain all its physiological processes. In the *regio olfactoria*, an area of the human nasal roof measuring about 25 mm.², the extensions of the *olfactory cells* are situated between yellow-pigmented supporting cells; they bear 6–8 ciliary-type hairs and are covered with a special watery mucus which, besides its rinsing function, could perhaps affect the selection of odiferous substances. Since breath passes chiefly over the second and third nasal muscles, the movement of air at the *regio olfactoria* is slight; the latter is thus protected against too strong a concentration of odors and too low an air temperature. The movement can be increased and accelerated by sniffing. Among the elements, only halogens smell, together with about thirty inorganic compounds; organic compounds also smell. Carbon monoxide and ammonium do not smell. We distinguish about ten thousand qualities of sensation. It is clear that this large number does not correspond to a similarly large number of receptors but that it is created by combination and by stimulation patterns. On the other hand there must be a definite

specificity of olfactory cells, for adaptation to individual odors is possible. H. Henning has postulated the existence of six basic smells (see *Odor prism*). The *stereochemical theory*, which proceeds from the molecular structure of smells, postulates a similar number of basic smells which do not, however, entirely coincide with Henning's. As with colors, an absolute threshold can also be distinguished from the specific threshold in the case of olfactory sensations. Olfactory sensations can combine, and smell changes with the concentration of the substance and the duration of its effect. Adaptation to a smell follows quickly at first, and then slowly. There are *hyposmias* (q.v.) and *anosmias* (q.v.).

Contact and touch sensations, pain, temperature sensation and taste have no *fields of projection* distributed according to the sense organs; instead, the primary sensory cortex is distributed according to organs so that, for example, touch and taste stimuli to a large extent overlap. Confusions are therefore not excluded.

Bibliography: Bauer, I.: Unsere gegenwärtigen Kenntnisse über den Geruchssinn und deren Prüfung. Diss. Med. Fac., Kiel, 1962. **Fröhlich, F. W.:** Die Empfindungszeit. Jena, 1929. **Gross, C. G. & Zeigler, H. P.** (Eds.): Readings in physiological psychology, Vols. 1–3. New York & London, 1969. **Gulick, W. L.:** Hearing: physiology and psychophysics. New York & London, 1970. **Haber, R. N.** (Ed.): Contemporary theory and research in visual perception. New York, 1968. **Hensel, H.:** Allgemeine Sinnesphysiologie. Hautsinne, Geschmack, Geruch. Berlin, 1969. **Keidel, W. D.:** Physiologie der Hautsinne. In: Handbuch der Haut- und Geschlechtskrankheiten. Suppl. Vol. I, Pt. 3. Berlin, 1963, 157. **Milner, P. M.:** Physiological psychology. New York & London, 1970. **Monjé, M.:** Empfindungszeit und zeitlicher Verlauf der Gehörempfindung bei Verwendung kurzdauernder Schallreize. Z. Biol., 1926, 85, 349. **Id.:** Ein Beitrag zur Frage der Richtungslokalisation von Schallreizen. Z. Sinnesphysiol., 1935, 66, 7. **Id.:** Physiologie des Auges. In: Handbuch der Zoologie, Vol. 8(2). Berlin, 1968. **Id.:** Lichtsinn. Physiologie des Auges. In: **Velhagen, K.** (Ed.): Der Augenarzt. Vol. 1, Leipzig, ²1969, 173. **Moray, N.:** Attention: selective processes in vision and hearing. London, 1970. **Noton, D. & Stark, L.:** Eye movements and visual perception. Scient. Amer., 1971, *6*, 35–43. **Polyak, S.:** The retina. Chicago, 1941. **Ranke, O. F. & Lullies, H.:** Gehör, Stimme, Sprache. Berlin, 1953. **Schober, H.:** Das Sehen. Leipzig, ³1960, (Vol. 1); 1964, (Vol. 2). **Trendelenburg, W.:** Der Gesichtssinn (Monjé, Schmidt, Schütz). Berlin, 1961. **Trincker, D.:** Physiologie des Hörens und die Reiztransformation im Innenohr. J. Audiological Technique, 1967, *6*, 158.

M. Monjé

Senses. See *Sense organs.*

Sense types. These are characterized by the preference of a certain sensory area for perception (q.v.), but also for imagination (q.v.) and for remembering and thinking (q.v.) (see *Ideational types*). J. M. Charcot distinguished the optic (visual), acoustic (auditive) and motor type.   *W.K.*

Sensibility. 1. *In psychology* sensibility is sensitivity, delicacy of or capacity for feeling. 2. *In physiology*, sensibility denotes the ability to feel and to process sensory stimuli. Sensibility may be either superficial (pressure, temperature, pain) or deep-seated (muscular tonus, etc.) (see *Sense organs*).

Disturbances of sensibility. Physiologically three forms may be distinguished: (*a*) *anesthesia* (q.v.): absence of sensibility; (*b*) *hypesthesia*: diminished sensibility; (*c*) *hyperesthesia* (q.v.): excessive sensibility (see also *Analgesia*).

H.-J.A.

Sensitive. Person with special ability for ESP (q.v.). In experimental parapsychology is often referred to as a "high scorer".   *J.B.*

Sensitive delusion of reference. Kretschmer used the phrase *sensitiver Beziehungswahn* to describe a delusion of reference occurring in a person who is self-conscious, easily upset and prone to feel that he is conspicuous or remarked upon. The delusion may or may not develop after some humiliating or upsetting experience, and is usually accompanied by other delusions and symptoms of anxiety. These delusional states may not be related to schizophrenia if they follow some traumatic experience and if they are not accompanied by personality disintegration.   *B.B.*

Sensitiveness; sensitivity. In general: the degree to which a person is capable of receiving influences from the outside world. *In sensory perception and psychophysics:* the capability of receiving sensory stimuli. *In technology:* the relation between output and input magnitudes of a measuring instrument or plant (cybernetics: a system), etc. G. T. Fechner (q.v.) defined the sensitiveness of the sensory organs as the reciprocal value of the stimulus which was just sufficient (in 50% of cases [threshold]) to produce a sensation. The number 1 in the counter (1/S, S = stimulus intensity) indicates the unit in experience, that intensity of sensation which is just perceptible. This makes the Fechner definition a special case of the definition in technology.

Sensitiveness is often divided into *sensitivity* (sensitiveness to some stimulus) and *sensibility* (sensitiveness to differences in stimuli). In general linguistic usage sensitive is also used in the sense of sentimental, and sensible in the sense of having delicacy of feeling. Psychophysics (q.v.) sometimes uses for sensitivity the expression *absolute sensitiveness*, and for sensibility the expression *relative sensitiveness*. *Sensitiveness functions* (function of spectrally clear sensitiveness, linear, logarithmic, etc.; graphs of sensory systems in bio- and psychocybernetics) show the rules governing the relation between stimuli and their effects on the sensory system. On change of sensitiveness see *Adaptation*.   *A.Ha.*

Sensitive reaction type. The almost schizoid personality. Manifests itself in oversensitive impressionability to the stimuli of experience and in defective, uneven power of expression and behavior, i.e. conscious complex formation. The impact of sthenic sensation, pride and ambition spurs the personality on in spite of its feeling of insufficiency (see *Experience of insufficiency*) to a struggle with agonizing experience. Self torture and moral scruple are the typical responses to "humiliating insufficiency" and "moral defeat". Development to sensitive delusion concerning relationships (q.v.) is possible.

Bibliography: Kretschmer, E. & Kretschmer, W.: Medizinische Psychologie. Stuttgart, 1970. *W.K.*

Sensitivity training. A method closely connected with group therapy which has entered into the sphere of industrial psychology and must be regarded as an important step toward widespread adult education in the pure communication of knowledge. Sensitivity training takes place today in group therapy sessions where completely free expression is encouraged of individual emotional reactions to a gathering of fellow participants. In this way those who undergo the training learn how to give themselves, and how others react to them. It is thus possible to break down fixed reactions (see *Communication*) toward other people and to achieve social sensitivity (Tannenbaum *et al.*, 1953).

Bibliography: Tannenbaum, R., Wechsler, I. R. & Massarik, F.: Leadership and organisation. New York, 1953. Corsini, R. J.: Methods of group psychotherapy. New York, 1957. *W.Sch.*

Sensorimotor activity or behavior. Field of research, oriented partly to behaviorism but recently more to cybernetics, concerning the connection between the sensory (q.v.) and motor systems. The chief problems of the sensorimotor are: (*a*) by which processes are sensory and motor information linked with each other (*sensorimotor coordination*, e.g., between sense of vision and ocular motor, sense of vision and hand motor, hand sense and proprioceptors of the hand, etc.)?

(*b*) Which stabilizing processes guarantee that information provided by the sensorium leads to the effect of motor action (sensorimotor adaptation processes)? (*c*) What role has movement (motor action) for perception, etc?

Bibliography: Ashby, W. R.: Design for a brain London, 1960. Taylor, J. G.: The behavioral basis of perception. New Haven & London, 1962. *A.Ha.*

Sensory. The sensory system of organisms (*sensorium*), consisting of peripheral receptors (q.v.) sensory nerves and central nervous processing planes, performs the task of transmission of information between the physical environment and the central nervous system. By way of numerous types of information processing, special central nervous arousal patterns occur which are collated in association centers and finally become conscious as primary acts of judgment. *M.S.*

Sensory-perceptual function. In C. Jung's theory, one of the four basic "functions" of behavior (the others being the *feeling, thinking,* and *intuitive* functions). Overdevelopment of this function is said to produce a sensory-perceptual bias of the personality. *J.M.*

Sensory physiology. The theory of the normal functioning of the sense organs (q.v.). A distinction is made between exteroreceptors and enteroceptors. The former process information from the body's general environment and include the senses dealing with distant sources, such as sight, hearing and smell, as well as those dealing with immediate sources such as taste and feeling (reception of temperature, vibration, contact, pain, burning and itching) and the organ of balance (q.v.). In contrast to the above, the enteroceptors are located inside the body and give information concerning the condition of the internal organs. They include the sinew and muscle spindles, the mechanoreceptors of the joints, the pressure receptors in the arterial vascular system and the heart as well as the osmo- and chemoreceptors in the different regions of the body; temperature receptors located in the central nervous system can also be grouped here. (See *Receptors*.)   *E.D.*

Sensualism. The doctrine according to which all our knowledge (including rational knowledge) originates in sensation. One of the possible forms of empiricism (Condillac, 1715–80; Dewey, 1859–1952).   *M.J.B.*

Sensuality. 1. Devotion to the senses, i.e., predominantly to sensory pleasure. See *Sensation*. 2. Addiction to or dependence on physical, especially sexual, pleasure. See *Alcoholism; Drug dependence; Sexuality*.

Sentence completion tests. These tests, published almost exclusively in English-speaking countries, belong to the group of verbal completion methods (e.g., projective questions, continuation of stories) and are based on the concept of projection. It is assumed that the spontaneous completion of incomplete sentences will reveal the attitudes, inclinations, needs of an individual. Experimental investigations (A. C. Carr, 1956) have shown that sentence completion tests with regard to their stimulus material (projection of unconscious material) come between personality inventories and picture interpretation methods. In the majority of sentence completion tests the results are interpreted subjectively (e.g. A. E. Payne, 1928; A. D. Tendler, 1930; OSS Assessment Staff, 1948). For some of them objective standards of assessment are available (e.g., A. R. Rohde & G. H. Hildreth, 1947; J. B. Rotter *et al.*, 1949). See *Projective techniques*.   *P.G.*

Sentiment (*Feeling, attitude*: W. McDougall). In R. B. Cattell's study of motivation by factor analysis, sentiment has the same significance as a motive aim through which various motives can be satisfied (e.g., the self, q.v., parents, marital partner, one's own profession, etc.).   *K.P.*

Sentimentality. A special form of emotional reaction which finds expression in an *excessive* degree of emotional excitability and response to experience.   *P.S. & R.S.*

Sequential analysis. A type of statistical test developed by A. Wald during two world wars. The basic principle is as follows: to establish errors of the first and second kind with a given difference of observed populations, the sample area which is necessary for the statistical recording of this difference, is confined to random variables with a definite expectation value. Thus the sample range necessary for the decision can be minimized. In sequential analysis one observation is made after another, and after each observation one of the three following decisions is reached: (*a*) accept H_0; (*b*) accept H_1; (*c*) carry out a further observation. Observations continue in this way until the decision turns out in favor of H_0 or H_1.

Bibliography: Wald, A.: Sequential analysis. New York, 1947.
                                          A.R.

Serial photography. A phototechnical procedure to represent movements: (*a*) by arrangement in series; (*b*) by superimposing several single shots on each other; the industrial and scientific uses of serial photography are as for cyclography. Both procedures are also used to good effect today by the media of visual communication (e.g. television, advertising). Sheldon's types were ascertained by superimposition.

Bibliography: Sheldon, W. H.: The varieties of human physique. New York & London, 1940.

G.R.W.M.

Serotonin (*5-hydroxytryptamine*), 5-HT, *Enteramine* (= previous name) belonging to the *Indoleamine* class. Substances peculiar to the body (see *Biogenic amines*) which are found up to 90–95% in Darminukosa. The substance already discovered in the thirties and called enteramine has been the subject of neuropsychiatric research since the middle fifties, when it was proved to be in the brain (chiefly in the hypothalamus, q.v., the limbic system and the epiphysis, q.v.). Serotonin is formed in the body with the participation of different enzyme systems by a catalyst (5-hydroxytrytophan) from tryptophan (q.v.). Certain psychotropic drugs (e.g. reserpine, q.v., LSD, q.v.), by the emptying of the central store, cause a serotonin deficiency in the tissue, which is accompanied by behavioral changes (e.g. depression q.v. and hallucinations, q.v.). Substances such as 5-chlorophenylalanine, which by a process of selection block biosynthesis, are theoretically significant. Biological inactivation of serotonin is brought about by monoaminoxydase (q.v.). MAO-inhibitor therefore increases the effect of serotonin. Since serotonin does not pass the blood-brain barrier, the element 5-hydroxytryptophan is used to manipulate the serotonin content of the central nervous system. Many experiments indicate that depressions are linked to a diminished content of serotonin in the brain (q.v.) (hypothalamus, nucleus amygdalae, septum nucleus). At the same time there are areas which produce a high content of biogenic amines.

The hypothesis of a relationship between lack of serotonin in the brain and schizophrenia (D. W. Woolley & D. A. Shaw) advanced in the fifties because of the ill-effects of LSD is totally rejected. Serotonin has the effect of increasing blood pressure and contracting blood vessels and is spasmogenic.

Small quantities have an inhibitory effect on the nervous system, large quantities a stimulating effect. It is certainly difficult to understand the effects of serotonin on the nervous system, since *inter alia* it scarcely passes the blood-brain barrier (q.v.) and many interactions with catecholamine (q.v.) occur. Animal experiments suggest that serotonin acquires significance in the consolidation of learned material. More plausibly serotonin plays an important role in the waking-sleeping rhythm and for the duration of sleep (REM-phases; see *Sleep*; Jouvet, 1969). During sleep a smaller quantity is produced in the brain than in waking hours. The role of serotonin as a transmitter substance (q.v.) is disputed. The assertion made by B. B. Brodie and P. A. Shaw (1957) that serotonin is the transmitter substance of the central parasympathetic nervous system (see *Autonomic nervous system*) is not yet sufficiently substantiated. There are many substances occurring in plants (alkaloids) which are related to and derive from serotonin; these have partly psychomimetic effects (LSD, q.v., bufotenin, ibogaine, psilocybin, harmine).

Bibliography: Erspamer, V. (Ed.): Handbuch d. expt. Pharmakologie, Vol. 19: 5-Hydroxytryptamine and related indolealkylamines. Berlin, 1966. Garrattini, S. & Valzelli, L.: Serotonin. Amsterdam, 1965. Jouvet, M.: Biogenic amines and the states of sleep. Science 1969, *163*, 32–41. Kawka, Z. M.: A review of the central actions of serotonin and its implications in schizophrenia. Amer. J. Pharmac., 1967, *19*, 136–54. Koe, B. K. & Weissman, A.: p-Chlorphenylanaline: a specific depletor of brain serotonin. J. Pharmacol. exp. Ther., 1966, *154*, 499–516. Lewis, G. P. (Ed.): 5-Hydroxytryptamine. Oxford, 1968. Scheving, L. E. *et al.*: Daily fluctuation (circadian and ultradian) in biogenic amines of the rat. Amer. J. Physiol., 1968, *214*, 166–73. Woolley, D. W.: The biochemical basis of psychoses. New York, 1962.   *W.J.*

Set. 1. A temporary orientation, expectation, or state of readiness to respond in a particular way to a particular stimulus situation: e.g. *Perceptual set:* readiness to perceive the environment in a particular way; *Motor set:* readiness to perform a particular muscular response; *Neural set:* a temporary sensitization of a particular neural circuit (usually hypothetical); *Instructional set:* a perceptual, cognitive, or motor orientation induced by instructions from the experimenter. (Cf. *Attitudes* and *habits* which are relatively enduring dispositions.)

2. A fixed or rigid mode of responding.

3. A group or aggregate. In mathematical *set theory*, the totality of objects or elements which satisfy a given condition: e.g. the set of all female depressives over the age of thirty.

G.D.W.

Sex. See *Sexuality.*

Sex chromosomes. In genetic sex determination, one pair of chromosomes differ (XY type) in one sex but are identical (XX) in the other sex. If a Y chromosome is present in the zygote chromosomes, the zygote will develop into a male (e.g. in the mammals) or female (many species of butterflies and birds). This Y chromosome is known as the sex chromosome.

H.Sch.

Sex cycle, in women. See *Menstruation.*

Sex differences. Members of the different sexes achieve varying results in personality and ability tests, as well as interest and attitude tests. The origin of these differences (e.g. better results achieved by men in tests of the coarse motor system, spatial orientation, mechanical understanding and by women as regards perception speed, accuracy and verbal flow) is as yet unexplained; presumably an interaction between biological and cultural factors is involved.

Bibliography: Anastasi, A.: Differential psychology. New York, ³1958.

G.K.

Sex education. Instruction (especially in schools) in the physiology of male–female differences and reproduction, and/or the social ethics relating to sexual behavior. The aim of such instruction is usually stated as helping the individual toward a happy, healthy and socially acceptable sexual adjustment.

G.D.W.

Sex, extramarital, postmarital, premarital. Extramarital sex is regarded as objectionable by many societies which demand monogamous marriage, in spite of the fact that it often occurs. When it is allowed, the man is nearly always given more rights than the woman. According to Kinsey and his collaborators, (See *Kinsey report*), extramarital petting (q.v.) occurs quite frequently (about 50% of married men and 25% of married women up to the age of forty). In working-class men extramarital intercourse decreases with age (from 45% at age 21–22 to 27% at age 36–40). In middle- and upper-class men, on the other hand, it increases (from 20% to 30%). Education and social class do not make significant differences in the figures for women. The percentage of women with extramarital sexual contacts was twice as high in those with premarital experience than in those without. This is probably due to an (acquired) stronger appetite for sex and to more liberal attitudes.

Postmarital sex refers to the sexual behavior and attitudes of separated living spouses, the divorced and the widowed. According to Kinsey and others, postmarital sexual behavior is not very different from behavior when married, the average frequency of intercourse being somewhere between the celibate and the married (according to their age, 85–54% of women and 96–82% of men had intercourse). Frequency of *masturbation* (q.v.) was above that of the married (29–13% of women, 56–33% of men). *Homosexuality* (q.v.) occurred in 10% of women and 28% of the men. Extramarital sex relations were more dependent on age than any other.

"Premarital sex" refers to sex relations before marriage.

Bibliography: Bell, R. R.: Premarital sex in a changing society. Englewood-Cliffs, N.J., 1966. **Gebhard, P. H.** *et al.*: Pregnancy, birth, and abortion. New York, 1958. **Kinsey, A. C.** *et al.*: Sexual behavior in the human male. Philadelphia, 1948. **Id.**: Sexual behavior in the human female. Philadelphia, 1953.   *J.Fr.*

Sex flush. Reddening of particular areas of the skin: e.g. stomach, breast, face, back, resulting from an increased blood supply caused by sexual stimulation. Sex flush is more common in women than in men.

Bibliography: Masters, W. H. & Johnson, V. E.: Human sexual response. Boston, 1966.   *V.S.*

Sex gland hormones. Hormones (q.v.) formed in the testes of man and the ovaries of woman which are of fundamental importance to the formation and development of primary and secondary sex features as well as for general growth. A distinction is made between female and male sex hormones on the basis of their effects. Androgens are produced not only in the testes but in the adrenal cortex, and to some extent in the ovaries. The formation of sex gland hormones is stimulated by the gonadotropic hormones of the HVL. The relationship between sex gland hormones and physical as well as personality development is undisputed, at least in terms of broadly parallel characteristics. Hypofunction or hyperfunction of the gonads or hypophysis leads to retarded or accelerated development. In adults, underfunctioning (e.g. castration) leads to reduced sexual activity in the male, although this is often not the case in the female. At an advanced age, the sexual drive in women is increased by androgens and reduced in men by estrogens. Little is known about the relationship between psychological characteristics and sex gland hormones in the case of

persons with a healthy hormonal balance. The correlation is, however, probably slight. It seems likely on the other hand that estrogens and androgens play a part in the general level of activity of an individual. This is confirmed by the higher noradrenalin content in the central nervous system after the administration of estrogen or androgen. Behavioral fluctuations in the menstrual cycle have also not been clearly associated with the production of sex gland hormones. There is also no certain link between androgen or estrogen administration in males and sexual behavior.

Bibliography: Broverman, D. M. *et al.*: Roles of activation and inhibition in sex differences of cognitive abilities. Psychol. Rev., 1968, *75*, 23–50. **Diamond, M.** (Ed.): Perspectives in reproduction and sexual behavior. Bloomington, 1968. **Düker, H.**: Leistungsfähigkeit und Keimdrüsenhormone. Munich, 1957. **Giese, H.** (Ed.): Die Sexualität des Menschen. Stuttgart, 1955. **Lloyd, C. W.** (Ed.): Human reproduction and sexual behavior. Philadelphia, 1964. See also *Androgens; Estrogens.*   *W.J.*

Sex offenses. Blanket term for all behavior contravening the current sexual laws of a state or country, by persons of indictable age. Legally, criminologically and socially this term covers an enormous variety of behavior, from rape to the—possibly socially damaging —"dissemination of obscene literature." At the centre of the legal, psychiatric and psychological research are the (usually male) delinquent, his personality traits, life history, (social background, psychic, sexual, social development), specific sexual offenses and their relation to the age of the delinquent or victim and to other variables (e.g. circumstances of the crime, behavior which preceded and followed it, etc., prognosis for its repetition, resocialization, pre-delinquent prognosis, q.v.). Different scientific disciplines are engaged in research and practice: psychology, psychiatry, sociology, criminology. In West Germany scientific research has been lacking. In the USA, Gebhard (1965), for example, has engaged in it.

Bibliography: Gebhard, P. H.: Sex offenders. New York & London, 1965. Karpman, B.: The sexual offender and his offenses: etiology, pathology, psycho-dynamics and treatment. New York, 1954.   *H.M.*

Sex roles. In every society, specific behavioral expectations and standards are applied to men and women; deviations are generally subject to negative sanctions. On the basis of biological and physiological differences between the sexes, psychological reactions and social behavior patterns are formed which in turn are dependent on the socio-economic organization of a society, in particular on the division of labor. As a function of this division of labor, research suggests that the sex roles can be traced back to a learning process in which an increasing range of activities are standardized as typical of a particular sex, without reference to biological differences being noticeable (D'Andrade, 1966). The sex roles almost always lead to unequal power relationships, expressed in property ownership laws, inheritance laws, residence after marriage and sexual standards.

Since the sex roles are learnt in the process of socialization and generally unconsciously internalized, they come to be taken for granted culturally. Intercultural comparisons (and comparisons between different social strata in a given society) show the extreme variability of the sex roles. The following activities are almost always pursued by men and rarely by women: hunting, metal working, weapon manufacture and boat building, mining; the opposite is true of: child rearing, housework, work in the fields, weaving and preparation of food (Murdock, 1949, 1967). Opposite examples are provided by societies in which women do all the physical work (cultures of Micronesia and Melanesia) or where the traditional, western sex roles are reversed (Tschambuli). The change in sex roles in industrial societies is reflected in the increasing economic equality of woman, sexual emancipation, a lessening of dual moral standards, i.e. in a reduction of all (male) privileges.

Bibliography: D'Andrade, R. C.: Sex differences and cultural institutions. In: Maccoby, E. E. (Ed.): The development of sex differences. Stanford, 1966. Ford, C. S. & Beach, F. A.: Patterns of sexual behavior. New York, 1951. Mead, M.: Sex and temperament in three primitive societies. New York, 1936. Murdock, G. P.: Social structure. New York, 1949. Id.: Ethnographic atlas. Pittsburg, 1967.   *J.F.*

Sex, science of. The application of the scientific approach (detached, logical, empirical, and usually quantitative) to the study of the physiological and psychological aspects of sex. Also called *sexology*.   *G.D.W.*

Sex skin phenomenon. Coloring of the labia minora pink or pale to dark red caused by the increased blood supply in sexual stimulation. Because of this reaction (which takes place during the plateau stage of the sexual reaction cycle, q.v., and is characteristic of the coming orgasm) the labia minora are called the *sex skin*.   *V.S.*

Sexual. Pertaining to sex. Broad and variable usage encompassing the biology of male–female differences, reproduction involving male and female gametes (as opposed to *asexual reproduction*), the behavior of organisms relating to reproduction and sex drive, and the conscious experiences relating to sex, e.g. *eroticism*.   *G.D.W.*

Sexual arousal mechanism (abb. SAM). A term from animal-experimental comparative psychology, and an element in a theory regarding the mechanisms of sexual behavior in male laboratory animals, "SAM" designates the hypothetical mechanism responsible for the onset or beginning of sexual behavior (AM = arousal mechanism; see *Arousal*). The measure of the AM is the time from the sight of a receptive female animal to the mounting and intromission response of the male animal (=ML = "mount latency": Beach & Whalen, 1959). By successive intromission, the AM and CM (=copulation mechanism) are sensitized and kept at full excitation level until the ejaculation threshold is reached after a critical period of time, and the male ejaculation ensues. Other researchers have postulated a further mechanism (EM = ejaculation mechanism, triggered off on ejaculation), which exerts an influence on the AM and prevents an immediate, renewed sensitization of the AM until the recovery phase of the EM (McGill, 1965). On renewed presentation of a receptive female, the sensitization of the AM (and CM) becomes manifest in reduced ML and reduced genital stimulation until a second ejaculation. Experiments shows that the AM (like the other mechanisms) is to a large extent dependent on genotype. See *Intromission–copulation–ejaculation mechanism; Drive; Instinct.*   *H.M.*

Sexual characteristics. A general designation for all external and internal physical features which distinguish between the male and female sexes. In general a distinction is made between two kinds of sexual characteristics: primary characteristics, i.e. the sexual organs as such (gonads: testicles, and sperm ducts in the man; womb, ovaries and fallopian tubes in the woman); accessory sexual organs: penis, vagina, vulva, etc., and secondary characteristics, i.e. specific male and female features of bodily development (e.g. beard, body hair in men; breasts and rounded hips in women). Apart from the different sexual organs, other differences are also classified as sexual characteristics and referred to by some authors as "tertiary" characteristics (e.g. physical size, bone structure, specific blood cells, development and position of the organs, cardiac and respiratory activity).

Bibliography: **Money, J.:** Sex research. New York, 1965.   *H.M.*

Sexual deviations. Various kinds of sexual behavior may be considered deviant in three different, though usually overlapping, senses: (*a*) abnormal in the statistical sense, i.e. relatively unusual, (*b*) abnormal in the pathological sense, i.e. as symptomatic of some physical or psychological disease, and (*c*) socially unacceptable, perhaps to the extent of being illegal. See *Perversions, sexual.*
                                                    G.D.W.

Sexual disorders. Disorders of procreative (*impotentia generandi*) and coital (*impotentia coeundi*) capacity. Both forms of impairment frequently occur together, but only disorders of sexual efficacy (functional sexual disorders) are relevant to psychology. These may be divided into two main groups: (*a*) symptoms of physical and mental sickness; (*b*) symptoms of disturbed partner relationships. The most important functional sexual disorders are inadequate libido control, isolated libido reduction (see *Libido*), disorders of erection (q.v.), and of ejaculation (q.v.), anorgasmy (q.v.). Functional sexual disorders are often delimited by the terms *impotence* (q.v.: in men), and *frigidity* (q.v.: in women). In general, sexual disorders are separated from *unconventional* sexual behavior (see *Perversions; Sexuality*).   *F.Ma.*

Sexual economy. A theory of sexuality developed by Wilhelm Reich in connection with psychoanalysis (q.v.). According to Reich, it is an independent discipline comprising psychological, physiological, biological and sociological approaches. In a narrower sense, the term refers to the regulation of the energy flow of the organism (regulation of the "life energy" or "sexual energy"). The orgasm (q.v.) is considered most important in this regard. A reduced capacity to make love ("orgasmic potency") is said to bring about a disturbance of the total energy flow resulting in neurotic disorders or a "deformed character structure". The so-called psychotherapeutic technique recommended in "sexual economy" is "character-analytic vegetotherapy". Reich's importance would seem to have been his emphasis on the socially-conditioned nature of mental disorders.

Bibliography: Reich, W.: Character analysis. New York & London, 1950. Id.: Selected writings. London & New York, 1960. Id.: The sexual revolution. London & New York, ²1969. Rycroft, C.: Reich. London, 1971.   *F.Ma.*

Sexual inheritance. If sex is determined by hereditary factors (as opposed to phenotypical sex determination, i.e. development into male or female organism determined by different environmental influences), the sex is determined either by the YX type or XO type; in the latter case the decisive factor in determining sex is the presence of one or two X chromosomes in the zygote.   *H.Sch.*

Sexuality. Biologically, sex is the combination of characteristics that differentiate the two forms or parts of organisms reproducing themselves by the fusion of gametes and hence of genetic material from two different sources. Female gametes are eggs and male gametes sperms. They may be produced by a single individual (hermaphrodite) or by the sexes separately.

Psychologically, sex is the behavior directly associated with the meeting of the two sexes, and in some species their copulation, to allow the fusion of the gametes (fertilization) to take place. In humans, sex may refer specifically to the act of copulation or heterosexual intercourse, but may extend to the related behaviors of two individuals of the same morphological sex (homosexuality).

Genetically, sex is determined by the presence or absence of the smaller Y chromosome in the relevant chromosomal pair. In mammals (including humans) females have the XX pair of chromosomes and males the XY form.

Sex identification by inspection ranges from impossible in some species, to unmistakable, as normally in humans. Five methods of sex identification are: (i) assay of the chromatin content of cell nuclei—the additional X chromosome in women forming an identifiable chromatin body not found in men with the Y chromosome; (ii) examination of the sex organs—external genitalia; (iii) examination of the internal accessory sex organs; (iv) examination of the gonads, the gamete-producing organs, ovaries and testes; (v) investigation of hormonal state. Since human sexual morphology is distinctly bimodal, errors of sex assignment are rare. Genetically determined anomalies do, however, occur, giving a continuum of maleness–femaleness and individuals in whom there is inconsistency of sex as determined by the above methods. These difficult cases provide investigators with evidence on the development of psychological awareness of sex.

1. *Psychosexual differentiation and gender role.* There are behavioral differences between the two sexes, apart from actual sexual activity, which give rise to the concept of sex or gender role. Clearly, men and women have different roles in society, in reproduction and the associated family structure, and in their occupational choices and ambitions, their peer groupings and social behavior. That sex roles differ markedly from one society to another even to the extent of reversal indicates the importance of culture as a determinant of sex role behavior. Nevertheless, the problem of the assimilation of sex role is raised by individuals who do not adopt the sex-appropriate behavior of their society.

Cases of intersexuality and hermaphroditism, including some brought up with incorrect gender assignment by parents puzzled by the sexual morphology, show instances of unquestioning acceptance of the sex of upbringing—even when contrary to biological sex. This led to statements of the paramount importance of environmental over biological factors of sex determination where the two were at variance. It has been proposed that human sexuality is essentially neutral at birth, and develops as male or female according to the environmental pressures which bring about learning of the gender rôle. This view has been criticized because evidence from intersex abnormalities may not apply to normal individuals. Moreover, there are intersex individuals who rebel against their assigned sex. It is now generally agreed that environmental factors in sex role determination are important, but that powerful hormonal influences operate and all factors interact with genetic sex.

2. *Development of sexual behavior.* Because sexual behavior in lower animals is seen as instinctive, and because in human society, owing to prudery and ignorance, there are few formal lessons in sexual and reproductive behavior, human sexual performance has also been thought to be instinctive. However, mammalian sexual behavior is generally found to become more efficient with experience and the effects of learning are apparent here also.

Freud (1934) employed the instinct (q.v.) concept in his theory of infantile sexual development, with implications for normal and abnormal personality formation. His major achievement was to reintroduce the notion of a continuity of sexual development throughout the life of the child, including the "latent period" in which sexual behavior had been thought to be absent. In the earliest infantile stage of sexual development the child takes pleasure in oral exploration—sucking and chewing. In the second stage the child develops his strength and power; with increasing sensitivity of the anal region sexual responsivity becomes anal and aggressive (see *Sadism*). In the final stage of sexual development, the centre of sexual awareness moves to the genital regions.

Freud adds hypotheses of personality and

pathology development based upon the normal progression through the stages stated, or alternatively, a fixation at, or regression to, earlier, inappropriate stages of sexual development. This theory of pathology and the link between sexuality and pleasure derived from non-genital zones of the body have not remained unquestioned scientifically. Much remains speculative or has been discredited for lack of confirmatory evidence. For example, the lack of major sexual abnormality in neurotic patients argues against the Freudian position.

Since human experimentation is fraught with difficulties, studies using non-human subjects can advance our knowledge of the development of sexual behavior. Animals reared in social isolation from others of their own kind show later deficiencies of sexual behavior. Harlow has reared rhesus monkeys in isolation from infant peer groups, combined with isolation from the mother. This was found to be much more disruptive of adult socio-sexual behavior than was isolation from the mother only. Reared in complete isolation from infancy, neither sex showed the normal sexual approach behavior nor the mounting or presenting behavior characteristic of males and females respectively. Females mated with normal males could conceive and give birth but were inadequate and cruel in the secondary sexual behavior of infant care. Hence, at least for infrahuman primates, experience of peer contacts and early sexual play with other infants is a necessary prerequisite for normal development of sexual behavior.

3. *Evidence on human sexual behavior.* Despite the difficulties of studying the intimate and until recently largely taboo topics of human sexuality, methods have gradually progressed from insecure clinical generalizations to large-scale surveys giving factual data. Kinsey pioneered the use of trained interviewers with very large samples in the United States, and achieved a remarkable degree of

cooperation from his interviewees. The results, mainly tabulated to show sexual outlets including intercourse, masturbation, nocturnal emissions and perversions (q.v.), show a marked discrepancy between social expectations and actual behavior. These surveys provide normative data for many human sexual activities and have not been seriously disconfirmed in the numerous smaller replications carried out in other countries.

4. *Disorders of sexual behavior.* Homosexuality ranks first in popular view as a major disorder of sexual behavior and yet Kinsey (1948, 1953) showed clearly that incidents of homosexuality in the population are frequent (males, 37%) and that there is no clear distinction between the homosexual and the heterosexual. The findings suggest that there is a continuum from pure homosexuality to pure heterosexuality with the majority of men showing interest in both directions. The same is true of women homosexuals, or lesbians. Although homosexuals rarely wish to change their sexual orientation, society exerts such pressures towards heterosexuality—the social norm—that sexual reorientation may be desired to relieve the psychiatric distress and depression thus caused. While psychoanalytic or another psychotherapy (q.v.) can offer a greater acceptance of the self, behavior therapy (q.v.) is increasingly able to effect a change of sexual interests in selected patients.

As with homosexuality, other disorders of sexuality are notably more frequent in men than in women. This is more than a greater societal tolerance for female deviation and may be related to a sex difference in sexual arousal. Males are more arousable generally and by visual stimuli in particular.

5. *Research.* Research into sexuality is in its infancy. There is currently a growth of serious interest, and surveys are more ably carried out than formerly, but problems of theory and of measurement remain. Little true experimentation has been carried out but the therapeutic application of findings from comparative and general psychology gives hope of further rapid developments in the future.

Bibliography: Beach, F. A. (Ed.): Sex and behavior New York, 1968. Broadhurst, A.: Abnormal sexual behaviour female. In: Eysenck, H. J. (Ed.): Handbook of abnormal psychology. London, [2]1971. Diamond, M.: A critical evaluation of the ontogeny of human sexual behavior. Quart. Rec. Biol., 1965, 40, 147–74 Ellis, H. & Abarbanel, A. (Eds.): The encyclopedia of sexual behavior. 2 vols., New York, 1961. Feldman, M. P.: Abnormal sexual behaviour male. In: Eysenck, H. J. (Ed.): Handbook of abnormal psychology. London, [2]1971. Id. & MacCulloch, M. J.: Homosexual behaviour: therapy and assessment. Oxford, 1970. Freud, S.: Collected papers. London, 1934. Gagnon, J. H.: Sexuality and sexual learning in the child. Psychiatry, 1965, 28, 212–227. Green, R. & Money, J. (Eds.): Transsexualism and sex reassignment. Baltimore, 1969. Harris, G. W. & Levine, S.: Sexual differentiation and its experimental control. J. Physiol., 1965, 181, 379–400. Kenyon, F. E.: Homosexuality in the female. Brit. J. Hosp. Med., 1970, 3, 183–296. Kinsey, A. C. et al.: Sexual behavior in the human male. Philadelphia, 1948. Id.: Sexual behavior in the human female. Philadelphia, 1953. Maccoby, E. E. (Ed.): The development of sex differences. London, 1967. Masters, W. H. & Johnson, V. E.: Human sexual response. Boston, 1966. Rheingold, H. L.: Maternal behavior in mammals. New York, 1963. Sackett, G. P.: Abnormal behavior in laboratory-reared rhesus monkeys. In: Fox, M. W. (Ed.): Abnormal behavior in animals. Philadelphia, 1968, 293–331. Winokur, G. (Ed.): Determinants of human sexual behavior. Springfield, Ill., 1963.

A. Broadhurst

Sexual neurosis. A form of neurosis (q.v.) in which the sexual functions are disturbed and a cause of distress. The patient who becomes uncertain of his sexuality (q.v.) reacts oversensitively to a demand for sexual performance. The causative factor may be the situation, the partner or the patient himself. The most frequent symptom of a sexual neurosis is impotence (q.v.).

Bibliography: Wolman, B. B.: Handbook of clinical psychology. New York & London, 1965.   *F.Ma.*

Sexual reaction cycle. According to Masters & Johnson (1966), the physiological reactions to a sexual act such as coitus (q.v.) or masturbation (q.v.) go in a cycle which can be arbitrarily divided into four phases: excitement (q.v.), plateau phase (q.v.), orgasm (q.v.), detumescence (q.v.). These phases, even the orgasm, cannot be exactly defined either in terms of objective reactions or of subjective experience.

Bibliography: Masters, W. H. & Johnson, V. E.: Human sexual response. Boston, 1966. Sigusch, V.: Exzitation und Orgasmus bei der Frau. Stuttgart, 1970. *V.S.*

Sexual socialization. This is the adaptation of the individual to society by internalizing its values and learning the appropriate modes of behavior. Sexual socialization is made more difficult by the gap between the age of puberty and the attainment of social adult status. This brands youthful sex relations ("premarital") as deviant. Sexual socialization is also made more difficult by the gap between the sexual norms of a bourgeois society (taboo on sex, denial of instinct, monopolizing of sex by marriage), and the need to satisfy sexual drives, which is particularly strong in youth. It is paradoxical that children brought up to respect these inhibiting standards before they marry are expected to achieve a full flowering of sex within marriage: that is to say, they are expected at a single moment to become experts in a skill which they were forbidden to learn. The tone of sexual explanations and education is correspondingly ambivalent. *N.S.-R.*

Sexual symbolism. The representation by any object or event of the sex organs or sexual behavior. Thus in psychoanalytic dream interpretation, narrow, pointed objects, such as knives, keys, chimneys and snakes, are often taken as *phallic symbols*, while soft, round and indented objects, such as hats and vases, are treated as female symbols. Intercourse is said to be represented by many activities, such as climbing stairs and riding horses. According to Freudian theory, this kind of symbolism has the function of disguising the sexual meaning from the conscious mind where it would otherwise be unacceptable. *G.D.W.*

Sexual trauma. General definition: a trauma is an experience or event which (directly or indirectly) has a damaging influence in the psychological and/or psychosexual sphere. The term "sexual trauma" is used in two branches of science with a slightly different meaning: in psychoanalysis, where it has undergone a number of changes for empirical and theoretical reasons, in the context of the theory of neuroses, and in forensic psychology and psychiatry, where it is the subject of empirical research in the special sector of victimology, concerned with children who are victims of sexual offenses.

1. *Psychoanalysis.* The notion of the sexual trauma was first introduced specifically by Freud in 1896 ("Weitere Bemerkungen über die Abwehr-Neuropsychosen"). Freud assumed at the time (on the basis of thirteen analyses of cases of hysteria) that a predisposition toward neurosis (q.v.) may occur as a result of actual sexual experiences in early childhood (between the second and tenth years of life). However, he considered that the traumatic effect did not lie in the early experiences themselves but in subsequent recollections of them after puberty; these recollections are not conscious but lead to emotional ties and repression. These sexual traumata of childhood, accompanied by "real irritation of the genitalia", consisted, in the case of hysteria, in sexual passivity of the child (which was sexually seduced: frequently sibling incest) and, in the case of a compulsion neurosis, in sexual activity of the child, i.e. in "aggression performed with pleasure and pleasurable participation in sex acts" (Freud).

The theory that sexual traumas of early

childhood were the etiological bases of defense neuroses had to be abandoned, however, as experience of analysis grew: Freud realized that these childhood recollections of his adult patients did not entirely correspond to genuine experience. The pathogenic memories which repeatedly come to light during analysis are (wish) phantasies consisting of a blend of reality and imagination. The real aspects of these phantasies are events which the child is as yet unable to understand: (*a*) "with the seduction phantasy when there has been no actual seduction, the child generally conceals the auto-erotic period of its sexual activity. It spares itself shame over masturbation by inventing the existence of a desired object in this early period." (*b*) The child deduces the threat of castration "from his knowledge that auto-erotic satisfaction is forbidden and under the impression of his discovery of the female genitalia" and builds up a corresponding phantasy. (*c*) The primal scene, i.e. observation of sexual intercourse between the parents, is considered a historical fact which is then embellished "on the strength of observations of intercourse in animals (dogs), motivated by the child's unsatisfied voyeurism in the years of puberty". The trauma is always triggered by a conflict between drive stimuli and drive-inhibiting ideas. (*d*) The attempt to master the traumatic libido energy by repetition in order to re-establish satisfaction at an earlier, pleasurable stage of libido development cannot succeed and makes a decisive contribution to neurotic development.

2. *Victimology*. Although a number of case studies have been made on the subject of the harmful effects of sexual crimes against children, there have so far been no methodical studies of sexual trauma and their consequences in the case of sexual crimes. Results obtained so far are contradictory and of differing value.   *H. Maisch*

S factor. The specific ability factor in Spearman's two-factor intelligence theory,

according to which there is a "g" or general factor common to all performance, and every individual performance possesses an "s" or specific factor. See *Abilities.*   *H.J.A.*

Shadow. A term found in the complex psychology of C. G. Jung (q.v.) for the totality of those personal and collective-unconscious tendencies (see *Unconscious*) which are incompatible with the conscious life form and are therefore not integrated into the ego (q.v.). The shadow functions as a relatively autonomous partial personality which acts as compensation for the consciousness; however, it embodies not only negatively repressed influences but also tendencies pointing to the future. To make the shadow conscious is the first task of any Jungian analysis.   *W.Sch.*

Shannon-Wiener entropy formula. See *Information; Communication.*

Shape constancy. The perceived shape of an object is relatively independent of changes in the stimuli exciting the retina (q.v.) brought about in the projected image by spatial adjustment. Usually the set of stimuli furnish information about the spatial situation, e.g. through the distribution of brightness, perspective, texture, and above all the surroundings of an object. Shape constancy is impaired when such information is withdrawn.

Bibliography: Epstein, W. & Park, J.: Shape constancy; functional relationships and theoretical formulations. Psychol. Bull. 1963, *60*, 265–88.   *J.Z.*

Sheldon types. Sheldon (1942) distinguished three dimensions of physical constitution, or three main clusters of traits of temperament, each cluster consisting of twenty traits: *viscerotonia, somatotonia* and *cerebrotonia.* Each cluster was related to bodily functions. See *Type; Traits.*

Bibliography: Sheldon, W. H.: The varieties of temperament. New York & London, 1942. **Id.:** The varieties of delinquent youth: an introduction to constitutional psychiatry. New York & London, 1949.   *M.H.*

Shock. A complex syndrome with physical and psychic components brought about by a sudden, intense influence on the organism. The main characteristic of shock is the vascular crisis (an acute circulatory insufficiency). There is frequently a disturbance of consciousness, or a loss of consciousness. Two basic forms are distinguished: organic shock (e.g. in a cardiac infarction, or *commotio cerebri*), and shock as a general reaction (e.g. anaphylactic shock brought about by inappropriate protein; insulin or hypoglycemia shock— reduction of blood sugar; psychic shock).

Since a shock can cause long-lasting alterations, especially of a psychological nature, it is used, as "shock therapy", to treat psychoses artificially. See *Psychoses, functional; Schizophrenia.*   *F.Ma.*

Shock, apperceptive. In his characterology, Lersch places this among the "excitations of feeling directed toward self-preservation" (as a sub-group of the excitations of emotion of the individual as he exists for himself), a "shock condition of fright", a disturbance in grouping perceptional material into some orderly connection based on experience and accompanied by a loss of orientation and diminished capability of performing a purposive act. *A.G.*

Shock inducer. An instrument on the principle of electro-magnetic induction (induction coil) which makes it possible to produce a variable aversive stimulus whose intensity can be regulated; it is used especially in learning and conditioning experiments (q.v.).   *J.M.*

Shock therapy. Treatment of severe mental illness by inducing some kind of shock to the nervous system. At one time drugs which induced an epileptic fit were used for this purpose. Since the late 1930s an electric current passed through the brain has been found to produce the same effect with less unpleasantness for the patient. Used mainly for the treatment of severe depression, and less often for schizophrenia or mania.   *R.H.*

Shortsightedness. See *Myopia.*

Short-term memory. In interpreting the findings of memory psychology, the model of a short and long-term memory has been adopted. W. James already spoke of a primary memory which is used for short-term retention and a secondary memory corresponding to the psychological past. Tests of immediate retention capacity generally show little correlation with tests of the long-term memory. Time estimates of the short-term memory range from 2–3 to 10 seconds (Rohracher, 1968; Frank, 1969). Frank developed a model which showed a short-term memory with an intake speed C of 16 bits per second and a capacity of 160 bits, a short memory ($C = 0.4 - 0.8$ bits/sec) and a long-term memory ($C = 0.05$ bits/sec). See *Memory.*   *R.R.*

Short-term therapy. In many neuroses, analysis or other forms of long-term psychotherapy are not necessary. For this reason, and also because of the actual therapeutic requirements, short-term therapy has been introduced for less severe neuroses in which it is generally necessary to defuse the conflict situation and disintegrate it without the need for long-term analysis of the past.   *J.L.I.*

Sight. The faculty of vision; seeing; the sense mediated by the eyes. The visual modality is often considered the dominant one in humans and is characteristically and especially concerned with the perception of space and spatial relations. See *Eye; Visual perception.*   *G.D.F.*

Sigmatism. Incorrect formation of the S sound. The most prevalent forms are: *sigmatismus interdentalis* (tongue between rows of teeth); *sigmatismus addentalis* (tongue on upper row of teeth); *sigmatismus lateralis* (air escaping on either side of tongue). The most difficult to treat is lateral sigmatism.   *H.B.*

Sign. A sign is usually understood as a perceptual content effected by a signal (q.v.) which refers beyond itself to a referent—a cause or meaning. Signs are distinguished as indicators (signs *of* . . .) and representational signs (signs *for* . . .). When a sign indicates, the referent is the cause of the sign: hence a higher body temperature is a sign (indication) of an infection. When a sign represents, the referent is the meaning of the sign: hence a spoken word is a physical signal sequence which becomes a sign only by virtue of the associated meaning. A common repertoire of signs (letters, words, etc.) is the prerequisite for information exchange and transmission. Three sign functions are distinguished: the *syntactic, semantic* and *pragmatic,* whose study is the object of semiotics (q.v.), or semiology. See *Sign and symbol; Communication.*
    P.-B.H.

Sign and symbol. Signs and symbols are information bearers which, by virtue of their meaning, stand for that which they symbolize or designate; they *represent* that which they designate. Both terms may be used synonymously or in different acceptations; there is no one mind in the diverse research traditions as to the definition or psychological function of the words.

1. *Behaviorism* (q.v.). In this area, signs and symbols are considered predominantly in regard to their function as signals. Under the influence of Pavlov's first and second signal systems, H. Mead and O. H. Mowrer described those stimuli that elicit responses as signs, and those stimuli that stand for stimuli eliciting responses as symbols. According to C. E. Osgood, a stimulus becomes the sign of a stimulus object when it exerts a mediating, fractional response exerted originally by the stimulus object. Osgood calls signs that stand for other signs, "assigns". In neo-behaviorism (q.v.) it is emphasized that the part response released by a symbol is not an instrumental action but serves merely to "stimulate" further responses (D. E. Berlyne). The production and association of such symbolic part responses are known as symbolic processes; they are adduced to explain information processing in learning and thinking.

2. *Depth psychology.* Symbols are viewed as isomorphic and usually pictorial manifestations of the unconscious, and are studied in order to analyze pathological states, dreams and myths. For Freud, a symbol is (*a*) a mental representation of physical processes, e.g. an hysterical symptom (see *Hysteria*); (*b*) a disguised expression of repressed objects and wishes, especially in infantile, primitive or regressive thinking (O. Rank, T. Reik, W. Stekel, M. Klein). For Jung, a symbol is the individual concretization of an archetype, and does not merely serve to mask something but unites the conscious and the unconscious, the productivity-favoring flow of the libido (q.v.) and the manifestation of phylogenetic experiences.

3. *Cognitive psychology.* Signs and symbols are considered to be of major importance in perception (q.v.), thinking (q.v.) and memory (q.v.), and to be means of understanding these processes as well as characteristics of diverse levels of thought and abstraction. Whereas the term "sign" is usually applied to representations with a denotative, and conventionally fixed meaning, the term "symbol" is used to characterize representation by means of

convention, isomorphisms, expressive traits, associations, and so on. Piaget (1959), for example, speaks of *social* symbols (with an acquired meaning), and of *private* symbols (which are understood since they are a part of, or like, that which is designated). Extending K. Goldstein's classification (concrete, asymbolic and abstract, symbolic thinking), J. S. Bruner distinguishes between *enactive* representation (which forms part of an action and controls further actions), *iconic* representation (which serves concrete description and apprehension), and *symbolic* representation (i.e. signs to represent abstract relations). Gestalt psychologists (W. Köhler, H. Werner) take into account especially the implications for the psychology of thinking of the fusion (in concrete representations) of the symbol and that which is symbolized, and consider even abstract symbols to be expressive agents. The level of abstraction of the designatum (Kahn's symbol test), or of its representativeness (R. Brown), are used to classify thought processes. See also *Language; Grammar; Semantics.*

4. *Synthesis.* The agreement about the term "sign" and the chaotic state of definition of the term "symbol" would seem to be conditioned, among other things, by the fact that symbols are viewed as *bearers of connotative meaning*, so that on the one hand a specific symbol symbolizes various things, and on the other hand a specific designatum can be variously symbolized. The consequent large number of forms of symbolization allowed research workers to take into account only those kinds of symbol that accorded with their intention. For the purpose of a more unified classification of different forms of symbol, and to allow the study of their interrelations, symbolization experiments were carried out, and the means of symbolization in each case was analyzed: ten symbol categories resulted (Kreitler, 1965). Most like the sign are symbolizations whose meaning is afforded by lexical explanations (category 1), e.g. Osgood's "assign", Piaget's "social symbol", Gold-

stein's and Bruner's "abstract symbols", etc. Predominantly isomorphic symbolizations, e.g. by representation of the referent by means of an individual case or detail, a situation, a scenic action or real consequence (categories 2, 3, 4 and 6), correspond to Bruner's "enactive" and "iconic", Piaget's "private" and von Domarus' "*pars-pro-toto*" symbols. Symbolization by means of the sensations elicited by the referent (category 7) correspond to gestalt-psychological criteria. The symptoms of hysteria conceived by Freud as symbols are symbolizations by means of physical expression (category 5), whereas his dream symbols are isomorphous allegories (category 9). Jung's archetypal symbols are in part verbal or pictorial indications (category 8) of individual or collective behavior patterns, and in part the synthesis of a contradiction and its resolution in a good gestalt (category 10) as the representation of an immanent dynamic.

Bibliography: Jacobi, J.: Complex, archetype and symbol in the psychology of C. G. Jung. Princeton & London, 1959. Kreitler, S.: Symbolschöpfung und Symbolerfassung. Munich & Basle, 1965. Piaget, J.: La formation du symbole chez l'enfant. Neuchâtel, ²1959. Werner, H. & Kaplan, B.: Symbol formation. New York, 1963. *S. Kreitler & H. Kreitler*

Signal. A stimulus in any modality intended to convey information; often contrasted to *noise* used in the sense of conveying no information. *C.D.F.*

Signals, animal. Communication within or between species in animals employ signals which are bodily structures, sounds, smells and specific patterns of behavior. Signals usually have a releasing function, e.g.: The red breast of the robin releases aggression in males of the same species. When signals are copied from other species this is called *mimicry*. Non-stinging hymenoptera are avoided as if they were wasps when they have a black and yellow striped body. *V.P.*

Signal transformation. By the process of signal transformation a given signal (q.v.) is transformed into another. The transformation must take place in such a way that the original signal can be reconstructed (through "reversed transformation"). Signal transformation is a physical process which makes use of a clearly understood transformable *code* (q.v.). It is used, e.g., to transform the signals of a sender to suit a given channel of communication.   *P.B.H.*

Significance. Statistical (q.v.) tests are also called significance tests, because they test the significance (that is to say relevance) of differences. We distinguish between *statistical* and *practical* significance. Statistical significance (provable by a test) is a necessary but not a sufficient condition of practical significance. Very large samples may reveal very small practically insignificant differences, in which case the taking of a smaller sample is quite sufficient to reveal the same practically significant differences.   *A.R.*

Significance level. The probability of error which is allowed for in a statistical (q.v.) test is called the significance level. In psychology this is usually set at 5%.   *A.R.*

Significance, limits of. The numbers in statistical tests which at a given significance level (q.v.) must be exceeded or fallen short of to make these tests significant (q.v.).   *A.R.*

Significant. When a hypothesis is adopted from observed data, the probability of error is calculated as a number which is called the significant difference.   *A.R.*

Sign language. A means of communication based on signs for use in cases where normal speech must be replaced. Sign languages developed among the North American Indians (to enable different tribes to communicate), Neapolitans (as a secret language) and Trappist monks (because of the rule of silence). These languages form the basis of the sign language used for deaf and dumb people which, however, has been enlarged by conventional signs (the French Method was founded by Abbé Charles Michel de l'Eppée in about 1770). Recently the American Sign Language has been successfully used to train chimpanzees and establish a broader means of communication between men and chimpanzees (attempts to teach spoken language proved unsuccessful).

Bibliography: **Gardner, R. A. & B. T.**: Acquisition of sign language in the chimpanzee. Progr. Report, Reno, 1967.   *F.Ki.*

Simplicity structure. A concept from factor analysis. If, following extraction, all common factors (q.v.) are rotated according to the criteria of simplicity structure, the following characteristics are attributed to the factor matrix: (*a*) the factorial solutions rotated in this way (see *Rotation*) are, given certain assumptions, unspecific for random samples. (*b*) This structure makes possible a particularly simple content interpretation of the factors. According to the criterion of the simplicity structure, rotated factor matrices are usually no longer orthogonal.   *W.H.B.*

Simulation. See *Lie scale*.

Simulation of psychological (mental) processes. The process by which pseudo-empirical data are produced from an abstract psychological theory. The familiar representation of psychological regularities (laws) as curves in a Cartesian coordinate system stand for statistics already calculated from observations but not the data themselves (e.g. see *Learning* *curves*). Individual observations are dispersed around these mean values in a way that is generally not closely considered. All oppositions of theory and observation consist mainly in the comparison of theoretical with empirical statistics. The simulation of psychological processes enables any desired number of learning curves to be produced. Their points are pseudoempirical since they represent a set of data which, although produced theoretically, should correspond to experimental data. It is therefore evident that the simulation of

By its use as an instrument for validation of a theory, or in prognosis, simulation is itself used as a *medium in the construction of theories*. Psychological regularities often do not allow of a mathematical representation in a consistent form. In the areas of cognitive psychology (see *Thinking*) and social psychology, for example, the theoretical consequences of an aggregate of individual mathematical-logical assertions are sought for by the use of simulation. Newell, Shaw & Simon (1957) compiled their deliberations in the process of solving a

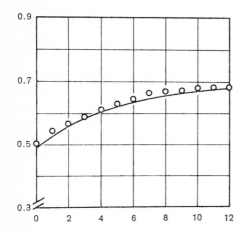 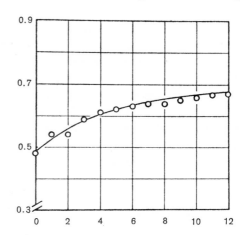

Empirical results (Fig. left) and simulation data (Fig. right) for a learning experiment. In the ordinate direction, the cumulative total of mistakes improved on spontaneously by the subject is set off against the actual errors (abscissa). The simulation data were obtained using the Bush-Mosteller model and parameters estimated from experimental data (Drösler, 1964).

psychological processes can be applied to the validation of theories. The pseudoempirical data produced can be contrasted item for item with the experimental data. The prerequisite for the use of simulation is a non-contradictory formulation of psychological theory. This is usually impossible if one is restricted to natural languages (e.g. German, English, etc.). In order to formulate theories, special languages are used: e.g. mathematics (cf. Atkinson, Bower & Crothers, 1965), or a computer or program language (Algol, Fortran, etc.). A simulation whose set of pseudoempirical data cannot be distinguished from a set of genuine experimental data even by an expert has passed the "Turing test".

simple logical problem. The system shows such a high degree of complexity that its consequences can be surveyed only by means of simulation. Hence extensive theoretical constructions show the useful application of electronic data-processing installations (see *Computer*). Simulation is often used with mainly pragmatic aims: human working potentials must be mechanized for industrial purposes. Here the criterion for realization consists only of successful automation, whereas the psychologist is just as interested in the errors of the "automaton", in order to compare them qualitatively with human errors. Hence in the simulation of letter recognition not only success in the form of probable score is considered, but all the mistakes that occur. A psychological theory is needed which in practice would (through simulation) produce an error matrix which is indistinguishable from an empirical one.

The first experiments in simulation related to the behavior of parts of the organism (individual nerve cells—"neuron models"—and reflexes). Electronic control circuits were used for simulation in these instances. Later, an electromechanical simulation of conditioned responses was produced. The availability of electronic data-processing makes a wide variety of behaviors, such as perception (q.v.), learning (q.v.) and thinking (q.v.) accessible to simulation. The search for the widely ramified consequences of a developed simulation model is in itself tantamount to being an empirical pursuit. This may have contributed to the fact that in published work on simulation the experimental aspect is sometimes too restricted.

The emphasis of present-day research is on the field of perception and the psychology of thinking. Sign recognition is of major importance in perception (cf. Uhr, 1966). The incentive for such investigations is to be seen in the fact that each item of information still has to be prepared manually before it is accessible to electronic data-processing, and because an army of workmen has to be employed for this purpose in industry and administration. The gain to psychology in the use of simulation in sign recognition is still small, since the procedures applied are oriented more toward technological than psychological data. In the psychology of thinking, approaches to simulation have led to the first precise formulations of certain extensive areas, and a clear view of the connections between learning, concept formation and problem solving (Hunt, 1966). With the help of simulation, for example, an exact analysis of heuristic behavior is possible for the first time. The realization of similar programs on electronic computers leads to pseudo-data in areas which not long ago were

quite impenetrable: for example, the use of arguments in elementary logic or the practice of two-dimensional geometry, problem solving, or the course of dialogues.

Developments of this kind are occasionally known as "artificial intelligence", though this term is misleading, and threatens to divert us from the scientific aim of simulation. Simulation generates fallacies as soon as aspects of pseudo-empirical sets of data are uncritically generalized. Details peculiar to the simulation may easily be mistaken for psychological regularities. Precautions are necessary so that pseudo-empirical data are compared in as many aspects as possible with experimental results. This requirement is often not observed today. It is therefore sometimes difficult to estimate the psychological-theoretical content of simulation findings as they are reported in the literature. Nevertheless, the heuristic value of the simulation of psychological processes is recognized as high (Gregg & Simon, 1967). See *Communication; Cybernetics and psychology; Machine learning; Instructional technology.*

Bibliography: Anderson, A. R. (Ed.): Minds and machines. New York, 1964. **Atkinson, R. C., Bower, G. H. & Crothers, E. J.:** An introduction to mathematical learning theory. New York, 1965. **Bernstein, J.:** The analytical engine: computers—past, present and future. **Bush, R. R. & Mosteller, F.:** Stochastic models for learning. New York & London, 1955. **Drösler, J.:** Ein besonders empfindlicher Indikator für den Lernfortschritt und der Bush-Mosteller-Operator. Z.f. exp. angew. Psychol., 1964, *11*, 238–253. **Id.:** Künstliche Intelligenz. In: **Irle, M.** (Ed.): Bericht über den 26. Kongress der DGP. Göttingen, 1969, 37–52. **Gregg, L. W. & Simon, H. A.:** Process models and stochastic theories of simple concept formation. J. of mathematical Psychol., 1967, *4*, 246–76. **Hunt, E. B., Malin, J. & Stone, P. J.:** Experiments in induction. New York & London, 1966; **Loehlin, J. C.:** Computer models of personality. New York, 1968. **Meltzer, B. & Michie, D.** (Eds.): Machine intelligence 4. Edinburgh, 1969. **Minsky, M.:** Artificial intelligence. Scientific American. 1966, *215*, 246–63. **Id.** (Ed.): Semantic information processing. Cambridge, Mass., 1968.   *J. Drösler*

Simultaneous contrast. See *Contrast*.

Sitter. Person at a *séance* (q.v.) who is the recipient of a communication from the medium (q.v.).   *J.B.*

Situation, social. A general term for the field of reference (stimuli, objects, fellow men, groups, values, including those of the individual self) of the orientation of a person acting in society. Looked at from this standpoint, the social situation may be defined by three categories of data and the manner in which they are linked: (*a*) the actual data which influence the acting person, (*b*) the attitudes (q.v.) which are brought into play at the time of the act, and (*c*) the degree of ego involvement (q.v.) or awareness of the actual data and attitudes on the part of the acting person. T. Parsons and E. A. Shills designate all those data of the environment which have some meaning for the acting person as constituents of the social situation.   *W.D.F.*

Sixteen Personality Factor Questionnaire. (*16 PF*). R. B. Cattell devised this representative test of factor analytical personality research with subjective tests. Among the 16 factors designated by the letters A–O (without D) and Q_1–Q_4 can be found: B = intelligence; C+ = emotional stability; E+ = dominance; O+ = trust; L+ = composure; N+ = naïveté. Each factor is represented by 20–26 items. The standard form for adults consists of the forms A and B (of 6 possible forms A–F) each with a different half of the items. The forms A and B can be regarded as *parallel tests* (q.v.). (Equivalence coefficients lie between r = 0.34–0.76 when N = 230). For the test ratings calculated per factor different norms are available. For interpretation of the factors the manual can be consulted, where descriptions of them will be found. By means of a special calculation, scores can also be obtained for the secondary factors: (i) anxiety; (ii) introversion/extraversion; (iii) emotionality; (iv) submission versus independence. The test-retest reliability of the factors ranges between r = 0.78–0.93 (6 days; N = 146) and r = 0.63–0.88 (2 months; N = 132), the bisection reliability between r = 0.06–0.78 (form A), r = 0.12–0.81 (B) when N = 218. The factorial validities (multiple correlation of the items [q.v.] with the factor representing them) lie between r = 0.74–0.92.

Bibliography: Cattell, R. B. & Eber, H. W.: Manual for forms A and B Sixteen Personality Factor Questionnaire (16 PF). Champaign, Ill., ⁵1962.   *P.G.*

Size perception. An important and much studied phenomenon in the psychology of optical perception (visual perception). Size perception in human beings cannot be described and explained by physical laws: in spite of the identical size of different *retinal* (images) the corresponding objects can be perceived as different in size. The phenomenon of size constancy (q.v.) in spatial perception (q.v.) is involved here.   *R.Hä.*

Skaggs-Robinson hypothesis. Formulated by E. B. Skaggs and E. S. Robinson, this hypothesis deals with the effect which the similarity of two amounts of material to be learned (when presented successively) has on the retention performance (retroactive inhibition, q.v.). The effect of the inhibition of the retention performance is maximal when there is "average similarity" between the interpolated and the original material and it decreases towards the poles of maximal and minimal similarity, the retention performance with minimal similarity not equalling that with maximal similarity.   *F.-C.S.*

Skepticism. The name of a school of Greek philosophy whose teaching was taken up again by M. de Montaigne and P. Charron ("What do I know?") and later by L. Klages, G. Jünger *et al. Absolute* skepticism considers man to be incapable of arriving at the truth in any area of knowledge whatsoever; those who believe this recommend the suspension of all judgment. *Relative* skepticism excludes from some areas any possibility of knowing the truth (metaphysical, religious, scientific skepticism, etc.). The word is commonly used to signify the attitude of a person who does not regard some datum as certain, and to indicate the basic attitude of a mind inclined to doubt.

M.R.

Skewness. A measure for the deviation of a distribution from symmetry. Most commonly used in the moment coefficient $a_3 = m_3/m_2{}^3/^2$: (m_2 and m_3 are the second and third powers of the distribution based on the arithmetic mean). The Pearson skewness coefficients are now only of historical interest, as in more recent times the percentile coefficients are more commonly used.

A.R.

Skiascopy. A method taken from ophthalmology to determine *refraction anomalies* (see *Refraction*) and astigmatism (q.v.). It consists of moving a perforated convex mirror in front of the eye of the person being examined and observing the movement of the light ray and its shadow in the red illumination of the pupil.

E.D.

Skin. The skin (*integumentum commune*) consists of three main layers, the *epidermis*, *corium* and *tela subcutanea*. The skin provides protection against physical, chemical and microbiological influences; it is also involved in the process of water and temperature regulation.

G.A.

Skin diseases. The skin (as the external boundary of a human being) has always been considered as a privileged centre of expression for emotional processes (blushing, losing color, goose pimples). Many psychological factors may be involved in the various disturbances of the functional relationship between the skin gland reaction and the vascular and pilo-activity; however, the assumption of a direct psychological cause seems inexact. It is simply possible to observe multifactorial complementarity functions between personality variables and skin diseases. It is difficult to make a distinction between psychological changes which have contributed to the skin disease and those which are merely a result of the latter (e.g. feeling of inferiority).

Psychosomatic symptoms: acne occurs primarily at puberty as a result of abnormal secretion by the sebaceous glands due to a disturbance of the endocrine equilibrium. If the condition continues, adult patients frequently show a delay in reaching effective and psychosexual maturity. Traumatic conflict situations are often responsible for the sudden occurrence of acne. This also applies to skin diseases which become secondary symptoms as a result of intense itching and scratching. Diseases of this kind include *acne excoriée des jeunes filles* (L. Brocq) encountered frequently among female patients. The skin is damaged by crushing or scratching and large flat scars develop which are liable to become inflamed. These forms of self-aggression have a compulsory character and serve to break down mental stress in the case of neurotic patients. In patients suffering from neurodermatitis (= endogenous eczema) in which organic factors played an important part (constitution, nutritional and metabolic disorders, allergy factors), the following psychosyndrome has been observed: heightened irritability, unsociable behavior and depression, strong attachment to the mother and masochistic trends. These mental factors play a decisive part in the reappearance or disappearance of the neurodermatitis but they need not necessarily be psychological causes of the disorder.

In the case of urticaria (chronic nettle-rash) whose organic factors have not yet been clearly determined, psychopathological changes may be observed: repressed aggression, exhibitionist (see *Exhibitionism*) and masochistic (see *Masochism*) trends.

Because of their demonstrative social protest against the withdrawal of affection and love (skin as an organ of contact and expression), patients tend to inflict punishment on themselves. Highly unspecific psychological changes (heightened anxiety, feelings of inferiority) are found in the case of psoriasis, alopecia, etc. Some patients develop phobias, e.g. zoophobia (illusion of small animals penetrating into the skin, and particles which must constantly be scratched out), luophobia and gonococcal phobia (fear of venereal disease), or cancerophobia (fear of cancer).

Treatment: medication and changed diet, supported by psychotherapy (psychoanalytic focal therapy, client-centered discussion therapy, autogenic training). See *Psychosomatics*.

D. *Vaitl*

Skinner box. A wooden box for experiments with animals in *operant* conditioning (q.v.). A lever device is fitted to it and when this is depressed, a pellet of food drops into the cage or a door is opened through which the test animal can escape. The Skinner box is a variant of the experiment, vexation (q.v.) or problem cage (q.v.) developed by E. L. Thorndike, and owes its name to R. F. Skinner, the American researcher into behavior and learning. *H.Ro.*

Skin resistance. I. The resistance to a direct current flowing through the skin corresponds in very small measure only to a true ohmic resistance (13–95 kohms). It is caused primarily by a combination of several different kinds of variable polarization voltage (1.5–800 kohm polarization resistance). The reflectoral changes in the skin resistance caused by sen-

sory stimuli or motor reactions are due solely to changes in the adsorption and permeation characteristics of membranes or to changes in polarization capacities. The capacitative proportion of the skin impedance consists of a "diffusion capacity" and a "double layer capacity" and can be determined by alternating current measurements or by recording the cut-in characteristic of a DC current. *M.S.*

II. *Skin potential:* the resistance and potential difference vary as a function of the subject's condition. At different times in the day, when solving problems and in conjunction with emotional changes, long-term alterations may be noted (basal values, basal level). In addition external or internal stimulation leads to brief reductions in the skin potential and multiphase fluctuations (skin galvanic or psychogalvanic reactions, phenomena, reflexes). In psychophysiology short-term changes are used to demonstrate orienting and defensive behavior.

Bibliography: Venables, P. H. & Martin, I.: Skin resistance and skin potential. In: **Venables, P. H. & Martin, I.** (Ed.): Manual of psycho-physiological methods. Amsterdam, 1967. *W.Sch.*

Skin vision. The alleged capacity to be able to discriminate brightness and colour by means of touch. Also known as "finger vision" and "dermo-optical perception" or DOP (G. Razran). See *Eyeless sight*. *J.B.*

Slavery, reflex of. Pavlov's term for an "inborn reflex of slavish submission" opposed to the reflex of freedom (q.v.), related to appeasement gestures (q.v.) in animals, and having a similar effect in decreasing the destructive ambition of the strong. Pavlov suggests that insight into the condition, and systematic measures, will enable the reflex to be controlled and suppressed, whereas ineffective resistance will only increase aggression (q.v.). *J.C.*

Sleep is a recurrent, healthy state of inertia and unresponsiveness. Observable responses are less easily elicited, and so also, it would appear, are the internal responses underlying perception. Sleep must be distinguished from hibernation, in which activity declines during long periods of low body temperature. Sleep should also be distinguished from the hypnotic trance, in which responsiveness to external stimuli (from the hypnotist) is not reduced, and in which the physiology is that of wakefulness.

In recent years, it has become known that there are two different kinds of sleep (Oswald, 1962) which alternate throughout mammalian sleep. The normal human passes from wakefulness into "orthodox" sleep, and later into the "paradoxical" phase of sleep. These phases will be described subsequently. There appears to be a physiological and psychological continuum embracing intense alertness, relaxed wakefulness, drowsiness and the successive stages of orthodox sleep. The transition into paradoxical sleep, however, usually appears abrupt and discontinuous.

1. *Historical perspective and methods*. Sleep can be studied by simple observation, an approach that still provides interesting comparative data (Hediger, 1960). Questionnaires too can provide subjective estimates of delay to sleep, duration of sleep, number of awakenings and so on. The method of intermittent stimuli, to which the subject must respond, has the disadvantage of potentially interfering with the sleep process. Motility during the night was for long a principal tool, but the advent of the electroencephalograph (EEG) has stimulated extensive research.

Bremer (1935) made a cut through the lower medulla oblongata of the cat, producing the *encéphale isolé*, in which EEG and ocular signs of alternating wakefulness and sleep persisted. A cut made through the upper mesencephalon resulted in the *cerveau isolé*, in which signs resembling perpetual sleep were seen. Bremer's belief that the signs of wakefulness were contingent solely on greater afferent inflow was discounted following the finding by Moruzzi & Magoun (1949) that electrical stimulation of the central core of the brainstem would cause signs of wakefulness to replace those of sleep in the *encéphale isolé*.

There came the formulation of the concept of the ascending activating reticular formation (Delafresnaye, 1964). The brainstem reticular formation, in the central core of the brain stem, from medulla to thalamus, was found to receive collateral afferent nervous inflow from all the main sensory pathways. Impulses arriving by these afferents, or descending from the cortex, would exite the reticular formation, from which activating impulses would then ascend to the cerebral cortex. These impulses did not convey specific information but increased the cortical vigilance or efficiency, making possible perception and controlled response, together with EEG signs of wakefulness. Sleep was conceptualized as a negative state resulting from a decline in the up-flow of activating impulses from the reticular formation.

The concept of the activating reticular formation can still be considered valid for orthodox sleep but not for paradoxical sleep. The controlling-mechanisms for the latter are in the pons (Jouvet, 1965). Sleep induced by drugs such as barbiturates has been explained in terms of a depressant action on the reticular formation. It is now realized that such drugs cause an enhancement of orthodox sleep but a suppression of paradoxical sleep.

There is currently no comprehensive theory of the sleep mechanism. A possible chemical hypnotoxin is still the subject of conflicting reports. Any satisfactory theory will need to embrace the rapid provocation of sleep by intense, repetitive, sensory stimuli; the provocation of sleep by electrical stimulation of some forebrain areas (Clemente & Sterman, 1967); the circadian rhythmicity of the desire for sleep; and the probability that there is a delicate balance between the two different kinds of sleep.

2. *The present state of knowledge*. Sleep is accompanied by characteristic EEG features. In man the waking alpha (Berger) rhythm, at 10 c/sec. gives way in drowsiness (stage 1 sleep) to irregular low voltage waves of 4–6 c/sec. with rolling eyeball movements, succeeded by stage 2 sleep with sleep spindles at 12–14 c/sec. and high voltage slow wave complexes, and then stages 3 and 4 with predominant high voltage 1–2 c/sec. waves (Rechtschaffen & Kales, 1968). These are all stages of orthodox sleep (or NREM, slow-wave, or synchronized sleep). Paradoxical sleep (or REM, desynchronized, or activated sleep) is accompanied by a low voltage EEG with 4–10 c/sec. waves and frequent bursts of conjugate rapid eye movements. A burst of eye movements is often preceded by a few "saw-tooth" EEG waves at 2–3 c/sec.

In orthodox sleep, the breathing, heart rate and blood pressure are regular, the brain blood flow is reduced and the brain temperature falls slightly. The skeletal muscles retain some tone, and the penis is flaccid. The thresholds for arousal (q.v.), and for respiratory response to carbon dioxide are raised, but electrically induced reflexes of the lower limbs are still present.

Paradoxical sleep in man makes up about 20–25% of total sleep and recurs about five times per night. The first period, after about one hour of orthodox sleep, is brief, but later periods are longer, lasting some 20–40 minutes. In paradoxical sleep the breathing, heart rate and blood pressure are irregular, and more brief body and facial movements are made. A major body movement often precedes by a minute or two each period of paradoxical sleep, which again often terminates with a movement. The penis is erect unless there is accompanying severe dream anxiety (Karacan *et al.*, 1966) and most skeletal muscles are flaccid. There is abolition of limb reflexes because of descending inhibitory impulses in the spinal cord. The inhibition is maximal at the moment of each rapid eye movement

burst. The brain blood flow is greater than in wakefulness, and the brain temperature rises, whereas the blood flow through red muscles is greatly reduced.

The total duration of sleep is about fourteen hours per twenty-four in the newborn human. The proportion spent as paradoxical sleep is greatest just before birth, declines in the weeks after birth, declines steeply again in senility, and is low in mental defectives. Stages 3 and 4 are accompanied by increased secretion of human growth hormone, are enhanced after physical exercise, but are much reduced in middle and old age. In old age, total sleep is somewhat reduced and is frequently interrupted.

In wakefulness, sporadic galvanic skin responses will occur "spontaneously" but these are reduced during drowsiness, are occasional in stage 2 and in paradoxical sleep, but in some people become very large and almost continuous in stages 3 and 4 sleep.

Total deprivation of sleep leads to diminished ability to sustain attention (Williams *et al.*, 1959) and, after about sixty hours, to occasional visual and auditory hallucinations or paranoid ideas. Selective deprivation of paradoxical sleep causes it to be subsequently enhanced in both its duration and its intensity. Selective deprivation of stages 3 and 4 sleep is followed by similar enhancement.

3. *Psychological features of sleep*. The terms "light" and "deep" sleep are no longer valid: in paradoxical sleep especially, concordance between differing criteria is lost. Progression from wakefulness through stages 1 to 4 of orthodox sleep is associated with progressive decline in responsiveness to auditory stimuli, but in paradoxical sleep responsiveness is governed by the meaningfulness of the stimuli (Williams *et al.*, 1966). Meaningful stimuli are often woven into dream content on an assonant basis without causing awakening (Berger, 1963). Complex auditory discriminations and selective responses can be made during sleep (Oswald *et al.*, 1960).

Memory of the psychological events of sleep, or of external stimuli presented during sleep, is poor (Hoskovec & Cooper, 1967), but awakenings from any stage of sleep can usually elicit recall of some immediately preceding mental life. In drowsiness there occur *hypnagogic hallucinations*, namely brief, disconnected and often bizarre sensory experiences, coupled with internal verbal productions of schizophrenia-like nature. Awakenings from orthodox sleep usually elicit fragmentary reports, often characterized as "thinking", whereas awakenings from paradoxical sleep usually elicit lengthy, colorful and adventuresome reports often characterized as "dreaming" (Dement & Kleitman, 1957). The experienced observer can discriminate the type of sleep from which the dream was elicited (Monroe *et al.*, 1965). (See *Dream*.)

4. *Aberrations of sleep*. Insomnia is the commonest complaint about sleep. It occurs in association with older age, especially in women, with introversion, with anxiety and depression, or with states of mood elevation, whether spontaneous or caused by drugs such as amphetamine. The consumption of drugs to promote sleep is widespread and increasing. Many drugs, including alcohol, suppress paradoxical sleep, and if the individual has grown accustomed to a drug and it is then withdrawn, a "rebound" increase of paradoxical sleep occurs which takes up to two months to resolve (Oswald, 1969) and is accompanied, in the case of hypnotic drugs, by insomnia, restless sleep and vivid dreams.

Sleep-walking, sleep-talking, and enuresis are phenomena of orthodox sleep, whereas head-banging, body-rocking, and nightmares can occur in either kind of sleep. Among these only the nightmares are recallable by the subject, and he may remember the paralysis that accompanied a period of paradoxical sleep. Idiopathic narcolepsy is characterized by short periods of irresistible day-time sleep and, often, cataplectic attacks, namely sudden loss of muscular tone following an emotional stimulus specific to the individual. The cataplexy is probably a form of partial paradoxical sleep. The narcoleptic is unusual in that he will often pass immediately into paradoxical sleep instead of first into orthodox sleep.

Sleep is important in psychology because its study shows that the degree and the quality of a response are governed by a generalized state of the nervous system which can vary between extreme alertness and profound unresponsiveness. The role of sleep in the physiological economy is uncertain, but it is probable that the two kinds of sleep subserve different restorative functions, and that paradoxical sleep, with its intense brain blood flow, is especially related to synthesis for growth, plasticity and renewal in the brain (Oswald, 1969).

Bibliography: Berger, R. J.: Experimental modification of dream content by meaningful verbal stimuli. Brit. J. Psychiat., 1963, *109*, 722–40. Bremer, F.: Cerveau isolé et physiologie du sommeil. C. R. Soc. Biol. (Paris), 1935, *118*, 1235–41. Clemente, C. D. & Sterman, M. B.: Basal forebrain mechanisms for internal inhibition and sleep. Res. Publ. Ass. nerv. ment. Dis., 1967, *45*, 127–47. Delafresnaye, J. F. (Ed.): Brain mechanisms and consciousness. Oxford, 1954. Dement, W.C. & Kleitman, N.: The relation of eye movements during sleep to dream activity, an objective method for the study of dreaming. J. exp. Psychol., 1957, *53*, 339–47. Fisher, K. C. *et al.* (Eds.): Mammalian hibernation III. Edinburgh, 1967. Foulkes, D.: The psychology of sleep. New York, 1966. Hediger, H.: Comparative observations on sleep. Proc. roy. Soc. Med., 1969, *62*, 153–6. Hoskovec, J. & Cooper, L. M.: Comparison of recent experimental trends concerning sleep learning in the USA and the Soviet Union. Activ. nerv. sup. (Prague), 1967, *9*, 93–6. Jouvet, M.: Paradoxical sleep. In: Akert, K. *et al.* (Eds.): Sleep mechanisms. Amsterdam, 1965, 20–62. Kales, A. (Ed.): Sleep: physiology and pathology. Philadelphia, 1969. Karacan, I. *et al.*: Erection cycle during sleep in relation to dream anxiety. Arch. gen. Psychiatr., 1966, *15*, 183–9. Monroe, L. J. *et al.*: Discriminability of REM and NREM reports. J. pers. soc. Psychol., 1965, *2*, 456–60. Moruzzi, G. & Magoun, H. W.: Brain stem reticular formation and activation of the EEG. Electroenceph. clin. Neurophysiol., 1949, *1*, 455–73. Oswald, I.: Sleep mechanisms recent advances. Proc. roy. Soc. Med., 1962, *55*, 1910–1912. Id.: Human brain protein, drugs and dreams. Nature, 1969, *223*, 893–7. **Id.: Sleep**. Harmondsworth, 1970. **Id., Taylor, A. M. & Treisman, M.**: Discriminative responses to stimulation during human sleep. Brain, 1960, *83*, 440–53. **Rechtschaffen, A. L. & Kales, A.** (Ed.): A manual of standardized terminology, techniques and scoring system for sleep stages of human subjects. Washington, D.C., 1968. **Williams, H. L., Lubin, A. & Goodnow, J. J.**: Impaired performance with acute sleep loss. Psychol. Monogr., 1959, *73*, No. 14. **William, H. L., Morlock, H. C. & J. V.**: Discriminative responses to auditory signals during sleep. Psychophysiology, 1966, *2*, 208–15.   *I. Oswald*

Sleeping pills. See *Hypnotics*.

Sleep-walking (syn. *Somnabulism*). Sleep-walking may occur spontaneously; the somnambulist acts unconsciously in a kind of semi-conscious state. Sleep-walkers used to be referred to as "moonstruck" but it has been impossible to demonstrate any real influence of the moon on their behavior. Somnambulism can be generated artificially by hypnosis (q.v.). The concordance between depth hypnosis and sleep-walking was already discovered by J. M. Charcot and H. M. Bernheim. Holzschuher (1955) has a bipolar interpretation of sleep-walking as action and reaction in the purely primitive consciousness, while the ego-consciousness is eliminated in sleep. In this state, the primitive person functions quasi-independently. Sleep-walking is observed in neurotic personalities and is fairly common in children.
E.U.

Smell. See *Sense organs*.

Smelling, colored. An example of *synesthesia*. The spontaneous tendency found in some people to interpret smells consistently in terms of certain colors.   *C.D.F.*

Smell, intensity of. The intensity of a smell is dependent on the concentration of the gas carrier and is particularly important from the methodological angle, since quality perception is influenced by intensity. Other qualities are modified in addition to the intensity, e.g. by adaptation. The absolute thresholds of smells —examined primarily olfactometrically (see *Olfactometer*)—are very low (= high sensitivity of the sense of smell (see *Sense organs: sense of smell*). On the other hand the ability of human beings to differentiate between pure gradations of intensity seems very poor. *F.N.*

Smile, first. An expressive movement which appears above all on perception of a human countenance between about the third and sixth months. According to A. Gesell, it occurs in ninety-eight per cent of six-month-old infants. The first smile underlies positive and negative reinforcement. C. Bühler (1921) saw it as the first social reaction. According to investigations carried out by Spitz (1946) and R. Meili, it is, less specifically, an expression of pleasurable states. These effects are clearly heredity-conditioned responses to specific stimuli, above all to the eye-nose-forehead schema, which acts as a releaser (q.v.) or key stimulus.

Bibliography: Spitz, R.: The smiling response. Genet. Psychol. Monogr., 1946, *34*.   *H.J.K.*

Snellen charts. Charts with letters of a certain shape and varying in size to test visual acuity.
R.R.

Sociability. 1. Literally, the capacity of the individual to adapt himself to social conditions; more generally, the inclination or the need for social life and human contact.

2. Also "gregariousness"; the desire for friendly relations with other people or for participation with them in common activities. Sociability was described by Cattell and Guilford as a motivation factor defined in factor-analytical terms.

Bibliography: Cattell, R. B.: Personality and motivation structure and measurement. New York, 1957.
D.B.

Social anthropology. A term used in association with cultural anthropology (q.v.), ethnology (q.v.), and ethnography to signify the study of the early history of forms of human society. Under the influence of E. Durkheim it has come to mean specifically and in contrast to ethnology the science of the general laws which are to be found behind the development of cultures (syn.: *Socio-cultural anthropology*).
W.D.F.

Social desirability. This is one of the most important response sets (q.v.). It contains the tendency to answer an item independently of the reply which would be appropriate for the individual by giving that which, in the individual's opinion, is the most desirable by the criterion of social norms. In order to check this reply tendency, suitable scales of social desirability (SD) were constructed, e.g. the SD scales of A. L. Edwards, O. P. Corwen & D. Marlowe.
P.Z.

Social hygiene. The science dealing with health in social life. See *Mental hygiene.*   *W.Sch.*

Socialization refers to the process whereby individuals develop the qualities essential to function effectively in the society in which they live. As indicated in this definition, socialization is concerned with the characteristics that individuals acquire and the psychological mechanisms through which the desired changes are brought about. These issues have been studied most extensively in the context of child socialization.

1. *Outcomes of socialization.*

(*a*) *Primary socialization.* During early childhood, efforts at socialization are principally directed at developing in children basic psychological functions that are necessary for acquisition of more elaborate patterns of behavior. Among other things, children must develop cognitive skills that will enable them to deal intelligently with complex and changing requirements of everyday life; they must gain proficiency in verbal communication by which they can influence others and be influenced by them; they must become adept in intricate social behaviors that are conducive to reciprocally satisfying relationships; and they must learn to value social approval and other symbolic rewards which make them amenable to social influence.

As children become more versatile, their wishes inevitably come into conflict with those of other group members. No longer can they express their desires when and how they please, but they must learn to regulate their actions partly on the basis of the consequences these can have for others. Whereas self-controlling behavior contributes to the well-being of other people, it generally detracts from the person's own rewarding outcomes. For example, self-control often involves relinquishing expedient means of gaining satisfactions because, for one reason or another, they are socially prohibited. At other times it requires postponing rewarding activities in the pursuit of goals requiring expenditure of considerable time and effort. On most occasions, the performance of desired activities must be channeled through irksome routines and time schedules. Because of the unfavorable immediate consequences associated with self-controlling behavior it is difficult to establish, even though in the long run it may benefit all group members in varying degrees.

(*b*) *Internalization and self-regulatory processes.* The ultimate aim of successful socialization is the substitution of internal controls for external sanctions. Once a self-regulatory system is developed, a person's self-demands and self-reactions to his own behavior serve as his main guides and deterrents. At this level of development, adherence to societal norms occurs in the absence of external pressures and social surveillance.

It is commonly assumed that self-regulatory systems are established through internalization of attitudes and values. This type of explanation, however, rarely specifies the manner in which attitudes govern action. There is, in fact, some dispute whether attitudes control behavior or whether a change in behavior produces attitudinal accommodations. Experimental evidence (Festinger, 1964; Bandura, 1969a) favors the latter causal sequence. Behavior is also sometimes spoken of as being internalized. Actually, after behavior has been acquired it cannot undergo any further interiorization. The process of internalization is, therefore, less concerned with the locus of behavior than with the manner in which it is maintained. See *Attitude*.

According to social learning theory (Bandura, 1970), internalized control is largely mediated through anticipated consequences for prospective actions. These self-produced consequences may take two major forms. As a result of experiencing differential outcomes in conjunction with different patterns of behavior, a person eventually comes to expect that a given course of action will be rewarded, ignored, or punished. Anticipated reward facilitates performance of behavior, whereas anticipated punishment usually has an inhibitory effect. Through symbolic representation, future consequences can be converted into current events that are functionally similar to actual outcomes in their capacity to influence action.

Behavior can be self-regulated not only by anticipated external consequences but by self-evaluative responses to one's own actions. People typically set themselves certain behavioral standards, and respond to their own performances in self-rewarding and self-punishing ways in accordance with their self-imposed demands. Anticipation of self-disapproval for personally devalued actions provides an additional motivating influence to keep behavior in line with adopted standards. Self-generated and externally occurring consequences often conflict, as when certain behaviors are approved and encouraged by others, but if performed would give rise to self-critical and self-devaluative reactions. Under these circumstances, the effects of self-reinforcement may prevail over external influences. Conversely, response patterns may be maintained by self-reward under conditions of minimal external support.

It is not difficult to explain why people might reward themselves for praiseworthy accomplishments. A more challenging, but inadequately explored, question is why they punish themselves for transgressive behavior or for performances they judge to be inadequate? There are several factors that may cause people to punish themselves. Reprehensible or self-disappointing performances provoke distressing thoughts that are likely to persist until amends have been made. Self-punishment can thus provide relief from self-generated distress that is enduring and often more painful than the self-administered reprimand. This phenomenon is most vividly illustrated in extreme cases where people torment themselves for years over relatively minor transgressions and do not achieve equanimity until they have made some kind of reparation. Having criticized or punished themselves for undesirable actions, individuals are likely to stop upsetting themselves by thinking about that behavior.

Although self-punishing behavior is partly maintained because it can stop self-generated distress, it often receives external support as well. Self-censure can serve as an effective means of reducing reprimands from others that might otherwise be even more unpleasant. In this case, self-punishment is the lesser of two evils. Moreover, adherence to high standards of behavior is actively supported through a vast system of societal rewards, whereas few accolades are bestowed on people for rewarding themselves on the basis of reprehensible performances. Self-regulative behavior is most effectively sustained when the standards adopted for self-reinforcement result in selective association with persons who share similar behavioral norms, thus providing social support for one's own system of self-evaluation.

(c) *Socialization as a reciprocal influence process.* When socialization is discussed in terms of psychological changes occurring in the learner, it provides a one-sided view of the process, which may erroneously convey the impression that individuals merely learn to conform to societal requirements. A number of writers (Cottrell, 1969; Goslin, 1969; Inkeles, 1968) have therefore stressed socialization as a two-way process. Although behavior is regulated to some extent by environmental influences, equally, individuals play an active rôle in altering their environment. In primary socialization, for example, children exercise some degree of control over parents as well as being influenced by them. Socialization therefore involves a continuous reciprocal influence between individuals' behavior and societal demands. Because of reciprocal control societal agencies often encounter formidable difficulties in inculcating in their members the characteristics they value. Not infrequently the social system fails to surmount the counter-control exerted by its members, and is then altered in accordance with their wishes.

(d) *Transmission of cultural patterns by familial and other social systems.* Socialization is often depicted as a process that is largely achieved in childhood, with the family serving as the principal agency. In fact, socialization is a life-long process in which a wide variety of social agents plays an influential role. As Brim & Wheeler (1966) point out, childhood experiences do not adequately prepare one for meeting the demands of adult life. New modes of behavior have to be learned in later years as individuals assume various marital, occupational, and social roles. Even at the adult level, under conditions of rapid social and technological change, behavior patterns that had functional values may have to be replaced by new skills appropriate to the altered circumstances. Moreover, when cultural discontinu-

ities exist, early social learning must be modified; sometimes drastically, in later years. In American society, for example, childhood sexual behavior is negatively sanctioned, but adults are expected to engage in appropriate sexual activities without anxiety or guilt. Hence, the more successfully parents inhibit their children's sexual behavior, the more likely sexual disorders are to occur in adulthood. Other cultures similarly involve training discontinuities (Hsu, 1961), notably in the areas of dependency, aggression, and affectional behavior, which necessitate re-socialization experiences.

It is evident that the diverse outcomes of socialization cannot be established solely within the family agency, no matter how versatile its members may be. Social, legal, educational, and religious organizations, mass media influences, and a host of other extra-familial agents, contribute, in varying degrees, to the types of values and response patterns instilled in group members. Socialization is further complicated by the fact that these multiple sources of influence frequently act in conflicting directions.

2. *Modes of socialization.* Socialization outcomes are achieved through a variety of means.

(a) *Differential reinforcement.* There is abundant documentation in psychological research (Bandura, 1969a; Staats & Staats, 1963) to show that human behavior is largely controlled by its consequences. Behaviors that produce rewarding outcomes tend to be adopted, whereas those that are punished or ignored are generally discarded. Differential reinforcement is, therefore, widely employed by socialization agents to promote desired patterns of behavior.

(b) *Vicarious reinforcement.* In everyday life, people repeatedly observe the actions of others and their consequences for them. As will be shown later, observed rewards and punishments can play an influential rôle in regulating behavior in much the same way as outcomes which are directly experienced (Bandura, 1970; Kanfer, 1965).

Observed consequences also provide a reference standard that determines whether a particular outcome will assume positive or negative value. The same compliment, for instance, is likely to be punishing for persons who have seen similar performances by others highly acclaimed, but rewarding when others have been less generously praised. Thus, observation of other people's outcomes can drastically alter the effectiveness of direct reinforcement.

(*c*) *Verbal guidance.* Socialization would be exceedingly laborious if individuals had to discover the appropriate cultural patterns solely through trial and error responses and their associated consequences. Other forms of influence are therefore used to accelerate the process of social learning. Verbal guidance is one such technique. After children have acquired linguistic skills, they can be taught, by verbal instructions, advantageous ways of behaving, and the societal rules and prohibitions.

Instructional control and reinforcing sanctions are most effective when combined. The power of sanctions is often enhanced if the reinforcement contingencies are verbally specified (Aronfreed, 1968); conversely, instructions have no enduring effects or go unheeded if they are not backed up with appropriate sanctions.

(*d*) *Modeling.* Socialization is to a large extent effected through modeling processes. Research conducted within the framework of social-learning theory (Bandura, 1969a, b; Flanders, 1968) demonstrates that virtually all learning phenomena resulting from direct experiences can occur on a vicarious basis through observation of other people's behavior and its consequences for them. Intricate response patterns can be acquired by observing the performances of live or symbolic models; emotional and attitudinal responses can be developed observationally by witnessing the affective reactions of others undergoing painful or pleasurable experiences; fearful and defensive behavior can be eliminated vicariously by observing others perform the threatening behavior without experiencing any adverse consequences; inhibitions can be induced by witnessing the behavior of others punished; and, finally, the incidence of group members' engagement in given activities can be socially regulated through the actions of influential models.

The provision of models not only serves to accelerate the learning process but, in cases where errors are dangerous or costly, becomes an essential means of transmitting behavioral patterns. Social behavior, of course, is most rapidly acquired and modified through the combined influence of modeling, verbal guidance, and differential reinforcement.

Bibliography: Aronfreed, J.: Conscience and conduct. New York, 1968. **Bandura, A.:** Principles of behavior modification. New York, 1969a. **Id.:** Social-learning theory of identificatory processes. In: **Goslin, D. A.** (Ed.): Handbook of socialization theory and research. Chicago, 1969b, 213–62. **Id.:** Vicarious and self-reinforcement processes. In: **Glaser, R.** (Ed.): The nature of reinforcement. Columbus, Ohio, 1970. **Brim, O. G. & Wheeler, S.:** Socialization after childhood, two essays. New York, 1966. **Cottrell, L. S.:** Interpersonal interaction and the development of self. In: **Goslin, D. A.** (Ed.): Handbook of socialization theory and research. Chicago, 1969, 543–70. **Festinger, L.:** Behavioral support for opinion change. Publ. Opin. Quart., 1964, *28*, 404–17. **Flanders, J. P.:** A review of research on imitative behavior. Psychol. Bull., 1968, *69*, 316–37. **Goslin, D. A.:** Handbook of socialization theory and research. Chicago, 1969. **Hsu, F. L. K.:** Psychological anthropology. Homewood, Ill., 1961. **Inkeles, A.:** Society, social structure, and child socialization. In: **Clausen, J.** (Ed.): Socialization and society. Boston, 1968, 74–129. **Kanfer, F. H.:** Vicarious human reinforcement: a glimpse into the black box. In: **Krasner, L. & Ullmann, L. P.** (Ed.): Research in behavior modification. New York, 1965, 244–67. **Staats, A. W. & Staats, C. K.:** Complex human behavior. New York, 1963. *A. Bandura*

Social motivation test (SMT). A method published by Müller in 1966 for diagnosing the structure of social motivations and the social awareness of values in children whose ages range from nine to fourteen years. The method which is available in two parallel forms consists of twenty-four items (q.v.) in which social problem situations differing in clearness and closeness to experience are verbalized. An objective evaluation according to six different motivational forms is guaranteed by a choice between several responses. There are differential norms in percentage ranks and test scores. The objectivity of the evaluation and interpretation is assessed as follows: parallel test reliability when $N = 309$ individuals is $r = 0.71$. With high *content validity* there are some indications of construct validity based on age and sex differences.

Bibliography: Müller, R.: Der soziale Motivationstest. Weinheim, 1966.   *G.P.*

Social neurosis. Social illnesses are said to occur when the affective life of the members of a society is either excessively stimulated or repressed. Under the heading of social neuroses may be grouped, for example, compensation neuroses (q.v.) as well as the neurotic reactions which may be caused by social mobility of one kind or another that the individual finds unbearable (retraining late in life, unemployment among older workers, removal to an uncongenial district due to work requirements (see *Neurosis*).   *J.L.I.*

Social norms. These *denote* (*a*) behavioral patterns which the population regards as of positive worth and which are to be striven for because they represent a *value*, an *obligation* or an *ideal*; social norms *describe* (*b*) as real norms what individuals know or imagine they know about the actual behavior of the other members of the population. *Statistical* social norms are data obtained by a selected sample of individuals which describe in figures the extent or distribution of the real behavior investigated.   *I.M.D.*

Social perception. Social perception as a branch of social psychology (q.v.) may be defined in narrow or wide terms: the narrower definition takes as its theme the influence by personal and social factors while the wider definition not only considers the dependence of perception on social environment but also its relationship to that environment (in particular to man, i.e. person perception). The discrepancy between these two definitions is continued in the interpretation of the notion of perception. In the narrower definition, in spite of all methodological difficulties, emphasis is still placed to a greater extent on the direct experience of the senses whereas in the wider definition the concept of perception is used in a very loose sense to include all processes of information acquisition and processing right up to the most complex judgment processes. In the wider version, social perception therefore represents a very vague sphere of study. But even if the narrower definition is adopted, studies often go beyond the range of perception based on direct experience. Allport (1955) draws attention to the fact that social perception is frequently taken to denote the whole range of the individual's understanding of his social situation. The difficulty of setting down a precise definition was accurately described by Taijfel (1969, 316) when he pointed out that the transition from perception to such cognitive activities as drawing conclusions, establishing categories or making judgments was always difficult. There is in fact a continuum with no sharp distinctions. In the central area of perception, attempts to make a clear distinction between perception and non-perception will probably fail, all the more so as in recent years the rôle of establishing conclusions and categories has been considered centrally important to the act of perception. The result is that in many studies, the precise point of reference cannot be identified (for instance in many studies of distortions of perception the question arises as to whether it is in fact perception and not memory which has been distorted). This may be one of the reasons why many studies are not classified under the heading of social perception, but considered primarily from the angle of the social variables. Example: the problem raised by Asch (1952) of the distortion of perception under group pressure is certainly a problem of social perception but is frequently dealt with under the heading of "conformity", i.e. as a special example of influence of the group on the individual, and in this genuine example of perception, the same explanations are given as for the problem of attitude changes under group pressure (see *Group dynamics*). The lack of integration of the object sphere is apparent in a particularly important area which is generally dealt with separately, namely that of language. B. L. Whorf has developed the theory that language shapes perception of the environment (see *Whorf's hypothesis*). We therefore arrive at a new principle of relativity indicating that observers will not arrive at the same images of the universe through the same physical evidence, unless their linguistic background is similar or could be calibrated in some way (Whorf, 1940). But the majority of existing studies do not differentiate between cognition and perception.

While it is apparent that different languages cannot represent the environment in the same way (e.g. have different color differentiations), this does not mean that the perceptions themselves must therefore be different too. Whorf's theory is, however, confirmed by the classical work of Brown & Lenneberg (1958) who showed a correlation between the codability of colors (i.e. the association between individual colors and the names given to them) and the repeated recognition of these colors, i.e. a positive relationship between linguistic and non-linguistic behavior.

In the nineteen-forties and fifties, social perception was referred to by many authors as the "new look" because—by contrast with gestalt psychology—it placed great emphasis on motivational factors which had hitherto received little attention in perception psychology. A considerable step forward was taken by comparison with the theory based on inherent factors of the perception process (such as stimulus, nerve excitation, etc.) as is shown by some of the hypotheses developed in this connection:

Physical needs determine what is perceived. Studies did, however, show that while physiological needs influence perception, this influence cannot be heightened at will; on the contrary as needs increase, the influence may be reduced. Values which are characteristic for the individual influence the speed with which words associated with these values are perceived. Some authors did, however, attempt to reduce the significance of values to the variable of word frequencies. According to this assumption, the value structure of an individual leads to heightened interest in the relevant stimuli and therefore to a greater degree of familiarity with these stimuli. A more recent study (Johnson *et al.*, 1960) has, however, shown both the influence of the degree of familiarity and that of the value in lowering the recognition thresholds. At the same time this study revealed a clear relationship between the value of a word and the frequency with which this word is used in a particular country.

The influence of value attributes was also found in the sphere of distortion of perception. In a perception experiment conducted by Wittreich & Radcliffe (1956), authoritative personalities showed less distortion than non-authoritative personalities; the variable of familiarity was controlled during this experiment.

Verbal stimuli which are emotionally disturbing or threatening to the individual, require a longer perception time than neutral words and are sometimes perceived with such heavy distortion that their significance is radically changed and characteristic emotional reactions provoked before they are perceived.

This phenomenon assumed a central position in the discussion of social perception and led to the concept of perceptual defense. While the phenomenon of defense against memory contents was well-known from depth psychology (q.v.), the problem was encountered in a paradoxical formulation here in the sphere of precisely defined perception psychology: how is it possible for an individual to repress, distort or delay perceptions which he has not yet perceived? Put like this, the problem can only be solved by postulating a "homunculus theory", i.e. the existence of a kind of "censor" in the percipient individual which checks the contents of perception before allowing them to be "perceived". To avoid this dilemma, hypotheses were developed which were based essentially on the availability of response patterns and confirmed experimentally. One of the few portmanteau theories in social perception was developed by J. S. Bruner and L. Postman; it takes into account considerations of probability theory as well as motivational factors (see the summary report by Allport, 1955). The idea underlying this hypothesis testing theory is that perception consists essentially in testing specific hypotheses. Perception is based on a process of experience which leads the individual to expect certain objects and specific characteristics for these objects. According to this theory, the strength of a hypothesis is determined by: (a) the frequency of the confirmations obtained of it; (b) the number of simultaneously available hypotheses; (c) the motivational backing; (d) the cognitive backing. While these factors determine the strength of a hypothesis, the strength itself is defined by the quantity of corresponding stimulus information needed to confirm or refute the hypothesis.

Criticism of social perception concentrates on three points: (a) Most studies do not take into account personality differences while differential psychological (see *Differential psychology*) studies have tried to demonstrate that subjects include both sensitizers (i.e. subjects who react with heightened attention and can therefore be described as sensitized) and repressors (subjects who tend to be characterized by perceptual defense). The general and differential psychological theories have not as yet been integrated.

(b) Jones and Gerald (1967) have drawn attention to the fact that previous studies of perceptual defense have failed to take the experimental situation adequately into account in the interpretation. In their opinion, perceptual defense is only present beyond dispute when perception itself is the ultimate objective; if, however, perception has an instrumental function in a decision on action, the categories both for preferred and rejected values by comparison with neutral categories will be more easily available to the observer, i.e. the perception threshold will be lowered both for positive and negative values as opposed to neutral ones. This theory can be confirmed experimentally.

(c) The third point of criticism concerns the importance to be attributed to the theory of social perception. It must be remembered that the theory cannot explain social perception as such but can only attempt to clarify the influence of social factors on perception. In many experiments the emphasis is therefore not placed on the accuracy of perception but on the social factors which influence it. An extreme example is provided by Sherif's autokinetic effect, where testees are required to describe in the dark, without any aid to structuration, the position of a point which does not move but is experienced as moving because of the experimental set-up; in a situation of this kind, social influences can become the dominant factor. In order to ensure the action of social factors, the perception process is often made quite difficult, and, e.g., images have to be reconstructed from memory, which in many studies raises the question as to which particular psychological function has in fact been tested. In addition many studies were organized from the outset in order to demonstrate the influence of social factors and clearly reflect their origins. As a result the theory of social perception has ceased to be of immediate importance and the phenomena involved are grouped together under social factors (e.g. reference group, stereotype, q.v., prejudice, q.v., conformity, etc.).

Bibliography: Allport, F. H.: Theories of perception and the concept of structure. New York, 1955. Asch, S. E.: Social psychology. Englewood Cliffs, 1952. Brown, R. W. & Lenneberg, E. H.: Studies in linguistic relativity. In: Maccoby, N., Newcomb, T. & Hartley, E. L. (Eds.): Readings in social psychology. New York, [3]1958. Carpenter, B., Wiener, M. & Carpenter, J. T.: Predictability of perceptual defense behavior. J. Abn. Soc. Psychol., 1956, 52, 380–3. Eriksen, C. W.: Defense against ego threat in memory and perception. J. Abn. Soc. Psychol., 1952, 47, 230–5. Graumann, C, F.: Social perception. Exp. Angew. Psychol., 1956, 3, 605–61. Hörmann, H.: Psychologie der Sprache. Berlin, 1967. Johnson, R. C., Thomsen, C. W. & Frincke, G.: Word values, word frequency, and visual duration thresholds. Psychol. Rev., 1960, 6, 67. Jones, E. E. & Gerald, H. B.: Foundations of social psychology. New York, 1967. McDavid, J. W. & Harari, H.: Social psychology. New York, 1968. Secord, P. F. & Backman, C. W.: Social psychology. New York, 1964. Sherif, M.: Group influences upon the formation of norms and attitudes. In: Maccoby. N., Newcomb, T. & Hartley, E. L. (Eds.): Taijfel, H.: Social and cultural factors in perception. In: Lindzey, G. & Aronson, E. (Eds.): Handbook of social psychology. Reading, Mass., 1969. Whorf, B. L.: Science and linguistics. In: Maccoby, N., Newcomb, T. & Hartley, E. L. (Eds.): Wittreich, W. J. & Radcliffe, K. B.: Differences in the perception of an authority figure and a non-authority figure by Navy recruits. J. Abn. Soc. Psychol., 1956.   J. Schenk

Social power. The extent to which an individual has the ability or authority through his position or status in a group, to control other individuals, prescribe forms of behavior for them and demand obedience.

Social power is determined less by special personality features than by the type of social relations in the group. It is therefore considered as a decisive aspect for explanation of social interaction and the distribution of costs and rewards among members of the group (see *Group dynamics*). At present three variables are generally mentioned which determine the extent of social power: (*a*) the resources which enable an individual to influence the subjective rewards and costs of others. The value of these resources is in turn determined by (*b*) the extent of dependency of others on this individual, which in turn is a function of (*c*) the number of possible alternatives for other individuals which are reward sources.

Bibliography: Cartwright, D. (Ed.): Studies in social power. Ann. Arbor, Mich., 1959. Emersin, R. M.: Power-dependence relations, Amer. sociol. Rev. 1962. 27, 31–41.   A.S.-M.

Social psychology. I. Social psychology is identified as a branch of psychology, and as a branch of sociology. Anthropologists are also concerned with this field, most commonly calling it the study of "culture and personality". It has been variously defined as a function of the prevailing conceptions concerning the nature of man and the theoretical orientation of the particular writer. Thus, when human behavior was thought of as representing an essentially physiological process, social psychology was the analysis of social factors that influenced the individual, as in the heredity-environment controversies in the study of intelligence. The more sociologically oriented conceive of social psychology as representing those aspects of behavior defined by the participation of the individual in a structured society. The more behavioristic students emphasize the study of interaction, or responses to social stimuli. In essence, the field may be defined operationally by noting that study of the following topics tends to be identified with social psychology: social influences on abilities and behavior, attitudes, social norms, group dynamics, communication, role and status, leadership, conflict and co-operation, intergroup relations, crime and delinquency, authoritarianism and machiavellianism, belief systems and value orientations, socialization, person perception, social learning, and conformity.

As with other fields of psychology, we find some authors making a molecular and others a molar approach; some emphasizing learning theories, some using a cognitive orientation, and others relying on conative processes to explain behavior. There is currently little interest in social philosophy or theoretical speculation. In order to secure reliable information, instead of opinions, about important issues, the almost universal concern is with empirical analyses of problems, preferably using experimental methods with the requirement that variables be identified and controlled, with manipulation of the independent variable by the experimenter, the assignment of subjects to treatment categories by chance, and the objective assessment of the dependent variables with proper statistical treatment of the data. There are, of course, field studies as well as laboratory studies, correlational as well as experimental analyses, studies of simulations as well as of significant social processes and matrices. As might be expected, there is considerable emphasis on the applied aspects of social psychology as well as on the development of the scientific principles. Here we can only offer a very brief introduction to a few of the special topics in social psychology, in order to illustrate what might be found if one explored more broadly and more deeply in the field.

1. *Social attitudes*. The early traditions of modern psychology included experimental analyses of reaction time. In these studies, the importance of "set" (*Einstellung*) as a determinant of performance was clearly established. Subjects who were paying attention to the motor response they were going to make (a response set), responded more rapidly than those who were focusing on the stimulus that would set off the response (stimulus set). In the research on the laws of association, the in-structions given the subjects, for example "opposites" or "part-whole relations", determined what word was associated with the stimulus word. The early studies of the reliability of testimony indicated that people "saw" what they were set to see. In such a context, it was not surprising that the early decades of the nineteenth century saw the concept of "attitude" as the core concept for social psychology. Attitudes were the determiners of behavior; they were thought of as enduring sets which accounted for the consistencies in behavior. When behavior was not consistent, or when the behavior did not correspond to what was expected on the basis of verbalized attitude, it was because the attitudes could not be expressed in the particular situation. After the war of 1914–1918, psychology was marked by the development of psychometrics. During the war, a notable achievement by psychologists was the successful development of group intelligence testing. After the war, this success led to applications in personal selection in industry as well as to the extension of the concepts of measurement to a wide array of skills and personal attributes. By the nineteen thirties several different methods of measuring attitudes had been developed, demonstrated, and used in research. The increased attention paid to social psychology during the economic collapse of the time led to the widespread use of these new techniques in many different areas of study. Studies of morale, race prejudice, and liberalism-conservatism in economic and political affairs, were undertaken with objective measuring instruments. With the development of the war of 1939–1945, new researches were defined on the basis of applied problems, and new measurement techniques were devised. Public opinion study flourished, but it was almost completely descriptive and unrelated to any theory.

With the post-war trend towards an emphasis on observable behavior rather than on mentalistic events, the importance of attitude study declined. The neo-behaviorists had little use for the construct. Those having a conative orientation tended to conceive attitudes in the form of ego defense systems. The cognitively oriented often established attitudes as another way of referring to the perceptual structuring of a field. That mental images of the people of other nations, or stereotypes, existed, was unquestioned. But what the significance of such stereotypes was in psychological theory was completely uncertain. The prevailing emphasis on empirical investigation could not lend itself to encouraging preoccupation with the definition of attitudes as such. Instead, a new development emerged in the form of studies of attitude change—and the problem of what is an attitude was subordinated to the question of how attitudes are modified.

The learning theorists presented their particular emphases in their analyses of attitude change. Studies demonstrated the importance of classical conditioning and of reinforcement theory. Similarly, the field theorists demonstrated the modification of attitudes by the manipulation of the field forces impinging on the individual. The psychoanalytically oriented elaborated the rôle of tension reduction and the functions of attitudes in facilitating responses which reduce tensions and resolve conflicts among motives. However, it was largely among the cognitively oriented that the studies of attitude change developed most significance, for these studies established a motivational component within the cognitive domain. The fundamental proposition is that inconsistent cognitions lead to activities which contribute to the reduction of the inconsistency, the establishment of consistency. The consistency theories are varied and are known by various names, e.g., cognitive inbalance, congruity theory, cognitive dissonance. The research generated by the consistency theories has been very extensive and their contributions have implications for the understanding of a broad range of social behavior. With respect to attitude change, they have analyzed such

problems as the effects of information at variance with one's own position on an issue (if it varies too much, it loses credibility), the effects of taking a public position at variance with private beliefs (under what conditions do one's opinions change?), the effects of failure of prophecies, and so on.

2. *Group processes.* The study of collective behavior is a specialization within sociology. The study of differentiations within a group, the behavior of individuals in a social group, the analysis of the effects of group membership on the individual, the development of group norms and group productivity all illustrate concerns of social psychology. In the nineteen thirties, J. L. Moreno introduced sociometry with a technique for studying the patterning of interpersonal attractions and repulsions among the members of a group. This led to the study of "real" groups with analyses of their psychological structures. At about the same time, K. Lewin extended his field theoretical approach by establishing small groups in the laboratory and exposing them to various kinds of experimental manipulation. Both approaches had profound impacts on subsequent developments of social psychology. Moreno's work, however, overlapped with his contributions to group psychotherapy and seemed to find more of a place in the clinical setting, whereas the students of Lewin remained identified with social psychology and contributed to the founding of the specialization in group dynamics.

An aggregate of individuals interacting to achieve a common goal form a group. In time, the differentiations within the group become stabilized, and a pattern of relations emerges which defines the group structure. The behavior expected of an individual occupying a particular position in a group is known as a social rôle. Some rôles derive from the activities needed to achieve the group goal, and are known as task rôles. Other rôles have the function of maintaining the cohesiveness of the group and are known as group maintenance rôles. The various rôles in a group are perceived as forming a prestige hierarchy or status system; and some rôles, and some individuals, achieve relatively high status, whereas others are perceived as having lower status. Stratification in small groups is paralleled in the larger society by the ranking of occupations, people of different ethnic and religious backgrounds, degrees of affluence and education.

The difficulty in achieving a sound understanding of group processes is illustrated in the efforts to solve the applied problems of selecting leaders for business and industry, the military, educational systems, and so on. Early researches studied leaders in an effort to identify those attributes which differentiated them from others and which could account for their success. Literally hundreds and hundreds of studies were done without significant success. Not until the nineteen forties did the theoretical conception of group structure and function, combined with the failure of the earlier approaches, lead to the appreciation of the fact that one could not be a leader without followers. It became clear that the question of leadership was in part the question of what the followers were seeking. Therefore, the problem was transformed from a study of characteristics of individuals, to the analysis of processes with an emphasis on the consequences of the leadership behavior for the group.

3. *Communication.* Early studies were concerned with the development of language in the child, verbal imagery in mental content, bilingualism and intelligence, language and thought, the influence of naming on perception, the influence of propaganda on attitudes. Only quite recently, however, has communication been confronted as the field for study. As might be expected from the heterogeneity among social psychologists, a complex field like communication study has not been given simple and uniform treatment. In some discussions, for example, communication is

examined with a cybernetics model emphasizing a feedback system in interpersonal relations; other approaches examine varieties of communication materials to study social influence; and others use mathematical models, and apply information theory with the reduction of uncertainty as their point of departure. And of course there are those who study language, psycholinguistics (and sociolinguistics and ethnolinguistics), and semantics. The applied problems of persuasive communication in industrial advertising, political campaigning and international maneuvering have led to considerable research. These studies have tended to focus on such variables as one-sided versus two-sided presentations, primacy and recency factors in the comparative effectiveness of arguments, "sleeper" or delayed effects of communication materials, factors associated with enhanced communicator credibility. However, this research has contributed little to the development of general theory.

Much attention has been paid in recent years to the effects of the mass media in shaping the perceptions, values and behaviors of the mass audiences, particularly children. The recent attacks of concerned community groups on the television industry are very similar to those made on the motion pictures and radio in earlier years. Content analysis of the media reveals a large component of violence in the entertainment offered. The lay concern is that such presentations brutalize the audience and encourage children in such display. Some controlled laboratory studies have demonstrated a modeling effect which might lead one to suspect that the pictured violence could increase the violence behavior of the audience. However, field studies show no such effects on the normal child, and more careful analyses of the laboratory studies show many significant differences between the naturalistic setting in which programs are commonly seen and the controlled laboratory conditions.

4. *Methodology*. The problem of extrapolation from the laboratory to the community has been considered in various contexts, but never really settled. Laboratory studies of social attitudes show that they are readily manipulated, easily influenced. The field studies, particularly in the political and economic realms, find attitudes very resistant to change. Laboratory studies of group dynamics often fail to be confirmed when findings are extended to the community. Apparently there is a social psychology of the experiment that has to be further explored in order that we may understand more fully the true meanings of our findings. There may well be a "guinea pig role" adopted by subjects in an experiment which alters the relations that may obtain when subjects are playing other roles. In addition, the ego involvement in real decision making is very poorly reflected in the laboratory decision making.

Methodological improvements have been sought along many lines. In the laboratories, advanced technology has been used for instrumentation. Great ingenuity has been used in devising "games" and social simulations in order to provide analogs for the processes deemed of significance in the larger community. The social psychological literature can hardly now be read unless one is familiar with the "prisoner's dilemma", a game which permits the study of trust-distrust and is used to analyze the bases for co-operation. In addition, there are simulations that represent international relations, inner city functions, land use, and generalized societal organization. These simulations have become useful teaching devices and are also advanced as research techniques in that they permit representation in the laboratory of important societal variables that are commonly excluded from the conventional small group research.

Research developments in the field have been proceeding along two significant lines. On the one hand, there have been ingenious experiments designed in natural settings—sometimes by intervention in the community, and sometimes by complete formal experiment building. Another development of particular interest is the use of unobtrusive measures of behavior. In these studies, the design involves focusing observations and collecting data so that the entire study is perceived as part of the natural setting, yet without the invasion of privacy of the subjects being observed. Illustrative of these studies, for example, is the one in which stamped, addressed envelopes were dropped on the street in different parts of a city. It was possible easily to observe the comparative proportions of "letters" picked up and mailed in the different sections (with their known social characteristics), and thus to study a form of helpfulness and co-operation.

Another development of promise has been in the field of cross-cultural research. Though using subjects from different cultures is old in the history of psychology, the modern approach includes increased sophistication. Though it is true that there is still interest in simple comparative studies, a number of studies are devised because of the search for social variables in a context where they may not be confounded as they are in Western society. Though it is still too early in the emergence of this field to predict with confidence, it seems likely that this specialization will have much of significance to contribute in the future.

As we head into the nineteen-seventies, peace and conflict research is becoming more accepted as a focus for research and theory. In the past, social psychology has addressed itself to the study of competition and co-operation, to the nature of industrial conflict, race relations, and in times of crisis to the problems of human nature and enduring peace. These, however, have tended to be relatively transitory and specialized concerns. In recent years, however, there has been a growing peace research movement and academicians in increasing numbers are dedicating themselves to systematic work in this field. Social psychologists are extending their professional field and addressing themselves to the systematic analysis of conflict resolution, of problems in international relations. While it would obviously be the height of academic imperialism to claim that war is a psychological problem, wars do begin in the minds of men—and, increasingly, social psychologists are implementing their social concerns by means of professional and scientific applications toward the construction of the defenses of peace.

Bibliography: Asch, S. E.: Social psychology. Englewood Cliffs, 1952. Bales, R. F.: Interaction process analyses. Cambridge Cliffs, 1952. Dexter, L. A. & White, D. M.: People, society and mass communications. London, 1964. Deutsch, M., Katz, J. & Jensen, A. R.: Social class, race and psychological development. New York & London, 1968. Deutsch, M. & Krauss, R. M.: Theories in social psychology. New York & London, 1965. Dohrenwend, B. P. & Dohrenwend, B. S.: Social status and psychological disorder. London & New York, 1969. Edward, E. J. & Harold, B. G.: Foundations of social psychology. New York & London, 1967. Eysenck, H. J.: The psychology of politics. London, 1963. Feldman, S.: Cognitive consistency. New York & London, 1966. Festinger, L., Schachter, S. & Bach, K.: Social pressures in informal groups. London, 1963. Fiedler, F. E.: A Theory of leadership effectiveness. New York & London, 1967. Flavell, J. H.: The development of role taking and communication skills in children. New York & London, 1968. Freedman, J. L., Carlsmith, J. M. & Sears, D. O.: Social psychology. London & Toronto, 1970. Gnetzkow, H.: Groups, leadership and man. New York, 1963. Graumann, C. F. (Ed.): Hdb der Psychol., 7. Göttingen, 1969. Greenstein, F. J.: Personality and politics. Chicago, 1969. Grennwald, A. G., Brock, T. C. & Ostrom, T. M.: Social status and psychological disorder: A causal inquiry. New York & London, 1969. Grey, A. L.: Class and personality in society. New York, 1969. Harvey, O. J.: Motivation and social interaction. New York, ⁴1963. Heidner, F.: The psychology of interpersonal relations. New York & London, ⁵1967. Hofstätter, P. R.: Einführung in die Sozialpsychologie. Stuttgart, 1963. Kretch, D. S. & Crutchfield, R. S.: Theory and problems of social psychology. New York & London, 1948. Lewin, K.: Feldtheorie in der Sozialwissenschaften. Stuttgart, 1963. Lindgren, H. C.: Contemporary research in social psychology. London & New York, 1969. Lindzey,

G. & Aronson, L. J.: The handbook of social psychology, vols. 1–5. Reading, Mass. & London, ²1969f. Proshanky, H. & Seidenberg, B.: Basic studies in social psychology. London & New York, 1969. Secord, P. F. & Backman, C. W.: Social psychology. New York, 1964. Sherif, M. & C. W.: An outline of social psychology. New York, 1956.

E. L. Hartley

II. The literature that goes under the title of "social psychology" is now quite vast and yields numerous definitions of a fairly diverse nature. It is not easy to offer a satisfactory inclusive definition of social psychology. Nevertheless, most specialists in the field would certainly admit that the notion of *social interaction*—a concept mediating between individual and group qualities—is central to their interests. It is justifiable to describe the essential object of social psychology as the study of interaction processes: interaction between individuals, between individuals and groups, and between groups.

The following are some of the research areas: *communications* in a group (discussion) (interactions between individuals); *attitudes and opinions* (interactions between the individual and the group); *co-operation or competition* between two or more groups (interactions between groups). In most cases the three varieties of interaction occur simultaneously.

1. *History.* The term "social psychology" dates from the beginning of the present century. A notable user of the concept was Durkheim (1858–1915): "As for the laws of collective ideation, they are still wholly . . . ignored. The 'social psychology' which should be used to ascertain what they are is only a phrase which denotes all kinds of generalities. . . ." (1901). The first books using the term as a title appeared in 1908 (E. A. Ross: *Social Psychology. An Outline and Source Book*, New York, and W. McDougall, *Introduction to Social Psychology*, London). But the real work in social psychology only came after 1925.

Admittedly, people from very different

fields (dramatists, philosophers, historians, economists, politicians, and so on) have always addressed themselves to the problems with which social psychology is now concerned. Yet those earlier "studies" lacked the objectivity and precision of scientific work. For a long time, social psychology was considered only as an appendix of psychology or of sociology. This considerably delayed the development of investigations into psychosociological questions.

The mutual lack of understanding between psychologists and sociologists had to cease before social psychology could become an independent discipline. The French sociologist Marcel Mauss (1872–1950) bears much of the credit for this. His paper to the French Psychological Society in 1924 ("Actual and practical connections between psychology and sociology", published in the *Journal de Psychologie* in the same year) stated that psychology and sociology enjoy major common ground, and that close collaboration between the two disciplines was not only desirable but necessary in this area of mutual interest. At about the same time, Max Weber (1864–1920) and Max Scheler (1874–1928) in Germany, and Charles H. Cooley (1867–1929) and George H. Mead (1863–1931) in the United States, bore witness to the same desire to coordinate the viewpoints of psychology and sociology. Mead's contribution was especially important: his theory proved effective in empirical research, and his posthumous work, *Mind, Self and Society* (Chicago, 1934), exerted (and continues to exert) considerable influence on American research-workers. The diffusion of his ideas probably had much to do with the advance won by American social psychologists over their European equivalents.

The experimental work which most obviously contributed to awareness of the autonomy of social psychology may be attributed to Americans, or to researchers who lived and worked in the USA. The change of consciousness would seem to have occurred in the nineteen thirties, for the first sociometric inquiry was conducted by Moreno (born 1892) in 1930, in the Hudson Institution, a delinquents' home near New York. The famous Hawthorne experiments (q.v.) were carried out by Elton Mayo (1880–1949) at the Western Electric Company at almost the same time, as was the study of aggressive behavior in four groups of five ten-year-olds, by Kurt Lewin (1890–1947) and co-workers (results published in 1939). The first opinion polls were in action around 1936. The main effort of these pioneers of social psychology related to the development of concepts, methods and techniques appropriate to the study of the specific problems facing the young science. Social psychology became an autonomous human science in its own right once it had a proper conceptual apparatus and adequate research instruments.

2. *Main research areas.* The general definition already offered reveals the gamut of ambitions of social psychology. All the levels and aspects of human activity can, in fact, provide socio-psychological research subjects. This great variety of problems has brought about a certain diversification of methods, and it is now legitimate to distinguish different areas whose limits vary according to one's viewpoint. Methodologically, these are:

Sociometry, which uses two specific approaches, the sociometric test, a quantitative technique employing statistical procedures to describe attractions and repulsions, and modes of indifference between individuals in a small group; and psychodrama (q.v.) and sociodrama, psychotherapeutic techniques in which a group of individuals directed by a play-leader (who should be an experienced clinical psychologist) becomes the essential therapeutic instrument.

Group dynamics (q.v.), which studies the play of forces and takes into account the formation and transformation of restricted groups. It draws on ideas developed by gestalt psychology, and uses mathematical models. Group practice and discussion have served to popularize this branch of social psychology. Some specialists in group dynamics are much indebted to psychoanalytic concepts.

The *study of opinions and attitudes*, which makes use of psychological and statistical surveys.

The *study of communication processes*, which is based on information theory (q.v.), is certainly the most promising of the branches of contemporary social psychology.

The following, according to the French social psychologist Jean Stoetzel (born 1910) are the main centers of interest:

Problems of relations between the individual and culture (civilization); the study of psychological behavior under social conditions; personality (q.v.) from the psycho-social viewpoint; the study of various aspects of interindividual interaction; behavior in large groups.

But the ambition of social psychology is not restricted to the acquisition of theoretical knowledge. It also seeks *practical* knowledge which might help men to resolve actual problems. In addition to general social psychology, there is an *applied* social psychology which now extends into almost all the major spheres of contemporary social life: politics, management, medicine, religion, mass media, leisure, consumption, publicity, etc.

Social psychology, of all the branches of psychology, would seem to be the most alive today and to have made the greatest progress. This is probably the result of two factors: the relatively unresearched state of this area, despite the historical stirrings already noted; and the richness of the instruments available to social psychology. In fact the late appearance of social psychology enables it to benefit, apart from its own methods, from all those developed in other areas, and in particular from those proper to psychology and sociology.

Bibliography: Klineberg, O. & Christie, R. (Eds.): Perspectives in social psychology. New York, 1965. Lazarsfeld, P. F., Berelson, B. & Gaudet, H.: The people's choice. New York, 1948. Mead, G. H.: Mind, self and society. Chicago, 1934. Moreno, J. L.: Who shall survive? New York, ²1953. Stoetzel, J.: La psychologie sociale. Paris, 1963.   *D. Victoroff*

Social medicine. A term used in many senses. In his "Lectures on the tasks and aims of social medicine" L. Teleky (1909) uses the term principally for social hygiene (q.v.); social medicine was the term used in England, "preventive medicine" in the USA. The term is often used in contrast to individual medicine to mean "public health", "communal hygiene". Sociologically, social medicine covers the social security of the individual in sickness, accident and disablement.   *H.W.*

Social sciences. The totality of sciences which seek to use experimental methods of studying the behavior of man in society. Historically, they were preceded by the work of the humanists and the great syntheses of the nineteenth century. They attained a scientific status only in the twentieth century, particularly through World War II (industrial development, ideological conditions, integration of minorities, decolonization, etc.). Methods were refined (quantitative methods, field studies), branches became specialized (economics, political sciences, sociology, social psychology, ethnology, anthropology as a natural science, linguistics, etc.). Nowadays these separate disciplines are coming together again, as man is seen more and more as a totality.   *M.J.B.*

Social structure. All the social relations of a formal (organization) or informal (group dynamics) nature, between individuals and groups (q.v.) in businesses. See *Management*.   *G.R.W.M.*

Social system. The kind and form of mutual relations (interactions) of the members of a group or larger community of a certain system of action, in the context of which the individual group members orientate themselves as acting according to compulsory norms or expectations connected with them. This concept occurs especially in the work of Parsons & Shils (1951) where it includes interaction, orientation towards another person with his aims and norms and the consensus in respect of norms and norm expectations between the individual(s) and others. Norm and norm expectations define the roles (q.v.) of the individual member so that the social system can be represented as *role structure*. See *Group dynamics*.

Bibliography: Parsons, T. & Shils, E. E.: Towards a general theory of action. Cambridge, Mass. 1951.

W.D.F.

Social therapy. Therapy which seeks to make changes in the patient's environment or conditions of life (*milieu* or *situation therapy*). The term is also sometimes used in the sense of *group therapy* (q.v.) or *psychodrama* (q.v.).

W.D.F.

Social type. One of the six *life forms* described by E. Spranger. A person who loves his fellow men, who finds his chief satisfaction in being of service to others. Its opposite is the misanthrope who has been disappointed in love.

W.K.

Sociatry. A term is used in the branch of psychiatry expecially concerned with conflicts of a socio-psychological nature. During World War II, sociatry was understood as a form of "spiritual counseling". At the moment, sociatry is being vigorously developed as psychiatry is influenced more and more by socio-psychological and sociological viewpoints: e.g. in research into psychiatric communities (clinics, institutions for treatment and care, hospitals).

J.L.I.

Society. A term used with increasing frequency since the development of sociology as a separate branch of science in the mid-nineteenth century, but for which no general definition is available; society is held to be an entity which is "more" than a mere social aggregate. If a distinction is made between a specific society and "society" as such, most definitions are based on descriptions of the given structures of social relations or cultural peculiarities. Accordingly social sciences are those which are concerned with the organizational and relational structures as well as the cultural and institutional differences between cultures or cultural groups.

W.D.F.

Sociogram. Illustration or diagram representing the findings of sociometric tests (Moreno, 1953): the (desired) relationships of a positive or negative nature or interaction frequencies of the members of a group (q.v.). (See *Sociometry*.)

In a sociogram, individuals are represented as circles or squares connected by lines or arrows of varying lengths. The length of the line or arrow is analogous to the social (emotional) distance between two individuals. The arrows show the direction of choice. In this way some of the distinguishing factors of the sociometric structure of a group (outsiders, central figures, clique formation, group comparisons, etc.) are illustrated. In large groups, a representation by sociogram is not easy to read, and so in these cases other methods of representation (matrix analysis, index analysis) are used.

Bibliography: Moreno, J. L.: Who shall survive? New York, 1953. **Proctor, C. H. & Loomis, C. P.:** Analysis of sociometric data. In: Jahoda, M., Deutsch, M. & Cook, S. W. (Ed.): Research methods in social relations, Vol. 2. New York, 1951.

A.S.-M.

Sociolinguistics is virtually identical with "sociology of language", and comprises the relations of language (q.v.) to culture; sociolinguisticians may be said to study the relations between language and social structure.

The only contemporary sociolinguistic theory founded on empirical evidence, Bernstein's "language barrier" (q.v.) theory, distinguishes between a "restricted code" possessed by all social classes but spoken mainly by the lower (or working) class, and an "elaborated code" spoken only by (a) privileged class(es). A man's code is the socio-culturally determined inventory of meanings, signs and rules that controls his language. Characteristics of the restricted code are: simple, often incomplete sentences in the active form, a rigid sentence structure, abrupt orders and questions, simple adjectives, adverbs and conjunctions ("then", "and"), conventional locutions, gestures. Characteristics of the elaborated code are: complex sentence structure, conjunctions and prepositions with logical functions, impersonal pronouns, a highly differentiated vocabulary, individual usage. According to the theory, these differences and their consequences for thought development are conditioned in childhood by class socialization processes. The resulting linguistically disadvantaged condition of the underprivileged may sometimes (it is thought by some) be improved by compensatory or even "emancipatory" English teaching. Problematic aspects of the theory are: the underlying class concept (an impermissible degree of?), generalization from imprecise samples, the use of an implicit middle-class language norm in the selection of linguistic characteristics, and an absence of socio-theoretical foundation in the definition of the goals of compensatory language work. See *Language; Psycholinguistics.*

Bibliography: Bernstein, B.: Class, codes and control, Vol. 1. London, 1972. Crystal, D.: Linguistics Harmondsworth, 1971. Douglas, M.: Natural symbols: explorations in cosmology. London, 1970. Lawton, D.: Social class, language and education. London, 1968.   *G.S.*

Sociology. The study of society. The term comes from A. Comte: the overlap between sociology and social psychology (q.v.) is so substantial that the two disciplines must be regarded as two aspects of the same field. Social psychology starts with the individual and tries to ascertain how he reacts upon his environment, influences other people and is in turn influenced by them, whereas sociology starts with the group (q.v.), its specific forms, structures and norms, and then tries to tackle the laws of human community directly. Sociology also has close ties with cultural anthropology (q.v.) and folk psychology. Sociology may be described as the cultural anthropology of industrial societies, whereas cultural anthropology is often understood as sociology applied to illiterate (or "primitive") societies.   *W.Sch.*

Sociometry. A blanket term for techniques, particularly the *"sociometric test"* (Moreno, 1953) used to make a quantitative analysis of the emotional structure of a group (q.v.). The emotional structure is measured on the basis of mutual choices of the group members, what they feel and think about one another.

Two components are of crucial importance for the results of a sociometric test: (1) the prescribed form of choice, and (2) the criteria of choice. The resulting emotional structure is a function of the criterion employed.

At the present the term is used not only for the analysis of emotional structure but for the assessment of other aspects of the relationships between group members. See *Sociogram.*

Bibliography: Moreno, J. L.: Who shall survive? New York, ²1953.   *A.S.-M.*

Sociopath. A term often used as a synonym for *psychopath*, but suggests that anti-social behavior is caused primarily by socio-cultural factors rather than constitutional elements. Two main kinds of sociopath have been described. The first group are of extravert personality and have difficulty in forming conditioned responses. The second group condition normally but are exposed to an abnormal delinquent subculture which shapes their behavior anti-socially. *D.E.*

Sodomy. In some countries, the term signifies sexual intercourse between men and animals (see *Bestiality*). In English-speaking countries "sodomy" is mainly used for *anal coitus.* From ancient times, there have been laws (Hittite Book of Laws, Old Testament, Talmud) which expressly tabooed sodomy.

H.M.

Solipsism. That position in the theory of knowledge according to which reality exists only in cognition by the individual. Only the individual ego (q.v.) and its psychic states really exist; neither others nor the outside world have any reality. Max Stirner is the most famous solipsist. The standpoint reappears in the neo-positivistic (see *Neopositivism*) concept of *elementary experience. M.R.*

Somatic. Pertaining to the body, bodily; ant.: "psychic", mental, referring to the psyche.

H.W.

Somatization. It is supposed that the "transformation reaction", the "conversion reaction" (see *Conversion*) presupposes the transformation of an experience together with its emotional charge into a somatic change. This may consist of some change in the nervous system, when, for example, a hysterical paralysis appears, or of some psychosomatic disorder, e.g. diarrhea, dysuria, asthma, etc. The expression somatization is preferred when referring to this kind of relations between the psychic events and the accompanying somatic correlates. *J.L.I.*

Somatogenic. In *biology*: changes in individuals due to body cells (not from hereditary factors); in *medicine* and *psychology*: conditioned or produced by bodily causes. Ant.: *psychogenic*, conditioned or caused by the mind. *H.W.*

Somatology. The science of the general properties and characteristics of the body. Ant.: *psychology* *H.W.*

Somatopsychology. The branch of psychology which investigates the bodily phenomena accompanying and following psychic events. (See *Psychosomatics*.) *H.W.*

Somatotherapy. A treatment for somatic disorders which may be accompanied by pathological psychic changes as is the case, for example, with the exogenous psychoses (q.v.). It is used also in cases of endogenous psychoses when a somatic cause, although not definitely known, is suspected none the less. In cases of neurosis (q.v.), too, somatotherapeutic methods are currently being used together with psychotherapy (q.v.) as, for instance, in aversion therapy (see *Behavior therapy*), and where special psychopharmaceuticals (q.v.) such as ataraxics (see *Tranquilizers*) and thymeretics (see *Antidepressants*) are being tried.

J. H. Schultz uses the word "somatization" to signify the integration of the individual body, which can be undertaken with the help of hypnosis (q.v.), *autogenic training* (q.v.) or under other conditions. *J.L.I.*

Somatotonia. A temperament related to the mesomorphic growth tendency: extraverted, energetic, fond of exercise, straightforward and simple.

Bibliography: Sheldon, W. H.: The varieties of temperament. New York, 1942. *W.K.*

Somatotropic hormone (*Somatotropin, growth hormone*, abbreviation STH). A polypeptide formed in the adenohypophysis (see *Hypophysis*) and carried from there in the blood stream to the peripheral tissue. The secretion of somatotropic hormone is stimulated, *inter alia*, by hypoglycemia (heightened level of insulin, q.v., in the blood) and physical and mental stress. STH, like the androgens (q.v.), has an anabolic action. It stimulates, *inter alia*, the formation of ribonucleic acids (q.v.) and the synthesis of protein and mobilizes fat (in the form of free fatty acids). In adolescents it increases the activity of the epiphysis (q.v.) and thus promotes growth. STH deficiency in childhood and adolescence results in pituitary dwarfism, over-production of the growth hormone in adolescents results in gigantism. In adults overproduction is responsible for the condition known as acromegaly (q.v.). STH acts synergistically to numerous other hormones, especially gonadotropic hormones (q.v.) and catecholamines (q.v.)

Bibliography: Pecile, A. & Müller, E. E. (Eds.): Growth hormone. Amsterdam, 1967.   *W.J.*

Somatotropin. A term for somatotropic hormone (q.v.) (STH).

Somnabulism. Sleepwalking in a state of partial consciousness, followed by amnesia (q.v.) and often accompanied by other complex activities.   *W.S.*

Sophistry. 1. Sophistic argument (sophism)—literally: inference which has been falsely drawn but which is given out as correct with the intention to deceive; in a wider sense, "paralogism": inference which has been drawn falsely but unintentionally; or "paradox": an inference starting from correct premises and rightly drawn, but leading, however to an unacceptable and irrefutable conclusion.

2. Sophistic attitude (sophist)—this is the attitude of the person who (*a*) has skilfully mastered the tricks of speaking, (*b*) gives out that he is teaching the truth, and (*c*) uses sophisms: a charlatan who seeks rather to persuade than to find the truth.

3. Sophistic school—its teaching set out to impart by the use of language (q.v.) (formal science of language) a practical (political) affectiveness with a skeptical and pragmatic perspective (fifth to fourth centuries B.C.).

                                              M.-J.B.

Sorting. In sorting, Ss. have to select from a series of comparison stimuli the one which most readily accords with a predetermined standard stimulus. Sorting techniques are used both in language-free and in verbal tests, but hardly at all in psychological scaling, where the results would be affected by the conditions of similarity varying from instance to instance within the pool of comparison stimuli.

                                              W.H.B.

Soul (Gre. *psyche;* Ger. *Seele;* Fre. *âme*). In the widest sense, the "soul" is all states of consciousness of an individual or a group. It also designates the principle of moral or religious life. More specifically, among "primitives" and in ancient philosophy, the soul was conceived as the vital principle, or principle of life (Lat. *anima*): that which animates bodies and departs at the moment of death. This belief conditions the *animist* attitude and *vitalist* doctrines. It recurs in the concept of a "world soul" or dynamic principle of unity of the sensible world (Plato, Plotinus). But, in the same context, the soul is also conceived as the seat of feeling, of volition (will) and thought (*animus*), which is contrasted with the body and vegetative functions (the Aristotelian theory of the soul: see *Entelechy*). This conception grounds "spiritualistic" doctrines according to which the soul dominates the body and, being immortal, seeks to escape from it (Plato), and those "dualisms" which address themselves to the problem of the union of the soul and the body (Descartes). See *Mind-body problem; History of psychology; Philosophy and psychology.*   *F.B.*

Sound. Mechanical vibrations in a given medium (e.g. air) conduct energy in the form of longitudinal waves.

We become sensitive to sound within a definite frequency (16–20,000) and field of amplitude (lower or higher hearing threshold). According to the number of frequencies and the regularity of the phase vibrations various kinds of sound occur. Sound localization is the localization of the distance and direction of a sound wave. Localization of the direction of a sound wave is rendered possible by: (*a*) the time difference between both ears; (*b*) the left-right intensity difference. See *Auditory perception; Noise.*   *M.B.*

Bibliography: **Bekesy, G. v.:** Experiments in hearing. New York, 1960. **Stevens, S. S.:** Bibliography on hearing. Cambridge, Mass., 1955.   *B. Schmidt*

Sound image theory. Theory of auditory perception (q.v.) formulated by G. Ewald. Ewald stretched a rubber membrane over a frame and made this vibrate by means of a tuning fork. Waves formed on the membranes, which produced an image characteristic of a particular sound, the so-called sound image. Ewald assumed that the basilar membrane operated in the same way and that appropriate receptors conducted the structure of vibrations into the brain, where the individual sound images were distinguished by central processing.   *R.Hä.*

Source traits. Traits (q.v.) are the descriptive attributes of personality research. They may appear as *surface* traits or as *source* traits. Source traits constitute the elements of personality theory, forming the major constructs for models of personality. Source traits are latent variables accounting for the covariation between observed scores on personality tests, and may be regarded as "sources" or "causes" of the observed scores (Cattell, 1957). Thus an observed act of hostility would be regarded as resulting from several more fundamental sources of variance: perhaps anxiety, some learned pattern favoring aggressive responses, and extraversion, to name three possible sources.

An important issue is the extent to which the same source traits may be identified in different areas of measurement (e.g. questionnaires, morphological measures, performance tests, ratings). The evidence on this is still incomplete.

Whether some score is to be regarded as a measure of a source trait must be resolved on empirical grounds. Some criteria of source trait measures that have been suggested (Hundleby, 1970) are: (1) aspects of factor validity; (2) consistency over situations and persons; (3) circumstantial relations to other constructs; and (4) predictive validity in terms of personality-relevant criteria.

There is not, as yet, complete agreement on a set of source traits, though in some areas, notably questionnaires, much integration is taking place. Works by R. B. Cattell, H. J. Eysenck, and J. P. Guilford may be consulted to appreciate links between systems.

Bibliography: **Cattell, R. B.:** Personality and motivation structure and measurement. New York, 1957. **Hundleby, J. D.:** The structure of personality: surface and source traits. In: **Dreger, R.** (Ed.): Multivariate personality research. Claitor, 1970.

J. D. Hundleby

Soviet psychology. I. In the USSR, psychology is defined as the study of mental ("psychic") activity viewed as a function of the brain, determined by the conditions of life, reflecting objective reality, and regulating the interaction between man and his environment. It incorporates the dialectical materialist concept of the unity of the physical and the mental, inseparability of the mind from the physiological processes of the brain, and the vital role of the mind. Man's consciousness is regarded as the product of a prolonged historical development in which a decisive rôle was played by man's work and by verbal communication (Kostyuk, 1966).

The results of psychological research are considered to have a theoretical and a practical significance. The scientific knowledge of the mind (*psikhika*) constitutes an important component of our understanding of the nature of man. Psychology contributes to the theory of knowledge and to the formulation of a philosophical view of the world. It shares in the scientific organization of human work and is an essential ingredient of the theory and practice of education, both as regards the acquisition of information and skills (*obuchenie*), and the development of personality (*vospitanie*).

In the sense of political geography, Russian psychology became a "Soviet psychology" overnight, so to speak, as a result of the 1917 October political revolution. Russian psychology and, in its early years, the psychology of the USSR, were not essentially different from equivalents abroad. Psychology of this period, in and out of Russia, was characterized by a multiplicity of approaches and points of view.

Although it was, indeed, a branch of European psychology, Russian psychology developed in a distinct intellectual, political and socio-economic environment. Intellectually, this environment was characterized by a long-lasting struggle between "materialism" and "idealism". Historically, in Russia, "idealism" stood for metaphysical speculation, "materialism" for science. This was a local, autochthonous tradition, which can be traced back to M. V. Lomonosov (1711–1765), a many-sided scientist, scholar and man of letters, and A. N. Radischchev, a revolutionary writer. In the nineteenth century, materialism was the philosophical credo of the influential group of revolutionary democrats (A. J. Gertsen, V. G. Belinsky, N. A. Dobrolyubov, N. G. Chernyshevsky) and of such influential scientists as I. M. Sechenov (1829–1905), the "father of Russian physiology" and a proponent (*Reflexes of the Brain*, in Russian, 1863) of a physiologically oriented psychology. Materialism, historical and dialectical, is one of the bases of Marxism-Leninism, which became the sole and official philosophy of the Soviet Union. The question of what constitutes a "truly Marxist-Leninist" psychology was not answered readily in the Soviet Union. In fact, the issue represented the focus of search and debate, frequently acrimonious, for many years. There was a whole file of "candidates", including several varieties of "objective psychology": Bekhterev's reflexology, Vagner's biopsychology (human psychology as a part of comparative psychology), Blonsky's behavioral human psychology, and Kornilov's reactology.

In the nineteen-twenties and early thirties, Pavlov's (and I. M. Sechenov's) views on the reflex nature of the mind tended to be rejected by Soviet Marxist psychologists as "mechanistic". Only later, Pavlov's concept of mental activities as the processing of signals by the brain became regarded not only as compatible with Marxism–Leninism but as a premiss (*predposylka*) of the interpretation of the mind (*psikhika*) in the framework of (Soviet) dialectical materialism. But it could be argued that the R in the S-R (stimulus-response) formula is an artificial "interruption of what is uninterruptable"; consequently, the concept would be contrary to the principles of dialectical materialism. It was the physiologist, P. K. Anokhin (1935), anticipating the cyberneticists' concept of feedback, who pointed out that each R is followed, in turn, by afferent impulses ("return afferentation") which constitute information concerning the response act. At about the same time N. A. Bernstein formulated the concept of the "reflex circle", replacing the traditional "reflex arc". These were important new ideas in the physiology of behavior, but it was some time before they were incorporated, as its organic parts, into Soviet psychology.

In the nineteen-thirties *consciousness* was affirmed, *ex officio*, as the subject matter of orthodox Marxist psychology. In those years the Soviet psychologists began to consider in earnest the implications for psychology of the thought of V. I. Lenin, especially as formulated in his *Materialism and Empiriocriticism* and *Philosophical Notebooks*. It is the express acceptance of Lenin's theory of reflection as psychology's philosophical basis that contributes, in part, to the distinctiveness of Soviet psychology. The theory, not to be confused with I. P. Pavlov's theory of conditional (conditioned) reflexes, views mind, a product of highly organized matter, as an active (not passive, not mirror-like) *reflection* of external reality.

Also in the nineteen-thirties, L. S. Vygotsky stressed an historical, socio-cultural approach to the study of man's mind. The thesis of socio-historical conditionality of human consciousness became one of the basic tenets of Soviet psychology.

In 1940 S. L. Rubinstein published his *Foundations of General Psychology*, with emphasis on the dialectical *unity* of consciousness and activity (all mental processes not only manifesting themselves in activity but having their origin in activity).

Hence the reconstruction (*perestroika*) of "bourgeois" Russian psychology as truly "Soviet" psychology, based on Marxism-Leninism, proved to be a complex undertaking stretching over years and decades. In Payne's formulation (1968, p. 168) this has meant "not merely adherence to its [Marxism-Leninism's] principles but even to the very words used by the 'Classics'—Marx, Engels, Lenin—when referring to psychological subjects. This has acted as a brake on the normal development of psychological theory, has forced Soviet psychology into a theoretical straightjacket

and produced a vast crop of purely exegetical problems."

The Soviet authors view the issue differently. To Petrovsky (1967), Marxism-Leninism represents the only theoretical (philosophical) platform that could provide a unifying framework and could have led Soviet psychology out of the "crisis" of the nineteen-twenties, initially shared with the West and expressed in the chaos of the warring "schools" of psychology. In view of the dissolution and virtual disappearance of the schools and global systems in the West, without the benefit of a universally shared philosophical underpinning, Petrovsky's argument is not convincing.

In any case, the general methodological (philosophical) "foundations" of Soviet psychology in Marxism-Leninism are a *sine qua non*, and will remain so in the visible future. A non-partisan, comprehensive assessment of the effects of the insistence on ideological uniformity and orthodoxy on the development of psychology in the Soviet Union has yet to be attempted.

In the mid 'thirties, psychology began to dry on the vine. One after another, the psychological journals withered away. The July 4, 1936 decree of the Central Committee of the Communist Party, directed against "pedology", originally conceived as an interdisciplinary study of child development, had disastrous effects on applied psychology in general, and suppressed psychometrics for decades. Psychologists, lacking a journal of their own for some twenty years, sought refuge in the journals of education and philosophy.

In the early 'fifties, the insistence on the "Pavlovization" of psychology created further confusion and stress. In this "general-methodological" crisis, dogmatic Pavlovism threatened to "liquidate" psychology, since, it was argued, psychology lacked a valid subject matter. For ideological reasons, the development of whole fields of psychology (e.g., social and animal) were suppressed as "reactionary" and "lacking promise". Animal psychology was charged with being out of tune with Pavlovian principles. Stalin's death in 1953 provided relief from the pressures of "the cult of personality".

The outward symbols of rapid recovery were the foundation of a scientific journal of psychology (*Voprosy psikhologii*, in 1955) and of a scientific society (*Obshchestvo psikhologov*, in 1957), the first all-Union psychological congress (in 1959), and the publication of a two-volume, historically oriented handbook reviewing the accomplishments of Soviet psychologists (Ananjev *et al.*, 1959, 1960).

Contacts with colleagues abroad were re-established, and Soviet psychologists familiarized themselves, through an impressive number of translations, with the work accomplished during their isolation from the "West". The new trends, including a rapid advance in the area of engineering psychology and a hesitant exploration of the area of social psychology, were clearly visible in the program of the second all-Union congress held in 1963 in Leningrad.

The culminating event in this process of "opening the windows to the West" (and vice versa) was the eighteenth International Congress of Psychology, held in Moscow in August 1966. The same year saw the establishment, in Moscow and in Leningrad, of the first Colleges of Psychology—first not only in the Soviet Union but in the world.

Current research activities are reflected in the program of the third all-Union congress of the Soviet Psychological Society, held in Kiev in June 1968 (Brožek, 1969). The percentages ($N = 906$) of papers presented in different areas were as follows: philosophical-theoretical topics, 1.0; history, 1.2; psycho-physiology, 2.2; general experimental, 20.7; personality and differential psychology, 5.9; engineering and industrial, 12.8; medical (incl. neuropsychology, psychopathology, and abnormal child psychology), 15.2; social, 3.8; comparative, 0.7; and physical education and sports, 7.8.

A major advance in the status of psychology was represented by the establishment, in 1968, of doctoral degrees in psychology. Prior to this, psychologists could receive a doctoral degree (denoting a substantially higher level of demonstrated competence than the European or the American Ph.D. degrees) "in pedagogical sciences, with specialization in psychology". Administratively, the 1968 decree marked psychology's coming of age in the Soviet Union.

Bibliography: Ananjev, B. G. *et al.* (Eds.): Psikhologicheskaya nauka v SSSR. Moscow, Vol. 1, 1959; Vol. 2, 1960 (Eng. trans.: Psychological science in the USSR. Washington, D.C., Vol. 1, 1961; Vol. 2, 1962). **Bauer, R. A.:** The new man in Soviet psychology. Cambridge, Mass., 1952. **Id.** (Ed.): Some views on Soviet psychology. Washington, D.C., 1962. **Brožek, J.:** Spectrum of Soviet psychology: 1968. Model. Amer. Psychologist, 1969, *24*, 944–6. **Id.** (Ed.): Fifty years of Soviet psychology: An historical perspective. Soviet Psychology, 1968, *6* (3–4), 1–127 und *7* (1), 1–72. **Id.** (Ed.): Special issue on Georgian psychology. Soviet Psychology, 1968/69, *7* (2), 1–55. **Cole, M. & Maltzman, M.:** A handbook of contemporary Soviet psychology. New York, 1969. **Kostyuk, G. S.:** Psikhologija, Vol. 3. In: Pedagogicheskaja entsiklopedija. Moscow, 1966. **Molino, J. L.:** Is there a new Soviet psychology? In: **Simirenko, A.** (Ed.): Chicago, 1969, 300–27. **O'Connor, N.** (Ed.): Present-day Russian psychology. Oxford, England, 1966. **Payne, T. R.:** S. L. Rubinstejn and the philosophical foundations of Soviet psychology. New York, 1968. **Petrovskij, A. V.:** Istorija sovetskoi psikhologii. Moscow, 1967. **Razran, G.:** Russian physiologists' psychology and American experimental psychology. Psychol. Bulletin, 1965, *63*, 42–64. In: **Rubinstein, S. L.:** Psychology. In: Social Sciences in the USSR. New York, 1965, 120–6. **Slobin, D. I.** (Ed.): Handbook of Soviet psychology. Soviet Psychology and Psychiatry 1966, *4* (3–4), 1–146. **Wolman, B. B.** (Ed.): Historical roots of contemporary psychology. New York, 1968,

J. Brožek

Brožek, J.: Soviet contributions to history. Contemp. Psychol., 1969, *14*, 432–4. **Golann, S. E.:** Ethical standards for psychology, Ann. New York Acad. Sci., 1970, *169*, 398–405.   *J.G.*

II. The main task of psychology as it has developed in the USSR is the scientific (materialistic) investigation of the highest forms of human psychic (mental) activity, of their evolution in the process of socio-historical development, and of the fundamental laws of their operation. Consequently psychology in the USSR has always stood in a close relationship to the social sciences on the one hand, and to the physiology of higher nervous activity on the other, and has always been subject to the guidance of the philosophy of dialectical and historical materialism.

The most important task of psychology in the USSR has always been the investigation of the process of the development of the highest forms of psychic activity, in other words, their differentiation in the process of socio-historical development. A decisive part in the performance of this task was played by the work of the prominent Soviet psychologist L. S. Vygotsky (q.v.) (1896–1934), who established the scientific analysis of the development of the highest mental processes.

Vygotsky's initial thesis, which has decisively influenced the further development of psychology in the USSR, was the realization that the highest mental processes in man are to be viewed as *complex functional systems*, which are socio-historical in origin, mediated in structure (i.e. dependent on corresponding aids, e.g. language), and self-regulating as far as their mode of operation is concerned. A child always develops in the course of exchanges with adults. Even relations to things are mediated for the child by relations to adults. Through language acquisition, the child begins to organize its own behavior. The highest mental functions then arise; they are social in origin and dependent on a system of signs that comes into existence in the process of human intercourse, and—above all—on language.

In the further course of development, the child interiorizes slowly developed behaviors, i.e. they now depend not on external aids and on external, audible language but on inner language (inner speech, q.v.) and the concep-

tual system formed in language. A process begins: i.e. the appropriation of universal human knowledge and of modes of behavior which have developed in history and have now become the major human behavior patterns. This approach to research has been extended by a great number of investigations carried out by Soviet psychologists and pre-eminently by A. N. Leontiev, A. V. Zaporozhec, P. J. Galperin and D. B. Elkonin, who have made a major contribution to the extension of the theory of the structure of human activity with its complex motives and needs, and auxiliary operations leading to the production of complex "inner behaviors". The investigation of different stages in the gradual development of "inner behaviors" proved to be very productive not only in regard to theory, but in regard to educational practice, and became the basis of a scientifically grounded transformation of educational methods put into effect in a number of Soviet schools. The psychological theory of the gradual development of intellectual activities and concepts is also at the basis of the principles of programmed learning (see *Instructional technology*) as elaborated in Soviet psychology.

The second characteristic of psychology in the USSR is the constant search for the physiological mechanisms of complex psychic processes. This direction of research was established by I. M. Sechenov and realized in the investigations of I. P. Pavlov (q.v.), A. A. Uchtomskii and V. M. Bekhterev, who developed the theory of the reflexive basis of psychic processes. In the last few decades, a number of physiologists and psychologists have actively developed this field. P. K. Anokhin has established a theory of functional systems and of a behavior "acceptor", which play an active part in the regulation of complex behaviors. S. V. Kravkov elaborated a theory of the organization of sensory processes and their interaction; L. A. Orbeli grounded the theory of the interaction of afferent systems, which was further developed by his pupils, in particular by G. V.

Gershuni, who worked out an unusually precise theory of the construction of sensory (and above all auditory) functions, and was the first to establish the scientific basis for an objective investigation of subsensory processes. An important part in the investigation of the reflexive bases of sensory processes was played by E. N. Sokolov's studies of the orienting reflex (q.v.) and those of complex forms of orientation and information-seeking behavior by A. V. Zaporozhec and co-workers.

Also important for the development of Soviet psychophysiology was the research work of B. M. Teplov and co-workers, who developed exact methods for the investigation of the main characteristics of nervous processes, and a concept for the objective study of types of human nervous activity and interindividual differences.

A new branch of neuropsychology developed by A. R. Luria and co-workers has also won considerable importance: it is concerned with the investigation of the changes in psychic processes occurring with local lesions of the brain (see *Aphasia; Brain pathology; Restitution of psychological functions*).

Further important contributions to the development of psychology in the USSR have been made by, e.g., P. A. Blonskii, S. L. Rubinstein, A. A. Smirnov and B. G. Ananiev.

Present-day psychology in the USSR is a complex and differentiated research system extending throughout general psychology (q.v.) (A. N. Leontiev, A. A. Smirnov, B. G. Ananiev, A. N. Sokolov, etc.), genetic and child psychology (q.v.) (A. V. Zaporozhec, L. I. Bozhovich, N. A. Mechinskaia, D. B. Elkonin), psychosomatic disorders (J. M. Soloviev, M. I. Zemcova, Z. S. Sif), medical psychology (B. V. Zeigarnik), psychophysiology (E. N. Sokolov, V. D. Nebylicyn), and engineering psychology (B. D. Lomov, V. D. Zinchenko).

The most important work in psychology is carried out in the Psychological Institute of the Academy of Educational Sciences in Moscow, and in the Faculty of Psychology of the Universities of Moscow and Leningrad. Original work is also produced in Georgia—in the D. N. Uznadze Institute for Psychology of the Academy of Sciences of the Georgian SSR and by the Professors of Psychology at the University of Tiflis. Another important center is the Psychological Institute of the Ukrainian Ministry of Education in Kiev.

Bibliography: Psichologicheskaia nauka v. SSSR. Edited by the Academy of Educational Sciences. Moscow. **Leontiev, A. N., Luria, A. R. & Semivnov, A.** (Eds.): Psychological research in the USSR. Moscow, 1966. **Masucco Costa, A.:** Psicologica Sovietica. Turin, 1963.   *A. R. Luria*

Space perception. The study of space perception is concerned with our registration of sensory information about the spatial layout of the environment: that is, the distance and directions of objects from one another. This is ordinarily accomplished by seeing, hearing, and/or feeling. Interest in the subject can be traced to Greek philosophers who worried about how things at a distance could be sensed. However, it was not until British associationism of the seventeenth and eighteenth centuries that a systematic and, in fact, quite contemporary analysis was made. Berkeley proposed a solution to the paradox that distance or depth, i.e. the third dimension, is registered, although stimulation from the world falls on a two-dimensional surface such as the retina of the eye, or the skin. His answer was that cue sensations, such as the strain of convergence of the two eyes, are associated with the distance one must reach or walk towards an object. For example, one learns that when the eyes strain to converge on an object, it must be close, whereas if they are relaxed in converging, the object is more distant.

During the mid-nineteenth century, when psychology as a self-conscious discipline was born, problems of space perception were among the first to be tackled. The perception of visual distance and depth was studied by severely restricting all stimulation from the environment that could possibly provide information about distance. Then specific stimulation was provided to see how much perception of distance was possible. The use of eye convergence, for example, was studied by estimating the distance of a single point of light in the dark. Accurate judgments on the basis of convergence were possible only up to a few meters. In a similar manner, a number of other "cues" for depth were identified, for example: binocular disparity—the disparity between the images in the two eyes from a single object due to the slight difference between the eyes in viewpoint; and motion parallax—the different rates of apparent motion of near and far objects with head movement. Certain pictorial cues were identified also, for example, linear perspective—the convergence of pictorial representation of parallel lines as they recede from us.

In the study of the perception of the *direction* of objects in space, local sign was a central concept during the nineteenth century. Every point on a receptor surface such as the skin or retina of the eye was said to have a unique quality which innately, or through experience, specified direction in vision, or locus in touch. The concept of local sign generated much careful research into the acuity of our sense of direction.

Contemporary work on perception of distance and of direction has shifted from assessment of acuity or of capacity to analysis of process. Consider binocular disparity again: that two slightly different views of an object to the two eyes do provide depth information can be demonstrated with a Wheatstone stereoscope. With this device, a slightly different flat picture can be presented to each eye: a solid three-dimensional object is vividly perceived. The two disparate views are fused as one if the amount of disparity is small. If the amount of disparity is too large, double images are perceived. When the eyes are

stimulated by radically different pictures, rivalry occurs and one sees, in alternation, first the right eye picture, then the left, or a constantly changing intermixture of the two.

Closely related to binocular disparity is the problem of visual direction. Since the two eyes are at slightly different positions in space, the direction of an object from each eye will be slightly different. How is the direction of an object from us determined? Research indicates that visual direction is judged as if from a point between the two eyes. It may be, but is not generally, exactly midway.

Our ability to register the direction of sounds has been shown to depend on the fact that there are time and intensity differences in the stimulation reaching the two ears. If a sound source is to our right, the right ear receives a slightly stronger sound signal, slightly sooner than the left. As in vision, two similar sounds to the two ears are fused in perception. There is no auditory phenomenon exactly like binocular rivalry. However, if two different messages are presented one to each ear, we cannot perceive both as well as we could one alone.

Little is known about the mechanism of distance and direction perception by feeling (haptic perception), except that it is probably mediated primarily by neural receptors in the joints rather than by muscle receptors. Haptic directional perception, as evidenced by pointing, is good, but not as precise as visual or auditory. Haptic is also less precise than visual, but probably better than auditory distance perception, and, of course, it only functions close to the body.

There has been considerable interest in the calibration between the visual, haptic, and auditory modes of distance and direction perception. It has been found, for example, that we are very precise in aligning a light with a sound, or in pointing to either. One technique for studying the mechanism underlying this calibration is to disturb it by optical distortion. Errors made initially in pointing after optical distortion may be quickly corrected as our directional systems recalibrate to such disruption. See *Visual perception.*

Bibliography: Bekesy, G. von: Sensory inhibition. Princeton, N.J., 1967. **Boring, E. G.:** Sensation and perception in the history of experimental psychology. New York, 1942. **Broadbent, D. E.:** Perception and communication. London, 1958. **Gibson, E. J.:** Principles of perceptual learning and development. New York, 1969. **Gibson, J. J.:** The perception of the visual world. New York, 1950. **Harris, C. S.:** Perceptual adaptation to inverted, reversed, and displaced vision. Psychological Review. 1965, 72: 419–444. **Hochberg, J. E.:** Perception. Englewood Cliffs, N.J., 1966. **Howard, I. P., Templeton, W. B.:** Human spatial orientation. New York, 1966.   *H. L. Pick*

Spaltbarkeit; Spaltungsfähigkeit (Ger.). The analytical ability, inherent in one's constitution, to dissect impressions and acts or to analyze several separate intentions in juxtaposition; said to be most marked in schizothymes.   *W.K.*

Span of consciousness. 1. The consciousness of incoming information is severely limited. Experiments in the awareness of several streams of incoming information (e.g. several speakers) suggest that people can be conscious of little more than one such source at a time, although additional information may be stored temporarily below the level of consciousness. There is a similarly limited span of consciousness with regard to time. See *Psychological moment.*

2. Studies of immediate retention show that the extent of simultaneously apprehended conscious contents is limited. Tachistoscopic experiments revealed a span of approximately five to eight units (figures, letters, geometrical shapes, etc.). The degree of redundancy of sign sequences plays an important part in the phenomenon. Sequences containing less information are identified more readily (Miller, Bruner & Postman, 1954). By appropriate coding, larger quantities of data can be consciously surveyed for a short period of time. See *Memory; Reminiscence.*

Bibliography: Miller, G. A.: The magical number seven, plus or minus two: some limits on our capacity of processing information. Psychol. Rev., 1956, *63*, 81–97. **Miller, G. A., Bruner, J. S. & Postman, L.:** Familarity of letter sequences and tachistoscopic identification. J. gen. Psychol., 1954, *50*, 129–139.   *B.R.*

Spasm (*cramp*). An increased, involuntary state of tension (*tonic* spasm) lasting for some time and, or, a quick succession of irregular, involuntary contractions (*clonic* spasm) of a muscle or group of muscles, especially in diseases of the brain or spinal cord (lesion of the pyramidal tract).   *F.-C.S.*

Spasmolytics. Substances which produce a decrease in tonus of the smooth musculature, in particular of the gastro-intestinal tract. The chemistry and pharmacology of the different spasmolytics varies; most of them belong to the anticholinergic (q.v.) or sympathicomimetic (q.v.) substances. Depending on their points of attack, there can frequently be disagreeable side-effects (e.g. anticholinergic substances can cause dryness of the mouth).

Bibliography: Miller, S. W. & Lewis, S. E.: Drugs affecting smooth muscle. Annals of the Pharmacological Review, 1969, *9*, 147–72.   *W.J.*

Spastic (*convulsive*). Contracting after the manner of a spasm (q.v.). Impairment of the normal coordination of movement.

Spastic paralysis: paralysis in which the ability of a large skeletal musculature to move at will is lost although the muscle is not slack, but tonically contracted.   *F.-C.S.*

Spatial symbolism. Theory applied particularly to graphology, according to which spatial grouping of features in handwriting, drawings, sculpture, etc., give a key to expression and coordination of individual personality traits of the author. Thus in handwriting the lower half of a letter corresponds to the area of desire and affect and the upper half to intellectual interests. Spatial symbolism also plays a part in the interpretation of dreams (q.v.) in many depth psychology schools (see *Depth psychology*) (e.g. C. G. Jung), which usually hold that the unconscious is allied with the lower, the conscious (q.v.) with the upper, the past with the left and the future with the right.

W.Sch.

Spatial threshold. The necessary minimum distance between two stimulus points, such that they are experienced as two different stimuli. The spatial threshold is measured in the optical and tactile sensory modalities. In the measurement of simultaneous spatial thresholds, the stimuli are simultaneous; in the measurement of successive spatial thresholds (successive threshold) they are successive.

F.Ma.

Spearman, C. E. B. 10/9/1863 in London; d. 17/9/1945 in London. It was only relatively late, in 1897, after leaving the English army where he had served as an officer, that Spearman turned to psychology. He subsequently spent several years in Germany, first under W. Wundt (q.v.), under whom he graduated in 1904 with an investigation of spatial perception (q.v.), and subsequently at the universities of Würzburg, Göttingen and Berlin, where he completed his studies of physiology, experimental psychology and philosophy. While in Germany he published in 1904 his famous article "General intelligence objectively determined and measured", in which for the first time he clearly expounded the fundamental ideas of factor analysis (q.v.). In 1907, Spearman was appointed to a lectureship, and in 1911 to a professorial chair, at University College, London. which he occupied until 1931.

Spearman's historical significance can be seen in two facts which are closely interrelated: on the one hand the development of the factor analytical method, the beginnings of which can admittedly be found in K. Pearson's work but which Spearman was the first to set out explicitly, and, on the other hand, the two-factor theory of intelligence (q.v.) which, together with A. Binet's work, represents the starting point for the development of the theory and measurement of intelligence in the twentieth century. The basic assumption of the two-factor theory is that every cognitive performance represents a function of two factors: (*a*) a *general intelligence factor* g which underlies every performance of the intelligence and (*b*) specific ability factors which only come into play at any time in particular kinds of tasks. In subsequent revisions of his theory Spearman recognized in addition the existence of individual group factors, without however abandoning his basic concept of g and s factors. (See *Abilities*.)

Other significant contributions by Spearman were the development of Spearman rank correlation (q.v.) and Spearman–Brown formula (q.v.). On the other hand, his attempts to state fundamental laws of psychology and the human mind on the basis of his g factor concept ("The nature of intelligence and the principles of cognition", 1923; "G and after —a school to end schools", 1930) must be regarded as somewhat exaggerated.

Other works: The abilities of man, their nature and measurement. London, 1927. Creative mind. London, 1930. Psychology down the ages. London, 1937.

Bibliography: Murchison, C. (Ed.): A history of psychology in autobiography, Vol. 1. Worcester, Mass., 1930, 299–333.   *W.W.*

Spearman–Brown formula. If the reliability (q.v.) r_{tt} of a test of a given extent is known, then the reliability of a test extended *n*-fold can be calculated according to this formula. It is as follows:

$$r_{nn} = \frac{n \cdot r_{tt}}{1 + (n-1)r_{tt}}$$

Of special importance is the case where $n = 2$, which occurs when calculating the reliability according to the *split-half* method (q.v.).

Bibliography: Guilford, J. P.: Psychometric methods. New York, 1954. *A.R.*

Spearman rank correlation coefficient. A method of comparison of two rank orders for agreement. In the following, r_s = correlation between ranks over things ranked:

$$r_s = 1 - \frac{6(\sum_i D_i^2)}{N(N^2 - 1)}$$

when N = number of things observed, and D_i = the difference between ranks associated with a specific observed object i. This computational method applies when no ties in rank exist. r_s is, therefore, a normal correlation coefficient calculated on ranks (see *Correlational techniques*).

Bibliography: Kendall, M. G.: Rank correlation methods. London, 1962. *A.K.*

Special school. An institution, either private or run by the State, which has as its object to care both for the health and the education of children and adolescents who because of some organic or mental defect can respond only inadequately or not at all to primary school instruction and yet are *capable of development*. The term special schools embraces institutions of the most diverse kinds, such as schools for the deaf and hard of hearing, schools for children with language difficulties, for the blind and partially blind, schools for those with learning disabilities and the mentally handicapped (see *Mental defect*), and in addition institutions for those with behavioral disorders, for the subnormal, adolescents serving a sentence, the physically handicapped and those suffering from some disease. The first special schools were for the deaf (Paris, 1770; Leipzig, 1778), then followed those for the blind (Paris, 1780). It was only in about 1900 that institutions for those with learning disabilities began really to appear as a result of the psychological and psychiatric discoveries of the nineteenth century. Schools for those serving a prison sentence have been in existence since 1921. Quite recently dyslexia (q.v.) has also begun to be treated in special classes. The organization of the special school system varies; for some types there are preparatory institutions, primary and intermediate schools, senior sections, vocational classes, and courses for adults. Instruction at special schools is an educational problem of the first order since it makes great demands on teachers' skill and requires outstanding human qualities (leader figures). See *Child psychology; Educational psychology.* *E.U.*

Species. 1. A natural class, a single order of beings. **2.** Any class, sort, or subdivision of a general term. **3.** In particular: a class narrower than a genus, yet wider than a variety.

Specific energy of sensations, law of. A doctrine proposed by Müller in 1826. He stated that each sensory nerve has its own characteristic type of activity, so that the optic nerve signals light and color, the auditory nerve sound and the olfactory nerve odor, and so on. In accord with this theory is the fact that most receptors respond to electrical stimulation in just this way, resulting in reports of light, sound, and smell respectively. The current view is that the specific activity depends not so much on the nerve, but on the locality in the brain at which the signal the nerve is transmitting eventually arrives. Hence electrical stimulation of the occipital lobe gives an experience of light. *C.D.F.*

Spectrum. 1. In general: periodic but also aperiodic fluctuating partial oscillations distributed in time or space can be split up into harmonic partial oscillations, of differing frequency. If, in a system of coordinates, the amplitudes of the partial oscillations (ordinates), for example, are plotted as a function of the frequency (abscissa), a representation is obtained which is known as a spectrum. In the case just mentioned, the spectrum is called the *amplitude spectrum*. If, instead of the amplitude, the amplitude squared is plotted on the ordinate, a *performance spectrum* is obtained.

2. In a literal sense the concept of spectrum is used for the range of electromagnetic oscillations with a wavelength between 380 and 780 nm, which is also known as *visible spectrum*. In this case the radiation energy (light current, etc.) as ordinate is plotted as a function of the wavelength (lambda) on the abscissa.

The energy-like spectrum in all wavelength ranges (visible) has a constant energy. A spectrum can be made from a reflected radiation: *reflection spectrum*. Also analogous are: emission spectrum, absorption spectrum, etc. (see *Absorption*). Sound spectra are also referred to in the field of acoustics when the frequency range between 16 Hertz and 20, sometimes, as much as 40 thousand Hertz (20 k Hertz): is understood (above 20 kHz, *ultrasonic spectrum*). In this case a performance spectrum is usually meant (pressure fluctuations in microbar or dyn/cm² as a function of the frequency). **R.R.**

Speculative psychology. A branch of philosophical psychology which dispenses with experiments (q.v.) and systematic observations and describes the essential dimensions of mental life in connection with a comprehensive philosophical system. Thus Thomism, for example, includes a speculative psychology. See *Philosophy and psychology*. **P.M.**

Speech (syn. *Speaking; Linguistic behavior; Verbal behavior*). In everyday usage, "speech" appears to be a clearly demarcated form of behavior. In varying conceptions of language (q.v.), however, speech (whether as a whole or in part) is variously conceived theoretically: e.g. as the emission of verbal responses, as encoding, as communication, as performance (see *Psycholinguistics; Expression; Verbal behavior, establishment and modification of*).

The linguistic concept of "competence" unites the most diversely nuanced ideas of the dispositional bases of language acquisition (see *Grammar;* Miller & McNeill, 1969). The complementary concept of "performance", in the sense of language use, is any processual application of competence in language or in the reception of linguistic utterances, and requires correspondingly differentiated ideas of speech and speech perception (Bierwisch, 1966; Wales & Marshall, 1966). Accordingly, a psychological theory of linguistic performance would have consistently to interpret at least the following part functions individually and in their functional interactions (Hörmann, 1970; Osgood & Sebeck, 1965): (*a*) in speech *production*: the actualization of meanings and meaningful linguistic units (see *Semantics*); the selection, formation and arrangement of such units according to grammatical rules (see *Grammar*); and the vocal realization of available linguistic structures (see *Phonemics*) in the interaction of respiration, phonation and articulation (or graphic realization by means of writing). In speech *perception*: the perception of sound sequences (or of written sequences) and their decoding as phoneme sequences (or grapheme sequences); the constitution of meaningful units (morphemes, words), including the actualization of meanings, the decoding of their grammatical relations, the construction of integrative meaningful contexts (e.g. of sentences and more extensive linguistic structures).

Psychological theories and investigations are concerned primarily with some of the performance components (Goodman, 1968; Lashley, 1951; Morse, Ballintine & Dixon, 1968; Wathen-Dunn, 1967); and in addition with specific aspects of speech and speech perception, such as the effect of emotional conditions and/or social interactions down to the most varied formal and substantial parameters of speech, interactions between speech and non-verbal forms of communication (body postures, movements, visual contact), between speech and thought (see *Inner speech*), and the identification of affective states, social and individual-specific characteristics in the partner in communication by means of perceived utterance and/or intervals and disturbances in the same (Argyle, 1969; Davitz, 1964; Ellingworth & Clevenger, 1967; Ervin-Tripp, 1969; Goldman-Eisler, 1968; Knapp, 1963; Paivio, 1965; Wiener & Mehrabian, 1968), and effects of the limited nature of the actual storage capacity and processing speed on linguistic performance. For methodological and theoretical reasons, speech and speech perception are usually treated together, since both processes would seem to include common part processes or, to some extent, to imply one another. Under differential-psychological and individual-diagnostic-pathognostic aspects, in addition to content (Gottschalk & Gleser, 1969), the most diverse formal characteristics of speech production and its voiced or graphic realization come into play: e.g. tempo, duration, duration and type of pauses and disturbances, pitch, volume, intensity, intonation, accentuation, breathing, and so on (Ellingworth & Clevenger, 1967; Rudert, 1965). The formal variables of graphic realization are studied in the psychology of handwriting (see *Graphology*). Techniques for the detection of the interindividual variability of speech perception can also be used for the differentiation of such aspects as readability, comprehensibility, etc.

Bibliography: Argyle, M.: Social interaction. London, 1969. **Bierwisch, M.:** Strukturalismus. Kursbuch, 1966, *5*, 77–152. **Davitz, J. R.:** The communication of emotional meaning. New York, 1964. **Ellingworth, H. W. & Clevenger, T.:** Speech and social action. Englewood Cliffs, N.J., 1967. **Ervin-Tripp, S. M.:** Sociolinguistics. In: **Berkowitz, L.** (Ed.): Advances in experimental social psychology, Vol. 4. New York & London, 1969, 91–165. **Goldman-Eisler, F.:** Psycholinguistics. London, 1968. **Goodman, K. S.** (Ed.): The psycholinguistic nature of the reading process. Detroit, 1968. **Gottschalk, L. A. & Glese, G. C.:** The measurement of psychological states through the content analysis of verbal behavior. Berkeley, 1969. **Hörmann, H.:** Psychologie der Sprache. Berlin, ²1970. **Knapp, P. H.** (Ed.): Expression of the emotions in man. New York, 1963. **Lashley, K. S.:** The problem of serial order in behavior. In: **Jeffress, L. A.** (Ed.): Cerebral mechanism in behavior. New York, 1951. **Miller, G. A. & McNeill, D.:** Psycholinguistics. In: **Lindzey, G. & Aronson, E.** (Eds.): Handbook of social psychology, 3. Reading, Mass., 1969, 666–794. **Morse, W. C., Ballantine, F. A. & Dixon, W.:** Studies in the psychology of reading. New York, 1968. **Osgood, C. E. & Sebeok, T. A.** (Eds.): Psycholinguistics. Bloomington, 1965. **Paivio, A.:** Personality and audience influence. In: **Maher, B. A.** (Ed.): Progress in experimental personality research, Vol. 2. New York, 1965, 127–73. **Rudert, J.:** Vom Ausdruck der Sprechstimme. In: **Kirchhoff, R.** (Ed.): Hdb. d. Psychol., Vol. 5. Göttingen, 1965, 422–64. **Wales, R. J. & Marshall, J. C.:** The organisation of linguistic performance. In: **Lyons, J. & Wales, R. J.** (Eds.): Psycholinguistic papers. Edinburgh, 1966, 29–80. **Wathen-Dunn, W.** (Ed.): Models for the perception of speech and visual form. Cambridge, Mass.), 1967. **Wiener, M. & Mehrabian, A.:** Language within language. New York, 1968.

                                                G. Kaminski

Speech center. A cortical field in the left cerebral hemisphere (in the right-handed) the destruction of which leads to an inability to speak (see *Aphasia*). The motor speech center was described by P. Broca (see *Broca's area*) in the *pars opercularis* of the inferior frontal gyrus. Its destruction leads to motor aphasia with an inability to translate thoughts into spoken words. The sensory speech center was discovered by K. Wernicke in the rear temporal area. Its destruction leads to sensory aphasia, an inability to understand words. But see *Brain pathology; Localization of psychological functions.*   *E.D.*

Speech disorders. See *Aphasia; Aphrasia.*

Speech types. A division of modes of speech according to body posture, rhythm, clang, tension, etc. Sievers (1912) and Drach (1928) offer elaborate categorizations.

Bibliography: **Drach, E.:** Sprechausdruck und Charakterkunde. Päd. Zbl., 1928. **Sievers, E.:** Rhythmisch-melodische Studien. Heidelberg, 1912. *W.K.*

Speed test. A test of psychological performance in which the rapidity with which one or several tasks are solved is the crucial criterion. As far as possible the difficulty of the tasks should not enter into consideration and it is therefore kept uniformly low. To determine the score for the performance there are two possibilities: either the time required for a certain number of tasks or the number of tasks performed for each unit of time. The tests of this kind currently in use select chiefly the second alternative. Speed tests are usually employed in the diagnosis of attentiveness and concentration, endurance and motor skill.

P.S.

Spence, Kenneth Wartinbee (1907–1967) "demanding of others, . . . much more of himself," a personality "drawn in bold lines; strong attitudes, powerful opinions, prodigious worker" (Kendler, 1967). Born in Chicago, Illinois, Spence was raised in Canada, was educated at McGill University, Montreal (B.A., 1929; M.A., 1930) and Yale (Ph.D., 1933), worked as National Research Council Fellow at the Yale Laboratories of Primate Biology, Orange, Florida (1933–37), the University of Virginia (1937–38), and the University of Iowa (1938–64) (Professor and Head of Department in 1942). From 1964 he was Professor at the University of Texas. Both alone and in collaboration his experimental output was formidable, which for some may

have obscured his vital contribution to theory: "I do not consider myself a philosopher, even an amateur one," said Spence (1960, 7). This denial suggests an awareness evident in a careful theoretical progress from the identification of events deemed unitary and elementary to theory which can be extended to more complex, "higher" behaviors. Often regarded as a reviser of Hull's learning theory, Spence appears instead a theorist of a superior class, especially in his views on contiguity and reinforcement (1960, 185–201). His most visible scholarly monuments are his Silliman Lectures (*Behavior and Conditioning*, 1956), and the later collection *Behavior Theory and Learning* (1960). The latter covers methodology (five papers), learning theory extending to, e.g., anxiety (ten papers) and discrimination learning (seven papers), including an outstanding handling of the intervening variable. In his distinction between earlier and later behaviorism (1960, 40), exposition of developing views of the subject matter of psychology (1960, 72), and discussion of the shift of interest from complex to simple learning (1959, 89), there is more historical insight than has been commonly allowed. Spence was explicitly laboratory oriented, but appears more aware of applied psychology and more balanced in approach than has been sometimes thought. Hence, on learning theory and educational technology: "We psychologists have been asked to solve practical problems before we had the laws of behavior necessary to do so . . . the applied psychologist has found it necessary to proceed in much the same fashion as the basic research psychologist instead of operating in the manner of the typical engineer" (1959, 87); on "cultural" psychology: "knowledge . . . based on introspective observation or empathic projection . . . differs from scientific knowledge." This may be developed, e.g. regarding personality, but it should not be represented as being one of the natural sciences (1960, 81). Balanced contribution deserves balanced evaluation: Spence's position with psychologists, whether scientific or humanistic, remains secure.

Works: Behavior theory and conditioning. New Haven, 1956. The relation of learning theory to the technology of education. Harvard Educ. Rev., 1959, *29*, 84–95. Behavior theory and learning. Englewood Cliffs, N.J., 1960.

Bibliography: Kendler, H. H.: Kenneth W. Spence. Psychol Rev., 1967, *74*, 335–41.   *J.A.C.*

Sphere (*sphere of consciousness*). A concept of Schilder (1920) and E. Kretschmer which is related to the "marginal consciousness" (M. Prince) and "marginal zone" (M. Dessoir). E. Kretschmer describes the sphere as the "periphery of the field of consciousness" with "its beclouded orbit of associated conscious notions and feelings which has some obscure influence at the birth of every action and spoken sequence". These imprecise processes are indispensable not only for empathy and tact, but for intuitive, productive and artistic thinking.   *W.K.*

Sphygmograph. An instrument for graphical recording of the strength and frequency of the pulse.   *G.D.W.*

Sphygmography. A technique for recording changes in pulse beat with the aid of suitable measuring devices and the partly mechanical, partly pneumatic, partly electrical or optical transference of the fluctuations of blood pressure on to a writing system. A *sphygmogram* is the record of the fluctuations of pulsatory blood pressure.   *E.D.*

Sphygmomanometer. An instrument for measuring arterial blood pressure (both *systolic* and *diastolic*). A rubber tube connected to an air bulb is wound tightly around the upper arm

and air pumped into it until circulation is blocked off (heart sounds are no longer heard through a stethoscope placed on the arm just below the tube). As pressure is released, a pulse is heard first (the systolic pressure), but this disappears again as the blood begins to course more freely (the diastolic pressure).

G.D.W.

Spinal cord. That part of the central nervous system (*medulla spinalis*) located in the spinal canal of the vertebral column. Its function is on the one hand to provide links in the shape of nerve pathways between the brain (q.v.) and the body's periphery and on the other hand to form reflex centers as well as synapses for coordinating simple series of motor movements. Accordingly it consists of white (pathways) and grey matter (collections of nerve cells) which are absolutely separate from one another. When a cross-section of the spinal cord about as large as a small coin is examined, the pathways outside the butterfly-shaped grey matter can be easily recognized and assigned to the different cords (e.g. pyramidal anterior and posterior cord, Flechsig, Gower, Burdach and Goll cords). See *Nervous system.*   *E.D.*

Spinal ganglion. See *Ganglion.*

Spiritual exercises. Ignatius of Loyola (1535) developed the medieval "*Exercitia spiritualia*" as the classical "spiritual exercises" of the Catholic Church. Under the guidance of a leader, a few days (originally four weeks) are spent in examination of conscience, followed by meditation on the life of Jesus and his grace. With the general tendency to intellectualization, the ability of meditative devotional prayer to change the personality has become very rare. See *Meditation.*   *K.T.*

Spiritualism. A cult centered upon belief in survival (q.v.), and upon the practice of communicating with deceased persons through a medium (q.v.). Hence "spiritualist" = devotee of spiritualism.   *J.B.*

Spirometer. An instrument which measures the volume of air that can be expired at one breath (usually taken as an indication of lung capacity).   *G.D.W.*

Split-half method. A method of assessing the reliability (q.v.) of a psychometric test. The items are arbitrarily split into two equal parts (e.g. by taking all the odd and all the even numbers) and a score given to each half of the test. The correlation between the two halves of the test gives a reliability assessment which is half as great as the original test. By means of the Spearman-Brown formula this reliability score can be converted to apply to the original test. This method can only be used for power tests. Reliability tested in this way is called split-half reliability. See *Test theory*.

Bibliography: Guilford, J. P.: Psychometric methods. New York, 1954.   *A.R.*

Spontaneous psi phenomenon. A paranormal phenomenon (q.v.) that occurs spontaneously in the real-life situation as opposed to an experimental psi-phenomenon of the parapsychological laboratory.   *J.B.*

Sport, psychology of. The investigation of the psychological processes and their manifestations present in people during and after sporting activity. It tries to investigate the causes and effects of these processes but not the sport itself; it investigates the player not the game. In every sporting performance the personality is involved as a whole, both with the physical and psychic factors of ability to

perform, and with the affective and voluntary factors of willingness to perform (see *Motivation*). Every sporting activity is also the behavior (q.v.) of an individual in an environment (q.v.).

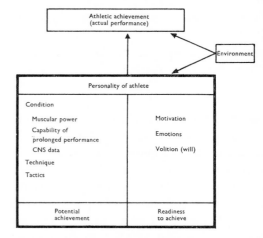

Athletic achievement is the result of a whole personality. The environment affects personality and performance.

Psychosomatic medicine and pediatric psychology are still working on the fundamental soul-body problem which concerns us in every sporting activity. New incentives came from various attempts continually to improve sporting performance and bring it to perfection. Sports medicine has contributed to this process of improvement, but the physical readiness of top athletes is approaching an optimum. The technical contribution to sport (biomechanics, equipment and apparatus) is also approaching perfection. The task of the psychology of sport is therefore to use the findings of general psychology (q.v.) and its own researches to help the performer to develop his sporting capacity and preparation to the full, so that he can be at his best at the critical moment.

The relationship between the practice and psychology of sport is mutual. The practice of sport can be perfected through the findings of psychology, and psychological knowledge can be increased by the practice of sport. Sport allows the observation of behavior which cannot easily be studied in everyday life. Questions of skill, for example, or the socio-psychological problems of group dynamics (q.v.) are of great importance in sport. The athlete, particularly in sport of a high standard, experiences psychologically extreme conditions with corresponding drives, e.g. aggression (q.v.), self-approval, fear. The athlete in training subjects himself to ordeals (see *Stress*) and makes demands upon himself which reach the limits of his personal capacities. "Neither in professional work nor in psychological studies in general can such an unreserved commitment of all a man's capacities be found, not only bodily but also psychic capacities." (Feige, 1964.) The psychology of sport investigates psychic behavior and capacity at the limits of normal performance" (Feige, 1964). This special task makes the psychology of sport a special branch of psychology.

Methods. The psychology of sport employs the usual methods of general psychology: the observation of experience (self-observation), the observation of others through questioning (see *Exploration*), and free association (see *Psychoanalysis*). Experiments (q.v.) and tests (see *Psychodiagnostics; Objective tests; Intelligence tests*) may be conducted in direct conjunction with sporting activity. Experiments and tests in the laboratory must always be ratified by field studies because the laboratory cannot reproduce the competitive situation very closely.

Aims. Basic research seeks through work which is not practice-directed to reach a deeper understanding of the psychic phenomena of sporting activity. In this sphere are the mind-body problem (q.v.), developmental psychology (see *Development; Maturation*), psycho-mechanics, high-performance psychology and depth psychology (q.v.): problems concerning biology and physiology on the one hand, and psychology on the other. Research directed toward the practice of sport seeks to reach a deeper understanding of the participant, and proceeds as in traffic psychology (q.v.) or occupational psychology (q.v.). It is particularly concerned with problems of adaptation of the player, motivation, performance and social psychology. There is a constant interchange between the basic and applied research. The relationship between research and practice is most important. Research, particularly applied research, must be directed toward practice, yet must not only describe but explain psychic phenomena, and pass on findings to the practice of sport. In a teaching department, the psychology of sport aims to give teachers and trainers a basic psychological knowledge. They are also shown what psychic factors are involved in a sporting performance. The attempt is made to arouse their interest and sense of responsibility, and to develop their understanding of problems in the psychology of sport.

As well as this research and teaching work, the psychology of sport is also directly engaged in the practice of sport, particularly in counseling. This counseling may be individual, or (in groups and clubs) a form of group therapy (q.v.).

Bibliography: Bally, G.: Vom Ursprung und von den Grenzen der Freiheit. Eine Deutung des Spiels bei Tier und Mensch. Basle Stuttgart, ²1966. **Feige, K.:** Aufgaben und Bedeutung der Sportpsychologie für die Theorie der Leibeserziehung. Die Leibeserziehung, 1964, *4*, 111–25. **Fischel, W.:** Psychologie. In: **Arnold, A.** (Ed.): Lehrbuch der Sportmedizin. Leipzig, 1960, 374–299. **Hegg, J. J.:** Tiefenpsychol. des Hochleistungssportes. Schweiz. Z. für Sportmedizin, 1969, *3*, 89–112. **Kleibert, G. & Elssner, G.:** Einige grundlegende Bemerkungen zur Entwicklung einer wiss. Psychol. des Sports. Theorie und Praxis der Körperkultur, 1954, *4*, 318–30. **Kohlmann, T.:** Die Psychologie der motorischen Begabung. Vienna, Stuttgart, 1958. **Kunath, P.:** Psychologie. Leipzig, 1965. **Lorenz, K. & Leyhausen, P.:** Antriebe tierischen und menschlichen Verhaltens. Munich, 1968. **Lotz, F.:** Sport–Leibeserziehung–Psychol. Die Leibeserziehung, 1965, *8*, 280–5. **Macak, J.:** The psychological aspects of the control of the prestart state and the possibilities of its valuation. Bratislava: Acta facultatis educationis fisicae, *VI*, 1967. **Neumann, O.:** Die leibseelische Entwicklung im Jugendalter. Múnich, 1964. **Ogilvie,**

B. & Tutko, T. A.: Problem athletes and how to handle them. London, 1966. **Puni, A. Z.**: Abriss der Sportpsychologie. Berlin, 1961. **Singer, R. N.**: Motor learning and human performance. New York & London, 1968. **Steinbach, M.**: Über konkrete Möglichkeiten einer Zusammenarbeit von Ärzten und Psychologen im Sport. Schweiz. Z. für Sportmedizin, 1968, *3/4*, 145–55. **Vanek, M.**: Medelovan trénink. Psychologické priprava sportovce, Metodicky dopis CSTV, 1963. **Widmer, K.**: Das sportliche Training in psychologisch-soziologischer Sicht. Jugend und Sport, 1967, *10*, 277–83. **Winter, E. de & Dubreuil, J.**: La relaxation comme psychothérapie sportive. 1st International Congress of Sports Psychology, 1965.

G. Schilling

Square illusion. The illusion by which a square standing on one corner looks larger than an

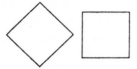

objectively equal square standing on one side.

C.D.F.

Squinting (*Strabismus*). When an object is fixated, the visual axes of both eyes are directed at it. Thus the image-forming rays fall on the identical retinal positions (q.v.). If a person is unable to direct the visual axes of both eyes simultaneously on a fixated object, he suffers from squinting. Squinting can occur when the pivots of both eyes are in their normal position and also when this position is abnormal (caused by tumors). In the following four cases of squinting the pivots of both eyes and hence both eyes themselves are in the normal position with respect to the orbits: (*a*) "eccentric fixation"; identical retinal positions: especially the foveae are located anomalously. (*b*) "Simple squinting". (*c*) "Paralytic squinting" (*strabismus paralyticus*), due to paralysis or contraction (shortening) of one or several muscles. (*d*) Anomalous attachment of the muscles at the bulbus, as a result of which the pull of the eye muscles acts at the wrong place physiologically.

The visual axes can deviate from one another both in a horizontal and in a vertical direction. When there is deviation in the horizontal plane, a distinction is made between inward squinting (*strabismus convergens*) and outward squinting (*strabismus divergens*). In the vertical plane (elevation squinting) one visual axis may deviate *upwards* (*strabismus ascendens*) or *downwards* (*strabismus descendens*). Usually the visual axis of one eye is directed correctly at the object fixated (the leading eye), whereas the visual axis of the other eye deviates. If the *leading eye alternates*, the term "*strabismus alternans*" is used. When both eyes squint, the case is one of *strabismus binocularis*. *Strabismus concomitans* occurs with hyperopia (q.v.) and myopia (q.v.). The eye tries to compensate for the hyperopia, for example, by near accommodation (see *Accommodation*). But, because of the nervous displacement caused in this near accommodation, the visual axes simultaneously turn inward (see *Convergence*).

Vision in the squinting eye is frequently poor (see *Amblyopia*). This amblyopia can be either the cause (absence of fusion stimulus) or the result of the squinting.

Strabismus latens indicates a tendency to squint. The squinting is irregular and varies in degree. "Heterophoria" is a term also used for such cases; it may be *esophoria* (deviating inward), *exophoria* (deviating outward), *hyperphoria* or *hypophoria* (deviating upward or downward).   *R. Rix*

S-R, S-R-S, S-S models. The attempt is made through the *S-R model* to explain all behavior of organisms as a response to preceding stimulation. It forms the basis of all behavioristic theories of learning (q.v.) and behavior (q.v.). The basic units of S-R theory are the innate S-R associations, which are known as *unconditioned reflexes*. If the association of S and R is produced because they repeatedly occur together or close in time to one another, then a conditioned reflex is formed by the method of classical conditioning (q.v.). The model which is adduced to explain how the association comes about in this way is known as the *S-R contiguity model*. If the association is explained as having occurred because a reward followed the appearance together of S and R, then the case is said to be one of a *S-R reinforcement model* or—particularly since the reinforcement represents the action of a stimulus—an *S-R-S model*. According to the so-called S-S theory of E. C. Tolman, it is not the associations between the S and the R which are learned, but those between the external stimuli leading to the reward (S_1) and the desired stimulus of the reward (S_2). E. R. Guthrie is famous as the proponent of the S-R contiguity theory and C. L. Hull (q.v.) as the proponent of the S-R reinforcement theory. See *Behaviorism*.   *H.Ro.*

S-R psychology. An inclusive term for most psychological research activities with a scientific orientation. This term was given to them because of their common theoretical basic model, according to which all behavior is explained as a response (R) to a certain stimulus (S).   *H.Ro.*

S-R relation. The connection between stimulus and response in an individual, where the stimulus represents a condition for the response. Study of the S-R relation is at the center of stimulus-response psychology, or S-R psychology, which is especially concerned with problems of learning (q.v.). See *Behaviorism; Conditioning, classical and operant; Learning theory*.   *F.Ma.*

Stabilized retinal image. Using special experimental techniques (e.g. an extremely bright flash inducing long-lasting afterimages) it is possible to stabilize a visual image so that it stimulates only one fixed part of the retina.

Viewed under these conditions, the visual image disappears within a few seconds. The exact nature of this disappearance depends on the structure of the stimulus, some parts of the stimulus remaining visible longer than others. These results show that normal vision depends on continual small movements of the eyes, thus revealing a particular inadequacy in the analogy between the eye and a camera. *C.D.F.*

Stammering. A speech impediment involving blockages and hesitations which interrupt the even flow of words. Is sometimes equated with *stuttering*, with which it is often associated. Normally distinguished from disorders of articulation such as *dysarthria* and *anarthria* which result from lesions in the speech areas of the brain. Believed to be influenced by psychological factors, although some emotional conditions may be secondary results of the stammering, e.g. shyness and withdrawal.
G.D.W.

Standard. The mean measure or *norm* (q.v.).

Standard deviation (abb. SD; syn. *Variation; Mean square deviation*). A measure for the standard deviation of a distribution from the arithmetic mean:

$$SD = \sqrt{\frac{\Sigma\, x^2}{N}}$$

x being a score minus the mean, N = the number of items, and Σ = sum of.   *A.R.*

Standard error. Measure of the sample error (q.v.). It is the standard deviation (q.v.) of a statistic (q.v.) expressed from a sample calculated to the size N. Simple relations are often valid between the standard deviation of a feature in the population, the N size of the sample and the S.   *A.R.*

Standardization. Sometimes used as a synonym for *normalization*; transformation of rough data into units of measurement which fulfil certain conditions (e.g. they have a given mean value and given deviations).   *A.R.*

Standard score. A numerical value derived from a raw value, which plays an important part in test construction. Standard scores have the mean value 0 and the standard deviation 1; they have no dimensions. If x is a raw value, x̄ the arithmetic mean of distribution of x and s its standard deviation, then $z = (x - \bar{x})/s$. Standard scores allow the comparison of performances in different tests, but only in relation to a standard sample applied to the calculation of x̄ and s; they are therefore dependent upon distribution. See *Test theory*.   *A.R.*

Standards, sexual. Attitudes and values which define sexual behavior. The term and classification of sexual standards were originated by Reiss (1960) and are based on attitude data from empirical surveys in the USA. Reiss distinguishes from sexual standards: (*a*) *abstinence* (q.v.), (*b*) orthodox and traditional *dual morality* (q.v.), (*c*) *permissiveness with affection*: heterosexual relationships are permitted on the basis of love without having to be directly connected with marriage. (*d*) *Permissiveness without affection*: heterosexual relationships are accepted unconditionally. In a later publication (1967) Reiss reduced the standards to a one-dimensional scale: "restrictiveness-permissiveness".

Bibliography: Reiss, I. L.: Premarital sexual standards in America. Glencoe, Ill., 1960. **Id.:** The social context of premarital sexual permissiveness. New York, 1967.
    J.F.

Stanford Intelligence Test. Stanford-Binet tests in the 1937 edition. The procedure applies the well-known Binet model of arrangement of tests according to age order. The calcula-

tion of intelligence age and intelligence quotients likewise takes place in the traditional form. The tests are used for children from 3–14, and without differentiation for adolescents and adults.   *P.S.*

Stationary wheel illusion. If a moving object is illuminated intermittently at such a rate that it is always in exactly the same position during the illumination, then it will appear to be stationary. This stroboscopic technique is used in industry to obtain a stationary view of moving parts without having to stop them moving. Before the availability of stroboscopic light, this phenomenon was sometimes observed when a wheel happened to move at the right speed behind a fence, the slits in the fence providing the intermittent view. *C.D.F.*

Statistic. Statistics are units of measurement which are calculated from sample observations. The parameter which can be estimated by statistics corresponds to statistics in the population. Statistics often in use are, for example, the arithmetic mean x̄ and the standard deviation s.   *A.R.*

Statistical sign test. A non-parametric technique by means of which two independent samples may be tested for differences in regard to their central trend. It is indicated when the samples are observed under different conditions, and these observational data can be grouped in pairs.

Bibliography: Dixon, W. J. & Mood, A. M.: The statistical sign test. J. Amer. Statist. Assoc., 1946, *41*, 557–66.
    H.-J.S.

Statistical certainty. The probability which an estimate or an assertion made on the basis of statistical methods has of being correct. The opposite of statistical certainty is probability of error. They are mutually complementary to 100%.   *A.R.*

Statistical inference. That branch of mathematical statistics (q.v.) concerned with the inferences possible in respect of a population on the basis of sample observations. Procedures for estimating credibility intervals and hypothesis testing form part of statistical inference.   *A.R.*

Statistics. 1. *General.* Given a set of elements and a variable, the association of a specific number or percentage of elements from the set with each value of the variable in such a way that only one value of the variable corresponds to a particular element is a basic aspect of statistics. A distinction is made between descriptive and inductive (analytical or sample) statistics. Descriptive statistics is concerned with finite values of real quantities, e.g. the number of workers in a country classified by profession or region, whereas inductive statistics considers the actual quantities as samples taken from a basic group (in the form of random samples) to allow the methods of probability calculation to be used.

Three developments in the history of statistics deserve especial mention: the theory of measurement errors formulated in the law of P. S. Laplace and F. K. Gauss, F. Galton's application of statistical concepts to the biological sciences, and Fisher's theoretical innovations. More recently, computers have facilitated the development of complex methods.

2. *Fundamental concepts of statistics.* (*a*) Distributions of a variable. Given a set of elements E and a variable x, the distribution of x in E is represented graphically by plotting a *histogram* (q.v.). It is assumed that the values are discontinuous either because of their effective nature or by dividing them into categories. The values are entered on an axis, and each of them corresponds to a segment which forms the base of a rectangle whose height is proportional to the number of associated elements E. A number calculated from the values X in E is a statistic (this term was proposed by Fisher; it is often referred to as a *parameter*). For a cardinal variable, the commonest statistic is the mean $\bar{x}$ of the values for X from all the elements of E. With ordinal variables, we consider the *median* (*central value*), i.e. the value of X on either side of which there are identical numbers of smaller and larger values. These statistics are said to measure the *central trend* (or tendency). There are also *dispersion statistics. Variance* is the mean value of the squares of the deviations from the mean; its square root, which has the advantage that it can be expressed in the same unit as the variable, is the *standard deviation*. Other dispersion measurements must be used for non-cardinal variables, e.g. entropy in the case of a nominal variable (see *Information theory; Communication*): $H = -\Sigma f_i \log f_i$, where f_i is the frequency of the values for X; this number is alone in having the properties expected of a dispersion measurement in this case. In addition, the central moment can be defined for a cardinal variable; the central moment of the order r is the mean value of the r-th power of the deviations from the mean, i.e. μ_r; the quotient μ_3/σ^3 is often taken to measure the asymmetry of the distribution (gestalt parameter).

Let us consider E from the standpoint of inductive statistics as a random sample, extracted from a basic set U; we can then define the distribution of X in U by working from a frequency distribution in which the area located between the curve and the ordinates of two random points X_1 and X_2 on the abscissa corresponds to the proportion of elements X of U for which X is situated between X_1 and X_2 (this is the case with a cardinal and continuous variable). We then define the mean μ as the mathematical expectation of X, the variance as the mathematical expectation of $(X - \mu)^2$, and the centered moment of the order r as the expectation of $(X - \mu)^r$. These concepts can also be applied to the discontinuous case by associating the corresponding frequency with each value X. Among the frequency distributions (q.v.), standard distributions are particularly important. Their density function is dependent on the two parameters μ and σ (see *Standard deviation*); μ is also the abscissa of the axis of symmetry of the distribution and $\mu \pm \sigma$ the abscissa of the points at which its direction changes. The curve is asymptotic to the X axis. If the variables X are replaced by the variables $\dfrac{X - \mu}{\sigma}$, we obtain the standardized distribution (mean = 0, standard deviation $\sigma = 1$), for which tables are drawn up showing, e.g., that 95% of the elements have values between -1.96 and $+1.96$, and 99% of the elements values between -2.58 and $+2.58$. Other highly important distributions can be derived from the standard distributions: the sum of the squares of ν standardized independent standard variables is known as the χ^2 distribution with ν degrees of freedom; if χ_ν^2 with ν degrees of freedom and $\chi_{\nu^1}^2$ with ν^1 degrees of freedom are distributed independently, the function

$$F(\nu, \nu^1) = \frac{\chi_\nu^2 / \nu}{\chi_{\nu^1}^2 / \nu^1}$$

is known as Snedecor's distribution with ν and ν^1 degrees of freedom; the distribution of the variables $t = \sqrt{F(1, \nu)}$ is a Student distribution with ν degrees of freedom.

(*b*) Special *discontinuous distributions*. If n balls with two colors and invariable composition are drawn from an urn, the probability of drawing r balls of one color with proportion p is $C_n^r p^r q^{n-r}$, in which $q = 1 - p$; the distribution of the value r is known as the *binomial distribution* (q.v.); its mean is np and its variance npq. Poisson's curve is another

significant distribution. It is obtained by assuming that $p = \dfrac{m}{n}$ with m constant and n tending to infinity; it is then clear that

$$C_n^r p^r q^{n-r} \rightarrow \frac{m^{r-m} e}{r}$$

The mean and variance of a Poisson distribution are both equal to m.

In applied psychology (q.v.), special methods of standardization are frequently applied to empirical distributions (stepped scaling); the variables, e.g. test performance results, are often only ordinal. This fact is utilized to convert the distribution into a step scale by suitable methods of conversion. If the distribution has a rectangular form and ten subdivisions are sufficient, we obtain a decile scale. This is obtained by fixing the criterion X_1 in such a way that ten percent of the testees have a better performance, X_2 in such a way that twenty percent have a better performance, and so on. Greater precision can, of course, be obtained with a centile scale. If the selected form is a standard distribution, we obtain a standardized scale; for example, with the following percentages: 4.0%, 10.6%, 22.7%, 40.2%, 59.8%, 77.3%, 89.4%, 96.0%, we should obtain a standard scale with nine classes (stages). This procedure enables, e.g., the *profile* of an individual to be recorded in a set of variables. Comparison of the performances for two variables is meaningful since it expresses the classification in a given population. The stepped scale provides an interpretation of an isolated performance result with reference to the population as a whole.

(*c*) *Multivariate distributions*. Let us first consider an example with two variables X and Y. In the (X, Y) plane, each element in the set E is represented by a point M and the resultant system of points is the dispersion or correlation diagram. The distribution of Y values corresponding to a given X value is known as the *partial* distribution of Y for this particular X value; the distributions of all X or Y values are *marginal* distributions. If we have a straight line D on the surface and consider the distance Mm, i.e. from M to this line, calculated parallel to OY, the line for which the Σ Mm^2 values are least is known as the line of least squares; its gradient is:

$$a = \frac{\Sigma (X - \bar{X}) (Y - \bar{Y})}{\Sigma (X - \bar{X})^2}$$

in which $\bar{X}$ and $\bar{Y}$ are the means of the marginal distributions. This gradient is the regression coefficient from Y to X. If the variance of the distribution of Y is given, the lines of the least squares will match all the more accurately, the closer the absolute value of

$$r = \frac{\Sigma (X - \bar{X}) (Y - \bar{Y})}{\sqrt{\Sigma (X - \bar{X})^2 \Sigma (Y - \bar{Y})^2}}$$

approximates to 1. r is known as the *correlation coefficient*. Inductive statistics distinguishes between the area of the frequency distribution of (X, Y), the partial distributions and the marginal distributions. If $\bar{Y}_x$ is the mean of the partial distribution of Y for a value of X, the equation $\bar{Y}_x = f(X)$ is the *regression equation* from Y to X, and the curve representing it is the regression line from Y to X. The most important distribution of two variables is the *bivariate standard distribution*. In addition to the product-moment correlation coefficient referred to above, there are other measurements of dependence, e.g. the *biserial*, *tetrachoric* and *Spearman's* correlation coefficients (see *Correlational techniques*). The regression equation from Y to X also enables Y to be forecast from X. If the regression is linear, the quality of the forecast is measured by the correlation coefficient r. Generalizing, a forecast is made of a variable z—starting from n variables—when the distributions of these variables are standardized and the regression is linear. The coefficients of the regression equation are the standardized coefficients of the partial regression and the accuracy of the forecast is measured by the multiple correlation coefficient. Partial correlation coefficients measure the association

between two variables when the influence of one or more variables has been eliminated. Let us assume n variables in a set of N elements (designated in this case as subjects). Using matrix terminology, let Z be the matrix (n, N) of the values of the standardized variables and R the matrix of the intercorrelations (with 1 in all the fields of the diagonals). We now obtain $R = \frac{ZZ'}{N}$ (X' is the transposed value of X). Let R* be a symmetrical real matrix with the order (n, n) of rank r (which need not necessarily only contain 1 in the diagonals); the determination of a real matrix F so that FF' = R* is then defined as factorizing R. F necessarily has the rank r. In factor analysis we look for diagonal elements which reduce r to a minimum. Thurstone and Hotelling have proposed solutions to the above equation. We obtain the solution by linear rotation (conversion) of the axes.

(*d*) *Methods of estimation.* From now on we shall be concerned solely with the statistics of samples. Let us assume a basic set, in which a variable X is present in standard distribution, with a mean value and a standard deviation. These are parameters which we wish to estimate by starting from a sample of N elements. This sample is one of the random samples of N elements which can be taken from the basic set under consideration. Let $\bar{X}$ be the (statistical) mean value of such a sample. For the population as a whole, $\bar{X}$ is normally distributed around the mean value μ, with a standard deviation $\frac{\sigma}{\sqrt{N}}$. If N is infinitely great, $\bar{X}$ tends toward μ. In such a case, $\bar{X}$ is said to be a *consistent* estimation of μ. In addition the mean value of the distribution of $\bar{X}$ is the parameter μ. In such a case, X is said to be an estimation of μ which is true to expectation.

The standard deviation $\frac{\sigma}{\sqrt{N}}$ is known as the mean error (standard error) of the mean value, and gives information on the effectiveness of the estimation. For 95% of the samples, the interval $(\bar{X} - 1.96 \frac{\sigma}{\sqrt{N}}, \bar{X} + 1.96 \frac{\sigma}{\sqrt{N}})$ contains the parameter μ. This interval is known as the confidence range, with a threshold of $P = 0.05$, and its limits are known as "confidence limits" on this threshold. In practice these limits are calculated by replacing σ by its estimated value $\hat{\sigma}$. Fisher has developed a technique known as the *maximum likelihood method* for obtaining the most effective statistic, if it exists. It can be shown, e.g. that to obtain an estimate of variance σ which is true to expectation, $\Sigma (X - \bar{X})$ must be divided by $N - 1$ rather than by N.

(e) *Statistical significance tests.* Let us now consider the difference d between a statistic and a norm, or between two statistics. Let us assume that $d = X - \bar{X}'$ is the difference between the means of two samples. We now make the *null hypothesis*, i.e. we assume that the basic sets of the two samples have the same mean value. If we use additional hypotheses (e.g. that the two basic sets follow a standard distribution and have the same variance) to determine the sample distribution of d, it is possible to indicate the limits of an interval in such a way that 2.5% of the subjects are situated outside it on the right and 2.5% on the left (bilateral test). If the empirical value of d is situated outside this interval, we say that the null hypothesis is rejected or that the difference on the $P = 0.5$ threshold is significant (by which we mean the risk that the null hypothesis is correct and that the empirical value is one of the 5% groups which would normally fall outside the limits). A test of significance has been made. Some significance tests require no additional hypotheses concerning the forms of distribution; they are referred to as "*non-parametric*" tests (q.v.). Conventional parametric tests use the standard distribution, the "Student's distribution" (comparison of mean values), the Snedecor distribution (see *Variance, analysis of*) and the X^2 distribution (frequency comparison).

Statistics are particularly important in psychology because of the variability of psychological measurements (especially interindividual measurements). See *Mathematical psychology; Test theory; Factor analysis.*

Bibliography: **Cramer, H.:** Mathematical methods of statistics. Princeton, 1945. **Faverge, J. M.:** Méthodes statistiques en psychologie appliquée. Paris, 1960. **Ferguson, G. A.:** Statistical analysis in psychology and education. New York & London, [3]1971. **Fisher, R. A.:** Statistical methods for research workers. Edinburgh, 1954. **Glass, G. V. & Stanley, J. C.:** Statistical methods in education and psychology. New York & London, 1970. **Guilford, J. P.:** Fundamental statistics in psychology and education. New York, 1958. **Kendall, M. G. & Stuart, A.:** The advanced theory of statistics. London, Vol. 1 1963; Vol. 2 1961; Vol. 3 1966. **Lewis, D. G.:** The analysis of variance. Manchester, 1971. **McCall, R. B.:** Fundamental statistics for psychology. New York & London, 1970. **McNemar, Q.:** Psychological statistics. New York, 1955. **Minium, E. W.:** Statistical reasoning in psychology and education. New York & London, 1970.

J. M. Faverge

Stato-acoustic sense organ. Fluid-filled parts of the inner ear (cochlea and basilar membrane) and of the organ of balance (the semicircular canals, sacculus and utriculus). Starting at the corresponding sense cells (ear: organ of corti; organ of balance; *cristae* or *maculae*) nerve fibers (*nervus cochlearis* and *nervus vestibularis*) meet in the *nervus statoacusticus*, the VIIIth brain nerve. The central nervous processing areas are, however, separate in respect of sense of balance and hearing.   *M.S.*

Statoliths. The statolithic organ consists of a sack (*sacculus*) in the petrosal bone of the skull, which is linked with the semicircular canal system and is full of *statoliths* (small grains on the sensory cilia of the statolithic organ). When the head is in a perpendicular position these press on the cilia of their base on the floor of the sack.   *E.D.*

Status arises in the process of group formation, and is based upon the differentiation of roles (q.v.) and the division of social power (in animals it is called the "pecking order"). It has a decisive influence on the interaction and communication of the group.

Through his status each individual is allotted a sphere of action. According to the type of group, status may be one-dimensional, i.e. based on a single criterion of status (e.g. military ranks) or multi-dimensional, i.e. based on several criteria of status (e.g. "high" society).

In groups with multi-dimensional status criteria, a member may have a high status in one respect and a relatively low status in another. In these cases there is usually a tendency for the two positions to draw together (Benoit-Smullyan, 1944), i.e. an attempt is made to bring the lower position up to the level of the higher (e.g. a newly rich person seeks to raise his educational and cultural level to that of his purse.)

Variables which determine the social status of a person are similar to those which determine his level of *social power*.

Bibliography: Benoit-Smullyan, E.: Status types and status interrelations. American sociological Review, 1944, *9*. Whyte, W. F.: Street corner society. Chicago, 1943.   *A.S.-M.*

Status orgasmus. Sigusch gave this name to an orgasmic form of reaction, first recorded physiologically by Masters & Johnson, which objectively and subjectively accompanies the highest intensity. *Status orgasmus* was observed only in women, lasts 20 to more than 50 seconds and is to be conceived as either a series of orgasms rapidly succeeding each other or as a long-drawn-out orgasmic episode.

Bibliography: Masters, W. H. & Johnson, V. E.: Human sexual response. Boston, 1966. Sigusch, V.: Exzitation und Orgasmus bei der Frau. Stuttgart, 1970.   *V.S.*

Stencil Design Test. A non-verbal intelligence test (individual test) developed by G. Arthur.

Tests are available with various difficulty gradings and may be used on subjects above the age of six. S. must reproduce geometrical patterns (designs) by superimposing paper stencils. There are two forms of test, one with colored and one with black and white materials. Standard values are available for each age group.   *F.Ma.*

Step size. A term for the size of a learning step which can be measured in (typewriter) strokes in the average time taken to work through it or by the contents seen as transinformation of the basic text.

Step size in teaching programs (q.v.) of the Skinner type (non-branching q.v.) amounts to an average of 200 typewriter impressions, or to 20–40 seconds for working through, or to 10–15 bits (q.v.) of medium semantic information. With teaching steps in branching programs the size is on average five times as large. See *Instructional technology.*   *H.F.*

Stereokinesis. The perception of the three-dimensionality of an object induced by its movement. Experiments have shown that the shadow of certain three-dimensional solids will only be perceived as three-dimensional when the object is in motion. It has also been found that for the moving shadow to have this three-dimensional quality it must contain contours or lines which change length and direction simultaneously.   *C.D.F.*

Stereophonia. The sensation of the direction of sounds and hence three-dimensionality in the experience of sounds depends on the subtle difference in the sounds reaching the two ears (see *Differential running time*). Hence an illusion of fully three-dimensional sound (stereophonic sound) can be produced by sounds recorded by two microphones simulating the two ears.   *C.D.F.*

Stereoscope. A viewing instrument through which two different stimuli (e.g. pictures) can be presented simultaneously, one to each eye. If the two stimuli are *anaglyphs*, i.e. disparate in the same way that the two retinal images are when a three-dimensional scene is viewed, then they will fuse to give an impression of *visual depth*. The easiest way to obtain anaglyphic pictures is by use of a *stereoscopic camera*, which takes two slightly different pictures of the same scene simultaneously through lenses separated by the same distance as the two eyes are apart. *G.D.W.*

Stereotactic techniques (syn. *Stereotaxic methods*). Methods used in human medical diagnosis and therapy by which potential variations from predictable structures, located by means of a probe, can be traced back and eliminated. The method is based on a pattern used in animal experiments, developed by Horsley & Clark around 1910 and introduced to human medicine in 1947 by Spiegel & Wyels.

Atlases of the brain provide the basis of stereotactic techniques derived from opened brains. Points can be selected from a map which are related to certain basic lines. After the patient's cerebral ventricle has been filled with air, the relationship between point, basis and lines is ascertained with standard X-rays. When the patient's brain and the atlas brain have been arranged in relation to each other, real values are obtained in respect of the patient's points. Two developments of stereotactic methods are (*a*) *focussed proton-beam elimination* of a point which in its precision resembles the usual stereotactic procedure, without any further surgical technique being necessary; (*b*) *"chronically" implanted electrodes:* with these a large number of electrodes, up to 60 per brain, with a diameter in each case of $100\mu t$ can be left in the brain for up to two years. During this time electric brain currents can be observed in

relation to behavior, and elimination can thus be controlled and followed more exactly.

Recently stimulation has been conducted telemetrically by these deep electrodes, i.e. without a wire connection, with patients living in completely natural circumstances. The indications are mainly in Parkinsonism (q.v.). Tremor and rigor experienced in this illness can be removed almost equally easily, but not drive disorders. Other disturbances of movement, e.g. *torticollus spasticus, hemiballism*, essential tremor, can also be treated by stereotactic methods. The procedure was used at an early stage in psychiatric disturbances and indeed in schizophrenia (q.v.), compulsive illnesses, etc. The non-specific therapeutic effect consists partly in a form of leucotomy: the original nuclei of the tracts, which are cut in leucotomy, are destroyed. Unlike the effects of leucotomy, the side-effects of stereotactic techniques are slight, with a somewhat similar therapeutic sequel. The possibilities of application in psychiatric disorders, however, relate to a specific effect in relatively easily isolated functional structures of the brain, e.g. within the so-called limbic system, when elimination takes place in the amygdalum, fornix, and other points.

Psychiatric indications will probably increase in the future. If this proves to be the case the method of chronic implantation, with its independence of the operating theater and with the possibility it allows of observing the patient under natural conditions, offers substantial prospects of psychiatric treatment. For example, methods have been devised which allow patients to stimulate themselves in different regions of the brain; these are similar to the methods used in animal experiments by Olds. With these, pleasurable and unpleasurable centers were found, as in animal experiments, but excluding the appearance of excessive additive excitation. Drugs (see *Psychopharmacology*) were injected by microcannulae, implanted chronically, and at the same time permanent electrodes were applied to diverse regions of the brain. The many individual results of these experiments show clearly the first elements of a coherent therapy (Heath & Mickle, 1960). Surprisingly, the side-effects of this technique are slight, and consist essentially in negligible and transient memory disturbances and in the possibility of bleeding, which according to past experiments (more than 10,000) occurs in less than 1% of cases. It has been said that side-effects in chronic implantations are less than in normal stereotactic treatment (Bechterewa et al., 1969). In addition to the direct clinical effects, new approaches to an understanding of the brain (q.v.) can result from these diagnostic and therapeutic techniques. Here anatomical, neurophysiological and psychological structural areas are directly linked with each other, and structural equivalences are already apparent between neurophysiological and psychological areas, for example in the sense that relationships exist on both sides which obey probability functions rather than deterministic controls. In this way, monistic conceptions capable of precise formalization form the basis of clinical and experimental "mind-body" research.

Bibliography: Bechterewa, N. P., Bondartschuk, A. N., Smirnow, W. M. & Trochatschow, A. J.: Physiologie und Pathophysiologie der tiefen Hirnstrukturen des Menschen. Berlin, 1969. Heath, R. G. & Mickle, W. A.: Evaluation of seven years experience with depth electrode studies in human patients. Electr. Studies on the unaesth. brain. New York, 1960. Mundinger, F. & Riechert, T.: Die stereotaktischen Hirnoperationen zur Behandlung extrapyramidaler Bewegungsstörungen und ihre Resultate. Fortschr. Neurol. Psychiat., 1963, 31, 1–120. Spiegel, E. A. & Wycis, H. T.: Stereoeucephalotomy. New York, 1962. Umbach, W.: Elektrophysiol. und negative Phänomene bei stereotaktischen Hirnoperationen. Berlin & New York, 1966.   M. Adler

Stereotype. A term whose meaning varies. It is most commonly used in the sense formulated by M. Jahoda among others, and according to which a stereotype denotes opinions about classes of individuals, groups or objects which are "preconceived", i.e. which do not derive from new judgments of each single phenomenon but are pattern-like forms of perceiving and judging. Accordingly, the Germans, for example, are hardworking and negroes are musical, etc. But beyond this common denominator, emphases differ.

Stereotypes can be examined as to origin, when expressly *defined as group judgments*, i.e. they are judgments on which a sufficiently large number of the members of a group (q.v.) or a social category are agreed; for this reason Sherif & Sherif, 1969 called them *a priori group stereotypes*, and placed them in the context of relations between groups.

Emphasis can also be placed on the element of truth in the stereotype. In this case stereotypes are often defined as over-simplified concepts which are false for the reason that they are over-generalized (Allport, 1955; Katz & Stotland, 1959; Lindgren, 1969; Hilgard & Atkinson, 1967; Morgan & King, 1966). Arguments against this are: (*a*) whether a reason is right or wrong can only be decided when there is sufficient knowledge. But this knowledge does not often exist. What, however, is certain is that all people's ideas, in so far as they have been generalized, are more or less false. One could however adhere to the evaluation of opinions from the aspect that as a rule certain knowledge of any subject is too scanty or that general experience shows that the subjects judged are as a rule too variable to justify a relatively simple and unchangeable judgment in the form of a stereotype (Katz & Stotland, 1959). Of course, the concept then becomes inflationary since it holds good for all everyday opinions.

(*b*) Investigations, however, show that stereotypes are by no means necessarily false. For instance, comparisons of studies of the intelligence of Americans seemed to show that American negroes on average have a lower IQ than whites (see *Abilities*). Admittedly, differentiated studies might show that this result is not due to race but, among other factors, to the conditions of life of the testees, for as a rule these are far more unfavorable for negroes. In this connection, Pettigrew (1964) speaks of a self-fulfilling prophecy: the opinion held about a population group influences the behavior shown to this group, and this behavior in turn provokes in the group the alleged behavior. For example, because negroes are held to be less intelligent, they do not need such good schools, and because they are not given such schools, they have less chance to develop and so stay less intelligent. It is clear that on the one hand opinions about others may be perfectly correct, but it is also clear that public opinion and the kinds of behavior resulting from it have a part in determining the behavior of the relevant group and thus bring their influence to bear on the social system.

(c) Whether a stereotype is appropriate is shown not only by its agreement with a fictitious "reality" but is dependent on the background to the judgment in a particular instance. For certain questions the precise knowledge of a certain subject may be necessary, for other questions it may be superfluous, indeed even confusing. It is certain that everyone must generalize, for events or persons do not return in all their detail, but as long as we cannot discern any repetitions, we cannot plan for the future and anticipate it (Brown, 1965). How sharply individual objects are to be delineated must therefore be determined by the aims of the individual concerned. In an extreme case a stereotype alone may be taken as a justification for the oppression of a certain social group; then very different evaluations are possible, depending on whether one thinks of the appropriateness to reality of the judgment or of the element of justification it possesses.

Empirical statistical studies as a rule are based predominantly on the approach of group psychology (Katz & Braly, 1933; Gilbert, 1951; Buchanan, 1953; Sodhi & Bergius, 1953), which has nevertheless been heavily criticized.

(a) Eysenck (1950) showed (from a study on the lines of the classical work of Katz & Braly, 1933) that many subjects admit they only repeat clichés which do not represent their own opinion. And, in fact, even when a certain group are agreed about what they say, this cannot be taken as a proof that the corresponding judgment is widely shared.

(b) As Asch (1968) showed, an inquiry does not lead to any unequivocal pronouncement. It may be that the pronouncement is based on all the members of the category; it may, however, for example, be based only on a higher percentage of the group in some particular respect. See *Prejudice; Attitude.*

Bibliography: Allport, G. W.: The nature of prejudice. Boston, 1955. **Asch, S. E.:** Social psychology. Englewood Cliffs, [8]1965. **Brown, R.:** Social psychology. New York, 1965. **Buchanan, W. & Cantril, H.:** How nations see each other. Urbana, 1953. **Duiker, H. & Frijda, N.:** National character and national stereotype. Amsterdam, 1960. **Eysenck, H. J. & Crown, S.:** National stereotype: an experimental and methodological study. Int. J. Opinion Attitude Res., 1948, 2. **Eysenck, H. J.:** War and aggressiveness. In: Pear, T. H. (Ed.): Psychological factors of peace and war. London, 1950. **Gilbert, G. M.:** Stereotype persistence and change among college students. J. Hbn. Soc. Psychol., 1951, 46. **Hilgard, E. R. & Atkinson, R. C.:** Introduction to psychology. New York, [4]1967. **Hofstätter, P. R.:** Einführung in die Sozialpsychologie. Stuttgart, 1966. **Jahoda, M.:** Stereotype. In: Gould, J. & Kolb, W. L. (Eds.): A dictionary of the social sciences. New York, [3]1965. **Katz, D. & Braly, K. W.:** Racial stereotypes of one hundred college students. J. Abn. Soc. Psychol., 1933, 28. **Katz, D. & Stotland, E.:** A preliminary statement to a theory of attitude structure and change. In: Koch, S. (Ed.): Psychology: A study of a science. Vol. 3, 1959. **Lindgren, H. C.:** Psychology of personal development. New York, [2]1969. **Lippmann, W.:** Public opinion. New York, 1922. **McDavid, J. W. & Harari, H.:** Social psychology. New York, 1968. **Morgan, C. T. & King, R. A.:** Introduction to psychology. New York, [3]1966. **Rice, S. A.:** Stereotypes: a source of error in judging human characters. J. Pers. Res., 5, 1926. **Sherif, M. & Sherif, C. W.:** Social psychology. New York & London, 1969. **Sodhi, Bergius:** Nationale Vorurteile. Berlin, 1953. **Wells, W. D., Goi, F. J. & Seader, S. A.:** A change in a product image. J. Appl. Psychol., 1958, 42. **Shuey, A. M.**: The testing of Negro intelligence. Lynchburg, 1958. **Pettigrew, T. F.**: A profile of the Negro American. Princeton, 1964.   *J. Schenk*

Sterilization. 1. Making aseptic. Freeing a part of the environment of bacteria and other living matter.

2. Rendering an organism incapable of sexual reproduction on a more or less permanent basis, usually by means of surgical intervention (cf. *contraception*). The most simple methods currently employed are *vasectomy* (cutting and tying the vas deferens in males) and *salpingectomy* (tying the fallopian tubes in females), but *castration* (removal of the gonads, particularly the testes) and *hysterectomy* (removal of the uterus) also prevent reproduction. Only the first two of these methods are ever used as *birth control* techniques with humans: neither interferes to any degree with sexual performance or enjoyment.
                                                                        G.D.W.

Stern, William Louis. B. 29/4/1871 in Berlin; d. 27/3/1938, in Durham (North Carolina). Stern studied in Berlin, became a lecturer in Breslau and was a university reader until 1916. But it was Hamburg which he made into a center for psychological research. In 1916 he succeeded Wundt's (q.v.) pupil E. Meumann at the Hamburg Lecture Institute, was one of those most active in founding Hamburg University in 1919, set up the Psychological Department and Laboratory of Hamburg University (which in 1930 became the Psychological Institute of Hamburg University) and was its director until 1933. Then he was obliged because of racial persecution to emigrate to the USA; he lectured at Harvard and Duke universities.

Works. Stern was one of the great pioneers of modern psychology. His work in three volumes *Person und Sache* (1916, 1918, 1924) was, as its enlarged title *"System der philosophischen*

Weltanschauung" says, primarily philosophical in essence, but formed the basis of his psychological thought; his *Allgemeine Psychologie auf personalistischer Grundlage* (1935) is proof of this. Stern attempted a synthesis of experimental and academic psychology, and defined psychology, in contrast to behaviorism (q.v.), as "the science of the individual as he experiences and is capable of experiencing", made a vital contribution with his theory of personalism to the solution of the problem of mind and mind-body (q.v.), disposed finally of "capability theory" with his concept of tendency, decided the problem of nature and nurture with his theory of convergence (q.v.), and built a bridge between elementarism and the theory of wholes, between natural science and philosophy. No less outstanding were his pioneer achievements in other departments of psychology; he was the founder of *Differentielle Psychologie* (1900, 1911); the term "intelligence quotient" (see IQ) was invented by Stern. Together with C. Stern he initiated research into developmental psychology with his study of child language (*Die Kindersprache*) 1907, and his psychology of early childhood (*Psychologie der frühen Kindheit*), 1914. Stern is regarded as the founder of applied psychology (q.v.): his two volumes *Beiträge zur Psychologie der Aussage* (Contributions to the Psychology of Testimony) 1903, belong to the history of the foundation of forensic psychology (q.v.); he advanced the cause of educational psychology (q.v.) by collaborating in the *Zeitschrift für pädagogische Psychologie* (joint editor, 1916) and the cause of the psychology of occupational and vocational by editing in part the *Schriften zur Psychologie der Berufseignung und des Wirtschaftslebens* (documents on the psychology of vocational aptitude and careers in industry), 1918.

Bibliography: Stern, W.: Selbstdarstellung. In: **Schmidt, R.** (Ed.): Die Philosophie in Selbstdarstellungen. Vol. 6, 1927; Das Psychologische Institut der Hamburgischen Universität in seiner gegenwärtigen

Gestalt. Leipzig, 1931. William Stern: Festschrift. Leipzig, 1931. **Stern-Anders, G.:** Bild meines Vaters und. **Cassirer, E.:** William Stern. In: Stern, W. (Ed.): Allgemeine Psychologie. The Hague, ²1950. **Pongratz, L. J.:** Problemgeschichte der Psychologie. Berne & Munich, 1967, 43 ff., 65 ff.   *L.J.P.*

STH. Abb. for *somatotropic hormone* (q.v.).

Sthenic type. "A predominant feeling of superiority, power, mastery and energy, a tendency to arrogance, activity, ruthlessness, aggressiveness." Conflicts are tackled head on. Ant.: *asthenic* (q.v.).   *W.K.*

Sthenoplastic type. Thin, fragile organism (see *Leptosome*).   *W.K.*

Stigma. *A general functional disorder* of the circulation or of certain organs, caused by an abnormal sensitivity and eccentricity of the autonomic nervous system (e.g. tendency to faint) and by hysterical reactions (anesthesia, paralysis, convulsions, etc.).

Stigmatization: special hysterical reactions in the shape of certain visible markings on the body (e.g. cutaneous hemorrhage), which often appear as an indication of identification—in Christian cultural circles with the crucified Christ and his stigmata—and are considered by believers to be of supernatural origin (e.g. in the case of saints).

Bibliography: Biot, R.: Das Rätsel der Stigmatisierten. Aschaffenburg, 1957.   *F.-C.S.*

Stilling test; Stilling charts. Devised by J. Stilling, an ophthalmologist in Strasbourg. Stilling-Hertel or Isihara charts are used to test color sensitivity in the normal eye. *K.H.P.*

Stimulants. Psychotropic drugs with a generally *activating effect*: they are *subjectively animating, tend to postpone sleep*, and usually *improve psychophysical performance*. Unlike the gradual and long-lasting effects of neurodynamics (q.v.), the effects of stimulants are rapid in onset, and limited to so many hours. When higher doses of stimulants are taken, appetite declines, tremor increases and longer sleeplessness can be induced. Chronic ingestion can lead to dependence (see *Drug dependence*) and psychotic states. Overdoses act to some extent like convulsive poisons. Stimulants possess a chemically diverse structure and are therefore difficult to classify; amphetamines (q.v.) are the most important group: e.g. methamphetamine hydrochloride = Desoxyn, Methedrine, Pervitin, etc., amphetamine sulfate = Benzedrine. Individual substances in other groups are: pemoline, caffeine (q.v.), methylphenidate hydrochloride (Ritalin), phenmetrazine hydrochloride (Preludin). Stimulants affect the central nervous system variously. Many stimulants also have effects on the autonomic nervous system (see *Psychopharmaceuticals and the ANS*); in this case the relationship of psychological to peripheral-autonomic effects varies considerably. Preparations whose main effects are on circulation and breathing are known as "analeptics" (q.v.). Substances which have a stimulating effect on the central nervous system but a convulsive effect even in relatively small doses (e.g. strychnine), are not counted as psychostimulants. Stimulants were used therapeutically before the development of antidepressives to improve mood and increase the motivation of depressive patients suffering from depression. They are now used mainly by healthy people to improve performance acutely (e.g. as a means of "doping") and temporarily to suppress fatigue and sleep, or to curb appetite. Psychological tests using stimulants (e.g. caffeine) were often carried out in the early stages of psychopharmacology (q.v.), but less after the development of antipsychotic and antineurotic drugs; they are now becoming useful again in research into learning and memory (see *Psychopharmacology*). Results in healthy people after one dose: mainly subjective activation; improvement of mood; feeling of improved performance, even when that is not so objectively (overestimation of one's own performance); in the sensorimotor field, effects are diverse. Activation is most clearly evident in purely sensory activities (e.g. flicker fusion frequency, afterimage sensitivity. The greater the degree of requisite motor security (e.g. steadiness of the hand), and the higher the dosage, the less performance is improved and the more it declines. The effects of stimulants depend on S.'s condition before administration, and particularly on the degree of previous stress and the amount of sleep deprivation (see *Sleep*). But they seem to be less dependent on habitual personality traits than the effects of tranquilizers (q.v.) and neuroleptics (q.v.). (See *Differential psychopharmacology*.)

Bibliography: Ehlers, T.: Zur quantitativen Differenzierung pharmakonbedingter Leistungsmotiviertheit. Arztneimittelforsch., 1966, *16*, 306–8. Wenzel, D. G. & Rutledge, C.: Effects of centrally acting drugs on human motor and psychomotor performance. J. Pharmaceut. Sci., 1962, *51*, 631–44.   K.-D.S.

Stimulation. The effect of an internal or external stimulus in activating the nervous system. The additional stimulation of the brain by micro-electrodes is sometimes used as an independent variable in learning experiments.   *H.Ro.*

Stimulus (Ger. *Reiz*). A variation in physical energy inside or outside an organism capable of influencing the afferent nervous system through receptors (when appropriate receptors exist), or (more narrowly defined) which activates a receptor (*stimulus transformation*). If the difference between these definitions is ignored, and it is assumed that a sensation must correspond to every external stimulus, a source of error (*stimulus error*) is present in

investigations. The entire process from the activation of a receptor up to sensation is *stimulus processing*. To activate a receptor the stimulus must be between *stimulus intensity thresholds* and within *stimulus quality thresholds*. *Stimulus generalization* occurs when a conditioned response does not clearly succeed a narrowly defined stimulus intensity but a specific area on the stimulus continuum; *stimulus response generalization*, on the other hand, occurs when every stimulus of a distinct area of the stimulus continuum can evoke a specific response from an area of similar responses. If an individual stimulus is insufficient to release a sensation or a reflex, stimulation repeated over a certain period of time, or a combination of individual stimuli in the sense of *stimulus summation*, finally sets off the process. However, a diminished stimulus effect can occur by reason of *stimulus habituation* arising from, e.g., repeated presentation. (See *Arousal; Nervous system; Learning; Conditioning, classical and operant*.)

H.Ro.

Stimulus conduction. The transmission of excitation from a receptor; arousal (q.v.).

Stimulus continuum. A hierarchical series of stimuli.

Stimulus sensation. See *Selective perception*.

Stimulus summation rule. Dummy experiments show that external and internal stimuli and excitations are calculated equivalently. Hence, given a state of acute readiness, minor external stimuli, such as dummies with a reduced number of apparent features, suffice for a response to be given. Movement seldom improves ineffective dummies significantly. The precise mode of calculation is unknown, but it is not a question of simple summation.

Bibliography: Seitz, A.: Die Paarbildung bei einigen Cichliden I. Z. Tierpsychol., 1940, *4*, 40–84. **Tinbergen,** N.: The study of instinct. London, ²1969. *K.Fi.*

Stimulus word. A word requiring a response and presented acoustically or optically to S.

Stochastic dependence. The connection between two or more random variables. An investigation of stochastic dependence will lead to regression and correlational analysis. Two random events A and B are stochastically independent if the probability of their incidence is: $P(AB) = P(A)P(B)$. See *Correlational techniques.* *A.R.*

Stochastic process. A process is stochastic when the sequence of events or procedures is governed by laws of probability. The events may be stochastically independent (e.g. radioactive decay) or stochastically dependent (e.g. the probability of a consonant occurring after a vowel). In communications theory the production of symbol sequences is analyzed by a stochastic process. Sequences of signs in which each sign preceding *r* codetermines the probability of the following sign constitute a Markov-chain *r* order. In 1913, A. Markov made statistical studies of associations of letters in printed texts. Letter sequences, like word sequences, are brought about by syntactic or semantic associations. Stochastic processes are characteristic of stochastic automata, whose behavior is not determined solely by momentary condition and input signals, so that output signals are determined to a greater or lesser extent by random processes. If no part is played by random processes, the stochastic automaton becomes a determined automaton. The theory of stochastic processes and of stochastic automata concerns psychology inasmuch as it allows models to be constructed which approximate behavioral

phenomena. See *Communication; Correlational techniques; Information theory; Machine learning.* *K.W.*

Storage capacity. The maximum input capacity of a store (q.v.) is expressed in terms of the storage (the number of words or "bits") it can accommodate. *B.R.*

Store; storage. A store retains information for recall. Its function corresponds to that of memory (q.v.).

Analogue storage is distinguished from *digital* storage. In the former, items of information are preserved as analogue measurement values, in the latter as series of digits. Punched cards and strips represent *permanent* storage. After verification their contents can no longer be changed. The contents of impermanent storage media can be changed. *B.R.*

Strain. 1. In general, a process in a biological system accompanying any changed stability in relation to the maximum stability of that system (stress). **2.** In a narrower sense, a biological process which may be experienced as psychic tension and is manifested physiologically in vegetative tonus in connection with response to particular psychic demands. Psychic strain is sometimes understood more in the sense of response to a specific demand, and sometimes as a state of fatigue (q.v.) in the sense of a debilitation of powers and functions. Investigations suggest that biological systems tend to avoid prolonged over- as well as under-strain. Apart from use to refer generally to tension in or injury to a muscle or joint, the term is, however, restricted to popular usage. See *Stress.* *J.N.*

Strata theory (syn. *Layer theory; Levels of personality theory*). The strata concept was introduced into psychology in about 1920. It follows the principle of the Platonic theory of the mind, according to which the *logos* is associated with the head, the *thymos* ("heart") with the breast, and the *epithymia* (desire) with the abdomen. As early as 1916, Scheler (1923) distinguished (in reverse order) a *vital* or *body stratum*, a *psychovital stratum of emotions* and aspirations, and a stratum of *intellectual activities*. Freud (q.v.) tended not to use this image of "strata" or "layers", yet in his demarcation of a *sub*conscious, and not simply an *unconscious*, he implicitly postulated a layer theory (see *Id; Ego*). Klages, again not explicitly a strata theorist, adopted a similar approach. Kraus of Vienna (1926) postulated the existence of two personalities in one: the "*depth personality*" (born of the genetically older, "more original" "sectors" of the central nervous system) and the "*cortical personality*" (controlled by the genetically recent central nervous area, the cortex). In his theory of the character and person (after Plato), Lersch (1966) united the approaches of Scheler, Kraus and Freud and opposed the "endothymic basis" (q.v.) to the "noetic" or (more broadly conceived) the "personal superstructure" (1942). Later (1951), like Scheler, he added another "*vital basis*" beneath the "endothymic basis". The theory of stratification (analogously with geology) was taken to an extreme by Scheler's pupil Rothacker (1938), who based his approach mainly on Kraus's "dual personality". Rothacker divided the "depth personality" into "life-in-me", "animal-in-me", "child-in-me", and an emotional layer; the "cortical person" into a person or character layer, and an ego layer, the latter being a mere organizational center, expressed as an "ego point". Rothacker stressed his belief that stratification represents a developmental process in which the personality's early stages are not dissolved or replaced by later phases, but are superimposed upon, and effectively retained. Correspondingly, the "deep personality" (the "id", the "uncon-

scious") must be regarded "as an independent creature, which, though 'below' higher centers, is in many cases directly expressed in the behavior of the whole person". On this supposition, Rothacker's theory (as he admits) conflicts with the hypothesis of the unity or wholeness of the personality.

Strata theory in these more recent formulations is partly accepted by such American authors as G. W. Allport and A. Gilbert. A. Wellek pointed out in 1941 that the image of a stratified pattern of personality must not be related unequivocally and unilaterally to the analogy of earth stratification, but to that of an onion (onion skin model): the "deep" layers ought to be called "*primitive layers*", and—if the term "person(ality)" were to be used at all—"*primitive person(ality)*" would be more appropriate. This term has been used by L. Holzschuher as the basis of a theoretical and "practical psychology" in which both the "deep" and the "primitive" person(alities) are invoked.

Wellek emphasized a "core character" or "kernel of personality" corresponding to the onion model, and divided it into four areas: *disposition (Gemüt)*, conscience, *refined intuition (Gespür)* and *taste*. The "existence" of such "nuclei" is, according to him, demonstrated by the fact of a "character barrier" observable in hypnosis experiments when a conflict occurs between hypnotist and hypnotized, and the latter reacts to a suggestion that his "character" finds unacceptable (particularly one that is criminal or distasteful), by breaking even the most profound rapport. The existence of "disposition" cannot be wholly comprised in the statement that man "lives from" a deep or primitive personality; it is not a matter of the "higher life of the mind" in any quasi-vertical sense. The personality condition described as "heartlessness" or coldness of disposition signifies neither a lack of cortical control nor a lack of emotionality. For example, in the case of a murderer neither the "deep" person(ality) nor the cortical person(ality) is to be held responsible: i.e. there is no lack of control (which may on the contrary be superbly exercised, as in the case of malice), or of emotionality, not to mention still "deeper", i.e. lower, "strata". Affects in particular can "simmer", so to speak, "under the surface" of an apparently "cold" individual, who may be touchy, mistrustful, envious, jealous, prestige-conscious, spiteful, irascible and even—in certain circumstances—sentimental. When viewed as "stratified" in the conventional (one-dimensional) sense, such people (especially the insignificant petty criminal—can seem quite "all right". The inadequacy—the "gap" in the structure—does not appear in the simplistic schema.

In double stratification it is a question not only of two (or more) different strata, but of two further diverse dimensions: double stratification is "two-dimensional", i.e. "vertical-horizontal". "Superstructure", "animation", "intensification" and "profundity" depend on the "disposition", or "core", of personality. This is to be understood not only on the level of individual psychology but in terms of social structures. Like most other strata theorists, Rothacker tends to identify deep (i.e. primitive) strata with the "unconscious" (q.v.). Admittedly, in Rothacker's, and certainly in Scheler's sense, the "deep layers" are less precise and less conscious; in many ways consciousness is even inimical to them, as—above all—in Freud's theory. But this does not apply to the "core": disposition (as well as conscience and taste: both are connected with temperament) is a consciously protected and respected area in a well-formed personality. Disposition and refined intuition, however, are to some extent comprised functionally in Rothacker's "deep areas", e.g. in the "need for tenderness".

On the other hand, lower strata or layers are not in a position to formulate "prospective" intentions but only to take them over and carry them out at an appointed time. The locus of intention is that of *insight:* the ego

(q.v.). As an interpretative model, "strata theory" has nevertheless been useful in many ways. By this method authentic and spurious expression (q.v.) and character have been traced by Lersch to agreement or disagreement between basis and superstructure, and by Wellek to accord or lack of it between core and casing, depths and surface. In addition, the concept of *identity* in recent American theories presupposes the stratification or even reconciliation of conscious and subconscious, though not in the sense of "pure" strata theory. A. Gilbert does adopt a stratification concept in his "*stratification discrepancy*", which is alleged to correspond to neuroticism (q.v.).

The present position of strata theory in regard to personality (q.v.) may be summarized as follows:

(*a*) Strata theory is a *genetic* theory: the strata develop out of one another.

(*b*) There are two basically different concepts of "depth" in use. The only legitimate candidate is the older one, which intends a "core" or "kernel" model.

(*c*) Equal attention to both dimensions of "depth" leads to a so to speak "two-dimensional" stratum uniting the *vertical* and the *horizontal.*

(*d*) A merely one-dimensional, "vertical" arrangement does not accord with the complexity of personality and its most decisive aspects.

(*e*) The conventional theory of a "deep person(ality)" confuses aspects of vertical and horizontal stratification.

(*f*) The (supposed) depth of a deep, i.e. primitive, person(ality) is *not identical* with the *unconscious.* The primitive layers and their functions may be conscious, and the high (like the core) layers and their functions may be unconscious.

(*g*) The "cortical person" is active even in deep hypnosis (as in deep sleep).

(*h*) It would seem to be unanimously accepted among "strata theorists" that the concept of a "stratum" or "layer" is an image of restricted applicability. See *Depth psychology; Dream; Consciousness; Traits; Type.*

Bibliography: David, H. P. & Bracken, H. von (Eds.): Perspectives in personality theory. New York, 1957. Gilbert, A. R.: On the stratification of personality. In: David & Bracken, *op. cit.*, 218–41. Kraus, F.: Allgemeine und spezielle Pathologie der Person, II. Leipzig, 1926. Lersch, P : Aufbau der Person. München, [11]1966. Id : The levels of the mind. In: David & Bracken, *op. cit.*, 212–7. Rothacker, E.: Die Schichten der Persönlichkeit. Leipzig, [2]1941. Scheler, M.: Wesen und Formen der Sympathie. Bonn, 1923. Wellek, A.: Die Polarität im Aufbau des Charakters. Berne, [3]1966. *A. Wellek*

Stratton's experiment. 1. A classical experiment on perceptual learning conducted by G. E. Stratton, using himself as subject. For many days he went about wearing a pair of spectacles which inverted the visual world. One of the most remarkable findings was that as he began to reorient himself and regain visual-motor coordination, he reached a stage when the world no longer looked upside-down. When he eventually removed the spectacles he experienced a certain degree of disorientation again. Stratton's technique has since been widely adopted as an approach to the investigation of the developmental basis of perception. *G.D.W.*

2. The spectacles experiment as a method is described by Kohler (1951, 1956) In general, it consists of the transformation of visual signals by optical means (lenses, mirrors, prisms, color filters, etc.). The optical media are maintained for relatively a long time in front of the eyes by means of spectacles. The state of perception (q.v.) and behavior while looking through the spectacles (acquisition of new constancy standards), and for a brief period while looking without spectacles (negative aftereffects, spectacle effects), are observed and measured. A distinction is made between the experiment in which spectacles are worn continuously for days and weeks, while the subject goes about his affairs, and that in which habituation varies from a few minutes to several hours in a controlled stimulus situation According to the nature of the questioning, a spectacles experiment can be a reaction experiment (the criterion of observation and measurement is the improvement in the testee's sensorimotor behavior), or a perception experiment (acquired perceptual constancy), or both. Since the nineteen fifties, spectacles methods have been applied to new problems: sensorimotor coordinations (Held, 1962), problems of form and figure perception (Kohler, 1951; Hajos, 1965), etc.; major contributions have been made to perception theory, and a bridge has been built between perception research and biological and biocybernetic models (e.g., reafference principle, q.v., homoeostasis models, etc.).

Bibliography: Hajos, A.: Nacheffekte unter kovariierenden Reizbedingungen und deren interoculare und intersensorische Auswirkungen. In: Heckhausen, H. (Ed.) Bericht 24. Kongress Deutscher Gestalt Psychologen. Göttingen, 1965. Held, R.: Adaptation to rearrangement and visual-spatial aftereffects. Psychol. Beitr. 1962, *6*, 439–50. Helmholtz, H. von: Handbuch der Physiologischen Optik, Vol. 3. Leipzig, 1910. Kohler, I.: Über Aufbau und Wandlungen der Wahrnehmungswelt. Österreichische Akademie der Wissenschaften: philosophisch-historische Klasse 227/1. Vienna, 1951, 1–118. Id.: Der Brillenversuch in der Wahrnehmungswelt mit Bemerkungen zur Lehre von der Adaption. Zeitschrift experimenteller und angewandter Psychologie, 1956, *3*, 381–417. Id.: Interne und externe Organization in der Wahrnehmung. Psychol. Beitr., 1962, *8*, 259–64. Stratton, G. M.: Upright vision and the retinal image. Psychol. Rev., 1897, *4*, 182–7. *A.Ha.*

Stream of consciousness. Experiences, recollections, feelings, aspirations, fancies, etc., seem to the individual to be a "stream" which, in the last resort, is independent of him. James calls this the "stream of consciousness".

Bibliography: James, W.: The principles of psychology. *V.M.*

Stress. The term "stress" has been widely and indiscriminately used; its most precise definition is that of Selye (1950). He restricts the concept of stress to a characteristic physiological response, differentiating this from "stressors"—the agents which produce stress.

This bodily reaction is manifested through the symptoms of a general adaptation syndrome. When the stress is prolonged, the syndrome typically includes three stages: (*a*) an alarm reaction, including an initial shock phase of lowered resistance and a countershock phase, in which defensive mechanisms begin to operate; (*b*) a stage of resistance in which adaptation is optimal; and (*c*) a stage of exhaustion, marked by the collapse of the adaptive response.

The features of this reaction are organized around the pituitary-adrenal cortical axis. Selye describes the triad of the alarm reaction as enlargement of the adrenals, shrinkage of the thymus and lymph nodes, and gastrointestinal ulceration.

This, like Cannon's earlier proposal of a sympathetic nervous system/adrenal medulla stress reaction (Cannon, 1932), was made within the concept of systemic equilibration. The general effect of the stress syndrome appears to be the modification of bodily processes so as to make available the energy resources normally kept in reserve or used for other functions such as digestion or anabolism (Cofer & Appley, 1964). Selye describes antecedents of the stress concept in the Hippocratic view of disease not only as suffering but as toil: the fight of the body to restore itself. A recurring theme is a finite amount of "adaptation energy" which gets "used up" (Selye, 1950); or physiological and psychological integrative capacities which are taxed to the limit (Basowitz *et al.*, 1955).

The nature of pituitary-adrenal involvement has been much debated, and the physiological (hormonal, metabolic, and so on) mechanisms involved in the stress reaction have been extensively investigated (Goldstein & Ramey, 1957; Oken, 1967).

Attempts to extend Selye's idea of systemic stress to include psychological aspects have met with many problems. Firstly, the nature of stressors is very different: Selye discussed such systemic stressor agents as heat, cold, infections, intoxicants, injury, shock, and surgical trauma. The range of psychological stressors is so wide as to be virtually endless. Cofer & Appley argue that these are effective only when they threaten the life or integrity of the individual exposed to them. They offer a definition of stress as "the state of an organism when he perceives that his well-being (or integrity) is endangered and that he must elevate all of his energies to its protection" (Cofer & Appley, 1964, p. 453).

Secondly, the nature of the physiological reaction is not now seen as a general, well-defined pattern. The results of decades of research suggest that individual differences, styles, patterns of response and pre-potent tendencies lead to idiosyncratic response patterns. These may relate to inherited responsivity (for example, of the sympathetic nervous system [Eysenck, 1967]) and possibly to various personality characteristics which determine stress thresholds and stress tolerance.

Central issues in psychological stress are the conditions and processes (*a*) that lead the individual to differentiate between benign and damaging conditions, and (*b*) that determine the kind of coping behavior which ensues. Recent analyses emphasize the role of cognitive appraisal (Lazarus, 1966). Once a stimulus has been appraised as threatening, various methods of coping are adopted. Pribram (1967) has suggested that cognitive re-evaluation may obviate the necessity for overt behavioral adjustment: that is, an individual's appraisal of the situation can reduce the stress reaction.

When examined in a psychological context, the stress reaction must therefore take account of complex cognitive processes as well as physiological reactions, and feedback from the effects of these reactions. In such circumstances it is difficult to retain Selye's clear though perhaps over-simplified view of stress, and of late the meaning of the term has tended to widen again. For example it is often undifferentiated from anxiety, conflict, emotion, frustration, and arousal (q.v.).

Perhaps some order could be restored if more attention were paid to the time course of the physiological reactions, and to the original implication of a balance between catabolic and anabolic processes. We should discriminate between the immediate physiological disturbance produced by a stimulus, and a chronic, long-term stress reaction where basic physiological changes are produced which result in a detrimental shift in equilibratory processes. Psychological stresses of an inescapable kind may lead to a sustained stress reaction eventuating in tissue damage, disruption of adreno-cortical functioning, and psychosomatic disorder. This type of reaction differs from a neurotic reaction in which sustained tissue damage is avoided by some behavioral solution—for example, the use of escape mechanisms.

Bibliography: Basowitz, H., Persky, H., Korchin, S. J. & Grinker, R. R.: Anxiety and stress. New York, 1955. Cannon, W. B.: The wisdom of the body. New York, 1932. Cofer, C. N. & Appley, N. H.: Frustration, conflict, and stress. In: Motivation: theory and research. New York, 1964, 412–65. Eysenck, H. J.: Biological basis of personality. Springfield, 1967. Goldstein, M. S. & Ramey, E. R.: Nonendocrine aspects of stress. Perspectives in Biol. & Med., 1957, *1*, 33–47. Lazarus, R. S.: Psychological stress and the coping process. New York, 1966. Oken, D.: The psychophysiology and psychoendocrinology of stress and emotion. In: Appley, M. H. & Trumbull, R. (Eds.): Psychological stress. Issues in Research. New York, 1967. Pribram, K. H.: The new neurology and the biology of emotion. A structural approach. Amer. Psychol., 1967, *22*, 830–8. Selye, H.: Stress. Montreal, 1950. *I. Martin*

Stress type. This type burdens the ego (q.v.) aspect of consciousness with slow or stubborn objection, especially noticeable in schizothymes. *W.K.*

Striate body (syn. *Corpus striatum*). A term applied collectively to the *nucleus lentiformis* (lenticular nucleus) and its parts, the *putamen* and *globus pallidus*, and the *nucleus caudatus* (caudate nucleus), all of which form part of the brainstem (q.v.). *E.D.*

Strivings (syn. *Aspirations*). According to Lersch (1954), "strivings" are human drives originating in the "endothymic basis" (q.v.) and directed to the attainment of definite aims; thus they are not indefinite instinctual impulses. Lersch speaks of strivings as the highest degree of drive experience. See *Strata theory*.

Bibliography: Lersch, P.: Aufbau der Person. Munich, ²1962. *B.H.*

Stroboscope. An instrument for producing and observing *stroboscopic effects*, i.e. illusions of movement resulting from intermittent stimulus exposure such as that produced by a light flashing on and off. The most familiar example of this effect is that seen in Western movies when the wheels of a wagon are perceived to be moving backward. This occurs because the interval between successive picture-frame exposures is of such a length that each new position of the spokes is more parsimoniously seen as just behind the previous one, rather than in front of it. The stroboscopic effect can be employed as an indicator of the speed of rotation of an object, e.g. the ring of radial stripes surrounding the labels of some gramophone records which provide a check on the turntable speed. *G.D.W.*

Strong Vocational Interest Blank. One of the most widely used American *tests of vocational interests*, the 399 items of which (careers, preferences, career-related activities, etc.) have to be answered, chiefly along the lines of like-dislike, or to be placed in order of preference, after which they are evaluated diagnostically on the basis of their correlation with the relative answer requirements of a large number of different career groups.

Bibliography: Strong, E. K. & Campbell, D. P.: Manual for Strong Vocational Interest Blanks. Stanford, 1966. *H.H.*

Stroop word-color test. See *Color-word test.*

Structuralism. 1. Any theory (e.g. *strata theory*, q.v.) which conceives mind or personality in terms of its structure (q.v.). **2.** Atomism (q.v.). **3.** Gestalt psychology. **4.** A science of signs, and of systems of signs (see *Semantics; Sign and symbol*). **5.** The study of that which has a systematic nature: of any whole, one element of which cannot be altered without bringing about an alteration in all the other elements (see *Ganzheit*).

Bibliography: Ducrot, O., Qu'est-ce que le structuralisme? Paris, 1968. Lévi-Strauss, C.: Structural anthropology. New York, 1963. Piaget, J.: Structuralism. New York & London, 1971. *J.G.*

Structure. The underlying organization of components. Structure usually refers to the relationship between the components that make up some complex stimulus. These relationships are independent of the nature of the component parts: e.g. a melody has the same structure even if played in different keys. The concept of structure is central to gestalt psychology, since it emphasizes the organization of complex wholes rather than their component parts in isolation. Structure in its more general sense is also used in other areas of psychology, e.g. personality and memory. See *Ganzheit; Strata theory.* *C.D.F.*

Strychnine. A substance which stimulates circulation and breathing; an alkaloid, obtained from the seeds of *nux vomica*, it produces convulsions when taken in large doses. Because of this danger, strychnine is of very restricted therapeutic value. It has a strongly exciting action on the central nervous system, probably because it blocks inhibition systems. Recently it has been shown that strychnine, administered in subconvulsive doses, improves the retention performance of rats, but so far the mechanism of these improvements in memory has not been explained.

Bibliography: Dusser de Barenne, J. G.: Mode and site of action of strychnine in nervous system. Physiol. Rev., 1933, *13*, 325–35. McGaugh, J.: Drug facilitation of memory and learning. In: Efron, D. (Ed.): Psychopharmacology, 1957–1967. Washington, 1968. *W. Janke*

Study of values. A method devised by G. W. Allport and P. E. Vernon in 1931 to cover the range of interests, attitudes and values to be found in an individual. The test is based on the value philosophy of E. Spranger (life forms, 1925) with its six *a priori* value areas: theoretical, social, economic, political, esthetic and religious. The test consists of two parts with thirty or fifteen alternative or multiple choice questions. The six test scores, which can be combined to form a profile are interpreted according to standardized norms. The test-retest reliability ranges from $r = 0.84$ to $r = 0.93$. *Pointers of validity* are: the clear discrimination of selected careers by the test and successful predictions of the behavior of individuals in different tests.

Bibliography: Allport, G. W., Vernon, P. E. & Lindzey, G.: Study of values. Boston, 1960. *P.G.*

Stumpf, Carl. B. 21/4/1848 in Wiesentheid; d. 25/12/1936 in Berlin. Stumpf studied philosophy under Brentano (q.v.) in Würzburg and Lotze in Göttingen; he received his doctorate in Göttingen in 1868, was a lecturer in Göttingen from 1870 to 1873, and from then on held the following posts: 1873, professor in

Würzburg; 1879, professor of philosophy in Prague; 1884, in Halle; 1889, in Munich; from 1894 to 1921, in Berlin. In Berlin he founded the Psychological Institute of Berlin University, with F. Schumann and N. Ach as his assistants. When he retired in 1921, W. Köhler succeeded him in his Chair.

Stumpf was influenced by Brentano's act psychology (q.v.); his theoretical approach was directly opposed to that of Wundt (q.v.) and, together with Brentano, he ranks as the founder of *functional psychology*. He made a distinction between the act of hearing and the heard content. The study of functions was in his opinion the sole province of psychology, whereas the study of contents belonged more to phenomenology (q.v.). Going beyond Brentano, he subjected act psychology to experimentation for the first time. His functional approach was diametrically opposed to Wundt's emphasis on contents, and Stumpf was in continual conflict with Wundt. One such controversy was in regard to differing views of the nature of the introspective method (see *Introspection*).

Stumpf's most significant contributions to knowledge were in the field of the psychology of music (q.v.) and comparative musicology, which he may be considered to have established as a sub-discipline. He won special recognition for his treatise on the songs of the Bellakula Indians (*Lieder der Bellakula Indianer*, 1886), a pioneer study in comparative musicology, for his main two-volume work on the psychology of sound (*Tonpsychologie*, Leipzig, 1883–1890), and for his later work on the beginnings of music (*Die Anfänge der Musik*, Leipzig, 1911). His other contributions to psychology, however, are less important. He wrote, *inter alia*, a treatise on the psychological origin of the idea of space (1873), and he was responsible for a theory of emotion (q.v.), in which, proceeding from the James-Lange theory, he reduced the emotions to a special form of organic sensations—the "emotional sensations".

Among Stumpf's pupils (many of whom were opposed to his basic scientific position, which they criticized very strongly) were W. Köhler (q.v.), K. Koffka (q.v.), M. Wertheimer (q.v.), C. J. von Allesch, W. Poppelreuter and H. S. Langfeld.

Other writings: Psychologie und Erkenntnistheorie. Leipzig, 1891. Erscheinungen und psychische Funktionen. Leipzig, 1907. Die Sprachlaute: experimentellphonetische Untersuchungen nebst einem Anhang über Instrumental-Klänge. Berlin, 1926. Gefühl und Gefühlsempfindung. Berlin, 1928. Erkenntnislehre, Vols. 1, 2 (Ed. F. Stumpf). Leipzig, 1939–40.

Bibliography: Langfeld, H. S.: Carl Stumpf: 1848–1936. Amer. J. of Psychol., 1937, **49,** 316–20. **Murchison, C.** (Ed.): A history of psychology in autobiography. Vol. 1. Worcester, Mass. 1930, 389–441.
W.W.

Stupor. An inhibited or suppressed ability to respond due to psychic causes, although consciousness remains clear (and reflexes can be demonstrated). The most diverse inner states may underlie the external symptoms: apathy, inhibitions, terror; but there may also be a high degree of ambivalence and ambitendency. An "examination stupor" (see *Examination anxiety, neurotic*) is a recognized condition. Stuporous syndromes can be caused reactively or psychogenically, but they also occur in cases of brain diseases, epilepsy (q.v.), depression (q.v.), and schizophrenia (q.v.).   *A.Hi.*

Stuttering. A speech impediment, sometimes equated with *stammering*, but strictly consisting in the rapid repetition of consonants and vowels at the beginning of words. Believed to be strongly influenced by emotional factors if not entirely psychogenic in origin. The incidence of stuttering is considerably higher in males than females, and there is some evidence that it is also associated with right hemispheric cerebral dominance.   *G.D.W.*

Style. Mode of presentation. The term has a specific meaning in the "individual psychology" (q.v.) of Adler (q.v.), where "life-style" stands for the way feelings of inferiority are handled. Far-reaching attempts to rationalize personal style have been made only in regard to verbal style. E. Mittenecker attempted to develop the degree of perseveration of style as an instrument in clinical diagnosis. The use of computers to quantify stylistic characteristics in written tests has become a major feature of linguistic and literary research in recent years. See *Experimental esthetics; Literature and psychology; Music, psychology of.*

Bibliography: Wisbey, R. A. (Ed.) Uses of the computer in literary research. Cambridge, 1972. *B.H.*

S type. A characterization according to the typology elaborated by Jaensch (1929). The central concept is synesthesia (q.v.). It is a question of the simultaneous response of two senses to a single stimulus. "S" indicates an ability of this type to associate color and auditory impressions, i.e. to "hear" colors. Jaensch differentiates the "S type" from the "I type", or *integrated type* (q.v.), because of the more intense inner coherence in experience of the environment. The inner world dominates absolutely and is projected onto the outer world, hence the S type is also (as a "projective type") contrasted with the "receptive type" of the integrative series. *M.H.*

Subconscious. The subconscious is sometimes assumed to be identical with the "preconscious", and is then a part-system of the psyche (in addition to the system of "conscious" and "unconscious"). It includes all psychic contents, memories, motives and readiness to act which are (momentarily) not activated, but when required can always be reactivated. Unconscious psychic contents, on the other hand, can be activated only with difficulty and against the inner resistance of the person in question (Freud). The subconscious as the "co-consciousness" (Rohracher)—as a consciousness without an attention cathexis (Freud)—comprises those psychic contents which exist among already conscious contents and in cases of necessity are made conscious more readily than other subconscious contents. See *Consciousness; Unconscious; Depth psychology.*

Bibliography: Freud, S.: Introductory lectures on psycho-analysis. London, ²1959. *W.T.*

Subject (abb. S.). The person or animal upon whom the experiment is being conducted. The subject is not expected to benefit personally from any treatment applied in the course of the experiment; at least if he does so it is purely incidental. *G.D.W.*

Subjective colors. If the eye is stimulated by intermittent white light at a frequency of approximately five impulses per second, it begins to see colors which are not highly saturated, and which follow one another with a certain regularity. A similar phenomenon, but with brighter color tones, results when a color top with white and black sectors is rotated at a speed of about forty r.p.s., i.e. in the stage before fusion (colored flicker).

Bibliography: Cohen, J. & Gordon, D. A.: The Prevost–Fechner–Benham subjective colors. Psychol. Bull., 1949, *46*. *G.K.*

Subjective stage. In dream interpretation, according to Jung (q.v.), the elucidation of dream images and events as representations of factors and situations within the dreamer. *W.T.*

Sublimation. According to Sigmund Freud (q.v.) a psychic process; according to Anna Freud, an inner defense (q.v.) mechanism, by means of which more primitive and socially less acceptable forms of motive gratification are replaced and then further developed by socially more acceptable forms. Hence a dauber may become an artist, a dissector of toys a surgeon, or a bawler a singer. If sublimation is to mean something more than the process of uninterrupted motive differentiation and correction of this process by people in the environment, then demonstrably greater renunciations of motive gratifications must be linked with especially unusual forms or degrees of sublimation. In practice, proof of this is often not possible in cases where sublimation is said to be present. Sublimation is related to socialization (q.v.) and enculturation: "We believe that civilization has been built up, under the pressure of the struggle for existence, by sacrifices in gratification of the primitive impulses, and that it is to a greater extent for ever being re-created, as each individual, successively joining the community, repeats the sacrifice of his instinctive pleasures for the common good. The sexual are amongst the most important of the instinctive forces thus utilized . . ." (Freud, 1929).

Bibliography: Freud, A.: The ego and the mechanisms of defence. London, 1937. Freud, S.: Introductory lectures on psycho-analysis. London, ²1929. W.T.

Subliminal. Appertaining (e.g. "subliminal perception") to stimuli which cannot be perceived or distinguished under the given conditions; in particular, those which, though they cannot be consciously apprehended or named (e.g. because presented for too short a time), nevertheless give rise to either conscious or unconscious stimulus-specific effects.

Bibliography: McConnell, J. V. et al.: Subliminal stimulation: an overview. American Psychologist, 1958, 13, 239–42. W.H.

Substance. 1. *History of the substance problem.* From the time of the Greek philosophers of nature, various aspects of this problem have come to the forefront of discussion: the material element as a bearer of substance; motion, change and development, especially in regard to living creatures; the question of essence (*ousia*). In addition to the theory of substance, the history of philosophy also features a substrate (*substratum; hypokeimenon*) theory. Heraclitus (536–470 B.C.) wrote of a substrate-less succession of things, and thought of it as most clearly "embodied" in the consuming movement of fire. Parmenides (*c.* 6th century B.C.), on the other hand, distinguished being from consciousness and explained thinking and being as wholly identical. Descartes made a distinction between conscious and spatial substances; Locke, as an empiricist, declared substance to be unknowable; Kant used it as a category and allowed it a metaphysical character; and Fichte gave it a secondary position in his theory of ideas.

2. *Substance and substrate.* Wundt (q.v.) brought about a change in the conception of substance by subjecting it wholly to a natural-scientific treatment. In physics and chemistry the term is used for any kind of matter. Such material substances, whether atoms, molecules, or compounds, are always entities. In biochemistry, substances which are changed in cell metabolism under the influence of enzymes, are known as substrates. In psychology, the substrates of cerebral and nerve cells are the most important.

3. *Present situation.* Recently, substantial being in the inorganic, organic and mental spheres has been more closely related. Physics does not stop at the detection of elementary particles, whose real existence can be revealed by special methods, but is constantly intent on passing new limits—possible only in terms of ever smaller hypothetical particles. This is a search for "what lies behind things"—for substance.

Similarly, biochemistry looks for the elements of living substance. Modern gene research has revealed the fundamental significance of desoxyribonucleic acid (DNA) for the individual development of all forms of life, and hence as a supportive principle for biological and psychological occurrence. But, here too, it has proved necessary to look for further bases, since DNA, like any other chemical compound, comes to be only by virtue of energy. The search for a prime base constantly comes up against certain limits; hence in modern psychology the substance problem has been obscured though not resolved, for it persists existentially. Inasmuch as characteristics of the nervous substrate have been detected which go to explain certain personality traits, and these characteristics have a general character, both somatologically and psychologically, the substance problem recurs for both areas simultaneously. Recent findings of Soviet psychological research conducted by B. Teplov emphasize this: "Whereas Pavlovian psychology postulated three main characteristics of the nervous system, i.e. intensity, mobility and equilibrium, with excitation and inhibition processes", recently the dominant conception has been that of an "equilibrium of the excitation and inhibition process as a relationship of two intensity characteristics of the nervous substrate". This "nervous substrate" is seen as a psychophysiological model of personality (q.v.); the characteristics of intensity, mobility and equilibrium are ascribed to it.

Independently of this Soviet research, in 1970 W. Arnold published a formula that arrived at the same basic factors in the motivational sphere: emotional tension (E), motivational intensity (I), inhibition (R). This gives the formula $I = E/R$, which is demonstrable in various modalities. The fact that these three factors tend in the same direction (and even coincide nominally) in neuropsychological research, i.e. empirically, and in theoretical considerations based on psychophysics (q.v.), allows one to suggest that the different scientific aspects derive from one and the same substantial unity and whole, which has specific rules within one and the same ordered system, different aspects of which are apprehended from time to time by research workers in diverse fields.

4. *Self, person and substance.* Dynamic psychology has tended to disregard the substantial approach. In reality, neither a functionally nor a motivationally oriented psychology can be concerned only with experience and behavior patterns, without taking into account the foundation that supports these modes of happening. Experiences and responsibilities are inconceivable without substance and substrate. Today, too, man is a questioner and a seeker in regard to the problem of substance. That and how he questions are psychological facts; why he questions is a philosophical question. Man seeks for causes and grounds of being and occurrence: in psychological terms, for the supportive principle of experience and behavior. In this perspective, it is not enough to see only drive (q.v.)—say, sexual drive—as a "spiritual" extreme from which all experience and behavior would develop; nor would reflexes or primary motives, or behavioral dispositions, suffice to explain the case. Neither molar nor molecular behaviorism (q.v.) can offer a satisfactory answer. From all these viewpoints there has been continual reflection and "self-observation" in an attempt to discover the substantial basis of things. Humanistic psychology (q.v.) identifies the *person* (q.v.) (Stern, C. Bühler), as a constitutional basis, with the self that bears all subjective experiences.

What are we to understand by "substance" in contemporary psychology? A supportive basic principle for all individual being and happening, the unity that establishes and makes observable in spatial and temporal reality all drives and motives, all action and permission. It is consistent in the true sense of the word. Within this consistency all these events and occurrences are related or diffugient. In the phenomena observed and described by psychology one thing persists: the individual person with his or her thus-ness (basic character) and specific constitution, with his or her self-ness, with his or her individually specific communication with the world of others, the co-world, and the world of objects, the environment. The many traits that the individual personal being displays in this process are externalities, or behavior patterns, which would, however, be impossible without a basic supportive principle: "*Substantia est id quod substat accidentibus*" (substance is that which underlies the accidents). See *General psychology; History of psychology; Philosophy and psychology.*

Bibliography: Arnold, W.: Person, Charakter, Persönlichkeit. Göttingen, ³1969. **Id.:** Ein vorläufig-theoretisches Motivationsmodell more psycho-physico. Psychol. Beitr., 1970, *12*, 2. **Jordan, P.:** Schöpfung und Geheimnis. Oldenburg, ²1971. **Monod, J.:** Chance and necessity. London & New York, 1972. **Nebylizyn, W.:** Die Haupteigenschaften des Nervensystems. Ideen des exakten Wissens, Wissenschaft und Techniks in der Sowjetunion. Stuttgart, 1971, *8*, 545–54. *W. Arnold*

Substance P. A polypeptide isolated from extracts of tissues (brain, viscera) whose biological significance has not yet been explained. Substance P possibly acts as a transmitter (q.v.) in the central nervous system. High concentrations are found in the hypothalamus (q.v.), thalamus (q.v.) and basal nuclei. Substance P is one of those substances which most dilate the blood vessels; it also influences the smooth musculature. Its central effects have not yet been established, because not many investigations have been carried out with pure substance P. It probably plays a part in the transmission of sensory information. Pointers in this direction are an increase in substance P concentration under sensory stimulation, and the high content of substance P in the dorsal roots of the spinal cord.

Bibliography: Stern, P.: Substance P as a sensory transmitter and its other central effects. Ann. N.Y. Acad. Sciences, 1962, 403–14. *W.J.*

Substitute formation. The formation of a substitute motive, action or satisfaction (gratification) to replace something that is intolerable for reasons of external situation or internal defense. Tolerance of this process is limited in the neurotic (see *Neurosis*), who is also less able to accept a substitute. According to psychoanalytical theory (see *Psychoanalysis*), a repressed motive is constantly searching for substitute objectives to allow its continuation. The conversion of the original motive, etc., into the substitute is effected with the aid of the mechanisms described in connection with "dream work". The "normal" individual generally has different appropriate and possible substitutes for an "urge" which cannot be satisfied for the time being, neurotic substitutes on the other hand, usually prove inadequate. This fact, as well as the neurotic individual's helplessness in a failure situation because of his inflexibility in the matter of choice, may be used to establish a distinction between the normal and neurotic structure. The neurotic symptom is a substitute for something which has been repressed or cannot be faced in reality because of a specific neurotic structure. See *Depth psychology; Dream; Instinct.*

U.H.S.

Substitute reactions (syn. *Substitute movements*). Not only intention movements and redirection activities but substitute reactions appear frequently in conflicts. The reaction is inhibited in regard to the initiator, and is abreacted onto a substitute: e.g. the appearance of a human in a herring-gull colony triggers off unmotivated attacks on other herring gulls. See *Conflict; Aggression.*

Bibliography: Bastock, M., Morris, D. & Moynihan, M.: Some comments on conflicts and thwarting in animals. Behaviour, 1958, *12*, 234–84. *K.Fi.*

Substitution therapy. Treatment by means of the substitution of substances which the body itself is failing to produce, e.g. the administration of thyroxine (q.v.) in cases of cretinism (q.v.). *E.D.*

Substrate (syn. *Substratum*). **1.** Substance (q.v.). **2.** The subject of prediction. **3.** The "matter" underlying a "form". **4.** A foundation, in the sense of one layer underlying another. (See *Strata theory*.)

Success. The positive confirmation of hypotheses. In subjective experience it appears as an activating variable and as such influences motivation (q.v.), cognition and behavior. Success can be represented as a function of actual performance capability, of the degree of difficulty of the task set and of the standard aimed at. See *Achievement motive; Achievement motivation*. *P.S. & R.S.*

Successive. E.g.: as in *successive contrast, successive gestalts,* = following upon one another.
Successive contrast: Contrast (q.v.): influence exerted upon a phenomenon by a perception directly preceding it in time, e.g. an *afterimage* (q.v.) appearing in the complementary color of a previously perceived object.
Successive gestalts: Successions, whose characteristics are determined from the specific temporal order of their elements, e.g. the melody obtained from a sound sequence. *E.H.*

Successive intervals (syn. *Successive categories; Methods of absolute scaling*). A procedure in scaling (q.v.), in which a subject is invited to categorize stimuli in a sequence of given categories. It is assumed that these categories are classified. The arrangement of the test corresponds to that used in the method of apparently equal intervals. But it is not supposed that the categories cover equally large areas of the subjective continuum. The procedure depends on the "law of comparative judgment"; Stevens includes it as one of the "confusion" methods. See *Mathematical psychology; Psychophysics*.

Bibliography: **Sixtl, F.:** Messmethoden der Psychologie. Weinheim, 1967. **Torgerson, W. S.:** Theory and methods of scaling. New York, 1958.
A.R.

Suggestibility. The individual degree of susceptibility to influence by suggestion (q.v.) and hypnosis (q.v.). The correlative connections between suggestibility and personality do not yet permit clear conclusions on a definite dimension of suggestibility. In 1947, H. J. Eysenck suggested three factors: *primary suggestibility, secondary suggestibility* and *"prestige suggestibility"*. States of heightened suggestibility can be induced by means of hypnosis and drugs. If by suggestion we understand the insinuation of ideas into the unconscious, then suggestibility may be aroused and heightened by ceremonial ritual, by the Carpenter effect (mass suggestion), by persistent repetition of the same word ("Hitler", "Stalin"), or by conversation in a subdued, agreeable atmosphere (colors, music), by appealing to sexuality (sex appeal), which are methods used by political and commercial propaganda. In medicine, suggestibility is eliminated during the testing of pharmaceuticals by the placebo effect (q.v.). When both suggestibility and credulity (or superstition and magic) combine, "faith cures" can occur. Learning processes are probably linked with suggestibility.

Bibliography: **Guilford, J. P.:** Personality. New York, ⁴1970. **Hull, C. L.:** Hypnosis and suggestibility. New York, 1933. **Schjelderup, H.:** Das Verborgene in uns. Stuttgart & Berne, 1964. **Schmitz, K.:** Was ist, was kann, was nützt Hypnose? Munich, 1964. *E.U.*

Suggestibility, primary and secondary. *Primary suggestibility* is susceptibility to influence by (autosuggestion and) heterosuggestion, as demonstrated in Hull's Body Sway Test of Suggestibility (q.v.), Chevreul's sway test, and the "press-and-release" test.

Secondary suggestibility signifies susceptibility to influence by heterosuggestion, as demonstrated in the ink-blot suggestion test, Lindberg's smelling test, the picture-report test, Binet's test of progressive lines and weights, and the heat illusion test.

Bibliography: **Eysenck, H. J. & Furneaux, W. D.:** Primary and secondary suggestibility: an experimental and statistical study. J. exp. Psychol., 1945, *35*, 485–502. Ferguson, L. W.: An analysis of the generality of suggestibility to group opinion. Char. and Person., 1944, *12*, 237–44. **Hull, C. L.:** Hypnosis and suggestibility. New York, 1933. **Stukat, K. G.:** Suggestibility: a factorial and experimental analysis. Stockholm, 1958. *S.M.D.*

Suggestion. A process of communication during which one or more persons cause one or more individuals to change (without critical response) their judgments, opinions, attitudes, etc., or patterns of behavior. The process can take place without being noticed by the individual to be influenced; non-hypnotic differs from hypnotic suggestion by being practised in a waking state. There is no consistently close connection between individual suggestibility in the hypnotic and in the waking condition.

Occasionally "suggestion" is also used to denote the communication content of social suggestion. See *Hypnosis; Suggestibility.*

Bibliography: **Stukat, K. G.:** Suggestibility. Stockholm, 1958. *H.D.S.*

Suggestion therapy. Interhuman influence whereby suggestions appealing to the emotions but lacking rational foundation are made to another person; preconditions are trust and "experience of community" (B. Stokvis). Many psychological and physical processes are more effectively influenced by suggestion than by conscious intention (see *Hypnosis*). *Suggestion therapy* consists in communicating to the patient positive suggestions which change according to his condition. Therapeutic suggestions must always be positively formulated. A less passive attitude in the patient than in pure (hetero-) suggestion therapy is sought for in autosuggestive techniques (see *Relaxation therapy; Autosuggestion*), which are often coupled with formal autosuggestions (e.g. *Autogenic training*, q.v.). Suggestion therapy is probably the oldest form of treatment of mental sickness; it is closely related to magic. Magic may be understood as suggestion transposed outside the individual, and suggestion as magic confined to the range of an individual nervous system. See *Psychoanalysis; Attitude; Stereotype.*

Bibliography: **Schultz, J. H.:** Die Seelische Krankenbehandlung. Stuttgart, 1963. **Schmidbauer, W.:** Schamanismus und Psychotherapie. Psychologischer Rundschau., 1969, *20*, 29–47. *W.Sch.*

Suicide. In most countries suicide is among the ten most frequent causes of death; however, official statistics are not always accurate or clear. They show the relative frequency of suicide in big cities (especially Berlin), and in certain countries (Austria, Switzerland and Sweden).

Methods of suicide are significant (in attempted suicide, usually pills; in successful suicide, forty percent by hanging).

Certain philosophical theories attempt to explain the phenomenon of "freely-chosen death" (in reality a sick compulsion). Psychoanalytic, sociological, pathologico-anatomical and theological theories can only offer suggestions. Those who threaten suicide are not acting in accordance with a Freudian "death instinct" (q.v.), but nearly all (ninety-six percent) are making a dramatic call for help.

E. Ringel advanced the psychiatric theory of a presuicidal syndrome (withdrawal, aggression, flight into unreality), particularly in his "International Union for the Prevention of Suicide". Some universities in the USA teach a course in the theory of suicide, i.e. "suicidology".

Suicide is the only destructive action in which actor and victim are one and the same person. As actor, a suicide is mentally sick (and therefore not responsible or sinful); as victim, he requires protection from himself. Hence the most important problem in connection with suicide is its *prevention*.

Among five thousand threatened suicides, we found fifty percent depressives and thirty-three percent neurotics, and the remainder schizophrenics, manics, psychopathics, etc. Nearly all were at the time in a state of conflict: more than fifty percent through love, marriage or sexual conflict; the rest, in authority, family, money, legal or vocational conflicts. Many seek religious, philosophic or similar answers (meaning of life and death; forgiveness of guilt, and so on).

Suicide prevention means psychiatric or psychoanalytic treatment, then a psychological approach to conflict resolution, including pastoral care (care by telephone helps to establish contact but cannot act as treatment). See *Aggression; Accident research; Alcoholism; Conflict; Criminality; Neurosis.*

Bibliography: Camus, A.: The myth of Sisyphus. London & New York, 1955. Durkheim, E.: Suicide. London & New York, 1952. Kessel, N. & McCulloch, W.: Repeated acts of self-poisoning and self-injury. Proc. Roy. Soc. Med., 1966, *59*, 89. Stengel, E.: Suicide and attempted suicide. Harmondsworth, 1964. Watson, A. S.: Psychiatry for lawyers. New York & London, 1968. Williams, G.: The sanctity of human life and the criminal law. London, 1955.

K. Thomas

Sulcus. The *sulci cerebri* are groove-shaped hollows between the cerebral convolutions. In human beings they grow from the second half of the embryonic period. The cortex is considerably enlarged because of them. On the cerebellum (q.v.) fissure-type hollows can be observed: *fissurae cerebelli*. The *sulcus centralis* runs diagonally over the cerebral hemisphere (see *Central convolution*). The visual cortex is situated in the occipital lobe in the area of the *sulcus calcarinus*. See *Neuroanatomy*. *G.A.*

Summated rating. One of the fundamental types of test. The test value is formed as the sum of the response items, or of response importance, without the items being clearly arranged in a basic continuum. The items indicate the existence of a definite feature. See *Test theory*. *P.Z.*

Summation (syn. *Summativity*). **1.** Any aggregate or total. **2.** A term from gestalt psychology. The opposite is suprasummation (q.v.). The first definition of summation is found in the work of W. Köhler (q.v.): "A whole is a pure sum of 'parts' or 'fragments' only when it can be produced from them, one after the other, without one of the parts changing because of the combination . . ." By analogy, this applies to the separation of parts. A comprehensive description of the theory is given by Rausch (1937). See *Ganzheit*.

Bibliography: Köhler, W.: Die physischen Gestalten in Ruhe und im stationären Zustand. Brunswick, 1920. Rausch, E.: Über Summativität und Nicht-summativität. Psychol. Forschung, 1937, *21*, 209–89.

A.R.

Summation curves. Graphic representations of the distribution function in constant random variables. A summation curve rises steadily. With a normal distribution it is S-shaped. Mean values and deviations, as well as deviations from the norm, can be derived from a summation curve. *A.R.*

Summation tone. The combined tone resulting from the simultaneous sounding of two tones at a frequency corresponding to the sum of frequencies of primary tones. Summation tones were discovered by H. von Helmholtz in 1857. See *Difference tone*.

Bibliography: **Helmholtz, H. von**: Die Lehre von den Tonempfindungen. Brunswick, 1896.   *R.S.*

Summativity. See *Summation*.

Superego. The superego is one of the aspects of personality which Freud (q.v.) described in his second theory of the psyche. Its role is comparable with that of a judge or censor in regard to the ego (q.v.). Among its functions, Freud includes the formation of a moral *conscience* (q.v.), and that of ideals and self-observation (see *Self-knowledge*). It is an inheritance from the Oedipus complex (q.v.), since it is constituted by the incorporation of all parental prohibitions. Klein (1948) suggests that the formation of the superego occurs in the pre-Oedipal stage.

Bibliography: **Freud, S.**: The ego and the id. London, ²1962. **Klein, M.**: The importance of symbol-formation in the development of the ego. London, 1948.
                                         J.L.I.

Superformation. The formation of *supersigns* (q.v.). Because of the reduction of information, superformation permits both a restriction of reaction times, and a scanning of relatively complex information despite a restricted span of consciousness (q.v.).   *A.R.*

Superposition effect. In 1941, E. von Holst discovered that the rhythmic fin movements of a fish feature a special automatism. The individual rhythms can be linked with one another by relative coordination. Hence the rhythms of the pectoral fins are independent and influence the beat frequency of the dorsal fin by *superposition*. The independent rhythm can respond to the dependent rhythm to the extent of almost complete dominance.

Bibliography: **Holst, E. von**: Entwurf eines Systems der lokomotorischen Periodenbildungen bei Fischen. Ein kritischer Beitrag zum Gestaltproblem. Z. vergl. Physiol., 1941, *26*, 481–529.   *K.Fi.*

Supersign. Created by the combination of several signs of a simple sign repertoire (complex formation or classification) by the receiver. For example, sounds or letters are formed by complex formation into a word as a supersign of the first order, and words into a sentence or proposition as a supersign of the second order. Details of a printed letter are not distinguished when one reads, but are formed into a class and perceived as one and the same letter. The information of the supersign is always less than the total information of the subsigns.   *H.R.*

Superstition. 1. An inappropriate or unnecessary fear or scruple requiring the observance of a rite or practice that it is supposed will ward off a usually non-existent danger. **2.** Such a rite or practice. **3.** The postulation of cause-and-effect relationships without good reason. **4.** Religion without morality, or tradition, or faith, or philosophy, etc. (pejorative usage). See *Attitude; Obsession; Religion, psychology of*.

Bibliography: **Jahoda, G.**: The psychology of superstition. London, 1969.

Suppression. Effective repression (q.v.), sublimation (q.v.), defense (q.v.), or censorship (q.v.). See *Depth psychology; Psychoanalysis*.

Suppressor fields. Areas of the cerebral cortex (e.g. *gyrus cingularis*), whose stimulation (electrical, chemical or mechanical) leads (*a*) to an *inhibition* or suppression of a motor activity evoked *simultaneously* by stimulation, and (*b*) to a transient inhibition occurring *shortly thereafter*, or to a diminution of spontaneous, local electrical activity in the cortex.

The postulation of the existence of these areas and their effect goes back to Dusser de Barenne and his school (1941), and especially to McCulloch (1944), but the experimental evidence for the regions has been called in question (Meyers & Knott, 1953). *Neurologically*, the suppressor effect may be interpreted as regulation of cortical activity; and *psychologically*, as an attention (q.v.) mechanism (inhibition of receptiveness to other sensory impressions).

Bibliography: Dusser de Barenne, J. C. & McCulloch, W. S.: Suppression of a motor response obtained from area 4 by stimulation of area 4 S.J. Neurophysiol., 1941, *4*, 311–23. **McCulloch, W. S.:** Corticocortical connections. In: **Bucy, P. C.** (Ed.): The pre-central motor cortex. Urbana, Ill., 1944, 211 ff. **Meyers, R. & Knott, J.:** On the question as to the existence of a suppressor mechanism. 5th Intern. Neurol. Congr., Lisbon, Vol. 2, 1953.

F.-C.S.

Suppressor variable (syn. *Suppressor test*). A test in a battery which indicates high correlation with a part test and no correlation with the criterion. Hence it suppresses a part of the variance (q.v.) which is without significance in the criterion. *R.M.*

Supranormal stimuli. Stimulus situations which exceed the "natural" key or signal stimulus of an innate releasing mechanism (IRM) in effectiveness. Example: the male *Eumenis semele*, or grayling, responds more intensively to black butterfly models than to naturally colored ones. The oyster-catcher rolls into its nest giant eggs which it prefers to its own. The capacity of the central evaluation apparatus would seem to be greater than necessary. See *Dummy sign stimuli; Instinct; Releaser.*

Bibliography: Magnus, D.: Zum Problem der überoptimalen Schlüsselreize (Versuche am Kaisermantel Argynnis paphia). Zool. Anz. Suppl. 1954, *18*, 317–25. **Tinbergen, N.:** The study of instinct. London, [2]1969. *H.H. & K.Fi.*

Suprarenin(e). Epinephrine hydrochloride (adrenalin, q.v.) obtained synthetically.

Suprasummation (syn. *Suprasummativity*). The effect by which it is supposed that the perception of a gestalt cannot be predicted from the perception of its individual parts. This is because perception depends on the relationships between the components of a gestalt rather than on the components themselves. See *Ganzheit; Transposition of gestalts; Structure.* *C.D.F.*

Surface colors. Katz (1911) distinguished various modes of appearance of colors according to their location in space. In addition to *film colors* (endowed with a loose spatial structure) and *solid colors* (occupying three-dimensional space), he speaks of "surface colors" localized at the site of the object bearing them, e.g. colored paper. Surface colors have a firm surface "structure".

Bibliography: Katz, D.: Die Erscheinungsweisen der Farben und ihre Beeinflussung. Z.f. Psychol., 1911, *7*. *A.Ha.*

Surface traits. When several personality measures show some degree of cohesion or correlation with each other, such a cluster is called a surface trait (Cattell, 1957). A score on such a trait may be obtained by forming a simple linear composite of the measures. An added refinement would be to extract a factor from the intercorrelations between the measures and then obtain scores on the factor by one of the several factor estimation methods.

Surface traits can be useful in the description of personality. However, they are not considered to be fundamental in the development of theoretical models of personality. It is in this sense of not being basic to theory that they are distinguished from *source traits* (q.v.). Use of a surface trait is often determined by practical and conventional considerations.

The variance of a surface trait is to be thought of as potentially reducible to a set of more basic explanatory constructs. Thus, it might be observed that several different tests of, say, "cautiousness" co-vary together. A set of trait scores, based on these tests, could be generated. This new variable could then be introduced into a factor analysis (q.v.) including measures known to be associated with source traits. It would be expected that if the test of cautiousness involves a surface trait, its variance will be distributed among several different factors. In this way, many of the variables in common usage in personality research—such as the clinical scales of the MMPI—may be expressed in terms of more fundamental influences. See *Personality; Traits; Type.*

Bibliography: Cattell, R. B.: Personality and motivation: structure and measurement. New York, 1957.

J. D. Hundleby

Surprisal value. The surprise evoked by an item of information (news) depends not only on the actual information but on the rest of the field. In information esthetics, Frank's (1964) surprisal value gives the relation of the information (q.v.) of an item to the uncertainty that this item removes. Information with the value s > 1 is described as "surprizing" and that with s < 1 as "banal".

Bibliography: Frank, H.: Kybernetische Analysen subjektiver Sachverhalte. Schnelle, 1964.   *H.R.*

Survey. The determination of characteristics and their prominence in units of a whole. If not all the units of a whole but only a random sample of units selected on representative, statistical principles, are covered, we speak of a *representative survey.* See *Area sampling; Demoscopy; Opinion polls.*   *E.N.-N.*

Survival. The doctrine that the individual person may continue to exist in some form after destruction of his body. Life after death. See *Spiritualism.*   *J.B.*

Susceptibility tests. Tests to measure the susceptibility of a subject to hypnotism. Recent susceptibility tests have been published by Hilgard & Weitzenhoffer. The researcher notes on prepared report sheets S.'s reactions to various hypnotic suggestions; S.'s susceptibility is obtained from the sum of reactions to different items. On the basis of his experiments, Hilgard rejects the stages of hypnosis (q.v.) as understood by, say, A. Forel.

Bibliography: Weitzenhoffer, A. M. & Hilgard, E. A.: Revised Stanford profile scales of hypnotic susceptibility. Palo Alto, 1967.   *G.L.*

Swarming. Animals in groups of at least two to three thousand individuals can display synchronous behavior, especially when in swimming or flight formations. Usually individuals in a swarm remain at a certain distance from one another, but this tends to diminish when there is any sign of danger. Shoals of fish or swarms of birds, e.g. starlings, can envelop predators and prevent them from attacking. The survival value of swarm formations lies in the increasing difficulty of mounting attacks on individuals. The swarm has no leader; instead movements are usually carried out as a result of optical mood signalling, which is reinforced by striking patterns.

Bibliography: Eibl-Eibesfeldt, I.: Grundriss der vergleichenden Verhaltensforschung: Ethologie. Munich, 1967. Horstmann, E.: Schwarm und Phalanx als überindividuelle Lebensformen. J. Forsch. Spiekeroog. Id.: Schwarmstudien unter Ausnutzung einer optomotorischen Reaktion bei Mugil cephalus (CUV.) Pubbl. Staz. Zool. Napoli, 1967, *XXXI/I*, 25–35.   *K.Fi.*

Symbiosis. The "cohabitation" of two, generally quite different, forms of organism, both of which obtain advantages from this association. In the intestines of termites, for example, there are unicellular organisms which produce cellulose-splitting enzymes which enable the termites to digest wood, their main item of diet; at the same time, the termites' intestinal tract, with its ideal environmental conditions and adequate food intake, is a paradise for the unicellular organisms. *H.Sch.*

Symbol. 1. In information theory (q.v.), usually synonymous with sign (q.v.), or with a sign whose referent is a part signal. If all disjunctive part signals are codes by means of symbols proper, statistical statements about signal sequences may be replaced by statements about symbol sequences. **2.** An abstract or compendium. **3.** That which figuratively represents something else. **4.** A sign that relies upon a convention accepted by its users. See *Sign and symbol; Communication.* *K.W.*

Symmetrical distribution. A frequency or probability distribution, for which the following applies: $f(X - \bar{X}) = f(\bar{X} - X)$. In symmetrical distributions, the arithmetic mean $\bar{X}$ and the median (q.v.) coincide (see *Normal distribution*). A non-symmetrical distribution is a skew distribution. *A.R.*

Sympathicolytic (syn. *Sympatholytic*). Appertaining to the mode of effect of chemical substances which inhibit or block sympathetic activity (see *Autonomic nervous system*). The sympathicolytic effect of drugs vary according to the basic mechanisms of action and varied physiological systems. A common characteristic of sympathicolytic substances is neurophysiological and chemical inhibition of the effect of biogenic catecholamines, especially noradrenalin (norepinephrine), in the peripheral ANS. According to the active mechanisms, the sympathicolytic substances which directly affect the receptors (q.v.) can be distinguished from those which influence biosynthesis or catecholamine storage. Alpha or beta receptor inhibitors can be distinguished according to the site of action. The effects of sympathicolytic substances on behavior vary considerably. Both stimulating and sedative effects are found.

Bibliography: See *Psychopharmaceuticals and the ANS.* *W.J.*

Sympathicolytics (syn. *Sympatholytics*). Chemical substances with a predominantly sympathicolytic effect. For examples, see *Psychopharmaceuticals and the ANS.*

Sympathicomimetic. Appertaining to the mode of effect of chemical substances which arouse the sympathetic division of the ANS. Effects differ according to whether the alpha or beta receptors are aroused. Stimulation of the alpha receptors (e.g. by adrenalin) induces, *inter alia:* contraction of blood vessels (only in a few parts, e.g. the skeletal muscles, skin, kidneys), reduced salivation, inhibition of gastric juice secretion, localized (adrenergic) sweating and the mobilization of glycogen. Excitation of beta receptors (e.g. by isopropylnoradrenalin) leads, *inter alia,* to increased heart rate, enlargement of the heart beat volume, dilation of the blood vessels of the skeletal muscles, and reduced intestinal motility.

Bibliography: See *Psychopharmaceuticals and the ANS.* *W.J.*

Sympathicomimetics. Substances whose predominant effect is to stimulate the sympathetic division. The comparison of sympathicomimetics to adrenergics (q.v.), though often made, is problematic since (*a*) the sympathetic system is not aroused only by noradrenalin and adrenalin (q.v.) or related substances, and (*b*) adrenergic substances also affect the central nervous system without arousal of the peripheral sympathetic system. Many sympathicomimetics also have strong central effects, and may be classed as stimulants.

Bibliography: See *Psychopharmaceuticals and the ANS.*   *W.J.*

Sympathicotony. A clinical syndrome described by Eppinger & Hess (1910). A shift (induced by unilateral heightening of sympathetic tonus) of equilibrium in the autonomic nervous system to the sympathetic side with increased sympathetic excitability, so that normally subliminal stimuli capable of sympathetic arousal cause abnormally increased reactions (increased vasomotor excitability, dilated pupils, tachycardia, q.v., and increased secretion of sweat). The reactions correlate with psychological traits: according to Birkmeyer & Winkler, increased psychological excitability and lability of affect, disturbances of concentration and sleep, inclination to anxiety states. Ant. *Vagotonia* (q.v.).

Bibliography: Eppinger, H. & Hess, L.: Die Vagotonie. Berlin, 1910.   *F.-C.S.*

Symptom. In the psychological sense, an attitude, thought or subjective experience with a significance beyond or different from itself. As a rule, unconscious though not wholly suppressed wishes and motives are indicated by symptoms (Freud, 1929). Hence sudden states of anxiety are alleged possibly to show that an individual is at a crucial stage in regard to a forbidden motive, or that he was prevented from avoiding such situations in his usual way or from using the necessary inner defense mechanisms. Compulsive washing is supposed to indicate aggressive impulses, stuttering a power conflict with relatives, and a hysterical paralysis a (forbidden) wish to touch a certain person.

Symptomatic actions are actions which are said to indicate something more than, or other than, the mere conscious and intended object of behavior. Unconscious motives and impulses are supposed to have contributed to their origin. "Freudian" slips (q.v.) are also symptomatic actions in this sense. See *Syndrome.*

Bibliography: Fenichel, O.: The psychoanalytic theory of neurosis. New York, 1945. **Freud, S.:** Introductory lectures on psycho-analysis. London, ²1969.   *W.T.*

Synapses. Nerve fibers (axons) of other nerve cells or receptors terminate at several points (*end feet*) of the nerve cell body, or neuron(e), and at the dentrites. These fibers transmit excitation (nerve impulses) by way of *synapses*; similarly, the link between nerve and muscle is formed by a kind of synapse. A synapse is, therefore, a *transfer point*. Essentially, a neuron can be regulated by a few up to several hundred synapses. A structural distinction is made between the *presynaptic fiber* terminating in an extension on the cell body, the *subsynaptic membrane* (membrane part of the cell), and the narrow gap (*synaptic cleft*) between them (width 200–300 Å).

1. *Excitatory synapses* with chemical transmitter substances. In spite of the narrow gap, pre- and postsynaptic structures are thoroughly linked by electricity. The chemical *transmitter substance* molecules (q.v.) stored in the presynaptic part, and released in appropriate quantity by the incident electrical excitation has, after diffusion through the gap, the effect of depolarizing that part of the subsynaptic membrane near the synapse; the excitatory postsynaptic potential (EPSP), delayed by about 0.3–0.6 ms, arises intracellularly. EPSP is not identical with the action potential (q.v.), which represents the further conducted excitation of the neuron, but stands primarily for a purely local change of potential (about 10 mV). EPSP follows a characteristic course: a rapid rise (1–20 ms), an approximate exponential drop (1–20 ms). The amplitude, and not the course, is influenced by the sequential frequency of the impulse: *summation* (decoding), to be explained by repeated secretion of

transmitter substance and a corresponding rise in concentration. If the amplitude of the EPSP, or the integral above the amplitudes of all EPSPs in the neuron, reaches a critical threshold, then excitation of the whole neuron takes place and an action potential (80–140 mV) is created as an input signal to the conductor axon. Hence the excitation of the whole neuron depends on the number of excited afferent fibers and their action potential frequency.

2. *Excitatory synapse; electrical transmission.* Synapses of this relatively infrequent type have a narrower gap, and almost no latency of EPSP in relation to presynaptic action potential (< 0.1 ms). A direct transmission of the depolarizing current from the presynaptic to the subsynaptic membrane is assumed to occur here, though only in one direction.

3. *Inhibitory synapse with chemical transmitter substance.* The excitation which generally arrives by way of an intermediate neuron with a short axon creates (by means of a chemical transmitter substance, e.g. γ-aminoperbutyric acid in invertebrates) a hyperpolarization of the synaptic membrane and an inhibitory postsynaptic potential (IPSP). The latter is directed electrically against EPSP and reduces the excitability of the nerve cells.

4. *Inhibitory synapse; electrical transmission.* In a few nerve cells (Mauthner cells), the axon is surrounded by a fine nerve tissue which exerts an electrotonic influence on the excitation conducted in the axon, and in certain cases inhibits it. (See *Axon; Nervous system.*)

Bibliography: Eccles, J. C.: The mechanism of synaptic transmission. Ergebnisse der Physiologie, 1961, *51*, 300–429. Grossman, S. P.: Physiological psychology. New York, 1967. Pritbam, K. H. (Ed.): Brain and behavior. Harmondsworth, 1969. *M. Spreng*

Synchronicity. Jung (q.v.) introduced the concept of synchronicity to describe the correlation between external and internal facts, which cannot be explained "causally". According to Jung, this correlation is based on archetypes (q.v.). Coincidences often occur between certain factors in an individual's life and mythological patterns, where at first sight a causality may be inferred. Yet it is a question not of strict causality but of a special synchronous variation. Jung and his disciples, above all E. Neumann, gave the theory a chronological, "evolutionary" dimension.

J.L.I.

Syndrome. A concurrence of a set of abnormal signs and/or symptoms. Syndromes are given names which are either descriptive or eponymic (that is, they bear the name of one or more individuals who described or clarified them).

J.P.

Synesthesia. In some people, sensory systems other than the one actually being stimulated can share in the perception of the stimulus. Hence musical notes may give rise to the perception of colors or odors. *C.D.F.*

Synop(s)ia. A subvariety of synesthesia (q.v.) in which the visual modality is influenced by non-visual stimuli or images See *Mental imagery.* *F.Ma.*

Synthesis, creative. According to Wundt (q.v.), a universal principle of psychic activity. It indicates that a "psychic structure" represents more than the sum of its elements ("pure feelings" or "pure sensations"). The product of several elements is something wholly new in relation to its parts. The principle of creative synthesis refers not to objective circumstances but to subjective values and goals; nevertheless it does not contradict physical laws. The creative synthesis is most evident in the "higher" psychic processes ("apperceptive synthesis"). See *Ganzheit.*

Bibliography: Wundt, W.: Grundriss der Psychologie. Leipzig, [12]1914. *F.Ma.*

Syntonia. A term coined by Bleuler in 1922 to replace cyclothymia (q.v.), and meaning that "affectivity toward the outside world . . . is in harmony with that of the human environment and corresponds to the conditions of the outside world; actual emotions are harmonious within, and—like aspirations—are unified." Kretschmer's concept of a "midpoint" of the diathetic proportion (q.v.) of adequately balanced, non-extreme feeling and thought has been more influential; "healthy human understanding, traditional manner, practical instinct . . . skill . . . in friendly communication."

Bibliography: Bleuler, E.: Die Probleme der Schizoidie und Syntonie. Zschr. ges. Neur. Psychiatr., 1922, *78*, 373 ff. Kretschmer, E. & W.: Medizinische Psychologie. Stuttgart, [13]1970.   *W.K.*

Systematic error. See *Bias*.

Systole; diastole. *Systole:* contraction of a hollow muscular organ, in particular of the heart. Part of the cardiac cycle; contraction of the heart muscle rhythmically alternating with diastole: pumping out of the blood.

Diastole: enlargement of the heart muscle alternating with systole; phase of refilling of ventrical with blood.   *H.W.*

Szondi test. Devised by L. Szondi and published in 1947. The original purpose of the test was to discover the motivational nature of the "familiar unconscious", but experience shows that it throws more light on questions of individual motivation. The test consists of forty-eight pictures (six series of eight) of persons lacking in motivation; these the testee is required to arrange in two groups (four pictures per group) in terms of relative attractiveness or unattractiveness. These sympathy/antipathy choices are projections (q.v.) of inner need and motive tensions. The reliability of the test is difficult to assess. Its validity, despite much research, is doubtful.

Bibliography: Heinelt, G.: Bildwahlverfahren. In: Heiss, R. (Ed.): Handbuch der Psychologie, Vol. 6. Göttingen, 1963.   *P.G.*

T

Tabes dorsalis (syn. *Locomotor ataxia*). A third-stage sequel of syphilis (and rarely due to other causes): posterior spinal sclerosis. It appears five to fifteen years after the first infection with *Treponema pallidum* (*Spirochaeta pallida*) and is characterized by degeneration of sensory neurons in the spinal cord, sensory ganglia, and nerve roots. Characteristic symptoms are: alterations in pupils (see *Argyll-Robertson pupil*); disturbances of sensibility, such as lightning pains; analgesia (q.v.) and heat sensations in particular areas of the body; disturbed movement (see *Ataxia*) and especially gait, as a result of faulty information to the brain about the position of the limbs and the contact of the soles of the feet with the ground; failure of tendon (ankle and knee) reflexes; and personality changes. The disease develops slowly, and over the years leads (if the causative syphilis is untreated) to tabetic paralysis and *dementia paralytica*.   *E.D.*

Table. An arithmetic representation of scores, so arranged as to reveal relations of time, frequency, etc.

Taboo (syn. *Tabu*). Originally a term for a "primitive", solemn prohibition of certain actions (e.g. looking at or touching certain objects or persons). From this arose the magical religious belief that violation of a taboo brings harm to a community. Punishment for ignoring the taboo was often violent expulsion from the (tribal) group, or death.

In social psychology, the term "taboo" is applied to certain usually unofficial but highly regarded norms in a group or society. It is applied in particular to social prohibitions of an irrational nature when punishment is threatened if they are violated. There are many similarities between "taboo" objects in modern and in primitive societies (e.g. the tabooing of aspects of certain vital functions such as some forms of eating, drinking, elimination, sexual taboos, taboos on strangers and property, etc.)

Freud held that taboos arose through an instinctual conflict, with a resulting repression of the attractive but forbidden behavioral tendencies into the "unconscious" (q.v.). The repression had features in common with neurotic compulsions not to touch certain things. Social psychology, however, sees the taboo as a special instance of group norms by which the community can control an individual's behavior—sometimes very strictly (e.g. the increased effectiveness of a religious or military group through certain sexual taboos. See *Incest*).

Bibliography: Freud, S.: Totem and taboo. New York & London, 1918.   *H.D.S.*

Taboo death. The sudden or gradual death of a person who knows (or thinks he knows) he has offended against a taboo and therefore must die. Because he believes himself bewitched or guilty—excluded from the law, and therefore from life—he dies. His responsibility is wholly bound up with the observance of the prohibition.

This phenomenon is observed almost exclusively in archaic cultures, in which the psychosomatic connection is very close. The individual is subject to an almost pure affectivity, which can pass directly from excess to exhaustion. He can die through the effect of a shock of joy or fear, or of a death wish. If he is bewitched and cast out of society, he can avoid sudden death or pining away only through exorcism or the conjuration of "counter magic". For the physiological effects of these phenomena and the clinical causes of such deaths, see C. Lévi-Strauss's *Structural Anthropology* (New York, 1963). They are due to a kind of paralysis of the sympathetic nervous system.   *M.R.*

Tachistoscope. An apparatus for presenting visual stimuli for very brief and accurately timed periods. Various mechanisms have been employed, but most operate either on a shutter system like that of a camera, or on a principle of selective illumination. The instrument has a wide variety of uses in the field of *perception*, but it best known in connection with studies of *pattern recognition* and the influences of motivation upon perception, e.g. *perceptual defense. Tachistoscopic projector:* A slide projector with the addition of a shutter mechanism for timing brief presentations of the slide on the screen, and usually also the interval between slide presentations. *G.D.W.*

Tachycardia. An increased heart beat above the rate of a hundred beats a minute is normal in bodily exertion and in childhood. Tachycardia, or an abnormally rapid heart beat, is unhealthy in the case of heart attack (*paroxys-*

mal tachycardia); in cases of acute or chronic occurrence through psychic excitement, heart weakness, endocarditis and myocarditis; and in hormone poisoning, and poisoning from drugs and eating and drinking, and in long-term infections. There is no fixed boundary between heart flutter and the mortal heart murmur.   *E.D.*

Talbot-Plateau law. If the eye is stimulated by a light flickering at a frequency above that of flicker-fusion frequency, the brightness created by the flickering light is the same as that which would result if the total amount of light had been uniformly distributed over the whole period of the intermittence. In other words: a light of intensity *a*, shining for the period *t*, has the same effect as a light of intensity *a/n* shining for the period *nt*. If the flickering lights are colored (i.e. of different wavelengths), the resulting color tone is that to be expected from a summative color mixture (q.v.), and its brightness (q.v.) conforms to the Talbot law. See *Flicker photometry.*   *G.Ka.*

Talent. Great or outstanding ability. See *Giftedness, research into; Abilities; Creativity.*

Talisman. An object which is supposed to bring its owner luck or give him protection (see *Fetishism*).   *J.L.*

Tapping. An experimental or test procedure in which S. has to carry out simple tapping movements or depress keys with the fingers and hands as rapidly as possible, or at a speed convenient to him. Tapping is a psychomotor test which has been introduced in several variations: for instance, as simple tapping (knocking with the bare finger, a pencil on a paper pad, etc.), and as purposive tapping, when S. has to hit target points (circles, parts of figures, etc.) at a prescribed speed, or at any speed he chooses. Usually a tapping test serves to determine "personal tempo", that is, the speed of work preferred by the individual, and to test delicate motor precision. See *Motor skills; Practice.*

Bibliography: Whipple, G. M.: Manual of mental and physical tests. Baltimore, ²1914.   *A.T.*

Tapping test. A test to measure the abilities requisite to learn typewriting and similar activities, and to predict individual scores.
                                                         F.Gr.

Tarchanoff phenomenon. See *Galvanic skin response.*

Target. In parapsychology (q.v.): the particular object, symbol or property that has to be identified in an ESP experiment.   *J.B.*

Taste nerves. The taste receptors are longish cells with a diameter of 3 to 8 μ, combined in groups of ten to forty in taste buds. The latter are situated in elevations of the mucous membrane of the tongue, or papillae, and also in isolated groups on the hard and soft gum, the pharynx and even the larynx. It may be assumed that there are four different kinds of receptors for the four qualities of taste, i.e. *sweet*, *sour*, *salt* and *bitter*, since sweet tastes are detected primarily by the tip of the tongue, bitter tastes by the base of the tongue, and salt and sour tastes on the edges of the tongue (the former at the front and the latter further back). Thin, afferent (myelinated) nerve fibers of the Aδ group according to Erlanger & Gasser, are synaptically connected to the bases of the taste buds and lead into the central nervous system. The fibers originating in the front two-thirds of the tongue lead through the *nervus lingualis* (*n. trigeminus* 3/1) to the *chorda tympani*, and with the latter through

the middle ear to the *n. facialis*; the fibers from the base of the tongue lead to the *n. glossopharyngicus* and those from all remaining areas which are sensitive to taste to the *n. vagus*. All these nerves lead in turn to the *nucl. terminalis tract. solitarii*, which is located in the bulbo-pontine cerebrum in the vicinity of the *vestibularis nuclei*, and is frequently referred to as the *nucl. gustatorius*. Above the thalamus (*nucl. ventr. posteromedialis*) Brodmann area 43 is reached at the lower end of the *gyrus postcentralis* in the immediate vicinity of the primary somesthetic projection of the tongue and mucous membrane of the mouth (Brodmann areas 1, 2 and 3); Brodmann area 43 is considered to be the primary cortical taste center. Previous assumptions that the taste center was located in the *gyrus* and *uncus hippocampi* or in the *insula Reili* or *operculum* have been superseded.

Bibliography: Plattig, K. H.: Über den elektrischen Geschmack, Z. Biol., 1969, *116*, 161–211.   *K.H.P.*

Tau effect. See *Gelb phenomenon.*

Taxis. The response in space of freely moving living creatures to external stimuli. There are the following subforms:

(*a*) Grouped according to the basic tendency of the movement: (i) *positive taxis* (seeking, turning toward); (ii) *negative taxis* (avoiding, turning away from).

(*b*) Grouped according to the quality of the operative stimulus: (i) *phototaxis:* irradiation by light; (ii) *chemotaxis:* concentration of diverse substances; (iii) *thermotaxis:* temperature, drops in; (iv) *geotaxis:* gravity; (v) *rheotaxis:* direction of current; (vi) *thigmotaxis:* tactile contact with solid bodies, etc.

(*c*) Grouped according to the kind of movement evoked, or the relation to the stimulus source striven after by the organism: (i) *phobotaxis*—movement of flight on the principle of trial and error, on the basis of a time-differential intensity. Success is shown by the time spent in a zone of optimal conditions. (ii) *topotaxis:* directional movements in the stimulus field on the basis of a spatial difference of intensity. According to the final position achieved by the body with respect to the stimulus source, subgroups are distinguished among which are: (*a*) *tropotaxis:* the object is an excitation equilibrium between two receptors (q.v.), arranged symmetrically like a mirror-image (e.g. left and right eye); (*b*) *telotaxis:* heading in a straight line for a target that can be fixed; (*c*) *menotaxis:* the object is the maintenance of a certain angle between the axis of the body and the direction of stimulus action; (*d*) *mnemotaxis:* the orientation movement is directed toward a number of stimulus sources (e.g. path markers), which are headed for in succession and whose space and time relationships are stored in the memory. But it is a matter of controversy whether such complex orientation behavior should be included under taxis.

Whereas taxis was formerly regarded as a reflex-like set of movements with some direction in view, modern behavioral research separates the directive component, taxis in the more limited sense, from the automatic movement controlled by the central nervous system. Only the combination of the two (successively or joined simultaneously) will produce the space-oriented action.

Bibliography: Kühn, A.: Die Orientierung der Tiere im Raum. Jena, 1919. Tinbergen, N: The study of instinct. Oxford, ²1969.   *I. Lindner*

Taxonomy. The *taxonomy of learning goals* dispenses with the description of teaching content in instruction. Instead it endeavors to take account of all the elementary psychological processes of the pupil and to classify the instruction according to them. See *Educational psychology; Instructional technology.*
                                                        G.B.

Taylor system. Methods and principles of organization worked out by F. W. Taylor (1903) for scientific management: the first attempt at a global concept for solving human problems in large-scale industry. The system went through the following phases: (*a*) increase of individual productivity by a differential wage-system (until 1895); (*b*) investigation of work by time-and-motion studies (part-time work was measured but the workers concerned were specially picked); (*c*) reorganization and division of work between shop-floor and office on a functional basis (until 1903); (*d*) change of the whole factory organization by substituting for overseers a system of several foremen with special functions.

Taylorism: the further development of the Taylor system, especially by F. B. Gilbreth, H. L. Gantt, J. Hopkins, C. G. Garth, H. K. Hathway, etc. See *Industrial psychology; Occupational psychology.*

Bibliography: Taylor, F. W.: Shop management. New York, 1903. Id.: Principles of scientific management. New York, 1911.   *W.F.N.*

t distribution. A distribution for average values of samples from normally distributed populations; devised by W. S. Gosset in 1908, but under the pseudonym "Student". The t distribution allows, e.g., significance testing of average value differences in the case of smaller samples.

Bibliography: Student: The probable error of a mean. Biometrika, 1908, *6*, 1–25.   *D.W.E.*

Tea. A beverage brewed from the dried young leaves, buds and blossom of the tea shrub contains the stimulating substance *theine*, which is identical with caffeine (q.v.). *H.-D.S.*

Teaching machines. See *Instructional technology; Programmed learning; Machine learning; Cybernetics and psychology; Cybernetic education.*

Teaching program. In the sense of programmed instruction, a number of complex steps which unequivocally determine a teaching algorithm. A *linear program* is the type of program devised by Skinner (1960), in which the learner has to work through short frames (steps) according to a pre-determined sequence. An individual frame or a group of frames cannot be repeatedly circumvented, and in any case only under special conditions. Usually only those assignments are linearly programmed that allow of one possible solution. The *branched* form of program derives from Crowder (1960). In contrast to the linear method, this method uses remedial tracks and branches allowing repetition, circumvention of frames, and other possible solutions. The remedial tracks depend on a series of alternative questions or selective answers (multiple-choice responses), which anticipate total and partial erroneous solutions. In the case of a false answer, the learner is led out of the main program, informed of his error, and referred back to the initial question. The branching technique allows for individual learning speeds, and is specially suited to assignments capable of several modes of solution. Linear and branched programs are now often found in combination. See *Instructional technology.*

Bibliography: Crowder, N. A.: Automatic tutoring by intrinsic programming. In: **Lumsdaine, A. A. & Glaser, R.** (Eds.): Teaching machines and programmed learning. Washington, 1960. **Skinner, B. F.:** The science of learning and the art of teaching. In: **Lumsdaine & Glaser,** *op. cit.* *H.F. & E.U.*

Team. A form of division of labor in which (in contrast to the traditional *hierarchical* organizational model) cooperation of formal equals takes the place of orders received from a superior. See *Democracy; Group.* *P.B.*

Teamwork. 1. A term for any work done by a group (q.v.). 2. A special form of direct co-operation where every member of the group is a specialist but has constantly to rely on coordination and communication with the others, and where success cannot be achieved by anyone alone. *G.R.W.M.*

Tectum opticum. The terminus of the optic pathway in fish, amphibians, reptiles, and birds. It is here that optical, olfactory, static and somatic items of information are integrated and converted into behavioral patterns. In mammals the visual cortex dominates over the *tectum opticum.* *K.Fi.*

Telekinesis. In parapsychology (q.v.), the exertion of a psychological influence on external objects. Driesch (1967) places telekinesis in the group of paranormal "physical" phenomena, which he distinguishes from "intellectual" paranormal phenomena. In a series of studies, Rhine (1962) tried to demonstrate individual telekinetic activities using "psychokinetic" tests, e.g. when testees were asked to roll dice, any significant deviation from random results could be explained by a psychic influence.

Bibliography: Bender, H.: Parapsychologie: ihre Ergebnisse und Probleme. Bremen, 1970. **Driesch, H.:** Parapsychologie. Munich, 1967. **Rhine, J. B. & Pratt, J. G.:** Parapsychology. Springfield, 1962. *K.E.P.*

Telencephalon. The human brain (q.v.) is divided into the telencephalon, diencephalon (q.v.), mesencephalon (q.v.), metencephalon (consisting of the pons, q.v., and cerebellum, q.v., and myelencephalon (see *Medulla oblongata*). From the evolutionary point of view the telencephalon is the most advanced; in man it has reached the highest point of development. It can be divided into a *pars basalis* (basal brain) and a *pars palliaris* (pallium, q.v.). The telencephalon consists of the hemispheres of the cerebrum, the *corpus callosum,* the *fornix cerebri,* lateral ventricles and the *corpus striatum*. Between the two hemispheres of the cerebrum is the longitudinal fissure of the brain, the *fissura longitudinalis cerebri*. See *Neuroanatomy*.   G.A.

Teleology. In philosophy, the science of *finality*. In a wider sense, *finality* itself, i.e. the fact of striving for some goal—whether intentional (*volition*) or unintentional (*entelechy*—a purpose which is realized by organic development, the arrangement of the parts in a whole). The term can also mean *finalism*, i.e. the doctrine according to which the world is thought of as a system of relations between means and end. In the Aristotelian theory of "four causes", teleology refers to the "*causa finalis*", or final cause. *Vitalism* is one of the forms of finalism (H. Bergson); it is opposed to any mechanistic interpretation.

Bibliography: Monod, J.: Chance and necessity. London & New York, 1972.   *M.J.B.*

Telepathy. A form of ESP (q.v.) where the information acquired by the subject is assumed to derive from the mind or brain of some other person (see *Clairvoyance*). A term introduced by Frederic Myers which has superseded earlier expressions such as "thought-transference" or "teleasthesia".   *J.B.*

Television. An audiovisual mass medium whose importance and effectiveness have undergone extensive empirical investigation since the beginning of the nineteen-fifties. The assumption that prolonged viewing as such is harmful (e.g. impairs concentration or encourages crime) has not been established in general either for children and juveniles or adults. The effectiveness of the medium in spreading knowledge appears to be greatest in combination with other media communication. In this respect the importance of television for education is constantly increasing.

The question of the beneficial or harmful effects of television obviously depends on the view held of the esthetic value and/or educative, moral, etc. value of the ethic, information, etc., of a specific program in regard to a specific age group, personality type, environment, and so on.

Bibliography: Benton, C. W. et al.: Television in urban education: its application to major educational problems in sixteen cities. New York, 1970. **Eysenck, H. J.:** Television and the problem of violence. In: Report of the Committee on broadcasting, Vol. 2. London, 1962, 1116–20. **Hancock, A.:** Planning for educational television. London, 1971.

H.D.S. & W.A.

Temperament. A basic characteristic of the personality as a whole. The classical descriptions of temperament (melancholic, phlegmatic, choleric and sanguine) derive from ancient cosmology and pathology. According to Kretschmer ([13]1970), temperament is "the overall attitude of the affectivity characteristic of an individual . . . measured by sensitivity and impulses" or "the profile of activity and sensitivity, the dominant ranges and outlets". It is the result of the "combination of affective, vegetative, humoral and morphological factors". See *Personality; Traits; Type*.   *W.K.*

Temperature. See *Body temperature*.

Temporal lobe. The *lobus temporalis* of the brain (q.v.) is situated in the center of the cranial cavity, and bordered above by the lateral cerebral fissure (*Sulcus lateralis*) and connected posteriorly and above to the parietal and occipital lobes (q.v.). The convolutions of the temporal lobe are the *Gyrus temporalis superior, medius et inferior* (the superior, middle and inferior temporal convolutions) and the *Gyri temporales transversi* (the transverse temporal convolutions = Heschl's gyrus), which are responsible for hearing. In the *gyrus temporalis superior* is the sensory speech center; its removal or failure produces aphasia (q.v.). In the right-handed, the sensory speech center is on the left-hand side, and in the left-handed, it is on the right of the *gyrus temporalis superior.* **G.A.**

Temptation. Guilt (q.v.) is said to arise after the commission of a previously punished act. Temptation corresponds to the anxiety (q.v.) and conflict (q.v.) experienced before the commission of forbidden acts. Guilt feelings can occur if they occur independently of the direct threat of external punishment (q.v.). If corresponding feelings are associated with an external source of punishment, one speaks of *shame.* See *Conscience; Criminality; Traits; Type.*

Bibliography: Mowrer, O. H.: Learning theory and the symbolic processes. New York, 1960. **F.Ma.**

Tenacity. Used of attention (q.v.): a difference between individuals in the length of time for which they can perform correctly tasks which require a high degree of attention. Tenacity is generally measured by crossing-out tests (q.v.). **K.P.**

Tendencies (determining, anticipatory, persevering). **1.** *Determining tendencies:* A term in the psychology of thinking and volition invented by N. Ach. Thought (q.v.) does not proceed in any direction, like association (q.v.), but is given a firm direction by attitudes to, or ideas of, a goal or task; sometimes these are part of observable experience, and sometimes unobservable and unconscious.

2. *Anticipatory tendencies:* If a learning process is divided into a sequence of individual associations, it is found that the steps in the sequence are not independent of one another. For example, if when memorizing nonsense syllables a particular response to a stimulus is

learnt, subjects show a tendency to react before the stimulus if the response is demanded.

3. *Persevering tendencies:* Reproductive tendencies: the dependence of one step in a learning process on its predecessors. Appears in experiments with nonsense syllables, when a syllable recently learnt is reproduced instead of the correct one, which was learnt earlier. **H.W.**

Tendermindedness. An idealistic attitude toward social, political and philosophical problems; ant.: *toughmindedness.* Whereas the tenderminded person will make judgments and perform actions according to principles, and try to solve problems by reason or argument, the toughminded person adopts a position based on facts and tries to solve problems by manipulation or the use of force (pragmatism). H. J. Eysenck (1963) claims a correlation between tendermindedness and introversion, and between toughmindedness (q.v.) and extraversion. See *Traits; Type; Authoritarian personality.* **I.L.**

Tension. 1. *Muscular tension* (*hypertension:* increased tension; *hypotension:* reduced tension). **2.** *Condition of an organism:* restless, tense activity (see *Stress*). **3.** Emotional condition resulting from unsatisfied needs or blocked desires (see *Conflict; Frustration*). **F.-C.S.**

Tension, psychic. Psychoanalytic term referring to a state or condition marked by high arousal, anxiety, restlessness, and undirected drive. Also called *psychentonia.* Similar to popular concepts of "nervous tension" and "emotional tension". **G.D.W.**

Tension system. According to K. Lewin, mental activity can be visualized in terms of topological concepts, such as *region, path* and *boundary* (see *Field theory; Topological psychology*). The ego and life-space can be regarded as an internally differentiated field in a number of regions interconnected by paths. Under extreme stress the tension systems, or part-regions of the differentiated personality, "de-differentiate": i.e. energy levels in the various tension systems are equated because of the flow from one to the other, and there is something like (e.g. when a man loses his head in a fit of rage) a return to the poorly differentiated child personality.

Bibliography: Lewin, K.: A dynamic theory of personality. New York, 1935. **Id.:** Principles of topological psychology. New York, 1936.   *P.M.*

Terman, Lewis Madison. B. 15/1/1877 in Johnson County (Ind.); d. 21/12/1956 in Stanford. Ph.D. 1905, under Stanley Hall at Clark University; 1910, assistant Professor in the Department of Education at Stanford University; 1916, full Professor; from 1922, until his death, Professor of psychology at Stanford University.

Terman was a very prolific scholar, and his bibliography lists over two hundred publications. He is mainly known, however, for his famous investigations into the measurement and development of intelligence (q.v.).

In his *The Measurement of Intelligence. An explanation of and a complete guide for the use of the Stanford revision and extension of the Binet-Simon Intelligence Scale* (1916) he took a revised form of the Binet-Simon intelligence test and adapted it to North-American conditions. This "Stanford Revision", which was later revised a number of times, acquired great importance, particularly through its use by the US Army during World War I for the selection of gifted personnel.

Besides his work on intelligence tests, Terman devoted particular attention to famous and gifted people. In the second volume of his *Genetic Studies of Genius* (1926) (together with U. Miles) he examined the lives of three hundred famous historical figures and awarded them intelligence quotients based on an examination of their letters, sayings and actions. Sample assessments are: Goethe, 210; Descartes, 180; Napoleon, 145. The remaining four volumes of *Genetic Studies of Genius* (1925–29) describe a longitudinal investigation (q.v.) of the development (q.v.) of over 1000 gifted children with an IQ of over 140 into adulthood (age 45). Among Terman's conclusions was that, contrary to previously held beliefs, gifted children were open, effective and socially active, and retained these characteristics throughout development.

Other studies of Terman's were concerned with the relation between masculinity and femininity in groups of different age, sex and occupation (*Sex and Personality*, 1936), and with the contribution of psychological factors to marital happiness (*Psychological Factors in Marital Happiness*, 1938). In the presentation of his research findings, Terman generally remained on the purely descriptive level and avoided general theoretical statements.

Bibliography: Boring, E. G.: Lewis Madison Terman: 1877–1956. In: National Academy of Sciences, Biographical Memoirs, Vol. 33. Washington, 1959, 414–61. **Hilgard, E. R.:** Lewis Madison Terman: 1877–1956. Amer. J. of Psychol., 1957, *70*, 472–9. **Lewis, W. B.:** Professor Lewis M. Terman. Brit. J. of Stat. Psychol., 1957, *10*, 65–8.   *W.W.*

Terminal depression. A depression (q.v.) which appears after the discharge of some difficult task or a release from worry or deprivation. The decisive factor is that those affected were initially wholly absorbed in some task, and feel "empty" after its completion.   *A.Hi.*

Termination of pregnancy. See *Abortion*.

Terminology. In the strict sense, the *study of technical terms* used by any theoretical discipline concerned to reduce a totality of contents to a logically ordered and systematic form. In general, terminology is also the *total* *range of such terms*, or the technical vocabulary of such disciplines. A "term" is an expression which defines an object of thought by describing its specific content. "Term" is sometimes also used to mean "word" in contexts where the content in question is loosely described.   *M.J.B.*

Test. 1. *Definition.* The term "test" has several meanings in psychology. In addition to specific mathematical and statistical test methods (see *Statistics*), the test material used in all studies and the process of testing, considerable importance attaches to psychodiagnostic testing (see *Psychodiagnostics*). Lienert defines the latter as "a routine scientific method of studying one or more empirically defined personality traits in order to draw quantitative conclusions on the relative importance of the particular features in the individual." In this sense, psychodiagnostic testing is a specific form of psychological experimentation. (See *Traits*).

2. *History.* Diagnostic psychology employing tests was not founded by a particular individual or publication. Interest in differential psychology (q.v.) led certain research workers in the late nineteenth century to develop and use measuring instruments to determine interindividual differences; interest centered first on intellectual differentiations (see *Abilities*) and intelligence tests, for educational (McK. Cattell, 1890; H. Münsterberg, 1891; H. Ebbinghaus, 1897; A. Binet, 1905, etc.), psychopathological (C. Rieger, 1888; E. Kraepelin, 1896; T. Ziehen, 1897, etc.), or philanthropic (F. Galton, 1883, who already used fundamental statistics in his work) reasons. It is significant that many of these psychologists were influenced directly (e.g. Cattell, Kraepelin and Münsterberg), or indirectly (e.g. Binet through his colleague V. Henri), by W. Wundt and his experimental psychology. Binet's test methods (the "échelle métrique" for individual testing) were used in many countries (USA, Germany, Switzerland,

Sweden, etc.) and the development after 1917 of group testing methods (see *Army Alpha Test; Army Beta Test*) in the USA (L. M. Terman, G. M. Whipple, R. M. Yerkes *et al.*), which proved extremely useful in the selection of soldiers, played an important part in earning recognition for prediction of performance by means of tests. The simultaneous development of the classical test theory (H. O. Gulliksen) made it possible to provide a full theoretical foundation for these methods.

The development of methods to determine emotional, motivational and—in the broadest sense—characterological components (see *Projective techniques*) began with psychoanalysis (q.v.). Jung's word association test (1904) may be considered the starting-point of this development, which culminated in Rorschach's shape interpretation method (1921).

Today psychodiagnostic tests form an essential part of practical and scientific psychology. They are used for individual diagnosis and in the academic sector for developing, verifying and refuting theories.

3. *Test criteria.* Literature on the subject (Anastasi, 1966; Cronbach, 1971, *et al.*) lists criteria which must be met by a test: (*a*) *standardization:* the test material, instructions and the test situation must be standardized sufficiently for each subject to be confronted with identical conditions, so that his own behavior is the only variable; in this way, interindividual comparability of the test results is guaranteed; (*b*) *norms:* to make quantitative statements on the degree of development of a given feature in an individual, comparable results from other individuals are needed in order to determine the relative position of an individual on a scale. A number of different normative scales are used in psychodiagnostics. The requirement of standardization is met only by *psychometric tests*, i.e. test methods which allow a particular feature to be measured (numerical determination); (*c*) the *objectivity* (one of the main quality criteria, in addition to *reliability* and

validity) of a test is defined in a variety of ways in the literature. Lienert understands this term to denote the degree to which different evaluators are in agreement, i.e. arrive at the same results; Watson, on the other hand, suggests (1959) that the test material should have the same stimulus value for every testee, while Cattell (1957) stipulates that subjective, distorting influences on the part of the subject must be eliminated; (*d*) *reliability:* for proper interpretation of a test value, it is necessary first of all for this value to be characteristic of an individual. Reliability determines the accuracy of the measurement, regardless of what is measured. Reliability (generally represented in numerical terms by a reliability coefficient) characterizes the proportion of interindividual dispersion for a test result which is explained by "true" interindividual differences, by comparison with the proportion of total variance which can be explained by measurement errors and intervening factors in the test record (*error variance*). Two different sources of error must be taken into consideration here: the inaccuracy of a test as a measuring instrument (lack of consistency and inadequate evaluative objectivity), and changes in test conditions (inadequate objectivity in test arrangements, motivational influences, situational interference, etc.). The effect of these sources of error varies as a function of the different operational possibilities of determining a reliability coefficient. When tests are repeated with the same or an equivalent test form, the two sources of error come into play, whereas when reliability is determined by a method of test halving, the conditions of implementation may be considered more or less constant, so that any lack of consistency and objectivity in evaluation are particularly important here. Test halving gives a more optimistic estimate of reliability than determination of repeat reliability. *It is impossible to speak of the reliability of a test in an absolute sense.* The commonest techniques to determine reliability are:

(i) *test repetition:* (with the same test form —test-retest; with equivalent test form— parallel test); (ii) halving techniques (split-half): halving as a function of the test time— in speed tests; random halving; odd-even-split-half—division into items with odd and even indexes; halving on the basis of analysis data—items of identical selectivity and difficulty in each test half (inter-item consistency).

In the English-language literature, reliability coefficients determined by halving techniques are generally referred to as *consistency coefficients*, whereas coefficients obtained by repetition with the same test form are *stability coefficients;* if there is repetition with a parallel form, we speak of *equivalence.*

Reliability coefficients enable the standard measurement error of a score to be calculated, and the confidence interval to be estimated (taking into account also the mean value and test dispersion); in this interval there is a specific probability that a "true" test value can be found.

(*e*) *Validity.* Whereas reliability concerns only the formal accuracy of measurements, validity determines the degree of accuracy with which a test measures the parameters it is designed to measure. A distinction is made between three different validation concepts: *criterion-related validity, content validity* and *construct validity* (q.v.); for diagnostic practice the most important of these is criterion-related validity. Here validity is defined empirically as the correlation with a criterion; many different comparisons may be used as criteria, ranging from objective notations of performance (e.g. production figures) to subjective appraisals (e.g. by a superior).

In the case of criterion-related validation, a distinction is made between *concurrent validity* and *predictive validity*. In concurrent validity, the test values are measured simultaneously with the criterion values; this allows a diagnosis to be made. A prognosis of anticipated behavior is not possible from this validation. In the case of predictive validity, psychological test results are used to predict criterion values measured after the test values. The period of prediction may vary widely, as may the validity coefficients determined for different time intervals. Under certain circumstances validation of a test may not be necessary, i.e. when the validity of a test is logically or psychologically evident (e.g. a spelling test for the criterion "spelling"), if a test is more comprehensive than a criterion (e.g. the task of continuing a series of numbers gives a better impression of the "ability to abstract" than a score in mathematics), if no practical criterion exists (e.g. in interest questionnaires), or if the criterion is much less reliable than the test (e.g. a teacher's appraisal of intelligence). In all these cases it is assumed that the test problems are themselves the best possible criteria. We then speak of *content validity*.

A third, more theoretical than pragmatic, concept of validation is that of *construct validity* (q.v.). This is concerned less with practical-diagnostic relevance than with the clarification of the actual factors measured in a test.

In addition to these main criteria of quality, a test must be comparable, economical and useful.

4. *Classification of psychodiagnostic tests.* Psychodiagnostic tests can be classified on the basis of a range of factors concerning *content* or *form*. Performance tests are sometimes contrasted with personality tests, although this dichotomy is rarely encountered in personality psychology. This division corresponds to Cronbach's (1971) distinction between maximum and typical performance tests. The classification of psychometric and projective methods does not take into account the fact that different classification standpoints are used, and that these two possibilities are certainly not mutually exclusive. Clearer classifications may be established from formal criteria: e.g. standardized—non-standardized tests; one-dimensional—multi-dimensional tests; speed tests; power tests; individual tests; group tests; etc.

5. *Test construction.* We cannot examine in detail here the many theoretical and technical problems of test construction, and confine ourselves to the individual stages of construction: (*a*) *Planning* covers the selection of the type of problem best suited to the aim of the study (correct—wrong, free answer, multiple choice, etc.), as well as the test time and test length. (*b*) *Test design:* bearing in mind the range of applicability of the test (which also determines to some extent the type of validation), the plan must be provisionally implemented. Very great importance attaches here to the content of the test problems, the structural design of the test (questionnaire, test battery, etc.), the test instruction and problems of test evaluation. (*c*) *Construction of the test problems:* problem concepts are designed having regard to the aim of the study and then broken down into concrete individual problems. These are subsequently built up into a first provisional test form. (*d*) *Problem analysis:* an analysis sample is used to check the test problems for utility (with regard to reliability and validity). The criteria for a good test problem are difficulty, selectivity, and—less frequently—the validity relationship between individual problems and the degree of characterization of a particular feature). Item analysis is used to eliminate unsuitable problems, and the problems as a whole are revised as far as necessary. The instructions are also tested under practical conditions. (*e*) *Distribution analysis* of the raw values. A standard distribution is generally the aim, but in special cases an oblique distribution may be desirable because of the better differentiation obtained in specific areas. (*f*) Preparation of the *final test form.* The nature of the material, problem arrangement, test time and instructions, instructions for arranging and evaluating the tests are now defined in detail. (*g*) Check on *quality criteria, reliability* and *validity* by various methods. (*h*) *Test calibration,* as the final stage in standardizing a test, is carried out on a calibrated sample; the results are

then to draw up test norms. See *Objective tests; Test theory*.

Bibliography: Anastasi, A.: Psychological testing. New York, ²1966. Bormuth, J. R.: On the theory of achievement test items. Chicago & London, 1970. Cattell, R. B.: Personality and motivation: structure and measurement. New York, 1957. Cronbach, L. J.: Essentials of psychological testing. New York & London, ³1971. Lyman, H. B.: Test scores and what they mean. New York & London, ²1971. Rapaport, D. *et al.*: Diagnostic psychological testing. New York & London, ²1971. Thorndike, R. L.: Personal selection test, and measurement methods. New York, 1949. Watson, R. I.: Historical review of objective personality testing: the search for objectivity. In: Bass, B. M. & Berg, I. A. (Eds.): Objective approaches to personality assessment. New York, 1959, 1–23.   *D. Pfau*

Test battery. A group of different tests designed to test a broad ability (general intelligence level, aptitude for specific schools or professions, etc.). The intercorrelations between the individual tests should not be too high, but the correlation between the overall result and the criterion should be higher than that of the individual test. See *Test theory*.   *R.M.*

Test economy. One of the secondary quality criteria for a test. A distinction is made between three major aspects: implementation, evaluation and interpretation economy. In general all three economy conditions are more stringent for objective than for projective methods. They constitute an important criterion in selecting tests for routine and group purposes.   *P.Z.*

Testicles (*testes; testiculi*). See *Gonads; Sex gland hormones*.

Testicular feminization. See *Hermaphroditism*.

Test norms. In the methodological context, the term "norms" usually denotes *test norms* (= standardized raw score). In psychology, on the other hand, the "norms" refers to different aspects of behavioral "normality".

1. *Significance of test norms.* The score (raw score) calculated initially in a test evaluation consists of units chosen arbitrarily with a zero point selected at will. The raw score in test (A) is not directly comparable with the score obtained in test (B). The raw score usually does not enable the relative position of a testee in his group to be determined directly. To eliminate these drawbacks, test psychology has developed transformation methods by means of which the raw score can be converted into standardized values. The task of establishing norms is one of the main problems of calibration in the final test construction phase. It should be noted that test norms acquire major importance only if the reliability of the test is sufficiently high, as this is the only way of obtaining statistical references for interindividual and intraindividual differences along a test scale. The lower the empirical reliability, the less accurate the standardization scale need be, and *vice versa*.

2. *Classification of test norms:* depending on the particular problem, test norms may be classified in a variety of ways.

(a) *Simple* and *multiple norms:* if separate norms are established for the overall sample (standardized sample) and/or for individual subgroups within it, we refer to simple norms. If both overall and group norms are formed, we refer to multiple norms. Representativity (because of small samples) is particularly important for group norms.

(b) *Equivalent* and *variability norms:* while equivalent norms refer to the mean values for different groups which can be classified according to a sociologically relevant criterion (e.g. age, school year, etc.), the most common variability norms are based on variability within a given standardized sample.

(c) *Non-parametric and parametric norms:* from this formal angle, a distinction may be made between test norms as a function of the transformation process on which they are based.

(i) *Non-parametric norms* are used for raw scores which do not conform to a standard statistical distribution. Percent rank norms are obtained by converting the raw score into a rank between 1 and 100. Although these norms are still used, they have the drawback that the actual individual test differences are exaggerated in the medium scale range, and under-estimated in the extreme ranges. Percent rankings therefore undergo further transformation. From the statistical angle, test norms merely require an asymptotic raw score distribution.

(ii) *Parametric norms* are used for scores following a standard statistical distribution of the type normally encountered in carefully constructed psychometric procedures. These linear transform methods always refer to a basic distribution, i.e. to the standard or z transformation, based on the well-known equation $z = (x - \bar{x})/s$. To avoid negative values, preference is given to the following test norms: Z norms, obtained through $Z = 100 + 10z$; IQ (intelligence quotient) norms, obtained through $IQ = 100 + 15z$; school mark norms, obtained through $S = 3z$. See *Test theory; Objective tests.*

V. Sarris & G. A. Lienert

Testosterone. The most important male sex hormone. The administration of testosterone often leads to an improvement in persons with a disturbed endocrine metabolism. The effect in healthy persons is uncertain. Extensive studies by H. Düker show an improvement in performance in slightly exhausted individuals, whereas the improvement is only temporary in completely normal subjects. Only a small percentage (about 1%) of active testosterone is excreted unchanged in the urine. The percentage differs from individual to individual, but is relatively constant. Under stress (q.v.) conditions, the amount of testosterone excreted in urine appears to be reduced.

Bibliography: Rose, R. M.: Androgen excretion in stress. In: **Bourne, P. G.** (Ed.): The psychology and physiology of stress. New York, 1969. See also *Sex gland hormones.* *W.J.*

Test profile. A graphic representation of test results. Test profiles are popular because of their clarity and generally make for much easier interpretation. Specific forms of intelligence, professional profiles, etc. are associated with the individual profile forms, as a function of the particular test concerned. *H.J.A.*

Test projectif d'intérêts vocationnels. A test developed by F. Bemelmans to clarify vocational interests. The test is designed on the TAT principle. It consists of two series of thirty small photographs, differing according to sex; the testee is asked to answer six questions concerning the activity of the persons illustrated in each photograph.

Bibliography: Bemelmans, F.: Test projectif d'intérêts vocationnels. Schweiz. Z. f. Psychol., 1953, *12*, 283–94. *H.J.A.*

Test theory. 1. *A basis for definition.* As it is used in psychology and related behavioral sciences, the term "test theory" has a number of quite distinct connotations. At the core of the most widely accepted meaning, however, there is reference to conditions under which numbers are assigned to objects in ways that will ensure that the numbers will reliably and validly represent amounts (i.e. magnitudes) of an attribute of the objects. In specifying these conditions, many theories are elaborated: test theory refers to a collection of theories developed under the headings of reliability, standardization, levels of measurement, validity, item characteristic curves, corrections for chance success, scaling, and norms. Entire books (see bibliography) are written to explicate these various theories. There is thus a domain of test theory. But because the elements of this domain are quite diverse, are sometimes in competition, and are not closely interlocked in a single unifying system, it can be a bit misleading to imply that there is *a* (singular) test theory. Here the term is defined by referring to some of the important kinds of theories considered under headings such as those mentioned above.

2. *Axioms and levels of measurement.* In one important set of test theories, the focus is upon specifying fundamental relationships between meta-theories of mathematics, and procedures whereby numbers may be assigned to objects to represent amounts of an attribute. In such theories the position of formal axiomatics is implicitly accepted. It is assumed that number systems and number operations defined within subsections of mathematics exist quite independently of empirical observations (including those which, historically, led to the development of the system of mathematics). The task of measurement is then viewed as one of forming a one-to-one (isomorphic) link-up between magnitudes of an attribute and the numbers of an established system of numbers.

Four characteristics of the number system of scalar algebra are singled out as having particular relevance for defining the essential nature of measurement. These are referred to as the properties of identity, order, order of difference, and true zero. By *identity* is meant simply that a number symbol, such as 5, is distinct from all other number symbols, and represents the same thing regardless of the context in which it appears. The order *property* refers to the fact that of all numbers that are not identical, one is either larger or smaller than another. It is sometimes convenient to think of an ordered number as representing magnitude of an attribute of numerosity of the number system. The order of *difference characteristic* then represents the fact that differences (and sums) of numerosity are defined explicitly as numbers which, as all other numbers, are ordered. The *zero characteristic* refers to the fact that the number

system contains a unique number, zero, which represents the idea of no numerosity, or none of the attributes represented by other numbers.

Levels of measurement are defined by specifying which of these characteristics of a number system are, or (as is more common) are assumed to be, isomorphically related to magnitudes of an attribute of objects. If, when all of a set of objects have the same amount of an attribute, the same number is consistently assigned, the identity property is used. If only this property is used, a nominal level of measurement is said to obtain. To use the order property, it is necessary that the order of numbers assigned to objects be the same as (or the exact reverse of) the order of magnitudes of an attribute. This kind of an assignment of numbers is referred to as an ordinal level of measurement. The order of difference property is used when numbers are assigned to objects in such a way that the order of differences between numbers is consistently the same as the order of differences in magnitudes of an attribute of the objects. When numbers are assigned in this way, theorists speak of an interval level of measurement. If an object has none of an attribute, or such an object can be conceived of as an extrapolation from observations, and the zero number is assigned, then either ordinal level measurement with a true zero, or interval level measurement with a true zero, is said to obtain. The latter is most often referred to as the ratio level of measurement.

3. *Combinative models and item characteristic theories.* The basic element of most psychological measurements is a response to an identifiable stimulus. In itself, however, a response is usually too small a sample from the responder's repertoire of possible responses to be a reliable and valid indicator of a magnitude of an attribute: a single response is usually a rather unstable, complex, and trivial indicator of many attributes. In most behavioral measurement, therefore, it is necessary to combine several responses. There are

many ways to do this, and therefore many combinative models, but by far the most commonly used procedure is merely to count the number of responses of a particular kind (e.g. "correct responses") to a set of stimuli all of which are assumed to provoke responses that are indicative of the attribute in question. The measurement obtained by counting the number correct in an ability test is typical. This procedure is part of what is frequently referred to as the summative model.

A theory about the relationship between the probability of responding in a particular way to a stimulus and magnitude of an attribute is an item characteristic theory. Several of these are considered in books on test theory. They are usefully cross-classified as either monotonic or non-monotonic and as either probabilistic or deterministic. The theory implicit in most applications of the summative model, and therefore the one most commonly accepted, belongs to the class of monotonic probabilistic theories. According to this kind of theory, as magnitude of an attribute increases, the probability of a response counted to measure that attribute should increase: if several responses to a stimulus are recorded and assigned different numbers (such as 1, 2, 3 and 4) before being summed with numbers representing responses to other stimuli, then there should be a positive monotonic relationship between the item numbers assigned and the total sum-score.

4. *Error theory and concepts of reliability.* If the assumptions of the summative model and a monotonic item characteristic theory are warranted, then it is reasonable to suppose that, in summing responses, the indications of irrelevant attributes will function as random errors which cancel out; and that there will be an accumulation of information on the non-random influence represented by the positive relationship between stimulus response and total score. This idea of a cancelling of random influences and convergence in a non-random influence is basic to many theories of reli-

ability. In the particular application outlined here, the concept of internal consistency reliability is indicated: a set of stimuli is said to be internally consistent if response to each stimulus reliably indicates the same attribute as does response to all other stimuli of the set. A measurement operation may be reliable in this sense without being reliable in the sense that a subject obtaining a high score on one day would obtain a correspondingly high score on another day. Consistency in measurements obtained at distinctly different times is referred to as "stability" reliability. Measurements of thirst might show high internal consistency reliability, but low stability reliability. Consistency in measurements obtained with distinctly different measurement operations— as, for example, different tests—indicates equivalency reliability. When measurements depend upon complex judgments made by raters, it is useful to assess consistency across raters. This is referred to as "inter-rater" or "conspect" reliability. Conspect reliability and equivalency reliability can be high when internal consistency and stability reliability are low. (See also *Construct validity*.)

5. *Dynamic nature of test theory.* This sampling of some of the basic concepts of test theory can only adumbrate the outlines of a broad and complex field within the behavioral sciences. There is much activity and change within this field. The assumptions outlined above are being considered evermore carefully by an increasing number of investigators; a variety of non-linear, non-Euclidean and multivariate theories for representing responses in measurements are being studied; unusual theories of error are being tried out; attempts are being made to specify more clearly the conditions required to assume ratio-level measurement; and many other basic questions are being asked. Yet in much of this activity there would appear to be a trend toward conceptual integration of poorly related areas. Test theory, a complex medley of loosely related theories, is developing into

an even more complex but perhaps symphonically arranged set of theories.

Bibliography: Cattell, R. B.: Validity and reliability: a proposed more basic set of concepts. J. Educ. Psychol., 1964, *55*, 1–22. Id. & Tsujioka, B.: The importance of factor-trueness and validity versus homogeneity and orthogonality, in test scales. Educational and Psychological Measurement, 1964, *24*, 3–30. Ghiselli, E. E.: Theory of psychological measurement. New York, 1964. Gullicksen, H.: Theory of mental tests. New York, 1950. Horn, J. L.: Equations representing combinations of components in scoring psychological variables. Acta Psychologica, 1963, *21*, 184–217. Id.: Integration of concepts of reliability and standard error of measurement. Educational and Psychological Measurement, 1971, *31*. Horst, P.: Psychological measurement and prediction. Belmont, Calif., 1960. Lord, F. M.: A theory of test scores. Psychometric Monographs, 1952, *7*. Id.: An approach to mental test theory. Psychometrika, 1959, *24*, 283–302. Nunnally, J. C.: Psychometric theory. New York, 1967.   *J. L. Horn*

Tetanus. 1. The rhythmic contraction of the striated skeletal muscle which occurs under normal conditions. As a function of the frequency of contraction, a distinction is made between incomplete tetanus with visible tremor, and complete tetanus with uniform, flowing movements.

2. Lockjaw: an acute, severe infection caused by the toxic influence of the tetanus bacilli, characterized by tonic muscle cramps which begin in the face (*risus sardonicus*) and spread throughout the muscular system, so that there is a risk of asphyxia and of bone fractures. Passive and active vaccination is possible and advisable.   *E.D.*

Tetrachoric correlation. An estimate of the relationship between two normally distributed, continuous variables obtained from the information contained in a two-class table. The tetrachoric correlation is a two-class correlation coefficient. See *Correlational techniques.*   *D.W.E.*

Thalamus. The largest subdivision of the diencephalon, consisting chiefly of an ovoid mass of nuclei in each lateral wall of the third ventricle, and divisible into an anterior and medial group of nuclei constituting the paleothalamus; concerned with primitive correlations in connection with the *corpus striatum* but not the cerebral cortex, and a center for the crude perception of pain and affective qualities of other sensations: it is the major relay center between the cerebral cortex and various sensory and optic pathways.   *E.D.*

Thanatos instinct. See *Death instinct.*

Thematic Apperception Test (*abb. TAT*). A psychodiagnostic (q.v.) procedure developed by Morgan & Murray and published in 1935. The TAT is based on the hypothesis that, in imaginary stories centering upon pictorial material open to several interpretations, an individual expresses motives (q.v.), needs (q.v.), attitudes (q.v.), and conflicts (q.v.), which throw light on his own personality. Procedures of this kind are known as "thematic apperception techniques" (Kornadt, 1964). The widely circulated test material from the TAT revision published by Murray in 1943 consists of a manual describing the test, its use and evaluation, and thirty picture cards with a simplified representation in black and white of mainly social and human situations, together with a blank card. The cards were selected according to a clinical test (which is not precisely defined), and some of them are intended for certain reference groups (male or female—under or over fourteen years of age), and bear appropriate markings. It is allegedly possible for the test to be used with subjects from the age of approximately eight years (Revers & Taeuber, 1968). In each of two sessions S. is given ten picture cards in a predetermined sequence, and is asked to tell an exciting story about each picture; at least twenty-four hours should elapse between the two sessions. Because time is limited, it often happens in practice that only a smaller number of cards is used (Bell, 1948; and others). Very different techniques have been developed to evaluate TAT stories; they can be put into three groups: (*a*) evaluation by content; (*b*) formal counting methods based on content; (*c*) purely formal counting methods. In practice, techniques belonging to the third category are chiefly used, whereas methods of the second and third kind have become particularly relevant in research.

First technique: Murray himself has proposed an evaluation technique based on content and going back to a general personality model which he devised in 1938 and which has become known as "need-press analysis": the needs (q.v.), feelings, wishes of the principal figure in each story, and the environmental influences ("press") to which he is exposed, are recorded with a numerical weighting; the sum of these loadings in the whole test then gives for each variable a numerical value which expresses its prominence. Other evaluative techniques based on content have been proposed by Tomkins (1947), Stein (1955) and Rapaport (1943). Bellak with his "inspection technique" (Bellak, 1954), and an outline evaluation schedule (Bellak, 1947), responded to the need for a less time-consuming interpretation. A proposal for a shortened evaluation has been made by Revers (Revers, 1958; Revers & Taeuber, ²1968).

Second technique: Proposals for a formal counting method based on content were made by Dana (1959). McClelland *et al.* (1953). The technique of motive measurement—especially in the area of performance motivation—as developed by McClelland and others, was taken up and elaborated in German-speaking countries by, among others, Heckhausen (1963), Sader & Keil (1968) and Vontobel (1970).

Third technique: the purely formal counting methods exclude considerations of content in evaluating the story and are based solely on structural characteristics. One of the most extreme proposals taking this line comes from Balken & Masserman (1940).

The development of *norms* for TAT was neglected for a long time (Kornadt, 1964), although as early as 1943 Murray had published norms for "need-press" analysis; other attempts to construct norms were directed to the formulation of "common stories", frequent stories concerning certain cards (Stein, 1948, etc.) and the identification of cliché stories and deviations from them (Rapaport, 1943).

The results of investigations to determine reliability and to validate TAT findings are not unanimous (Kornadt, 1964), and are so strongly influenced by the questions or picture selection forming the object of the particular study that general pronouncements are not possible. See *Protective techniques.*

Bibliography: Balken, E. R. & Masserman, J. H.: The language of phantasy. J. Psychol., 1940, *10*, 75–86. **Bell, J. E.:** Projective techniques. New York, 1948, 207–38. **Bellak, L.:** Thematic Apperception Test blank. Psychological Corporation, New York, 1947. Id.: The Thematic Apperception test and the children's apperception test in clinical use. New York, 1954. **Dana, R. H.:** Proposal for objective scoring of the TAT. Perceptual and Motor Skills, 1959, *9*, 27–43. **Heckhausen, H.:** Hoffnung und Furcht in der Leistungsmotivation. Meisenheim, 1963. **Kornadt, H. J.:** Thematische Apperzeptionsverfahren. In: **Heiss, R.** (Ed.): Handbuch der Psychologie, Vol. 6. Göttingen, 1964, ²1966. **McClelland,** *et al.*: The achievement motive. New York, 1953. **Morgan, C. D. & Murray, H. A.:** Method of investigating fantasies: the Thematic Apperception Test. Arch. Neurol. Psychiatr., 1935, *34*, 289–306. **Murray, H. A.:** Explorations in personality. New York, 1938. Id.: Thematic Apperception Test manual. Cambridge, 1943. **Rapaport, D.:** The clinical application of the Thematic Apperception Test. Bull. Menninger Clin., 1943, *7*, 106–13. **Revers, W. J. & Taeuber, K.:** Der Thematische Apperzeptionstest. Berne, ²1968. **Sader, M. & Keil, W.:** Faktorenanalytische Untersuchungen zur Projektion der Leistungsmotivation. Arch. Ges. Psychol., 1968, *120*, 25–53. **Stein, M. I.:** The Thematic Apperception Test. Cambridge, 1948. **Tomkins, S. S.:** The Thematic Apperception Test. New York, 1947. **Vontobel, J.:** Leistungsbedürfnis und soziale Umwelt. Berne, 1970.

F.J.B.

Thematic sign tests. Tests in which S. is asked to draw a specific theme (e.g. tree, man, family, house, person, etc.). The test is then used to reach conclusions concerning S's. social behavior, intelligence, etc., on the assumption of personality projection. See *Projective techniques.*   *H.J.A.*

Theoretical frequency. Theoretical frequencies are frequency indices calculated on the basis of hypotheses or known basic entities. Distributions of theoretical frequencies can always be described by distribution functions.
                                                  D.W.E.

Theoretical type. One of Spranger's six "forms of life", denoting persons who are always concerned to find the truth and arrive at general laws. They are interested in intellectual matters and not in "a bed to sleep in" (Helwig, 1957, 82). They search for truth as the sole value, and their emotions are oriented to this goal.

Bibliography: Helwig, P.: Charakterologie. Stuttgart, 1957.   *W.K.*

Theory. In philosophy, a construct deduced logically by the intelligence and isolated from action; a consistent group of concepts and statements derived from principles, built up methodically and systematically and detached from their application. In science, laws expressed in a systematic form, which are based on observation and remain true until they are superseded by new data; they are therefore dependent on a specific state of knowledge. The purpose of a theory is not only to explain the known but to forecast the unknown. In the narrower sense, a theory is a system of axiomatic mathematical statements which serves as a model for a set of empirical laws (hypothetico-deductive theory). Examples: theory of reminiscence (q.v.); theory of relativity.   *M.J.B.*

Thermoreceptors. There are two kinds of receptor in the skin which respond to heat; they are known as *cold spots* and *hot spots.* Respectively, these respond to temperatures above and below skin temperature.   *C.D.F.*

Thinking. I. Thinking is defined operationally as the establishing of order(s) in the apprehended world. This ordering relates to objects as well as to representations of the world of objects. Thinking is also the ordering of relations between objects, and the ordering of relations between representations of objects.

The figurative or pictorial representation (imagery) of what has been perceived makes it possible to order according to *equality*, *similarity*, or *difference:* objects with the same visual, acoustic, haptic or kinesthetic qualities are treated as belonging together; inequalities lead to separation from the grouping of similar objects. The action of ordering with figurative and pictorial images is called *intuitive thinking.*

The younger subjects are, the more stubbornly they adhere to intuitive orders, and are unable to classify the material or representations of it in any new way (principle of reversibility: Piaget, 1948).

Thought is said to be *"autistic"* (but see *Autism*) if the ordering of the experienced world takes place according to states conditioned by feeling or motivation so that it *arbitrarily* links persons, things or objects coinciding fortuitously with these inner states. If *wish-fulfilment* tendencies determine the results of thinking, the thought processes are defined as *primary*; if, on the other hand, *rational* ordering techniques determine the result of thinking, the thought processes are defined as *secondary* (S. Freud).

Magical thinking orders the relations of image, sign or symbol to the object as if objects, animals or plants, as well as representations of them, were capable of acting like human beings. This way of thinking is frequently found in younger children, uninformed adults, and in exceptional existential states.

If the representations, thoughts and their relations which are being ordered can no longer be expressed in imagery or figuratively, then thinking is non-intuitive, abstract or conceptual (Selz, 1913). An experimental example is searching for words which are subordinated, co-ordinated, or superordinated to a given stimulus word. In such thinking activity the *task* determines the direction thinking will take: "determining tendency" (Ach, 1905), or "convergent and divergent thinking" (J. P. Guilford). The simulation of thinking processes by means of binary-functioning electronic models makes use of the thinking steps expressed audibly by testees.

The establishing of ordered relations between representations or thoughts is conceptual behavior. Rules, thought patterns and operators are developed, or those already known are applied in a formalized model (orientation experiment on maps, Bartlett, 1958) (actualization of knowledge). An experimental example: Kendler (1970): testees learn that the choice of two large squares, then that the choice of two small squares and finally that the choice of two black squares, is correct. The relearning required to change from the concept "big" to the concept "small" can be managed by adults; that from big to black by children up to the age of six; then the verbalization of rules of thinking enables them to proceed like adults. In the response method, different objects are given words until the testee defines the order set with a comprehensive concept. Both reinforced and non-reinforced reactions lead to the formation of concepts; concepts are verbal mediators between perceived material and attempts to arrange the material (C. E. Osgood). In the mechanized or electronic stimulus-response experiment of complex thinking behavior, the testee orders stimuli in classes, and simultaneously decides verbally or in accordance with stimulus what he supposes to be the order system stored in the sequence of stimuli. A success or a mistake is indicated or corrected as the case may be, so that with each reaction one "bit" (q.v.) of information-growth can be used. The quotient of the optimal and the observed increment of knowledge indicates the strategy of information-assembly. Multiple response-sequence analyses with fixed alternating selection possibilities reveal individual styles of deciding and thinking.

Bibliography: Ach, N.: Über die Willenstätigkeit und das Denken. Göttingen, 1905. **Bartlett, F.:** Thinking. New York, 1958. **Bruner, J. S.** et al.: A study of thinking. New York, 1962. **Duncan, C. P.** (Ed.): Thinking: current experimental studies. New York, 1967. **Graumann, C. F.** (Ed.): Denken. Berlin, 1965. **Hedinger, U.:** Die Faktorenstruktur komplexer Denkaufgaben. Zschr. exp. angew. Psychol., 1965, *12*, 337–403. **Kendler, H. H.** et al.: Stimulus control and memory loss in reversal shift behavior. J. exp. Psychol., 1970, *83*, 84–8. **Külpe, O.:** Versuche über Abstraktion. Ber. l. Kongr. exp. Psychol. Giessen, 1904. **Selz, O.:** Über die Gesetze des geordneten Denkverlaufs. Stuttgart, 1913.
E. Jorswieck

II. In the USSR, psychological research into thinking is developing on the bases of cognition theory (q.v.), dialectical materialism, logic, the physiology of higher nervous activity, information theory (q.v.), cybernetics (q.v.), and other sciences adjacent to psychology. Soviet psychology rejects all idealistic and metaphysical interpretations of thinking as "purely mental" or "spontaneous activity", and supports instead the Marxist socio-historical theory of the development of thinking in the process of practical activity and human intercourse. The production of ideas, notions and of the consciousness is primarily interwoven directly with the material activity and the material intercourse of human beings; it is the language of real life (Marx & Engels). In the further course of socio-historical development it becomes possible to abstract from real actions, to replace them with mental actions, or those described with words (other, different signs are also used for this purpose).

On this foundation the highest—abstract and generalized—form of thinking arises. Simultaneously, a separation of cognition takes place: it becomes a special theoretical activity, which nevertheless remains linked to practice as the source and criterion of accuracy, and the place where the results of thinking will be used. From the start, thinking is an active, purposeful process of cognition, a creative activity, a search for the solutions to practical and subsequently to theoretical problems.

These general principles relate not only to the socio-historical but also to the ontogenetic development of thinking, which from the time proceeds by paths of its inception goes along ways different to those of the biological evolution of thinking in the animal world. The latter is only the "prehistory of the intellect", which remains restricted by the limits of biological needs, these being satisfied by elementary forms of intuitive-practical thinking (practical analysis and practical synthesis). But social factors are of crucial importance in the onto-genetic development of thinking, a child's conversation with adults, social forms of play, participation in ongoing work, school instruction, etc.; their influence determines not only the content but the structure of thinking operations. Age "norms" for the mental development of the child are relative, and can vary within a very wide range—independently of any system of education and training. In this connection, Soviet psychologists criticize the formal evaluation of the intellect with the aid of tests which usually do not consider the possibilities of a child's mental development during training and practical activity. Hence long-term observation of children undergoing instruction at school remains the principal means of determining mental development and its prognosis. The use of short-term intelligence tests can have only a limited significance. (See *Abilities*).

From the psychological angle, thinking is characterized as a complex analytical-synthetic activity of the brain, its cortical and subcortical mechanisms, which process all the objective and linguistic information reaching the brain (the first and second systems, according to I. P. Pavlov) and correct it with the mechanisms of *feedback* (q.v.) or *retroactive afference*. In this process, according to Pavlov, different degrees of correlation between the first and second signal systems are possible; different types of thinking can then develop (intuitive or "artistic", abstract or "verbal", or mixed). This difference of types of thinking (q.v.) is, however, relative, and depends on many factors (e.g. the kind of objects being thought about, experience, diverse subjective attitudes, etc.). Such conditions apply also to the early ontogenetic stages of thinking, which are termed merely "sensorimotor" or "intuitive-practical", since in reality even in the second year of a child's life not only direct sensorimotor influences but verbal stimuli and verbal responses from the child himself which are bound up with them, become increasingly important in the development of his intellect. Soviet psychological research reveals the complicated and contradictory nature of the relations between thought and language (q.v.), and proves that language is not only a means for expressing thoughts but *a basic element or mechanism of thinking*, with the aid of which abstractions are made from immediate objective impressions and behaviors, which are replaced by thought-images and schemata in combination with outer or inner language.

The most complete presentation of these theoretical theses will be found in the works of L. S. Vygotsky (1934; Eng. trans., 1962), S. L. Rubinstein (1946, 1958) and A. N. Leontiev (1959, 1964), in which early and modern theories of the intellect, the theories about thinking of the Würzburg school (q.v.), of gestalt psychology, behaviorism (q.v.), and J. Piaget's approach are critically analyzed. Experimental research into thinking follows various paths in the Soviet Union, the most important of which are: (*a*) the *phylogenetic* investigation of the mental development of animals, including the genetics of higher nervous activity, animal psychology, ecology and ethology (I. P. Pavlov and his school, N. N. Ladyna-Kots, N. J. Voitonis, N. A. Tich, A. D. Slonim, L. V. Krusinski); (b) ontogenetic research into the mental development of children (P. P. Blonski, A. V. Zaporozhek, D. N. Usnadze, B. I. Chashapuridze, N. Ch. Shvashkin, M. M. Kolzova); (c) *structural-functional and operational* research into thinking in different kinds of teaching and practical activity (P. A. Shevarev, G. S. Kostiuk, P. J. Galperin, N. A. Menshinskaia); (d) research into *heuristics* and the *model construction* of thinking operations with electronic computers (V. N. Pushkin, D. A. Pospelov, O. K. Tichomirov); (e) *psycho-physiological and clinical research* (A. R. Luria, V. N. Miasichshcev, E. I. Bojko, B. V. Zeigarnik); (f) psycholinguistic investigations into the problem of the interrelations of language and thought, the psychological foundations of nomenclature and the understanding of meaning, the acquisition of foreign languages and translating (D. N. Usnadze, V. A. Artemov, N. I. Zhinkin); (g) *defectological* research specializing in the specific nature of thinking, and the ways in which it is compensated with different defects of mental development (L. V. Zankov, I. M. Solovev), and when there is either damage to hearing or some other defect (N. G. Morozova, Z. I. Shif). The results of this research work are published in psychological and other reviews, monographs and volumes with different contributions on special topics; they are also announced at scientific symposia, conferences and meetings.

Bibliography: Bartlett, F.: Thinking. London, 1958. Blonski, P. P.: Memory and thinking (Russian). Moscow, 1935. Duncan, C. P.: Thinking: current experimental studies. New York, 1967. Graumann, C. F.: Denken. Cologne–Berlin, 1965. Humphrey, G.: Thinking. London, 1951. Ladygina-Kots, N. N.: Research into the cognitive abilities of the chimpanzee (Russian). Moscow, 1923. Id.: Prerequisites for human thinking (Russian). Moscow, 1965. Leontiev, A. N.: Problems of psychic development (Russian). Moscow, 1959. Luria, A. R.: The human brain and psychological processes (Russian). Moscow, 1963. Pushkin, V. N., Pospelov, D. A. & Sadovski, V. N. (Eds.): Problems of heuristics (Russian). Moscow, 1969. Rohr, A.: Komplexes Denken. Weinheim & Basle, 1968. Rubinstein, S. L.: Thinking and research (Russian). Moscow, 1958. Sokolov, A N: Inner language and thinking (Russian). Moscow, 1968. Usnadze, D. N.: Psychological research (Russian). Moscow, 1966. Voitonis, N. J.: Prehistory of the intellect (Russian). Moscow, 1934. Vygotsky, L. C.: Thought and language. Cambridge, Mass., 1962. Watson, P. C. & Johnson-Laird, P. N. (Eds.): Thinking and reasoning. Harmondsworth, 1968. Werner, H. & Kaplan, B : Symbol formation. New York & London, 1963. *A. N. Sokolov*

Thinking, abstract. From the viewpoint of association (q.v.) psychology, any thought process makes use of "images" or raw ideational material presented pictorially in the conscious mind. Since the Würzburg school's research into thought processes, non-pictorial or abstract thinking has been supposed to be characteristic and constitutive of thought processes. Images are often only the stimulus and starting-point of a thought process; they are accompanied by specific abstract contents (or elements of consciousness) and determinative tendencies which exert a decisive effect on the course of thinking. *H.W.*

Thinking function. According to C. G. Jung (q.v.) one of the four basic functions of the psyche. Like the feeling function, it helps us to understand our own significance and that of the world. *W.L.*

Thinking, psychology of. A collective term for several lines of research into cognitive functions, especially in solving human and animal problems. The Würzburg School (q.v.) showed (in experiments with introspection, and departing from the Aristotelian view that thinking is only a linking of images) that thinking is possible non-intuitively and without images, being controlled by "determining tendencies" defined by the task. Gestalt psychology explained the experience that a problem is often solved suddenly by a flash of insight (see *Aha experience*) in terms of a successful restructuring of the individual parts of the problem. Systematic problem-solving is investigated in terms of concept (q.v.) formation. The development of early thinking in the child and of concept formation into a higher complexity has been investigated and described in detail by J. Piaget (q.v.).   *W.L.*

Thinking type. Thinking is the "principal function", as "active", "directed", "rational" thinking. The "extraverted thinking type is guided by objective data", "objective facts" or "universally valid ideas", the "introverted" by subjective ideas. The latter strives to "study in depth and not to widen his range".

Bibliography: Jung, C. G.: Psychologische Typen. Zürich (1921), 1960.   *W.K.*

Thirst. A primary, not an acquired need. The regulating system for the intake of water is supposed to be in the hypothalamus. The controlling part is stimulated principally by the osmotic state of pressure of the cells as well as by the degree of tension of the stomach wall, and this is expressed psychologically as a sensation of thirst or as a motive to drink. In addition to physiological effects (e.g. loss of weight, changes in blood pressure), thirst has been shown to have an influence on cognition, motivation and behavior.

Bibliography: Weinert, F.: Hunger und Durst. In: Handbuch der Psychologie, Vol. 2. Göttingen, 1965, 465–512.   *P.S. & R.S.*

Thomson, Godfrey Hilton, Sir. B. 1881; d. 1955. Thomson received his Ph.D. in 1906 at the University of Strasbourg; from 1925 to 1951, he was professor of educational psychology at Edinburgh University and at the Moray House training college (also in Edinburgh). Thomson was largely responsible for the development of the Moray House Tests, a series of group verbal tests of intelligence for the selection of gifted children. In addition to his research into giftedness, and his immense part in establishing psychology and especially educational psychology on a proficient footing in Scotland, Thomson became widely known for his factor-analytical model of the structure of intelligence, which—as the "sampling theory"—posed an alternative to Spearman's two-factor theory and Thurston's multiple factor theory. Thomson contended that all cognitive achievements were determined by a large number of independent, elementary ability factors, only a limited "sample" of which ever enter into a particular operation. The extent of the correlation between different achievements depends on the degree to which the same elementary factors take effect in them.

Main works: The essentials of mental measurement (with W. Brown). London, 1911. Instinct, intelligence and character. London, 1924. The factorial analysis of human ability. London, 1939.   *W.W.*

Thorndike, Edward Lee. B. 31/8/1874 in Williamsburg (USA); d. 10/8/1949 in Montrose, N.Y. Thorndike studied under William James (q.v.) at Harvard, where he began his experiments in animal learning. He continued his learning experiments with cats and dogs (using the mazes and problem boxes, or puzzle boxes, he had constructed for the purpose) at J. McK. Cattell's instigation at Columbia University, New York. He presented his findings in 1898 in a dissertation entitled "Animal intelligence: an experimental study of the associative processes in animals". The learning theory presented in this study remained for nearly fifty years the dominant theory in the USA and decisively influenced the development of American learning psychology. From

1899 Thorndike worked at Columbia Teachers' College, where he concerned himself increasingly with problems of human learning, education and intelligence. The Thorndike bibliography contains five hundred and seven published items, among which are some major psychological monographs.

Thorndike's learning theory. The basis of learning, i.e. of the formation of habitual behaviors, is the association (q.v.) of stimuli and responses (S-R theory). The characteristic form of learning is by trial-and-error: the individual who finds himself in a problematic situation (e.g. in a problem box) draws on his existing behavioral repertoire until by chance a behavior leads to a successful outcome. Certain laws are responsible for the choice of a response and its association with the stimulus situation:

The *law of effect*, which in the original version states that the intensity of a connection arising between a stimulus situation and a response is increased if the connection is followed by a satisfying state, and that the intensity of the connection decreases if it is followed by an unsatisfying state.

Thorndike formulated the law thus: "Any act which in a given situation produces satisfaction becomes associated with that situation, so that when the situation recurs the act is more likely than before to recur also. Conversely, any act which in a given situation produces discomfort becomes dissociated from that situation, so that when the situation recurs the act is less likely than before to recur."

The *law of exercise* (or of "use and disuse") stated that, independently of their consequences, S-R connections could also be exclusively reinforced by practice, whereas they became weaker without "frequency".

Thorndike to some extent revised the theory in his post-1930 publications. The law of exercise was all but rejected. The law of effect was also thoroughly revised so that the effect of negative was played down in favor of positive behavioral consequences, and punishments appeared inappropriate to any substantial weakening of connections. Punishment made the learner go on trying until he discovered a response that was rewarded and thus associated positively with the situation.

Thorndike introduced some other principles to explain the mechanisms of learning, among which the principle of "belongingness" has a major place: it states that a stimulus-response connection is learned the more easily the more closely and naturally the response suits the stimulus situation and the behavioral result the response. The principle of "spread of effect" states that the influence of a satisfying state is exerted not only on the connection which it directly follows, but on stimulus-response connections that are close in time ("recency").

Major works: Animal intelligence: an experimental study of the associative processes in animals. Psychol. Rev. Monogr. Suppl., 1911, *8*. Mental social measurements. New York, 1904. The elements of psychology. New York, 1905. The psychology of learning. New York, 1913. The psychology of arithmetic. New York, 1922. The measurement of intelligence. New York, 1926. Human learning. New York, 1931. The fundamentals of learning. New York, 1932. An experimental study of rewards. New York, 1933. The psychology of wants, interests and attitudes. New York, 1935. Edward Lee Thorndike. In: Murchison, C. (Ed.): A history of psychology in autobiography, Vol. 3. Worcester, 1936, 263–70. Man and his work. Cambridge, Mass., 1943.

Bibliography: Hilgard, E.: Theories of learning. New York, ²1956. *W.W.*

Thread test. A test associated especially with W. Wundt and used in some quarters to estimate depth perception. The subject observes through a slit a number of threads horizontally suspended against a grey background. Some are made to approach or removed to a greater distance from the eye, until all appear equidistant from it.   *J.G.*

Three-sided intercourse (syn. *Triangular sex*). Heterosexual or homosexual contacts between three individuals. One of the three partners may act as a voyeur. A variation consists in one partner being heterosexually selected but homosexual, and engaging in homosexual relations with a third partner of the same sex while the first watches the activity. The association of three-sided intercourse and voyeurism is quite often a feature of genuine perversions (see *Perversion*); however, three-sided intercourse is not intrinsically perverted, but a variant sexual activity subject to strong societal taboos, and therefore less well-known.
                                                          H.M.

Threshold. The value of a quantitative variable (e.g. sound intensity) at which a stimulus is just detectable (*absolute threshold*) or the minimum difference between two stimuli on either a quantitative or qualitative variable (e.g. hue) that is detectable (*difference or differential threshold*). In both cases it is usually necessary to express the threshold as a statistical average even for an individual subject. Also called *limen*; hence abbreviations AL and DL for absolute and difference thresholds respectively, and *subliminal perception:* referring to stimuli below the threshold of conscious perception which are nevertheless supposed to influence behavior. The *psychophysical methods* were developed originally as means for determining thresholds. See also: *Signal-detection theory*, which is a modern approach to the problem of measuring sensory thresholds.
                                                          G.D.W.

Thurstone, Louis Leon. B. 29/5/1887 in Chicago; d. 29/9/1955 in Chapel Hill, USA. Thurstone studied electrical engineering at Cornell University and worked as an assistant of Edison's at the East Orange (N.J.) laboratory. In 1914 he began to study psychology at Chicago and at the Carnegie Institute of Technology. His initial interest was research into learning. In 1923 he worked for a year at the Institute of Government Research in Washington, and returned in 1924 to Chicago as Associate Professor of psychology; three years later he was appointed a full professor; he established a psychometric laboratory. Thorndike was among the founders of the "Psychometric Society" and its journal *Psychometrika*; in 1932 he became president of the APA, and in 1936 first president of the Psychometric Society.

Thurstone was essentially a psychometrician, and in this capacity made important contributions to many areas of psychology. In intelligent research he became well-known for his factor-analytic approach: he came out against Spearman's "g" and tried instead to derive cognitive performance from several group factors (see *Abilities; Intelligence*). After a considerable amount of factor-analytic work, he postulated his seven "primary mental abilities": verbal comprehension, numerical ability, spatial visualization, perceptual ability, memory, reasoning and word fluency. He was able to extract similar factors in corresponding investigations in other areas, e.g. in perception.

Beyond the field of intelligence, Thurstone is best known for his work on "simple structure" and many other contributions to the development of multiple factor analysis, and for the construction of modern scaling techniques and their use in attitude (q.v.) measurement. See *Factor analysis*.

Main works: The measurement of attitude: a psychophysical method and some experiments with a scale for measuring attitude toward the church. Chicago, 1929. The vectors of mind: multiple-factor analysis for the isolation of primary traits. Chicago, 1935. Primary mental abilities. Chicago, 1938. A factorial study of perception. Chicago, 1944.

Multiple-factor analysis: a development and expansion of the vectors of mind. Chicago, 1947. L. L. Thurstone. In: Boring, E. G. *et al.* (Eds.): A history of psychology in autobiography. Vol. 4. Worcester, Mass., 1952, 295–321. An analytical method for simple structure. Chicago, 1954. A method of factoring without communalities. Chicago, 1955. The measurement of values. Chicago, 1959.

Bibliography: Atkins, D. C.: Louis Leon Thurstone: creative thinker, dedicated teacher, eminent psychologist. In: Frederiksen, N. & Gulliksen, H. (Eds.): Contribution to mathematical psychology. New York, 1964, 1–39. *W.W.*

Thymeretics. A subgroup of the antidepressives (q.v.).

Thymoleptics. A subgroup of the antidepressives (q.v.).

Thymopsyche. A term used in A. Gemelli's personality psychology. The thymopsyche forms the layer of the personality in which drives and inclinations are formed. It lies between the layer of organic functions (constitution) and that of higher feelings, thought and will. See *Strata theory*. *W.K.*

Thymus. An endocrine organ (see *Endocrine glands*) behind the breast-bone which grows only until the individual reaches sexual maturity and then gradually degenerates into fatty tissue. Its function affects growth, calcium balance, and the development of the gonads and the entire lymphatic system. Recent research shows that the thymus is also very important for the development of immunities. *E.D.*

Thyrocalcitonin. A thyroid gland hormone which normalizes the extracellular calcium level when it becomes too high. Thyrocalcitonin is an antagonist of parathyroid hormone. The secretion and effect mechanisms of thyrocalcitonin are as yet unexplained.

Bibliography: Russell, R. G. G. & Fleisch, H. (Eds.): Thyrocalcitonin. London, 1967. *W.J.*

Thyroid gland (*Glandula thyreoidea*). A dual inner secretory gland situated on the anterior side of the neck, to the right and left of the larynx, and producing the hormone thyroxin. Histologically, it consists of epithelial follicles. Many thyroid diseases are connected with the formation of a goiter. *E.D.*

Thyroid hormones. Hormones stored by the thyroid gland. The most prominent effect is that on *metabolism*. Hyperfunction leads to increased basal metabolism. Substantial hypofunction characterizes the myxedema syndrome. In the case of innate hyperfunction, or where it appears during early youth, cretinism occurs. Slight hyperfunction often leads to adiposity. The primary thyroid hormones are *thyroxin* (tetraiodthyroxin) and the more active *triiodthyronine*. The storage of thyrotropin(e) is inhibited by both hormones. Recently, a further thyroid hormone, *thyrocalcitinon*, which causes a drop in blood calcium, was discovered. There have been few psychological tests of thyroid hormone. Under stress (q.v.) conditions, slight variable increases in storage after initial decrease have been demonstrated.

Bibliography: Klein, E.: Die Schilddrüse. Berlin, 1969. Mason, J. W.: A review of psychoendocrine research on the pituitary-thyroid system. Psychosom. Med., 1968, *30*, 666–81. Pitt-Rivers, R. & Trotter, W. R.: The thyroid gland. Washington, 1964. *W.J.*

Thyrotoxicosis. See *Basedow's disease*.

Thyrotropic hormone (TSH). See *Thyrotropin*.

Thyrotropin (*Thyropar*). A glandotropic hormone which stimulates the secretion of thyroid hormones. Secretion is regulated under the influence of the neurohormone TRH (thyrotropin-releasing hormone) produced in the hypothalamus, and by the quantity of thyroid gland hormones present in the blood.   *W.J.*

Tic. A brief jerk in the muscles usually of the upper part of the body such as the face, neck or shoulder. May be due to psychological causes but may also be associated with brain damage.   *P.Le.*

Time-and-motion study. The methodical investigation, analysis and synthesis of movement (using appropriate recording devices) during some work process. See *Time study*.

Time, estimation of. All reactions to the discrimination of the duration of (or between two) events, whether through comparative or absolute judgment, production or reproduction. As a specific process, time estimation is the direct assessment of duration with the aid of a subjectively numerical scale (e.g. seconds or minutes). Sometimes the term is used for events of longer duration (more than the directly experienced present of a few seconds), and thus set over against time perception. But this phenomenal distinction is not functionally straightforward.

Bibliography: Fraisse, P : Psychologie du temps. Paris, ²1967.   *A.L.*

Time, experience of. The experience of time may be defined as the representation of time in the human consciousness (q.v.).

The perception of temporal duration requires a simultaneous apprehension of successive aspects of an occurrence without the participation of memory (q.v.). The process of learning to harmonize physiological processes without environmental changes makes possible orientation in time (the "internal clock") and the anticipation of external events. "Empty" stretches of time are perceived as shorter than "full" ones. The perception of "empty" and "full" periods of time is influenced by stimulus intensity, frequency, duration and location of stimuli. Psychic (psychological) time does not elapse continuously but discretely. The shortest perceptible form of temporal duration is the "moment".

A temporal perspective develops out of the interaction of recurrent needs with environmental influences in the sense of *conditioning* (q.v.). The expectation of a need gratification already experienced at an earlier date produces the connections between past, present and future. The separation of temporal from spatial succession is a prerequisite for the perception of time. Around the eighth year of age, the ability to reconstruct events in correct time sequence and the idea of an abstract unit of time as the basis for a perspective of time corresponding to the adult level come into being. The stability of time assessment increases with age.

Old people assess a given stretch of time as shorter than young people would. For older people, time passes — subjectively — more quickly. This tendency becomes more obvious with increasing age. Women tend to be less proficient than men in the exactitude and stability of their estimation of time, and are more inclined than men to overestimate.

Time seems to pass more quickly, the higher the activation level of the organism. Low motivation for an actual event (boredom) accompanies spontaneous overassessment of periods of time, just as high motivation for a future activity accords with momentary inactivity (waiting). Spontaneous underassessment occurs with high motivation for actual events. These conditions are reversed in reminiscence (q.v.).

The variable length of hypothetical inner units of time conditions interindividual variations in the processing of temporal information. The length of these units can be altered by external circumstances (e.g. stress, q.v.).

Hallucinogens (mescalin, psilocybin, LSD-25) and thyroxin, caffeine and methamphetamine can cause overestimation of periods of time. Phenothiazine, tranquilizers (e.g. chlorpromazine), quinine and laughing gas can produce underestimation.

Phenomena of pathological time perception are: (*a*) extreme acceleration or deceleration of time perception; (*b*) loss of temporal sense of reality: absence of any awareness of a temporal continuum; (*c*) the proportions of past, present and future are displaced: one or more of these dimensions may be missing.

The perception of temporal sequences may be traced to fluctuations of attention (q.v.), whose intermediate periods are experienced as "present", and whose rhythm may depend on motivation. The hypothesized existence of a subcortical "pacemaker" center dependent on the relation between excitation and inhibition processes explains the ability of the nervous system to reproduce a series of excitations as sequential experience. See *Arousal*.

Time perception alters with fluctuations in body temperature: the basis for this process is thought to be the speed of chemical processes. Personality-dependent differences in time perception are explicable in terms of a hypothetical, individually diverse input level of chemical processes in the organism. See *Time, psychology of; Memory; Reminiscence*.

Bibliography: Fraisse, P.: Psychology of time. New York, 1963. **Id** : Zeitwahrnehmung und Zeitschätzung. In: **Metzger, W.** (Ed.): Handbuch der Psychologie, Vol. 1/1. Göttingen, 1966, 656–90. **Orme, J. E.**: Time, experience and behaviour. London, 1969. **Ornstein, R. E.**: On the experience of time. Harmondsworth, 1969.   *J. Wittkowski*

Time, psychology of. As an object of psychology, time is bound up with happenings as they appear to an individual (*awareness of time*), which affect or influence him (*relation to time*), or in relation to which he orientates his action (*time perspective*). *Psychic* or *psychological time* designates the totality of before-and-after relations between the individual and such events. The events are thought of as foreseen or planned (*future*), or engaged in, or accomplished (*present*), or remembered or stored (*past*). They can arise in the organism or its environment, and may be noticed or unnoticed. In their temporal aspect, all events for an individual follow an irreversible order. A given event in this series can only occur once, lasts for a shorter or longer time (*duration*), and stands in a particular relationship of order to other events (*simultaneous* or *successive*). This series and the socio-culturally conditioned relationship of its elements to each other make possible the *temporal orientation* of the individual in the world and in society.

The psychology of time does not seek to establish the philosophical nature of time, but to determine the means by which it is possible to form a concept of, and relationship to, time. It also seeks to discover the laws underlying this means, and its diverse modes of operation. Traditionally, time is real though mysterious (Augustine), but in the calendar and the clock as well as the parameters of Newtonian physics it has been made successfully operational.

Kant defined time as a "form of perception", and thus made it a central problem of psychology. The ordinary procedure of the psychology of time is to compare and contrast "objective" clock time and "subjective time", which is understood in many different ways.

1. *Duration.* The early psychophysics (q.v.) of duration investigated the awareness of time as a "sense of time" (E. H. Weber, Czermak) which, by analogy with the other senses, apprehended duration as its object. The researches of Vierordt, E. Mach, G. J. Fechner, W. Wundt and their disciples showed that

subjective time is related in a peculiar way to clock time. Hence the *difference threshold* (between time as a sense object and clock time) is smaller the shorter the duration to be apprehended. At 0.6–1 seconds it is at a minimum of 1.5–15%, according to conditions and the methods employed; it increases irregularly as the duration increases. Under optimal conditions (training and repeated presentation of the sense object), the minimum difference threshold becomes about 1% at about 100 milli-seconds.

The relation between subjective and objective duration is also unclear because the methods most frequently used of comparing, reproducing and verbally communicating the processes of apprehension (q.v.) and attention (q.v.) are various and uncorrelated.

Pronounced individual differences make the usual averages and the subjective scales derived from them appear artificial. In most studies the shorter intervals are presented in relationship to the longer, and the longer to the shorter. (Concepts of over- and under-estimation are ambivalent because the relative difference is not the same in different cases.) The rate of constant error in the assessment of a length of time so that clock time agrees with subjective time is *indifference point*. This was at one time held to be a constant in the order of 0.6–0.8 seconds, or up to 1.5 seconds. More recent research shows that it is not constant but relative to the interval in question. Therefore the time or "tempo" of the "internal clock" is *dependent on the duration* of the objective length of time to be assessed. Frequent repetition of objectively the same interval effects cumulative changes in subjective duration. Unlike the immediate experience of duration, a period which seemed to pass slowly can seem in retrospect to have been short, and *vice versa*. The apprehension of, and relationship to, time can be influenced in uncertain ways by *situational conditions*, such as instruction, a context of aspiration, the nature of the stimulus, the intensity of the

stimulus, a change of stimulus, a changed interpretation of the stimulus, and *organic conditions* such as the mode of apprehension, hormonal condition, psychopharmacological factors, the time of day, body temperature (q.v.), activation level (q.v.), motivation, age, intelligence (q.v.), personality traits (q.v.), psychopathological categories, and so on. The hope of using the apprehension of time as a diagnostic element in personality psychology and psychopathology, has not been fulfilled.

In the peculiar relationship between subjective and objective time there is also a phenomenological difference between immediately experienced duration (psychic *present time*, in the range of 0.5 to a few seconds; W. Stern) and longer, apparently cognitively apprehended (or not immediately experienced), periods (Fraisse, 1967). This difference cannot be functionally ascertained. With respect to the *cognitive process* (in the apprehension of duration), it is clear that under conditions of sleep (q.v.) or hypnosis (q.v.), and in animals, the relationship to time is more exact. At any rate in rhythmic behavior and experience, a frequency of one to two heart beats (corresponding to periods of 1.5 to one second) appears in many cases to be acceptable, comfortable and natural.

Early theoretical studies stressed the eventual fading of a sense impression; the extent to which a memory had faded was regarded as a temporal sign (T. Lipps). They also described apparent continuities (with the smallest difference threshold, indifference point, personal tempo, etc.) as playing a time-structuring role. In obvious analogy to the mechanical clock, the "internal clock" was thought of as the *measure of individual duration* (H. Münsterberg, W. James).

2. Simultaneity and succession. Under optimal conditions a practiced listener can distinguish an acoustical stimulus as two sounds with an interruption between them of a minimum of 2 msec. With optical stimuli on the same retinal image, about 50 msec are necessary. In order to distinguish clearly between two signals distinct in place, nature of stimulus or the sense by which it is to be apprehended, a pause of 100–60 msec is necessary. Practiced observers can reduce this to about 20 msec (F. Exner, D. J. Hirsch). Events occurring at objectively different times can (within a certain span which has not been clearly determined) be subjectively experienced as simultaneous. Numerous serial interactions, usually dependent upon *temporal integration*, can be distinguished in the reception of two or more signals at a short interval.

Although the question of an absolute threshold between simultaneity and succession cannot be given a clear and general answer, the functional apprehensibility of the time dimension is of great importance for the renewal of the unitary single-number theory of the "internal clock", which is held today either explicitly or implicitly by most authors. According to this theory, subjective time is made up of a series of elements, by the "counting" of which the duration of events can be assessed and reproduced. The units are defined as apprehended internal or external occurrences in themselves (Fraisse, 1967; M. Frankhaeuser), numerous biological oscillatory and subsidiary processes of a (quasi-) periodical (for example the Alpha-rhythm: N. Wiener) or excitatory (Creelman) nature. The most commonly advanced theory (von Baier, H. Bergson, von Uexküll, Stroud) is of a cumulative series of so-called "psychic moments", together with assumed additional mechanisms to explain the special articulation of the duration dimension and its functional dependencies. These additional mechanisms are, e.g., a variable length of psychological moments, distortion of the counting process in storage, etc. (Triesman, 1963; Michon, 1967; Cohen, 1967). The discontinuity of one's apprehension of the sense object is thus assured. However, there is no proof of the relevance of this series of moments to the problem of coping with time.

3. *Orientation in time*. Research is being carried out into the so-called *time perspective* (K. Lewin; H. Frank), particularly into time span, but also into articulation, intensity, consistency and division (particularly in the experience of the future: R. Bergius), factors which are psychically active in present experience and behavior. Such research uses questionnaires and many projective (q.v.) tests both as functions and determinants of diverse social, cultural, constitutional, personal and developmental factors. The results of research to date show the relevance of temporal orientation, particularly in motivational and social psychology. But empirically tested detailed knowledge is still lacking because of the lack of any real consistency of method.

In contrast to the functional discrepancy and irregularity of subjective time, the *subjective concept of time* takes the form of an idealized, homogeneous continuum. Subjective time narrows the distant past and future to the point of immobility; the conceptual continuum continues both ways everlastingly. Accordingly, the concept of time in classical physics takes time-and-space as an absolute presupposition of the rapidity of movement dependent on them. Researches into the ontogenesis of the concept of time (J. Piaget) and the complex relationships between time, distance and speed known as the *tau phenomenon* (q.v.) and kappa effect, are undertaken on the basis of relativist physics. According to this, psychic time is constituted by the tempo of endogenous life processes, and the processes in the environment which they use for the purpose of synchronization.

Bibliography: Bindra, D. & Waksberg, H.: Methods and terminology in studies of time estimation. Psychol. Bull., 1956, *53*, 155–9. **Cohen, J.:** Psychological time in health and disease. Springfield, Ill., 1967. **Fischer, R.** (Ed.): Interdisciplinary perspectives of time. Ann. N.Y. Acad. Sci., 1967, *138* (2), 367–915. **Fraisse, P.:** Psychologie du temps. Paris, ²1967. **Fraser, J. T.** (Ed.): The voices of time. New York, 1966. **Michon, J. A.:** Timing in temporal tracking. Soesterberg (Holland), 1967. **Mönks, F. J.:** Zeitperspektive als psychologische

Variable. Arch. ges. Psychol., 1967, *119*, 131–61. **Treisman, M.**: Temporal discrimination and the indifference interval: implications for a model of the "internal clock". Psychol. Monogr., 1963, *77* (13). No. 576. **Wallace, M. & Rabin, A. I.**: Temporal experience. Psychol. Bull., 1960, *57*, 213–36. **White, C. T.**: Temporal numerosity and the psychological unit of duration. Psychol. Monogr., 1963, *77* (12), No. 575.   *A. Lang*

Time sampling. A systematic or "fractionated" short-term observation method in which a subject is observed repeatedly for only a few minutes at a time in the course of a longer investigation, and the observed behavior is simultaneously or subsequently recorded. Distribution of the observations for each subject takes into account the comparability of conditions in the observation situation. Multiple short-term observation allows of a higher reliability of observational data. See *Observation; Test theory.*

Bibliography: Cronbach, L. J.: Essentials of psychological testing. New York & London, ²1960.   *J.O.*

Time sense. The mechanism by which people can estimate the passage of time is still obscure. "Primitive" time estimation, i.e. during sleep and hypnosis, is more accurate than conscious estimation. Time sense is affected by the activity being carried out during estimation and also by drugs, fever and certain psychiatric states. These latter effects suggest that metabolism may play a role in time estimation.
                                                          C.D.F.

Time-sharing systems. A computer is a time-sharing system (abb. TSS) when it is accessible simultaneously to several users by way of their own on-line service devices ("on-line" means that the user's requirements are directly processed by the computer's central unit).
                                                          K.-D.G.

Time study. Part of a work study or analysis. Among other things, a time study ascertains the time required for human work. The time spent on the task is measured and assessed experientially. Various kinds of stop watch and recording device may be used that are actuated by the worker or observers (industrial engineers), or even automatically. Cinematic records may also be made. See *Industrial psychology; Occupational psychology.*
                                                          G.R.W.M.

Titchener, E. B. Edward Bradford Titchener (1867–1927) "donned his gown, the assistant brushed his coat for fear of ashes from the ever-present cigar, the staff went out the door for apparatus and took front seats, and Titchener then appeared on the platform from the office door" (Boring, 1927). This was Titchener at Cornell, where he *was* psychology from 1892 until his death. His psychology was intellectually pure and professionally separatist. Titchener left no school behind him, though he deeply influenced many in American psychology. The determining force in his intellectual life was his time at Leipzig with Wundt (1890–92). Though he spent more years at Oxford (1875–90), taking a double first in Greats (classics and philosophy) and reading physiology, this period furnished background rather than professional orientation. Yet his English university and public school (Malvern) background and the long-established status of his family in Chichester, Sussex, probably combined to furnish a feeling for history and a scholarly exactitude which appear in his *Experimental Psychology* (1901–05), a book which Boring was inclined to accept as "the most erudite psychological work in the English language", "astonishingly accurate". Probably Titchener's most seminal theoretical doctrine was that the point of view is basic to psychology, that in it experience is treated as "dependent upon the experiencing individual" (1950, p. 417), so that a psychologist who deserts the psychological point of view commits the stimulus-error. His contributions to feeling, attention, and thought were also notable. In Titchener's immense production (7 books, 216 articles, 176 publications from the Cornell laboratory, 54 doctorates supervised), there is only one comprehensive outline of his doctrine, the *Text-book* (1909-10). His proposed systematic work never appeared, though Weld was able to put together its *Prolegomena* (1929). Of this, the opening section, on Wundt and Brentano (also in *Amer. J. Psychol.*, 1921) is now seen to be historically important. Himself a redoubtable translator (e.g. of Külpe and Wundt) Titchener was much translated. His life and work appear as a series of dualisms: psychology and not-psychology; mental process and meaning; structure and function, graciousness versus dominance; experimental rigor versus delight in music and tennis—not to mention numismatics; American residence versus British nationality (plus German appearance); a certain exclusiveness versus controversial editorship and informal leadership of the group known as the "Experimental Psychologists": a paradoxical and great man.

Bibliography: Boring, E. G.: Edward Bradford Titchener, 1867–1927. Amer. J. Psychol., 1927, *38*, 489–506. Id.: A history of experimental psychology. New York, ²1950, 410–20; 435–7. Titchener, E. B.: A primer of psychology (rev. ed.). New York, 1903 (1899). Id.: Systematic psychology: prolegomena (Ed. H. P. Weld). New York, 1927.   *J.A.C.*

Titchener's illusion. A contrast illusion. Two identical circles are surrounded by large and small circles respectively. The one surrounded by large circles appears smaller.   *C.D.F.*

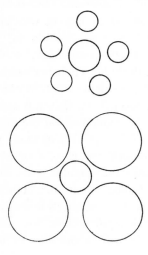

Toilet training. See *Bowel training*.

Token-object (syn. *Inductor*). Object used to elicit paranormal information concerning its owner. Sometimes used at a *séance* (q.v.) as a proxy for an absent sitter (q.v.)   *J.B.*

Tolerance. A term descriptive of social attitudes and/or behaviors of an individual which —in contrast to intolerant attitudes or behaviors—show no offense at the opinions, attitudes and so on of other individuals (e.g. members of minority groups), which are divergent in substance and objective from those of the majority; "tolerance" also indicates an active seeking to prevent the rejection or repression of other or alien ways of thought and behavior.

E. Frenkel-Brunswik's (1949) term "tolerance of ambiguity" is restricted to a specific cognitive style characterized by a more or less limited ability to offer nuanced judgments and balance them in ambiguous situations. "Intolerance of ambiguity" occurs, e.g. as a tendency to prejudge an issue prematurely (see *Prejudice; Stereotype*); and to withdraw, or to resort to an authority rather than try to understand and cope with a situation.

Investigations indicate positive relations between intolerance of ambiguity and "authoritarian personality" (q.v.) traits; but these findings have not yet been confirmed.

Bibliography: Frenkel-Brunswik, E.: Intolerance of ambiguity as an emotional and perceptual personality variable. J. Pers., 1949, *18*, 108–43. Martin, J. G.: The tolerant personality. Detroit, 1964.   *A.S.-M.*

Tolman, Edward Chace. B. 14/4/1886 in Newton, Mass.; d. 19/11/1959 in Berkeley. Tolman received his doctorate in 1915 at

Harvard. He taught until 1918 at North-western University, where he became inter-ested in abstract thought, retroactive inhibition and similar phenomena of memory. From 1918 (with only short breaks, when he taught at Harvard and Chicago) he was Professor at the University of California at Berkeley. His investigations of learning and goal-directed behavior made him one of the most prominent representatives of neobehaviorism and American learning psychology. In 1937 he became president of the APA.

Cognitive learning theory. Tolman's theory of cognitive learning is distinct from the other behaviorist learning theories in a number of features: (*a*) it describes behavior not on the molecular but on the molar level; (*b*) all behavior is seen as purposive; (*c*) the individual learns not sequences of movements but *expectations*, i.e. meaningful connections be-tween two given stimuli: the actual situation S1 (sign) and the situation arising in the course of the action (the signified, the goal); (*d*) reinforcement (q.v.) is replaced by the prin-ciple of "confirmation".

In addition to objectively measurable stimulus and response variables, Tolman postulates a series of (not directly observable) factors: "intervening variables", which as internal processes in the organism establish connections between factors: the need (q.v.) system, the "belief-value matrix", and immed-iate actual "behavior space".

In contrast to C. L. Hull (q.v.), who experi-mented mainly with problem boxes and runways, Tolman used the most diverse maze situations in his investigations. For an individual in the maze, the situation is sub-divided by means of "choice points": signs which denote the way to the goal and allow orientation. On repeated trials the animal develops specific "expectations" for the different signs, i.e. differences in the proba-bility that specific behaviors in this situation will lead to the goal. If the expectation that the way taken leads to the goal is "confirmed",

the probability of its occurrence (and there-fore, indirectly, the probability of the behavior in question) is increased. If the expectation is not confirmed, its probability is reduced. All that is required for confirmation is reaching the goal, and not a reduction of need tension in Hull's sense.

The signs encountered on the way to the goal are emphasized by the confirmation and become sub-goals which are themselves liable to confirm expectations. Ultimately the organ-ism establishes a kind of "cognitive map" of all the signs in the maze situation and their meanings, and then orientates its behavior by this map.

Main works: Purposive behavior in animals and men. New York, 1932. Drives toward war. New York, 1942. Cognitive maps in rats and men. Psychol. Rev., 1948, *55*, 189–208. E. C. Tolman. In: Boring, E. G. (Ed.): A history of psychology in autobiography, Vol. 4. Worces-ter, Mass., 323–39. Collected papers in psychology. New York, 1951. Principles of purposive behavior. In: Koch, S. (Ed.): Psychology: a study of a science, Vol. 2. New York, 1959, 92–157.

Bibliography: Hilgard, E. R. & Bower, G. H.: Theories of learning. New York, ³1966.   *W.W.*

Tone-deafness. The inability to recognize the different pitches of musical notes. The term is often generalized to include other musical disabilities, such as the inability to recognize tunes.   *C.D.F.*

Tone psychology, or the psychology of sound, is the theory of the psychophysical prerequi-sites for, and processes of, auditory perceptions and experiences, which originate as the result of diverse sound impressions, and in particular those with simple musical stimulus structures (e.g. clang, interval, rhythmical units). The real progenitor of tone psychology was H. von Helmholtz (1863); it was established as a discipline by Carl Stumpf (1883; 1890). The onesided nature of the study of psycho-acoustics in that era was followed after the turn of the century by the development of the psychology of music, which considered music and its effective context as a complex whole and tended to question the validity of a psychology of sound oriented to physiological psychology. Later, however, tone psychology became more important, not least as the necessary basis for a psychology of music, and as a relatively independent discipline open to the varied approaches of phenomenology (q.v.), information theory (q.v.), cybernetics (see *Cybernetics and psychology*), etc. See *Experimental esthetics; Music, psychology of; Auditory perception; Sense organs: the ear; Noise.*

Bibliography: Bekesy, G. von: Experiments in hearing. New York, 1960. **Stevens, S. S.**: Bibliography on hearing. Cambridge, Mass., 1955. **Stumpf, C.**: Ton-psychologie, 2 Vols. Leipzig, 1883–90, ²1965.   *B.S.*

Tonolytics. Syn. for *Spasmolytics* (q.v.) and *Muscle relaxants* (q.v.).

Tonus (syn. *Tonicity*). A state of slight muscular tension. In striate skeletal muscles tonus is known as "contractile tonus" when produced by tetanic contraction, i.e. by rhythmic contractions of individual muscle fibers. Tonus in this case depends on the number of nervous impulses emanating from the spinal cord, is higher in a waking state, and (especially) under arousal (q.v.), and lower in sleep (q.v.). In the case of the smooth musculature (of, e.g., the blood vessels), there is a "plastic tonus", which depends on the particular regular state of arousal of the individual muscular fibers and their mutual location.   *E.D.*

Topological and vector psychology. A comprehensive psychology of behavior developed by K. Lewin (q.v.).

1. *Basic principles.* Working on the basis of gestalt psychology, Lewin devised a "field theory", which he described as a "method for the analysis of causal relations and the synthesis of scientific constructs".

An essential component of this theory is Lewin's "constructive" or "genetic method" of concept (q.v.) formation. In contrast to the classificatory method, it attempts to explain phenomena by way of their conditions, and to group them according to their conditions: i.e. "genotypical identity" is posited as fundamental to concept formation. In this way one attains to functional concepts ("function" is conceived here as a relational concept—analogously to the mathematical concept of function), which comprise the dynamic aspect and can be represented mathematically. It is possible in this way to bridge the gap between the general and the particular, since the essence of the constructive method lies "in the representation of an individual case with the aid of a few constructional elements". Lewin looked for psychological concepts that would adequately comprehend not the "objective" (physical) but the *behaviorally relevant* facts.

Lewin oriented the construction of his theories toward the findings of the "philosophy of science". A system of empirical constructs is allocated to a specific formal system by means of coordinate definitions. For his formal system Lewin drew on a few fundamental terms from topology and vector mathematics, and evolved "hodology" (a "theory of the way").

(*a*) *Topology* is a science of spatial relations based on the relationship between the "part" and the "whole." It is concerned with the reciprocal locations of areas (regions). Lewin uses topology to represent the structure of a psychological field.

(*b*) In order to explain the changes in, and hence the dynamic characteristics of, a psychological field, Lewin uses mainly the concepts of vector mathematics. Associated vectors are determined by size, direction and point of access. The psychological forces from which changes in field structure derive, are ascribed to vectors.

(c) Hodology represents a substantial union of both formal systems. It extends topology by defining the (topologically non-apprehensible) concepts of "direction" and "distance".

2. *Topology of life space.* (*a*) *Structure.* The behavior (B) of an individual is dependent on (a function of) all the psychological facts, the psychological field, or life space (L): B = f(L).

The life space of an individual comprises all that which, at a specific point in time, has "psychological life" for this person: "that which is real is that which is effective". Life space (L) is a function of the person (P) and environment (E):

L = f(P, E); applied to behavior:
B = f(L) = f(P, E).

Life space is divided into regions (areas). The regions represent possible events (in most cases, possible behaviors). Life space may therefore be characterized as an inclusive concept of all possible occurrences, "containing the person and his psychological environment".

(*b*) *Structural change and dynamics.* If a person moves from one region to another, then psychological "*locomotion*" is said to occur. However, other forms of restructuration are possible: e.g. those in which other regions are moved. These are equivalent to locomotion. Locomotion is the most important structural alteration of life space, and depends on the individual's pattern of movement. Within the area of freedom of movement the boundaries between the individual regions are relatively easy to cross. However, the sphere of movement itself is determined by especially rigid and almost impassable boundaries, or "*barriers*". A barrier is defined by the resistance it offers to locomotion. The degree of resistance of a barrier varies according to the kind of locomotion and the point of approach to the

barrier, and also depends on the direction in which the barrier is to be crossed. Barriers, and therefore freedom of movement, are conditioned primarily by two aspects: specific goals cannot be reached, (i) because they are forbidden (the intensity of prohibition determines the fixedness of the boundary, the extent of the prohibition the inaccessible area), and (ii) because of a lack of intellectual and physical ability.

The direct cause of locomotion is the "*power*" with which an individual aspires to a goal. This power is the resultant of all field forces which exert an effect on the individual at a given point in time. This force is represented mathematically by a *vector*. The access point and direction are obtained from the topological structure, and the degree of force from the "*valence*" of the goal object and its (psychological or topological) distance.

A region has valence when it attracts or repels the individual (positive or negative valence, symbolized by + or −). Valence is determined by the perceived quality of the goal region and the total state of the individual (tension conditions within the individual).

3. *Topology of the person*(*ality*). (*a*) *Structure.* Like the environment, personal structure can be represented topologically. This is necessary, since behavior is conditioned not only environmentally but, to the same extent, personally. Lewin distinguishes between the "inner personal" and "sensorimotor" areas. In the topological schema, the sensorimotor area is the transitional zone between the inner personal area and the environment. The sensorimotor area comprises, e.g.: language and expression (efferent) and the whole perceptual system (afferent). In the inner-personal area, Lewin distinguishes between central (e.g. drives, emotions) and peripheral (e.g. thoughts, attitudes) regions.

(*b*) *Structural change and dynamics.* In contrast to the environment, locomotion in the person is not a fundamental dynamic quantity (for determination of structure). In the case of the person, another dynamic relation is applied—the degree of dynamic dependence (degree of communication). Dynamic dependence is the greater the more intensely the state of the area affects the other. Lewin calls the dynamic characteristics of the individual personal areas "*tension*". Tension is the state of an area in relation to the state of another area. Tension is dependent on, e.g. *needs* and *quasi-needs* (see *Need; Tension system*).

(*c*) *Interindividual differences.* The most important topologically apprehensible interindividual differences are obtained from the degree of individual difference (a child compared with an adult has less part-areas), and the type of personal structure (arrangement of part-areas and the intensity of their association).

4. *Criticism.* (*a*) *Critique of mathematical bases.* An objection often brought against topological and vector psychology is that it uses only a few of the terms but not the propositions of topology (London, 1944). Basically, Lewin uses an incomplete formal system of his own construction (Madsen, 1958) that is not explicit (Koch, 1941). According to Lewin (1963), it is not a matter of the extent to which a formal system is invoked for interpretation, but of the utility (e.g. predictive value) of the presupposed coordinations.

(*b*) *Formal critique.* Here criticism is directed against the terminology and the whole propositional system. The key concepts of topological and vector psychology are not precise enough (Deutsch, 1954), since they are largely without empirical substantiation (Estes, 1954). Individual propositions cannot be deduced unequivocally (London, 1944; Estes, 1954).

(*c*) *Substantial critique.* The practical value of the life space concept is questioned, since it is scarcely possible to represent all behaviorally-relevant facts as components of life space (London, 1944). Brunswick (1943) criticizes the inadequate attention paid to external (physical) factors. He calls life space "post-perceptual" and "pre-behavioral", and indicates the danger of the phenomenal "encapsulation" of the field. Lewin counters this criticism in his emphasis on the necessity for a psychological *ecology*, which has the task of determining the peripheral zone of life space (or of the individual personality), i.e. the relevance of all external factors for life space.

Bibliography: Brunswick, E.: Organismic achievement and environmental probability. Psychol. Rev., 1943, *50*, 225–72. **Cartwright, D.:** Lewinian theory as a contemporary systematic framework. In: **Koch, S.** (Ed.): Psychology: a study of a science, Vol. 2. New York, 1959. **Deutsch, M.:** Field theory in social psychology. In: **Lindzey, G.** (Ed.): Handbook of social psychology. Reading, Mass., 1954. **Escalona, S.:** The influence of topological and vector psychology upon current research in child development: an addendum. In: **Carmichael, L.** (Ed.): Manual of child psychology. New York & London, 1954, 971–83. **Estes, W. K.:** Kurt Lewin. In: **Estes, W. K.** *et al.* (Eds.): Modern learning theory. New York, 1954. **Koch, S.:** The logical character of the motivation concept. Psychol. Rev., 1941, *48*, 15–38. **Lewin, K.:** Der Richtungsbegriff in der Psychologie: Der spezielle und der allg. hodologische Raum. Psychol. Forsch., 1034, *19*, 249–99. **Id.:** Dynamic theory of personality. New York & London, 1935. **Id.:** Principles of topological psychology. New York, 1936. **Id.:** The conceptual representation and the measurement of psychological forces. Contr. Psychol. Theory, Vol. I, 1938. **Id.:** Frontiers in group dynamics. Human Relations, 1947, *1*, 5–41; 143–53. **Id.:** Resolving social conflicts. New York, 1948. **London, I. D.:** Psychologists' misuse of the auxiliary concepts of physics and mathematics. Psychol. Rev., 1944, *51*, 266–91. **Madsen, K. B.:** Theories of motivation. Copenhagen, ⁴1968. **Marx' M. H. & Hillix, W. A.:** Systems and theories in psychology. New York & London, 1963.

F. Mattejat & E. G. Wehner

Topological mnemonics (syn. *Topological learning*). The "art" of remembering, used as an aid in spatial and situational recall. The assignment is made more accessible by (imaged or actual) spatial arrangement, or made more imprintable by associative pictorial images (e.g. diagrams). *H.W.*

Totem. Totemism is a principle of social organization among "primitive" peoples. The cohesiveness of a group (clan) is attributed to a mythic process in animal form (sometimes also a plant or some other natural object). The members of the group are under the protection of the totem as long as they obey certain commandments (e.g. exogamy) and prohibitions (e.g. that of killing the totemic animal). See *Taboo*.

Bibliography: Freud, S.: Totem and taboo. New York & London, 1918. Lévi-Strauss, C.: Totemism. London & Boston, 1963.   *I.L.*

TOTE units. According to Miller *et al.*, TOTE units are elements of behavioral process. As an alternative to reflex arcs, they may be thought of as more flexible "foundation stones" in the hierarchical structure of a behavior. "TOTE" is the abbreviation for the characteristic course of events: *"Test operate test exit"*. "Test" is the comparison of an actual value ("state of organism") with a desired value ("state to be tested"). Should both stages prove incongruent, a correction takes place in the shape of a reduction of difference (operate), a new test, and in the case of adequate congruence the end response ("exit"). TOTE units are used to study behavior on various levels of abstraction from the operation of simple cellular membranes all the way to cognitive processes. See *Cybernetics and psychology*.

Bibliography: Miller, G. A., Galanter, E. & Pribram, K. H.: Plans and structure of behavior. New York, 1960.   *W.H.B.*

Touch receptors. Receptors for the sensation of contact. See *Sense organs*.

Tough-mindedness. A pragmatic attitude (q.v.) to social, political and philosophical problems, associated with more extraverted personality traits. See *Traits; Type; Authoritarian personality; Prejudice.*   *J.L.*

Tourism. Tourism research came into being some forty years ago, but at first was concerned only with economic questions. With the rapid development of modern tourism since the nineteen-fifties, there has been growing interest in a psychologically and sociologically oriented form of tourism research. The object of psychological research in this area is not the "journey" or travel as such, but "psychological traveling time" as a whole (Böhm), which includes all activities and influences (before and after setting out) conditioned by traveling. Among the main topics are: analyses of the conditions for travelling (including motivational and social emphases); analyses of experience and behavior during a tour (specific vacation habits, role playing, role expectations, etc.); effects of the holiday (e.g. on educational, leisure and consumption interests; changes in attitudes to other nations; changes in experience of self). Apart from these questions of individual and social psychology, there are other aspects of tourism which come into the areas of medicine (the psychophysical value of traveling), education, and economics (advertising and publicity).

Bibliography: Hahn, H. (Ed.): Motives, Meinungen, Verhaltensweisen. Starnberg, 1969. Id. (Ed.): Jugendtourismus. Munich, 1965.   *B.S.*

Tracing test. A test of fine motor co-ordination involving the tracing of life drawings and measurement of the resultant deviations.
                                                    C.D.F.

Traction effect. One of Michotte's experiments on mechanical causality. An object A approaches and passes a stationary object B. Thereafter the two objects move together. Under the right conditions, object A appears to observers to be pulling object B in its wake.   *C.D.F.*

Tractus opticus. The two *tractus optici*, or optic tracts, begin at the *chiasma opticum* or chiasma in the region of the *sella turcica* (behind the optic groove) and divide near the geniculate bodies into a lateral and a medial root, which then pass into the lateral and medial geniculate bodies. Fibers are carried in the *radiatio tractus optici*, or optic radiation, to the sight center in the occipital cortex. Injury to an optic tract can cause blindness of the corresponding half of each eye.   *R.R.*

Tradition. The (or a) totality of opinions, attitudes, habits and customs handed down (primarily informally) by oral communication or imitation from one generation to another, in such a way that the self-obviousness and accepted value of such traditions usually increase with their age. The term "traditionalism" stands for tendencies to overvalue traditional opinions, etc., or to exclude them from (rational) evaluation. See *Attitude; Habit; Authoritarian personality; Social psychology; Prejudice; Stereotype.*   *A.S.-M.*

Traffic psychology. Traffic psychology may be thought of as a subdivision of applied psychology (q.v.). It is concerned with the scientific study of psychological problems arising from conditions of motor, rail and air travel (see *Aviation psychology*). The main emphasis of research is on motor traffic. The driving of motor vehicles (driving behavior), which is the primary concern of traffic psychology (the behavior of pedestrians and others has received less attention), is considered as a comprehensive *man-machine system* (MMS) consisting of *street* (roadway), *driver* and *vehicle* and symbolically represented as in Fig. 1. In cybernetic terms, this is a dynamic system of interactive elements, and with multiple feedback (q.v.). Although it seems appropriate when describing the problems of traffic psychology to begin with the input of the system and then progressively to discuss its components, it is in fact advisable to start with an analysis and description of driving behavior, i.e. with the *output* of the driver or of the whole system, in order initially to appreciate the object of traffic psychology, i.e. *traffic behavior.*

Whereas a few investigations have tried to evaluate drivers' statements on driving behavior, most studies are based on direct

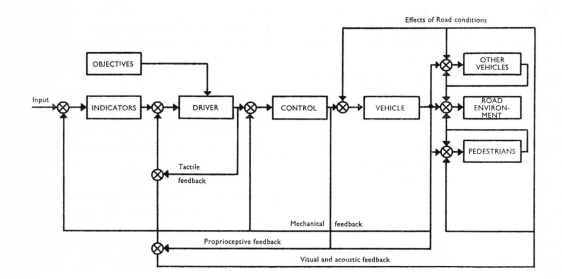

observations of the driver or the vehicle, usually by passenger observers. Scales have been devised for systematic recording of observed driving behavior. In part, control movements (e.g. braking) are recorded by instruments with simultaneous registration of the vehicle's position in relation to the roadside or other vehicles.

Observations in normal traffic are complemented by observations in simulated traffic situations. Simulated studies are especially suitable for the investigation of behavior in dangerous situations, under the effect of alcohol, etc. Some large simulators, especially in the USA, attempt optimal truth-to-life, and represent reality by means of TV pictures of a miniature landscape, or movies, the subject being able to exercise control. In many cases, only selected aspects of traffic are simulated, e.g. a roadway.

A description of driving behavior is meaningful only when it is judged in regard to the goals or aims of the MMS, among which traffic safety and traffic flow are the main criteria. Both criteria have to be brought into an optimal reciprocal relation, since, e.g. increased traffic safety correlates with impaired traffic flow, and *vice versa*. The evaluation of traffic behavior in terms of safety is very difficult since few indices for traffic safety are available, and the accessible criteria, such as accidents, near-accidents and offenses against regulations, can be recorded only imprecisely and have unfavorable psychometric characteristics. Therefore indirect criteria are also used, such as maintaining distance, sign recognition, and so on. Traffic flow, on the other hand, is more precisely recorded, since it can be estimated from the capacity of a streetcar (tram), the average speed of the stream of traffic, the throughput of a crossing, etc.

Input is the most important of the determinants of system-output. It consists of street, traffic signs, and other vehicles, pedestrians, etc., and of feedback signals from the vehicle.

From the ergonomic viewpoint, the question of the configuration of traffic routes, signals, etc. on system performance is of primary interest. Little is known about the visual characteristics of traffic routes, yet basic findings of the psychology of perception may be applied to roadway design. The concept of optical direction—by special guidelines, etc.—is especially important. For future traffic design, it will be important to give warning of not directly visible sections of roadway by means of better indicators.

On the other hand, the legibility of signs and plates of all kinds has been thoroughly investigated, and the excessive demand on the driver made by the conventional forest of signs has often been pointed out. Other vehicles produce relevant visual input as a leading vehicle, as an obliquely crossing vehicle, and so on. The brake warning lights (stop lights) of preceding vehicles indicate speed changes in the leading vehicle. Response speed is improved if three pairs of rear lights are used (green: maintenance of uniform speed or acceleration; orange: moderate braking; red: sharp braking). The driver receives a great deal of information if he directly observes the roadway and uses the rear view mirror. Further information—especially regarding the condition of the vehicle—is supplied by indicators (e.g. the speedometer) which are being intensively studied at present with a view to optimal improvement (e.g. by indication of the distance from a preceding vehicle, or of stopping distance). Since the information relevant for the driver is for the most part visual (acoustic and tactile information essentially inform him only of the state of the vehicle), the functions of the optical apparatus (resolution, accommodation, sensitivity to dazzle and glare, day and twilight vision, color vision, depth vision) are of basic importance, but are not solely determinative of safe driving behavior, since inadequacies can to a large extent be compensated. A normative variable, which has been adequately assessed only recently, is the driver's active detection and scanning performance with the aid of eye movements. Significant variations in fixation were shown, e.g. between normal driving and overtaking. The change of fixation from distant to near space, and *vice versa*, is also important. Attempts have been made to assess the general channel capacity of the driver in information reception, and the not impressively high rate of 4–6 bits a second has been obtained.

The processing of received information takes place by means of the selection of relevant signals, comparison with known quantities, and reference to instructions, rules, etc. Processes of this kind were examined to some extent from the viewpoint of "mental load", distraction, and aspects of stress (q.v.). The driver's *reactions* (responses) consist partly of automatic, i.e. highly practiced and not consciously intended, behavior patterns, the nature of which is as yet inadequately explained. A large number of inputs require a decision in regard to the kinds of response. These decisions may be confined to limited aspects of driving (e.g. braking, overtaking), or may be of a basic kind (e.g. avoidance of night driving, or driving after taking alcohol) and are considered primarily in terms of the risk the driver is prepared to take (see *Risk taking; Alcoholism*). There is a broad variation in risk taking, the course of which may be interpreted according to standard decision models (see *Decision processes*), and the origin of which is examined in terms of the psychology of personality (see *Personality; Traits; Type*).

The above-mentioned processes give rise to *driving behavior*, which may be divided into several components. Among the cybernetic aspects, the transfer characteristics of the human part-system are of interest. The driver's actions are also influenced by the kind and arrangement of the control and operation devices to which he has access. The conventional motor vehicle is poorly constructed from an ergonomic viewpoint, since, for example, it requires movement in the same direction for opposed activities (acceleration and braking); the devices are often operated only with difficulty (there would seem to be no appropriate, relevant anthropometric measurements); and switches are poorly coded (functions may be confused).

The functioning of the "driver" part-system is of primary interest to the traffic psychologist, and is affected by several temporally variable and temporally constant conditions which have already evoked a considerable amount of research. One of the most consequential time-variable conditions is certainly drunken driving (see *Alcoholism*). The degree of drunkenness determines inadequacies in driving performance, but also in decision about erroneous judgment of internal and external magnitudes. In the field of decisions, it is necessary to investigate why individuals with restricted driving capacity actually take to their vehicles.

Analogous problems arise in regard to time-variable conditions, such as the influence of drugs, vigilance (q.v.), and fatigue (q.v.), and to a certain extent in regard to transient moods. Intelligence (q.v.) and mental abilities, motor abilities and personality variables of the most varied kind have been correlated with accidents and other data obtained from traffic and driving behavior; with only a few exceptions, however, only minor correlations have been revealed. Only biographical information on social characteristics has been shown to be a useful predictor of driving behavior (see *Accident research*). The relative failure of these investigations may be attributed in part to methodological difficulties. Since data from personality tests were usually compared directly with external criteria, it remains unclear where and how the functional structure can be influenced by a personality variable. On the other hand, the accident (on account of its inadequate psychometric aspects) is an uncertainty factor. Further studies will have to concentrate more on system analysis of the driver, and take new, improved criteria into account. Simulation experiments may be of use here. Some success would seem to be promised by attempts to detect the influence of sets and attitudes on driving behavior. Major attitudes deserving of research are those toward safety and authority.

The driver's age is an essential factor among influences on driving behavior. Young drivers and those of an advanced age have proved of especial interest to researchers. The adequately proven higher accident rate among members of the group up to age twenty-five is explainable largely in terms of inappropriate attitudes and sets, and a lack of experience in regard to the performance limits of the system. Older drivers frequently exhibit performance deficits which can considerably restrict driving fitness.

Bibliography: Arthur D. Little, Inc.: The state of art of traffic safety. Cambridge, Mass., 1966. Bena, E., Hoskovec, J. & Stikar, J.: Psychologie a fyziologie ridice. Prague, ²1968. Hoyos, C. (Ed.): Psychologie des Strassenverkehrs. Berne, 1965. Mittenecker, E.: Methoden und Ergebnisse der psychologischen Unfallforschung. Vienna, 1962. O'Day, J. (Ed.): Driver behavior—cause and effect. Washington, D.C., 1968. Selzer, M. L., Gikas, P. W. & Huelko, D. F. (Eds.): The prevention of highway injury. Ann Arbor, Mich., 1967. Wagner, K. & Wagner, H.-J. (Eds.): Handbuch der Verkehrsmedizin. Berlin & Heidelberg, 1968.

C. Hoyos

Training. Systematic and extensive practice (q.v.) in order to reach a state of optimal physical, manual and/or mental and spiritual capability, or to maintain the same. "Training on the job" is short though intensive systematic introductory practice at the work place itself.

G.R.W.M.

Training, animal. The acquisition of certain behaviors (by animals) using associative methods. The training procedure endeavors by frequent repetition and reinforcement (see *Conditioning, classical and operant*) to produce specific reactions to definite stimuli. A prerequisite for any attempt at training is a certain measure of "teachability" (or contionability). See *Behaviorism*.

Bibliography: Thorndike, E. L. : Animal intelligence; an experimental study of the associative processes in animals. Psychol. Rev. Monog., 1898, Suppl. 2.

K.E.P.

Training method. A procedure for controlling behavior. Desired behavior is "reinforced" (rewarded or praised); undesired behavior is punished. With this method any "breaking out" of the situation is prevented by the erection of real or social barriers. With the aid of a well-planned method, behavior can be selected and channelled at will. The acquisition of automated knowledge is most economically promoted with this method. See *Conditioning, classical and operant; Aversion therapy; Behavior therapy; Manipulation.*

B.L.

Training within industry (abb. TWI). A systematic technique of instruction used in connection with conversion from one form of production to another, or a change of processes.

G.R.W.M.

Traits. The concept of "personality" (q.v.) is too all-embracing to be of much direct use to the empirical investigator; we require more specific concepts which will point the way towards measurable entities. These are found in the concepts of *abilities* in the cognitive field, and in those of *traits* and *types* (q.v.) in the non-cognitive field. All these concepts presuppose some form of nomothetic approach; the idiographic approach would deny that traits or abilities appearing in any two individuals were in fact only *quantitatively* different, and would argue that the actual behaviors involved were unique. An alternative criticism, often made by behaviorists, insists that all stimulus-response bonds or habits are *specific*, and that consequently general traits cannot exist. As Thorndike

(1913) has put it, "there are no broad, general traits of personality, no general and consistent forms of conduct which, if they existed, would make for consistency of behavior and stability of personality, but only independent and specific stimulus-response bonds or habits." These criticisms will be considered after we have defined the concept itself more closely.

Language and the man in the street have always incorporated traits in their characterization of people; Allport & Odbert (1936) have listed some 4,500 trait terms in the English language. Many typologists, from Galen to Jung and Kretschmer, used trait terms to characterize their ideal "types". Among modern writers, Stern (1921) was perhaps the foremost advocate of a trait psychology; he wrote: "We have the right and the obligation to develop a concept of trait as a definitive doctrine; for in all activity of the person, there is beside a variable portion, likewise a constant purposive portion, and this latter we isolate in the concept of trait." Allport (1937) introduced this doctrine into the English-speaking countries; here is his description of how traits are discovered: "Traits . . . are discovered not by deductive reasoning, not by fiat, not by naming, and are themselves never directly observed. They are discovered in the individual life—the only place where they can be discovered—only through an inference (or interpretation) made necessary by the demonstrable consistency of the separate observable acts of behavior." This insistence on *behavioral consistency* is even stronger in another quotation: "Traits are not directly observable; they are inferred (as any kind of determining tendency is inferred). Without such an inference the stability and consistency of personal behavior could not possibly be explained. Any specific action is a product of innumerable determinants, not only of traits but of momentary pressures and specialized influences. But it is the repeated occurrence of actions having the *same significance* (equivalence of response) following

upon a definable range of stimuli having the same personal significance (equivalence of stimuli) that makes necessary the postulation of traits as states of being. Traits are not at all times active, but they are persistent even when latent, and are distinguished by low thresholds of arousal".

Consistency of behavior can be conceptualized best in terms of statistical *correlations;* consistency implies (1) test-retest reliability, that is, the same or at least similar behavior should appear on temporally separate occasions when the same stimuli are presented, and (2) inter-test correlations when different but functionally identical or similar stimuli are presented. Thus a person who is *persistent* in situation A should also be persistent in situation A', that is, the same situation on another occasion; he should also be persistent in situations B, C . . . N, that is, situations which call for and enable persistence to be shown. These are testable propositions, and their investigation should enable us to decide between this hypothesis and Thorndike's notion of *response specificity* mentioned above.

The literature on these points is now very large; a historically oriented account is given by Eysenck (1970). The first large-scale experimental attack on this problem was mounted by Hartshorne & May (1928, 1929; Hartshorne & Shuttleworth, 1930) in their Character Education Enquiry; their concern was with the problem of honesty and other morally and ethically desirable qualities, and with ways and means of improving these. They administered objectively designed tests to thousands of school children; these dealt with honesty (lying and cheating), co-operation, inhibition of impulses, and persistence. In devising these tests, they followed certain rules: the test situation should be natural as well as controlled, all subjects should have equal opportunity for showing the behavior in question, children should not be subjected to undue moral strain, and the tests should have low "visibility", i.e. they should not be recognized for what they were by the children. They also inquired into knowledge of moral conduct, and collected "reputation" scores for their children; finally, they assessed the "integration" of the children, a term by which they mean "consistency of performance"—"by *integration* is often intended a certain dependability or stability of moral conduct". The statistical treatment of the data was beyond cavil, and in view of the brilliance of the design and the technical excellence of the execution, this study has rightly been regarded as crucial in respect to the theory of specificity. When therefore Hartshorne & May found very low intercorrelations between their tests (averaging 0.20–0.25), and discovered that children who were honest, or persistent, or co-operative in one test-situation were not always so in another, their conclusion that these alleged qualities were "groups of specific habits rather than general traits" was very widely accepted as finally settling the issue in favor of specificity.

Eysenck (1970) has re-examined the detailed results, and argues that the conclusion does not follow from the data. Single tests do not correlate very highly, but if they are regarded as parts of a battery it can be shown that the battery is in fact a very reliable measure. The reliability of a battery of nine tests of honesty is 0.72, that for a battery of five service tests was only slightly lower. Validities of these batteries were investigated by correlating scores with ratings; these were 0.4 for honesty, 0.6 for service, figures which are not all that much lower than correlations between intelligence test results and teachers' ratings for IQ. Finally, the batteries intercorrelated positively, correlations going up to as high as 0.5, thus giving some support for the concept of "integration"; integration itself was shown to be quite highly correlated with honesty, co-operation, and the other desirable moral qualities. Hartshorne & May may have been misled by certain assumptions which is fact do not hold. Thus they find that a given child may succeed in one test of honesty and fail on

another; this, they argue, is evidence of specificity. But this is not necessarily true; a child may succeed with an easy IQ problem and fail with a difficult one, without demonstrating that intelligence does not exist! A child may cheat (in the schoolroom situation), but may not steal, in another test; this demonstrates merely that the tests differ in the amount of stress which they put on a child's moral nature. Most children find it easier to cheat than to steal; little (often no) blame attaches to the former, but a great deal to the latter. Thus the tests may be ranged in order of "difficulty", much like intelligence tests; some children "pass" many items, others few, others yet are intermediate. All this does not prove the specificity of moral behavior.

Another argument relates to the age of the children; moral behavior has to be learned, and young children are still in the early stages of learning; older children and adults may show greater consistency of conduct. McKinnon (1933) later showed that this was in fact so, and that with older subjects very high correlations were found. It would thus seem that consistency may develop through a process of learning or conditioning, and evidence should be looked for in older rather than in younger subjects. Even so, work with very young children of two years or younger has shown marked consistencies in such behavior traits as activity, or withdrawn behavior, or frequency of crying, and some of these consistencies correlate with behavior many years later; this suggests that much of behavior depends on inherited patterns of conduct, a point to be taken up presently.

The ready acceptance of Hartshorne & May's proposition regarding specificity of conduct was probably due to the wide recognition of Thorndike's associationist position; if all learning was of specific S-R bonds, then general traits should not exist. There was also Thorndike's disproof of the doctrine of "transfer of training", associated with his doctrine of identical elements; when transfer of learning took place, this was supposed to be due to the presence of identical elements in the original and the second task. Modern learning theory has effectively abolished the first of the positions; not only do we have many alternatives to a simple S-R model (which indeed is put forward by fewer and fewer people), but in addition stimulus and response generalization provide means by which simple S-R connections could be built up into general traits. The second of these positions has been heavily criticized by Allport (1937), and is now of purely historical interest. Theoretical support for the specifist position has been dwindling, at the same time as its main empirical support has been shown to be wanting; nowadays it would be difficult to find any proponents of it among experts in the personality field. This fact, however, should not cause the pendulum to swing too much in the opposite direction; conduct certainly is less general than the man in the street imagines, and there is a considerable degree of specificity about it. What was wrong in Thorndike's position was its denial of *all* generality; this whole question has been shown to be a graded, dimensional problem, not an all-or-none one. There are both generality and specificity; it becomes an empirical research problem in each case to decide for a given trait, and for a given population, at a given time, just how general and how specific conduct really is.

The same conclusion may apply to the idiographic argument; as Spinoza already pointed out, everything that exists is unique, and personality is thus not exceptional. But there are also similarities and identities between persons, and only in so far as these exist can we begin to treat personality as an experimental problem. It is unnecessary to lay down on an arbitrary and *a priori* basis just how much of personality can be suitably treated in this way; such information will emerge at the end, not at the beginning of scientific work. Even in the study of sub-atomic particles, the Heisenberg principle sets

limitations to prediction and accuracy of measurement; it seems likely that in due course we shall understand better than we do now the limitations placed on the accurate measurement of human traits. But the idiographic position is wrong in so far as it declares impossible all nomothetic investigations; the success of many such studies adequately proves this point (Eysenck, 1970).

Research into traits has in the main used the following lines of research: (1) Personality inventories (self-ratings); (2) Ratings by peers, teachers, and other persons with knowledge of the candidate; (3) Miniature situations, i.e. laboratory replicas of life-situations calling into action the trait to be measured; (4) Laboratory situations making use of some hypothetico-deductive system to predict objective manifestations theoretically linked with a given trait. Personality inventories and ratings are perhaps most frequently used because they are particularly easy to collect; laboratory studies are more laborious but more objective, and possibly in the long run more fruitful. The differentiation between (3) and (4) is not always easy, but an example may make the matter clear. Persistence is a personality trait or quality calling for continuance of effort against fatigue, pain or boredom; it is easy to set up in the laboratory a situation requiring persistence in this sense. We may instruct the subject to pull against a dynamometer at half his full strength, or ask him to solve problems some of which are insoluble; great differences are observed between people in the length of time during which they pull against the dynamometer (although their strength differences have been averaged out), or the length of time which they spend on insoluble (but not obviously so) problems. Furthermore, such tasks correlate together to form a general factor of persistence, and do not correlate with IQ, thus ruling out the possibility that we are merely measuring intelligence. As an example of a hypothetico-deductive test, consider the work of Witkin *et al.* (1962) on the assumed trait of field dependence—field independence; they used tests such as the rod-and-frame and the embedded figures test, neither of which would have been thought of as a measure of a personality trait in the absence of Witkin's theory. Thus a theoretical framework may provide the basis for the experimental testing of laboratory tests as measures of personality traits.

It cannot of course be assumed that because a trait name exists, a corresponding trait must also exist; statistical methods are required which will translate observations into scientifically meaningful and objective concepts. The main method in use at present is factor analysis (q.v.); starting with a matrix of intercorrelations between all measures used, this method condenses the existing pattern of covariation into orthogonal factors which, after rotation, may or may not resemble the hypothetical traits postulated by the investigator. It is sometimes objected that "you only get out of a factor analysis what you put into it", but this is only partially true. If no tests of certain traits or abilities are contained in the battery, then of course these will not emerge from the analysis; just in the same way, qualitative analysis in chemistry will not disclose the presence of substances not contained in the sample. But the obverse is not true; in most cases we do not in fact know what we "put into" the analysis, and the statistical treatment often gives results not anticipated. Several outcomes are in fact possible when a series of tests supposedly measuring a given trait is intercorrelated and factor analyzed. (1) The tests form a matrix of rank one, thus confirming the hypothesis that they all measure the same trait; we also obtain information in this case about the degree to which each test measures the hypothetical trait (through its factor loadings). (2) The tests fail to intercorrelate, thus disproving the hypothesis completely. (3) The tests show patterns of intercorrelations suggesting the existence of two or more independent traits. (4) The tests

intercorrelate as in (1), but with an additional breakdown into smaller factors which suggest further subdivisions of the hypothetical trait.

Examples of these various outcomes are given by Eysenck (1970); a few of these are quoted here. (1) is illustrated in the work of Gould (1939) on level of aspiration; he found that several tests of this trait intercorrelated in such a way as to give rise to one single general factor. (2) is relatively rare, as tests seldom fail to intercorrelate completely; usually something can be salvaged, unless the original choice of tests was exceptionally poor. A good example of complete failure is the work of Payne (1955) on Kretschmer's conception of the trait of "*Spaltungsfähigkeit*". (3) is illustrated by the work of Eysenck and Furneaux (1945) on suggestibility; instead of one single factor they found two independent ones, called primary or ideomotor and secondary or perceptual suggestibility, with a possible third type, tertiary or social suggestibility, less well established. (4) is illustrated by work on persistence, McArthur (1955), where a general factor is found, but also additional factor differentiating "ideational" persistence and "physical" persistence, i.e. persistence on cognitive and on physical (endurance) tests respectively. This type of solution merges into a multiple-factor one, in which a larger number of sub-factors are found; personal tempo is a good example of this. Rimoldi (1951), using 59 tests, obtained 9 factors which were, however, not independent; their intercorrelations in turn gave rise to 4 second-order factors (motor speed, speed of perception, speed of cognition, reaction time). Thus the outcome of a factor analysis is not predetermined by the hypotheses to be tested; it can and often does deviate very considerably from the preconceptions which led to the setting up of the experiment. Factor analysis is indispensable in the testing of hypotheses regarding traits, as without it there is no proper statistical check on the experimenter's preconceptions;

it also serves the additional purpose of generating new and previously unconsidered hypotheses.

Within factor analysis Cattell has drawn a distinction between surface traits and source traits. A surface trait is defined as "a set of personality characteristics which are correlated but do not form a factor, hence are believed to be determined by more than one influence or source". A source trait is defined as a "factor dimension, stressing the proposition that variations in value along it are determined by a single, unitary influence or source". Statistically, the distinction is between rotation of factors through clusters (surface traits) or through hyperplanes (source traits). This view is not widely held, and it may be regarded as doubtful if factor analysis by itself can ever decide about the presence or absence of "a single, unitary influence or source". More specialized hypotheses and experimental designs are likely to be required for this purpose.

Traits are not independent; they tend to correlate and give rise to higher-order factors (superfactors) which resemble the *types* of writers like Jung and Kretschmer (see notation on *Type*). American writers tend to concentrate on the trait level; European and British writers tend to concentrate on the type level. This sometimes gives the impression that factor analysis does not give identical results in different hands, and that it is therefore not an objective method. This is not true; Eysenck & Eysenck (1969) have analyzed correlations between tests used by Cattell, Guilford & Eysenck, and have shown that considerable similarities (almost amounting to identity) exist at the higher-order level. Analyses should always include both levels, as otherwise the study is incomplete and difficult to interpret; American studies have in the past often sinned in this respect, in spite of the categorical statements to this effect by Thurstone and other pioneers of the statistical methods employed in these studies.

Are traits determined by heredity or by environment? Such a question is meaningless; all observed behavior is of course *phenotypic*, that is, determined by genetic causes acting in interaction with environmental ones. Nevertheless it is permissible to try to assess the relative importance of these two factors in particular cases, i.e. particular traits, in a particular environment, for a particular sample, at a particular time. Extrapolation beyond these limitations is dangerous. The method used in the majority of studies is that of comparing the intraclass correlations of monozygotic and dizygotic twins, of identical sex; better methods are now available, thanks to the efforts of biometrical geneticists. Cattell & Scheier (1961) review the extensive work of the former author, and Fuller & Thompson (1960) give a good review of the general field. Unlikely as it may seem, animal work has also been prominent in this field (Eysenck & Broadhurst, 1964; Scott & Fuller, 1965); it is of course more difficult to measure and interpret "personality traits" in dogs or rats, but it is much easier to conduct breeding experiments (e.g. diallel crosses) in animals, thus enabling proper genetic analysis of such factors as dominance to be made. The outcome of such studies in humans or animals is too complex to be reviewed here; heredity certainly plays an important part in the genesis of many traits, but the respective contribution of environment and heredity differs from trait to trait, and much further work is required before any very definitive generalization becomes possible.

The whole notion of traits is sometimes attacked (e.g. Lundin, 1961) on the same grounds as that of instincts. We start with some piece of behavior which we class, say, as sociable; we then explain it by inventing an instinct, or trait, of sociability. But nothing has in fact been explained by this circular bit of argument; all the evidence we have for our "trait" is still the behavior, which thus remains unexplained. This type of criticism is not admissible; trait psychology does not in fact try to give a *causal* analysis, but rather a *descriptive* one. Before we can say what *causes* a given trait, we must analyze the myriad items of ordinary, everyday behavior into meaningful units which can be measured and handled with sufficient ease to permit further analysis. To analyze physical entitles into elements, as in Mendeleff's Table, does not tell us *why* these elements are as they are; it merely describes them in a systematic fashion. That is all that trait analysis sets out to do, and it is unreasonable to blame it for not doing more. Nor is it correct to suggest that the argument is circular; we use the term "sociability" as if it were a unitary trait, but Eysenck & Eysenck (1969) have shown that there are at least two quite separate types of sociability; introverted lack of sociability (I don't care to be with other people) and neurotic lack of sociability (I am afraid to be with other people), and there is perhaps yet a third type (psychotic lack of sociability—I hate other people). These are factual results of statistical analysis of behavior; they are not implicit in the term "sociability" or in the simple observations which formed the lay use of that term. We conclude that this type of criticism is not damaging to the concept of "trait", which remains fundamental to the analysis and discussion of personality.

Bibliography: **Allport, G. W.**: Personality. London, 1937. **Allport, G. W. & Odbert, H. S.**: Trait names: a psycho-lexical study. Psychol. Monogr., 1936, *47*, 171. **Cattell, R. B. & Scheier, I. H.**: The meaning and measurement of neuroticism and anxiety. New York, 1961. **Eysenck, H. J.**: The structure of human personality. London, ³1970. **Eysenck, H. J. & Broadhurst, P. L.**: Experiments with animals. In: **Eysenck, H. J.** (Ed.): Experiments in motivation. Oxford, 1964. **Eysenck, H. J. & Eysenck, S. B. G.**: The structure and measurement of personality. London, 1969. **Eysenck, H. J. & Furneaux, W. D.**: Primary and secondary suggestibility. An experimental and statistical study. J. exper. Psychol., 1945, *35*, 485–503. **Fuller, J. R. & Thompson, W. R.**: Behavior genetics. New York, 1960. **Gould, R.**: An experimental analysis of "level of aspiration". Genet. Psychol. Monogr., 1939, *21*, 3–15. **Hartshorne, H. & May, M. A.**: Studies in deceit. New York, 1928. **Id.**: Studies in service and self-control. New York, 1929. **Hartshorne, H., May, M. A. & Shuttleworth, F. K.**: Studies in the organization of character. New York, 1930. **Lundin, R. V.**: Personality. New York, 1961. **MacArthur, R. S.**: An experimental investigation of persistence in secondary school boys. Canad. J. Psychol., 1955, *9*, 47–54. **McKinnon, D. V.**: The violation of prohibitions in the solving of problems. In: Ph.D. thesis: Harvard University Library, 1933. **Payne, R. W.**: Experimentelle Untersuchung zum Spaltungsbegriff von Kretschmer. Z. exp. angew. Psychol., 1953, *3*, 65–97. **Rimoldi, H. J. A.**: Personal tempo. J. abnorm. soc. Psychol., 1951, *44*, 283–303. **Scott, J. P. & Fuller, J. L.**: Genetics and the behavior of the dog. Chicago, 1965. **Stern, W.**: Differentielle Psychologie. Hamburg, 1921. **Thorndike, E. L.**: Educational psychology. New York, 1913. **Witkin, H. A., Dyke, R. B., Goodenough, D. R. & Harp, S. A.**: Psychological differentiation. New York, 1962.

                                                                    H. J. Eysenck

Trance. 1. A state of dissociation in which the individual is oblivious of his situation and surroundings. Can be induced by hypnosis, drugs, meditation, and so on. Sometimes associated with ESP (q.v.) experiences.

2. A transition (Lat. *transitus*) into a state of psychic abstraction characterized by restricted consciousness and (often) subsequent amnesia. Studied experimentally largely in connection with hypnosis (q.v.), and induced by concentration on a fragment of experience, possibly together with monotonous, rhythmic stimulation, physical exhaustion and emotional strain or expectation, as in the "archaic ecstasy" techniques described by Mircea Eliade (dancing to a drum or to rhythmic singing). Trance has a close connection with religious ecstasy or rapture and visionary experiences (see *Meditation; Religion, psychology of*). In functional terms, it is related to the normal, reality-oriented state as a mutation is to inheritance. It enables the affected individual to obtain release from everything he has learned to date, and makes possible achievements (both mental and physical) that he would not otherwise attempt.

Bibliography: Eliade, M.: Patterns in comparative religion. London & New York, 1958. Ludwig, A. M.: Trance. Comprehensive psychiatry, 1967, *8*. Schmidbauer, W.: Zur Psychologie des Orakels. Psychol. Rdsch., 1970, *21*, 88–98.   *J.B. & W.Sch.*

Tranquilizers (syn. *Anxiolytics; Ataractic drugs; Relaxants; Happy pills;* etc.). Psychopharmaceutical substances used in pharmacotherapy on account of their anxiolytic and relaxing effects. In contrast to the neuroleptics (or *major tranquilizers*), which also have a tranquilizing effect in low doses, but are primarily anti-psychotic, the tranquilizers proper (or *minor tranquilizers*) are used mainly for the treatment of neurotics, and healthy individuals under emotional stress. Tranquilizers have much in common with hyponotics in low doses, which (as "sedatives") in the past fulfilled the function of the tranquilizers and neuroleptics at present in use. An essential difference is the absence of the sleep-inducing, unpleasant effects of high doses of tranquilizers. Chemically, the tranquilizers are divided into the therapeutically important glycol derivatives (meprobamate, tybamate, phenylglycodol) and benzodiazepine (chlordiazepoxide, oxazepam, diazepam, nitrazepam), and into the less important glycerine derivatives (mephinisine), diphenolmethane derivatives (phenyltoloxamine, captodiamine, hydroxycine), and the carbonols (emylcamate). Neurophysiologically, the primary result is an attenuation in the limbic and thamamic system, and in high doses an extension to other areas, but no narcotization. Autonomic effects are hardly noticeable. Central muscle-relaxant and spasmolytic effects are frequent. A large number of psychological investigations in healthy individuals have been carried out for meprobamate and chlordiazepoxide. With low to middling doses there are no, or only slight, impairments of performance, and to some extent improvements in motor functions (tremor tests), and emotional stabilization without (or with only slight) fatigue.

Differences in effect are related to neuroticism, extraversion (in the Eysenckian sense; see *Drug postulate, Eysenck's; Trait; Type*) and situative factors (stress, mental strain).

The tranquilizing effect is reinforced if the individual condition is habitually or situatively oriented to emotional lability. Sedation is emphasized in the case of mental strain (see *Differential psychopharmacology*). Factorial test plans have been used in investigations.

Bibliography: Barret, J. E. & Dimascio, A.: Comparative effects on anxiety of the "minor tranquilizers" in "high" and "low" anxious student volunteers. Dis. nerv. Syst., 1966, *27*, 483–6. Berger, F. M.: The relation between the pharmacological properties of meprobamate and the clinical usefulness of the drug. In: Efron, D. H. (Ed.): Psychopharmacology, 1957–1967. Washington, 1968. Berger, F. M. & Potterfield, J.: The effect of antianxiety tranquilizers on the behavior of normal persons. In: Evans, W. O. & Kline, N. S.: The psychopharmacology of the normal human. Springfield, 1969. Eysenck, H. J.: Experiments with drugs. Oxford, 1963. Janke, W.: Expt. Untersuchungen zur Abhängigkeit der Wirkung psychotroper Substanzen von Persönlichkeitsmerkmalen. Frankfurt, 1964. Janke, W. & Debus, G.: Experimental studies on antianxiety agents with normal subjects. Methodological considerations and review of the main effects. In: Efron, D. H. (Ed.): Psychopharmacology 1957–1967. Washington, 1968. Rickels, K.: Antineurotic agents: specific and non-specific effects. In: Efron, D. H. (Ed.): Psychopharmacology 1957–1967. Washington, 1968. Zbinden, G. & Randall, L. O.: Pharmacology of benzodiazepines: laboratory and clinical correlations. In: Garattini, S. & Shore, P. A (Eds.): Advances in pharmacology, 1967, *5*, 213–91.   *G. Debus*

Transaction, social. In relation to "interaction", a social transaction is a process presupposing individual dynamic participation, which is not necessarily the case with interaction.   *W.D.F.*

Transducer. An instrument which converts energy from one form into another. Hence the human ear is a transducer because it converts sound waves into nerve impulses.
          G.D.W.

Transfer occurs if the acquisition of an assignment (material B) is influenced by the previous learning of another assignment (material A). The influence of the assignment learned first on that learned second, may be an improvement (positive transfer) or an impairment (negative transfer: see *Proactive inhibition*). The positive transfer effect is the more emphatic the greater the similarity between learning assignments. A negative transfer occurs if the stimulus situation for both assignments is similar, but differing responses are required (Osgood, 1953). A negative transfer is noticeable, e.g. if a new, like task is to be solved in a way different from the first. But the "similarity" of learning assignments is quite variously defined.

In the case of conditioned learning, the notion of positive transfer is identical with that of *stimulus generalization* (q.v.). See *Conditioning, classical and operant.*

One may distinguish between the transfer of elements (e.g. in serial learning), when the elements of an assignment learned first make the learning of the second easier, and the transfer of rules (e.g. in problem-solving, when the principle for solving one task is transferred to the other ("learning set"). These specific transfer effects are to be distinguished from non-specific transfer effects, which consist merely of an increased general readiness to learn ("warming-up effect", or "learning to learn").

An unproven theory of formal education derives positive transfer from the improvement of individual functions, e.g. from the extension of memory (q.v.), will (q.v.), and logical thinking (q.v.). See *Memory; Reminiscence; Learning; Instructional technology.*

Bibliography: Kintsch, W.: Learning, memory and conceptual processes. New York, 1970. **Osgood, C.:** Method and theory in experimental psychology. New York, 1953. *H. Hofer*

Transference. A general phenomenon of the perception or interpretation of current situa-

tions in the light of past experiences or similar past situations. Approximately identical with the concept of generalization (q.v.) in learning theory. In psychoanalytical terminology (see *Psychoanalysis*), the term indicates primarily the phenomenon of emotional adjustment of the patient to the psychotherapist in analogy to the emotional adjustment of the patient to his early and earliest (intrafamilial) reference persons. Feelings of love, devotion, respect (*positive transference*), but also of hate, fear, or abasement (*negative transference*) are directed to the psychotherapist without the latter having actually given any "cause" to elicit them. Hence, as a rule, specific emotions of the patient toward the psychotherapist, and his ideas of the psychotherapist's feelings, are interpreted as transferences from past relations. They are referred to as such during treatment, if the patient uses them (inwardly) to resist an acknowledgement of his or her own unconscious motives, desires and aspirations.

If the psychotherapist has given the patient some concrete occasion for such feelings, he may find himself in a state of *counter-transference:* the psychotherapist misinterprets his relation to the patient in the light of his own irrational needs and his own unresolved conflicts. If the psychotherapist succumbs to such tendencies to counter-transference, he can seriously endanger the proficiency of psychotherapy and psychoanalysis. Hence one of the most important aspects of a psychotherapist's training is control of his own tendencies to counter-transference, ensured by an appropriate training analysis.

In psychotherapy and psychoanalysis, positive transferences of the patient in regard to his past are requisite. Extremely positive and negative transferences often impair the process.

Transference neuroses (in contrast to "narcissistic neuroses"; see *Neurosis; Psychoses, functional*) are psychic illnesses, the analytical treatment of which includes transference, or development of an emotional relation to the psychotherapist. Those said to be suffering from narcissistic neuroses are hardly capable of such an emotional relationship, since they are scarcely (or not at all) capable of it "in reality". Therefore treatment by Freudian psychoanalysis (q.v.) is not possible. Transference neuroses are said to be quite accessible to therapy; their interpretation uncovers the infantile factors in a disturbed development. See *Depth psychology; Psychotherapy*.

Bibliography: Freud, S.: Introductory lectures on psychoanalysis. London, 1922. Toman, W.: Introduction to psychoanalytic theory of motivation. London & New York, 1960. *W. Toman*

Transfert (Fre.). According to J. M. Charcot, the treatment of hysteria (q.v.) consists in an alteration of the moral medium, and in mental hygiene, and physical therapy. It seemed clear to him that treatment with static electricity should have an assured place among such methods. His basic idea was the production of an analogy ("*transfert*") between suggestion and hypnosis (q.v.), and such treatments. The basic conception of *transfert* goes back to the notion of a psychic fluid, as postulated by Mesmer (q.v.). *J.L.I.*

Transformation. The conversion of data in accordance with a prescription (usually simple functions), so that a transformed value corresponds to every initial value. The purpose is an alteration of a measurement scale, usually in order to correct empirical data according to the demands of the selected mathematical model, and to simplify data processing, mainly in the comparison of relative with theoretical frequencies. *D.W.E.*

Transformation, area. The transformation (q.v.) of raw values on the basis of the relative portion of the area lying between a particular raw value and a reference value derived from a theoretical or observed distribution. Hence in a distribution that has undergone area transformation the new scale units correspond to units of area of the distribution that has not been transformed. An example of area transformation is percentile rank. *W.H.B.*

Transformed standard values are obtained from a z scale by means of linear transformation, in order to avoid negative values and to compare scores with differing average values and dispersions. Example: IQ scores. *D.W.E.*

Transinformation. The amount of information (q.v.) correctly received in data transmission, and thus the information common to the transmitted and received signal sequences. In the absence of interference or noise, transinformation can equal information sent; the information flow, however, is limited by channel capacity.

Semantic transinformation is the amount of meaning common to two signal sequences, or that correctly transmitted in data transmission. A special case of semantic transinformation in cybernetic education (q.v.; see *Instructional technology*) is *didactic transinformation*—the didactic information conveyed by instructional techniques and acquired by the student. Didactic transinformation is employed as a measure of learning achievement in the information-theoretical process of "transinformation analysis". See *Sign and symbol*. *K.W.*

Transmitter substances. Transmitter substances (sometimes known as *neurohormones*) are substances formed in the organism which make possible or assist a transmission, and/or further transmission, of nervous excitation in the ANS or CNS (see *Nervous system*). The transmission may be from neurone to effector or from neurone to neurone (see *Synapses*). It is generally acknowledged nowadays that the transmission of impulses occurs chemically by means of the release of transmitter substances in the synapses. Since the identification and demarcation of transmitter substances from other body substances is relatively difficult, the following criteria for the characterization of a substance as a transmitter have been formulated: (*a*) the substance must be detectable in neurones whose action is transmitted to another neurone or effector; (*b*) the neurone must contain the enzyme system requisite for synthesis; (*c*) the transmitter is stored in the neurone in a physiologically inactive form; (*d*) an impulse entering the neurone releases the transmitter substance; (*e*) the transmitter substance reacts with specific receptors of the effector organ; (*f*) the application of the transmitter substance in the immediate neighborhood of the receptor must imitate the action of neurone stimulation; (*g*) an inactivation system must be present to make possible a limitation of duration of effect.

For the peripheral ANS, the transmitter substance in the pre- and post-ganglionic fibers of the sympathetic is acetylcholin(e) (q.v.). In the postganglionic fibers of the sympathetic, the transmitter substance is noradrenalin(e) (noreprinephrine), and possibly also adrenalin(e) (with a few exceptions). For some years the major emphasis of interdisciplinary transmitter research (biochemistry, pharmacology, clinical medicine, comparative psychology) has been on the search for transmitters in the CNS. The most important (and certainly present) transmitter substances in the CNS are acetylcholin(e) and noradrenalin(e). There is as yet no adequate information on the extent to which other substances (see *Biogenic amines*) definitely act as transmitters in the CNS (see *Serotonin; Gamma-amino-butyric acid; Histamine; Substance P*). Synthesis and inactivation of transmitters usually occur in several stages by means of various metabolites, with the participation of diverse enzymatic systems. Transmitter research is of considerable practical importance in the following respects: (*a*) the

attribution of transmitter systems to specific behavior patterns; (*b*) disturbance of the synthesis or decomposition of transmitters and psychoses; (*c*) the replacement of natural transmitters by substances which take over or alter their functions (false transmitters, substitute transmitters, e.g. alpha-methyldopa, q.v.); (*d*) the alteration of the function of transmitters by psychopharmaceutical means.

Bibliography: Eccles, J. C.: The physiology of synapses. New York, 1964. **Ehrenpreis, S. & Solnitzky, O. C.:** Neurosciences research, Vol. 1. New York, 1968. **Kappers, J. A.** (Ed.): Neurohormones and neurohumors. Amsterdam, 1969. **McLennan, H.:** Synaptic transmission. Philadelphia, 1963. **Phillis, J. W.:** The pharmacology of synapses. Oxford, 1970. See also: *Biogenic amines.*   *W. Janke*

Transparency. If the rays emanating from an object penetrate a second object lying on top of it, e.g. a sheet of glass, there is transparency in a physical sense, as contrasted with a transparency which is either psychic or experienced when objectively non-transparent things are perceived as transparent. To explain this, one has recourse to the gestalt laws of perception, and especially the law of pregnance (q.v.).

Bibliography: Kanizsa, G.: Die Erscheinungsweisen der Farben. Handbuch der Psychologie, Vol. 1/1. Göttingen, 1966, 161–91. **Michotte, A., Thinès, G. L. & Grabbe, G.:** Die amodalen Ergänzungen von Wahrnehmungsstrukturen. Handbuch der Psychologie, Vol. 1/1. Göttingen, 1966, 978–1002.
P.S. & R.S.

Transport effect. A phenomenon studied by Michotte whereby a transported object, e.g. an apple on a plate, appears stationary because it is seen only in relation to the object transporting it. It is difficult to demonstrate the effect experimentally since it is crucial that the transported and the transporting objects be seen as separate entities. Michotte achieved this by having a white screen and a black patch moving together horizontally while the black patch made irregular vertical oscillations in relation to the screen. The black patch was then seen as transported by the screen.

C.D.F.

Transposition of gestalts. Since a gestalt is a pattern of relationships between components, the components can be changed without altering the gestalt. Thus a gestalt can be transposed into a different set of components. For example, a tune can be recognized in many different keys. See *Structure; Ganzheit. C.D.F.*

Transsexualism. A term first used by Benjamin for physically normal people who are convinced that they belong to the opposite sex. They are driven by a compulsion to have their sexual organs, ordinary appearance and social status changed to those of the opposite sex. Several transsexuals are not homosexuals; many have little interest in sexual activity. Hormonal treatment and psychological support are usually helpful. In appropriate cases plastic genital surgery after surgical castration in the male usually gives satisfactory results. In several parts of the world, after castration and plastic surgery, such patients have obtained a change of name certificate. After a so-called change-of-sex operation a few cases are known to have married in their new sex role. See *Hermaphroditism.*

Bibliography: Green, R. & Money, J.: Transsexualism and sex reassignment. Baltimore, 1969. **Hamburger, C., Stürup, G. K. & Dahl-Iversen, E.:** Transvestism. Hormonal, psychiatric and surgical treatment. J.A.M.A., 1953, *152*, 391–6. G.K.S.

Transvestite. The term used for those who derive pleasure from wearing the clothes of the opposite sex. In practice mostly applied to a male who uses female dress. First described by Hirschfeld (Germany, 1910); called (by Havelock Ellis) Eonism, after Chevalier d'Eon de Beaumont (famous French T., 1728–1810). The need to dress thus is not always of the

same strength, and is often activated by a sexual stimulus. Both heterosexual and homosexual T.'s are met with. Transvestism should not be confused with fetishism, or with homosexuals using the dress of the opposite sex as an element in erotic situations. See also *Transsexualism; Hermaphroditism.*

Bibliography: **H. M.:** Die Transvestiten. Eine Untersuchung über den erotischen Verkleidungstrieb. Berlin, 1910. **Ellis, H.:** Eonism. Studies in the psychology of sex, Vol. 7. Philadelphia, 1928.

G.K.S.

Trapezium illusion. See *Segment illusion.*

Trauma, psychic. A psychic trauma may be any painful individual experience, especially if that experience is associated with permanent environmental change(s). As a rule psychic trauma involves a loss of possible motive gratification. This is "painful", i.e. it evokes an anxiety-aggression state that some claim can be cancelled only by aggressive restoration of the threatened possibilities of gratification, or by the development of inner defense (q.v.) mechanisms and an ultimate renunciation of possible gratifications (see *Object cathexis*).

W.T.

Traumatic neuroses are neuroses that derive from for the most part unexpected and short-term, frightening or painful environmental influences (e.g. accident neuroses, war neuroses, animal phobias, etc.). Despite the short-term nature of the environmental effect and the speedy restoration of the original objective state, the frightening or painful experience and the expectation of a recurrence of such occasions (e.g. that an accident will happen any moment, that a bomb will fall or a dog bite are retained). The neurotic behavior (say an hysterical paralysis, or an excessive anxiety reaction to every kind of noise or to dogs) is promoted by secondary advantages by illness (see *Defense; Object cathexis;*

Advantage by illness; Psychopathology, psycho-analytic schema of).

Freud assumed initially that all psycho-neuroses were preceded by traumatic events (the trauma hypothesis). He rejected this supposition in favor of the "wish theory" of neurosis, according to which infantile wishes can introduce psychoneuroses after traumatic events. It is, however, a matter for debate how some individuals of this type develop such infantile desires when others do not.

Today it is assumed that traumatic factors may also be present at the commencement of psychoneuroses, but that the severity of the trauma depends on the extent of painful change in the affected individual's environment. See *Family; Psychoanalysis; Depth psychology.*

Bibliography: Freud, S.: Inhibitions, symptoms and anxiety. London, ²1936. **Toman, W.:** Introduction to psychoanalytic theory of motivation. London & New York, 1960.   *W.T.*

Tremograph; tremometer. Devices for testing and measurement of tremor (q.v.). Tremo-graphs are used to record the tremor as a curve on a kymograph by applying the device to the bodily organ. With a tremometer a pin has to be inserted in a small aperture, or retained there so that it does not touch the sides of the hole. The number of times it does touch the edge is a measure of the intensity of tremor of the organ in question. In his factor-analytical studies, E. A. Fleishman tried to isolate an "arm-hand steadiness" factor.

Bibliography: Fleishman, E. A.: Dimensional analysis of movement reactions. J. exp. Psychol., 1958, *55*, 438–53.   *A.T.*

Tremor. Shaky movements of individual parts of the body caused by varying contraction of antagonistic muscle groups. Tremors can occur in conditions of cold, intense fatigue, stimulation, in the aged as *tremor senilis*, and

in various cases of poisoning (by alcohol, lead, mercury and nicotine); it may be inherited and is a symptom of various diseases, such as Parkinsonism (q.v.), *paralysis agitans*, multiple sclerosis (q.v.), and Basedow's disease (q.v.).
                                          E.D.

Trend. A systematic variation in time in a basic variable, in terms of a rise, drop, or a constant, intermittent, monotonous or phasic change. Dispersions and other parameters can underlie a trend.   *D.W.E.*

Trend analysis. An analysis made at different points in time in order to establish the significance of a trend (q.v.)   *D.W.E.*

Trial and error. A term applied by L. Morgan to behaviors which occur when an organism is presented with tasks which it is unable to solve because of its lack of appropriate behavior patterns. C. L. Hull (q.v.) called such behaviors "operants". Complex behavior patterns are developed by means of directed, positive reinforcement (q.v.) of desired, and negative reinforcement of non-desired, trials (operant conditioning, or "shaping"). See *Learning, trial-and-error; Conditioning, classical and operant.*   *H.Ro.*

Triangular conflict (syn. *Three-sided conflict*). In many animals courtship arises from a conflict between urges to aggression, flight and sex, but others such as the urge to build or care for the young may also be activated. Conflicting instincts led during phylogenesis to typical compromises, which are represented in typical intensities of movement patterns.

Bibliography: Morris, D. L.: The function and causation of courtship ceremonies. In: Grassé, P. P. (Ed.): L'Instinct dans le comportement des animaux et de l'homme. Paris, 1956, 261–87.   *K.Fi.*

Tribadism. Lesbianism; sapphism; female homosexuality. *Tribade:* a woman with an abnormally large clitoris who adopts the male role in homosexual behavior.   *G.D.W.*

Trichromatism. Normal color vision.

Triple-X Syndrome. A sex chromosome abnormality in which an extra X chromosome is added to the usual XX structure of the female. Occurs in about 0.12% of the female population, and tends to be associated with mental retardation. Yet more Xs are possible (e.g. XXXX), and with each addition the probability of retardation is increased. Only two cases of pento-X chromosome structure have been reported.   *G.D.W.*

Tritanomaly. A defect of color vision in which the third, blue-violet sensitive cone pigment is only moderately effective.   *K.H.P.*

Tritanopia. Color blindness, in which the third (blue-sensitive) cone pigment is wholly absent.   *K.H.P.*

Tropism. The directive response of an organism to a stimulus or a stimulus source. The absolute stimulus intensity is less decisive than the spatial or temporal intensity. *Positive tropism:* toward; *negative tropism:* away from. Other distinctions are made according to the kind of stimulus: toward light radiation: *phototropism;* the sun: *heliotropism;* a concentration of various substances: *chemotropism;* temperature: *thermotropism;* and so on. The term "tropism" is usually applied to fixed plants, immobile animals, etc. *Taxis* is the term for freely mobile organisms. Sometimes, however, both terms are used synonymously.
          I.L.

True value. A term occurring mainly in test theory, where it indicates the expectation value of an observed variable obtained by measuring an individual with a specific test. As a rule the true value is not identical with the observed value, since measurements include an error. Therefore the true value may be characterized as the difference between the observed value and the error in measurement. In principle, the concept of true value may also be applied to other parameters of a variable.   *H.-J.S.*

Truth drug. A chemical substance supposed to compel an individual to disclose all information. Experimental studies on the validity of information given oppose the existence of such drugs. In 1932, House asserted of scopalamine (q.v.), a drug related to atropine (q.v.), that no one under its influence could lie, and introduced the term "truth drug". See *Narcoanalysis; Lie detector.*   *E.L.*

Tryptamine. A neurohormone and biogenic amine formed from the aromatic amino-acid tryptophan(e) (q.v.) by decarboxylation. Tryptamine passes the blood-brain barrier and can therefore be administered extracerebrally. It has sympathicomimetic (q.v.) qualities (e.g. increased heart rate and blood pressure). Related drugs (dimethyltryptamine) have psychotomimetic (q.v.) qualities.

Bibliography: Dewhurst, W. G.: On the chemical basis of mood. J. Psychosom. Res., 1965, 9, 115–27. See also *Biogenic amines.*   *W.J.*

Tryptophan(e). An aromatic amino-acid from which serotonin (q.v. = 5-hydroxytryptamine) is formed by way of the intermediate substance 5-hydroxytryptophan(e) (see *Biogenic amines*). Tryptophan(e) is also to some extent transformed by decarboxylation into tryptamine, which counts as a neurohormone. Oral administration of tryptophan(e) to healthy subjects can induce very slight parathymia after a short time (app. one hour). *W.J.*

Tsédek test. A test by H. Baruk for moral insight. S. has to judge the behavior of persons from the moral viewpoint in a series of summarized everyday situations. The judgments offered are assessed in order to arrive at S's moral attitude. *H.J.A.*

TSH. Abb. for *Thyroid stimulating hormone.* See *Hormones.*

T-technique. A factor-analytical technique based on correlation coefficients determined by means of the correlation of the measurements of a characteristic at t different times in regard to n individuals, in which $n > t$. The factors extracted are interpreted as situational. The technique is applied in developmental psychology and learning studies. See *Factor analysis.* *G.Mi.*

Tunnel effect. An example of a *kinetic screen effect* similar to the *piston effect* (q.v.). Two lights appear successively at points some distance apart. A screen is placed between and in front of the lights. In these conditions observers see one light travelling from one side of the screen to the other as if it had gone through a tunnel. This effect continues even after the screen has been removed. However, if the observer is never aware of the existence of the screen, the effect does not occur. *C.D.F.*

Turner syndrome (syn. *Albright-Turner syndrome; Morgagni-Turner syndrome; XO syndrome*). An intersexual syndrome named after the American physician H. H. Turner (b. 1892) and featuring dysgenesia (= underdevelopment) or agenesia (= complete absence) of sex glands (see *Gonads*). The classic genetic sex-chromosome constitution is XO; there are, however, also mosaic structures (XO/XX, XO/XY). Further symptoms are: physical appearance usually female; internal and external genitals usually female, but infantile; secondary sex characteristics often underdeveloped; sex chromatin more often negative (male) than positive (female); inadequate growth or dwarfism; multiple deformations; *ptergyium colli;* primary amenorrhea (q.v.); often increased gonadotrophin and decreased estrogen excretion in urine; average intelligence.

Bibliography: Jores, A. & Nowakowski, H.: Praktische Endokrinologie. Stuttgart, 1968. Leiber, B. & Olbrich, G.: Die klinischen Syndrome. Munich, ⁴1966. Overzier, C.: Intersexuality. New York, 1963. *V.S.*

t value. A normalized standard value from non-normal distributions named after L. Terman by McCall (1939). See *Test theory.*

Bibliography: McCall, W. A.: Measurement. New York, 1939. *D.W.E.*

Twilight sleep. A state of dream-like semi-consciousness which is associated with some psychopathological conditions such as hysteria and epilepsy, and may be induced by certain drugs. It is normally transitory, but is of highly variable duration. *G.D.W.*

Twin studies. When Galton (1875, 1883) introduced twins into scientific research toward the end of the nineteenth century, they already had a rich history in mythology, legends and superstition. In the age of Darwinian theorizing and research, a major question was that of the "supremacy" of heredity; recourse was had to twins in order to substantiate this supremacy.

1. *Classic method of twin research.* Classically defined, the method of twin study used in scientific research is very simple. The basis

is the existence of two kinds of twins: namely, one-egg and two-egg twins. Genuine one-egg (*monozygotic*) twins (*MZ twins*) come from a single zygote—a single egg cell (or ovum) fertilized by a single sperm cell (spermatozoon). They represent two copies of a single individual. Their inherited basis (*anlage*, q.v.) is wholly identical.

Two-egg (*dizygotic*) twins (*DZ twins*) come from two zygotes (i.e. from two egg cells (ova), fertilized by two sperm cells). Genetically, their similarity is like that between two usual (genuine) siblings. But, in both MZ and DZ twins, the members of a pair are of the same age and depend upon the same environment. The only difference is that in one kind the genetic inheritance is identical, and in the other it is not.

The classic twin study method consists of taking a given (intellectual or physical) characteristic or trait and comparing the average differences between individuals from MZ and DZ pairs. The difference noticeable in MZ twins is to be ascribed only to the very small difference in environmental influences. The difference between DZ twins is attributable to the same influences, but also (and above all) to the difference in genetic inheritance. If one then demarcates the differences between MZ twins from those between DZ twins, the role of inheritance in regard to the characteristic under examination should be clear.

Numerous research projects have been carried out in accordance with this classic method. Nevertheless, they have been unable to answer the following question: "What are the respective contributions of inheritance and environment in the formation of individual differences?" The reason is simply that the question is wrongly put. There is no real "contribution" or "share", but a complex interaction between genetic and environmental factors. This interaction varies according to the characteristics under investigation, the age of the subjects, and the methods of comparison used. On the other hand, this method has made it possible to draw the main lines of the structure of mental and physical characteristics from the viewpoint of inheritance.

Body build and intelligence (defined according to the Binet-Simon test) are the characteristics most closely associated with inheritance. The correlation in regard to intelligence is of course zero between individuals who are not related and who have no environmental influences in common. It is approximately 0.25 between non-related children who were nevertheless reared together, and 0.50 between parents and their children and between siblings. The correlation reaches a value of some 0.55 for DZ twins reared together, and a value of almost 0.90 for MZ twins who have grown up together. School success also depends on inheritance, but to a much less noticeable degree. On the other hand, the hypothesis according to which there are genetically conditioned special abilities for mathematics, science, literature, history and so on, could not be verified. The results in regard to affective or volitional characteristics are often uncertain, and are contested. This is perhaps attributable to the fact that in this area the concepts are unclear and the test methods insufficiently validated.

Newman, Freeman & Holzinger, who were the first to use the twin method to any real point, came to the following conclusion (1937): in so far as personality and temperamental traits are concerned, MZ twins are hardly any more alike than DZ twins.

By using more complex methods (mainly factor analysis, q.v.), more recent studies have nevertheless been able to demonstrate the essential role of inheritance for certain personality factors. Hence, e.g. Vandenberg (1962) found very significant differences between MZ and DZ twins for the four factors of Thurstone's temperament inventory ("active", "vigorous", "impulsive", "sociable"), and for four factors of one of Cattell's inventories ("emotional sensitivity", "nervous tension", "neuroticism", and "will control").

Eysenck's (1952) work on neuroticism is, however, by far the most convincing and fruitful in this area. Eysenck defines neuroticism (q.v.) as a normal personality (q.v.) variable, extending from extreme stability to extreme instability. There is no difference between the MZ and DZ groups in regard to neuroticism. On the other hand, the correlations between DZ pairs are 0.21, and between MZ pairs 0.85. Variance analysis shows that, for the neuroticism factor, 80% of the individual differences are to be attributed to inheritance and only 20% to environmental influences.

2. *Control method.* The "co-twin control method" is associated with the name of a major child psychologist, A. Gesell (1941). The method consists in comparing MZ twins by subjecting one (experimental) partner to intensive training, whereas the (control) partner continues in his "spontaneous" development, i.e. without any special training. It is no longer a question, as in the classic method of twin studies, of comparing the respective parts played by inheritance and environment, but of comparing the effects of maturation (q.v.) and education (upbringing) (q.v.). In other words: Can learning and training—in short, education—accelerate the child's maturation process? This method has not often been used, and only with children of pre-school age, and most often in the areas of motor and linguistic development (q.v.).

Gesell's central experiment is well known. It consists of training the experimental twin in stages over a period of several weeks. The training gives the experimental twin an incontestable advantage, yet by the end of the experiment this head start is compensated by the control twin thanks to mere maturation.

The co-twin control method has tackled the old problem of "nature" and "nurture" in terms of the more dynamic concepts of maturation and learning, and usefully questioned the American ideology of the nineteen-thirties, which ascribed predominance to education.

The essential point of Gesell's observation is to be found elsewhere, however: namely in the demonstration that the maturation process of MZ twins is never wholly identical. Hence MZ twins no longer appear as a single being divided into two exemplars, but as two individualities. The twin method allows clarification of the maturation process (as a multiplicity of factors subjected to a general regulative principle), and simultaneously poses (yet again) the question of the inheritance and genesis of the human individual.

3. *Twin pair method.* The twin pair method is concerned predominantly with the genesis of individuality. It is a matter of a new problem whose formulation, however, puts in question the other problems of inheritance and maturation. The twin pair method starts from a critique of the other research methods.

The control and the classic twin study methods treat the partners of each pair of twins as two independent individuals, and not as a pair. It is, however, obvious (or at least a hypothesis is feasible) that life in a pair-bond has certain consequences. This form of existence determines similarities which have nothing to do with genetic inheritance (mutual imitation), and differences which are not attributable to environmental differences (role difference, dominance and submission relations, etc.). Hence it would seem possible to explain why in certain personality tests genuine twins are not more, and sometimes even less, alike than usual siblings.

But here, as in the foregoing perspectives, the interest of twin studies is that (thanks to their specific characteristics) they provide a generally applicable research method. The complete identity of MZ twins grounds the investigation of inheritance in classic twin research.

Twins—as complete pairs—offer the unique opportunity not only of carrying out research into the psychology of the pair, but of investigating the fundamental processes of the development of human individuality. Child psychologists have long been aware that it is not the individual in the sense of the *I* or *ego* (q.v.) that is "original" or "fundamental", but the undifferentiated "we", the "confusion" between mother and child; and that a consciousness of the self and of others forms only gradually (though simultaneously). (See *Self-knowledge*.) Whereas, however, a fundamental difference lies at the basis of the mother-child pair (as in the case of every other freely-formed pair), in a pair of twins (above all in a MZ pair) there is, at first, practically no difference between the partners. For this reason, any ascertainable differences between partners may be ascribed to the (direct and indirect) consequences of living in the pair bond.

The twin pair method is relatively new. Its rough lines were suggested by Gedda (1948), applied by von Bracken (1934) before it had been developed in its own right, and have been defined and developed by Zazzo (1960). This method makes it possible to investigate the negative or positive (and differentiating) effects of existence in the pair bond on the development and structure of personality. The noticeable delay in language development and the frequent occurrence of secret languages—chiefly with MZ twins—clearly indicate the danger of alienation in or through the pair. Both partners are their mutual prisoners, and social needs are gratified and exhausted in the twin relationship. In spite of this "mirror effect", and in spite of identity in regard to inheritance and environment, an individualization process does take place. The fact that a pair is a structure allows it a differentiating effect. Above all, it is possible to observe how oppositions, rivalries and completions occur, and how role division and ego-consciousness are formed; in short, it is possible to observe the formation of a specific individuality in the case of each partner.

Twin studies are not restricted to one method. A distinction has been made here between three methods, which correspond to the many problems and to the historic sequence of questions raised by scientific psychology. The methods of twin research are not the only ones that allow investigation of such problems. Nevertheless, the application of a "naturally" available method in an area where experiment research proper was impossible, enabled at least an entry to be made into some of the most difficult areas of human psychology.

Bibliography: Bracken, H. von: Mutual intimacy in twins. Char. and Pers., 1934, 4, 293–309. Id.: Zwilling und Psychologie des Gemeinschaftslebens. Report of 14th German Psycho. Soc. Jena, 1935. Burlingham, D. T.: The relationship of twins to each other. Psychoanal. Stud. Child, 1939, 3–4. Burt, C.: The genetic determination of differences in intelligence: a study of monozygotic twins reared together and apart. Brit. J. Psychol., 1966, 57, 137–53. Cattell, R. B.: Methodological and conceptual advances in evaluating hereditary and environmental influences and their interaction. In: Vandenberg, S. G. (Ed.): Methods and goals in human behavior genetics. New York, 1965. Day, E. J.: The development of language in twins. Child Developm., 1932, 179–99; 298–316. Eysenck, H. J.: The scientific study of personality. London, 1952. Id.: The biological basis of personality. Springfield, 1967. Id.: Intelligence assessment: a theoretical and experimental approach, Brit. J. Educ. Psychol., 1967, 37, 81–98. Galton, F.: The history of twins as a criterion of the relative powers of nature and nurture. Fraser's Magazine, 1875, 12, 566–76. Id.: Inquiries into human faculty and its development. London, 1883. Gedda, L.: Psicologica della società intrageminale. Riv. di Psicol., 1948, 4, 10–44. Id.: Studio dei gemelli. Roma, 1951. Id.: Twins in history and in science. New York, 1961. Gesell, A. & Thompson, H.: Twins T and C from infancy to adolescence: a biogenetic study of individual differences by the method of co-twin control. Provincetown, Mass., 1941. Gottschaldt, K.: Das Problem der Phänogenetik der Persönlichkeit. In: Lersch, P. & Thomas, H. (Eds.): Handbuch der Psychologie, Vol. 4. Göttingen, 1960. Husén, T.: Analyse de facteurs héréditaires et de milieu determinant la réussite scolaire par l'étude de jumeaux élevés ensemble. Bull. Psychol., 1967, 20, 772–81. Id.: Über die Begabung von Zwillingen. Psychol. Beitr., 1953, 1. Luria, A. R. & Yudovitch, F. I.: Speech and the development of mental processes in the child. London, 1959. Mittler, P.: The study of twins. Harmondsworth, 1971. Newman, H. H., Freeman, F. N. & Holzinger, R. J.: Twins: a study of heredity and environment. Chicago, 1937. Pire, G.: Application des techniques sociométriques à l'étude des jumeaux. Enfance, 1966, *1*, 23–48. **Vandenberg, S. G.**: The hereditary abilities study: hereditary components in a psychological test battery. Amer. J. Hum. Genet., 1962, *14*, 220–237. **Id.** (Ed.): Methods and goals in human behavior genetics. New York, 1965. **Zazzo, R.**: Les jumeaux, le couple, et la personne. Paris, 1960. **Id.**: Sur le postulat de la comparabilité dans la méthode des jumeaux. Acta genet. med. gemellolog., 1955, *4*.   *R. Zazzo*

Two-factor theory of learning. A theory of O. H. Mowrer's that he has since abandoned. It separates the areas of application of classical and instrumental learning: (*a*) *sign learning:* emotions, autonomic responses, movements of the smooth musculature are acquired in accordance with the law of contiguity (q.v.); (*b*) *solution learning:* voluntary responses, movements of the striate musculature are acquired by instrumental learning. See *Learning theory; Conditioning, classical and operant.*
                                                       H.W.

Tympanic membrane (syn. *Tympanum; Eardrum*). The tympanic membrane lies between the external auditory canal and the middle ear. The hammer of the first auditory ossicle is joined to it. Recent objective studies of middle-ear functioning have been carried out by measuring input wave resistance on the membrane. See *Auditory perception; Sense organs: the ear.*   *M.S.*

Type. In common parlance, the terms "type" and "trait" (q.v.) are used almost interchangeably. We may say that a person possesses the trait of sociability, or that he is "the sociable type", meaning in both instances that he is sociable, that is, behaves in a sociable manner. Many psychologists, particularly in the USA, make little difference in their usage of these terms, except with respect to the hypothetical distribution of the behavior in question; it is often said that the concept of *type* requires a bimodal distribution of test scores, or even a clear separation of members of the opposite sides of the typology, whereas the concept of *trait* requires a unimodal and probably even a normal Gaussian form of distribution. This point will be discussed presently; the best modern usage certainly distinguishes clearly between the two concepts, as will be pointed out later, but nevertheless much of what has been said about traits in this book also applies to types, and the two articles should be read together in order to clarify all the relevant points.

Typology may be said to have begun with Galen's theory of the four temperaments (choleric, sanguine, phlegmatic, melancholic) in the second century A.D., although the roots of this typology are said to go back to Hippocrates, and traces of it are certainly found in ancient Greece (Roback, 1931). In his *Anthropologie*, Kant adopted and adapted this doctrine, and his version became official doctrine until the end of the nineteenth century. One essential feature of this typology was its categorical character; a person belonged to one type or another, and no mixtures were allowed. It is this feature of the Galen-Kant view which gave rise to the mistaken notion that distribution of scores discriminated between types and traits; this is only true if we accept a categorical view of type concepts. As we shall see, none of the well-known exponents of modern typology (Jung, Kretschmer) has in fact adopted such a view.

The alternative to a categorical view is a dimensional one, and such a position seems to have been adumbrated by Wundt (1903), who argued that two of the four types were characterized by high emotionality (cholerics and melancholics), whereas the other two were characterized by low emotionality; he consequently suggested a dimension of "emotionality" along which people could be graded continuously. He provided a second dimension by noting that cholerics and sanguines were "changeable", melancholics and phlegmatics "unchangeable"; this dimension was independent of the first. Wundt's dimensional system thus locates the four temperaments in the four quadrants generated by these two dimensions; they have lost their categorical character, and normal or unimodal distributions along the two dimensions, while not a necessary feature of the model, would certainly not be counter to Wundt's thinking. Combining Kant's description of the personality traits characterizing the four temperaments, and the dimensional system of Wundt, gives us a picture of what might be called "classical typology" which is reproduced as Fig. 1 (Eysenck, 1967).

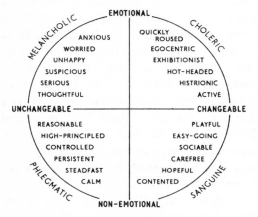

Fig. 1. Diagram showing combination of the Galen-Kant theory of the four temperaments and Wundt's dimensional hypothesis

Distribution of scores is thus not the distinguishing mark as between type and trait concepts; it would in any case be a meaningless one from a purely statistical point of view (Eysenck, 1970). Scores measure error variance as well as true variance; indeed in psychology, particularly the psychology of personality, they probably contain more error variance than true variance. But error variance is by definition normally distributed, so that even if the distribution of "true" scores happened to be bimodal, the addition of normally distributed error variance could easily make the combined distribution unimodal. Furthermore, arguments from distributions require a proper, rational metric; no such metric has ever been suggested for measures of person-

ality. Observed scores are arbitrary, and can be transformed in any desired way through the use of logarithms or other mathematical functions; none of the resulting distributions, however different they may be, can be said to be more correct than any other. Arguments from distributions are a quagmire which more cautious writers avoid; no possible conclusions could be drawn from them, even if the argument happened to be relevant, which it is not (Eysenck, 1970).

If the distribution of scores does not mark the distinction between type and trait concepts, what does? Eysenck (1947) has suggested that traits are the subordinate concept, type the supraordinate concept; typologies are created to account for the observed intercorrelations between traits. This suggestion forms part of a general hierarchical concept of personality structure, which is shown diagrammatically in Fig. 2, using the type "extraversion-introversion" as the example. At the lowest level we have specific responses to specific stimuli, i.e. isolated bits of behavior; these are integrated into habitual responses when they can be shown to be regular, i.e. to have statistical reliability. These habitual responses are in turn integrated into traits, such as sociability, impulsiveness, activity, liveliness, or excitability; evidence for the existence of such traits is provided by observed intercorrelations among habitual responses. If these traits themselves are found to intercorrelate in representative samples of the population, in the manner predicted by the theory, then we have evidence of the supraordinate type concept; in the case shown in diagram form in Fig. 2, the concept of "extraversion" implies, and is based on, positive intercorrelations between the various traits listed.

As in the case of traits (q.v.), the statistical technique best adapted to the exploration of typological hypotheses is that of factor analysis (q.v.). Thurstone's use of oblique primary factors, the intercorrelations between which can again be factored to give rise to second-order factors, fits the situation very well; traits are primary factors, types second-order ones, and both levels of the hierarchy can be investigated simultaneously by modern computerized rotation methods. Of these, varimax is often used but is not appropriate as it imposes orthogonality on the solution; this automatically rules out type factors conceived as second-order factors. Promax or some such program which allows the angles between primary factors to align themselves according

version and is based on certain pseudo-physiological speculations of the Austrian psychiatrist O. Gross (1902). Eysenck (1970), who gives a detailed account of these studies, has recalculated the original data and has shown that activity is in fact correlated quite highly with primary-secondary function, so that the only two independent dimensions which emerge are emotionality and primary-secondary function, or extraversion; this result is in good agreement with Wundt's

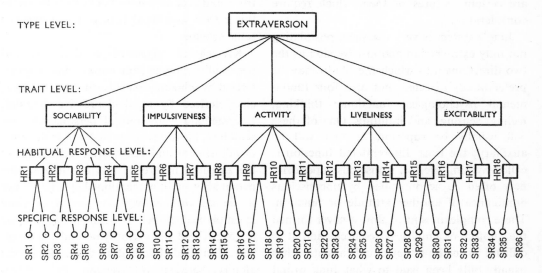

Fig. 2. Diagram showing hierarchical hypothesis of type and trait concepts

to simple structure principles without additional requirements of orthogonality is mandatory for the proper exploration of the factor space. Apparent contradictions between different writers can often be traced to the use of clearly inappropriate methods of rotation.

Historically, the first to use quasi-statistical methods for the elaboration of a descriptive system of personality were Heymans & Wiersma (1906–9); on the basis of ratings of some 2,523 individuals by their doctors on various personality traits, they arrived at a system of classification using three main dimensions: emotionality, activity, and primary as opposed to secondary function; this last dimension resembles extraversion-intro-

hypothesis as shown in Fig. 1. (It is assumed here that "changeableness" can be identified with extraversion; this seems likely from the personality descriptions given, and also from experimental work done, e.g. Eysenck, 1967.)

Better known than Heymans and Wiersma's typology (which is widely used only in South Africa at the present time) is the work of Jung (1921) and Kretschmer (1948). Jung's exclusively theoretical and speculative writing was not influenced by empirical studies, and his particular hypotheses did not give rise to much experimental work; Kretschmer's first book appeared in 1921, and ran into twenty-five editions by 1968, having inspired a tremendous amount of empirical research, and being changed in many ways by the results of this research, much of which was done by Kretschmer and his students. Detailed reviews are given of these theories in Eysenck (1970) and by Hall and Lindzey (1957); the latter work gives prominence to Sheldon's (1940, 1942) version of Kretschmer's teachings, mixed as it is with Jungian notions, and hardly does justice to Kretschmer's pioneering investigations. The details of these two typologies cannot of course be discussed here, but there are certain features of them which require consideration.

Jung's system is very complex, postulating not only extraversion and introversion as the two directions into which the libido may be preferentially directed, but also four fundamental psychological functions: thinking, feeling, sensing, and intuiting. One of these will usually be superior, another will be auxiliary; the least differentiated function is called by him inferior. Conscious superiority may often be accompanied by unconscious dominance of another attitude or function. These complexities have almost never formed the subject of empirical research, and it is difficult to see how they could; attention has usually only been paid to what Jung would consider an extremely superficial caricature of his system, namely the behavioral dimension of extraversion-introversion; this closely resembles Wundt's "changeableness" and Heymans and Wiersma's primary vs. secondary function, and is by no means original in conception.

Jung suggested that the two types of neurotic illness which emerged from Janet's investigations (hysteria and psychasthenia) were characteristically found in extraverted and introverted personalities respectively; this proposition was verified by Eysenck (1947). The same investigation tested another proposition implicit in Jung's account, but never discussed by him. If two types of neurotic illness are at opposite ends of the extraversion-introversion continuum, then we must posit

another dimension, orthogonal to the first one, ranging from neurotic to stable; this dimension was called "neuroticism", and is in nature very similar to Wundt's emotionality. Fittingly, psychasthenics (now more usually called "dysthymics", i.e. anxiety states, reactive depressions, obsessional and compulsive patients, and phobics) fall into the "melancholic" quadrant, hysterics and psychopaths into the "choleric" quadrant, as do criminals. Thus empirical results support the Wundtian doctrine, and accommodate Jung's hypothesis (in this rather superficial form) in one and the same scheme.

Kretschmer suggested a dimension of personality ranging from one extreme, characterized by schizophrenic disorders, to another, characterized by manic-depressive disorder. Intermediate were normal personalities, resembling, however, the extreme in their mode of adjustment and behavior. Figure 3 shows the essential nature of this continuum; the personality qualities mentioned by Kretschmer to demarcate his two types show a close resemblance between the schizothyme and the introvert, and the cyclothyme and the extravert. (Jung had already drawn attention to the affinity between introversion and schizophrenia.) Here too it is obvious that the existence of psychotic patients at both ends of the continuum requires the postulation of another dimension, orthogonal to the first, ranging from psychosis to normality; this dimension may be named "psychoticism" and there is considerable evidence for its existence (Eysenck & Eysenck, 1968).

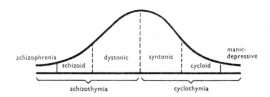

If we can identify, as is probably permissible, introversion with schizothymia and extraversion with cyclothymia, the question remains of whether we can identify, as the Freudians would do, neuroticism with psychoticism, regarding psychotic illness as a more serious form of neurotic illness. The evidence fairly conclusively suggests that this hypothesis is false, and that the two dimensions are in fact orthogonal (Eysenck, 1964; Cattell & Scheier, 1961). In general, tests which discriminate between normals and psychotics do not discriminate between normals and neurotics, and vice versa; discriminant function analyses demonstrate the existence of two significant latent roots. Hence at the type level a minimum of three independent dimensions seems to be required to represent human personality: extraversion, emotionality-neuroticism, and psychoticism. (The Heymans and Wiersma dimension of *activity* may be similar to psychoticism; the slowness and retardation of psychotics may appear as the opposite of activity.)

Kretschmer introduced the notion of body-build into his system, associating leptomorph, linear physique with schizothymia and pyknic, broad physique with cyclothymia. There is probably a low correlation of 0.3–0.4 between introversion and leptomorph physique, but the association with psychotic disorder is largely an experimental artefact, produced by the different ages at which schizophrenics and manic-depressives succumb to their respective illnesses; body build becomes more pyknic with age, and manic-depressive patients are considerably older than schizophrenic ones. Sheldon found a very high correlation between physique and temperament, but these have not been replicated by other investigators, and are almost certainly due to contamination of one measure by knowledge of the other.

Giese (1939), conscious of the multiplicity of typologies, pleaded for a single typology; his wish is gradually coming true as experimental studies and refined statistical techniques clear away many of the obstacles which have hitherto stood in the way of such a unified account of human typology. Cattell, Guilford

and Eysenck all find evidence for extraversion-introversion and emotionality-stability in their studies (Eysenck & Eysenck, 1969), and there is also a good deal of agreement on psychoticism, and on the position within this dimensional framework of various psychiatric diagnostic groups. Much still remains to be done, but better methods and more objective measures are gradually narrowing the range of dispute. Models are becoming more sophisticated, largely by becoming more quantified, and questions are being asked the answers to which were being taken for granted by earlier writers. Thus for instance the distinction between normals and neurotics, or normals and psychotics, may be quantitative, i.e. along a continuum, or qualitative, i.e. categorical; one answer or the other was usually assumed by psychiatric and other intuitive writers, but no method was available to provide cogent evidence one way or the other. The method of criterion analysis (Eysenck, 1950) was designed specially with this problem in mind, and has shown that the quantitative hypothesis is in fact the correct one, both for neurosis and psychosis.

Empirical work on typologies makes use of the same methods as work on traits (q.v.); ratings, self-ratings (questionnaires), miniature situation tests and laboratory tasks based on theoretical systems and deductions therefrom are all being used, as well as physiological recordings. As in the case of traits, the question arises whether a person's position on a typological dimension is determined more by hereditary or environmental causes. A detailed survey of the evidence is given by Eysenck (1967), who concludes that in the Western type of culture, at the present time, the average contribution of heredity to individual differences in extraversion, emotionality and psychoticism is roughly between 60% and 80%, with the majority of well designed studies giving values in the neighborhood of 75%, a value very similar to that found in the case of intelligence tests. There are many different methods in use, in addition to the study of monozygotic and dizygotic twins, and results are in good agreement. The same may be said of concordance studies of neurotic, psychotic and criminal twins; concordance of identical twins is considerably greater than that of fraternal twins.

A central problem in genetic studies of this kind is connected with the question of what is inherited—clearly we cannot inherit function, only structure. This raises the fundamental problem of causality; types, like traits, are merely descriptive, yet we would like to know more precisely why a particular person is situated at the extraverted end of the continuum, or at the stable end, or the psychotic. Such questions are difficult to answer, and attempts have been made either by using psychological concepts like Hull's reactive inhibition (Eysenck, 1957) or Pavlov's "excitation-inhibition" (Gray, 1964), or physiological notions like the ascending reticular activating system and the visceral brain (Eysenck, 1967). Such theories generate testable hypotheses, particularly the physiological types of theory, and many experiments have been reported in which such deductions have been subjected to test. Such deductions may be along physiological or psychological lines. As an example of the first type, consider the hypothesis that extraverts have higher thresholds of A.R.A.S. activity, so that cortical arousal will be lower in them; this leads immediately to the deduction that EEG alpha activity will be of greater amplitude, and characteristically of lower frequency. Similarly, it can be predicted that sedation thresholds are low in extraverts, high in introverts. Both predictions have in fact received strong support. Psychological predictions derive from knowledge of behavioral consequences of high and low arousal states; conditioning is facilitated by high arousal, impaired by low arousal, and introverts do as predicted show better conditioning than do extraverts on eyeblink or GSR conditioning. Many other predictions

relating to orienting responses, figural aftereffects, sensory thresholds, reminiscence, blocking, vigilance, tolerance of pain and sensory deprivation, rote learning, time errors, perceptual defense, motor movements, level of aspiration, autonomic reactions, and so on have been tested in efforts to provide evidence relating to the causal hypothesis mentioned, usually with positive results (Eysenck, 1967). It seems likely that work along these lines, i.e. using the hypothetico-deductive method, will succeed in the long run to put the whole study of typology on a higher level than the largely intuitive, subjective kind of impressionism which characterized the earlier writers. At present we have reached a half-way house, with a fair number of well established facts, but also with a number of puzzling discrepancies; with fair agreement on the outline of the general picture, but with disagreement on specific points. Resolution of these disagreements will be the next stage in the development of typological theories.

Types, like traits, may be investigated with animals as well as with humans; rats may be bred for emotionality, using the open field tests, and emotionally reactive animals compared with emotionally non-reactive ones on a variety of experimental tests, or with respect to physiological functioning and biochemical make-up. It cannot of course be assumed without proof that the meaning of emotionality is identical in humans and in animals, but the hypothesis that this is so can be experimentally tested, and predictions made on this basis have been largely validated. Experimental work along these lines promises to add considerably to our knowledge; animal analogues of human types offer advantages (breeding studies for genetic analysis; physiological analysis *in vivo*; biochemical analysis and anatomical study after dissection) which make them of considerable value to the experimenter. Possibly dogs and monkeys will in due course supplant rats, being closer to man in their make-up; to date, most work has in fact been done with rats (Eysenck & Broadhurst, 1964).

Although the various dimensions of personality which constitute the basis of modern typology are independent of each other, and of intelligence, nevertheless they may interact, and this interaction requires the use of special techniques of *zone analysis*. Consider as an example work done on expansiveness of movements; low N extraverts show much expansiveness, low N introverts little. High N extraverts show little expansiveness, high N introverts much. If the results are averaged over all high E vs. high I groups, no differences appear; similarly when all high N groups are contrasted with all low N groups. It is only when we plot all four zones (high E, high N; low E, high N; high E, low N; low E, low N) that highly significant results emerge. Taking only extremes of this kind, and using our three dimensions plus intelligence, we have sixteen sub-groups which require to be compared with each other; if we took three samples for each dimension (high, medium and low) in order to test linearity of regression (which should not simply be assumed), then we have 81 groups to compare. It will be clear that typological studies, properly carried out in line with the principles of zone analysis, require considerable thought, special design and complex statistical treatment; many failures to replicate previous studies, or to find results in line with hypothesis, may be due to insufficient care being taken with the design of the experiment. Typology is such an important part of psychology that greater care in this respect will undoubtedly repay the trouble taken.

Bibliography: Cattell, R. B. & Scheier, I. H.: The meaning and measurement of neuroticism and anxiety. New York, 1961. Eysenck, H. J.: Dimensions of personality. London, 1947. Id.: Criterion analysis—an application of the hypothetico-deductive method in factor analysis. Psychol. Rev., 1950, *57*, 38–53. Id.: The dynamics of anxiety and hysteria. London, 1957. Id.: Principles and methods of personality description, classification and diagnosis. Brit. J. Psychol., 1964, *55*, 284–94. Id.: The biological basis of personality. Springfield, 1967. Id.: The structure of human personality. London, ³1970. Eysenck, H. J. & Broadhurst, P. L.: Experiments with animals. Oxford, 1964. Eysenck, H. J. & Eysenck, S. B. G.: Structure and measurement of personality. London, 1969. Eysenck, S. B. G. & Eysenck, H. J.: The measurement of psychoticism: a study of factor stability and reliability. Brit. J. soc. clin. Psychol., 1968, *7*, 286–94. Giese, F.: Lehrbuch der Psychologie. Tübingen, 1939. Gray, J. A.: Pavlov's typology. Oxford, 1964. Gross, O.: Die cerebrale sekundärfunktion. 1902. Hall, C. S. & Lindsey, G.: Theories of personality. New York, 1957. Heymans, G. & Niersma, E.: Beiträge zur speziellen Psychologie auf Grund einer Massenuntersuchung. Z. Psychol., 1906, *42*, 81–127; *43*, 321–73; 1907, *45*, 1–42; 1908, *47*, 321–33; *49*, 414–39; 1909, *51*, 1–72. Jung, C. G.: Psychologische Typen. Zürich, 1921. Kretschmer, E.: Körperbau und Charakter. Berlin, 1948. Roback, A. A.: The psychology of character. New York, 1931. Sheldon, W. H.: The varieties of temperament. New York, 1942. Id.: The varieties of human physique. New York, 1940. Wundt, W.: Grundzüge der physiologischen Psychologie. Vol. 3. Leipzig, 1903.

H. J. Eysenck

Typical intensity. In order to reach a formal constancy of ritualized movements, a typical intensity which excludes ambiguity was "discovered" in the course of phylogenesis (Morris, 1957). The basis is variable intensity. In typical intensity there is constancy over a wide range and variability only with very low and very high frequencies. Constant intensity is independent of frequency: e.g. the telephone.

Bibliography: Morris, D.: "Typical intensity" and its relation to the problem of ritualization. Bevaviour, 1957, *11*, 1–12. *K.Fi.*

Tyramine. A neurohormone obtained from tyrosine by decarboxylization, which is counted among the biogenic amines (q.v.). It is also a substance with a sympathicomimetic effect; it is weaker though more long-lasting in effect than adrenalin, with a pronounced circulation effect, and especially increased blood pressure. Numerous similar substances are produced synthetically (phenylephrine-tyramine group) and are used as vasoconstrictors, bronchodilatators, mydriatic drugs (see *Mydriasis*), and therapeutically. Tyramine's sympathico-mimetic effect probably occurs indirectly through the release of noradrenalin(e) (nor-epinephrine).   *W.J.*

Tyrosine. An aromatic amino-acid, and an important protein component. A precursor in the formation of hormones, for instance in the catecholamines (q.v.; see also *Biogenic amines*). Tyrosine is introduced into the organism in food (protein); in the organism it is formed, e.g., from phenylalanine (q.v.).

Bibliography: Acheson, G. H. (Ed.): Second sympo-sium on catecholamines. Pharmacol. Rev., 1966, *18*, 1–804.

U

Ultrared. Also known as "infrared": electromagnetic radiation shorter in vibration frequency than the visible red portion of the spectrum. *W.P.*

Ultrasound; ultrasonics. Mechanical vibrations and waves above the frequency range that can be perceived by the human ear, on account of its mode of operation: from 2×10^4 to 10^9 Hz; beyond that is "hypersound" up to 10^{13} Hz. Some species (e.g. bats) hear in ultrasound, and locate objects in the environment by echolocation. Psychologically relevant experiments try to imitate the bat principle by technical means and use it in the service of the blind.

Bibliography: Griffin, D. R.: Listening in the dark. New Haven, 1958. **Kay, L.:** Ultrasonic mobility aids for the blind. In: **Clark, L. L.** (Ed.): Proceedings of the Rotterdam mobility research conference. Rotterdam, 1965, 61–71. *M.B.*

Ultraviolet. The electromagnetic radiation shorter than extreme violet and beyond the violet portion of the visible spectrum. *W.P.*

Unburdening type. This type unburdens the ego aspect of consciousness by a readiness to prepare and change objects; this is especially the case with the cyclothymic temperament. *W.K.*

Unconditioned inhibition. In Pavlov's behavioral theory: a collective term for inhibition phenomena which, in contrast to forms of conditioned inhibition, need not first be acquired by learning. Among the varieties of unconditioned inhibition are external inhibition or negative induction and protective inhibition. See *Inhibition; Conditioning, classical and operant; Pavlov.* *L.B.*

Unconscious. The *personal unconscious* is all those experiences and memories of situations of motive gratification which, from specific points in time in the development of the individual in question, were no longer available (or only with subsequent punishment), and were therefore repressed. It is all the object cathexes of an individual at a given point in his development; the sum of all opportunities for motive gratification that were once available but are so no longer. This repressed totality may be assessed directly by psychotherapy or psychoanalysis, and indirectly in terms of observable gaps or deficits in the reality concept of the individual concerned. According to Toman (1960) it may be defined in relation to the given age and motive differentiation rate of an individual as the extent by which that individual's knowledge is behind the optimal state (see *Energy, mental*).

The personal environment is clinically and socio-psychologically important. Experiences with individuals are (according to Freud, by the process of object cathexis; and, in general terms, by means of data storage and learning of meaning) precipitated as knowledge. Gaps in knowledge may relate to authority figures, individuals (of approximately the same age) of the other sex, of the same sex, children, and so on. Part aspects of individuals, such as their readiness to co-operate, conscientiousness or power, may be ignored.

By means of defense (q.v.) mechanisms, *subconscious* and *preconscious* experiences become unconscious (see *Preconscious*). The now unconscious motives may (according to Freud) become evident in behavior or in the conscious mind. In dreams, in fantasy (q.v.), and in mental illnesses, the individual's reduced control allows such unconscious motives to become manifest. Their indication in psychotherapy is supposed to help the patient reporting such dreams or fantasies to make these supposedly unconscious motives conscious, and to learn to some extent to gratify them in reality, and to some extent to find substitute gratifications for them if they are no longer gratifiable, or to do without them more successfully than hitherto.

According to Jung (q.v.) the *collective unconscious* is the totality of certain innate modes of response to typical objects and occasions, such as danger, death, woods, water, etc., but also to persons, such as the old man, the child, the woman, the man, the mother or the father. Certain discrepancies may arise between concrete experiences and archetypally pre-existent expectations; these may be attenuated by psychoanalysis of preferences and wishes arising from the collective unconscious. Analogous phenomena from comparative psychology would be instinctive behaviors (see *Instinct*) that can be evoked (without experience) by certain key stimulus schemata. In psychotherapy and psychoanalysis the term is sometimes used as a *deus ex machina*, and then prevents further analysis of the experiential components of supposedly archetypal responses.

The *familiar unconscious* is all those un-conscious wishes and tendencies at least in part taken over from parents and other members of the family (by identification or introjection). As a rule the familiar unconscious represents a part of the personal unconscious, and especially unconscious fragments of the superego (q.v.). See *Freud; Jung; Depth psychology; Dream.*

Bibliography: Toman, W.: Introduction to psychoanalytic theory of motivation. London & New York, 1960.   *W. Toman*

Unconsciousness. A condition in which the ability to perceive and to act consciously is in abeyance. The deepest state of unconsciousness is *coma.* Unconsciousness results from a threat to the whole organism (e.g. in fevers, heart attacks, cases of poisoning), or from a direct disturbance of brain functioning (*exogenous:* concussion, the paralysing effect of narcotics (q.v.), alcohol, etc.; or *endogenous:* epileptic fits).   *V.M.*

Underachievement. See *Overachievement.*

Understanding. 1. The ability to think, i.e. to apprehend being and relations non-pictorially. In this acceptation often synonymous with intellect (q.v.). Frequently conceived as the capability of purposeful, insightful behavior, though not necessarily connected with highly "conceptual" thought. **2.** Apprehension of a meaning. **3.** The awareness of a logical connection; the apprehension of a meaningful connection between sign and signified; the meaningful apprehension of a sign in semantics (q.v.). **4.** Knowledge of that which is not expressed. **5.** Automatic interpretation of an expression (q.v.). **6.** Thinking (q.v.).   *H.W.*

Undoing. An (inner) defense (q.v.) mechanism which allows appeasement of a guilt feeling about a forbidden motive gratification that has already occurred. It usually consists of the gratification of those introjected motives which in the past followed forbidden motive gratifications in the form of punishment by others. Examples: being particularly friendly to someone to whom one has already shown hatred; compulsive washing to compensate for supposedly unclean actions (even if only intended) or thoughts.   *W.T.*

Uroboros. According to Neumann (1956), the ur-archetype, represented by a serpent biting its own tail. The symbol of the primal situation, in which the consciousness and ego of the individual have still to develop. It includes contradictory principles—positive and negative, male and female—and represents primal chaos and the totality of the psyche.

Bibliography: Neumann, E.: Die grosse Mutter. Zürich, 1956.   *J.L.I.*

Urolagnia. A kind of sexual deviation in which urine, urination, or the sight of others urinating, are sources of erotic enjoyment. Drinking one's own urine is another behavior which usually comes under this label.   *G.D.W.*

Usnadze's volume illusion. This illusion discovered by Usnadze is the prototype of a series of demonstrations of *set* which is the basis of the Georgian (USSR) school of psychology. The illusion requires the repeated presentation to each hand of two spheres of unequal volume, the subject indicating each time which is the smaller. Finally, two equal spheres are presented, and it appears to the subject that the sphere in the hand that previously held the larger sphere is smaller than the other.

C.D.F.

Utopia. Thomas More's term for an imaginary world, and the title of his prose fiction *Utopia* (Latin version, Louvain 1516). Utopia aims at an ateration of society even though it can never be achieved; it strives to approximate to the ideal by (as far as possible) human means. Utopian socialism intends a better world than capitalist society without offering a concrete programme for its attainment. In general usage, a "utopia" is any system or project which seems incapable of realization; a "utopian" is an unrealistic dreamer.

Bibliography: Bloch, E.: The spirit of utopia. New York, 1972. More, T.: Utopia (first Eng. trans.). London, 1551.   *M.R.*

Utriculus. See *Statoliths*.

V

Vacation. A period of time free from work commitments and extending beyond the daily or weekly rest period; for the most part the minimum vacation is now legally determined. With the present increasing trend to solution of technico-economic problems there is a tendency toward longer vacations. The problem of the future in this regard will be the provision of appropriate activities for an "achieving society" during enforced leisure time. See *Aging; Industrial psychology.*

Bibliography: Kleemeier, R. W. (Ed.): Ageing and leisure. New York, 1957. McLellan, D.: Marx's Grundrisse. London, 1971. Mott, P. E.: Shift work: the social, psychological and physical consequences. Ann Arbor, Mich., 1965. Murrell, K. F. H.: Ergonomics. London, 1965. Sergean, R.: Managing shiftwork. London 1971. *G.R.W.M.*

Vacuum neurosis. A term sometimes used for what V. E. Frankl (Vienna) has called the "existential vacuum", which causes many, and especially young, people in most contemporary cultures to suffer from a feeling of essential meaninglessness: "Today we are no longer, as at the time of Freud, living in an age of sexual frustration, but in one of existential frustration" (Frankl, 1970).

Bibliography: Frankl, V. E.: Der Mensch auf der Suche nach Sinn. Universitas, 1970, *25*, 369–76. *G.H.*

Vacuum response. In behaviorism, a response which occurs in the absence of the stimulus which usually evokes it. *G.D.W.*

Vagina, artificial. An artificial vagina is supplied mechanically or surgically in cases of congenital absence of a natural vagina or if a "sex change" is thought possible and desirable. It is requisite that an artificial organ should allow almost the same physiological reactions to sexual stimulation as a natural vagina. See *Hermaphroditism.*

Bibliography: Masters, W. H. & Johnson, V. E.: The artificial vagina. Western J. Surg., 1961, *69*, 192–212. Id.: Human sexual response, Boston, 1966. *V.S.*

Vaginism (syn. *Vaginismus*). A contraction or spasm (adductor spasm) of the pelvic and vaginal orifice musculature which either prevents the introduction of the penis into the vagina (and therefore coitus), or hinders withdrawal of the penis during coitus. In very rare cases, the latter condition can be arrested only by narcosis of the woman.

Bibliography: Ellison, C.: Psychosomatic factors in the unconsummated marriage. J. Psychosom. Res., 1968, *12*, 61. Friedman, L. J.: Virgin wives: a study of unconsummated marriages. London, 1962. *H.M.*

Vagotonia. According to Eppinger & Hess (1910), a shift (brought about by unilateral increased tonus of the parasympathetic system) of equilibrium in the autonomic nervous system to the parasympathetic side. It tends to cause increased parasympathetic excitability, so that normally subthreshold, parasympathetically exciting stimuli evoke abnormally intensified responses (low blood pressure, inclination to cold hands and feet, increased assimilation, over-acidification of the stomach), which are also evident psychically (according to Birkmeyer & Winkler, 1951).

Bibliography: **Eppinger, H. & Hess, L.**: Die Vagotonie. Berlin, 1910. **Birkmeyer, W. & Winkler, W.**: Klinik und Therapie der vegetativen Funktionsstörungen. Berlin, 1951.   *F.-C.S.*

Vagus. The tenth cranial nerve; the motor and secretory fibers arise in the *medulla oblongata* and the sensory fibers in two ganglia on the nerve-trunk. Part of the parasympathetic nervous system.   *E.D.*

Valence. Lewin's term for the psychological attraction, or drawing-power, of a thing. Valence may be positive or negative. See *Lewin, Kurt; Tension system; Topological and vector psychology.*

Validity. A vitally important concept in the theory of psychological testing. A test is valid when it actually measures the characteristic it is supposed to. Accordingly the validity of a test can vary gradually. See *Test theory; Objective tests; Traits; Type.*   *W.H.B.*

Variability. See Dispersion.

Variable. In the mathematical acceptation, an alterable value, and frequently used as a short form of "random variable". A variable represents a basis for the notation of functions (in the function $x = f(y)$, x represents the independent and y the dependent variable). In general, "variable" is a term for a factor which has some effect or exerts an influence during the observation or measurement of some phenomenon.   *D.W.E.*

Variables, continuous. As opposed to discrete variables, these may assume any value within a certain interval of real even numbers. In practice the distinction between continuous and discrete variables is more a question of degree than of principle, since continuous variables, too, can be measured only in stages.
                                              A.R.

Variance. A measure of variability or dispersion; the square of the standard deviation (s^2) used to determine the degree of difference from one another of certain values (scores) in a set.   *D.W.E.*

Variance, analysis of, may be characterized as a collection of procedures by which the variation of a measure relative to its mean is resolved as the sum of two or more distinct sums of squares each corresponding to a source, real or suspect, of variation.

It may also be regarded as a family of linear regression models in which a single dependent variable is expressed as a linear combination of a number of independent variables. The independent variables represent either potential sources of variation (factors) or products of such factors (interactions).

These views lead to very piecemeal treatments of the subject in which the reader is confronted with a vast array of cookbook techniques each with its own computational formulae and set of rules of thumb for the determination of appropriate error terms.

Key papers by Eisenhart (1947), Mann (1949), and Bock (1963) as well as the book by Scheffé (1958) have led to a more unified treatment of the subject. Bock outlines in detail a general model which leads directly to powerful, flexible, yet highly efficient computer codes for the analysis of variance. Such programs perform univariate and multivariate linear estimation and tests of hypotheses for any crossed and/or nested design, with or without concomitant variables or covariates, and with equal, proportional, disproportionate, and even zero subclass frequencies. The multivariate tests for repeated measurements designs make much less unrealistic assumptions on the data than do the now standard univariate trend analyses in common use.

It should be emphasized, however, that the availability of such powerful programs is not an unmixed blessing. That very flexibility which allows the skilled and experienced worker to fit a carefully considered model to his data and to test its appropriateness also allows the naïve, inexperienced worker to fit a variety of ill-conceived and inappropriate models and to grasp at that one which just happens to yield statistical significance.

Yates (1964) has outlined the early development by R. A. Fisher of the analysis of variance in the context of agricultural field trials, and has emphasized the extent to which it developed concurrently with the study of the design of experiments. The reader is referred to the extensive bibliography in Scheffé (1958) for further reading.

Bibliography: Bock, R. D.: Programming univariate and multivariate analysis of variance. Technometrics, 1963, *5*. Eisenhart, C.: The assumptions underlying the analysis of variance. Biometrics, 1947, *3*. Mann, H. B.: Analysis and design of experiments. New York, 1949. Scheffé, H.: The analysis of variance. New York, 1958. Yates, F.: Sir Ronald Fisher and the design of experiments. Biometrics, 1964, *20*.   *O. White*

Variation. 1. A term for the possibilities of combining *n* different elements as *k* elements, including the possibility of repetitions of the elements. **2.** Any difference or change. *G.Mi.*

Variation coefficient (syn. *Variability coefficient*). A measure of relative variability given by the formula

$$V = \frac{100 \times S}{\bar{x}}.$$

The variation coefficient allows of comparison of dispersions of groups of differing sample size and scale units.   *D.W.E.*

Varimax method. An orthogonal analytic rotation method developed by H. F. Kaiser (see *Factor analysis*).

Bibliography: Kaiser, H. F.: The varimax criterion for analytic rotation in factor analysis. Psychometrika, 1958, *23*, 187–200.   *D.W.E.*

Vasoconstriction; vasodilatation. Constriction and expansion of the diameter of blood vessels.   *H.W.*

Vasolability. A weakness of the vascular muscles evident, e.g., in inadequate vascular contraction when standing up after lying down.   *E.D.*

Vasopressin (*Pitressin*). A posterior pituitary hormone; also known as *antidiuretic hormone*, or ADH, because it inhibits diuresis. Vasopressin tends to raise blood pressure (peripheral vasoconstriction) and is excreted more profusely under physical and psychic stress. See *Stress*.

Bibliography: Heller, H. (Ed.): The neurohypophysis. London, 1957.   *W.J.*

Vater's corpuscle (syn. *Pacinian corpuscle*). One of the oval, lamellated corpuscles (discovered by A. Vater in 1741, and rediscovered by F. Pacini in 1842) in the skin of the hands and feet, acting as terminal capsules for sensory nerve fibers and sense organs for depth sensibility and pressure. See *Sense organs*.   *E.D.*

Vector. A symbol representing a force or an abient or adient suasion toward an incentive. See *Topological psychology; Lewin*.   *D.W.E.*

Vegetative dystonia (syn. *Vegetative dystony*). A term introduced by B. Wichmann in 1934, and largely synonymous with "neurasthenia", "vegetative lability", "vegetative stigmatatization". It is an inexact collective term for disturbances of vegetative functions of the most varied etiology, and disorders resulting from faulty regulation or lability of an antagonistic "tonic equilibrium" in the autonomic nervous system formed by the *nervus vagus* and *nervus sympathicus*. There are many contributory factors in the etiology of the condition: it is affected by constitution and to a considerable extent psychogenically conditioned, but may also arise from non-physiological sources: e.g. work and environmental conditions. Vegetative dystonia is always the symptom of an underlying sickness.   *F.-C.S.*

Vegetative lability. A disorder of the autonomic nervous system (q.v.). See *Psychosomatics; Neurosis; Traits; Type*.

Ventricle. Any cavity within a body organ, but more especially one of the chambers of the heart.

Verbal behavior, establishment and modification of. This article is concerned with the establishment and expansion of verbal behavior, and the modification of inadequate verbal behavior in the impaired. Verbal behavior submits to Skinner's three-term contingency paradigm. A behavioral event, verbal or other, is seen in terms of the *stimulus setting* in which a *performance* occurs, and the following *consequential changes in the environment* of the performing organism. Unlike behaviors with which an organism operates *directly* on his physical environment (moving objects), verbal behavior effects changes through the agency of *other* organisms with a corresponding verbal repertoire. Since the

probability of emission of any performance in a specific stimulus setting is a function of the consequences, study of these consequences permits prediction and control of the probability of recurrence of a performance in a given stimulus setting. The primary data are the shifts in *probability* and *topography* of the behavior as functions of the relationships between *stimulus settings, performance* and *consequences*. Crucial is the discrimination of two discrete repertoires; a *receptive verbal repertoire* of behaviors of *any* class occurring under the stimulus control of some organism's *verbal* behavior, and a *productive repertoire* of verbal behaviors that control the behavior of any organism displaying a corresponding receptive repertoire. This discrimination allows issues of receptive repertoires to be viewed as problems of bringing behavior under specific *verbal stimulus control* ("understanding"), and issues of productive repertoires ("speaking") as problems of *shaping* verbal behavior having operant function in a verbal community. Primary principles include: analysis of response topographies in terms of *function* rather than form; rigorous management of stimulus settings and consequences relative to a performance; fine analysis of terminal behavior in terms of *requisite antecedent behaviors;* building complex behaviors through the successive establishment of antecedent behaviors.

Bibliography: Sapon, S. M.: Operant studies in the expansion and refinement of verbal behavior. Reports from the Verbal Behavior Lab., Univ. of Rochester, Rochester, N.Y., 1969. **Skinner, B. F.:** Verbal Behavior. New York, 1957.   *S. M. Sapon*

Verbal suggestion. Suggestion (q.v.) by means of spoken words. The patient's responsiveness to verbal suggestion is individually diverse. See *Hypnosis*.   *H.N.G.*

Verstehende Psychologie (Ger.). The "psychology of understanding" is an inclusive term for those human-scientific modes of interpretation which try to offer insight into the mental life of a human individual or the social configuration of a group (q.v.). The procedure of "understanding" is *deductive* and *descriptive*, and aims at the apprehension and knowledge of personality structures, of dispositions to certain abilities and levels of performance, and of social formations and "forms of life". The approach arose out of philosophical phenomenology and epistemology, yet is concerned primarily with practical human knowledge and life experience. Intuitive apprehension of essences and "mimpathy" are necessarily, in every act of understanding, under the control of critical understanding itself. The method emphasizes the importance of an attentive, wholly observant procedure in which the essence of a thing is fixated by means of analysis, formally ordered by synthesis, inserted in a meaningful context, and precisely described by means of appropriate concepts or symbols and unambiguous linguistic formulations. See *Geisteswissenschaftliche Psychologie*.

The principles and procedures of *verstehende Psychologie* play a dominant role in structural psychology (Dilthey, *et al.*; see *Ganzheit*), in characterology (Lersch), in typology (Spranger, Jung, q.v., Kretschmer, q.v.; see *Type*), and in strata theory (q.v.). It also has important consequences for the psychology of expression (Klages, *et al.*) and of achievement (Mierke). "Understanding" under specific conditions is characteristic of the empirical and analytic methods of experimental (Wundt), gestalt (Krueger) and social psychology (Lewin, Gehlen). Depth psychology (q.v.) attempts to describe and *understand* drive-conditioned behavior, elementary "urges" and needs, and reaction and compensation tendencies.

The cybernetic theory of information (see *Information theory*) adds natural-scientific explanations to human-scientific analyses. It orders experiences obtained in informational processes into a systematic pattern, and tries to examine their causal or final connections. Similarly, differential psychology (q.v.) and developmental psychology (C. Bühler) unite empathic understanding and "mimpathy" with inductive causistic or statistical methods. The same is true of Russian ability and achievement research (N. S. Leites, S. A. Samarin, L. J. Vygotsky).

Behavioral research, behaviorism (q.v.; see *Watson, Thorndike*), and operationism (see *Tolman*) basically reject the methods of *verstehende Psychologie*, since subjective moods and feelings, intuitions and self-observations offer diverse sources of error.

Nevertheless, the psychology of understanding still has an important position among diagnostic methods (see *Psychodiagnostics*), and would seem to be essential in areas where certain practical problems of human management arise (e.g. in learning and occupational psychology, in educational and forensic psychology, and so on. In practical psychology, "understanding" is invoked in terms of the evidence offered by studies of courses of human life (case histories), and analyses of abilities, behavior and expression.

Bibliography: **Dilthey, W.:** Ideen über eine beschreibende und zergliedernde Psychologie. Leipzig, 1894. **Hinde, R.** (Ed.): Non-verbal communication. Cambridge, 1972. **Mierke, K.:** Psychologische Diagnostik. **In: Ach, N.** (Ed.): Lehrbuch der Psychologie. Bamberg, 1944. *K. Mierke*

Vertical center line illusion. One of the geometric illusions. Although objectively equal, the vertical line looks longer than the horizontal line, especially if it starts from the center of the horizontal line. *C.D.F.*

Vertigo. 1. Subjective sensation after rapid and frequent rotation of the body round its own axis. After the end of the rotation one receives the impression that one is moving in the opposite direction or that the environment is turning in the same direction as the previous turning movement. Pronounced vertigo can indicate disturbances of balance (q.v.). Suitability as a pilot, suggestibility (q.v.), etc. can be investigated with the aid of the Barany (rotating chair) procedure.

2. A state characterized by a feeling of disturbed balance, an impression of a world oscillating and revolving, accompanied by an inclination to fall, a feeling of being ill, sweating, of nausea and other vegetative disturbances. In labyrinthine vertigo the feeling that one is turning round and round, that one is about to fall, and some characteristic symptoms such as nystagmus (q.v.) (rapid sideways movements of the eyes), and bending the head and body, are predominant. They occur as a result of the false information received from the organ of balance (q.v.) in the osseous labyrinth of the petrosal bone. Similar symptoms are caused by disorders such as inflammation and tumors in the nervous processing apparatus, e.g. in the cerebellum (q.v.) or brain stem. Attacks of vertigo with a circulatory origin should be regarded more as a decrease in functioning of cerebral activity, while in symptoms of brain pressure, feelings of vertigo are replaced by other autonomic disorders. As there may be many possible causes, treatment is correspondingly difficult.

M.B. & E.D.

Vestibule. A cavity forming part of the inner ear; the "vestibule" of the labyrinth, consisting of the saccule and utricle, two sacs whose hair cells convey sensations.   *E.D.*

Vibration, sense of. See *Sense organs*.

Vicarious instigation. A term from learning theory for a response to the evocation of

emotional responses. A human or animal subject observes the evocation of an unconditioned emotional response (EUR) in an "object" testee by an unconditioned stimulus (UCS). The perception of the UCS and the consequent UER leads to an emotional response (ER) in the observer. The concept of vicarious instigation enables socio-psychologically interesting phenomena, e.g. empathy, or envy, to be assessed more proficiently.

Bibliography: Berger, S. M.: Conditioning through vicarious suggestion. Psychol. Rev., 1962, *69*.

F.Ma.

Vicarious trial and error (abb. *VTE*). Symbolic trial-and-error behavior. It occurs during discrimination and maze learning when subjects have to choose between several possible behaviors (e.g. between right and left-hand turns in the *T* maze). In such situations the subject delays, looks to right and left, before selecting an alternative (Muenzinger, 1938). These "symbolic" responses are interpreted as orientation and trial movements. Nevertheless there would seem to be no unambiguous support for Muenzinger's & Tolman's assumption that VTE behavior makes learning easier (Goss & Wischner, 1956).

Bibliography: Goss, A. E. & Wischner, G. J.: Vicarious trial and error and related behavior. Psychol. Bull., 1956, *53*, 35–54. Muenzinger, K. F.: Vicarious trial and error at a point of choice: 1. a general survey of its relation to learning efficiency. J. genet. Psychol., 1938, *53*, 75–86.   *M.H.*

Victimology is concerned with the victims of criminal acts from two main viewpoints: (*a*) victims of sex crimes, traffic accidents, suicide, deception and theft. The main question is what group of individuals with what traits is potentially in danger of becoming the victims of this or that criminal tendency? (*b*) The objectification of social, psychological, psychopathological factors of groups of individuals who have already become victims. The main problems here are the pre-disposing factors (post-hoc data) and personality traits, the attitude of the victim and his behavior toward criminals, and injury to the victim by the crime (immediate and delayed psychological damage).

Bibliography: Huffman, A. V.: Violent behavior—possibilities of prediction and control. Police, 1964, 8, 13–6. Maisch. H.: Inzest. Hamburg, 1968. Schönfelder, T.: Die Rolle des Mädchens bei Sexualdelikten. Beiträge z. Sexualforschung, 1968, No. 42.

H.M.

Vienna School. 1. *Philosophy:* the neopositivism (q.v.) and operationalism (q.v.) founded by K. P. Moritz and M. Schlick, which maintained that philosophy had no specific content, but, by means of mathematical logic, helped to clarify conceptual contradictions in the empirical and experimental sciences, and to improve their propositional systems. Some of Schlick's pupils are R. Carnap, K. Popper, P. Frank, H. Reichenbach, V. Kraft.

2. *Psychology:* that psychodynamic orientation of psychology dependent on the theories of Freud (q.v.), or that deriving from A. Adler (q.v.). See *Depth psychology; Psychoanalysis.* **W.T.**

Vieth-Müller circle. When an object is viewed with both eyes a certain angle of convergence between the eyes is required for a single image of the object to be seen. Thus for any given angle of convergence there will be a surface in which objects have a single image, while objects nearer than or beyond this surface have a double image. This surface is known as the Vieth-Müller circle or horopter. Theoretically it should be a sphere which passes through the point of fixation and the centers of revolution of the two eyes. In practice, however, the situation is found to be more complicated. **C.D.F.**

Vigilance (Lat. *vigilantia*). Literally: "wakefulness"; but "vigilance" is more precisely defined, and includes the maintenance of a specific activity for a fairly long period, usually accompanied by voluntary attention (q.v.).

1. *Various definitions and acceptations.* Behaviorally, vigilance is most simply defined as performance in observational and inspection tasks. Since attention processes undoubtedly play a considerable part in vigilance, the term may also be applied to the central process which determines achievement in various vigilance tasks, and which may be characterized as long-term or extended *attention* (Haider, 1962). Finally, a specific state of the organism may be described as vigilance in either a physiological or a psychological sense. Physiologically, Head (1926) defines vigilance as a state of the CNS which makes possible a speedy and purposive reaction. Psychologically, Mackworth (1957) defines vigilance as readiness to detect and respond to specific, restricted environmental changes which occur at randomly distributed intervals. This readiness may be characterized by performance criteria, such as percentages of non-observed signals, reaction latencies for observed signals, and inappropriate reactions to non-signals (neutral stimuli).

2. *Historical survey.* Systematic investigations of this special kind of signal detection over fairly extended periods of time were first carried out during World War II in connection with problems of radar observation. Vigilance research has also won practical significance in automated industrial processes and in traffic and space travel. Neurophysiological investigations into cerebral vigilance were carried out mainly in the course of developing electroencephalographic techniques.

3. *Present state of research.* In vigilance tasks, the probability of signal detection decreases over the course of time and the length of reaction latencies increases. The decrease in performance can begin after even a few minutes, and usually reaches a plateau after about 30 to 60 minutes, when stabilization occurs. Rest pauses can keep observational

performance at a higher level. Total performance and course of performance depend on many variables, which can both be environmentally determined and derive from the organism itself.

(a) *Environmental variables and vigilance.* Most important here are the characteristics of the task situations. Complex task situations with several indicational elements usually lead to a reduced total performance, but to less emphatic drops in performance than simple vigilance tasks. Increased intensity and length of signals bring about improvements in vigilance, but do not always prevent the drop in performance. Increased signal frequency and the introduction of "random" stimuli increase the probability of detection. If the signals occur regularly (removal of temporal uncertainty) and only in a specific location (removal of spatial uncertainty), the probability of detection is high. The relation of neutral stimuli ("non-signals") to signals is also significant.

General environmental influences are also important. Hence noise and temperature have differential effects on vigilance with an optimum in the comfort range. Isolation tends to bring about a decrease in performance, whereas, e.g., the mere presence of the experimenter can prevent drops in vigilance.

(b) *Organismic variables and vigilance.* Individual differences are very great. Nevertheless, despite several investigations, no reliable methods of prediction were elicited. Age and experience show little influence. Introductory signal frequency and information about one's own performance play an important part. Sleep deprivation leads to an intensified reduction of performance. The effects of drugs have been demonstrated. Evoked potentials obtainable from EEG by computer analysis may be selectively analyzed as correlates for detected and non-detected signals, but also for neutral stimuli. In vigilance situations, pulse rates tend to drop, whereas activities requiring movement (spontaneous movements) tend to increase. See *Activation; Arousal.*

4. *Theoretical considerations.* (a) *Attention and vigilance.* The vigilance situation may be considered as an extended controlled attention situation without warning of the occurrence of signals. This situation has to be distinguished from, e.g., attention tasks with warning of the occurrence of the signals and free attention situations. Errors in detection may perhaps be ascribed in all situations to similar mechanisms, in terms of distractions, blocks, fluctuations, and so on, using, e.g., the filter theory model (Broadbent, 1958).

(b) *Expectation, learning and vigilance.* Mainly in view of the temporal distribution of signals, it can be shown that observers extrapolate to the future on the basis of their individual experiences. This may be conceived as the "construction of expectation structures."

Traditional conditioning experiments were drawn on for inhibition (q.v.) (thought to play a similar role in extinction processes) as an explanation (Mackworth, 1950), and for the concept of "reactive inhibition" (Frankman & Adams, 1962). The efficacy of instrumental learning in influencing behavior was demonstrated for observational reactions (Holland, 1958).

(c) *Activation and vigilance.* Activation processes play a role in vigilance (as in many other aspects of performance) in the sense that optimal arousal (q.v.) is associated with good performance, and hyper-arousal and non-arousal with performance deficits. The simple assumption that vigilance is dependent on the number and variation of neutral stimuli has not been confirmed. More complex approaches are more appropriate to the empirical findings. Among such theories is the postulate that arousal variables can follow divergent courses during vigilance experiments (Groll, 1966). A hierarchical theory of arousal (Haider, 1969) offers neuropsychological approaches to attention, expectation and vigilance processes, and a common basis for physiological and psychological vigilance research. See *Attention; Arousal.*

Bibliography: Broadbent, D. E.: Perception and communication. London, 1958. **Buckner, D. N. & McGrath, J. J.:** Vigilance: A symposium. New York & London, 1963. **Frankman, J. P. & Adams, J. A.:** Theories of vigilance. Psychol. Bull. 1962, *59*, 257–72. **Groll, E.:** Zentralnervöse und periphere Aktivierungsvariable bei Vigilanzleistungen. Z. exp. angew. Psychol., 1966, *13*, 248–64. **Haider, M.:** Ermüdung, Beanspruchung und Leistung. Vienna, 1962. **Id:** Elektrophysiologische Indikatoren der Aktivierung. In: **Schönpflug, W.** (Ed.): Methoden der Aktivierungsforschung. Berne, 1969. **Haider, M., Spong, P. & Lindsley, D. B.:** Attention, vigilance and cortical evoked potentials in humans. Science, 1964, *145*, 180–82. **Head, H.:** Aphasia. Cambridge, 1926. **Holland, J. G.:** Human vigilance. Science, 1958, *128*, 61–3. **Jerison, H. J. & Pickett, R. M.:** Vigilance: A review and re-evaluation. Human Factors, 1963, *5*, 211–38. **Mackworth, N. H.:** Researches on the measurement of human performance. M. R. C. Spez. Rep. Ser. N. 268 (H. M. S. O.) London, 1950. **ders.:** Some factors affecting vigilance. The advancement of Science, 1957, *53*, 389–93. **Studies of human vigilance.** Human Factors Res. Santa Barbara, 1968. **Wyatt, S. & Langdon, J. N.:** Inspection processes in industry. Rep. Ind. Health Res. Vol. 63. London, 1932.

M. Haider

Vincent curves. Graphic representations of average learning processes, dependent on relativized individual learning scores. In learning experiments discontinued according to a specific criterion (e.g. after three faultless trials), in general individuals require a varying number of trials to reach the criterion. If the learning curves of individual testees are to be compared or summarized in a single learning curve, it was thought useful to establish a universal standard number of trials. An equal part of the total time or number of trials needed by an individual is treated as equivalent to the same part of another individual's total. The method is hardly ever used in modern research projects.

Bibliography: Hilgard, E. R.: A summary and evaluation of alternative procedures for the construction of Vincent curves. Psychol. Bull., 1938, *35*, 282–97.

Hunter, W. S. & Yarbrough, J. N.: The interference of auditory habits in the white rat. J. anim, Beh., 1917, *7*, 49–65. **Vincent, S. B.:** The function of the vibrissae in the behaviour of the white rat. Beh. Monogr., 1912, *1*, No. 5.

M.H.

Vineland Social Maturity Scale. A scale designed to assess social maturity in terms of the ability to come to terms with one's social needs and assume responsibility. Norms are available up to age twenty-five. One scale may also be used with younger or retarded people. A "social age" (SA) and a "social quotient" may be answered from the 117 items. *F.G.*

Virginity. The condition of never having had experienced sexual intercourse, particularly (though not necessarily) with reference to the female. *G.D.W.*

Virile. Manly. Possessed of *virility*, masculine characteristics generally, and especially strength, vigor, procreative power, and (most specifically) the capacity to repeat sexual intercourse at short intervals. *G.D.W.*

Virilism. The development by a woman of masculine secondary sex characteristics.

G.D.W.

Visceral nervous system. See *Autonomic nervous system.*

Viscerotonia. A temperament associated with the endomorphic type. Tolerant, peaceful, rather slow. See *Traits; Type.*

Bibliography: Sheldon, W. H.: The varieties of temperament. New York, 1942. *W.K.*

Viscous type. One of the three types of constitution in Kretschmer's typology. The viscous type has an athletic body-build. Psychically, he is characterized by vacillation between an explosive and a phlegmatic temperament. See *Kretschmer; Traits; Type*.

M.H.

Vision, angle of. Two points of an object appear in an optical system at a certain angle (angle of vision), the size of which depends on the ratio of the size of the object to its distance. Hence the angle of vision increases with the distance of the two points from one another and diminishes with the increasing distance of the object. R.R.

Vision test. Determination of visual acuity. In vision tests, use is made of charts with letters (Hess, Snellen charts, q.v., Landolt circles, q.v.), animal pictures or pictures with easily recognizable subjects of different sizes. A vision test is carried out at a standard distance (3–5 meters), and in standard illumination (according to H. Schober, 1000 lux). Visual acuity is stated in a common fraction. The denominator represents the distance (in meters), at which the test ought to be seen normally; the numerator gives the distance at which the test is actually seen by the person being examined. R.R.

Visual center. The end of the visual pathway (q.v.) in the areas of the *fissura calcarina*. The *corpus geniculatum laterale* (thalamus) is also known as the primary visual center. It is in these centers that the items of information received from visual perception (q.v.) are processed. R.R.

Visual focusing. The ability to bring perceptual objects into focus which develops gradually in the new-born child. There are normally four stages in this process of development: (*a*) diffuse eye movements; (*b*)

attraction by light stimuli of the line of sight; (*c*) reflex movement; (*d*) voluntary focusing.

K.E.P.

Visual illusions, unlike illusions of *memory* (q.v.), have nothing to do with the relation of an experiential content evoked by trace reactivation to a chronologically past event or phenomenon, or—like illusions of memory occurring during logical thinking—with the relation of an ongoing conceptual act to the appropriate logical content, but are concerned with the relation of (*a*) an actual perception to (*b*) a particular part-area of its actual causative complex. The following applies to both aspects of this relationship:

(*a*) The perception has two characteristics: it has a general phenomenal similarity to imagery, but is distinguished from images and ideas conditionally and genetically, in that (i) it is evoked by a sensory stimulus occurring simultaneously, and (ii) phenomenologically, in that it is oriented to something present at the same time and in the immediate spatial environment. As far as the spatial extension of the sensory stimulation occurring in visual illusions is concerned, a fundamental role is always played by the whole stimulus field, which is also in certain cases *factually* relevant: often, however, apprehension of a specific sector is enough. The analogy in the case of (ii) is experiential: as a rule the intention concerns a more or less extensive, figuratively effective part of the phenomenal field. The distinction between two modes of experience remains significant: an active-apprehensive mode and a passive-sensitive mode: in most cases of visual illusion the perception is of the first variety.

(*b*) If, in the functional analysis of a specific visual illusion, "correctness" is in question, only one area of the complex of conditions is taken into consideration. This is that providing the norm for a "correct" perception of the type in question, but absent in the case of an illusion. When such a norm and possible deviations of visual illusions from it exist, it is assumed that both aspects of functional content (the phenomenon and the part-area of conditions) are comparable and —under certain conditions—genuinely commensurable. In optical illusions, retinal data make a comparison with the phenomenon possible: for psychological purposes, however, it is usually more appropriate when seeking the norm to follow the causal chain right back to the stimulus *source* (enriched by the characteristics of the direction and distance of observation).

One may distinguish three main areas of visual illusion:

(*a*) Phenomena in the case of which there is objectively "absolutely nothing" to be seen at the intended position in the spatial environment. Such phenomena depend on central processes and include hallucinations. More frequent are the everyday experiences of (modal and amodal) completion: gaps are filled by the illusion, etc. In autokinesis (see *Autokinetic phenomenon*), the new product is formed not by figurative components but by movements. The same is true of the gamma phenomenon (see *Gamma movement*)—which has, of course, a different origin.

(*b*) Other effects may be classed as "exchange". In beta movement (q.v.) the aspect of movement instead of that of succession is actualized. In induced movement, of the two participating elements (one may be the observer's body-ego), the false one becomes the bearer of movement. Even (illusory) phenomenal causality, which is sometimes taken at first as absolute novelty, is an example of exchange, or confusion.

(*c*) In the third class, illusions of alteration, the illusion accords basically with the object, but not in specific details, which act as variables. Examples are contrast (q.v.) effects, or the geometrical-optical illusions. In such cases the phenomenon is "altered" in relation to the object.

Visual illusions should be considered not only as "erroneous" but as meaningful and purposeful; for example: the great significance of completion phenomena for the construction of the phenomenal world.

The theory of visual illusions has specific epistemological presuppositions. The dualistic approach that sets a phenomenon over against its presentation, depends on a critical form of realism. A purely phenomenalistic viewpoint does not do justice to visual illusions. This is true also when the illusions concern the observer's body, e.g. his orientation in space, the location of pressure or pain, etc. In such cases, one's own body belongs both to the phenomenal and to the presentational area. See *Geometrical-optical illusions; Perception; Visual perception*.

Bibliography: Aarons, L.: Visual apparent movement research: Review 1935–55; Bibliography 1955–63; Perc. Mot. Skills, 1964, *18*, 239–74. **Metzger, W.:** Gesetze des Sehens. Frankfurt a.M., ²1953. **Michotte, A., Thinès, G. & Crabbé, G.:** Die amodalen Ergänzungen von Wahrnehmungsstrukturen. In: Metzger, W. (Ed.): Handbuch der Psychologie, Vol. 1/1. Göttingen, 1966, 978–1002. **Rausch, E.:** Probleme der Metrik. In: **Metzger, W.** (Ed.): Handbuch der Psychol, Vol. 1/1. Göttingen, 1966, 776–865. **Royce, J. R.,** *et al.*: The autokinetic phenomenon: A critical review. Psychol. Bull., 1966, *65*, 243–60.   *E. Rausch*

Visual nerve damage. Complete or partial paralysis of the mimic muscles controlled by the *nervus facialis*. Generally one half of the face is affected; it is very rare for both sides to be involved. A distinction is made between central (supra-nuclear) and peripheral (nuclear and infra-nuclear) visual nerve damage, or (by etiology) between traumatic, toxic, rheumatic and inborn visual nerve damage.   *F.C.S.*

Visual perception. Perception through the sense of vision is one of the oldest research areas in the history of psychology. Both the phenomenological and psychophysical methods are used. Gestalt psychology had a great influence on the development of this area.

1. *Simplest visual perception.* The perception obtained through a uniform retinal stimulation may be regarded as the simplest form of visual perception. The sight of a cloudless sky covering the whole visual field, and visual experience in the midst of thick fog or in a completely dark room, are examples. We see neither a form nor a rigid surface, but a soft, filmy field of uniform color which is not localized at a definite distance.

2. *Emergence of a figure.* A heterogeneous area in the visual field produces the perception of a figure. A perceived figure in general differs from its background in that: the figure has form and the character of an object or thing, whereas the ground is formless and appears as a substance; the figure is localized at a definite distance and its surface looks hard, but the ground is soft and not definitely localized; the figure seems usually to stand out in front of the ground, which appears to extend continuously behind it; the contours are perceived as belonging to the figure, not to the ground.

3. *Interactions among figures.* When more than one figure appears in a visual field they interact in various ways. For example, if several figures or objects are presented simultaneously, they are perceived neither singly nor as a chaotic total mass, but in groups. The following factors are found important for such grouping: (*a*) objects relatively close together (proximity); (*b*) objects of the same color or shape (similarity); (*c*) objects constituting a closed area (closure); (*d*) objects constituting continuous sequence (good continuity); or (*e*) objects moving in the same direction (common fate) are readily seen as a group. In some circumstances, the shape or size of a perceived figure which is presented with other figures appears different to that of the same figure presented singly. Geometrical illusions may be regarded as such an interaction among figures or figural elements; and

figural aftereffects as a kind of interaction which occurs if two figures are presented successively. See *Afterimages; Aftersensation.*

4. *Perceptual constancies.* A figure or visual object generally has shape, size, color and brightness as its perceptual properties, and appears to be positioned with a certain slant, at a certain distance, and under the illumination of a certain color and brightness. When the slant, distance and illumination vary physically, the shape and size of the retinal image and the quality and intensity of light in it vary correspondingly, but the perceived shape, size, color and brightness usually do not vary so much. There are consistent tendencies which keep these perceptual properties constant. These tendencies are called shape, size, color and brightness constancies, respectively. They all make the perceptual world stable, in spite of the continuous change of the positions of many objects relative to the observer, and of the illumination affecting them. The cues for depth perception are thought to be important factors for constancies of shape and size, interrelations in the distribution of light in the visual field, and constancies of color and brightness.

5. *Perception of movement.* A figure or object may be seen as it moves. The displacement of a retinal image is neither a necessary nor a sufficient condition for the perception of movement. If we fixate a moving object, its retinal image will be stationary, but its motion will be perceived. On the other hand, if we move our eyes, the retinal images of stationary objects will move, but we will not perceive them as in motion. Rather, the displacement of an object relative to greater objects (frame of reference) is important for the perception of movement. However, the perception of movement occurs even without any relative displacement (apparent movement, autokinetic phenomenon, aftermage of movement).

Bibliography: Boring, E. G.: Sensation and perception in the hstoiry of experimental psychology. New York,

1942. **Gibson, J. J.**: Perception of the visual world. New York, 1950. **Graham, C. H.**: Vision and visual perception. New York, 1965. **Koffka, K.**: Principles of gestalt psychology. London & New York, 1935. **Metzger, W.**: Gesetze des Sehens. Frankfurt am Main, 2, 1953. **Vernon, M. D.**: The psychology of perception. Harmondsworth & Baltimore, 1962.   *T. Oyama*

Visual registration. Procedures for registering ocular movements and hence the path of vision have been developed by restricting experimental conditions until they have come close to *biotic* procedures (see *Biotic experiment*). Visual registration was first used in ophthalmology and reading psychology (B. Erdmann & R. Dodge), and was later taken over by other disciplines with more refined methods and increasingly less harm to the testee; such disciplines are industrial psychology (q.v.) (e.g. ocular movements of the pilot during blind-flying to establish the optimal arrangement of the instruments, forensic psychology (q.v.), and consumer psychology (e.g. advertising appeal, ocular response to packaging, etc.).   *B.S.*

Visual type. An imaginative type (q.v.) in whom the visual aspect is dominant.   *W.K.*

Vitalism. The assumption of a special force (*vis vitalis*) at the basis of the phenomenon of life, and inexplicable (in principle) in mechanistic or physicochemical terms.   *W.Sch.*

Vitality. Life-force; the energy required for the functions of life. In personality (q.v.) psychology, a popular term for a quality shown by more easily arousable individuals. See *Arousal; Traits; Type.*   *W.Sch.*

Vitamins. Substances which exert catalytic functions within the framework of normal metabolism. They are essential nutrients, but are only partly manufactured by the body itself. Therefore they have to be ingested with food, and in the case of some deficiencies administered in a concentrated form. Vitamin deficiencies are largely "vitamin-specific"

Vitamins of psychological interest

Traditional term	Short chemical designation	Selected physical symptoms in deficiency conditions
A	retinol	disturbed vision, debility and drying up of sebaceous and sweat glands, hyperkeratosis
B_1	thiamin	beri-beri, polyneuritis, oedema
B_2	riboflavin	arrested growth in babies; cracked lips; diminished visual acuity
B_6	pyridoxine	alterations in skin
P	pantothenic acid	myasthenia
PP	niacinamide	pellagra, dermatitis, diarrhea
H	biotin	alterations in skin and hair
B_{12} group	cyanocobalamin, etc.	anemia
C	ascorbic acid	scurvy, reduced capacity of resistance, loss of appetite, digestive disorders, inclination to bleeding, loosening of teeth, rheumatic pains, susceptibility to infections
D	calcipherol	rickets, disorders of growth, hypertonia, disorders of fertility
E	tocopherol	muscular dystrophy

and have largely physical, though also psychic symptoms. It is, however, usually unclear how far the effects in question are primary or secondary (resulting from somatic changes). The tabular summary above shows a selection of vitamin substances of interest to psychologists; both the traditional names are given and those introduced since 1960 as a result of international-level discussions. The table also gives physical symptoms for deficiency states. Influences on behavior have been investigated and demonstrated in animal experiments, primarily for pyridoxine and for cynanocobalamin. There has been no systematic investigation of the psychological effects of vitamins in normal individuals. See *Avitaminosis.*   K.-D.S.

Vocational guidance (Syn. *Vocational counseling; Careers advice*). One of the chief fields of applied psychology (q.v.). Advice and help are given to adolescents and those entitled to education, but also to enterprises in industry, commerce and trade, and to schools, and mainly to those seeking work or a career.

The organization of vocational guidance varies from country to country, e.g., in France it is linked with the school, in Germany with labor administration and charitable organizations, in England and the USA both with the labor authorities, and in large measure with independent bodies. But in all countries there is also vocational guidance in large industrial and administrative concerns and in banks (railways, aviation companies, insurance and the like). Qualified vocational guidance officers are mostly psychologists, but other professional experience is recognized as a prerequisite, to be accompanied by a recognized form of psychological-diagnostic training and training in vocational work.

By far the largest number of cases dealt with are adolescents about to leave school. The purpose of vocational guidance is to set them on the right vocational track, taking into consideration personality (q.v.), inclination and aptitude for a given vocation or employment (see *Abilities; Traits; Type*).

Over and above this, vocational guidance is concerned with the rehabilitated (e.g., the disabled who can be brought back into employment), with adults seeking another vocation (retraining, change of employer), with those aspiring to promotion (e.g., electricians anxious to become engineers by taking the necessary training). The function of vocational guidance is primarily to help. Unlike the school, it conducts no examinations to determine performance but uses aptitude tests (q.v.), nor does it at any stage make any selection of the best (vocational selection q.v.), but is interested in the normal distribution of ability. Vocational guidance has been established by law in most countries (freedom of vocational choice). Measures to control vocations are possible only in dictatorial state systems in which the supreme guideline is not the right of the individual but the priority of society.

In its diagnostic work, i.e. in its endeavors to establish vocational aptitude, vocational guidance uses verifiable methods and data (abilities, q.v., intelligence tests, q.v., specimens of work, interviews, exploration, q.v.). It must be able to substantiate its advice; for estimates of aptitude with a purely subjective value have no greater prognostic value than "expressions of opinion". Vocational guidance must be social and humane; but this can still be achieved only by a scientifically based psychodynamics (q.v.), aware not only of its possibilities but also of its limitations. Hence vocational guidance makes use of scientifically guaranteed investigation procedures; it is also aware of its educational and therapeutic functions (e.g. finding employment for those who haver eceived therapeutic treatment). Therefore it must always work in close conjunction with remedial medicine. Vocational guidance is closely connected with school and university counseling.

School counseling is guidance in the school career; its task consists in finding the kind of school suited for child or adolescent: whether private or state primary school, above all which specially oriented intermediate school, and secondary "technical" or "academic" course (classical, modern language, science, art). Investigations into readiness to attend school and into the aptitude and attainment needed for secondary or tertiary education are among the essential tasks of vocational guidance; since a child's real aptitudes are often revealed gradually, school counseling comes before vocational guidance both in time and content.

The object of university counseling is to help and guide during academic life. In content, university counseling is determined by vocational choice, then by the aptitude of the student (if he has already selected a profession) as well as by the educational facilities available for realizing the vocational decision taken and enabling one to enter a particular profession. Crucial prerequisites for school counseling are full expert information about the vocation in question, and plans of study approved by panels of experts, i.e. lists of studies necessary in each of the academic years (lectures, practical work, advanced tutorials).

In contrast to vocational guidance, school and university counseling have still not received full official recognition outside the USA, and their development is very restricted. But such counseling assumes special importance in view of the increasing differentiation of vocational tasks and the wider variety of schools, and because of the need to be able to change from one school system to another.

Experts constantly affirm that it is essential to develop an effective system of school and university counseling. See *Industrial psychology; Occupational psychology; Educational psychology; Traits; Type.*

Bibliography: Adams, J. F. (Ed.): Counseling and guidance. New York, 1965. **Armor, D. J.:** The Ameri-

can school counselor: a case study in the sociology of professions. New York, 1969. **Borrow, H.** (Ed.): Man in a world at work. New York, 1954. **Cramer, S. H.** *et al.:* Research and the school counselor. New York, 1971. **Crites, J. O.:** Vocational psychology. New York, 1969. **Holden, A.:** Teachers as counsellors. London, 1969. **Id:** Counseling in secondary schools. London, 1971. **Hopson, B. & Hayes, J.** (Eds.): The theory and practice of vocational guidance. Oxford, 1968. **Jackson, R. & Juniper, D. F.:** A manual of educational guidance. New York, 1971. **Johnson, D. E. & Vestermark, M. J.:** Barriers and hazards in counseling. New York, 1971. **Jones, A.:** School counseling in practice. London, 1970. **Jones, A. J.:** Principles of guidance. New York, 1970. **Kell, B. L. & Burrow, J. M.:** Developmental counseling and therapy. New York, 1970. **Ligon, M. G. & McDaniel, S. W.:** The teacher's role in counseling. Englewood Cliffs, 1970. **Ohlsen, M. M.:** Group counseling. Chicago, 1970. **Osipow, S. H.:** Theories of career development. New York, 1968. **Peters, R. J.:** The guidance process. A perspective. New York, 1970. **Peters, H. J. & Hanson, J. C.** (Eds.): Vocational guidance and careers development. New York, 1966. **Peters, H. J. & Shertzer, B.:** Guidance, program development and management. New York, ²1970. **Pietrofesa, J. J. & Vriend, J.:** The school counselor as a professional. New York, 1971. **Taylor, J. H. F.:** School counseling. London, 1971. *W. Arnold*

Vocational Interest Blanks. For the purpose of vocational guidance (q.v.) questionnaires have to list in as much detail as possible interests in special subjects, activities, etc., so that the most suitable vocational line can be deduced. There are numerous inventories of this kind, but in most cases the validation problem has not been solved. See *Kudor Preference Record; Strong Vocational Interest Blank.* *R.M.*

Vocational research. An area of industrial psychology (q.v.) dealing with requirements in individual occupations, vocational analysis, vocational guidance (q.v.), procedural techniques in vocational guidance, vocational training, and producing literature in which the mental and physical requirements of any particular occupation are described. See *Occupational psychology.*   W.Sp.

Vocational selection. A procedure which aims at a choice of a certain group and type of vocation, but usually a technique which presupposes a determination of the quality of the candidates for employment or a profession, and excludes those found unsuitable (negative selection) or prefers those found to be best suited (selection of the best). These decisions are determined by subjective and objective factors. *Subjective factors* are interest, inclinations, abilities and social prestige; *objective factors* are chiefly social security and economic vocational prospects (pay, salary, possibilities of promotion). Subjective factors depend on how far one is inwardly attracted by a certain vocational activity, its purpose, significance and value, and much less by the economic, material weighting. In choosing employment, firm location and colleagues, the worker is primarily concerned with optimum pay, social advantages and how easy the job is. Vocational and labor selection are controlled by industrial, commercial and trade enterprises. Parents, teachers and vocational guidance officers have only a subsidiary influence.

Vocational guidance experts or counselors, usually subsidized by the State, assist in deciding the choice of a vocation. The special facilities which may be offered by vocational guidance to adolescents seeking advice and to their parents are investigations of psychological aptitude; the determinants of professional aptitude established by research in the vocational field afford a certain normative decision criterion for vocational advice as well as for vocational decisions by employers, schools and parents. Vocational selection and choice presuppose specialist knowledge of vocational matters which is best supplied by trained officers but can also come from vocational literature, illustrations, films, etc. See

Abilities; Intelligence; Educational psychology; Industrial psychology; Occupational psychology.   W.A.

Voice key. An instrument which enables a vocal sound to start or stop some other mechanism.   G.D.W.

Volition. See *Will.*

Voluntarism. In philosophy: a metaphysical doctrine which conceives ultimate reality as "will": i.e. as an obscure, irrational, independent power, or one opposed to the idea of an intelligible ground of things (Schopenhauer). Also a moral doctrine which sees will as the source of action, and more specifically so than intellectual thought (Nietzsche); also an epistemological theory for which any judgment is true only inasmuch as it is affirmed voluntarily (Descartes). In psychology, voluntarists see cognitive and representational (linguistic) functions as subject to affectivity, feeling and voluntary commitment (psychoanalytic viewpoint). See *Will.*   F.B.

Voyeur; voyeurism. Voyeurs obtain sexual satisfaction and stimulation from the observation (in secret) of sexual objects or situations. Pleasure in sexual observation becomes voyeurism when it is the only, or the dominant, sexual goal in an individual's sexual behavior. The voyeur is usually male (average age about twenty-four years), and tries to preserve his anonymity when watching women naked or undressing, or acts of coitus, and thus (with or without masturbation) obtains sexual gratification. Most habitual voyeurs appear to lead an inadequate heterosexual life, are seldom married, and become delinquent at a relatively early age (Gebhard *et al.*, 1965). As a sexually deviant behavior, voyeurism evokes relatively weak social responses (compared with, e.g., incest), and is relatively infrequent (compared, e.g., with male homosexuality). See *Perversion; Sexuality.*

Bibliography: Gebhard, P., *et al.*: Sex offenders. London, 1965. **Giese, H.:** Psychopathologie der Sexualität. Stuttgart, 1962.   *H.M.*

Vygotsky, Lev Semenovich. B. 1896; d. 1934. A Soviet psychologist who developed one of the most highly-nuanced and influential socio-historical theories of language and concept (q.v.) development. Vygotsky studied at Moscow University and did research in educational and developmental psychology and psychopathology (q.v.). His major work, *Thought and Language*, was suppressed in 1936, inasmuch as it offended against the peculiar lines of the pseudo-psychology recommended by Stalinism (see *Soviet psychology*), but Vygotsky influenced and continues to influence some of the most fruitful Soviet psychological thinking. Vygotsky conceived of thought as deriving from overt action in an internalized form (see *Inner speech*), and particularly from the internalization of external dialogue. He based his work on K. Bühler, W. Stern and the early Piaget, and viewed inner speech as inner representation. Vygotsky's emphasis on the human ability to replace and revivify earlier conceptual structures is also an emphasis on the multiplicity of individual modes of linguistic, conceptual and personal development. See *Act psychology.*

Bibliography: Hanfmann, E. & Kasanin, J.: A method for the study of concept formation. J. Psychol., 1937, *3*, 521–40. **Vygotsky, L. S.:** Thought and language. Cambridge, Mass., 1962.   *J.C.*

Vygotsky test. A variant of Ach's method of studying concept (q.v.) formation, developed by Sakharov, a co-worker of Vygotsky's, for use especially with schizophrenic subjects. Twenty-two wooden blocks (Vygotsky blocks) have to be related conceptually to the same number of nonsense syllables.   *F.-C.S.*

W

Waking, artificial. Deprivation of sleep achieved by chemical effects or repeated waking in order to vary sleep requirement. An independent variable for investigation of the part played by sleep in the course of diverse mental functions. See *Dream; Sleep.* *H.Ro.*

Waking dream; waking vision. See *Daydream.*

Wald-Wolfowitz test. A non-parametric test for testing whether two independent samples differ in regard to their form of distribution (central trend, dispersion, skew, excess). The scores of both samples are ranked in a common series and characterized alternatively according to sample (e.g. A, B). The variable measured must be continuously distributed, and at least ordinally scalable.

Bibliography: **Wald, A. & Wolfowitz, J.:** On a test of whether two samples are from the same population. Annals of Mathematical Statistics, 1940, *11*, 147–62. *H.-J.S.*

Walking. In general, the first free step is observable at the end of the first year of life, and usually occurs by chance in place of previous walking "along" the wall or other objects. On acquiring an upright carriage, a child considerably extends his life space to date ("distance space") and begins the process of release from the mother-child bond. *M.Sa.*

Wallon, Henri. B. 15/6/1879 in Paris; d. Paris, 1962. French psychologist. Studied philosophy and medicine. He began his career as a psychiatrist, but later took up developmental psychology, and became its leading representative in France. He taught at the Sorbonne and at the Collège de France. In 1927 he founded the Laboratory of Child Psychobiology in Paris, and edited the journal *Enfance*. Wallon entered into many lively discussions with Piaget on development. Whereas Piaget was concerned primarily with the mental development of the child, Wallon was more interested in his emotional ("affective") development. He emphasized especially the importance of the degree of maturation of the CNS linked with social influences. Wallon believed that development was marked by "crises" involving a new organization of mental structures.

Main works: Evolution psychologique de l'enfant. Paris, 1941. De l'acte à la pensée. Paris, 1942. L'enfant turbulent. Paris, 1945. Les origines de la pensée chez l'enfant. Paris, 1947. Les origines du caractère chez l'enfant. Paris, 1949.

Bibliography: **Zazzo, R.:** Portrait d'Henri Wallon (1879–1962). J. psychol. norm. path., 1963, *60*, 386–400. *W.W.*

Walsh test. A non-parametric technique used to test two dependent samples for differences in central trend. Used when both sample distributions are symmetric (though not necessarily identical). See *Non-parametric tests*.

Bibliography: Walsh, J. E.: Some significance tests for the medium, which are valid under very general conditions. Annals of Mathematical Statistics. 1949, *20*, 64–81.   *H.-J.S.*

Ward-Hovland phenomenon. A phenomenon of reminiscence (q.v.) named after Ward (1937) and Hovland (1938): an increase in retention is observable after an interval of two to ten minutes after a rote-learning trial.

Bibliography: Hovland, C. I.: Experimental studies in rote-learning theory. I, II. J. exp. Psychol., 1938, *23*, 201–24, 338–63. **Ward, L. B.:** Reminiscence and rote learning. Psychol. Monogr., 1937, *49*, 4 (whole No. 220).   *F.-C.S.*

Warfare, psychological. A term introduced in the USA during World War II as part of military and political strategy on the basis of learning, social, advertising and depth psychology. Features: defense and attack ritual, optically and acoustically effective intimidation, propaganda with a view to changing existing structures. Planning for psychological warfare, and military propaganda, are determined by a large number of psychologically relevant reference variables. Psychological warfare is used primarily in the preparatory stages for war (diplomacy of dramatic intimidation), or as carefully planned support for military actions. A distinction is made between open (white), camouflaged (black), strategic, tactical and defensive, divisive and counter propaganda. Technical aids are provided by the mass media and also by balloons and rockets to distribute propaganda leaflets. The aim is to win the opponent over, or to outlaw and intimidate him (war of nerves), and to paralyze the opponent's will to fight and disintegrate the cohesion of the group by fostering uncertainty.

In peacetime, psychological warfare makes a contribution to the intensive presentation of state ideologies, and helps to provide immunity against outside influences, e.g. by "mental armament," by arousing trust in the leadership and in the protagonist's own ability to fight and to consolidate morale.

G.Mi.

Warming-up period. A short period before the actual activity (e.g. verbal or motor learning) is begun, which produces an introductory set and adaptation to the task, without direct reinforcement (e.g. of the S–R connection to be learned (or practice, q.v.). Warming-up leads to an increase of the total (learning or reproduction) performance.

Warm(ing)-up decrement: cessation or diminution of warming-up during a rest or retention interval. The effect of warming-up would seem to depend on the extent of the period, the similarity between warming-up activity and learning task, and the interval between warming-up and the task or reproduction (McGeoch & Irion, 1952). See *Memory; Reminiscence; Learning*.

Bibliography: Adams, J. A.: The second facet of forgetting: a review of warm-up decrement. Psychol. Bull., 1961, *58*, 257–73. **McGeoch, J. A. & Irion, A. L.:** The psychology of human learning. New York, 1952.   *F.-C.S.*

Warning cries, or cries of distress, draw the attention of members of the same or different species to the presence of a predator. The response to such a cry may be acquired or inborn. Unhatched chicks cease scratching the shell at the sound of a chicken's warning cry. Young snipe, on the other hand, must first learn to associate the warning with the enemy's image. Minnows warn other fishes by emitting warning substances.   *V.P.*

Watson, John Broadus. B. 9/1/1878 in Greenville; d. 25/9/1958 in New York City. Watson studied at Furman University and (philosophy) at the University of Chicago. He received his doctor's degree in 1903 under the functionalist James Angell and the neurologist H. H. Donaldson for a dissertation on "animal education". He then devoted himself largely to animal psychology (q.v.), and in 1908 became a full Professor in experimental and comparative psychology at the Johns Hopkins University (Baltimore), where he was also director of the psychological laboratory. He left the university in 1920, and pursued a career in consumer psychology until 1945, although he exerted considerable influence on modern psychology through his popular lectures and his widely-read books.

Watson is considered to be the founder of behaviorism (q.v.). His fundamental works *Psychology as the Behaviorist sees it* (1913), *Behavior: an introduction to animal psychology* (1914), *Psychology from the Standpoint of a Behaviorist* (1919), *Behaviorism* (1925), and *Psychological Care of Infant and Child* (1928) had a revolutionary effect on the traditional psychology of consciousness. Watson's provocative theses and his quasi-journalistic defense of them helped in their dissemination. In addition, his uncompromising assertion that psychology was to be conceived and practiced wholly as a natural science, and especially on the model of physics, that the introspective method (see *Introspection*) was pointless, that an objectivist terminology was to be used, and that psychology should be restricted to the examination of measurable, tangible, visible and audible behavior, accorded with the spirit of the times and the tendencies of young scholars. Even though it can be shown that Watson's decisive ideas were put forward before him (by, e.g., J. Rush, F. A. Lange, q.v., W. McDougall, q.v.), and especially by Russian reflexologists (W. Bekhterev, J. P. Pavlov, q.v.), his service to psychology is undiminished, since he was responsible for propagating this view of the science and for helping worldwide psychological research on objective lines really to get under way.

Watson's optimistic ideas about education relied on an extreme environmental theory, and amounted to a belief in human malleability. They also influenced the development of psychotherapy (q.v.). After Pavlov, Watson may also be considered as one of the founding fathers of modern behavior therapy (q.v.). See *Conditioning, classical and operant; Aversion therapy.*

Bibliography: Murchison, C.: History of psychology in autobiography. Vol. 3. London, 1936, 271–81. **Skinner, B. F.:** John Broadus Watson, behaviorist. Science, 1959, *129*, 197–8. **Woodworth, R. S.:** John Broadus Watson: 1878–1958. Amer. J. Psychol., 1959, *72*, 301–10.   *L.J.P.*

Weber, Ernst Heinrich. B. 24/6/1795 in Wittenberg; d. 26/1/1878 in Leipzig. Weber was Professor of anatomy (1818) and physiology (1840) in Leipzig, and is considered by many to be the co-founder of modern sensory physiology and psychophysics (q.v.).

Weber's investigations of touch and muscular sense formed the starting-point for the quantitative assessment of the relations between stimulus and response and hence for the development of psychophysics. The method of "just-noticeable differences" used in his investigations was the first psychophysical method. Weber tried to confirm the least difference that could be distinguished by a testee with two weights laid on the back of his hands. The results showed that stimuli that differ only insignificantly are experienced as equivalent, and that the ability to distinguish between two stimuli varies with their size or intensity, and is finer in the case of smaller than greater stimulus intensities. Analogous conditions were revealed in all the sensory areas that Weber examined. The quantitative formulation of this stimulus-response relation is presented in the law known (by G. T. Fechner, q.v.) as "Weber's law" (q.v.). Weber's experiments were continued and extended by Fechner (see *Fechner's law*).

In other experiments, Weber was able to show the distance between two pressure points on the skin at which the impression of two separate pressure sensations goes over into that of a single sensation. Weber was able to demonstrate therefore that tactile sensitivity is different at different points on the body surface ("two-point discrimination" or "two-point threshold"). He explained this in terms of "sensory circles", or skin areas where there is no perception of "doubleness" because of the stimulation of immediately adjacent tactile nerve fibers.

Main works: De aure et auditu hominis et animalium. Leipzig, 1820. De pulsu, resorptione, auditu et tactu. Annotationes anatomicae et physiologicae. Leipzig, 1834. Der Tastsinn und das Gemeingefühl. In: Wagner, R. (Ed.): Handwörterbuch der Physiologie, Vol. 3. Brunswick, 1846, 481–588. Über den Raumsinn und die Empfindungskreise in der Haut und im Auge. Berichte d. kön.-sächs. Ges. d. Wissenschaften z. Leipzig: Klasse 4, 1852, 87–105.   *W.W.*

Weber-Fechner Law. See *Fechner's Law.*

Weber's law. An early psychophysical generalization stating that a *just-noticeable difference* (q.v.) is a constant proportion of the magnitude of the original stimulus, i.e., the more intense the stimulus the greater the increase must be to be perceptible. Also called the *Weber fraction:* $\Delta R/R$, where ΔR is the change of stimulus that is just noticeable and R is the magnitude of the stimulus. This fraction has generally been found to be fairly constant at least for stimuli of middle-range intensity. Weber's basic law was elaborated later by Fechner; see *Fechner's law. G.D.W.*

We-break. A term from individual psychology (q.v.) for a suddenly experienced opposition between the ego and the community. A we-break is favored by a neglectful or authoritarian education, and is alleged to be a frequent precursor of neurosis (q.v.). *W.Sch.*

Wechsler-Bellevue Test. A test battery of ten subtests for general intelligence. The selection of subtests and their grouping in a verbal scale and a performance scale extended, according to D. Wechsler, the diagnostic possibilities of the battery in comparison with earlier intelligence tests, especially in the clinical sense. The test is for use between ages ten to fifty-nine. The author suggests that the retest reliability of the whole test is 0.94. See *Abilities; Intelligence.*

Bibliography: Wechsler, D.: The measurement of adult intelligence. Baltimore, 1939.   *P.S.*

Weighting coefficient. Coefficient attached to an observation (by multiplication or addition) in order that it shall assume a desired degree of importance in a function of all the observations of the set. A further example of the application of weighting coefficients is in predicting a criterion based on a multiple regression. In the process, the weighting coefficients of test data in the individual variables are obtained from the intercorrelations of the variables and the correlations between the criterion and the variables. See *Test theory.*   *W.H.B.*

Weight, sensitivity to. Sensitivity to weight depends on both the *haptic* and the *kinesthetic* senses. A passively felt weight will depend largely on the haptic senses such as pressure, whereas an actively lifted weight will depend on the kinesthetic senses of movement and muscular tension. See *Kinesthesia.*   *C.D.F.*

Weltanschauung types (syn. *World-view types*). Those manifesting a form of judgment of the environment characterized by personal emotions, aspirations, values and experiences as well as rational considerations, and described by Dilthey, Spranger, Jaspers, etc. See *Type*.   *W.K.*

Wertheimer, Max. B. 15/4/1880 in Prague; d. 12/10/1943 in New York. Wertheimer obtained his doctorate under Külpe (q.v.) in Würzburg in 1904 with a thesis on the investigation of credibility (q.v.), in the sense of the detection of guilty knowledge. Subsequently he carried out independent psychological research in Prague, Berlin and Vienna without any fixed academic post. From 1910 to 1916 he was a Reader in Frankfurt University, and met W. Köhler (q.v.) and Koffka (q.v.), who were assistants at the Psychological Institute. With his investigations of the perception of stroboscopic apparent movements (see *Phi-phenomenon*), Wertheimer provided the basis for the development of gestalt psychology. From 1916 to 1929 he was *Privatdozent* at the University of Berlin. Together with Köhler and Koffka and the neurologists K. Goldstein and H. W. Gruhle (the Berlin School), he continued his gestalt research and became the first editor of the journal *Psychologische Forschung* in 1921. In 1929 he returned to Frankfurt as Professor. In 1933, with the onset of the Nazi dictatorship, he left Germany, and after a short stay in Marienbad received a teaching appointment in the graduate school of the New School of Social Research, New York; he taught there until his death in 1943.

Together with Köhler and Koffka, Wertheimer is acknowledged to be one of the founders of gestalt psychology, which may be dated from the publication of his investigation into "Experimental Studies of the Perception of Movement" as a research paper in 1912. In this paper, Wertheimer examined the phi-phenomenon (an apparent movement which arises as a result of the suc-

cessive presentation of two usually equivalent optical elements in different positions), which became the starting-point of the holistic mode of examining psychological phenomena (a mode characteristic of gestalt psychology), and the associated critique of elementarist psychology. Wertheimer was able to show that the phenomenon could not be explained by the existing theories of perception: i.e. neither by reduction to local sensory sensations, nor by the assumption of summative associations of individual sensations; therefore he viewed the phenomenon as an example of the operation of a dynamic whole whose individual parts are influenced by the structural determinative constellation of the total form ("gestalt-as-a-whole"). See *Ganzheit, Gestalt, Structure*.

Associated with this experiment was Wertheimer's assumption regarding the neurophysiological activation processes basic to the phenomenon. He ascribed a unified, holistic character to these, as to the perceptions themselves. This conception of brain processes as physiological gestalts was later more precisely conceived and extended by Köhler in his theory of isomorphism (q.v.).

In an article of 1923 on "Investigations of gestalt theory", Wertheimer showed for the first time how, through a series of organizational principles (the gestalt laws of proximity, equivalence and closure), perception has a spontaneous tendency to configural structuration.

Wertheimer also detected the effects of tendencies to organization on gestalt principles in areas of behavior other than perception, as is evidenced in the posthumous publication *Productive Thinking* (1959). In particular, he attributed a significant role in the thinking process to the tendency to *pregnance* (q.v.), which he understood as essentially a transition from a bad to a good gestalt.

Main works: Experimentelle Studien über das Sehen von Bewegung. Z. Psychol. 1912,

61, 161–265. Untersuchungen zur Lehre von der Gestalt. Psychol. Forsch., 1921, *1*, 47–58; 1923, *4*, 301–50 (part-trans. in: Ellis, W. D. (Ed.): A sourcebook of gestalt psychology. New York, 1938, 12–16; and in: Beardsall, D. C. & Wertheimer, M. (Eds.): Readings in perception. Princeton, 1958, 115–35). A story of three days. In: Anshen, R. N. (Ed.): Freedom: its meaning. New York, 1940, 555–69. Some problems in the theory of ethics. Soc. Res., 1935, 2, 353–67. Productive thinking (Ed. Michael Wertheimer). New York, ²1959.

Bibliography: Helson, H.: The fundamental propositions of gestalt psychology. Psychol. Rev., 1933, *40*, 13–32. **Newman, E. B.:** Max Wertheimer: 1880–1943. Amer. J. Psychol. 1944, *57*, 428–35.   *W.W.*

White noise. Noise composed of a random mixture of sounds of many different wave lengths (term derived by imperfect analogy from white light, which occurs naturally as a mixture of spectral wave lengths). The sound of a waterfall approximates to a white noise, but in the laboratory it is electronically created by a *white noise generator*.   *G.D.W.*

Whole learning. An analytical method: a progression in teaching and learning from the given total units of sense, experience and objects to their constituent elements. Many teaching goals call for subsequent synthesis. Initial tuition in reading using the whole-learning method starts with whole sentence and word units and proceeds to analyze the individual letters in order to reassemble words and sentences.   *G.H.*

Whorf's hypothesis (syn. *Sapir-Whorf hypothesis*). A theory put forward by the linguisticians B. L. Whorf, E. Sapir and H. Hoijer. Whorf started from undeniable differences in the vocabularies and structures of different languages, especially those of American Indian languages (e.g. Hopi) and "standard average European" (SAE). He asserted that language (q.v.) determined thought, so that variations in languages were derivable from diverse world-views (the thesis of linguistic relativity), and therefore diverse cultures or civilizations. Whorf tried to demonstrate this in terms of the concepts of "time", "space" and "matter", and accordant behaviors. He compared (for the most part) individual word-thing relations in different languages, in a largely anecdotal and exemplary manner. The less emphatic version of the hypothesis states that language influences perception and memory by specific encoding of areas of reality. In the planning of experimental tests of the Whorf hypothesis, three criteria need to be taken into consideration (in terms of the example of color coding): (*a*) *Variation*. It is necessary first of all to confirm in the linguistic and in the non-linguistic behavioral inventory, areas of variation between which covariation is expected (e.g. color codability, i.e. codability of colors by means of color terminology, performance in recognizing colors). (*b*) *Universality*. The object under investigation must be present in each of the cultures under comparison (e.g. the universal pre-existence of the physical color spectrum). (*c*) *Simplicity*. The object of investigation ought as far as possible to be comparable in terms of some one-dimensional characteristic (e.g. the localization of colored areas on the color circle). A covariation of color codability/color recognition has been shown to be intra- as well as intercultural. A correspondingly positive association has been reported for mimic emotional expressions in perception. The testing of covariance between linguistic and behavioral criteria (e.g. between color coding and classification by means of free object sorting) provided only ambiguous or negative results.

Critics of Whorf's hypothesis emphasize the following points especially: (*a*) the association of influence between language and thought is to be seen as interactive and not unilateral. (*b*) The over-emphasis on the word-thing relation in Whorf's conception of language is accompanied by a neglect of over-lapping significant linguistic contexts (e.g. no attention is paid to the semantic dependency of the sentence on the context). (*c*) The universals of languages (linguistic universals) are undervalued in favor of their differences.

Bibliography: **Brown, R. W. & Lenneberg, E. H.:** A study in language and cognition. J. Abn. Soc. Psychol., 1954, *49*, 454–62. **Hymes, D.** (Ed.): Language in culture and society. New York, 1964. **Lenneberg, E. H. & Roberts, J. M.:** The language of experience. Bloomington, Ind., 1956. **Miller, G. A. & McNeill, D.:** Psycholinguistics. In: **Lindzey G. & Aronson, E.** (Eds.): The handbook of social psychology, Vol. 3. Reading, Mass., ²1969, 666–794. **Whorf, B. L.:** Language, thought and reality. Cambridge, Mass., 1956.   *H. Bosbach*

Wiggly-block test. A test by O'Connor for assessment of space apprehension. A rectangular block about 20 cm long is divided into nine smaller blocks each cut by irregular wavy lines. The testee has to reassemble them as quickly as possible.   *H.J.A.*

Wilcoxon's test. A non-parametric technique used to test two dependent samples for differences in regard to central trend. Its use is indicated when the individuals in both samples can be grouped in homogeneous pairs or there are two observations for each individual.

Bibliography: **Wilcoxon, F.:** Individual comparisons by ranking methods. Biometrics, 1945, *1*, 80–3.
                                                          H.-J.S.

Wilcoxon-White test. See *Mann-Whitney U-test.*

Will. Wundt considered "will" or "volition" to be a basic function of psychic existence, which he conceived of as a dynamic structure —in contradistinction to the substantial concept of mind put forward by association

(q.v.) psychologists. The theory of will ("voluntarism," F. Tönnies) he developed was experimentally founded, and has been extended by his many pupils and disciples, and especially by the Würzburg school (O. Külpe, N. Ach, J. Lindworski, K. Bühler, A. Messer, O. Selz). Voluntarism also influenced American motivational and behavioral research (C. L. Hull, q.v., J. B. Watson, q.v., E. L. Thorndike, q.v., E. C. Tolman, q.v., R. B. Cattell, G. W. Allport, q.v.), who nevertheless reject the method of self-observation as too prone to subjective error. *Verstehende Psychologie* (q.v.) either sees will as a formal principle (L. Klages, P. Lersch) or divides it according to effect: will to learn, will to life, will to achievement, will to value (E. Spranger). Empirical investigations have derived will from ideas and thought processes (T. Ziehen; E. Meumann, 1908) or elementary emotions (H. Ebbinghaus). In its structural psychological orientation (K. Lewin, q.v., H. Rohracher, G. W. Allport, q.v.), motivational theory is convinced that genuine volitional motives are conscious, or that hidden motives can be made conscious in an act of recall.

Ach (1905) showed in experiments that the concept of will indicates a special energy potential which is able to overcome strong contrary forces such as associative inhibitions, fatigue, etc. A motivational act results in a decision, which then gives rise to "determining tendencies" controlled by a goal or target idea, but remaining effective for long periods of time and despite intervals. The expenditure of volitional energy is measurable (Arnold, 1969). Weakness of volition may be innate or acquired, and may be compensated by educational or psychotherapeutic measures (see *Adler, Alfred*).

Ach (1935) discovered the law of difficulty of motivation and the effects of guiding ideas and motivational limits. The law of special determination indicates that an intention is the more easily realized the more specialized the determining target idea is.

Volitional impulses may increase achievement level for some time during continuous operations. They show that "will" is able to convert potential into kinetic energies, and that it may therefore be viewed as a genuine force (Mierke, 1955). The impelling and affective energies which arise from the "vital layers" can be sublimated by the central ego (q.v.), which represents the "spirit" and its value associations, and thus become a will to achieve. A value-oriented will is said to change the elementary "achievement eros" into an "achievement ethos". Volitional acts may be directed inwards; they are directed outwards when they mobilize abilities and achievement energies for spontaneous or persistent activity (A. Wellek). Many think that in the consciousness of "I will!", men experience the freedom of a personal decision. See *Conscience; Drive; Instinct; Emotions; Personality; Traits; Type.*

Bibliography: Ach, N.: Über den Willenakt und das Temperament. Leipzig, 1910. **Id.:** Analyse des Willens. Berlin, 1935. **Arnold, W.:** Person, Charakter, Persönlichkeit. Göttingen, ³1969. **Cattell, R. B.:** Personality and motivation structure and measurement. New York, 1957. **Hull, C. L.:** Principles of behavior. New York, 1943. **Klages, L.:** Der Geist als Widersacher der Seele. Leipzig, 1933. **Lewin, K.:** Vorsatz, Wille und Bedürfnis. Psychol. Forsch., 1920, 7, 330–85. **Lindworski, J.:** Der Wille. Seine Erscheinung und seine Beherrschung. Leipzig, 1923. **Meumann, E.:** Intelligenz und Wille. Leipzig, 1908. **Mierke, K.:** Wille und Leistung, Göttingen, 1955. **Wundt, W.:** An introduction to psychology. New York, 1912. *K. Mierke*

Wing Standardized Tests of Musical Intelligence. Tests of musical ability (see *Music, psychology of*).

Winzen's proposition. Put forward by Winzen in 1921: the formation of an association between two learning elements is made easier if the more impressive, better-known element appears (as a stimulus) in first place. F. D. Sheffield came to the opposite conclusion in 1947. *F.-C.S.*

Wire-bending test. A prescribed shape has to be copied with a piece of wire. The purpose is to measure the manual skill shown in adapting the material in order to reproduce the shape correctly. See *Motor skills.*

Bibliography: Lienert, G.: Drahtbiegeprobe. Die Drahtbiegeprobe als standardisierter Test. Göttingen, 1961. *R.M.*

Wish. According to Freud (q.v.), the concrete form (enriched by individual experience) of a drive (q.v.) or motive (q.v.). Wishes may be repressed and unconscious. (See *Energy, mental; Object cathexis*). According to Freud's original conception, a "wish dream" can be any dream. Later, he excepted anxiety dreams (at whose start the dreamer's positive wishes play a definite though small part). The function of such a dream is alleged to be the maintenance of sleep (q.v.) and the protection of sleep from disturbing external and internal stimuli. See *Dream; Depth psychology.*

Withdrawal symptoms. Physical or psychic symptoms which set in during or after the process of withdrawal from dependence on an addictive drug. Among the drugs which can cause effects of this kind are narcotics and certain opiates. In the case of the opiates, such symptoms can include: extreme pain, fainting, diarrhea, shivering, vomiting, sensation of coldness, violent yawning, discharge of watery mucus, sleeplessness, restlessness, fear and anxiety. The popular terms for withdrawal, "kicking the habit" and "going cold turkey", are indicative of the symptoms. See *Drug dependence.* *A.Hn.*

Witnesses. Evidence provided by a witness may be said to be not merely a recalling of an experienced action but a performance reflecting the whole personality (q.v.) of the witness. A witness is often able to remember only insignificant aspects of an event, which are unimportant for the judicial process. In some cases he is able only to recall certain fragments of a process, and cannot connect them chronologically. The ability of children and adolescents to act as witnesses is conditioned by the simplicity or complicated nature of the event and the development of the witness's intellect. For instance, a twelve-year-old boy with a passionate interest in cars (automobiles) can (under certain conditions) offer qualitatively better evidence than a much older person with a quite different orientation. The effectiveness of witnesses is much reduced by intense emotion (especially by anxiety or fear). See *Abilities; Child psychology; Forensic psychology; Credibility; Conscience; Guilt.*   *O.T.*

Bibliography: Davis, R. C.: Physiological responses as a means of evaluating information. In: **Biderman A. D. & Zimmer, H.** (Eds.): The manipulation of human behavior. New York, 1961. **Inbau, F. E. & Reid, J. E.:** Lie detection and criminal interrogation, Baltimore, ³1953. **Jung, C. G.:** Zur psychol. Tatbestandsdiagnostik. Arch. Krim., 1939, *100*, 123–30. **Tent, L.:** Psychologische Tatbestandsdiagnostik. In: **Undeutsch, u.** (Ed.): Handbuch der Psychologie, Vol. 11. Göttingen, 1967. **Wertheimer, M.:** Tatbestandsdagnostik. In: **Abderhalden, E.** (Ed.): Handbuch der Biologischen Arbeitsmethoden, Section 6. Berlin, 1933.   *F.M.*

Witte-König effect. A paradoxical fusion effect. If S's eyes are variously stimulated the sensations fuse into one percept. Either one stimulus dominates, or the percept alternates from one stimulus to the other. If *S.* is presented (by means of a stereoscope) with two circles one of which is incomplete, *S.* sees the break only if it is relatively small. A larger break in the circle is not perceived.

Bibliography: Helson, H. & Wilkinson, A. E.: A study of the Witte-König paradoxical fusion effect. Amer. J. Psychol, 1958, *71*, 316–20. **König, E.:** Experimentelle Beiträge zur Theorie des binocularen Einfach- und Tiefensehens. Meisenheim, 1962.   *F.Ma.*

Woodworth Personal Data Sheet. The prototype of all personality inventories or questionnaires, devised by R. Woodworth in World War I in order to single out neurotics unfit for military service. The test was not validated at the time. See *Questionnaires; Personality.*

Bibliography: Symonds, P. M.: Diagnosing personality and conduct. New York, 1931.   *R.M.*

Woodworth, Robert Sessions. B. 17/10/1869 in Belchertown, Mass.; d. 4/7/1962 in New York. Woodworth obtained his M.A. at Harvard in 1897, having studied philosophy and psychology. He received his Ph.D. under J. McK. Cattell (q.v.) in 1899 with a dissertation on "The Accuracy of Voluntary Movement". He widened the scope of his knowledge with studies in anthropology and statistics under F. Boas and in physiology under H. Bowditch in New York, Sarpey-Schafer in Edinburgh (1900), and as Sherrington's assistant in Liverpool (1902). He went to Germany in 1912, where he visited Külpe in Bonn and Wundt in Leipzig. From 1903 until his retirement in 1958 at the age of eighty-nine, he worked as Cattell's successor at Columbia. In 1956 he received the first Gold Medal award of the American Psychological Foundation for his exceptional contribution as an integrator and organizer of psychological science.

Woodworth achieved a worldwide reputation, above all by his publications, which have become standard works. Especially important are the following: the revised edition of Ladd's *Physiological Psychology* (1911); *Dynamic Psychology* (1918), the first systematic presentation of his scientific position; the introductory manual *Psychology* (1921), which went into five editions before 1947, and after Boring's work of 1950 was for twenty-five years the most frequently consulted textbook of psychology; *Contemporary Schools of Psychology*, which appeared in Mary R. Sheehan's revision two years after his death (1964); *Experimental Psychology* (1938), which in Schlosberg's revision (1954) is still among the standard works on experimental psychology; and his last work, *Dynamics of Behavior* (1958), which Woodworth published at the age of eighty-nine.

Woodworth's standpoint was essentially functionalist, even though he did not belong to the functionalist school of J. R. Angell and H. A. Carr. On the one hand, Woodworth was eclectic enough to shun the narrowness of partisan attachment to a school, on the other he integrated quite considerable elements of dynamic psychology into his functionalist conceptions.

His dynamic psychology was concerned with the conditions determining human behavior. He did not think it sufficient to explain behavior solely in terms of stimuli and responses without taking the living organism into consideration. Therefore, even in behavioral analysis, he recognized introspection as a legitimate psychological method. The concepts invoked by Woodworth to explain motivated behavior were drives and mechanisms. His decisive assumption in this regard, later taken over in the principle of functional autonomy by G. W. Allport (q.v.), was that a mechanism, as soon as it was aroused, itself represented a drive (q.v.), and was also in a position to activate other associated mechanisms.

Bibliography: **Poffenberger, A. T.:** Robert Sessions Woodworth: 1896–1962. Amer. J. of Psychol., 1962, *75*, 677–92. **Seward, G. H.:** Woodworth, the man: a "case history". In: **Georgene, H. & Seward, J. P.** (Eds.): Current psychological issues. New York, 1958, 3–20.   *W.W.*

Word association. A collective term for a number of psychodiagnostic techniques used to make diagnostic conclusions on the basis of subjects' responses to specific stimulus words. Reaction time is also measured. The method goes back to suggestions from C. G. Jung (q.v.) and L. Binswanger at the turn of the century. See *Association; History of psychology.*   *G.L.*

Word blindness. See *Alexia.*

Word-choice tests. Tests to assess part-aspects of verbal intelligence. Usually employed as subtests in larger general intelligence test-batteries. By definitions or synonymns, *S.* indicates his mastery of the term in question.   *P.S.*

Word fluency. A factor ("W") described by E. L. Thurstone (1938) and replicated on several later occasions. It is defined operationally by means of tests in which as many words as possible must be named which satisfy specific formal and symbolic conditions (e.g. those ending with specific letters).

Bibliography: **Guilford, J. P.:** The nature of human intelligence. New York, 1967.   *H.H.*

Word-salad. A disturbance of thinking with complete loss of the connection between individual words. Because of the absence of association, words—often from different languages—are related quite haphazardly. Above all a schizophrenic symptom. See *Schizophrenia.*   *A.Hi.*

Work-factor system. A time-study system from the USA, used to analyze a work process according to predetermined guidelines, to classify individual movements, and provide a tabular summary of their time or energy demands.   *G.R.W.M.*

World test; world technique. A therapeutic game devised by M. Lowenfeld, and standardized by C. Bühler (1941) in regard to material, directions and evaluation. The world test is a projective technique (q.v.) which allows some insight into the (pre-logical) world-picture of a child. The game contains, e.g., more than a hundred items (houses, trees, human, animals). The child is asked to build something. The process is recorded and finally photographed.   *P.G.*

Writer's cramp. Formerly called *scrivener's palsy*, this is a condition in which various muscles involved in writing go into spasm whenever the patient tries to write, or after he has been writing for a short time. It is one of many occupational cramps, another being violinist's cramp.   *P.Le.*

Wundt's napkin ring. See *Napkin ring figure.*

Wundt, Wilhelm. B. 18/6/1832 in Neckarau near Mannheim; d. 31/8/1920 in Grossbothen near Leipzig. After a year at Tübingen University, Wundt moved in 1852 to Heidelberg, where he obtained his medical doctorate in 1856, became *Privatdozent* in 1857, and was appointed Professor in 1864. From 1858 to 1871, H. von Helmholtz (q.v.) held the chair of physiology at Heidelberg. The two giants of scientific psychology lived at close quarters for thirteen years without any real personal or scientific contact. In 1874, Wundt was appointed to the chair of inductive philosophy at the University of Zürich, and in 1875 to the University of Leipzig, where he remained until his death forty-five years later. Wundt is considered to be the founder of modern psychology. He enabled psychology to become an independent discipline in terms of its object and methods, and developed it in accordance with the natural-scientific model. He defined it as the "science of inward and immediate experience", and grounded psychological research on experiments and "pure observation". He offered a systematic presentation of the principles and results of psychology. In 1874 he published the first version of the eventual three volumes of his

main work, *Principles of Physiological Psychology*. In 1883, he founded the first psychological journal under the title *Philosophische Studien* (Philosophical Studies). His ten-volume work *Völkerpsychologie* (Folk Psychology) was intended to complement individual, experimental psychology with a psychology of communal life and research into the higher products of human consciousness. This immense work (now largely outdated) bears witness to an immensely knowledgeable mind. In 1879, Wundt founded the world's first psychological institute, which soon achieved international rank. Psychologists went there from all leading countries in order to study experimental psychology under Wundt (see *Titchener; History of psychology*).

Main works: Lectures on human and animal psychology. London, 1894. Outlines of psychology, Leipzig, 1896; New York, 1897. Principles of physiological psychology. New York, 1904. An introduction to psychology. New York, 1912. Elements of folk psychology: outlines of a psychological history of the development of mankind. New York, 1916.

Bibliography: Boring, E. G.: A history of experimental psychology. New York, ²1957, 316–47. Id.: On the subjectivity of important historical dates: Leipzig, 1879, J. Hist. Behav. Sci., 1965, *1*, 5–9. Feldman, S.: Wundt's psychology. Amer. J. of Psychol., 1932, *44*, 615–29. Fernberger, S. W.: Wundt's doctorate students, Psychol. Bull., 1933, *30*, 80–3. Hall, G. S.: Founders of modern psychology. New York, 1912, 311–458. Petersen, P.: Wilhelm Wundt und seine Zeit. Stuttgart, 1924. Tinker, M. A.: Wundt's doctorate students and their theses (1875–1920). Amer. J. Psychol., 1932, *44*, 630–7. Titchener, E. B.: Wilhelm Wundt, Amer. J. Psychol., 1921, *32*, 161–78. Wolman, B. B.: Historical roots of contemporary psychology. New York, 1968, 275–97.   *L.J.P.*

Würzburg School. The school of thought psychologists deriving from the ideas of O. Külpe (q.v.). Other main representatives: N. Ach, K. Bühler, K. Marbe, A. Messer, O.

Selz. The Würzburg School opposed the sensualist and mechanist axiom of association psychology, and carried out experimental investigations of many acts that had until then been subjected to no such research, such as thought processes and forms of judgment, or goal ideas. See *Act psychology; History of psychology.* *H.W.*

X

Xanthocyanopsia. Yellow-blue vision, color weakness or blindness, in which the second and the third cone color substance is intact, and the functioning of the first is non-existent or limited. See *Color blindness.* *K.H.P.*

Xanthopsia. Yellow vision in digitalis, phena- cetin, santonin and other forms of poisoning, etc. *K.H.P.*

Xenoglossy. Speech occurring during a trance (q.v.) in a language ostensibly unknown to the speaker. "Responsive xenoglossy": ability to answer questions appropriately in the unknown language. *J.B.*

Y Z

Yates correction. A special continuity correction for fourfold χ^2 scores. An improvement on the Pearson χ^2 test only for 1 degree of freedom. Included in the equation for the McNemar test, the Yates correction is as follows

$$\chi^2 = \frac{(|b - c| - 1)^2}{b + c},$$

so that the difference between the observed and the expected frequencies is reduced by 0.5 for every category before squaring.

H.-J.S.

Yerkes-Dodson Law. A rule deriving from a publication of Yerkes and J. D. Dodson (1908), in which they reported on experiments in mice. With increased intensity of electrical shock, the mice learned more difficult assignments less readily than easy ones. The "law" was examined anew by H. J. Eysenck in 1955, and more generally formulated by, e.g., Broadhurst in 1959: the optimal motivation for a learning assignment decreases with the increasing difficulty of the task.

Bibliography: Broadhurst, P. L.: The interaction of task difficulty and motivation. The Yerkes-Dodson law revived. Acta psychol., 1959, *16*, 321–38.

Yerkes, Robert Mearns. B. 26/5/1876 in Bucks County, Pennsylvania; d. 1956. Yerkes studied zoology and psychology. He obtained his doctorate in 1902 at Harvard. From 1902 he was an instructor and later Professor at Harvard. From 1912 to 1917 he also worked at the Boston Psychopathic Hospital, and in 1917 he took up a Professorship in psychology at the University of Minnesota but was called up for military service in the same year. In the Army Medical Department, within eighteen months and together with a number of co-workers, he developed the Army Alpha Test (q.v.). From the end of the war until 1924 Yerkes was active in the National Research Council in Washington. In 1924 he became Professor at Yale. From 1930 to 1941 he was director of the Yale laboratories of primate biology, founded at his instigation in Orange Park, Florida, which was a research center for the comparative psychobiology of infra-human primates.

Yerkes was one of the founders of modern animal research, and of comparative primate psychobiology. His laboratories were a model for animal psychology (q.v.) laboratories throughout the world (see *Comparative psychology*). Yerkes stressed the importance of understanding the anatomical, physiological and neurological bases of animal behavior in psychological experimentation. Summaries of his ideas are to be found in his two most significant books *The Great Apes* (1929, with his wife Ada W. Yerkes) and *Chimpanzees: a Laboratory Colony* (1943). Further contributions to this area were: "The dancing mouse: a study in animal behavior" (1907); a report published together with J. Watson: "Methods of studying vision in animals" (1911); *Chimpanzee Intelligence and its Vocal Expressions* (1925, with B. Learned); and *The Mind of a Gorilla* (1927, 1928). Yerkes also wrote an *Introduction to Psychology* (1911) and together with G. V. Hamilton devised the multiple-choice method for psychological diagnostics. His Army-alpha research was written up in the two publications *Army Mental Tests* (1920, with C. Yoakum), and *Psychological Examining in the United States Army* (1921).

Bibliography: Murchison, C.: History of psychology in autobiography, Vol. 2. New York, 1932, 381–407.

                                                                    W.W.

Yohimbine (syn. *Quebrachine; Corynine; Aphrodine*). An alkaloid obtained from a West African tree, *Coryanthe johimbe*. Related to the rauwolfia alkaloids, yohimbine blocks the alpha receptors in the sympathetic division, and is therefore grouped as a sympathicolytic substance. However, physiological and psychological investigations offer no unified picture. In low doses, there are sympathicomimetic as well as sympathicolytic effects; only with a higher dosage are sympathicolytic effects readily obtained. The psychic effects are unclear. Several investigations report conditions approaching anxiety (q.v.). There is no experimental foundation for the frequent recommendations of yohimbine as an aphrodisiac.

Bibliography: Holmberg, G. & Gershon, S.: Autonomic and psychic effects of yohimbine hydrochloride. Psychopharmacologia, 1961, *2*, 93–106.   *W.J.*

Young-Helmholtz theory. See *Color perception*.

Youth. The terms "youth" and "adolescence" (q.v.) cover a section of the human life-span which has not been precisely defined, but extends from the age of about eleven to over twenty years. The German word "*Adoleszenz*" covers the period from eighteen to the mid-twenties.

1. *Cognitive performance.* Development of the intelligence begins to slow down at the beginning of the second decade of life and reaches its climax in many types of performance in adolescence (formal logical operations in the sense defined by Piaget, thinking with semantically denotative and connotative symbols). The differences in intelligence which develop in adolescence are generally final and can be traced back partially to inherited factors and partly to social conditions (sociological stratification, sex differences).

2. *Physical development.* Important physical changes occur in adolescence. At the beginning of puberty there is a strong tendency for fat to develop and about one year after gonadotropine secretion begins, a sharp growth is generally noted. Puberty itself is triggered by the influence of the hypothalamus, which must have reached a certain level of maturity (Tanner, 1962). However, sexual maturation and sudden growth are caused by hormonal processes. The interaction between endocrinal processes is still relatively obscure (Tanner, 1962). As a result of muscular growth physical strength and speed are increased and motor coordination improves. Early sexual and physical maturation or accelerated growth (see *Acceleration*) and late maturation or retarded growth (see *Retardation*) are dependent on dispositional factors (see *Twin studies*), cultural and civilization conditions, sociological factors and nutritional influences. They may promote or retard development of personality.

3. *Social development.* Sexual behavior in youth is largely dependent on social and cultural factors. The standard of sexual continence which prevails in our cultures leads to forms of behaviour which conflict with the norm, e.g. masturbation (q.v.) (in more than

90% of male adolescents) and petting (q.v.). Sexual behavior varies with the sociological group (Kinsey, 1948). In relation to personality development and social adaptation, adolescence is frequently marked by conflicts and crises. This is in particular the case when a young person is prevented by adults from substituting the adult role for the childhood role, and when there is a discrepancy between different influences (e.g. values enforced in and out of school). In our culture, the difficulties in making the transition to adulthood are greater than in primitive societies where the transition is often made in a matter of days or weeks (see *Initiation rites*). The development of attitudes (q.v.) in adolescence is marked less by a complete break and new structures than by revision and modification of values already accepted at an earlier stage. Efforts are noted on the one hand to develop independent opinions often associated with radicalism and remoteness from reality, and on the other by attempts to take over the adult culture—with some liberal and relativistic features. In his efforts for "self-achievement" (Maslow, 1954), the adolescent frequently moves towards a *peer-group culture*, i.e. a subculture in which factors (requirements, interests, values) are represented which distinguish the youth sharply from children on the one hand and adults on the other. The importance of *models* no longer seems so important in adolescence as in earlier periods of life. Many adolescents cannot even name a "hero" (Jaide, 1963). A distinction between phases and stages does not seem justified because these may occur at very different periods for typical features (such as lability).

4. *Abnormal development in adolescence.* In addition to social maladjustment (juvenile delinquence, neglect), mental sicknesses also first appear in a pronounced form in adolescence. See *Child psychology; Development; Educational psychology; Neurosis.*

Bibliography: Jaide, W.: Aus empirischen Untersuchungen über Vorbilder heutiger Jugendlicher. In: Schenk-Danzinger, L., and Thomae, H. (Eds.): Gegenwartsprobleme der Entwicklungspsychologie, Göttingen, 1963. **Kinsey, A.,** et. al: Sexual behavior in the human male, Philadelphia & London, 1948. **Kuhlen, R. G.:** The psychology of adolescent development, New York, 1952. **Maslow, A. H.:** Motivation and personality, New York, 1954. **Staton, T. F.:** Dynamics of adolescent adjustment, New York, 1963.

R. Oerter

Zeigarnik effect. A phenomenon named after Lewin's pupil Zeigarnik, who showed in 1927 that interrupted tasks are remembered more proficiently than uninterrupted tasks, depending on involvement in the dynamic field.   *I.M.D.*

Zero absolute. The point on a measuring scale at which a psychological variable ceases to exist. This point is supposedly analogous to absolute zero of temperature in physics.

C.D.F.

Zipf's laws. Zipf (1932) obtained data from the application of statistical methods to linguistic material from various languages and diverse literary genres, and asserted that they showed the following tendencies (usually referred to as "Zipf's laws"): the more frequently words are used in a language, the shorter they become; the most frequent words of a language are probably also the shortest, oldest, morphologically most simple, and those with the greatest semantic extension.

Bibliography: Lepschy, G. C.: Die strukturale Sprachwissenschaft. Munich, 1969. **Mandelbrot, B.:** Information theory and psycholinguistics. In: **Wolman, B. B.** & **Nagel, E.** (Eds.): Scientific psychology. New York, 1965. **Meyer-Eppler, W.:** Grundlagen und Anwendungen der Informationstheorie. Berlin, ²1969. **Miller, G. A.** & **Chomsky, N.:** Finitary models of language users. In: **Bush, R. R., Luce, R. D.** & **Galanter** (Eds.): Handbook of mathematical psychology, Vol. 2. New York, 1963. **Zipf, G. K.:** Selected studies of the principle of relative frequency in language. Cambridge, Mass., 1932. **Id.:** Psychobiology of language. An introduction to dynamic philology.

Boston, 1935. **Id.**: Human behavior and the principle of least effort. An introduction to human ecology. Cambridge, Mass., 1949.   *D.Vo.*

Zöllner illusion. One of the geometric illusions. The small diagonals make it difficult to perceive that the vertical lines are parallel.

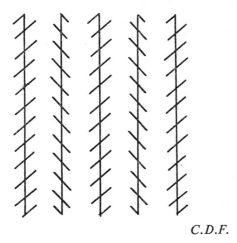

                                                    C.D.F.

Zoophilia. A term now seldom used and deriving from Krafft-Ebing: contact between humans and animals (stroking or beating) which give those concerned sexual pleasure (in contrast to direct sexual contacts with animals).   *H.M.*

z scale. A linear transformation of scores according to the formula

$$z = \frac{(X - \overline{X})}{s}.$$

The scale basic to the resulting standard distribution has a medium value of 0 and a standard deviation of 1. The z transformation is most often used for normally distributed scores.   *H.-J.S.*

z test. 1. A statistical test used as a test distribution for the standard normal distribution. It may be used as an approximation to various other statistical tests, since many test distributions are—with increasing degrees of freedom—transformed into a normal distribution.

2. A projective test (q.v.) procedure using screen projections and a Rorschach interpretative schema.   *H.-J.S.*

Zwaardemaker, Hendrik. B. 1857; d. 1930. Dutch physiologist. Worked as an army surgeon and then succeeded Engelmann as Professor of physiology at Utrecht University. Zwaardemaker became widely known mainly for his experimental research into smell, using large samples (*Physiologie des Geruchs*, 1895), and his invention of the olfactometer (q.v.). He also carried out investigations of acoustic perception, some in conjunction with his friend, the Belgian psychologist A. Michotte (q.v.).   *W.W.*

Zygote. A fertilized cell, which is always diploid, formed by the union of a male with a female gamete. A new individual develops from the zygote, which is therefore the starting-point of a new generation.   *H.Sch.*